SCENES FROM A REVOLUTION

SCENES FROM A REVOLUTION

THE BIRTH OF THE NEW HOLLYWOOD

MARK HARRIS

CANON‖GATE

Edinburgh · London · New York · Melbourne

For my mom and dad,
in loving memory

First published in Great Britain in 2008 by
Canongate Books Ltd, 14 High Street,
Edinburgh EH1 1TE

Published in the United States in 2008 by Penguin Press Ltd, 375 Hudson Street,
New York, NY 10014

1

British Library Cataloguing-in-Publication Data
A catalogue record for this book is available on
request from the British Library

ISBN 978 1 84767 102 8

Printed and bound in Great Britain by Mackays of Chatham Ltd, Chatham

www.canongate.net

BONNIE AND CLYDE

The actors
Warren Beatty (Clyde Barrow)
Faye Dunaway (Bonnie Parker)
Michael J. Pollard (C. W. Moss)
Gene Hackman (Buck Barrow)
Estelle Parsons (Blanche Barrow)
Denver Pyle (Frank Hamer)
Evans Evans (Velma)
Gene Wilder (Eugene)

Behind the scenes
Warren Beatty, producer
Arthur Penn, director
Robert Benton, screenwriter
David Newman, screenwriter
Robert Towne, special consultant (rewriter)
Burnett Guffey, cinematographer
Dean Tavoularis, art director
Theadora Van Runkle, costume designer
Dede Allen, editor
Robert Jiras, makeup designer
Elaine Michea, assistant to Beatty
Morgan Fairchild, driving double for Faye
   Dunaway
Elinor Jones and Norton Wright, producers
   (1963–64)
François Truffaut
Jean-Luc Godard
Jack Warner, head of Warner Brothers
Walter MacEwen, head of production at Warner
   Brothers
Benjamin Kalmenson, head of distribution for
   Warner Brothers
Richard Lederer, head of advertising and
   publicity for Warner Brothers
Robert Solo, assistant to Walter MacEwen
Eliot Hyman, head of Seven Arts

DOCTOR DOLITTLE

The actors
Rex Harrison (Dolittle)
Samantha Eggar (Emma Fairfax)
Anthony Newley (Matthew Mugg)
Richard Attenborough (Albert Blossom)
Peter Bull (Bellowes)

William Dix (Tommy Stubbins)
Geoffrey Holder (William Shakespeare X)

Behind the scenes
Arthur P. Jacobs, producer
Richard Fleischer, director
Mort Abrahams, associate producer
Leslie Bricusse, composer/lyricist/screenwriter
Robert Surtees, cinematographer
Ray Aghayan, costume designer
Herbert Ross, choreographer
Lionel Newman, conductor/orchestrator, head
   of 20th Century Fox's music department
Richard Zanuck, head of production at
   20th Century Fox, son of Darryl F. Zanuck
David Brown, New York-based
   20th Century Fox executive
Josephine Lofting, widow of author Hugh
   Lofting
Christopher Lofting, son of Hugh and Josephine
   Lofting
Bernard Silbert, Josephine Lofting's lawyer
Helen Winston, would-be producer of the film
Larry Watkin, author of an unused screenplay
   for the film
Alan Jay Lerner, Arthur Jacobs's original choice
   to write the screenplay
Rachel Roberts, Rex Harrison's wife
Joan Collins, Anthony Newley's wife
Natalie Trundy, Arthur P. Jacobs's girlfriend
   (later wife)

THE GRADUATE

The actors
Dustin Hoffman (Benjamin Braddock)
Anne Bancroft (Mrs. Robinson)
Katharine Ross (Elaine Robinson)
William Daniels (Mr. Braddock)
Elizabeth Wilson (Mrs. Braddock)
Murray Hamilton (Mr. Robinson)

Behind the scenes
Lawrence Turman, producer
Mike Nichols, director
Buck Henry, screenwriter
Calder Willingham, screenwriter
Charles Webb, author of the novel

Robert Surtees, cinematographer
Sam O'Steen, editor
Richard Sylbert, production designer
Joel Schiller, assistant production designer
Meta Rebner, script supervisor
Paul Simon and Art Garfunkel, composers
Joseph E. Levine, head of Embassy Pictures
William Hanley, author of an unused screenplay
Peter Nelson, author of an unused screenplay
Anne Byrne, Dustin Hoffman's girlfriend (later wife)
Mel Brooks, Anne Bancroft's husband
Leonard Hirshan, Anne Bancroft's agent

GUESS WHO'S COMING TO DINNER

The actors
Spencer Tracy (Matt Drayton)
Sidney Poitier (John Prentice)
Katharine Hepburn (Christina Drayton)
Katharine Houghton (Joey Drayton)
Cecil Kellaway (Monsignor Ryan)
Beah Richards (Mrs. Prentice)
Roy Glenn (Mr. Prentice)
Isabel Sanford (Tillie)

Behind the scenes
Stanley Kramer, producer/director
William Rose, screenwriter
Sam Leavitt, cinematographer
Ray Gosnell, assistant director
George Glass, associate producer
Robert C. Jones, editor
Robert Clatworthy, production designer
Marshall Schlom, script supervisor
Karen Kramer, Stanley Kramer's wife
Louise Tracy, Spencer Tracy's wife

IN THE HEAT OF THE NIGHT

The actors
Rod Steiger (Bill Gillespie)
Sidney Poitier (Virgil Tibbs)
Warren Oates (Sam Wood)
Lee Grant (Mrs. Colbert)
Larry Gates (Endicott)
William Schallert (Mayor)
Beah Richards (Mama Caleba)

Scott Wilson (Harvey Oberst)
Quentin Dean (Delores Purdy)
Anthony James (Ralph)
Jester Hairston (Endicott's butler)

Behind the scenes
Walter Mirisch, producer
Norman Jewison, director
Stirling Silliphant, screenwriter
John Ball, author of the novel
Hal Ashby, editor and Norman Jewison's right-hand man
Haskell Wexler, cinematographer
Quincy Jones, composer
Lynn Stalmaster, casting
Meta Rebner, script supervisor
Terry Morse, first assistant director
Martin Baum, Sidney Poitier's agent
Claire Bloom, Rod Steiger's wife
Juanita Hardy Poitier, Sidney Poitier's wife

The critics
Bosley Crowther, film critic for the *New York Times*
Roger Ebert, film critic for the *Chicago Sun-Times*
Penelope Gilliatt, film critic for the *New Yorker*
Pauline Kael, film critic for the *New Yorker*
Joseph Morgenstern, film critic for *Newsweek*
Andrew Sarris, film critic for the *Village Voice*
Richard Schickel, film critic for *Life*

The industry
Louis Nizer, chief counsel to the Motion Picture Association of America
Gregory Peck, president of the Academy of Motion Picture Arts and Sciences
Geoffrey Shurlock, head of the Production Code Authority
Jack Valenti, head of the Motion Picture Association of America

INTRODUCTION

When you talk about films, nobody agrees with anybody.
Guys get mad at each other and the air is full of screaming.
—David Newman and Robert Benton,
"The Movies Will Save Themselves," 1968

A few dozen reporters, wire-service men, studio publicity department employees, gossip columnists, and personal managers were gathered on Melrose Avenue in Hollywood outside the locked headquarters of the Academy of Motion Picture Arts and Sciences. It was the morning of February 20, 1968. At 10:00 a.m., the doors opened and the group was led inside and escorted to the Academy library, where each person was handed an unsealed, oversize manila envelope containing the names of the 1967 Oscar nominees.

The five films vying for Best Picture that year were *Bonnie and Clyde, Doctor Dolittle, The Graduate, Guess Who's Coming to Dinner,* and *In the Heat of the Night.* Some Academy Awards competitions offer an almost irresistible temptation to imagine that the Best Picture nominees represent a collective statement—a five-snapshot collage of the American psyche as reflected in its popular culture. But that morning, all that was illuminated by the list of contenders was the movie industry's anxiety and bewilderment at a paroxysmal point in its own history. *Bonnie and Clyde* and *The Graduate* were game changers, movies that had originated far from Hollywood and had grown into critics' darlings and major popular phenomena; *In the Heat of the Night,* a drama about race, and *Guess Who's Coming to Dinner,* a comedy about race, were middle-of-the-road hits that had, with varying degrees of success, extended a long tradition by addressing a significant social issue within the context of their chosen genres; and

Doctor Dolittle was a universally dismissed children's musical that most observers felt had bought its way to the final five. Of such mixed bags have countless Academy Awards races been made.

That winter, the question of who was going to win had taken on more urgency than usual. Not who was going to win the Oscars, which would shortly be decided by the usual blend of caprice and conviction, but who was going to win ownership of the whole enterprise of contemporary moviemaking. The Best Picture lineup was more than diverse; it was almost self-contradictory. Half of the nominees seemed to be sneering at the other half: The father-knows-best values of *Guess Who's Coming to Dinner* were wittily trashed by *The Graduate*; the hands-joined-in-brotherhood hopes expressed by *In the Heat of the Night* had little in common with the middle finger of insurrection extended by *Bonnie and Clyde*.

What was an American film supposed to be? The men running the movie business used to have the answer; now, it had slipped just beyond their reach, and they couldn't understand how they had lost sight of it. In the last year, the rule book seemed to have been tossed out. Warren Beatty, who looked like a movie star, had become a producer. Dustin Hoffman, who looked like a producer, had become a movie star. And Sidney Poitier, who looked like no other movie star had ever looked, had become the biggest box office attraction in an industry that still had no idea what to do with, or about, his popularity. The biggest hit among the five nominees, *The Graduate,* had been turned down by every major studio and financed independently. *Bonnie and Clyde* had been financed by Warner Brothers but loathed by Jack Warner, who rued the day he put even a small amount of his company's money into it. *In the Heat of the Night* was made because United Artists ran the numbers and realized the film could be produced so cheaply that it would never have to play in the South at all and might still break even. *Guess Who's Coming to Dinner* was green-lit only because Columbia Pictures owed its producer-director, Stanley Kramer, a movie. Together, the four films cost about $10 million. The fifth picture, 20th Century-Fox's *Doctor Dolittle,* cost more than twice as much to produce and promote as the other four combined; it was the only movie of the five that had been fueled by a studio's bottom-line goal to manufacture an immense popular hit, and the only one that flopped.

The *Los Angeles Times* looked at the list of nominees and called it a battle of the "dragons" against the "dragonflies." The dragons were Stanley Kramer and Katharine Hepburn and Spencer Tracy and Rex Harrison, the makers of *Guess Who's Coming to Dinner* and *Doctor Dolittle,* and what the paper termed the "armies of greybeard" technicians who had been making movies their way since the dawn of the sound era. The dragonflies—"nervous, rootless, hip"—were Beatty and Hoffman, Faye Dunaway, Rod Steiger, Mike Nichols, Hal Ashby, Norman Jewison, and Arthur Penn, all newcomers, nontraditionalists, or outsiders. The divide was generational, but also aesthetic—these were people who were rejecting what movies had been in favor of what they could be—and the fight was unabating.

In Hollywood, by the time the 1967 Best Picture nominees were made public, it was increasingly clear that something was dying and something was being created, but the transition between old and new is never elegant or seamless. The dragons couldn't quite believe that they were running out of firepower, and the dragonflies, still excited to have buzzed their way across the moat and through the palace gates, would have been very surprised to hear that they were about to achieve a great deal more than that. As iconic as the images of Bonnie and Clyde in their dance of death or Mrs. Robinson interposing herself between Benjamin and the bedroom door or Sidney Poitier demolishing Rod Steiger with the line "They call me *Mister* Tibbs!*" became the second they reached screens, they were still anomalies in a world that had just made *The Sound of Music* the highest-grossing film in history. What paid studio bills in the mid-1960s were James Bond extravaganzas, John Wayne westerns, Elvis Presley quickies, Dean Martin action comedies, and a long-standing willingness on the part of moviegoers to suspend disbelief. Now, suddenly, people also wanted *Blow-Up* and *The Dirty Dozen* and Clint Eastwood's *Man with No Name* and Bob Dylan in *Don't Look Back,* a title that could have served as a rallying cry for a generation of moviegoers that had emerged faster and more forcefully than the studios could have imagined. The old and the new existed in uneasy proximity, eyeing each other across a red-carpeted aisle that was becoming easy to mistake for a battle line. A fight that began as a contest for a few small patches of Hollywood turf ended as the first shot in a revolution.

All movies are gambles; each one begins with a prayer that what seems like a brilliant idea to its writers and directors and producers and actors at the moment it is kindled will still have meaning after years of fights and compromises and reconceptions and struggles, when it comes alive on a screen. The five movies up for Best Picture did have one thing in common: They had all been imagined for the first time many years earlier, in a world that bore little resemblance to the one in which they arrived in 1967. This is the story of what happened to those movies, to the hopes and ambitions of their creators, and to American filmmaking in the five years between their conception and their birth.

PART ONE

ONE

One afternoon in the spring of 1963, Robert Benton went to the New Yorker Theater to see François Truffaut's *Jules and Jim*. It was not his first time; it may have been his tenth or twelfth. Benton, then thirty years old and the art director of *Esquire* magazine, was using the movie both to nurse a romantic injury—the painful end of his relationship with his girlfriend, Gloria Steinem[1]—and to indulge a passion for European films, particularly those of the French New Wave, which was becoming something like a common language among young, smart, city-dwelling moviegoers.

Jules and Jim, with its delicate love triangle, its studied disregard for the moral and narrative strictures of Hollywood filmmaking (Truffaut himself called it "deliberately boring"),[2] and its equal doses of hopelessness and romanticism, was a perfect choice for Benton—and it's unlikely that he was the only one to travel that May afternoon up from midtown Manhattan to Dan Talbot's theater on Broadway and 88th Street so he could luxuriate in one more encounter with it. The movie, Truffaut's third, had opened in New York more than a year earlier to initial business that was only modest, but its cult was devoted, and the film was still holding on, playing one week on the Upper West Side, then a few days in the East Village on Avenue B, then a week on Bleecker Street. The deep chord of longing the picture sounded in many moviegoers was understandable—emotional ambiguity and grown-up sexuality were virtually black market

items in American movies of the time. And *Jules and Jim*'s calculatedly casual visual aesthetic, its diffused light and gentle nods to flickering silent-
film imagery, held particular interest for Benton as a magazine designer
who always had his eye on the next new thing, particularly when it was an
unexpected synthesis of old things.

But even if Benton hadn't happened to be so personally taken with
Truffaut's style, he would have had plenty of other places to go that day.
The last couple of years had brought an almost unimaginable wealth of
world cinema to the United States, starting, always, in New York City and
then moving west. Federico Fellini's *La Dolce Vita*—an immense explod-
ing flashbulb of a movie—and Michelangelo Antonioni's *L'Avventura*—
stone-faced, elliptical, unsolvable—had arrived within weeks of each
other; Antonioni's *La Notte* and *L'Eclisse* followed quickly, and that spring,
Fellini's *8 1/2* was just weeks from opening. The success of *The Magnifi-
cent Seven*, the American remake of Akira Kurosawa's *Seven Samurai*, had
spurred the release of five more of the director's movies—*Throne of Blood*,
The Hidden Fortress, *The Lower Depths*, *Yojimbo*, and *Sanjuro*—in the previous eighteen months, and despite mostly condescending dismissals from
Bosley Crowther in *The New York Times*, some of them were finding audiences. People were still talking about Jean-Luc Godard's *Breathless*—and
going to see it repeatedly—two years after its U.S. debut. The options were
so rich and varied: The mysteries of Alain Resnais's *Last Year at Marienbad*,
the almost punitive austerity of Ingmar Bergman's *Through a Glass Darkly*
and *Winter Light*, the begrimed, rough-hewn carnality thrown onto the
screen from England in *The Loneliness of the Long Distance Runner* and
Saturday Night and Sunday Morning. If Benton hadn't had to get back to
Esquire's offices that afternoon, where his colleague and comrade David
Newman, a staff writer and editor, was waiting for him, he could have
stayed at the New Yorker for the second feature, Luis Bunuel's *Viridiana*,
a portrait of a novice in the Catholic Church that was a long way from
Audrey Hepburn in *The Nun's Story*.

Whatever destination Benton had selected when he chose to sneak
away from work that day (a decision that wasn't hard, since *Esquire* was
a place where talent could excuse many varieties of midafternoon misbe-
havior), it's almost a certainty that he would not have ended up watching

a Hollywood movie. In the early 1960s, the American studio film had bottomed out: Even many of its own manufacturers and purveyors felt they had dragged the medium to a creative low point in the sound era. "It wasn't just that we were sick of the system," recalls the director Arthur Penn. "At that point, the system was sick of itself."[3] And with good reason: Though a handful of movies, as ever, either transcended convention or executed it with exhilarating skill, what Hollywood was primarily invested in turning out in 1963 were dozens of war movies and westerns (generally with aging stars and increasingly threadbare and recycled plots), biblical spectaculars of great scale and diminishing returns, musicals with an ever more strident sense of nostalgia, tinny, sexually repressive romantic comedies, and huge, unseaworthy battleships like *Cleopatra, The Longest Day,* and the remake of *Mutiny on the Bounty.* Many of these films would draw audiences, and every year, at least a couple of them would get Academy Award nominations for Best Picture, in stoic recognition of their bloat and expenditure. But nobody, not even their makers, was particularly inclined to defend them as creative enterprises.

When a filmmaker who was considered serious-minded would take on an adult subject (usually smuggled into Hollywood in the respectable packaging of a Tennessee Williams or Lillian Hellman play or a novel by John O'Hara), his work would be subjected to the censorious standards of the Production Code, which had barely changed in thirty years, and would end up stripped of meaning and sense. When the results arrived on screen—a *Butterfield 8* that was not quite about a prostitute, a remake of *The Children's Hour* that, twenty-five years after the first time Hollywood tried to adapt it, still couldn't refer to lesbianism, an adaptation of *Elmer Gantry* that had to shield timid sensibilities from the full content of a book that people had been reading since 1927—smart critics groaned, audiences applauded the actors and forgot the movies quickly, and the directors themselves expressed impotent disgust. "If you go to France nowadays . . . you are constantly involved in passionate discussions about the creative side of moviemaking," said the veteran Fred Zinnemann. "Here in Hollywood we are going in circles. We have moved into a trap, a self-imposed, self-induced trap with our dependence on best-sellers, hit plays, remakes, and rehashes."[4]

As it turned out, there was no need for Zinnemann or anyone else to go to France; the French, and the conversations he was envying, were coming to America in the form of the movies themselves. Godard and Truffaut had both written for *Cahiers du Cinéma*—Truffaut's reviews in particular were both deep appreciations and youthful, swaggeringly belligerent manifestos—and the movies they made were themselves implicit acts of film criticism. And ironically, if Zinnemann had gone to France in 1963, the conversation he would have heard was that the French New Wave was now *passé,* and the *cinematheques* he would have visited in Paris were filled with old work by Howard Hawks, Alfred Hitchcock, and underappreciated Americans like Samuel Fuller, Nicholas Ray, and Anthony Mann,[5] whose movies had been used to lay the cornerstones of the *auteur* theory that was becoming central to any movie discussion in the early 1960s. Those discussions filled the air at every cocktail party. Were Bergman's solemn, unsensual new movies a hermetic retreat from innovation or signs pointing toward a new formal rigor? Was *Marienbad* solvable, or was the whole point not even to try? Had Antonioni left Fellini in the dust with his defiance of narrative convention, and was he the cold-blooded moralist he seemed, perversely, to claim he was? People who cared about culture armed themselves for an evening out with an arsenal of stances, opinions, and positions that thickened the air as fast as cigarette smoke. Ten years earlier, the topic would have been literature or theater; these days, movies filled the agenda. "When *La Dolce Vita* and *L'Avventura* opened at about the same time, there were fights!" says Newman's widow, screenwriter Leslie Newman. "There were *Dolce Vita* people and *L'Avventura* people and you were one or the other. The average American movie at that time we didn't even go see, except for revivals. We were totally snobs! American movies meant Doris Day and Rock Hudson."[6]

But a hope that the studios could eventually incorporate some elements of European cinema and the French New Wave was very much on the minds of a new generation of directors trained largely in New York television production and theater—Penn, John Frankenheimer, Sidney Lumet. And the possibility that American movies could, one day soon, break the shackles of old-Hollywood thinking excited Benton and David Newman as well. At *Esquire,* they made a slightly Mutt-and-Jeff-ish pair, Benton low-key, precise, bespectacled, and single and Newman impulsive, hyper-kinetic, unruly, and already, at twenty-five, a husband and father. Newman had arrived in New York from the University of Michigan a couple of years earlier. Despite their differences in temperament, they made an exception-ally effective professional team. "He'd ask me to design a story he was writing, I'd bring him in to write the text for something I was working on," says Benton.[7] Their friendship became collegial and then personal. And it was fueled, as much as anything, by their compatible tastes.

By 1963, Harold Hayes was turning *Esquire* into the repository of a free-swinging style of writing that eventually became known as New Jour-nalism. It was a place where Norman Mailer could serialize his novel *An American Dream,* a home for Tom Wolfe, a reporter for the *New York Her-ald Tribune* who had just started publishing stories in the magazine that year, and a venue in which Gay Talese was reinventing the magazine profile with long takes on director Joshua Logan and the boxer Floyd Patterson that, in their language, their shaping of scenes, and their sense of drama, felt cinematic in precisely the way American films of the time didn't. But beyond its status as a home for influential prose, *Esquire,* under Hayes, was becoming the monthly exemplification of a way of thinking about what it liked to call "today's man": urban, sophisticated, unshy about sexual appetite and a love of "the good life," but also cynical, suspicious of cant, and contemptuous of mediocrity, conformity, and 1950s-style groupthink (not, however, of hyperbole). The scent of tobacco, Scotch, and heady after-hours arguments wafted off every page. And on many of those pages, style *was* content, which meant that a collaboration between someone with as keen and witty a sense of presentation as Benton and a writer as sharp as Newman (together, they were largely responsible for the look and tone of the magazine's famous Dubious Achievement awards) was bound to be fruitful. [8]

Benton and Newman had jobs to do at *Esquire,* but also time to spare and energy to burn. In 1963, the two of them spent many afternoons and evenings mapping out their own manifesto for the magazine: a massive, sweeping piece they planned to call "The New Sentimentality" that would define by brash dictum what was in and out, arriving and over, modern and hopelessly maudlin, in pop culture. "We were sort of bad kids," says

Benton. "Anything we could do to get attention, we did."[9] On afternoons when their absence might go unnoticed or be justified with a relatively straight face as "research," they would run over to the Museum of Modern Art, where their friend Peter Bogdanovich, who was helping to curate a six-month retrospective on the career of Alfred Hitchcock, would run the films for his friends at lunchtime. "We came away babbling, excited, thoroughly converted believers," they wrote later. "There wasn't a day spent . . . that didn't include at least one discussion on what *he* would have done."[10] Newman and Benton shared other tastes—an appetite for true-crime books, particularly John Toland's just published history of Depression-era outlaws, *The Dillinger Days*, and a ceaseless fascination with Godard and Truffaut (whose second movie, *Shoot the Piano Player*, was based on an American crime novel and had toyed knowingly with Hollywood gangster-film tropes).

The appendix to Toland's book made reference to two of the era's minor criminals, Clyde Barrow and Bonnie Parker. Benton had grown up in the small East Texas town of Waxahachie, and their exploits—they were killed in 1934, when he was two—were more familiar to him than to Newman. "Everybody in Texas grew up with Bonnie and Clyde," Benton says. "My father was at their funeral. You'd go to a Hallowe'en party as a kid and some boy would always be dressed as Clyde and some girl would be dressed as Bonnie. Nobody ever dressed up as Dillinger."[11]

Neither Benton nor Newman had ever read a screenplay, and they barely knew anyone in the movie business; a few weeks earlier, Benton had gone to a party at the comedy writer Herb Sargent's apartment and met Warren Beatty, but neither man had then made much of an impression on the other.[12] Nonetheless, high on everything they'd been watching and talking about, they decided that summer that the adventures of Bonnie and Clyde would make a great movie. From the afternoon they started working on the script after a midday screening of Hitchcock's *Rope*,[13] they thought, this could be the movie that brings the French New Wave to Hollywood, "a gangster film," says Benton, "that was about all the things they didn't show you in a gangster film." And if we do this right, they told each other, maybe we can get François Truffaut to direct it.

"We didn't know how to write a screenplay," says Benton, "so we wrote an extended treatment. We described a scene, including camera shots, and we'd write down what characters were talking about, but we didn't put dialogue in." Some of that writing took place in *Esquire*'s offices, behind closed doors, but much of it happened after hours, with Newman or Benton sketching out a scene at home, then giving it to the other in the morning. "The next day we would talk about the scene, and say, no, that's all wrong, and if David had written it, I would take it home and rewrite it, and if I had written it, David would redo it," Benton recalls. They would work together into the night, with Flatt and Scruggs and the Foggy Mountain Boys playing at full volume on the phonograph[14] and becoming, in effect, the sound track to their experience of writing the movie. "We had an enormous sense of freedom—and we didn't have skill, which was a good thing," says Benton. "If you have enough skill, when you get to a trouble spot, you can use that skill to skirt it, which can be dangerous. We didn't know how to do that."[15]

As they wrote, Benton and Newman tried to give themselves a crash course in both film technique and the gangster era. They'd return again and again to the Hitchcock retrospective, listening to what Bogdanovich, who at only twenty-four was about to publish a monograph on the director, had to say about the ways in which his movies were constructed. They would read and reread what Truffaut had written on the difference between creating shock and building suspense. Benton would leave the office to browse through used-magazine and old-book stalls on Sixth Avenue in the lower 40s, sometimes returning with treasures like the 1934 book *Fugitives,* written by Bonnie Parker's mother, Emma Parker, and Clyde Barrow's sister Nell Barrow Cowan, or vintage crime pulp magazines, including a 1945 issue of *Master Detective* that included photographs of Parker and Barrow and a story about how "adventure and bloodshed marked the Law's long pursuit of the Barrows and their murderous molls."[16] And as a touchstone, they kept returning to a sentence about Bonnie and Clyde from *The Dillinger Days:* "Toland wrote, 'They were not just outlaws, they were outcasts,' " says Benton. "That line was what hooked us."[17]

In some ways, Parker and Barrow were natural subjects for a movie. They were young—Barrow was twenty-five and Parker twenty-three when they were killed. They had a great hunger and flair for self-invention and self-promotion, taking photographs in which they posed as hardened out-laws as if they were playing dress-up and sending Bonnie's doggerel about themselves to newspapers. And although Barrow's record stretched back to his teens, their history together—a string of robberies that often led to murder, interspersed with periods in which they lay low—lasted only about a year and a half, ideal for the compressed narrative of a movie. Parts of their crime spree and relationship had already been appropriated for Fritz Lang's 1937 pre-noir drama, *You Only Live Once,* with Henry Fonda and Sylvia Sidney, and 1958's quickly forgotten *The Bonnie Parker Story,* which starred Dorothy Provine, had depicted a peculiar version of their lives that turned Clyde Barrow into "Guy Darrow."

Benton and Newman were interested in all the historical information they could get their hands on, but not in documentary realism. Already, they knew they were going to leave out certain unromantic details: Parker's early marriage to another man, Parker's and Barrow's separate stretches in jail, and the fact that Parker was severely and disfiguringly burned in a car crash almost a year before she and Barrow were killed.[18] Their version of Bonnie and Clyde's story would not be a history lesson, but a drama that entangled crime and passion, comedy and bloodshed. If Benton and Newman even knew of the Production Code's rules that "crimes against the law . . . shall never be presented in such a way as to throw sympathy with the crime," that "theft, robbery . . . etc. should not be detailed in method," and "that throughout, the audience feels sure that evil is wrong and good is right," hewing to those restrictions would have been the fur-thest thing from their minds. And the Code, which still maintained that "seduction . . . should never be more than suggested, and then only when essential" and that "suggestive . . . postures are not to be shown," didn't even have language, other than a general opprobrium on "sex aberration," that could have adequately expressed the futility of their plan to include a sexual ménage à trois (the *Jules and Jim* influence at its most apparent) involving Bonnie, Clyde, and their strapping male getaway driver.[19]

By November 1963, Benton and Newman were putting what they thought were the finishing touches on a seventy-five-page treatment of *Bonnie and Clyde* and, says Benton, "specifically writing it for Truffaut." The constant presence of the director's name in their bull sessions represented a combination of hubris, sky-high optimism, and a sliver of actual hope. Though neither writer was particularly well connected, Benton knew someone who knew someone who knew someone. While attending the University of Texas at Austin in the early 1950s, he had become friends with fellow undergrads Harvey Schmidt, an aspiring composer, and Tom Jones, a writer and lyricist. All three went on to serve in the army and then came to New York, where Schmidt and Benton roomed together and occasionally collaborated at *Esquire* and Schmidt and Jones worked on their first musical. That show, *The Fantasticks*, opened off Broadway in 1960 to mixed reviews but hung on with remarkable tenacity and was now starting the fourth year of its run. Jones's wife, Elinor Wright Jones, had gotten to know and admire Benton; she had even produced a short film he had created called *A Texas Romance 1909*, a chapter of his family history told through the paintings of four illustrators. "Bob called me one day and said, 'David and I want to tell you a story,'" she remembers. Benton and Newman went over to the Joneses' Central Park West apartment, bringing with them their treatment and their yellowed issue of *Master Detective*.[20]

Jones was dazzled by their enthusiasm and by their conviction that a movie based on their screenplay could bring a Nouvelle Vague aesthetic to as American a subject as Dust Bowl bank robbers. At the time, she was working as an assistant to Lewis Allen, a Broadway producer who was trying his hand at low-budget art films (that year, he had produced a movie of Genet's *The Balcony* as well as Peter Brook's adaptation of *Lord of the Flies*), and she was eager to start producing as well. Her younger brother, Norton Wright, then a twenty-eight-year-old production assistant, shared her ambition. "In the early 1960s, low-budget pictures were being made in New York City for $350,000, and some of them were good movies," says Wright, who had learned the ins and outs of working with a tight schedule and minimal budget as a production manager on a number of those films—"indies," before the term was in common use.[21] Wright and his sister shared Benton and Newman's reverence for the French New Wave and had accompanied Benton on some of his return visits to the New Yorker Theater. And the two writers made a good pitching team: "You kind of had the feeling that Benton had the history and the heart of it, and David, who was very funny, was the sparkplug, the live wire," says Wright.[22]

By the end of the meeting, it didn't seem impossible that, if the two would-be producers got the script into the right hands, they could raise the money to make a lean, no-frills, black-and-white version of *Bonnie and Clyde* themselves. And they had a well-placed ally: The Joneses' attorney was the powerful entertainment lawyer Robert Montgomery of the New York firm Paul, Weiss, Rifkind, Wharton & Garrison. Elinor Jones sent Montgomery the treatment for *Bonnie and Clyde* almost immediately. Montgomery agreed to send it to another of his clients, Arthur Penn.[23] Penn got the seventy-five pages, glanced at them, turned it down on the spot, and barely gave *Bonnie and Clyde* another thought for two years.[24]

By 1963, François Truffaut and Arthur Penn were already friendly acquaintances and admirers of each other's work. Early that year, while working on what was to become a seminal book about Hitchcock, Truffaut, whose English was tentative and whose insecurity about it was great, had asked Helen Scott, who worked for the French Film Office in New York, whether Penn might be able to review some of the technical passages in his manuscript to make sure the English translation was accurate.[25] A few months later, Penn had begun to direct *The Train*, a World War II suspense drama for United Artists that starred Burt Lancaster. Lancaster had just made a greater foray into European filmmaking than many of his Hollywood peers by starring in Luchino Visconti's *The Leopard*, a poorly edited and dubbed version of which had opened in the United States and flopped. Lancaster was now interested in making a hit, not in working with a director whose taste for sophisticated European moviemaking might get in the way of success. "He wanted a lot of hoopla and derring-do and I wanted a serious film with an ironic twist," said Penn a couple of years later. "He won."[26] Lancaster clashed with Penn and had him fired, replacing him with John Frankenheimer.[27] In September, Truffaut had dinner with the dejected Penn and his wife in New York and wrote sympathetically about his firing to Helen Scott, dismissing Frankenheimer as "someone Lancaster can manipulate as he pleases."[28] Soon after, when Penn was considering a film adaptation of William Faulkner's *The Wild Palms*, Truffaut recommended his *Jules and Jim* star Jeanne Moreau as a possible lead.

Penn, then forty-one, had cut his teeth on New York City's thriving television production business in the 1950s, working on episodes of *The Philco Television Playhouse* and *Playhouse 90*. His first feature, 1958's compelling revisionist western *The Left Handed Gun*, which starred Paul Newman as Billy the Kid, was an adaptation of a *Philco* one-act on which he'd worked. Penn shot the movie in just twenty-three days, only to have Warner Brothers take it away from him and add an ending he called "terrible. . . . I never heard 'Boo' from Warner Brothers, I never saw a cut, nothing. It got a bad review in *The New York Times* and bing, it was gone."[29] (The film was much more appreciated in Europe, where its maltreatment by a Hollywood studio only helped to burnish its status among critics and directors like Truffaut.)

Penn walked away from the movie business and went home to New York, where he began a robust career as a Broadway director. In less than three years, he mounted five successful shows, including Lillian Hellman's *Toys in the Attic* and the immensely popular *An Evening with Mike Nichols and Elaine May*. One of them, William Gibson's *The Miracle Worker*, became his return ticket to Hollywood. This time, working for a sympathetic producer, fellow TV veteran Fred Coe, and United Artists, a more director-friendly studio than Warner Brothers, Penn was able to make the movie largely on his terms, which included using the Broadway production's original stars, Anne Bancroft and Patty Duke. The result was a critical and commercial success that, in the spring of 1963, won both actresses Academy Awards and Penn a nomination for Best Director.

But Penn's luck soon started running cold again. His demoralizing experience on *The Train* indicated how little Hollywood capital his recent success had won him, and his return to Broadway resulted in two plays that ran for a combined total of eight performances after they opened. When the *Bonnie and Clyde* treatment landed on his desk, he says, he was trying to figure out what to do next, and "I was caught up in so many other projects, I just didn't take it seriously. I was sent that movie, but it was not 'that movie.' Yet."[30]

The rejection from Penn came so quickly that Benton and Newman may not even have known he saw their work in the first place. In any case, Elinor Jones wasted no time in trying to get a copy of the treatment to the director whom they had had in mind all along. This time, she used a different connection—her boss.[31] Lewis Allen and Truffaut already had a mutual friend in Helen Scott, a New York–born, Paris-raised former journalist and onetime Communist organizer whose remarkable résumé included everything from working as press attaché to the lead American prosecutor at Nuremberg to publicizing French films in New York.[32] Allen and Truffaut also had a mutual interest: Both men wanted to make a movie out of Ray Bradbury's dystopian book-burning novel, *Fahrenheit 451*, which Truffaut had already spent more than three years planning as his first movie in English.

Allen was preparing for a trip to France in a couple of weeks to discuss the Bradbury project with Truffaut. Before he left, Jones asked him to bring the director the *Bonnie and Clyde* treatment and asked Scott if she would set the table for its arrival. Scott agreed and wrote to Truffaut, "You know my embarrassment about these things, but I read it last evening and to my surprise—and for the first time—I was extremely excited. It has every evidence of being excellent. The scenario is created for you. . . . It's about Bonnie and Clyde—an authentic pair of young bandits who lived during the 1930s in Texas—the same period and locale as John Steinbeck's *Grapes of Wrath*. . . . May seem banal but for this ironic treatment. . . . At first I thought it was too American for you—but there are a thousand nuances that make it something special." Scott urged Truffaut to have his wife, Madeleine Morgenstern, read Benton and Newman's treatment and find someone to translate it into French for him.[33]

Allen, who was preoccupied with *Fahrenheit 451*, either forgot to bring the treatment with him or never showed it to Truffaut, but Scott's letter piqued Truffaut's interest, even though his only knowledge of Parker and Barrow came from a comic strip called *Un Ménage de Gangsters*[34] that he had seen in a newspaper a year earlier. "Allen didn't say a word about the script you described to me, *Clyde Barrow*," Truffaut wrote to Scott just before Christmas, "but I managed to get some *France Soir* comic strips on the subject, very interesting. Now there would be an interesting part for Jane Fonda. . . . Maybe. . . ."[35]

Elinor Jones mailed him the treatment without delay. Truffaut showed it to friends and colleagues and then asked Claudine Bouché, his editor on *Jules and Jim,* to prepare a translation. In early January 1964, the director wrote back to Scott, "I've had *Clyde and Bonnie* read by two or three friends here; everyone is enthusiastic and assures me I should make the film."[36] Truffaut himself hadn't read a word Benton and Newman had written—and if he had, he would have seen that the story whose title he still couldn't get quite right looked nothing like a filmable screenplay. But Benton and Newman believed that the movies coming out of France were so fresh in part because they were made without stultifying overpreparation. Maybe, they thought, making *Bonnie and Clyde* really was going to be as simple as getting their dream director to say yes.

TWO

At about the moment when Benton and Newman's treatment of *Bonnie and Clyde* was being sent to Arthur Penn, Warren Beatty was sitting in the living room of Stanley Kubrick's apartment on Central Park West, trying to convince Kubrick to direct his next movie. It was a meeting that Beatty would later recall only as a footnote, an answer to the question "Where were you when you heard that President Kennedy was shot?"[1] But on the morning of November 22, 1963, hours before the news broke, Kennedy wouldn't have been on Beatty's mind at all, except perhaps as a role that he'd recently turned down, in *PT 109*.

Beatty was used to turning things down. He was a movie star, a position at which he had arrived a couple of years earlier with almost no intermediate steps. There were no stories of protracted struggle, no doors slamming in his face, no dark nights of the soul. He had done a little work in television, gotten a recurring role on the situation comedy *The Many Loves of Dobie Gillis*, appeared in one Broadway play, and then signed for his first movie, starring opposite Natalie Wood in Elia Kazan's *Splendor in the Grass*. When Warner Brothers opened *Splendor* in 1961, Hollywood had not successfully launched a new young leading man in several years; the most recent of them to arrive on screen, Marlon Brando, Paul Newman, and Montgomery Clift, were all a dozen or more years older than Beatty, and although a new group of actors almost exactly Beatty's age—Robert Redford, Al Pacino, Jack Nicholson, Dustin Hoffman, Burt Reynolds—would become central to the movie business a decade later, none of them were remotely on the map yet. Beatty, just twenty-two when he was cast in *Splendor,* had a head start on the rest of his generation. Thanks to both his own magnetism on screen and a publicity and representation team that had worked shrewdly on his behalf, after the film's success the field was his for the taking.

In *Splendor in the Grass,* Beatty played a small-town high school star athlete so virile, tender, and handsome that Wood's character is literally driven mad by her desire for him. The movie had gone further than any film of the 1950s in presenting a male lead explicitly as an object of lust—Kazan hadn't even eroticized Brando as completely in *A Streetcar Named Desire* ten years earlier. Beatty was smart and observant enough to know that the adulation that followed was an opportunity that could easily turn into a booby trap. After *Splendor* opened, "I remember walking out of the Delmonico Hotel, and some teenage girls were leaning on my car looking at me, and one of them said, 'Oh my God, you're Warren Beatty! God, you're . . . nothing!' I thought, now I'm *her* size. When you were fifty times bigger than the person who was looking at you, you had an advantage."[2]

Beatty did what he could to stay larger than life. He conducted his romances with casual exuberance and serial enthusiasm but planned each professional move with hesitation, deliberation, and strategy. He was attracted to young, beautiful women for what he understatedly called "social fun"[3] and to older men—to writers, directors, and producers whose careers he admired—for work. Beatty had "a vision for himself," said Jane Fonda, who, just beginning to act and still uncertain of her own path and abilities, had lost the female lead in *Splendor* to Natalie Wood. "Very early on he made a list of the directors he would work with . . . it was just the existence of the list that fascinated me more than the names on it."[4]

"If I had any lists, they were lists of people that MCA [Music Corporation of America], who was my agent, were not aware of," says Beatty. "The movies that were really attracting the attention of people who were kind of smart were those of the Nouvelle Vague and the neorealists and all those guys in Woodfall* in London: Karel Reisz and Lindsay Anderson, Tony Richardson. Looking back, I realize how little I knew about movies then. But I did get interested. And it didn't take a Nobel Prize mentality to know that George Stevens or Kazan or Zinnemann or Wyler or Wilder or Lean or Fellini or Visconti or Bergman or Antonioni or Truffaut or Godard or Resnais were people to learn from."⁵

Beatty's aptitude for putting himself next to talent had paid off well initially. After he won a Tony nomination for his first and only appearance on Broadway, in William Inge's 1959 play, *A Loss of Roses*, Inge created the role of *Splendor*'s Bud Stamper for him, and Beatty put himself in Kazan's hands as willingly as any young actor in Hollywood who wanted to be taken seriously would have done. "I'm a bit scared and worried," he told *The New York Times* while filming *Splendor*, "but I'd try anything involving Bill and Gadge."⁶ By the time he arrived in Hollywood, Beatty had already done everything right. His press agent, John Springer, worked for Arthur P. Jacobs's company, one of the most important publicity firms of its time. His career was being guided by Hollywood's biggest talent agency. He met the right people at the right parties; one evening, when Rita Hayworth spotted him from the dance floor, she introduced him to her dancing partner, Clifford Odets, who in turn introduced him to Jean Renoir. And Beatty knew what he still needed to learn; he worked to steep himself in film history at a time when doing so meant using whatever connections he had to obtain undamaged 16-millimeter prints of Renoir's *Grand Illusion* and *Rules of the Game* so he could watch and rewatch them. "I thought they were the best movies I'd ever seen," he says.⁷

All of which made it even more puzzling that since *Splendor in the Grass*, almost nothing had gone as Beatty had hoped it would. By the time *Splendor* opened, he may already have had an inkling that he was about to stumble. His next two movies, *The Roman Spring of Mrs. Stone* (like *Splendor*, for Warner Brothers) and *All Fall Down* (for MGM), were already in the can, and neither one was particularly promising. The movies

---

*Woodfall was a British production company founded by Tony Richardson and John Osborne; between 1958 and 1963, it produced *Look Back in Anger, The Entertainer, Saturday Night and Sunday Morning, A Taste of Honey, The Loneliness of the Long Distance Runner,* and *Tom Jones.*

fulfilled contractual obligations—Beatty had signed a deal with MGM and turned down many movies the studio suggested before *All Fall Down*[8]— but they also represented the potential peril of gravitating toward theater-based talent rather than good material or strong roles. Beatty had courted Tennessee Williams for the chance to star opposite Vivien Leigh in *Roman Spring*, but the part, a callow, immoral gigolo, was poorly written and a less than ideal match for an actor who wanted the world to take him seriously despite an off-screen public image as a pretty boy and a hypereligible bachelor. *All Fall Down* gave him the chance to work with Inge again, as well as with New York–trained director John Frankenheimer, producer John Houseman, and Kazan-approved actors like Karl Malden and Eva Marie Saint. But the film itself turned out to be a sour variation on Inge's family dysfunction stage dramas of the 1950s, and Beatty's role, a sullen, womanizing rebel, was underwritten and unappealing. Neither movie did anything for Beatty's career or his standing in Hollywood.

For the rising star Frankenheimer, *All Fall Down* turned out to be a minor speed bump in 1962, a year that also brought the releases of his acclaimed *Birdman of Alcatraz* and *The Manchurian Candidate*. But Beatty seemed to take the experience as a warning: He didn't make another movie for sixteen months.[9] Part of the delay, he says, was due to the tireless pursuits that made him a gossip magazine mainstay: "There was an awful lot of fun to be had, and you kind of hate to think you're missing out on real life to put something on celluloid."[10] But Beatty was also learning to proceed with caution.

When he finally did decide to take a new role, it was, once again, in a project on which the roster of talent was far more impressive than the script. The film was *Lilith*, a Columbia Pictures drama about a sensitive young man who takes a job in a home for the mentally ill and falls under the spell of a disturbed young woman (Jean Seberg). In the movie's favor was a subject that, at the time, excited great curiosity in moviegoers (*David and Lisa*, with a similar theme, had been an out-of-left-field success in 1962) and a writer-director, Robert Rossen, who had made one of the best American movies of the last couple of years, 1961's poolroom drama *The Hustler*. But Beatty proved to be a bad match with Rossen, a troubled man who had been shattered by both sides of the Hollywood blacklist,

first refusing to name any names and then, after two years of unemployment, naming dozens.[11] By the time he made *Lilith,* Rossen was ill, and
ill-tempered, and Beatty bridled at his unwillingness or inability to talk
through nuances of the script and the role.[12]

Beatty's work on *Lilith* was an unhappy experience, and in the mess
of a film that resulted, which mixes some early-1960s experimentation
(double-image cinematography, expressionistic sound) with old-fashioned
and tedious Freudianism, the misery showed in his performance. For the
first time, Beatty appeared to be almost deliberately withholding and re-
tentive. By the time of *Lilith's* production, the actor was starting to acquire a clouded reputation in Hollywood. He was known to be obstinate,
overly painstaking, and sometimes argumentative on sets. His indecision
had angered at least one powerful studio chief, Jack Warner, when he
had waffled on an agreement to star in an adaptation of Herman Wouk's
Youngblood Hawke well into preproduction early in 1963[13] and resisted
Warner's strong-arming attempt to put him in *PT 109.*[14] And he was, to
the distress of his own management team, a profoundly unenthusiastic
interview subject.[15] *Lilith* would turn out to mark the moment when critics
collectively soured on him and used his performance to announce their
general exhaustion with Brandoesque Method mumbling. The reviewer
for *Variety,* the movie industry trade paper whose telegraphically written
notices generally expressed enthusiasm for any film that had good box office potential and reserved distaste only for the obscure, wrote, "Warren
Beatty undertakes lead role with a hesitation jarring to the watcher . . .
often the audience waits uncomfortably for words which never come while
Beatty merely hangs his head or stares into space." The review ominously
predicted that theaters would be reluctant to book the film at all.[16] And
Bosley Crowther, the aging but still influential lead movie critic for *The
New York Times,* who had not liked Beatty even in *Splendor in the Grass,*
called his work "muddy" and "monotonous."[17]

Lilith's poor reception was still almost a year away when Beatty paid
Stanley Kubrick a visit, but the shoot was already over, and Beatty wasn't
harboring any hopes that the poky, obscure film would turn his fortunes
around. After government antitrust laws forced MCA to drop its agency
business in 1962, Beatty decided to try a new approach: He would develop

his own material and try to handpick collaborators along the way. Decades before every actor in Hollywood had his own production company, Beatty's determination to take a hand in the architecture of his own career at a very young age was met by more than a few smirks, but he had little to lose by trying. Kubrick's new film, *Dr. Strangelove or: How I Learned to Stop Worrying and Love the Bomb,* wasn't due to open for two more months—some in Hollywood still couldn't believe that Columbia's black comedy, which went leagues further than any prior studio movie in its near nihilistic savaging of cold war politics, would open at all. But Beatty had been awed by an early screening, and the film's thirty-five-year-old director was now on his list.[18]

The movie Beatty wanted Kubrick to direct was *What's New, Pussycat?,* a comic take on sexual liberation and psychotherapy that Beatty's friend and mentor, the talent agent Charles K. Feldman, had been trying to produce for ten years. After four dark-spirited movies in a row, Beatty was aching for a change of pace, a broadening of his range, and an image tweak. "I wanted to play somebody who was *not* a neurotic, sensitive type," he says. "I thought the whole idea of sex and psychoanalysis was funny"—all the more after *Lilith*'s humorless take on the same subject—"and I wanted to play a compulsive Don Juan." The project had its earliest origins in *Lot's Wife,* an old script by a Hungarian playwright that Feldman had initially hired Billy Wilder's writing partner, I. A. L. Diamond, to overhaul. Beatty had since worked on the idea and made it his own, starting with the title, which was said to be one of the actor's signature off-camera come-ons, and he had handpicked a new writer, Woody Allen, after seeing him do a stand-up comedy routine. "I thought he was funny as hell, and I said, 'Charlie, let's get this guy.' Charlie was willing to spend $30,000. Woody wanted $40,000. I said to Charlie, 'Well, I'll pay him the extra ten, cheapskate,' and Charlie said, 'No, no, no, I'll pay him,' and then Woody said, 'I'll do it if I can be in the movie, in a little part.'" After that, with rewrites progressing nicely, Beatty started shopping for a director. At first, he talked to another comic performer, Mike Nichols, who was considering making his first foray into directing. "I wanted a guy who'd never done a movie," says Beatty. But Nichols, at that moment, had his eye on theater, not film, so they both moved on.[19]

Beatty was as skilled at courtship professionally as he was personally; alluring phrases like "It has to be you" and "You have to save this project" could work wonders when spoken by someone who could turn on ardor and charisma as effectively as he did. But Kubrick, not one to say yes precipitously, wasn't susceptible to charm—and he wasn't interested in directing *What's New, Pussycat?* The meeting ended pleasantly but inconclusively; a few minutes later, all thoughts of it were swept away by the day's news.[20]

As 1963 drew to a close, Beatty wasn't feeling a great deal of urgency about getting *Pussycat* into production. He felt as charged with excitement about the French New Wave as everyone else and had already committed himself to his next film,[21] a low-budget, black-and-white absurdist comedy-drama that would pay direct homage to the French style, entitled *Mickey One.* Once again—as he had done with Kazan and *Roman Spring*'s José Quintero—he would be working with a New York theater director: Arthur Penn. And after *Mickey One,* if *What's New, Pussycat?* still wasn't ready, there were other possibilities. Beatty had never bought a property to develop for himself before, but Inge had been urging him to read a first novel by a twenty-four-year-old writer that had just been published[22] and had a perfect part for him, comic, sexy, contemporary, and within his age range. The book was *The Graduate.*

Although it sounds unlikely, the protagonist of Charles Webb's novel appeared, on the page, to be tailor-made for Beatty. In *The Graduate,* Benjamin Braddock is the scion of an apparently WASPy family, a cocky, aloof college track star who returns home for the summer before beginning two years of graduate school, then announces to his parents that he has wasted his life, that he is sick of being their "goddamn ivy-covered status symbol," and that he is taking to the road; early in the narrative, he spends three weeks hitchhiking and fighting forest fires in northern California.[23] Beatty himself was the product of a Virginia Baptist upbringing, he had been raised to behave like a southern gentleman, and in high school he had been both a football star and senior class president before going on to spend a year at Northwestern University.[24] And he knew his way around alienated characters, perhaps too well. *The Graduate*, as written, made sense for him.

But somebody else also thought Webb's novel would make a good movie and moved swiftly to obtain the rights. Lawrence Turman first heard about *The Graduate* when he read Orville Prescott's mixed but appreciative review in *The New York Times* in October.[25] Prescott faulted the novel's "preposterous climax," in which Benjamin succeeds in getting to the church just in time to stop Elaine Robinson's wedding to another man, and he complained that the book "raises questions about the psychological motivation of its hero and makes no effort to answer them." Nonetheless, he wrote, the "sardonic comedy about the mysterious malaise that afflicts the spirits of some of the most intelligent of modern young people is written with exceptional skill. . . . He has created a character whose blunders and follies might just become as widely discussed as those of J. D. Salinger's Holden Caulfield."[26]

The Graduate was published by New American Library, a relatively new house under the editorial direction of David Brown, a former executive in 20th Century-Fox's New York offices who would return to the studio a couple of years later. Webb's novel represented an experiment for the publishing company, one of two books it was using to test the marketplace for hardcovers rather than the paperbacks that had been its specialty (the other was Ian Fleming's James Bond novel *On Her Majesty's Secret Service*, a minor gamble itself since the 007 movie franchise was not yet established in the United States).[27] But despite Prescott's warm (if qualified) endorsement of *The Graduate*, the book made little impact and quickly drowned in a sea of first-time literary fiction.

Its failure was no surprise. Webb's book arrived at an awkward moment for novels of its kind. *The Graduate* unfolds in a cool-temperatured, deadpan prose style that would likely have turned off any reader looking for an heir to the slangy, personalized voice of Holden Caulfield. Prescott's comparison to *Catcher in the Rye* notwithstanding, the book was a latecomer to the genre of adolescent and postadolescent anomie and a bit too early to be part of the shift from stories of individual alienation that flourished in the 1950s to novels in which alienation was used as the touchstone of an entire generation later in the 1960s. While not autobiographical, Webb's

novel clearly owed a strong debt to a wrenching episode in his life that
took place in 1960, when he was barely out of his teens and in his junior
year at Williams College. He had fallen in love with a Bennington sophomore named Eve Rudd. Rudd got pregnant, and she and Webb became
engaged; when her parents found out, they pulled her out of school and
she had an abortion. In the wake of his split from Rudd (whom he eventually married), he began his novel.[28]

Like his protagonist, Benjamin, Webb was a top student (the novel's
"Halpingham Award" was based on a prize for creativity that Williams
awarded Webb in his senior year), and like Benjamin, he was mired in
a sense of cultural, geographic, and emotional dislocation; once he had
finished at Williams, he moved to Brooklyn Heights, started and then
abandoned a novel, then moved to the West Coast and began *The Graduate* as a short story one morning in the Pasadena Public Library. Webb
wrote a first draft of the book while living in Berkeley, then moved back to
Cambridge, where he finished it.[29] Webb says he was inspired by the writing of Hemingway, Fitzgerald, and Katherine Anne Porter, and while
"J. D. Salinger did strike a particular chord, [it was] the stories, oddly,
more than *Catcher,* for some reason."[30]

The Graduate is told almost entirely in long passages of dialogue, with
no physical descriptions of the characters, no omniscient explorations of
states of mind, and only the barest, most unadorned language ("Two days
after he got home from the trip Benjamin decided to begin his affair with
Mrs. Robinson")[31] used to describe thought or action. Webb says he later
realized that the "particular style used in *The Graduate* . . . represented
the misdirection of an innate playwriting talent"[32] rather than an inherently novelistic approach.

Larry Turman, though, found the book haunting and droll, and he
thought the spare, dialogue-driven storytelling made it perfectly suited to
adaptation for the movies.[33] Turman was a latecomer to the business; he
had worked in his father's fabric company until he was twenty-seven, when
he left to make a new professional start on the bottom rung, working for
$50 a week at the Kurt Frings agency in New York. A decade later, he had
become a rising producer who, working with his partner, Stuart Millar,
had already made four films, including the Judy Garland vehicle *I Could*

Go On Singing and an upcoming adaptation of Gore Vidal's play *The Best Man*.[34] Now, he was ready to split with Millar and start producing by himself, albeit on a shoestring. *The Graduate*, which had sold only about five thousand copies, wasn't an expensive property, but Turman didn't have a lot of cash on hand. He swallowed hard and paid David Brown $1,000 out of his own pocket to option it, with an agreement that he would pay $20,000 if he decided to purchase the novel outright. Casting Beatty, or anyone else, as Benjamin Braddock, never crossed his mind: He would worry about actors later. First, he needed a screenwriter who could work quickly and cheaply and a director whose name could turn *The Graduate* into an attractive enough package to secure a studio deal and the financing that came with it.[35]

Turman didn't have immediate luck finding a writer, especially with the money he was offering. Having Webb adapt his own novel wasn't an option, since the young man was already ambivalent about his profession. "I wanted during my growing up to be an actor very badly," he said later, "and it was very painfully that I put this dream aside and took up writing, which in one sense was a second choice frustration for me."[36] Turman sent the novel to William Goldman, who was then a novelist, not yet a screenwriter; Goldman wasn't interested.[37] So, like many producers looking for low-cost writing talent, he turned to off-Broadway theater. A year earlier, Turman had seen a pair of one-acts at New York's Cherry Lane Theatre by a writer named William Hanley. "This guy came to me, Lawrence Turman. He said, 'I have this book and I'd like you to write the screenplay, and I've got $500 to pay you,'" says Hanley. "And I took it."[38]

In December 1963, another, much more high-profile pursuit of literary rights was also under way in New York; the quarry was Hugh Lofting's series of *Doctor Dolittle* books. Lofting's first novel about the extraordinary veterinarian of Puddleby-on-the-Marsh, *The Story of Doctor Dolittle*, had been published in 1920 to instant success; the author, a British civil engineer and World War I veteran who moved permanently to the United States with his first wife and children after serving in the Irish Guards, wrote a dozen Dolittle books before his death in 1947.[39] The rights to all of them were now in the hands of his widow, Josephine, who relied on her instincts, her twenty-seven-year-old son, Christopher Lofting, and her lawyer, Bernard Silbert, whenever a prospective buyer came calling.

The Dolittle books, with their plethora of animals and fantastical plots (including, in later installments, an extended trip to the moon), represented both ideal properties for children's movies and potentially insurmountable challenges for filmmakers. But other than a long-forgotten cartoon short made in Germany during the silent era, Dolittle had never reached the screen. The Fox Film Company, one of the two studios that eventually merged into 20th Century-Fox, had made Hugh Lofting an offer back in 1922. But in the decades after that, Lofting's primary suitor was Walt Disney.

"Disney tried to get hold of it for years," says Christopher Lofting, "but the cheap bastard wouldn't pay anything for it! Disney specialized in public domain properties—Snow White, Sleeping Beauty—that they didn't have to pay for. The Disney company offered a contract to my father back in 1940 or 1941, supposedly for a movie, but they were asking him to surrender everything: merchandising, television, which was in the contract even though it didn't really exist yet, and rights to everything that he had ever written and *would* ever write, for a flat fee of $7,500. My father's final line to them was, I only have one question—I have a four-year-old son and I wonder why Mr. Disney doesn't want him, too. What's wrong with him?"[40]

As Christopher Lofting grew up, the proposals to his father's estate kept coming. "I would say there was a serious offer every two to four months through the 1950s and early 1960s," he recalls. "They circled and circled. And we'd always say, 'How are you going to handle the animals?' And then it would collapse over creative issues."

In 1960, Josephine Lofting, on Silbert's advice, granted a short-term option on the books to Helen Winston, a former actress and neophyte producer who planned to commission a script for a live-action Dolittle movie and then shop it to studios. By 1962, Winston had a completed screenplay by a writer named Larry Watkin[41] but still found no takers for what was guaranteed to be an expensive production, given its fanciful nineteenth-century setting and the complexities inherent in working with a large cast of animals. "She had a lot of bad luck," says Lofting. "We kept extending and extending her option, but finally we had to say, 'Look, if you come up with a deal, fine, but you no longer have an exclusive option.'"

The Lofting family's decision to field other offers opened a window of opportunity for a far savvier and more competitive player. Arthur P. Jacobs—"Apjac" to his friends, colleagues, and clients—was, at forty-one, a pale, roly-poly, chronically tense, hyperactive chain-smoker, "a perfect cardiac profile," recalls Lofting. He had also, until recently, run one of the most successful public relations firms in the business, overseeing a bi-coastal self-titled company and a staff that served not just as publicists, but as career shapers, advisers, image makers, and crisis managers for Beatty, Otto Preminger, Marilyn Monroe, Judy Garland, and countless others.

With his motormouth, his stubby brown cigarillos, a bottle of Fresca always glued to his hand, and a set of omnipresent color-coded rectangular note cards on which he would jot down ideas, notes from meetings, phone numbers, and to-do lists (he even kept them in his bathroom),[42] Jacobs was easy to spoof as the picture of a Sammy Glick–style Hollywood hustler, but the man underneath all the perpetual motion was widely liked, funny, friendly, and very good at his job. In 1962, he had gotten out of the PR business and set his sights on becoming a producer. By the end of 1963, he had completed his first movie for 20th Century-Fox, *What a Way to Go!* The comedy was, in a way, a publicist's vision of what a studio motion picture should be—a big, colorful gift box the contents of which didn't matter as long as the wrapping looked fantastic. Jacobs had used his industry-wide connections and long client list to pull together a cast of big (if somewhat oddly matched) names—Shirley MacLaine, Paul Newman, Robert Mitchum, Dean Martin, Gene Kelly, TV stars Bob Cummings and Dick Van Dyke, even the venerable Margaret Dumont—for a movie that was little more than an extended series of blackout sketches about a hapless young woman (played by MacLaine) whose husbands keep dying on her. The film was extremely expensive, and even by generous assessments uneven in quality, but Jacobs had done at least part of a producer's job: The money was all up on the screen. Now, five months before *What a Way to Go!* opened, he was trying to line up his next project before any word of mouth on the last one could slow his momentum.

Jacobs first heard that the rights to *Doctor Dolittle* might be available on December 5, 1963. Six days later, he met with Silbert in New York, pitched the attorney the idea of doing the film as a musical, and dangled two names in front of him: writer-lyricist Alan Jay Lerner and Rex Harrison. By Christmas, Jacobs had met with Josephine Lofting,[43] and she and Silbert had agreed to give him an option without asking for a single dollar up front, on one condition. They were no longer willing to wait for a movie that never seemed to materialize. "Bernie Silbert said, 'You're not getting two years—you have six months,' " says Christopher Lofting. " 'If you don't have a deal [with a studio] by then, you're toast.' "[44]

Time pressure didn't intimidate Jacobs, whose years in publicity had taught him that sometimes the way to solve a problem was to move so quickly that everyone was on board before there was time for a second thought. That strategy allowed him to overcome the first of many hurdles he would face over the next four years: the fact that neither Lerner nor Harrison had committed himself to *Doctor Dolittle*, or even knew about it, at the time he floated their names to Silbert.[45] Jacobs gambled that the main lure of the project for each man would be the chance to work with the other again. Lerner was already a major force in both musical theater and Hollywood (he had won three Academy Awards, one for *An American in Paris* and two for *Gigi*), and Harrison was a well-respected stage actor who had finally broken through to stardom with Lerner and Loewe's *My Fair Lady*, which had run on Broadway for six and a half years and proved to be the biggest hit either Lerner or Harrison had ever had. The show's success had convinced Jack Warner to pay $5.5 million for the movie rights,[46] and expectations were high for the movie, which had just finished shooting and was due to open in 1964.

Lerner was the first to be approached,[47] and he said yes to *Doctor Dolittle* with a swiftness that Jacobs might have taken as a warning sign had he been more aware of the writer's volatility and propensity for over-enthusiastic commitment (Lerner was, at the time, battling through his fourth of eight marriages). Jacobs made a deal to co-produce the film with Lerner's company, and, acting as his own publicist, promptly planted an item in *The New York Times* announcing the movie, Lerner's participation, and a budget, apparently completely fictional, of $6 million on January 6, 1964.[48]

One week later, Jacobs met with Rex Harrison, who had arrived in New York City and was staying at the Colony Hotel.[49] Jacobs had plenty of experience dealing with the narcissism, ego, and insecurity of aging stars, and Harrison, not an easy man under the best of circumstances, was at a delicate moment in his career. His most recent movie, 20th Century-Fox's *Cleopatra,* had opened six months earlier, and although it was widely regarded as a creative debacle, Harrison, almost alone in the cast, had escaped with his reputation intact. And although the movie version of *My Fair Lady* was regarded in the industry as an almost sure thing, Harrison had not won the right to reprise his stage role as Professor Henry Higgins without enduring a serious measure of humiliation from Warner Brothers. The fifty-five-year-old actor had to sit by and wait, fuming, while Jack Warner pursued a fresher face, *Lawrence of Arabia*'s thirty-year-old Peter O'Toole, for the role. Harrison's feelings were understandably hurt, especially since he knew that Warner had earlier wooed Cary Grant, who was fifty-nine, to play Higgins: "I had heard that the film moguls were saying, 'Rex looks old,' " he wrote in his autobiography.[50] When negotiations with O'Toole finally fell apart, Harrison had to take a salary of $200,000 while his costar, Audrey Hepburn, got $1 million.[51] The experience left the actor bruised and paranoid.

Harrison could be explosive, impatient, capricious, and vain, but also charming, apologetic, and compliant, sometimes within the same conversation or at different points during the same stiff drink. That day at the Colony, the actor was apparently at his most amiable. Hearing that Lerner was involved, he agreed to do the picture on the spot. It was January 14, 1964.[52] Just five weeks after making his first inquiries, Jacobs now had a star, a writer, and enough publicity to make his rival for the material, Helen Winston, realize that she had been trumped. Now all he needed was a composer, a director, a leading lady, and a studio willing to foot a bill of $6 million, give or take. He had five months left.

THREE

rançois Truffaut was, it turned out, serious about *Bonnie and Clyde*. At least he seemed to be. Nobody knew if he really meant to make the movie. He was impetuous, his moods changed quickly, his marriage was disintegrating; push him too hard, and all would be lost. Truffaut had effectively taken the reins of the project the minute he received the treatment, well before it was even translated for him. "Please explain to me your precise relations with the writers of the script," he had written to Helen Scott in January. "Are they themselves the screenwriters or is there someone else? Did they offer it to anyone else? Do they want to sell it to a producer? Were they commissioned to write it? Was it their own idea to offer it to me?" Truffaut was already thinking about how the movie could be made—"It's such a simple and inexpensive film to shoot that I could [produce] it myself," he wrote—and about where to get the money to do it: He wanted to work with United Artists,[1] which at the time was alone among the major studios in offering great freedom to independent producers and directors to shape projects without taking away the right of final cut or forcing on them a studio house style, a crew, or contract players.

Simply by being the person on whom everybody else's hopes were hanging, Truffaut, with his take-charge tone and fusillade of questions, immediately became the de facto engine of *Bonnie and Clyde*; without having read a word of it, he was now the boss. Benton and Newman were exhilarated by the mere possibility of his involvement and did a couple of readings of their treatment for friends. "One of the people who came was a girl I was trying to get into bed with at the time," says Benton, "and I did, so I knew it was a good script!"[2] And they started mapping out their own idea for what the movie would be, earmarking the Flatt and Scruggs music they had played while writing as a perfect idea for the score of the film itself and fixing on Timothy Carey, a stone-faced character actor with a cult following from a couple of early Kubrick movies, to play Frank Hamer, the ex–Texas Ranger who tracked Bonnie and Clyde relentlessly in 1934.[3] But Truffaut wasn't ready to talk to Benton or Newman at all in January, much less to discuss ideas that specific.

In New York, Elinor Jones took steps to formalize her and her brother's role as producers. In February, she had Robert Montgomery start to draft a contract that would give them an eighteen-month option on *Bonnie and Clyde*.[4] Truffaut, unclear about whether Jones or her boss, Lewis Allen, was attached to the script, learned of Jones's involvement from Helen Scott and cautioned Scott, whom he was using as a go-between, not to overstate his commitment to the film, for which he still didn't have a completed French translation. "I won't speak to you about *Bonnie and Clyde* until I've read the script," he wrote on February 22. "Then I'll send a detailed note to the writers . . . in case they start taking it in another direction from the one I want; unless I'm disappointed by it and decide not to do the project."[5]

When Truffaut finally got his hands on a translation, he was interested enough to make time for Benton and Newman on his upcoming trip to New York. He had several reasons for coming to the United States: He wanted to continue researching his book on Hitchcock, he needed to meet with Allen about the still gestating *Fahrenheit 451*, and he was planning a side trip to Chicago to visit his friend Arthur Penn, who was there shooting *Mickey One* with Warren Beatty and Alexandra Stewart, a young French Canadian actress who was an intimate friend of Truffaut's.

Truffaut arrived in New York on March 26, 1964. Meeting Elinor Jones, he played it cool—"*Pas mal*," he murmured when he walked into the Joneses' eighteenth-floor apartment and saw their spectacular view of Central Park.[6] But with Benton and Newman, he was more openly enthusiastic and offered his time and advice in a way that profoundly affected the direction they took in turning *Bonnie and Clyde* from a treatment into a screenplay.

Truffaut invited "the boys," as he called them, to his hotel room, where, with Helen Scott translating and Elinor Jones taking notes, he spent two or three days working with them in a combination brainstorming session/tutorial. He had brought with him line-by-line suggestions. Taking each scene in order, he walked through the treatment with Benton and Newman and gave them a marathon seminar in writing for the movies. Some of his notes were technical: He recommended high-angle shots on Bonnie and Clyde's car for some of the getaway driving scenes.[7] Some were dramaturgic: He found places to add humor and sensuality, raising the stakes in a scene in which Bonnie and Clyde take Hamer hostage and humiliate him by having Bonnie force a kiss on him. "Truffaut said, 'It's got to be more than just catching a criminal—there's got to be a sexual aspect to it,'" says Elinor Jones. And some of his ideas were so fully thought through that it became clear he was already shooting and editing at least some sequences from the treatment in his head. His suggestion to cut from Bonnie scribbling out her self-aggrandizing poem for the newspapers to the newspaper itself in the hands of a Texas Ranger, then back to Clyde reading the paper delightedly to Bonnie, made it into the finished film virtually intact.[8]

Truffaut found the issue of historical accuracy even less compelling than Benton and Newman did. Before arriving in New York, Truffaut had broken their seventy-five pages into "what he called 'unities,' i.e., blocks of the film which stood as [separate] emotional and dramatic entities," Benton and Newman wrote later. "He demonstrated to us the difference between 'real time' and 'film time,' pointing out where we had goofed . . . in sacrificing the emotional curves of the film for factual or actual purposes."[9] Events could be elided or skipped, he told them; they were necessary sacrifices to the style that would define the movie.

That was exactly what Benton and Newman wanted to hear. Their original treatment had gone to Truffaut with a prefatory note of several pages from them, intended largely to provide historical context about Parker and Barrow to a director who might not have heard much about them. But it also contained an explicit announcement of the film's ideological intent: "Bonnie and Clyde were out of their time in the 30s," they wrote. "If Bonnie and Clyde were here today, they would be hip. Their values have become assimilated in much of our culture—not robbing banks and killing people, of course, but their style, their sexuality, their bravado, their delicacy, their cultivated arrogance, their narcissistic insecurity, their curious ambition have relevance to the way we live now. Of course, what makes them beautiful is they didn't know it. . . . They are not Crooks," the introduction finished with a flourish that Benton and Newman themselves later called pompous.[10] "They are people, and this film is, in many ways, about what's going on now."[11]

Truffaut got the point and helped the young writers move past the didacticism to which that statement of principle could have led and toward a kind of storytelling in which their concerns could be integrated organically. Though he was only a few months older than Benton, he proved to be a generous teacher, and Benton and Newman, elated to be in the presence of one of their idols, absorbed everything he had to say. Truffaut also let them know that, as much as they thought their idea was indebted to the French, they needed to look deeper into film history, particularly at some of the neglected American crime dramas that had inspired the directors of the Nouvelle Vague in the first place. While in New York, Truffaut arranged a screening of Joseph H. Lewis's *Gun Crazy*, a superbly unsettling B picture from 1949 about a thrill-seeking, amoral young couple (John Dall and Peggy Cummins) on a crime spree. The movie prefigures *Bonnie and Clyde* in several ways: its suggestion that the couple's criminal life begins almost as a game, its skillful depiction of violence and gunplay as a means of sexual excitement, and even the stylish beret that Peggy Cummins's remorseless Annie Starr wears cocked to one side. Truffaut watched the movie with Benton and Newman and also invited his friend Jean-Luc Godard, who sat in the front row with his wife, actress Anna Karina. "The boys" could scarcely keep their eyes on the screen. "I thought, this is the closest to heaven that I've ever gotten in my life," says Benton.[12]

What was going through Truffaut's mind at that moment is harder to discern; there's no knowing whether his decision to invite Godard to the screening was a gesture to a friend or something else—an attempt to find his own potential replacement. At the end of his week with Benton and Newman, Truffaut gave them marching orders to spend the next two or three months working on the *Bonnie and Clyde* screenplay[13] and was enthusiastic enough about its possibilities to mention to Marcel Berbert, a production manager, that he thought the script could be "terrific" and might even "substitute" for *Fahrenheit 451* on his schedule.[14] At the same time, he made it clear to Benton and Newman that *Fahrenheit,* the project he had long wanted to be his English-language debut, was his priority and that if financing and a cast came together for that movie, he could make no commitment to *Bonnie and Clyde.*[15]

That spring, both Truffaut and Godard flew to Chicago to see what Arthur Penn was doing with *Mickey One.* Their visits, which were made separately, were exploratory—Godard was almost as interested in making a movie in the United States as Truffaut, and both men were curious to see what an American director might do with their techniques. But the trip was also ambassadorial, an expression of respect for a director whose work was admired in France and who had already made clear his esteem for French moviemaking.

That *Mickey One* got financed by a major studio at all was a testament to the willingness of Mike Frankovich, the newly appointed vice president in charge of production at Columbia Pictures, to take a chance. In the early 1960s, Frankovich was the first studio head to pick up on the United Artists model of giving producers and directors control over their own movies as long as the budget was right. The price of *Mickey One* was low, though not nearly as modest as its commercial potential. Penn shot the wintry film in bleached, deliberately raggedy black and white, and it was assembled with muffled sound; an impressionistic, only semidiscernible plot that cast Beatty as a minor nightclub comedian on the run from a group of Detroit mobsters; jumpy, discontinuous editing; and a surreal climactic scene involving a performance artist whose work eventually bursts into flames and is destroyed, a reasonably appropriate metaphor for the movie itself.

What Truffaut and Godard encountered in Chicago was the production of a movie that, says Warren Beatty, "nobody wanted to make. Nobody."[16] And Truffaut came away disappointed. "Penn . . . films every scene from twelve different angles, <u>out of ignorance</u>," he wrote to Scott later that year.[17] Only the charge of ignorance was inaccurate. Penn, still feeling burned by his abrupt firing from *The Train*, was determined to make this movie his way. Although nothing in the script required elaborate setups, the shoot dragged on interminably. "Forty and fifty takes for some scenes!" says associate producer Harrison Starr. "Arthur was playing William Wyler, and God knows what role Warren had, but he had an opportunity that he might not have had when he was working with someone like Kazan to express himself more fully, and he took it."[18]

Coming off the noncollaborative experience of making *Lilith* with Robert Rossen, Beatty was no longer going to keep his mouth shut when he had something to say. He and Penn would argue daily: Beatty would tell his director that the movie's stew of symbolism, absurdism, and narrative ellipsis was "too fucking obscure," a point that Penn, years later, conceded. ("He now believes I was right?" says Beatty, laughing. "That's funny, because I now believe I was wrong.")[19] But their conflicts never became angry; rather, they were discovering a working rhythm that both men found nourishing. "Sometimes it was about who was gonna win, who was gonna get their way," says Starr. "But they weren't at loggerheads in a direct or personal way—it was just about the intensity with which they both worked on the film."[20]

Alexandra Stewart, Beatty's costar, saw the conversations between Beatty and Penn as productive, not problematic. "*Lilith*, I think, was not easy for Warren. He was very intelligent and had humor, but coming after Montgomery Clift and Paul Newman and Marlon Brando, you fear, maybe, that you are a 'sub' version of them, and with Rossen, the littlest thing . . . So he liked working with Arthur, who would talk and listen. And Arthur, because of his theater training, could maybe deal with Warren better than some other directors."[21]

Those involved in the production of *Mickey One* differ on how—and if—*Bonnie and Clyde* became part of the conversation. Stewart says Truffaut mentioned the treatment to her when he visited the set, which seems likely given the recent intensity of his involvement with Benton and Newman. "And I remember saying to Arthur and to Warren, 'Do you know who this couple is, Clyde Barrow and Bonnie whatever-her-name-was?' And they said, vaguely, not too much," she says.[22]

But when Godard visited the set, he seemed to be interested in directing *Bonnie and Clyde* as well. No evidence has been found that, this early on, Truffaut had talked to Godard about picking up the project if he dropped it. But a conversation between the two directors certainly could have happened after the *Gun Crazy* screening in New York, and it would not have been out of character for Truffaut—who at that moment was hedging his bets and about to debut his new film, *La Peau Douce*, at Cannes—to have been uncertain about his next move.

According to Harrison Starr, Godard had a copy of Benton and Newman's treatment in hand when he visited Chicago and, while there, told Starr he was considering directing *Bonnie and Clyde* as an extremely low-budget film with a quick shoot; Starr says Godard asked him if he'd be interested in producing it.[23] Starr believes that Beatty read the treatment of *Bonnie and Clyde* during the *Mickey One* shoot; Beatty says he vaguely remembers the movie being discussed but didn't read the treatment.[24]

If Beatty did get a look at Benton and Newman's work, it clearly didn't make much of an impression. At that moment, he was more concerned with other professional matters. *Mickey One* was turning out to be murkier than he had hoped, and Woody Allen's rewrites of *What's New, Pussycat?* had progressed in an unexpected direction ever since Allen had agreed to a lower writing fee in exchange for a small role in the movie. "Woody's part was little—a guy who jumps around on a pogo stick," says Beatty. "It was like five pages in his first draft, but I didn't think he had his mind around the pretty-boy Don Juan [Beatty's part] yet. In the next draft, the pogo-stick guy went from five pages to fifteen pages. By the second rewrite, the pogo-stick guy was thirty-five pages, and my character had turned into some neo-Nazi *Übermensch* who was unkind to women. The third rewrite was hilarious. His part was, of course, now *bigger* than my part—he was the lovable guy who found it hard to get laid and had all the really good jokes." Beatty was far from ready to give up on *What's New, Pussycat?*, any more than he was willing to stop pushing for what he believed would work best on *Mickey One*. Only three years into his movie career, he already felt he needed a comeback. But with Columbia still figuring out when and how to release *Lilith,* and *Mickey One* looking even less accessible, that prospect seemed a little further away every day.

If Columbia and United Artists were viewed at the time as the innovators and risk takers among the Hollywood studios, it was largely because of the men who ran them. In the preconglomerate era, studios often served as clear reflections of the tastes and passions of their leaders. At Columbia, a man like Mike Frankovich, who was genuinely interested in the films and directors coming out of England and Europe, could change the creative direction of the studio he ran and even the way it did business, setting up branch offices in London or Italy. The same was true of Arthur Krim and Robert Benjamin, who had assumed control of the flailing United Artists in the early 1950s and, over the next ten years, built a thriving creative and commercial structure in which independent producers would retain control of their work and share profits with the studio as long as they could reach agreements on cast, cost, director, and script.[25] Krim and Benjamin's dramatic rethinking of the old studio system not only resulted in better movies, but caught the attention of every other studio: From the beginning of the 1950s to the end, even as the overall number of Hollywood films declined sharply, so-called independent production at the majors quadrupled.[26]

For an unaffiliated producer like Arthur Jacobs who owned a property as valuable as *Doctor Dolittle,* that sea change both created an opportunity and limited his options. At a moment when the average studio picture cost around $3 million, *Dolittle* was without question going to shape up to be an expensive proposition. In the spring of 1964, Columbia had no interest in getting into the business of large-scale family musicals, and United Artists—whose executives were, at that moment, watching with alarm as the budget of George Stevens's long-in-production biblical epic, *The Greatest Story Ever Told,* soared past $20 million[27]—wasn't about to throw a lot of money at a *Dolittle*-size project. Disney was out of the question: Besides its long history failing to make a deal with the Loftings, the company's movies didn't even have producer credits; they would have undermined the notion that every foot of film came straight from the imagination of Walt Disney himself. Paramount and Universal weren't spending much money in the early 1960s; Universal was a great place to go if you wanted to make a Doris Day movie, but the studio was everybody's last stop, a second-rate empire that was becoming known more as a producer of television shows than a place to make movies, a reputation it wouldn't turn around until the 1970s.

That left three representatives of the old guard: MGM, Warner Brothers, and 20th Century-Fox. MGM had a well-respected new president, industry veteran Robert O'Brien, who had taken over in 1963. But the studio was still trying to wash off the red ink from the catastrophic failure of the 1962 Marlon Brando remake of *Mutiny on the Bounty;*[28] O'Brien had room on his slate for only one high-cost gamble and had already chosen to place his bet on David Lean's *Doctor Zhivago.*

Which meant that Jack Warner's office was a logical first destination for Jacobs. With the deaths of Louis B. Mayer and Harry Cohn in the late 1950s, the number of czars from the golden age of the studio system was dwindling, but the tenacious Warner, at seventy-two, was still holding on to his throne and the power that came with it. Warner was about to release *My Fair Lady,* a project he had pursued vigorously and on which he put his own name as producer; he believed in musicals, in Alan Jay Lerner, and in Rex Harrison. Jacobs flew to Los Angeles and met with him on February 7, 1964. But Warner may have been a little too familiar with the ever accelerating expenditure that making a Rex Harrison movie could entail. Though his investment would eventually pay off handsomely, he had, to his own shock, spent more than $22 million on *My Fair Lady,* making it the third most expensive movie in history; at one point, with George Cukor calling for reshoots and more reshoots, Warner ordered the Ascot racetrack set bulldozed rather than risk any further elevation of the budget.[29] He listened to Jacobs's pitch for *Doctor Dolittle* and passed.

The rejection didn't slow Jacobs down for a minute. Three days later, he met with Vincente Minnelli, who had worked with Lerner on *An American in Paris, Brigadoon,* and *Gigi,* and asked him to direct *Dolittle.* Minnelli said yes. On February 21, Jacobs took Julie Andrews to lunch "to discuss the picture," undaunted by the fact that he had no script to show her and that he had, in fact, no idea what kind of female lead a musical of *Doctor Dolittle* might have to offer her; Andrews, awaiting the release of Disney's *Mary Poppins,* understandably refrained from committing herself to a nonexistent role in an unscripted movie. A few days later, Jacobs met with one of Rex Harrison's representatives to secure his commitment more firmly.[30] And then he set up a do-or-die pitch meeting with the only studio left on his list, 20th Century-Fox.

The odds were not necessarily in Jacobs's favor. For the last four years, Fox's fate had been staked on one movie. At a cost of more than $40 million, *Cleopatra* was almost twice as expensive as any other studio film in history and the most heavily and lengthily publicized picture since *Gone With the Wind.* More than a year before it opened, as Fox's PR team funneled photographs from the set to the press, newspapers ran stories on the dramatic effect Elizabeth Taylor's kohl-eyed, striking makeup was already having on the fashion world. But the headlines quickly turned sour as the news of Taylor's affair with Richard Burton and impending divorce from Eddie Fisher caused a scandal that seriously damaged the popularity of a star whose box office clout was one of the primary reasons for Fox's big investment.

As production dragged on, as footage was scrapped, and as directors came and went, *Cleopatra*'s budget rose so dramatically that Fox's president, Spyros Skouras, was called on the carpet at a meeting of livid stockholders.[31] In 1962, with the studio projecting a loss of $10 million for the first half of the year alone, Skouras lost his job, and Darryl F. Zanuck, who had spent much of the last decade as a producer, found himself on the winning side of a boardroom showdown and returned to retake the reins of the business he had co-founded thirty years earlier. "I have no illusions about the present plight of the company," he said. "It has suffered disasters."[32] Zanuck quickly kicked *Cleopatra*'s director, Joseph L. Mankiewicz, out of the editing room, leading to more unwanted headlines.[33] When *Cleopatra* opened in the summer of 1963, Taylor and Burton, along with Mankiewicz, all but disowned the film, which drew large and curious audiences in New York and Los Angeles and then put them to sleep for much of its four-hour-and-four-minute running time. Cutting the movie, first by twenty-three minutes and then by an hour, only meant less of a bad thing.

Although 20th Century-Fox offered elaborate projections suggesting that *Cleopatra* might eventually break even (using studio math that involved plaintively exuberant predictions of lucrative rereleases and vast sums for TV sales that might take place years in the future), the studio continued to be defined by the film's failure.[34]

As Fox's financial crisis mounted, leading to a loss of nearly $40 million in 1962,[35] Zanuck had taken a step that was unprecedented in the history of Hollywood's major studios: He shut down the company. By the end of the year, he had laid off half of Fox's employees "for an indefinite period," and *The New York Times* reported that the only people left on the lot were "those actively engaged in completing . . . *Cleopatra* or assigned to future television or screen writing projects."[36] And, in a move that did not inspire renewed confidence, Zanuck handed the job of running Fox's movie production, or the little that was left of it, to his son Richard, a twenty-nine-year-old producer with only a handful of credits, and told him to start swinging the ax.[37] "Everybody was let go," recalls Dick Zanuck. "There was nobody left. I personally spoke to everyone who had been there over five years, but we closed everything. We were down to a janitor. Fox didn't even have anything ready to go, nothing even resembling a good script. They had one television show on its last legs—*Dobie Gillis*. That was it."[38]

Many in the industry dismissed Dick Zanuck as a Hollywood princeling whose father's nepotistic whim had landed him a job running a studio that no longer had a pulse. "A lot of people at the time said, oh, this is it—they'll never start up again and that's why he put the kid in charge," he says.[39] But neither Zanuck had any intention of presiding over the embalming of the family business, and Dick Zanuck's own ambitions for the studio were not to be underestimated. Though he was based in Los Angeles and his father spent most of his time in New York and Europe, the two were in frequent contact, and the younger Zanuck began hiring screenwriters and developing a slate of modestly budgeted comedy and action films that would bring some life back to the lot and get movies flowing through the pipeline to theaters again.

The Zanucks were taking Fox into a new era of moviemaking, but cautiously. They would sometimes bring in projects from outside producers, as United Artists and Columbia were doing, and they also moved Fox aggressively (and wisely) into television production. But *Cleopatra* did not occasion a fundamental rethinking of Fox's approach to movies: Like most studios, its lineup would continue to consist of westerns, war films, comedies, "filler" (usually low-cost horror flicks or beach party movies), and, once in a while, a bigger roll of the dice on a grand-scale historical epic or musical. These movies, known as road-show pictures, were long, large, and lavish: They opened initially in a limited number of huge movie houses, sometimes with two or three thousand seats, in engagements that offered reserved-seat tickets at significantly higher prices than the national average; only after those engagements had played out did the films move into first-run neighborhood theaters and smaller cities. Handled wrong, these movies could turn into *Cleopatra* or *Mutiny on the Bounty.* Done right, they were *The Ten Commandments* or *Ben-Hur,* money machines that could often play theatrically for more than two years before exhausting their audience.

When Arthur Jacobs showed up with his proposal for *Doctor Dolittle,* Fox was in the market for a road-show movie. The studio already had *The Sound of Music* in the works, but its release was still a year away, and Dick Zanuck knew he had to start thinking about another hard-ticket spectacular that could follow it, maybe in 1966. Zanuck liked the idea for *Dolittle,* he knew that Jacobs, with whom he had worked on *What a Way to Go!,* could deliver a movie, and he felt comfortable with the proposed budget: Although $6 million wasn't cheap, it was a long way from *Cleopatra.* On March 9, 1964, Jacobs met with him in Los Angeles, then flew to New York, where the following week he met with Darryl Zanuck at the St. Regis Hotel and finalized a deal for 20th Century-Fox to make the film.[40] Jacobs and the studio began to hammer out some early financial details: Alan Jay Lerner would, as the writer and co-producer, earn $350,000, the first $100,000 of which would come when he turned in a treatment; Rex Harrison would receive $300,000 (a 50 percent increase from *My Fair Lady*); Jacobs himself would take $100,000, plus $50,000 in overhead to set up shop for himself on the Fox lot. Since Lerner's longtime partner, Frederick Loewe, had decided to retire, an additional $50,000 to $100,000 was earmarked for a composer.[41] By May, Jacobs had found one: André Previn, who had written scores (and occasionally songs) for two dozen movies, agreed to compose and supervise *Doctor Dolittle*'s music for $75,000.[42]

On May 1, just two weeks before his six-month window of opportunity to make a deal was due to close, Jacobs nailed down an agreement with the Lofting estate. He now owned the exclusive movie rights to the Dolittle books, and Lofting's widow, Josephine, was to receive 10 percent of net profits from the film.[43] Fox's publicity department started drafting press releases immediately, trumpeting the involvement of Lerner, Harrison, and Vincente Minnelli and announcing that *"Doctor Dolittle* is planned for world-wide release for Christmas 1966!—Hollywood's Christmas present to the world! We visualize *Doctor Dolittle* as a classic international musical film which will be re-released in an orderly pattern every several years for many a year."[44]

Jacobs had only one thing to worry about: As the *Dolittle* deal was closing, one of the key members of his team was suddenly becoming a lot more famous. In May 1964, Alan Jay Lerner was making front-page tabloid news in New York City. The prospective writer of 1966's biggest fun-for-the-whole-family musical and his fourth wife, Micheline Muselli Pozzo diBorgo, were beginning a very public divorce battle that was about to provide local journalists with a year's supply of raw meat. He hired Louis Nizer. She hired Roy Cohn.[45]

On the 20th Century-Fox lot, Jacobs settled in for preproduction. He had an office painted for Lerner and a parking space reserved for him.[46] He wondered when he would get a call or a cable from Lerner and hear his co-producer say he was ready to begin work on the script for *Doctor Dolittle*. The call never came.

FOUR

When Mike Nichols sat down and started to read the copy of *The Graduate* he had received from Larry Turman, his first thought was that the story was "totally unoriginal."[1] His second thought was that he was going to make it into a movie.

Nichols didn't know who Turman was, only that a producer had sent the book to his agent, Robert Lantz, and asked him to forward it. He had never heard of the novel. He had never directed a movie; in fact, only recently had he started thinking of himself as a director at all. Twelve months earlier, he had been an improvisatory comedian facing the demise of the creative partnership that had made him famous and utter bewilderment about his next professional move. Now, he had become, for the second time in four years, one of the hottest commodities in New York.

Nichols's first round of celebrity came in October 1960, when he was twenty-eight and his show *An Evening with Mike Nichols and Elaine May*, directed by Arthur Penn, opened on Broadway. Nichols and May had met when he was a student at the University of Chicago. They started performing together with the Compass Players (which later evolved into Second City) in the mid-1950s. Though their backgrounds were dissimilar, the armature they had acquired along the way was oddly complementary. Nichols, born Michael Igor Peschkowsky, was an immigrant, the sickly child of a German mother and a Russian Jewish father who had escaped Europe just before World War II; he had arrived in the United States at the age

of seven and been educated in New York private schools and raised in a
European intellectual tradition.[2] May was born in Philadelphia to a family
of Yiddish theater performer-directors; they moved to Los Angeles when
she was young, and by the time she was nineteen, she was the divorced
mother of a two-year-old girl. Both Nichols and May were outsiders who
had endured stormy childhoods by sealing themselves behind walls of wit.
Both had the ability to stand just far enough apart from the culture around
them to observe it with the ruthless detachment of great comedians, and
both had an astonishing gift for improvisation; May could lampoon, on
the spur of the moment, the stylistic tics and affectations of writers she
had never actually read,[3] and Nichols, who had read all of them, knew
just how deeply he could tap his own intelligence without scaring the
audience away.

   Nichols and May's partnership took them to New York City, where they
began to gain a reputation with performances at the Village Vanguard and
other clubs, television appearances, and *Improvisations to Music,* a 1959
comedy album of two-character vignettes spoofing everything from cold
war spy thrillers to *Brief Encounter* (relocated to a dentist's chair). Nichols's talent for rooting out what he called "the secrets under the lines—the
secrets that aren't in the lines,"[4] and the almost flirtatious energy with
which he and May could lob the ball back and forth, each raising the
other's game repeatedly in the space of a four-minute routine, made them
media favorites, and the cult began to grow. Their move to Broadway, at
a time when Broadway success meant feature stories in *Time* and *Newsweek* and exposure on *The Ed Sullivan Show,* was a smash, and the ease
with which many of the show's language-rich routines translated to a hit
LP helped make Nichols and May into nationally known stars. For its
entire 306-performance run, *An Evening with Mike Nichols and Elaine
May* wasn't just a hot ticket; it was a showbiz magnet, attracting luminar-
ies not just in New York City, but from Los Angeles, as studio chiefs and
producers regularly made excursions eastward to scout new talent, and
from London, where new directors, young actors, and pop singers were
just beginning to assert their claim on America's attention. By the time
the show closed in July 1961, the list of celebrities who had knocked at

the stage door and paid their respects was staggering. Everyone wanted to know Mike Nichols.

Even when they were on Broadway, hunting for the laugh and then for the twist that would lead to the bigger laugh, Nichols and May had their share of rough nights and clashes; during one performance, they hit and scratched each other onstage as the audience, caught off guard, wondered nervously whether they were in character.[5] They were and they weren't. "We were both seductive and hostile people," Nichols said later, "and we were both very much on the defensive."[6] Perhaps inevitably, given the pressure to follow success with more success and the tension of working in so airlessly interdependent a dyad, their partnership took only a little more than a year to rupture after the show closed. Their rift, which Nichols called "cataclysmic,"[7] came soon after his agreement to take the lead role in May's play *A Matter of Position* in Philadelphia. The two fought furiously, and the transformation of their working relationship from that of collaborative performer-writers to one in which May did all the writing and directing and Nichols did all the performing was more than either could take. Nichols enjoyed being directed by Arthur Penn, but not by May. He quit, the show closed out of town, and although the two would eventually mend their relationship and work together again several times, Nichols was now on his own.

It was a producer named Arnold Saint-Subber who nudged him toward directing,[8] handing him *Nobody Loves Me*, a comic play about young newlyweds by Neil Simon that nobody, including Simon, thought was working particularly well. Nichols agreed to direct the play in summer stock. "In the first fifteen minutes of the first day's rehearsal I understood that this was my job, this was what I was preparing to do without knowing it," he said.[9] Nichols discovered within himself a natural talent for drawing good work out of actors and for guiding playwrights through rewrites without making them feel threatened or trampled. He also found, to his own surprise, a kind of emotional comfort in being at the center of the action. "I think people try to become famous because they think: If you can get the world to revolve around you, you won't die," he remarked to a reporter.[10] The comment typified the way Nichols handled himself with a press corps that was insatiably curious about his life with and without Elaine May—it was fast, funny, and so offhand that nobody could be certain whether it was self-revelation or just a good line.

Neil Simon, who didn't believe *Nobody Loves Me* was funny until he heard the audience laughing, came away flabbergasted by what Nichols brought to the table. His play, retitled *Barefoot in the Park,* opened in New York on October 23, 1963, to rave reviews that launched the careers of its two young stars, Robert Redford and Elizabeth Ashley, turned Simon into a brand-name playwright, and almost instantly made Nichols the comedy director at the top of every playwright's and actor's lists.

Larry Turman had been impressed by Nichols's work on *Barefoot in the Park,* which would shortly win him his first Tony Award. But when Turman sent him *The Graduate* and asked him to consider directing it, "I was really responding to the funny nervousness of his performances with Elaine May—I felt some connection there. When you read *The Graduate,* you feel the way I felt watching him: You laugh, but you're nervous."[11]

Nichols laughed when he read *The Graduate* and wasn't nervous at all. He had loved *The Catcher in the Rye,*[12] and he saw Holden Caulfield's literary descendant, slightly more grown-up but still utterly baffled, in the pages of Webb's story. "I thought it was a good, old gag," he says. "Kid, older lady—that's how everybody got started back then. It was a good subject. And I thought, I know how to do this."[13]

A few nights after he got the book, Nichols told Turman he was interested. The project and Nichols's involvement were announced in *The New York Times* on March 15. Soon after, the two men had lunch at the Plaza Hotel with William Hanley, who had completed a draft of the screenplay for *The Graduate,* been paid his $500, and was now moving on to considerably more lucrative work on action films. "I thought the book was terrific," says Hanley. "Charles Webb's dialogue couldn't be improved on—it was pointless to try. All the script needed was structure." At the lunch, Nichols expressed his desire for changes in a new draft. "I didn't want to make them," says Hanley. "I just knew it wasn't going to work with us, and I said to Larry Turman, 'I'm gonna back out—you need Mike Nichols more than you need me.'"[14]

With Hanley gone, Turman needed a new screenwriter who would be

SCENES FROM A REVOLUTION

willing to take Nichols's notes, but Nichols was in no rush to find one. He was flooded with offers to direct plays; moreover, he told Turman, *The Graduate* would have to be his second movie, not his first. Nichols had no desire to make a film version of *Barefoot in the Park* or of anything else he went on to direct in New York. "I couldn't! What would I do? They were dead for me," he says of the first four plays he staged. "There was nothing to discover. Unless I can be terrified and mystified and feel, 'I'm lost, this is the one that's going to destroy me, how could I have made this mistake' . . . that terror is the life of it."[15] But he did think that adapting a play to the screen might make for a logical first footstep into Hollywood, and he'd found a property he liked: *The Public Eye,* one-half of a pair of one-acts called *The Private Ear and the Public Eye* by British playwright Peter Shaffer that had opened on Broadway two weeks before *Barefoot in the Park.* Universal had announced that Nichols would direct the film, and Shaffer had recently begun to work with him on a screenplay for the three-character piece.[16] That bought Turman a little time, not only to get a viable screenplay drafted, but to use Nichols's name to lure a studio. Given all the buzz around his director, *The Graduate*'s future looked bright.

Over the next six months, every studio in Hollywood turned the film down.

On April 13, 1964, Hollywood took its annual Monday off for the Academy Awards. There had been no frantic winter campaigning season; the Oscars, though they drew a reliably huge television audience, were in some years a take-it-or-leave-it affair, even for the nominees. This spring, studio traditionalists were in a particularly glum mood: Twelve of the twenty acting nominees were from the United Kingdom or Europe; one company, United Artists, had dominated the major nominations, just as it had done for the last several years; and it was becoming apparent that, for the first time since the 1940s, the Best Picture Oscar was not going to go to an American picture—the winner would be Tony Richardson's raunchy smash *Tom Jones.*

"Wonder why we hate ourselves," Hedda Hopper snapped in her column.[17] The answer was evident: Even by its own declining standards, the

Hollywood studios had mustered an embarrassing lineup of films in 1963 and then failed to nominate the best of them, Martin Ritt's *Hud*. Two of the year's Best Picture nominees, Fox's *Cleopatra* and MGM's slow-moving Cinerama omnibus *How the West Was Won*, had been scorned by critics and were clearly the beneficiaries of bloc voting by the large roster of studio employees that, at the time, made up much of the Academy's membership. It was not a year for Hollywood to celebrate its own accomplishments. Some young stars—Steve McQueen, Tuesday Weld, Julie Andrews, Jack Lemmon—showed up as presenters, along with veterans like Edward G. Robinson and Ed Begley. Warren Beatty was in the audience with Leslie Caron; his sister, Shirley MacLaine, was also there, and up for Best Actress. But overall attendance among the nominees was sparse; three of the four acting winners—*Hud*'s Patricia Neal and Melvyn Douglas and veteran British character actress Margaret Rutherford for *The V.I.P.s*—didn't even show up.[18]

The fourth winner did, and provided the evening with its headline. Sitting in the audience, a nominee for Best Actor, Sidney Poitier, his palms sweating and his tension increasing with every category, thought, "I'm never going to put myself through this shit no more."[19] Poitier knew that all eyes were on him, that his win would provide a moment of genuine meaning for black Americans and an occasion for an avalanche of self-congratulation within his industry. He had been here before, five years earlier, when, as the costar of *The Defiant Ones*, he had become the first black man to be nominated for Best Actor. Now, he could be the first to win—a moment that he knew would make history and yet change almost nothing.

The movie for which Poitier was nominated, *Lilies of the Field*, was a sweet, thimble-size parable in which he had played a wanderer in the Southwest who stumbles across an isolated convent and helps a group of nuns from Germany build a new chapel. They don't share a culture, a homeland, or even a language, but they learn mutual respect through working together. Almost nothing of Poitier's character is revealed in the film's script; he is a holy stranger who arrives, helps, teaches, learns, and leaves. Poitier accepted a salary cut, taking just $50,000 plus a percentage of the gross to play a role that his friend Harry Belafonte had rejected.[20] Shrewdly handled by United Artists, which missed no opportunity to hard-sell the mild little movie as a beacon of tolerance and cross-cultural understanding, *Lilies* had become a minor success.

While nobody was claiming that the film was a masterpiece, much of Hollywood and the press were willing to laud it as a step in the right direction. More than a decade after the McCarthy era and blacklisting had caused many in the movie business to retreat from any public association with political issues, the civil rights movement was becoming the occasion for many in Hollywood to reassert their right to speak out on political issues. Actors like Paul Newman and Marlon Brando felt free to make their voices heard, and so did those considered industry leaders like Gregory Peck and Robert Wise.[21] The August 1963 civil rights march in Washington had been a galvanizing moment for the repoliticization of Hollywood, which *New York Times* columnist Murray Schumach wrote had "decided to rejoin the nation after nearly 16 years of spiritual secession."[22]

The content of *Lilies of the Field* was anything but political, but the fact that some movie houses in the South declined to book the film only added to its status as a good cause. And Poitier was a hard man to root against. Before Oscar night, one of his competitors for Best Actor, *Hud*'s Paul Newman, announced that he would be skipping the ceremony and pulling for Poitier to win. And even the part of the Hollywood establishment that still had one foot planted firmly in the era of red-baiting saw a chance, as columnist Sidney Skolsky wrote, "to telegraph to the globe that WE do not discriminate and thus give the lie to our so-called Communist friends."[23]

Poitier knew that was nonsense. He was well aware that, as much as the sight of a black man holding an Oscar statuette for the first time might move many black and white Americans, his win would be used to sell a preposterous falsehood, the spurious notion that the movie industry had solved its own race problem and was now pointing the way for the rest of America. "Did I say to myself, 'This country is waking up and beginning to recognize that certain changes are inevitable?'" he wrote, recalling the evening. "No, I did not. I knew that we hadn't 'overcome,' because I was still the only one."[24]

Nonetheless, when Anne Bancroft, who had won the Best Actress Oscar a year earlier for *The Miracle Worker*, took the stage, announced the nominees, opened the envelope, and, beaming, spoke Poitier's name, he strode to the podium with genuine excitement, telling the cheering audience, "It has been a long journey to this moment."

That much, at least, was true. *Lilies of the Field* was the thirty-six-year-old actor's nineteenth movie. Poitier was a native of the Bahamas who grew up in poverty; he moved to Miami as a teenager, then to New York, where he scraped by working in blue-collar service jobs and living in small rented rooms before he turned to acting. Poitier began his career as an immigrant who could barely read, an outsider wherever he found himself; the growing music and theater scene in Harlem in the late 1940s, and the indigenous black American experience from which it grew, felt and sounded, at first, as foreign to him as everything else in America. (He taught himself diction and grammar by listening to a white man on the radio.) He made his movie debut playing a doctor in Joseph Mankiewicz's 1950 urban melodrama *No Way Out*. The film established a template for Poitier's roles that was to provide him steady, if creatively constricting, employment for the next fifteen years: The character was a young professional surrounded by white bigots, a so-called credit to his race who achieved what white America was comfortable labeling "dignity" by at once demonstrating that he could feel anger and proving he was evolved enough to restrain himself from expressing it. Eventually, white characters in many of his movies would come to understand his finer qualities, meaning they would learn that he was exceptional and should therefore not be the target of prejudice: Often, for the sake of an imagined evenhandedness that made the films more palatable to white moviegoers, Poitier's character had to learn a lesson, too, usually something about the perils of being too proud or suspicious to accept a helping hand.

Poitier worked steadily after *No Way Out*: He was handsome, and his Roman-coin features made him castable across a broad age range (five years after playing a doctor, he played a high school student in *The Black-board Jungle*, the film that really ignited his career). And he had no competition, since in the 1950s the movie industry had room for exactly one black actor (Belafonte, who acted once in a while, was really more of a recording star). Hollywood needed an "Exceptional Negro" in the 1950s, and Poitier was perfect in the role. Aside from his talent and magnetism, he demonstrated a remarkable instinct for self-presentation; without anyone to emulate, he knew exactly how much he could say publicly without jeopardizing his status in either black or white America. In the press, he walked a fine line almost unerringly: He was humble but never servile, concerned but rarely intemperate, unwilling to pretend bigotry was anything other than an immense national problem, but optimistic that it would eventually give way. But as much as journalists liked to point out his unique status to him, Poitier didn't spend much time discussing the cost of that exceptionalism. He wouldn't let himself—couldn't let himself—play villains. Hollywood would never allow him to play a character with real sexual passion. And the possibility that he might one day be able to compete with white actors for roles in which race could be factored out wasn't even worth discussing.

In public, Poitier kept his own counsel about those issues, muting his frustration beneath a calm, consistent expression of personal responsibility. "While he disclaims being a crusader or a leader, Poitier acknowledges that he has made it a policy not to play any role that might offend Negro sensibilities or diminish the Negro's stature as a human being," noted *The New York Times* approvingly in 1959, on the eve of his first Oscar nomination and his ecstatically received performance as Walter Lee Younger in Lorraine Hansberry's *A Raisin in the Sun* on Broadway. "As I see myself, I'm just the average Joe Blow Negro," Poitier told the paper.[25] "But, as the cats say in my area, I'm out there wailing for us all." Poitier was not afraid to speak out about civil rights: The following year, when he went to Los Angeles to star in the film version of *A Raisin in the Sun* and ended up sequestered with his family in the Chateau Marmont, he went public about the fact that he couldn't rent a house for himself, his wife, and his daughters in a desirable neighborhood. "I speak about this with pain," he said, "because I would not like to say these things exist." Housing discrimination, he went on to say, "will yield only to time and pressure."[26] But his self-defined duty to be the one "wailing for us all" meant that Poitier had to keep his own complicated personal life under wraps. Elizabeth Taylor and Richard Burton could provide endless grist for talk-show jokes and gossip columns, but the news that Poitier, a married father of three, had long been having an affair with actress Diahann Carroll and was now headed for divorce would not have been welcome to moviegoers of any race.[27] Everything Poitier said and did had ramifications; the only real power he had was his control over the version of himself he chose to show the world.

How much had really changed, even in Hollywood, as Bancroft hugged Poitier, who took the trophy, made a jubilant acceptance speech, and left the stage to another round of applause? In New York, the actor was to be honored by Mayor Robert F. Wagner with a ticker tape parade. But he still had to endure appalling indignities like the *Time* magazine story that said he bounded to the stage to receive his Oscar "more like a great Negro high jumper than a great Negro actor" and, as a mark of approval, gushed that "he is so overpoweringly good looking that he quite literally pales the white actors beside him."[28] In his postvictory interviews, Poitier was, as always, grateful but judicious and precise, reminding people that the award was "not a magic wand" and saying, "I don't think that I'll ever be able to function as freely as a Marlon Brando, or a Burt Lancaster or a Paul Newman."[29]

Of course, he was right. In 1964, black Americans were still virtually invisible in filmed entertainment. "All we ask is that movies show the truthful American image," Edward W. Warren, head of the Los Angeles chapter of the National Association for the Advancement of Colored People (NAACP), had complained in 1961. "Any time [movies] have a crap game they show plenty of Negroes. But when do you see a Negro doctor or lawyer? . . . They will show you a scene with a baseball crowd and you don't see a single Negro. You will see city street scenes and not a single Negro. This is ridiculous."[30] At first, Hollywood simply didn't listen. When 20th Century-Fox was taken to task for making Darryl F. Zanuck's World War II epic *The Longest Day* without any close-ups of black soldiers,[31] Dick Zanuck was caught flatfooted, first announcing that the studio's research had shown that no black soldiers were involved in D-Day[32] and then, when that proved not to be the case, defending his father by pointing out that "one of his three secretaries was a Negro."[33]

In 1963, the movie and television industries finally began to take some real, if minuscule, steps toward integration, less out of the goodness of their corporate hearts than as the result of an extremely effective campaign waged by the NAACP, which threatened to go before the National

Labor Relations Board and attempt to have Hollywood's unions decertified if they didn't start integrating.[34] It took a sitdown between the NAACP and an alliance of producers before Hollywood would even commit to the principle that "more Negroes should be used in movies,"[35] both on screen and on crews. Later that year, Wendell Franklin became the first black man ever to hold the job of assistant director on a studio movie, *The Greatest Story Ever Told*, and publicly expressed his nervousness about how white crew members would react to being told what to do by him.[36] But despite the NAACP's attempt to urge more black workers to apply for jobs, Hollywood's unions remained largely closed shops,[37] and network television programmers were even more fearful than their movie studio counterparts. The pilot for the ABC sitcom *Bewitched* sat on the shelf for more than a year, a victim of complaints by the network's southern stations that its innocuous comic story of an advertising man whose wife is a witch was a veiled argument for racial intermarriage. In 1963, CBS became the first network to use a black actor as part of the ensemble of a drama series, casting Cicely Tyson as a secretary in the gritty, innovative New York–based drama *East Side/West Side*. But the network asked the show's producers to limit the number of scenes in which she appeared, and the series was canceled after one season, the victim of southern affiliates that refused to carry it at all.[38]

The NAACP's battles with Hollywood kept making news; the organization proved to be far more skilled than even the publicity-savviest Hollywood studios at taking the lead with the press and keeping its side of the fight in the headlines. Their strategy of repeated public complaints was so potent and widely recognized that, on Oscar night, Sammy Davis Jr., who was handed the wrong envelope as he was about to present an award, got the show's biggest laugh by ad-libbing, "Wait until the NAACP hears about this!"

Two days after Poitier's win, television critic Jack Gould commented dryly that Anne Bancroft's on-camera embrace of the actor, had it occurred in a scripted television series, "would have been written out lest Southern sensibilities be disturbed."[39] Gould called the actor's victory one of the few redeeming moments of the show. However, nobody was very specific about what, exactly, was being redeemed. Poitier's Best Actor win was widely taken as a breakthrough moment that was laden with symbolism. But what it symbolized was not a fundamental alteration in Hollywood's use of black actors, only an affirmation of what Poitier's career had always represented—his own status as the exception to the rule.

Sidney Skolsky's exultant headline OSCAR—CIVIL RIGHTS LEADER must have struck Poitier as ironic, given the one fact that everyone was politely declining to mention: This year's Oscar winner didn't have a job. Poitier had two films awaiting release—he had completed a cameo in *The Greatest Story Ever Told* and had a starring role as a Moorish prince in a period adventure film called *The Long Ships* that he already knew was going to be dreadful. He felt that his career was largely dependent on the grace and conviction of a handful of men—producer-directors Stanley Kramer and Richard Brooks and Columbia chief Mike Frankovich[40]—who kept him working and visible. His success was fragile.

Poitier's Oscar would turn *Lilies of the Field* from a modest hit into a major one and transform him into something he had never been before, a movie star with a box office following of his own. After the award, the film's business increased by as much as 500 percent in some theaters; the same southern movie houses that had refused to book *Lilies* now sought it,[41] and the movie played into the fall of 1964. But the week after the Oscars, when Poitier went to New York to receive a medal from Mayor Wagner, he was still wondering what would come next for him, and the dissonance between the celebration that surrounded him and his own internal turmoil must have been overwhelming. For one of the first times in his career, Poitier lost his temper in front of a reporter. Pressed to answer the same questions about the civil rights movement he had been fielding for days, he replied, "Why don't you ask me human questions? Why is it everything you ask refers to the Negroness of my life and not to my acting?"[42]

Poitier didn't need to wait for the answer: He had given it himself years earlier. He was still, as he had put it, "the only one." And with an Academy Award, Poitier was no longer just an actor, but himself a trophy, a successful progress report that the Academy had bestowed on the movie business and a name that Hollywood could invoke again and again as a way of telling itself that it had done enough, that a piece of unfinished business had finally been settled. Poitier had been in Hollywood long enough to know that the Oscar would be less useful to him than to the organization that handed it out. The prize was not a symptom of meaningful change, but a substitute for it; more substantial or widespread advances in the industry didn't appear to him to be on the horizon. In any case, Poitier certainly did not imagine that he had just been granted an opportunity for leverage. On the contrary, it seemed almost impossible for him to imagine any way that he would now be allowed to ask for more.

FIVE

In May 1964, almost a year after they had started to talk about *Bonnie and Clyde*, Robert Benton and David Newman became, for the first time, paid screenwriters. Elinor Jones and Norton Wright gave them $1,700, formalizing their own role as producers and buying themselves an eighteen-month window—until November 27, 1965—during which they had the right to try to secure a production deal for the movie.[1] Benton and Newman took some time off from their jobs at *Esquire* and used their payday for a trip to East Texas, where, guided by Benton, who knew some of the turf, they spent time visiting the sites of Parker and Barrow's crimes and getting a feel for the dusty, remarkably unaltered landscape. "Heighdy! See how I'm picking up the local jargon?" Newman wrote to Jones on a postcard. "Things going extremely well for us. Found the graves of Clyde and [Buck Barrow, his brother] in abandoned cemetery overgrown with weeds. One of the strangest sensations we ever had—standing six feet over Clyde. On Monday we'll see Bonnie's. . . . Bob is taking a lot of pictures. <u>Perfect</u> Bonnie and Clyde locations! Quite uncanny to see cities and towns that look like 1932 this year. So we are spending your money wisely and well."[2]

Benton and Newman often talked about the trip as a turning point—a journey during which they fell deeper into the world of Bonnie and Clyde and became fully committed to screenwriting. They kept their ears open for speech patterns and dust bowl slang.[3] Newman immersed himself in an idiom and an environment that he had never encountered. And it was in Texas that some of their ideas for the film's jolting changes in mood began to sharpen. "Bob and David had in their viscera some themes that they wanted to address," says Wright. "Bob in particular was always drawn to the thought that what is rollicking good fun one minute can, in the blink of an eye, turn into something violent and scary—it was in his blood."[4]

Jones and Wright became more excited with every new dispatch from Texas. Still convinced that the movie could be made for between $350,000 and $500,000, a budget range that had been confirmed by their conversations with François Truffaut, they were now trying hard to turn themselves into real producers. Wright, who had gotten a job as a production assistant on TV's *Captain Kangaroo* ("I was pickling my brains, but at least I had some income"), was taking a Directors Guild of America–sponsored class in production management,[5] and Jones was doing what she could to move Truffaut, their strongest link to legitimacy, closer to making a deal.

Truffaut, however, could raise her hopes with one sentence and dash them with the next. Before leaving New York, he met with Jones in the lobby of the Algonquin Hotel.[6] They talked about a due date for the script, settling on July 1, and Truffaut told her, "You have a very good thing here, you know—an excellent script for a director." When Jones told him he was the only director they wanted, Truffaut remarked casually that any good director, foreign or American, could make *Bonnie and Clyde* and that he would return to the United States sometime in July, when he would make a final decision about whether to direct the movie.

Knowing of Benton and Newman's trip, Truffaut asked Jones to have them send him as many photographs and postcards as possible from Texas. (They did, and he replied by sending them the gangster comic strips from *France Soir* that had helped spark his initial curiosity about Bonnie and Clyde.) Are "the boys" still following the ideas they had discussed during their hotel room marathons? he asked Jones. When she assured him that they were, he cautioned, "But not too faithfully. [I] don't want to . . . restrict them at this point."

During their meeting, Truffaut also suggested *Mickey One*'s Harrison Starr (whom neither Wright nor Jones knew) as a possible associate producer who might be able to help them secure financing. For his part, Starr wasn't happy to learn that the *Bonnie and Clyde* treatment already had producers attached; he had clearly had separate conversations with Godard and Truffaut about producing *Bonnie and Clyde* himself and, eager to prove his suitability for the job, had taken the initiative to meet with Mike Frankovich at Columbia to see if he would be willing to fund the film as part of a new program of low-cost European-style ventures the studio was setting up.[7]

After Benton and Newman returned to New York, they began work in earnest on turning their treatment of *Bonnie and Clyde* into a screenplay that incorporated everything they had learned from Truffaut and from Texas, reshaping their descriptive passages into scenes with dialogue. They also went back to *Esquire* (where Benton was no longer art director but had become the magazine's special projects editor) to oversee the completion of their grand statement of pop principle, "The New Sentimentality," the magazine's cover story in July 1964. Lofty and exuberant, hilariously arrogant, and irresistibly presented as an infallible index of taste, the article was a cultural call to arms—out with the old (except for those elements of the old approved by the young), in with the new. The "Old Sentimentality," exemplified by the Eisenhower era and values like "Patriotism, Love, Religion, Mom, The Girl," had given way, Benton and Newman argued, to a "New Sentimentality" about "you, really just you, not what you were told or taught, but what goes on in your head, *really*, and in your heart, *really*."[8]

"The New Sentimentality" was really about what was going on in Benton's and Newman's heads and hearts, which wasn't hard to decode. *Breathless*'s Jean Seberg and Jean-Paul Belmondo were a "Key Couple of the New Sentimentality," and their description of them ("He was destroyed because he let love carry him away . . . she was fragile, but hard") could have come straight from their *Bonnie and Clyde* treatment. Other favored representations of the New Sentimentality included *L'Avventura*, Malcolm X, Alfred Hitchcock, and, of course, Truffaut, who was shamelessly referenced four times. "He is Style over Content," they wrote, meaning it as high praise. Consigned to the ash heap as relics of the Old Sentimentality were *The Sound of Music*, Gene Kelly, and John Wayne. "What we were talking about," Newman wrote later, "was what is now known as 'the Sixties.' But as we were in the midst of living through them at the time, we didn't have a chronological name for what was happening."[9]

"The New Sentimentality" slowed Benton and Newman's work on *Bonnie and Clyde*, but not significantly: By August 1964, they had completed their first draft of the screenplay. Wright and Jones read what they had done and "flipped over it," says Wright. "It was just marvelous." The young producers were ready to spring into action, even though they weren't entirely sure what they were supposed to do next. "We really didn't have any idea other than that, if we got a budget together and then told [attorney] Bob Montgomery about it, we'd go to the major studios and tell them about François Truffaut and they'd come rushing to us," says Wright.[10]

Their first shock came when Wright, using the skills he had acquired in his production management class, went through Benton and Newman's script page by page, only to realize that the $350,000 they had tossed around as a budget was a fantasy. "I broke it down, added it up, and to my horror, it came to the catastrophically high figure of a million three," he says. "I kept checking my addition, thinking, 'This is terrible!' "[11] Wright's math was correct: He and Jones hadn't taken into account the fact that *Bonnie and Clyde* would require period automobiles, doubled and tripled costumes to account for all the blood and bullets the script now contained, and multiple locations. The film was no longer viable as the on-the-fly independent production they had envisioned.

The second, far worse piece of news came in a letter from Truffaut to Elinor Jones on September 7, 1964. "I have had the new script . . . read to me in French," he wrote of *Bonnie and Clyde*. "I thought all the modifications are excellent. I am, unfortunately, obliged to reply to you in the negative." Three weeks earlier, Truffaut had warned Helen Scott in a letter "that I want to curb the enthusiasm of Elinor Jones." Now, he was offering Jones a variety of reasons for turning down the film: He had decided that *La Marié Était en Noir* (*The Bride Wore Black*), a French-language adaptation of an American suspense novel, would be his next film; moreover, he wrote, Lewis Allen was insisting to him that his first American film would have to be *Fahrenheit 451*, which was now scheduled for production in the summer of 1965.[12]

"I would like you to know that, of all the scripts I have turned down in the last five years, *Bonnie and Clyde* is the best, but I hope that you will fully understand my reasons and that David Newman and Robert Benton will also understand them," Truffaut wrote. In fact his explanation was slightly slippery; it's not clear why he would suddenly have accepted a dictum from Lewis Allen, with whom he had now had a long and testy relationship, about the start date of *Fahrenheit 451*. Truffaut was, at the time of his letter, going through some problems he didn't share with Jones: He was in the middle of a divorce, and his latest film, *La Peau Douce* (*The Soft Skin*), had opened to poor reviews and mediocre business in France.[13] In the letter, he sounded self-conscious, formal, and somewhat overinsistent about his lack of remorse. "I do not think that I have caused you to waste too much time, nor have I broken my word," he wrote, "since I had always made it clear I would make my final decision when the second version of the script was finished."

But Truffaut seemed to know how crushing his abrupt about-face would be, because he had taken the time to arrange an extraordinary second chance for the movie. He had given Benton and Newman's script, he said, to Jean-Luc Godard, who "greatly liked" it, was "a very fast worker," "speaks English fluently," and "might well give you an American *Breathless.*" Truffaut didn't say whether he had ever talked with Godard about the possibility of taking over *Bonnie and Clyde* when both men were in New York. But he was telling the truth about Godard's reaction: Before he broke the news to Jones, he had sent the script to Italy, where Godard was showing his newest movie at the Venice Film Festival, and Godard had promptly cabled him back: "Am in love with Bonnie and also with Clyde. Stop. Would be happy to speak with authors in New York."[14]

Benton and Newman didn't have the time or the inclination to be devastated. They were now exchanging one leader of the French New Wave for the other, and hesitation was a luxury they couldn't afford: Two of Godard's newest movies were showing at the New York Film Festival the following week, and the director wanted to meet them during his visit to New York and make a decision about *Bonnie and Clyde* on the spot.

The festival, sponsored by the Film Society of Lincoln Center, was only a year old in 1964, but under the guidance of its respected and influential program director, Richard Roud, it was already starting to assert itself as an annual summit meeting for the world's leading filmmakers. Besides Godard, who was showing *A Woman Is a Woman* and *Band of Outsiders*, that fall's invited directors included Bernardo Bertolucci, Abel Gance, Luis Buñuel, and Satyajit Ray. An invitation extended to an American director signified approval by the auteurist critical community—thus the inclusion of Sidney Lumet's *Fail-Safe* and Robert Rossen's *Lilith* (the latter making its long-delayed and poorly received debut).[15]

As Truffaut had said, Godard worked fast: In the four years since *Breathless*, he had directed seven features as well as shorts in three different multidirector omnibus films, a format that enjoyed brief popularity in Europe in the early 1960s. "That was very much a Nouvelle Vague thing—get in there and do it quickly," says Elinor Jones. "Even Truffaut thought that way. But with Godard, it went to extremes."[16]

When he arrived in New York, Godard began his flirtation with *Bonnie and Clyde* by meeting with the two producers for lunch at the Algonquin. "Godard was somewhat cool, somewhat distant, but he said he was interested in the script," says Wright.[17] There was a bit of polite, detached discussion in which Godard advanced some of his ideas for the film and Jones and Wright discussed their own. Harrison Starr, whom Godard brought along to the meeting, says it didn't go well. "I literally saw the gate close in Jean-Luc's eyes, and that was it. I knew that he wasn't going to work with them."[18]

At lunch, the conversation turned to Arthur Penn's 1958 film, *The Left Handed Gun*. "We were all interested in how a western could be made a different way," says Wright. "And Godard turned to me and said, 'Could you arrange a screening for me by tomorrow?' I thought, this is a challenge—Godard is saying, I wonder if this kid has enough clout to set up a screening on short notice." Wright managed to book a showing of Penn's film, after which he says Godard warmed toward them a bit.[19] For their part, Benton and Newman had quickly transferred their enthusiasm to the director—whom, after all, they had already labeled a pillar of the New Sentimentality. "I think they were just so enamored of his work and of the possibility of getting another one of their film heroes," says Jones.[20]

"Bob and David just wanted to get it made!" says Leslie Newman. "To have people like Truffaut and Godard coming in—oh, my God, these were their idols, the people whose movies they worshipped."[21]

But the producers had as many doubts about what Godard would bring to Benton and Newman's script as Godard had about them. "The truth is that Norton and I didn't want Godard—we didn't like him for *Bonnie and Clyde*," says Jones. "I think that particularly upset David."[22]

It was in this context—one of growing tension, unarticulated concerns, and intense time pressure—that the key players in *Bonnie and Clyde* gathered at Elinor and Tom Jones's apartment on September 19 for a meeting that has since become one of the great gallows-humor moments in the film's history, although decades of embellishment and retelling have blurred some of the precise details.[23] Assembled in the living room were Godard, Jones, and Wright; Benton and Newman; and Helen Scott, who was continuing to act as a liaison on the project.*

After some pleasantries, they got down to business. "Everybody remembers that meeting differently," says Benton. But it began to go wrong almost from the start, when Godard, with little preamble, announced that he wanted to begin preproduction on *Bonnie and Clyde* in December— just three months away—and that he intended to shoot the movie in New Jersey in January, on a four-week shooting schedule. He also said he wanted to give the script to Columbia right away, information that took everyone by surprise.

Nobody in the living room had very much to say as Godard talked, but after a few minutes, Norton Wright's reservations boiled over into panic. "I said to him, you know, that's really not the way to do it. This is a period piece, it's an expensive piece, we should shoot it on location in the places where Bob and David had done their research. The spring would be good, or maybe the fall—but it's snowy and cold and wet in New Jersey."

Whatever Wright's exact words were—he had apparently referred to meteorological reports—they caused the temperature in the room to

---

*Starr says he was at the meeting as well, although neither Jones nor Benton recalls his presence, and Jones's notes from the time strongly suggest he is misremembering, conflating the meeting with the earlier lunch at the Algonquin.

plunge dramatically. According to Benton, Godard stood up, said, "I'm talking cinema and you're talking meteorology," and walked out of the apartment.

Others at the meeting don't recall Godard's departure as being quite so dramatic; he may have excused himself to use the restroom and said his good-byes and left soon after that. Norton Wright says Godard's comment about "matters *météorologiques*" was made not at the meeting, but to Benton and Newman the next day; over drinks, just before Godard left for Paris, he told the two writers, "Call me when the script reverts to your ownership." But nobody disputes the astonishing swiftness with which the meeting and Godard's involvement in *Bonnie and Clyde* were terminated.

Elinor Jones and her brother were ashen. Jones tried, the next day, to reconstruct what had gone wrong in a conversation with Helen Scott, who filled in a key piece of information that Godard hadn't shared with them: He had been trying to get out of a contract to shoot the film *Alphaville* for Columbia, and in order to have a chance of getting the studio to agree to a switch in projects, he needed *Bonnie and Clyde* to replace it in the exact same spot on his schedule. Harrison Starr, who was still hoping that he might be able to produce the film if Jones and Wright fell out of the picture, felt it could have worked on Godard's terms. "Mike Frankovich had worked in Europe, so he heard the beat of the drum—he could pick it up, that way of making movies," he says. "We could have done the picture very well for $350,000, and that's what Columbia was looking for."[24]

Godard, though nobody involved in *Bonnie and Clyde* knew it at the time, had been so serious about shooting the movie that, while in New York, he had met with Elliott Gould—then known only as the man who had recently married Barbra Streisand—and Buck Henry, who had both flown from Los Angeles to discuss making the film with him over dinner at the Algonquin. "I go into the restaurant, and there's Jean-Luc Godard, sitting cross-legged on a banquette," says Henry. "And we sit down and have a meal. It made no sense at all. Apparently, Elliott had talked to Godard about doing *Bonnie and Clyde*, and he was going to get him a writer to do it, and we had this strange conversation where I guess I told Godard how much I liked his films, and he said a lot of things to me that I didn't understand at all, culminating in, 'I will write things on legal pads and send them to you!' I said, 'Great.' I went off, spent the night in Barbra and Elliott's apartment, and I don't think I ever heard about it again."[25]

Godard was a "strange, mad guy," Helen Scott told Jones. But, she added, her and her brother's inexperience was what had really caused the problem. Producers more schooled in handling directors with volatile temperaments would have read the situation correctly and just rolled with whatever Godard was suggesting; they would have understood that all decisions made now could be altered later. Had Harrison Starr been present at the meeting, Scott told her, he would have known how to handle Godard. The director "wanted simple enthusiasm from us," Jones wrote in the notes she had begun to keep after important meetings. "But our cool response to giving the script to Columbia really turned him off, and the word 'meteorologically' really threw him. . . . He felt we were formal, slow, reserved [and behaved as if we were] 'not sure we really wanted Godard.' "[26]

When Truffaut heard what had happened, he called it "unfortunate." Wright and Jones, he said, shouldn't have shown their distress; "they should have known that Columbia would have decided when it could have been done."[27]

More than forty years later, Wright says, "I take great pride that I was the fella that prevented the movie being made by Godard, because he would not have made a good movie out of a marvelous, exceptional, groundbreaking script. We had just equated Truffaut and Godard with the New Wave in our minds, but the difference was immense—Truffaut had a huge humanitarian heart, and Godard was doing almost self-reflexive movies after that." But at the time, Wright was mortified by the cave-in his innocuous comment had caused and, like Jones, wondering what their next move could possibly be.[28]

Helen Scott encouraged Jones to shrug off the meeting, calling it "terribly funny." "Don't feel desolate!" she said. "You've had an experience with Godard."[29] But Jones and her brother were devastated; in the space of two weeks, *Bonnie and Clyde* had lost two directors. And Benton and Newman were no less glum. "After that, all the air seemed to go out of it," says Leslie Newman.[30] "It was really nobody's fault," says Benton, "but we thought, 'That's it. It's over.' "[31]

As the fall of 1964 began, *The Graduate* was no closer to finding a home at a studio than *Bonnie and Clyde* was. Larry Turman had pitched his movie to every studio executive on both coasts, assuring them that the film could be made for just $1 million, but he had overestimated the degree to which Mike Nichols's involvement would be a selling point. "I couldn't get to first base at the studios with Nichols," he says. "They didn't care about *Barefoot in the Park*—he had never directed a movie before."[32] The fact that Turman was trying to make a deal without having a script to show anyone may have made his task even more difficult. Paramount's production chief, Jack Karp, turned him down flat; so did Mike Frankovich, who, focused on Europe, had never heard of Nichols. Even when Turman went to United Artists to talk to David Picker, who at thirty-three was one of the youngest and most forward-looking studio executives in the business (he had been the first to recognize the potential value of the James Bond franchise), he got a flat no: Picker looked at the novel's sparse descriptions and uninflected dialogue and said, "What's funny about it?"[33]

While Turman was making the rounds, Nichols was in the middle of his own misadventure in Los Angeles, getting a taste of the difference between New York theater culture and the priorities of a Hollywood studio. He and Peter Shaffer had made good progress on the script for *The Public Eye*, working together in Nichols's New York apartment at the Beresford every morning—or, given Nichols's night-owl lifestyle, every afternoon. "He was so sweet," says Nichols. "We had a great time. He used to get very pissed off at me for oversleeping—he'd be there waiting, and I'd be late to a meeting in my own apartment!"

Nichols had not yet met the man who was to produce *The Public Eye* for Universal, Ross Hunter, the discreetly gay, indiscreetly extravagant, luxury-obsessed creator of what had become a house style for the studio's "women's pictures." The prolific Hunter was probably Universal's most important in-house producer at a time when the studio didn't have much to show for itself: He would deliver several films a year, usually a mix of very lucrative Doris Day pictures, *Tammy* movies, and melodramas like the remake of *Imitation of Life,* most of which shared a deep passion for interior decoration, hair, costume design, makeup, and scores drenched in Mantovaniesque strings. Nobody, including Hunter, made great claims for the film's scripts or performances, but his ability to deliver moneymaking movies had won him a measure of respect and power at the studio. "I have nothing against art," Hunter once said. *"Hiroshima Mon Amour* is great, but I wouldn't have produced it if I'd had the chance."[34] At Universal, there was no danger of that.

Hunter was an odd match for a project that came from a British play-wright and a New York director, but Shaffer, says Nichols, "was very funny and nice about it. I'd say, 'What will we do about this guy Ross Hunter?' And Peter would say, 'Well, I'll take care of him.' And he started doing things like writing, 'She appears at the top of the stairs' in the script, and then he would say, in parentheses, 'beautifully gowned.' He'd put in a lot of that shit to keep Ross Hunter happy."

When Shaffer finished the screenplay, Nichols was invited to Los An-geles to meet Hunter face-to-face. The two men had absolutely nothing to say to each other, but, determined to make the best of it, they spent the evening watching Norman Jewison's *Send Me No Flowers,* one of the rare Doris Day movies that Universal had made without Hunter's supervision, which was to open in October. When the screening ended, Nichols, feel-ing awkward, said to Hunter, "Did you enjoy the movie?"

"Well, it offended me as a producer," said Hunter.

"I said, 'How do you mean?' " Nichols recalls. "And he said, 'Well, as a producer, I was very offended by it.' I said, 'I don't understand, completely.' And he said, 'Well, as a producer, I wanted to rush up to the screen and just rip every bow off her dress.' And I said, 'Okay.' And I went back to my hotel and called my agent and said, 'I can't do this—I can't make this movie.' I mean, it would be hopeless. I knew I would kill him."[35]

Nichols got out of his commitment to make *The Public Eye;* there was a vague announcement in the press that the film would be postponed "for a while."[36] "I think there was something unpleasant, a deal in which I owed Universal a movie, and I think it cost me money, too. But anyway, it was over," he says.[37] *The Graduate* was now slated to be Nichols's first movie after all, if Turman could find anyone willing to make it—and just as *The Public Eye* was falling apart, he did: Joseph E. Levine, the founder of Embassy Pictures.

Embassy wasn't a Hollywood studio; it was, wrote Turman later, "the last stop on the line."[38] But the company was also a rarity in 1964: a well-financed American producer and distributor of movies that operated at the whim of one man independently of the studios (though he would sometimes produce movies for them). Levine had founded Embassy in the 1950s, using it as a pipeline through which he brought Italian movies to the United States—cheap, redubbed sword-and-sandals action films and Hercules pictures. "He was a great character, Levine," says Buck Henry. "For the Hercules movies, he hired me to be the voice of young Ulysses, the putz who trails after Hercules and keeps saying, 'No, Hercules! Don't go there! That's where the sirens live!'"[39]

Levine loved publicity; he'd call press conferences to announce nothing in particular and take out twenty-page ads in trade publications touting his upcoming films if he felt he was being ignored. No matter how often someone would call him crass or a philistine or even make fun of his enormous belly, he'd keep coming back for more; in 1963, he had allowed himself to be the subject of a documentary by Albert and David Maysles called *Showman* that depicted him in all of his overblown, hyperbolic glory. Levine didn't even seem to mind it when remarks like "You can fool all of the people all of the time if the advertising is right" were attributed to him, as long as the headlines kept coming.

"I never quite knew that Larry had been to every other outfit," says Nichols, "either because he didn't tell me or because I was still so naive. I certainly knew, though, that in every possible sense, Joseph E. Levine was scraping the bottom of the barrel."[40]

But like so many men in the movie business accused of being coarse or tasteless before and since, Levine also wanted to be thought of as a Medici. Every so often, Embassy would depart from its dub-'em-and-dump-'em distribution model; in the last couple of years, it had brought Fellini's *8 1/2* and Pietro Germi's *Divorce Italian Style* to U.S. screens, and Levine's knack for promoting the films with ads that played up their "forbidden" European sexuality, as blunt a tactic as it may have been, was also responsible for helping those films reach a much larger audience than they otherwise would have found. Levine himself had put up the money for Sidney Lumet's highly praised 1962 adaptation of *Long Day's Journey into Night* and was about to release Godard's *Contempt,* exploiting its star, Brigitte Bardot, for every millimeter of exposable skin he could get away with showing. "Levine was a vulgar vulgarian, but he wrote a check for the entire cost of *Long Day's Journey* without blinking," says Sidney Lumet. "He had Katharine Hepburn in a Eugene O'Neill play—it was just what he wanted, which was class with a capital K! We went out for the Academy Awards—I had never met him until then—and I remember him sitting in the Polo Lounge, so happy, a hooker on each arm, each hand on a different tit. But I ended up having a real affection for him—he really stuck by the film when it was doing no business. He didn't have taste, but he knew it when he saw it."[41]

"Joe was the king of the schlockmeisters,"[42] says Turman, "crude and crass, but not dumb."[43] Though publicly all Levine had to say about Fellini and Truffaut was that "some of these films are liked by the critics and nobody else,"[44] he enjoyed the Oscar nominations and the temporary luster that being connected with their work brought to Embassy. Levine, who was based in New York, knew Nichols's work and his reputation and was eager for the chance to associate himself with the director. He and Turman had a brief, tense standoff when Levine demanded executive producer credit. Turman refused, and Levine blinked first. On October 7, 1964, Embassy announced that it would finance *The Graduate* and that the film would begin production in the summer of 1965.[45]

Nichols was now back in New York, happy to know that *The Graduate* had a backer and happier still to be working in the theater again. That summer, he had directed his first off-Broadway play, Ann Jellicoe's *The Knack,* a British comedy that marked an early venture into the "swinging London" genre; his direction received rave reviews, and the play went on to run for more than eighteen months. In the fall, he returned to Broadway with another comedy, Murray Schisgal's *Luv,* an extended three-character sketch about neurotic New Yorkers in which Nichols had a cast that was up to his level—Alan Arkin, Eli Wallach, and Anne Jackson—and material that allowed him to exploit every possibility for a laugh. The play was a smash, running for more than two years and sending Nichols on his way to a second consecutive Tony Award for Best Director. With three hits now running in New York simultaneously, his reputation as a director started to outstrip his fame as a performer. "Things have reached such a monkey-see monkey-do situation that it is now incumbent upon anyone who has written a funny play or novel . . . to send the work to Nichols with a note exhorting him to direct it,"[46] said *The New York Times.* The same week, *Time* magazine called Nichols "one of the more gifted and promising new directors to take his place in the American theater since Elia Kazan left Constantinople."[47]

If studios hadn't known who Nichols was when Turman was trying to sell his movie, they did now, and one of them was about to make him an offer that would set *The Graduate* back more than a year. In March, Jack Warner had spent $500,000 to acquire the movie rights to Edward Albee's 1962 play, *Who's Afraid of Virginia Woolf?*[48] Warner thought the play—if its raw language could ever be sanitized enough to meet the stringent requirements of Production Code chief Geoffrey Shurlock—would make a great vehicle for Bette Davis and James Mason,[49] and he hired Ernest Lehman, who had adapted *West Side Story,* to write the script.

Though he had never overseen a movie before, Lehman somehow convinced Warner to let him produce *Virginia Woolf* as well and also won the right to cast and director approval. The studio thought briefly of Henry Fonda, who had admired the play (and who had lost a chance to originate the role of George on Broadway when his new agent preemptively turned down the "no-balls character").[50] Jack Lemmon and Patricia Neal were also considered.[51] But when Elizabeth Taylor and Richard Burton expressed interest, all casting questions came to an end, and what had been a chancy purchase of a controversial property suddenly became a gamble on which the potential risks and rewards were much higher. Fred Zinnemann[52] and John Frankenheimer[53] had both been mentioned as possible directors, but no deal had been made. Nichols had gotten to know Burton in 1961, when he was on Broadway with Elaine May and Burton was just down Shubert Alley playing Arthur in *Camelot;* he had spent time with Burton and Taylor in Italy during the filming of *Cleopatra,*[54] and the couple had talked about starring for Nichols in *The Public Eye*.[55] "Elizabeth Taylor and Richard Burton were pushing, really pushing, for Mike," says Larry Turman. "And I thought, let Mike do all his learning on *Virginia Woolf* and then he can do my movie second. I thought I was being smart."[56]

Once Taylor wanted him for *Virginia Woolf*, Lehman and Jack Warner wanted him, too. Nichols, who loved the play, jumped at the opportunity. In December, he signed on as director for $250,000.[57] Production was due to start in March. *The Graduate* would have to be postponed.[58] In early 1965, he headed for Los Angeles to begin preproduction. He had less than three months to learn how to make a movie, outmaneuver a notoriously combative studio head and a cautious, passive producer, and figure out how to direct the world's most famous couple. And, he says, "I wasn't entirely sure how a camera worked."[59]

SIX

etween August 1964 and March 1965, four new movies sold so many tickets and made so much money that, collectively, they pointed toward a dramatic shift in the tastes of American moviegoers and suggested an entirely new way for the studios to do business. Hollywood did not react well. Historically, the only event more disruptive to the industry's ecosystem than an unexpected flop is an unexpected smash, and, caught off guard by the sudden arrival of more revenue than they thought their movies could ever bring in, the major studios resorted to three old habits: imitation, frenzied speculation, and panic.

Three of the pictures were musicals—Disney's *Mary Poppins*, Warner's *My Fair Lady*, and Fox's *The Sound of Music*. By the end of their runs, each film was the highest grosser in the history of its company, and in 1966, *The Sound of Music* passed *Gone With the Wind* to become the biggest moneymaker ever.[1] Musicals had been reliably popular throughout the sound era, but the repeat business for this trio of films, the extraordinary duration of their theatrical runs, and the sheer amount of cash they yielded changed the industry's understanding of what the ceiling on a movie's potential grosses could be. The numbers seemed to point to an evolution of popular taste in road-show movies away from biblical epics and historical pageantry and toward lighter, song-packed family entertainment. This was an ominous turn of events for George Stevens, who had spent the last several years of his career pulling together *The Greatest Story*

Ever Told, and for John Huston, who had been working without end on *The Bible,* a film that seemed like a shrewd business idea when it was conceived in early 1963[2] and looked more like the last relic of a rusted-out genre by the time it opened in 1966. But it was generally good news for Hollywood, which had always known how to produce musicals and would now simply make them bigger, longer, and more frequently. Though they could be complicated and costly, musicals were a good fit for old-guard studios that were still wedded to a decades-old production model, holding on to their in-house costume construction shops, expanding their lots, and keeping music departments with seventy-five-piece orchestras on call. If the audience needed more musicals, the studios would just build more soundstages, buy the rights to every Broadway show that was still on the market, and, once that well ran dry, invent musical versions of old films from their own libraries.

The fourth movie to change the business represented a conundrum, since it seemed to contradict the message of the other three. United Artists' *Goldfinger* was the third James Bond movie to open in the United States in a year and a half. The first 007 vehicle, *Dr. No,* first arrived on American shores in the summer of 1963; it was shot cheaply, for $1.4 million,[3] and initially made a profit for the studio and for producers Harry Saltzman and Albert R. "Cubby" Broccoli that was too small to merit much attention. But even in 1961, when UA made its first deal with Saltzman and Broccoli,[4] executives Arthur Krim, Robert Benjamin, and David Picker had envisioned the Bond movies as a series that would build a growing audience with every installment. At a time when other studios simply hadn't considered that immense amounts of money could be made from movies with recurring characters (what would later be called "franchises"), UA's bet paid off staggeringly well. Working quickly, they brought out *From Russia with Love,* which cost $2.2 million and returned almost $10 million to the studio,[5] in early 1964. *Goldfinger,* which opened in December, cost $3.5 million to make—about average for a studio picture—and brought UA $23 million,[6] a then staggering sum that put the movie alongside the three musicals among the ten top grossers in history. And the money came fast: *Goldfinger* earned back its cost after just two weeks on sixty-four screens, a feat so widely publicized that it landed in *The Guinness Book of World Records*.[7]

With the next Bond installment, *Thunderball*, already promised for December 1965, the studios could no longer ignore the fact that United Artists, the company that didn't play by their rules, was beating them at their own game. The Bond films exemplified UA's strategy of bringing in strong independent producers, letting them make their movies their way, and splitting the profits when the money rolled in, and their immense success was a major factor in the erosion of the studio system by the end of the 1960s. But in early 1965, UA's competitors couldn't quite bring themselves to believe that the UA model would supplant a way of working that had been in place since the 1930s. Even Universal, then the most minor of the majors, was still signing a roster of young actors as contract players in the mid-1960s as if nothing had changed in decades.[8] The studios knew there was a lesson to be drawn from the success of the James Bond movies, but they chose the wrong one: In the next three years, they would release more than three dozen Bond rip-offs, spoofs, and second-rate copies.

If UA's success with the Bond series was an irritant to its rivals, the box office performance of *Mary Poppins, My Fair Lady,* and *The Sound of Music* proved to be a stimulant that led to the equivalent of gold rush fever. A year earlier, when Arthur Jacobs had started to chase the rights to *Doctor Dolittle*, he was a producer in search of a property that could serve as his calling card to studios. Now, suddenly, he owned the cornerstone on which 20th Century-Fox was building its hopes for 1966, and his leading man, Rex Harrison, was no longer *Cleopatra*'s aging Caesar, but *My Fair Lady*'s "sexy Rexy," the star of a box office smash that was on its way to winning eight Academy Awards.

All of which would have elated Jacobs except for one thing: Nine months after he had made his *Doctor Dolittle* deal with 20th Century-Fox's Dick Zanuck, the movie's screenwriter, Alan Jay Lerner, was not a day closer to turning in a first draft. Jacobs had known from the start that Lerner wouldn't be easy or exceptionally fast: He had been struggling for four years with the book and lyrics for a new Broadway musical, *I Picked a Daisy*, first attempting to collaborate with Richard Rodgers, who grew tired of his delays and distractibility and quit, and then with Burton Lane.[9] Lerner had made it clear to Jacobs that he would not begin work on *Doctor Dolittle* until he finished his own show.[10] But *I Picked a Daisy* still seemed to be in limbo, and Jacobs was driven mad by Lerner's tendency to drop out of communication with him for weeks or months at a stretch with no explanation.

Lerner's deadline to deliver a treatment of the *Doctor Dolittle* script to Jacobs was October 1, 1964,[11] a date that drifted by without a word from him. Aware of the pressure Lerner was facing from both his Broadway show and his impending divorce proceeding, Jacobs agreed to give him an extension until January 15.[12] A month before the new due date, Jacobs cabled Lerner and told him that it was "imperative" they meet to discuss the script before Lerner handed in his work.[13] Fox wanted a clear timetable, and Jacobs did, too: Their new plan was for Lerner to finish a thirty-page treatment in January, report to Los Angeles to begin work on the screenplay and lyrics in April, and turn in a full first draft by September 1, 1965.[14]

Just before the January deadline, Lerner finally responded—by asking for still more time to write the treatment. Jacobs was out of patience. He told Lerner he had ten more days, until January 25, at which point Jacobs himself would go to New York to pick up Lerner's completed work.[15] Lerner agreed. Ten days later, Jacobs boarded a plane, flew across the country, and took a car directly from the airport to Lerner's apartment. When he got there, he was told that Lerner had gone to Rome.[16]

Jacobs, now livid, sent Lerner a cable: "Extremely distressed by your failure to meet with me. . . . As you know I made special trip to New York for the express purpose of meeting you and receiving Dolittle treatment. . . . The entire arrangement including payment of your $100,000 is in complete jeopardy."[17]

That got Lerner's attention, and Lerner had Louis Nizer, his divorce lawyer, plead his case directly to Dick Zanuck, who was now concerned enough to demand a face-to-face meeting with the writer himself. Lerner was under intense pressure to finish *I Picked a Daisy*, Nizer told Zanuck, and there was also "the domestic relations matter,"[18] which was due to go before a judge in March. Around this time, Lerner's representatives made a counterproposal to Fox: Might he simply dispense with writing a treat-ment altogether if he agreed to hand in a screenplay by the end of April? After Lerner met with Zanuck in late February, the studio was temporarily mollified. "I was delighted with our meeting," Zanuck wrote in a cable on March 4, adding, "As I pointed out to you it is imperative that we have your first draft screenplay May 1ˢᵗ and I was greatly relieved when you guaranteed this Stop I am convinced more than ever that we are going to have a great picture."[19]

Fox's hope that *Doctor Dolittle* would, as the studio's publicity materi-als had promised, represent 1966's Christmas gift to the world had all but evaporated. But the studio still wanted to hold on to the film's creative team, and the bigger a box office hit *My Fair Lady* became, the stronger a hand Lerner had to play; soon after his meeting with Zanuck, he had his agent, Irving "Swifty" Lazar, finalize his $350,000 fee.[20] But by then, Lerner's missed deadlines were putting the whole project in jeopardy. Vin-cente Minnelli, Jacobs's original choice to direct the film, had long since departed, and Rex Harrison's participation was now up in the air. On April 5, 1965, Harrison won the Best Actor Oscar for *My Fair Lady* and found himself, for the first time in his long career, in demand as a movie star. Since the late-1965 start-of-production date that had originally been planned for *Doctor Dolittle* was now an impossibility, Harrison could have gotten out of his commitment to make the film, and he considered walk-ing away. Jacobs prevailed upon Lerner, who had caused the problem, to fix it, asking him to meet with Harrison in New York and get him to agree to a schedule in which *Dolittle* would begin production in May or June 1966.[21] In a moment of post-Oscar exuberance that he came to regret, Harrison had just decided to reunite with his *Cleopatra* director, Joseph Mankiewicz, on a comic update of *Volpone* that would start shooting in the fall of 1965,[22] so he was amenable to a later start for *Dolittle* and agreed to stay on board for the moment.

As Lerner's May 1 screenplay deadline approached, a familiar and un-settling silence set in once again, and in late April, Jacobs got in touch with Lerner's team and heard, one more time, that "because of Lerner's preoccupation with the writing of material for his play" (now retitled *On a Clear Day You Can See Forever*), not only would he miss his deadline, but

he "would not be in a position to do any work on the *Doctor Dolittle* treatment before the first of October."[23] Jacobs, perhaps for the first time, realized that he had wasted more than a year waiting for a script on which not
a word of work had been done. On May 7, he fired Lerner and demanded
the return of the $100,000 he had paid him to start writing the movie.[24]

In the 1960s, the producers of the Academy Awards began what eventually
became a tradition of inviting the previous year's Best Actor and Actress
recipients back to the show as presenters the following April. So in the
spring of 1965, one year after taking home his Oscar for *Lilies of the
Field,* Sidney Poitier found himself at the Santa Monica Civic Auditorium
again, this time handing a statuette to Julie Andrews for *Mary Poppins,* and
watching the prize he had won last year go to Harrison.

If some in the film industry had indulged themselves in the belief that
Poitier's Academy Award would create new opportunities for black actors in
Hollywood, or even for him, Poitier had not let himself be tempted by false
optimism. For all of Bob Hope's tinny jokes that evening about how the
Oscars looked more and more like the United Nations, Poitier's career in
the year since the success of *Lilies of the Field* had not changed markedly.
For six months after the award, he didn't work in movies at all but spent
much of the spring and summer of 1964 taking his most significant steps
yet toward civil rights activism. In New York, he appeared at an NAACP
benefit to honor the tenth anniversary of the Supreme Court's decision
ordering the desegregation of schools. He went to Washington, D.C., to
lobby for the landmark Civil Rights Act, which passed in July.[25] (Title VII
of the bill, which prohibited racial discrimination in employment, finally
provided the legal clout the NAACP needed in its ongoing struggle to in-
tegrate movie industry unions.)[26] And, urged on by Harry Belafonte, who
was far more politically engaged than Poitier and was forever pushing his
friend to join the movement more wholeheartedly, Poitier traveled with
him to Greenville, Mississippi, just days after the murder of three civil
rights workers, to meet with Stokely Carmichael and members of the Student Nonviolent Coordinating Committee (SNCC) at a small dance hall.
The two performers were followed the entire time they were there by

members of the Ku Klux Klan. "Don't worry," Carmichael assured them, "if they've got cannons, we've got cannons." They stayed only a few hair-raising hours, under heavy security, before returning to New York.[27]

Poitier, still deeply conflicted about the end of his marriage, his tumultuous relationship with Diahann Carroll, and the fact that, as he later wrote, "it was still just Sidney Poitier out there," was impassioned about the process of psychoanalysis at the time and spent four or five sessions a week on the couch, talking to his therapist.[28] He was less excited about returning to work. Professionally, he now resided in a netherworld that placed him somewhere between movie star and role model. America seemed most comfortable with him as an embodiment of nebulously defined dignity and incremental social progress, and the movie industry was happy to deploy him as a sort of international goodwill ambassador, sending him off to the Berlin Film Festival as a cold war exemplar of America's open society. But where were the great roles? At one point in the wake of his Oscar, Poitier complained that two-thirds of the parts he had played in movies were "triggered by the Negroness of my own life. I'd hate for my gift—or whatever—to be circumscribed by color. I'd like to explore King Lear, for instance."[29] But he also must have wanted a privilege of stardom that was routinely accorded his white contemporaries—roles created especially for him, which at the time almost certainly meant race-specific parts.

In late 1964, Poitier went back to work. He costarred with Richard Widmark—a friend with whom he had worked twice before—in *The Bedford Incident*, a drama set aboard a navy destroyer in which he played a visiting journalist and Widmark the tyrannical captain with whom he comes into conflict. The film, shot in black and white, was not particularly distinguished—Poitier himself called it "a bad movie"[30]—but it represented a $400,000 payday for Poitier (though half of it was to be deferred for more than a decade)[31] and a relatively rare chance to star in a movie in which race was not a central theme. *Bedford* was due to open at the end of 1965, along with a movie that Poitier had started shooting in March, just before that year's Oscar ceremony. The new film, MGM's *A Patch of Blue*, was, like *Lilies of the Field*, a racial homily, in which a young blind white woman (Elizabeth Hartman) falls in love with a black man. Poitier thought both movies were "fables" with "very little relation to objective reality," and he had little interest in his saintly, restrained character, who again kept his serenity and temper in the face of racist abuse and was not allowed to manifest more than a hint of sexual appetite or energy. By the time Poitier finished the movie, he said, "I was at my wits' end."[32]

No matter what kind of role he took, Poitier ended up feeling neutered. A race-blind part in a mediocre film like *The Bedford Incident* was more a step sideways than forward—in a country roiling with racial unrest, why make a film that averted its eyes from the problem? On the other hand, every time he played a character like *A Patch of Blue*'s Gordon Ralfe, whose race was integral to the plot, he seemed to end up becoming complicit in a fantasy designed to explain to white America that racism was wrong because it meant mistreating someone as free of human flaws and foibles as Sidney Poitier.

The actor's frustration was reaching a peak at about the time that his agent, Martin Baum, got his first look at the manuscript for a new mystery novel by John Ball called *In the Heat of the Night*. Ball's book had been shopped to several studios; the playwright and activist Larry Kramer, then a twenty-nine-year-old reader in Columbia Pictures' New York story department whose job was to scout outside material for the studio, recommended that Mike Frankovich (who had made *The Bedford Incident*) purchase the rights as a possible vehicle for Poitier, but Frankovich wasn't interested.[33] Ball's novel found a taker when Baum brought it to the Mirisch Company, which for the last several years had been the main independent supplier of movies to United Artists. The Mirisch brothers—"Harold was the older brother, who kind of made the final decisions, Walter was the production guy, and Marvin was the accountant," recalls director Norman Jewison—didn't develop their own material. "They were middlemen," says Jewison, "kind of wholesalers,"[34] whose strategy was to pursue material that already had a strong director or star attached to it and then take the projects to UA to work out a deal. The Mirisches didn't spend more money than they had to—budgets for the first forty films they made for the studio generally stayed between $1.5 million and $3.5 million. They were efficient, and they were remarkably productive; in the most recent renegotiation of their deal with

UA, in September 1964, they had promised the studio forty-eight films in ten years.[35]

When *In the Heat of the Night* arrived, the Mirisch Company was in the market for new material. And Ball's novel, which was published in March 1965 and received warm reviews, was new, although not as new as many in the movie business may have imagined. Poitier's decision to play Virgil Tibbs, who in the book is a polite, chatty Pasadena police officer who passes through a town in the Carolinas on the evening of a murder and stays to help solve the crime,[36] was noted as a Hollywood milestone: No black actor had ever starred in a detective movie before. But Tibbs was hardly a groundbreaker in mystery fiction, a genre in which black detectives and cops had already constituted a small but strong subcategory for years. In 1957, *Rebecca's Pride* by Donald McNutt Douglass, a novel narrated by a black police captain in the Virgin Islands, had won the Mystery Writers of America's Edgar Award for best first novel. The following year, Ed Lacy's *Room to Swing*, a first-person novel about a black private eye in New York, won the Edgar as the year's best mystery. And by the time *In the Heat of the Night* reached bookstores, the black writer Chester Himes had already published a half dozen of his lively, bawdy, richly textured Harlem novels featuring a black police team, Coffin Ed Johnson and Grave Digger Jones, books that would come to be viewed as classics of the genre.

Himes's novels came from a specifically urban, black perspective (it's no surprise that they were more attractive to Hollywood in the 1970s than in the 1960s). And although Ed Lacy was white (Lacy was the pseudonym for a political activist named Leonard Zinberg who was married to a black woman), *Room to Swing*, with its casual references to Marcus Garvey and black nationalism, its depiction of the intraracial class distinctions between light-skinned and darker-skinned African Americans, and its casual mockery of both patronizing white liberals and outright racists, was a good decade ahead of Hollywood in its thinking and far more sophisticated than anything *In the Heat of the Night* had to offer.[37] But what made those novels strong on the page—the specificity and "blackness" of their worldview— is exactly what kept filmmakers away. *In the Heat of the Night*'s take on race was easier for the studios to grasp. Virgil Tibbs is a foreigner in an unfriendly land, and Ball, who was white, wrote in a tone that was not omniscient so much as it was neutral; the novel simply observes Tibbs and the white cop and police chief with whom he is forced to work without attempting very much in the way of viewing things from Tibbs's vantage point or understanding his state of mind. As in *The Graduate*, the novel's relatively spare prose style allowed readers to fill in its blanks however they chose; and Ball's storytelling presented an opportunity to place Sidney Poitier in a position that seemed to please moviegoers—not as the master of his own fate, but as a low-key, unexpected, mostly affable presence in a predominantly white world.

Poitier liked the idea of playing Tibbs, but Mirisch, who was both a good liberal and a pragmatic businessman, knew the film might face resistance both from United Artists and from audiences, who were used to crime movies in which, as an article announcing Poitier's casting phrased it, "Negro actors [stay] on the sidelines . . . dogging the heels of the detectives as helpful servants or comedy relief."[38] Mirisch's solution was to sell UA on the film as a potentially profitable enterprise, not a worthy cause. "I made the argument [to UA] that, even if there was a great deal of exhibitor opposition to the picture below the Mason-Dixon line, it certainly would find a ready audience in the great northern cities," says Mirisch. "And I argued that the cost of the picture was not so great that it couldn't recoup, even if it were never to play in the South at all. But we had to make the picture for a reasonable price."[39] Coming off of the success of *Goldfinger*, United Artists also knew that the character of Tibbs—even though he had appeared in only one novel—might represent another potentially lucrative film series for the studio, and the Mirisch Company had included, in its deal with Poitier, an option for two sequels. When Mirisch agreed to keep the budget low—around $2 million—and convinced Poitier to take $200,000,[40] half of what he had received for *The Bedford Incident*, to play Tibbs, the studio gave the project its approval. In June 1965, soon after he finished *A Patch of Blue*, Poitier signed for the starring role.[41]

SEVEN

Robert Benton hadn't been thinking much about *Bonnie and Clyde* on the morning that Warren Beatty showed up on his doorstep, asking if he could read the screenplay. After the Godard fiasco, it had almost been a relief to stop hoping for anything, to drop it and move on. Even if he and David Newman had let themselves continue to cycle through one round after another of optimism and despair, there wouldn't have been any time to prepare for this one; Beatty had announced his interest in the movie just twenty minutes before he rang Benton's doorbell. The moment was disorienting: Movie stars didn't just arrive in one's living room after breakfast on a lazy Saturday. And it wasn't even clear who was supposed to be doing the courting.

Beatty had the advantage of surprise on his side and knew how to play the moment, but the last eighteen months had been somewhat humbling for him as well; he was no longer a cocksure star on the rise, but an actor trying to get his career back on track. Before he went to Chicago to start shooting *Mickey One*, Beatty had begun a serious affair with actress Leslie Caron. Caron was thirty-two, six years older than Beatty; she was married to the British theater director Peter Hall, and she was the mother of two young children. In June 1964, soon after the film was completed, their romance became public in the worst possible way, when Hall, who had already filed for divorce, charged Caron with adultery and named Beatty as corespondent.[1] Since she was now enjoined from taking her two children out of England, Caron promptly returned to London to be with them, and Beatty soon followed her.

Being seen as a robustly active bachelor in gossip columns was one thing; being depicted as a dilettantish home wrecker in tabloid headlines in both England and America was another. The middle of 1964 marked the start of a bleak stretch in the actor's professional life. *Lilith*'s poor reception at the New York Film Festival in the fall was, though not unexpected, still disappointing; Beatty knew that the oblique and experimental *Mickey One*, which was not scheduled to open for another year, would at best be received as an art-house curiosity. And his hope that he would finally have the chance to star in a comedy with *What's New, Pussycat?* had been dashed after a confrontation that left the actor feeling particularly stung.

Beatty had fretted about Woody Allen's *Pussycat* rewrites throughout the production of *Mickey One* and, after his move to London, found himself in a series of increasingly tense standoffs with his old friend Charles Feldman. Beatty still wanted to produce the movie with Feldman and star in it, but he was irked that his role had gotten smaller. When Feldman insisted on casting his girlfriend, the French actress Capucine, in a major role and, during contract negotiations, baitingly reminded the young actor that his "personal problem" with Caron was a potential liability,[2] the dispute between the two men became personal.* Angry about the way the movie had evolved, Beatty fussed over his billing,[3] then quit the project, gambling that Feldman would cave in to his wishes rather than let him go. He was mistaken. Feldman was already disconcerted that at least one studio to which he'd pitched *Pussycat* had dismissed Beatty as "not a 'top star' ";[4] he wrote Beatty off and moved on to what, at the time, was a much more bankable cast, signing Peter O'Toole as the Don Juan and Peter Sellers, hot from the success of *Dr. Strangelove*, as his psychoanalyst. "I diva'ed my way out of the movie," says Beatty. "I walked off of *What's New, Pussycat?* thinking they couldn't do it without me. I was wrong. And

*Although one recent biography of Beatty has suggested that Feldman also hurt Beatty's pride by reminding him of "your money problem," what Feldman actually wrote was "you too must be mindful of *our* economic and money problems"—he was warning Beatty that, given his history of balkiness and last minute departures from projects, he expected him to keep his word and show up on time for *Pussycat*'s September 1964 start date.

I was hurt. I was really hurt." Woody Allen, whose script Beatty still liked despite the degree to which he had augmented his own role, stayed on the film, and, says Beatty, "his part went from seventy-five pages to sixty to fifty to forty. By the time the movie was made, he might as well have been just a guy on a pogo stick again. They just went on to another guy and did another script. What the movie did was, it certainly caused me to be a producer. I really had been behaving as the producer of the movie and was unable to come to comity with the nominal producer. So I learned. Some things that you care about, you have to control."[5]

Beatty wasn't ready to produce yet, but he took a step in that direction on his next movie, *Promise Her Anything*. Arthur Hiller's film, which started production in early 1965 in London, gave him his first role in a contemporary light romance. The character of a charming, energetic, slightly reckless man brought up short by overexuberance or blind confidence—someone who doesn't have nearly the control of his own life that he imagines he does—was one to which Beatty was deeply attracted; it would define the majority of his best-known roles, no matter what the genre, for the next twenty years. While *Promise Her Anything* was only a minor comedy, it represented Beatty's first opportunity to present his own version of himself to the public. In the movie, which was released by Paramount, he plays an aspiring director who specializes in short "nudie" flicks but has too arty a touch to satisfy his boss (Keenan Wynn), who mocks him as "the Ingmar Bergman of the mail-order movie." The film was one of the first mainstream movies to acknowledge, albeit lightheartedly, a worry that had been hanging over Hollywood for years: The prudery of the Production Code had been causing the studios to lose a share of the audience to European films. "The customers are getting too hip! Times have changed!" Wynn complains.

"Sex never changes," replies Beatty.

"Only in America," says Wynn. "In Denmark it changes. . . . .Today if a guy wants to see some broads in bikinis, he don't need no mail-order movie—he just goes down to the corner supermarket. If he wants *real* kicks, he goes to an Italian movie!"

Promise Her Anything appealed to Beatty for several reasons. It allowed him to costar with Caron, who plays his girlfriend, the mother of a little boy. It kept him in England; Seven Arts, which produced the movie, agreed to shoot it at Shepperton Studios, building sets that doubled, none too convincingly, as Greenwich Village, so that Caron could be near her children while her divorce was pending. And it had a patient and easygoing director in Hiller, whose recent film, the sharp, dark antiwar comedy *The Americanization of Emily*, Beatty had admired. "On *Promise Her Anything*, you could *feel* Warren as a director and producer," says Hiller. "You could feel his grasp of movies increasing—he had an appetite for everything about it. I don't think that he wanted to be doing the actual directing or producing yet, but he was very strong. There were times when he wanted something different than I wanted, but we'd talk it out."[6]

When production ended in May 1965, Beatty, for the first time in a few years, could celebrate the end of a smooth and convivial shoot. And he liked living in London, which by then had transformed itself into a third entertainment capital. If Los Angeles was the home of movie and television production, and New York represented the energy of theater and publishing, London took the best of both cities and added to it a music scene that was having worldwide impact on fashion, photography, art, and, most of all, youth. A third of the city's population was between the ages of fifteen and thirty-four, and the never-ending party roved from coffee bar to discotheque to gallery to town house to boutique, with playwrights and photographers, rock stars and fashion models, actors and directors, all intermingling along the way. The Beatles had just finished shooting *Help!* for United Artists ("it's a rollicking, rollicking, happy, smash, uhh . . . what are the other words you say about films?" joked John Lennon).[7] The Rolling Stones had just come on the scene to challenge them for the rock-and-roll throne; the Bond films had made Sean Connery an international star; Albert Finney, Richard Harris, Terence Stamp, Julie Christie, Lynn and Vanessa Redgrave, Tom Courtenay, and Michael Caine were all emerging; and whatever fusty, embalmed image American pop-culture consumers had once had of England was giving way to a sense that it was the new center of freedom, style, and sexual openness. Since almost every American studio maintained a base of operations there, London by the mid-1960s was also a thriving hub of film production, whether they were scruffy homegrown dramas or expensive studio undertakings that drew talent from Hollywood and Europe. "In a decade dominated by youth, London has burst into bloom. It swings," declared *Time*. In such a spirited milieu, Caron became "unquestionably this season's most with-it hostess,"[8] and Beatty was right where he most enjoyed being—at the center of the action.

In the mid-1960s, real celebrity meant making it in all three cities, and as Warren Beatty was traveling across the Atlantic in one direction, Leslie Bricusse was working his way west. Bricusse was thirty-four, a composer and lyricist who had begun writing songs as a Cambridge University undergraduate, where his theater club collaborators included writer Frederic Raphael and director Jonathan Miller; their first effort together transferred to the West End when the three men were just nineteen years old. Bricusse met the rising pop singer Anthony Newley soon after that; they struck up a friendship and decided to write a musical together. They first tried adapting Ingmar Bergman's *Smiles of a Summer Night*, a project that foundered over their inability to obtain rights to the film (a problem that Stephen Sondheim was able to solve several years later with *A Little Night Music*). The effort left them each with a new nickname, obtained by dividing the last name of the director they so admired (Newley became "Newberg" and Bricusse became "Brickman"), and an undiminished determination to get a musical to the West End.[9]

Bricusse and Newley worked astonishingly fast. Ten weeks after they sat down together to begin writing *Stop the World—I Want to Get Off*, the show, starring Newley, opened in Manchester. The bare-bones production, budgeted at just £6,000,[10] moved to London soon after and became an immediate success, powered by the belted-out ballads "What Kind of Fool Am I" and "Once in a Lifetime." In 1962, Bricusse and Newley brought the musical to New York, where both men received Tony nominations. Bricusse and his wife, Yvonne, both enjoyed the party circuit, and given that Newley, his best friend, had just married Joan Collins, it was perhaps inevitable that the attractions of Los Angeles and the movie business started to tug at them.

Bricusse was not Arthur Jacobs's or Dick Zanuck's first choice to write *Doctor Dolittle* after Alan Jay Lerner was fired. With *Mary Poppins* making a tremendous amount of money, Jacobs had, even before dismissing

Lerner, checked on the availability of Richard and Robert Sherman, the songwriting brothers who had composed the score for *Poppins* and had just won the Best Song Oscar for "Chim Chim Cher-ee." But the Shermans were tied to Disney, and Jacobs realized that hiring Bricusse would solve a problem and save some money, since, unlike Lerner, he could write the film's music as well as its lyrics and screenplay.[11]

A week before he fired Lerner, Jacobs sent Bricusse the Dolittle books and sounded him out; on May 6, Jacobs spent the day with him in San Francisco, where Bricusse was working on material for an ill-fated musical called *Pickwick* (an adaptation of *The Pickwick Papers*).[12] Bricusse wanted to impress him—his second Broadway venture with Newley, *The Roar of the Greasepaint—The Smell of the Crowd*, had not received anything like the acclaim of *Stop the World*, and with *Pickwick* in trouble, the prospect of a Hollywood job and paycheck was auspiciously timed. Bricusse's only previous work on a movie had been the amusingly overwrought lyrics for Shirley Bassey's thunderous rendition of *Goldfinger*, but he knew how to work his way through a pitch meeting. During his meeting with Jacobs, Bricusse threw several suggestions for animal-related tunes on the table—many of which were actually concepts that he had come up with for an unfinished musical called *Noah's Ark*—and also recommended the addition of a character that could serve as a female lead. The delighted producer responded by telling him, "I am here to change your life!"[13]

"Yesterday he had more specific ideas than the other gent has had in 14 months to think about it," Jacobs told Zanuck in a memo. He added, perhaps too optimistically, that Rex Harrison "is a great fan" and also noted the approval of the man who had (very temporarily, it turned out) replaced Vincente Minnelli in the director's chair, George Roy Hill. While Jacobs cautioned Zanuck that, contractually, any replacement for Lerner would have to be approved by Hugh Lofting's widow, he felt it wouldn't be a problem.[14]

In June, Zanuck agreed to hire Bricusse on a sort of trial basis, making a deal to put him up in Los Angeles, where he would write two songs and the first twenty pages of the *Doctor Dolittle* screenplay. Bricusse and his wife drove down from San Francisco and took to Beverly Hills instantly, moving into a house off Coldwater Canyon. The day Bricusse began to work on the film, he wrote the song "Talk to the Animals," tailoring it to

Harrison's narrow vocal range and what he called his "unique *Sprechgesang* style."[15] Two weeks later, Bricusse was summoned to the Fox lot to give the song a test run in front of the studio's music director, Lionel Newman, and a full orchestra. Bricusse got the job. But somehow, everyone forgot to tell Rex Harrison.

In New York, *Bonnie and Clyde* was no closer to finding a director or a studio than it had been the day Godard had walked out of Tom and Elinor Jones's apartment. After the publication of "The New Sentimentality," Benton and Newman had left *Esquire* and moved into an office together. Benton was now married, Newman had a growing family to support, and both men felt it was time to see if they could make a living as a writing team. Inspired by a comic book that Newman's young son had left on his living room floor,[16] they had begun work together with composer Charles Strouse on a Broadway musical, *It's a Bird . . . It's a Plane . . . It's Superman,* which would, a year later, become their first produced work.

After Godard's departure, says Norton Wright, "Ellie and I wanted to shift into high gear and see if we couldn't make amends [to Benton and Newman] by using our connections to Bob Montgomery."[17] Montgomery, for the second time, sent the script to Arthur Penn, who, for the second time, rejected it. Penn was about to start shooting *The Chase,* a massive, murky southern crime-and-passion melodrama for producer Sam Spiegel at Columbia. The production was gargantuan, the cast—led by Marlon Brando—challenging, and the tone of Lillian Hellman's adaptation utterly at odds with the original material by Horton Foote. Penn, facing all he could handle, passed on *Bonnie and Clyde* in a note sent by his assistant, saying that he liked the material but that its young-outlaws-on-the-lam theme was too close to *The Chase,* which begins with Robert Redford running for his life and just barely escaping the reach of the law.[18]

In the spring, Montgomery managed to get Jones and Wright a meeting with Arthur Krim, Robert Benjamin, and David Picker at United Artists, with the idea that Picker, who was enthusiastic about the project, might be able to sell his bosses on it. "It was really just to get their reaction and their ideas about what directors they would favor," says Wright. "Picker was a young guy—he seemed to be happy and open—but Krim and Benjamin looked gloomy and troubled."[19] They had read the screenplay—at least, they had gotten as far as the scene, early on, in which Clyde and his accomplice both fall into a sexual relationship with Bonnie (in this version of the script, Clyde's partner in crime was still named W. D. Jones, who was one of the last surviving members of the Barrow gang).[20] "Mr. Krim said to me, 'Mr. Wright, I don't know how to say this, but am I to assume that Clyde Barrow and this character W.D. are, well, being sexually intimate with Bonnie Parker?' And I said, 'Oh yeah, they're both balling her. And maybe each other! It's a ménage à trois!'. . . It was as if I'd spit on the flag. He looked at me, and there was a sort of a shudder. That was the first time that we realized that the sexuality of the script could be something that would make people somewhat reserved."[21]

"Their reaction was, 'What the hell do you want to make this movie for? I mean, you've got naked women and homosexuals and violence—are you out of your mind?' " says Jones.[22]

"Without exception, it was turned down," wrote Benton and Newman, "with comments . . . along the lines of, 'Who could care less about characters like these? They are repulsive people.' "[23]

After United Artists said no to *Bonnie and Clyde*, the movie began to feel like used goods. Those who weren't disgusted simply didn't see anything fresh about it. "This is what he said," wrote Jones after a meeting with a potential production manager for the film. " 'Oh my. Oh boy. Oh God. All that violence—it's been done before a million times. I've read it carefully through a couple of times and I just can't see anything special about it. It's like a thousand TV gangster films—Public Enemy Number One and his tough moll and speeding cars and all that. I doubt a distributor's reaction will be good.' "[24]

With no takers at the studios, Wright went to London, where he wooed Desmond Davis, a young British director who had been the camera operator on *A Taste of Honey, The Loneliness of the Long Distance Runner,* and *Tom Jones* before directing his first feature, 1964's *Girl with Green Eyes,* an art-house hit in the United States. Davis liked *Bonnie and Clyde,* but Benton and Newman's deal with Jones and Wright gave the writers approval over the choice of a director, and they vetoed him.[25]

"As we moved on," says Wright, "you could kind of see the names move toward the bottom of the barrel." Their low point came when Benton, Newman, Wright, and Jones, in an attempt to secure private financing, paid a visit to the Manhattan apartment of jazz clarinetist Artie Shaw, the last big name that Bob Montgomery was able to offer up. "We sat down, and Artie Shaw told us how terrible the script was—he said it was like looking in a sewer," says Benton. "Literally nobody wanted to do it. David and I would laugh and tell each other that we'd be eighty years old, out on the street, and still peddling *Bonnie and Clyde*."[26]

As *Promise Her Anything* wrapped in London, Beatty still wasn't sure what his next job was going to be. Nothing in particular had excited him until he heard that François Truffaut had been thinking about making his first English-language movie. As soon as Beatty heard about *Fahrenheit 451*, he wanted to play Montag, the book-burning "fireman" who begins to question authority. Caron knew Truffaut, and during a postproduction vacation in Paris, Beatty asked her to set up a lunch for two—after which he would, with choreographed offhandedness, arrive for coffee.[27]

It's a safe bet that the outcome of that lunch was a surprise to all three of the participants in it. Beatty showed up, as planned, at the end of the meal, and according to Caron, who acted as a translator and interpreter when needed, he expressed his enthusiasm for *Fahrenheit 451*.[28] Truffaut politely rebuffed his inquiry, telling him that he had already earmarked the role of Montag for Oskar Werner, the Austrian actor who had played Jules in *Jules and Jim* and had since moved on to star as a world-weary physician, a part that would bring him an Oscar nomination, in Stanley Kramer's soon-to-open *Ship of Fools*. (Truffaut, in his desire to put Beatty off, may have been less than fully honest about Werner's hold on the role; at the time of the lunch, he had not yet signed the actor for *Fahrenheit 451* and was considering Terence Stamp as well.)[29]

Truffaut recommended *Bonnie and Clyde* to Beatty, praising Benton and Newman's script and telling him he should take a look at it. If Beatty had read the treatment a year earlier, when Harrison Starr and Godard had talked about making the movie while on the set of *Mickey One,* he either didn't remember or didn't reveal it. But Beatty came away from the lunch eager to get his hands on the screenplay, and he decided to contact Benton. Caron was also intrigued, imagining that *Bonnie and Clyde* might be a good opportunity for her to reteam with Beatty on screen. And, somewhat perversely, Truffaut, who had long since passed on the film, left the lunch with his own interest in *Bonnie and Clyde* rekindled, even though his brief encounter with Beatty had left him determined to avoid working with the actor.

Several factors, including the volatility of Truffaut's own enthusiasms, were probably responsible for his sudden reemergence as a possible director for the movie. The start of production on *Fahrenheit 451* was now facing yet another delay; Truffaut's own hard sell of *Bonnie and Clyde* to Beatty may have reminded him of what he had liked about the script in the first place; and perhaps most significant, Elinor Jones had stayed in touch with him for the last several months, determined to hold on to even the slenderest chance that he might reverse himself and make the picture after all. Jones had also kept in touch with David Picker, who saw great potential in the screenplay;[30] on June 5, 1965, unaware that Truffaut had just been talking about the screenplay to Beatty, she and Wright sent the director a letter, telling him that Picker was "very enthusiastic about the property and has indicated a willingness to put up full financing for the film in the neighborhood of $800,000." Jones and Wright asked Truffaut if he would permit them to tell Picker he was still considering the movie; they quickly followed up with a telegram inviting him back to New York to reopen the discussion.[31]

Picker's desire to make the movie was serious, and if Truffaut's was just a whim, it wasn't apparent from his behavior. On June 18, the director wrote back to Jones, telling her, "Your proposition concerning *Bonnie and Clyde* has come at just the right moment, provided . . . that we will be able to start shooting this summer." Truffaut was ready to talk specifics and went on to enumerate several conditions that had to be met as a prerequisite to continue negotiations: He wanted $80,000 plus 10 percent of the net profits to direct the film, he wanted Helen Scott hired as his personal assistant, and he wanted Alexandra Stewart, who had costarred with Beatty in *Mickey One,* to play Bonnie: "She would represent for me . . . [a] reassuring presence, since it is very important, in this, my first English-language film, that I have around me people with whom I can get along." If Jones and Wright were able to meet those requirements, he said, he would plan a trip to New York to discuss other issues—the choice of cinematographer, his hope that Benton and Newman would be available for rewrites before and during the shoot, and the casting of Clyde, for whom Truffaut now wanted Terence Stamp ("But I will not speak to him before hearing what you have to say," he wrote Jones).[32]

Jones blanched a little at the idea of Stamp, whose film *The Collector* was just opening in New York ("Terence Stamp?! He's an Englishman!" she wrote in her notes), but she was determined not to let Truffaut slip away again.[33] At the same time, Beatty had decided to pursue *Bonnie and Clyde* his own way. He flew to New York, telephoned Benton, whom he had met at a party years earlier, and reintroduced himself.

"I think he doubted me when I said who I was," says Beatty of Benton, who was indeed incredulous.[34] "Warren said he'd had lunch with Truffaut and had heard about the script, and could he see it? I said, yes, I'll bring it to you, and he said, that's all right, I'll come by your apartment. Twenty minutes later there he was. My wife was so angry—she hadn't even had a chance to put on makeup."

Beatty took the script and left. A little while later, he called Benton and said, "I'm on page 25 and I want to do it." Benton, knowing that he had yet to reach the scene in which Clyde's bisexuality was introduced, said, "Wait until you get to page 45." Beatty hung up. It didn't take long for the phone to ring again. "I'm on page 45," he said, "and I know what you're talking about, and I still want to do it. Who do you want to direct?"[35]

Beatty has often said that when he first read Benton and Newman's screenplay, he wanted to produce the film, not star in it: "I didn't want to play Clyde. I didn't think I was right for it. You know who I thought was right for it? Bob Dylan. And the person I could see the most as Bonnie was my sister. But I couldn't see her with Bob Dylan. And certainly not with me! So I was confused."[36] But Beatty soon learned that he was getting ahead of himself, since Elinor Jones and Norton Wright still had five months left on their eighteen-month option. Had Beatty truly wanted to star in the film at that point, he could have called Jones and Wright and told them he was interested, as Benton urged him to do. But as the project's would-be producer, he was their rival and decided that he would keep his endgame private while their time ticked away.

Benton and Newman were not so circumspect; given the way Beatty was talking about the script, they had every reason to believe he wanted to act in *Bonnie and Clyde,* not just produce it. "We kissed our wives and broke open a fresh six-pack and started playing Flatt and Scruggs again,"[37] they wrote. "I just remember the excitement starting again," says Leslie Newman. "All the more because it had sagged. This terrible low followed by this incredible high that you hadn't expected to have!"[38] Benton and Newman called Elinor Jones to let her know that Beatty had read the screenplay and liked it. Jones, thinking this might be a further selling point for Truffaut and an effective way to get him away from the improbable idea of casting Terence Stamp, immediately wrote to the director in Paris, asking him, "What do you think of Warren Beatty in the role of Clyde?" and "If [his] participation makes it easier to raise money, would that be an influence on your opinion?"[39]

Truffaut's reply was swift and stinging. He told Jones some of the details of his meeting with Beatty and Caron in Paris and said that he had recommended *Bonnie and Clyde* to them before he heard about Picker's interest in the movie. However, he added, "truly, I have much admiration for Leslie Caron, but none for Warren Beatty, who increasingly seems to me an extremely unpleasant person. He belongs for me, with Marlon Brando and several others, on a small list which I classify in my head under the heading, 'Better not to make a film at all than to make it with men like this.'" Truffaut went on to say that he had since spoken to Caron, who he felt was "too old to play Bonnie," and that he had been "obliged to be very frank with her and to explain to her that actually, this project had been offered to me again, but that it was out of the question that I would make it with Warren Beatty."[40]

Beatty may have picked up on Truffaut's distaste for him at their lunch. When Benton and Newman told him in their first conversation of their passion for Truffaut and Godard, he instantly replied, "You've written a French film—you need an American director."[41]

EIGHT

The man who wrote the battle scenes for *Spartacus* did not, judging by his credits, appear to be the ideal choice to try his hand at a new screenplay for *The Graduate*. Calder Willingham was Stanley Kubrick's poker buddy and go-to screenwriter, a southerner in his early forties who, aside from the patchwork he did on *Spartacus*, had written one screenplay that the director filmed (*Paths of Glory*), one that he rejected (for *Lolita*), and one, for Marlon Brando's western cult oddity *One-Eyed Jacks*,[1] that Brando disliked so much, he ended up having both Willingham and Kubrick fired. Willingham was a guy's guy with enough inherent swagger to be able to look Brando in the eye and tell him, "You've gotta have faith in my God-given gifts as a writer."[2] Larry Turman, looking for someone to take on *The Graduate*, liked the fact that he was a published novelist and that he lived with his family in New England, a proximity that would make a potential collaboration with Mike Nichols easier.

But Nichols, at the moment, had his hands full. When he wasn't busy preparing for *Who's Afraid of Virginia Woolf?*, he was working with Neil Simon, directing the author's first Broadway play since *Barefoot in the Park*. *The Odd Couple*, with Walter Matthau as Oscar Madison and Art Carney as Felix Ungar, opened in March and extended Nichols's winning streak; he now had four hit shows running simultaneously in New York, and that spring, he won, for the third straight year, the Tony Award for Best Director of a Play. Almost as soon as Willingham signed on and *The*

Odd Couple opened, Nichols was back in Los Angeles to supervise rewrites and preproduction on *Virginia Woolf,* and *The Graduate*'s new screenwriter was on his own. Willingham had already adapted one of his own novels, *End as a Man,* into the 1957 military drama *The Strange One,* a film about repressed homosexuality that, thanks to the Production Code, ended up becoming an example of it. He told Turman that the experience had taught him that "doing an adaptation of your own novel is like performing an appendectomy on yourself."[3] But Willingham felt no compunction about doing surgery on someone else's novel; he took the sexual triangle at the center of *The Graduate* and coarsened it, turning in a draft that both Nichols and Turman felt was "vulgar."[4] "It was in every way unacceptable," says Nichols. "And when I asked him if he'd like to work with me on it, he said no. So that was the end of his screenplay."[5]

Knowing Nichols was displeased with the progress the script was making, Turman took two paths at the same time: He held on to Willingham, urging him back toward Charles Webb's novel, its scenes and its dialogue, in the hope that his screenplay could be rescued.[6] And when that began to appear less likely, he hired another screenwriter for *The Graduate,* a newcomer named Peter Nelson. Turman had represented Nelson before quitting his job as an agent to become a producer, and Nichols, while he was directing *Barefoot in the Park,* had read and enjoyed a spec script by the novice writer called *The Surprise Party Complex.* "Mike Nichols said, 'I read your script and I think it's funny and touching. Call Sam Cohn,'" says Nelson. "It was one of those wonderful calls that you hope to get as a writer. I never got Sam on the phone. But I think [Nichols] liking my script impressed Larry enough to use me."[7]

Nelson remembers taking the job, for which he was paid $5,000, with the understanding that it was urgent work. "When Mike was going to do *The Public Eye,* and then when that fell through but he took *Who's Afraid of Virginia Woolf?,* Larry was scared shitless that he was going to lose him, as any producer would be," says Nelson. "When somebody takes a movie before your movie, you have no idea what that movie is going to lead to. He knew it was important to have a script ready when Mike came back."

Soon after he got the assignment, Nelson was temporarily derailed by the illness of his young son, and it took him longer than he expected to turn in a draft. Turman never showed him Willingham's script, only Webb's novel. "I just went right to the book," he says. "My script was faithful, and sort of kicky and long." But Turman was no happier with this version than he had been with Willingham's. Nelson was off the project before he even had a chance to meet with Nichols. "I don't think my script was even considered," he says.[8]

Although Nichols would eventually play a strong role in the shaping of the screenplay for *The Graduate,* that spring he had to face an even larger and more pressing crisis involving Ernest Lehman's script for *Who's Afraid of Virginia Woolf?* The decision to retain Albee's scabrous dialogue was already an issue. Phrases like "screw you," "goddamn," "hump the hostess," "monkey nipples," and the like had never been heard in a motion picture that received the Production Code's seal before, and in 1963, before the Code's powerful chief administrator, Geoffrey Shurlock, had even seen a draft of the script, he had warned Warner Brothers that all the profanity would have to come out. Lehman, terribly nervous about running afoul of either the studio or Shurlock, had written several early versions with no profanity, but Nichols told him to go for close to broke, eliminating just a few words and pushing as hard as they could to keep the rest. "Ernie, for example, changed 'you son of a bitch' to 'you dirty lousy dot dot dot,' " he said. "[But] disguising profanity with clean but suggestive phrases is really dirtier."[9]

Lehman had taken it upon himself to identify another "problem": the death of the imaginary baby over which George and Martha quarrel throughout the play. On Broadway, the nonexistence of the baby had generated reams of what-does-it-all-mean discussion; many critics embraced the then voguish notion that *Virginia Woolf* was really an encoded play about a homosexual couple with only an imaginary child to show for their "false" marriage—an idea that Albee himself repeatedly dismissed but that Lehman believed[10]—and others expressed honest uncertainty about the viability of introducing a metaphor or symbol and then turning it into a concrete plot point. Lehman decided that what *Woolf* needed was a third-act rewrite: In the screenplay he first presented to Nichols, George and Martha's child had become real, a son who had hanged himself on his eighteenth birthday in the family's living room closet, in which George says "the whole rotten truth of our lives is hidden."[11] His grieving parents had then sealed it forever.[12]

If Lehman had imagined that his dual role as writer and producer would give him the upper hand with an inexperienced movie director in creative disagreements, he was soon disabused of that notion. Nichols, feeling the new twist was closer to *What Ever Happened to Baby Jane?* than to *Who's Afraid of Virginia Woolf?,* immediately vetoed his alterations and, over the course of two months in early 1965, supervised a rewrite that, step by step, took the screenplay back toward Albee's original dialogue and vision. *Virginia Woolf* still needed to be cut—even at 131 minutes, it omits large sections of Albee's three-act play. But in the course of making those trims, Nichols got to know the text intimately; it started to belong to him. Lehman, he said later, "wasn't suited to the Albee stuff, and he wasn't used to being a producer. And I didn't have the patience. I would get pissed off and probably be rougher than I needed to be."[13]

Nichols had spent his time in Los Angeles well, screening European movies (Fellini's 8 1/2 was a favorite) to help him find a look for the film and learning everything he could about camera movement and technique, an area in which he was self-conscious about his lack of knowledge. His reputation as a New York theater hit maker alone would have made him something of a visiting eminence in Los Angeles, even at the age of thirty-four, but coupled with the enthusiastic endorsement of Richard Burton and Elizabeth Taylor, he landed at the top of everybody's invitation list. He got to know his way around a Hollywood party, and, never lacking confidence, he discovered with remarkable alacrity that once he stepped onto the Warner lot, he had some weight to throw around.

Nichols insisted on three weeks of rehearsal time with his stars, an almost unheard-of luxury in the movie business then and now, and he got it. He also won a major showdown with Warner Brothers over the way the picture would be shot. In 1965, some of the rules of the old studio system were still firmly entrenched, and one of them was that first-time directors didn't select their own crews. On *Virginia Woolf,* Warner simply assigned Nichols a cinematographer, Harry Stradling. Stradling was sixty-four; he had shot over 120 movies, the first of them in 1920, and had received a dozen Academy Award nominations. Though he had photographed the black-and-white *A Streetcar Named Desire* for Kazan fifteen years earlier, most of Stradling's notable work since then had been in color—brightly lit amusements like *Guys and Dolls, The Pajama Game, Gypsy,* and *My Fair Lady.* In Hollywood, black-and-white films and color movies had coexisted for twenty-five years in an increasingly uneasy aesthetic détente (complete with separate but equal Oscar categories for Art Direction, Cinematography, and Costume Design). Although the decision about which way to shoot a movie was sometimes monetary, it was just as often based on a set of shaky artistic principles in which color was reserved for musicals, westerns, scenic spectacles, and fantasy, and black and white, which was considered more "realistic," was used for anything serious, adult, or controversial.

This unwritten rule, a division often forced on filmmakers by the fact that the inconsistencies of color-processing labs were still yielding sloppy, overbright, unrealistic hues, was followed by directors until 1966, when the conversion of network television to color (and the refinement of processing techniques) led studios to abandon black and white entirely within a matter of months. But given that most color films in 1965 still looked more like *That Darn Cat!* than *Lawrence of Arabia,* Nichols had no interest in breaking with tradition. Fellini's films were in black and white; so were Truffaut's and Godard's; so were the social-issue dramas of Stanley Kramer, and theatrical adaptations like Arthur Penn's *The Miracle Worker,* and Production Code envelope pushers like Sidney Lumet's *The Pawnbroker.* Nichols wasn't about to shoot *Who's Afraid of Virginia Woolf?* in color—aside from everything else, he felt that the heavy makeup that would be used to turn the thirty-three-year-old Taylor into a harridan in her late forties would be too evident in color. But Stradling, an old-fashioned guy who had little use for European films and thought *8 1/2* looked like "crap,"[14] was insistent, and Nichols suddenly found himself at loggerheads with Jack Warner, fighting him one-on-one as his producer sat by silently.

"Warner said to me and Lehman—who never spoke—'I'm sorry, boys, but New York says it has to be in color.' There was no 'New York.' He owned the whole studio! I said, 'I'm sorry, Mr. Warner, it's not possible, it's way too late, the sets are built, everything is designed for black and white.'

We went back and forth forever with all that shit, and he finally said, all right, black and white.' "[15] A week after that, however, Stradling came back to Nichols with a final proposal to shoot the film in color but print it in black and white; Nichols, with no particular animosity, fired him and replaced him with his own choice: Haskell Wexler, who was twenty-five years younger than Stradling and had recently shot striking black-and-white films for Kazan (*America America*), Franklin J. Schaffner (*The Best Man*), and Tony Richardson (*The Loved One*).[16]

The day he started production on *Who's Afraid of Virginia Woolf?*, Nichols finished one of his first shots, and a first assistant director sauntered by him, muttering, "Oh, well—it's just another picture." Nichols fired him on the spot. "I had to prove I was going to be strong," he said later.[17] That may have been the case, but Nichols also had to prove that the first AD wasn't right. If *Virginia Woolf* turned out to be "just another picture," his career as a movie director would begin with a failure on a massive scale, and he knew it.

"You would think that as a director, slowly, as you got to be a geezer, you would become more and more irascible," says Nichols, "until you ended up like George Cukor, screaming at Candice Bergen and Jacqueline Bisset for an entire movie [*Rich and Famous*]. But with me, it was the other way around. I started out as a prick on the set. Not to the actors so much, but by and large to everybody. I don't know who I was then or what was happening. And I got nicer as time went by. But I was a prick."[18]

On July 4, 1965, Jane Fonda threw a party in the oceanfront home in Malibu that she had recently rented with the man she was about to marry, director Roger Vadim. The party spilled out of the house, which had once belonged to Merle Oberon, and onto the beach, where she had set up a giant tent and laid down a dance floor.

Fonda wrote in her autobiography that the party was one of the first occasions on which old Hollywood and new Hollywood came face-to-face, and her guest list—with one faction represented by William Wyler, Gene Kelly, Darryl Zanuck, Lauren Bacall, Sam Spiegel, and her father, Henry, and the other by Warren Beatty, Tuesday Weld, Jean Seberg, Dennis Hopper, and her brother, Peter—bears that out.[19] Fonda was in the mood to celebrate; after a half-dozen films in which the young actress had seemed to try on different personae—ingenue, seductress, rebel, hellcat—without finding anything that quite fit, she had just opened in her first hit, playing the title role in the comic western *Cat Ballou,* a movie that arrived just when the clichés of an aging genre were becoming ripe for parody. Now she was shuttling between France, where Vadim seemed to be building his body of work around her (actually, around her body), and Los Angeles, where she was suddenly being offered a better class of project: She was currently working with Robert Redford and Marlon Brando in Arthur Penn's *The Chase.* Her father, who had just turned sixty, roasted a pig on a spit and, surrounded by his own friends, enjoyed the event as a belated birthday party; her twenty-five-year-old brother hung out with the Byrds, the band he had hired to play for the crowd. The group's electrified version of Bob Dylan's "Mr. Tambourine Man" had reached the number one position on *Billboard*'s singles charts the week before; by the end of the month, Dylan would take his own song electric at the Newport Folk Festival.

Few people were better suited to broker a summit meeting between the Hollywood establishment and its upstarts than Jane Fonda, who even in 1965 had a foot in both worlds. She had not yet been stirred by political activism; that would happen, for the first time, a few days after the party, courtesy of Penn, who invited her to a Hollywood fund-raiser for the Student Nonviolent Coordinating Committee that he was co-hosting with Brando.* But her life in Europe had begun to give her a currency beyond her status as a second-generation movie actress, and perhaps because her own sense of identity was far from settled, she knew how to blend in anywhere, from an old-guard industry function to an all-night talking-and-smoking French house party to an L.A. "happening."

The party Fonda threw that Fourth of July was a little bit of all three, plus a taste of the New York underground in the form of Andy Warhol, a perfect witness to the spectacle of celebrity, who arrived on a visit from

---

*Although the spring of 1965 had brought the start of anti-Vietnam "teach-ins" and the first major antiwar protest in Washington, D.C., the war was not, at that point, on the political agenda for Hollywood, which was concentrating almost all of its activist efforts on the civil rights movement and on individual political campaigns.

New York with two of his self-created "stars" in tow. "Hollywood's social events were very compartmentalized in those days," wrote Vadim. "We decided that ours would be more democratic."[20] There's no question that Fonda and Vadim succeeded in that goal, but the party was not, and could never have been, a conscious intermingling of old Hollywood and new, since in 1965, "old Hollywood" did not yet know it was soon to be over-thrown, and "new Hollywood" was nothing more than a cast of players who didn't yet realize that they were about to start running the show. But the two groups were aware of each other, and there seems to have been a sense of unspoken but mutually-agreed-upon territoriality.

"I remember the party, as does everyone who went near it, very well," says Buck Henry, who was in Los Angeles working with Mel Brooks to cre-ate a new comedy series, *Get Smart,* that would make its debut on NBC in the fall. "I'm not even sure I was invited, but I went anyway, because I knew a lot of people. What I recall was the feeling that there was the adults' room and the kids' section, where it was really fun to be. There was a space for [Henry] Fonda and the establishment in the back, but there was certainly a large percentage of young Hollywood—because there were all of Jane's friends. People got into big trouble, people left and came back, there was a lot to drink, a large segment of the group was going outside to do drugs of one level or another. And of course, the Byrds were playing, and they moved me almost beyond words."[21] At one point, Henry Fonda went over to his happily stoned son and yelled, "Can't you get them to turn it down?"[22]

Although the term *generation gap* was beginning to come into popular use, the question of who belonged to old Hollywood and who didn't was not one that could be resolved by age alone. About some of the guests, there was no doubt: Old Hollywood, defiant, resistant, and crotchety, was William Wyler, who after thirty years behind the camera was trying to stay abreast of contemporary material with an adaptation of John Fowles's sadistic thriller *The Collector* but couldn't hide his disgust at the increas-ing popularity of movies like *8 1/2* and *Last Year at Marienbad.* "What is it?" he fumed. "It's just another talking radio show with pictures. No-body acts! . . . The public wants to know what a story is all about. It does not want to leave a theater wondering what it saw."[23] Old Hollywood was

Darryl Zanuck and George Cukor, both staring dumbstruck as a barefoot young hippie began to nurse her baby in front of them.[24] Old Hollywood was, as Sydney Pollack put it, "the same people doing the same things they had been doing for the last twenty-five years."[25]

Others, though, weren't so easily labeled. Warren Beatty, who had been groomed for movie stardom by the well-oiled workings of the old studio system, had returned to the West Coast with Leslie Caron for a visit. He hadn't yet won control of *Bonnie and Clyde,* but he was already thinking about casting, and the party offered up at least three possibilities for Bonnie: Tuesday Weld, Natalie Wood, and Fonda herself. Weld was new Hollywood, trapped in a series of sex-kitten parts but bringing a highly charged, troubled element to her screen personality that occasionally broke through to the surface of even a banal role. Wood, although she was a year younger than Beatty, had made her film debut as a child in 1943 and was old Hollywood to her core; it was the only world she could imagine. "The whole routine about submerging your personality [while acting] is a lot of bunk. You have to bring your personality to every part you play," she had said at twenty, airily dismissing what she called "the nose-picking 'Method' fringe group, who never got closer to the Actors Studio than Sunset Boulevard."[26] Even if the term *new Hollywood* had been in use, Wood certainly would have considered herself no part of it; and in 1965, it's doubtful that Beatty, watching his contemporaries get high on the beach, would have identified himself as part of the counterculture. He would have been more likely to head for the back room in the hope that he'd find the people with whom he really wanted to work—Wyler, George Stevens, Fred Zinnemann.

The "kids' section" of Fonda's party was populated by people who would come to define new Hollywood and yet, at that time, were barely inside the door—Peter Fonda and his friends Jack Nicholson and Dennis Hopper, all of whom were scraping by on a combination of episodic television gigs and low-budget movies and were now entering the orbit of American International Pictures (AIP) and exploitation-movie king Roger Corman. Vadim described the boys as being "particularly cheerful" that night, and as the sun went down and the celebration escalated, Peter Fonda climbed onto the roof of the house of another son of Hollywood, Robert Walker Jr., and, blissed out, watched the action below, thinking, *"God bless grass."* (A

couple of months later, when the Beatles played the Hollywood Bowl for
the first time, Peter Fonda and the Byrds would go to an afterparty with
the Fab Four, where he would take one of his first acid trips.)[27]

In the "adults' section" sat Sam Spiegel, who was, that summer, Jane
Fonda's boss and Arthur Penn's as well. Spiegel was sixty-five, a hands-on
producer whose name (or self-chosen pseudonym, "S. P. Eagle") had been
on *The African Queen, On the Waterfront, The Bridge on the River Kwai*,
and *Lawrence of Arabia. The Chase* was his first movie since *Lawrence* had
won him his third Best Picture Oscar in 1962; although David Lean's film
had marked a career high point for him, in the wake of its success Spiegel's
arrogance and autocracy were alienating even longtime colleagues. During
production of *The Chase*, Spiegel was making Penn's life so miserable that
the director would leave Hollywood after the shoot vowing never to work
for a studio again.[28] Penn, who already felt the script was a "dog's breakfast," later said that he had "never made a film under such unspeakable
conditions," which included the daily delivery of script rewrites that were
so clumsy and incoherent, he suspected they must have come from the
pen of Spiegel himself.[29] After seeing a cut of Penn's difficult little passion
project, *Mickey One,* a Columbia executive said, "No more artsy-smartsy
pictures."[30] Now he was back working for the same studio and was, ironically, trapped by Mike Frankovich's willingness to leave creative decisions
in the hands of an independent producer. With Spiegel calling all the
shots from casting (he apparently made liberal use of the couch) to location shooting (there would be none, despite the movie's southern setting
and multiple outdoor scenes) to rewrites, there was little Penn could do
but report to the set and shoot the screenplay—whatever it happened to
be that day. (In postproduction, Spiegel would take *The Chase* away from
Penn and edit it himself, to the satisfaction of almost nobody involved.)[31]

On his own at the party, Sidney Poitier, at thirty-eight, belonged to neither old nor new Hollywood; once again, he was a category unto himself,
liked by all but claimed by nobody. His fifteen-year marriage to Juanita
Hardy was finally at an end; Hardy, who was herself becoming an active
and engaged civil rights fund-raiser, was three thousand miles away, living
in the home she and her husband had once shared in the New York suburb
of Pleasantville and raising their four daughters. After the divorce, Poitier

later wrote, "I remember feeling liberated—but from what?" He had not been happy in his marriage, but with his relationship with Diahann Carroll far from settled, there were lots of "empty, lonely times" ahead.[32] That evening, missing his kids, Poitier naturally gravitated toward Roger Vadim's little girl, Nathalie, and he and Gene Kelly spent part of the night playing with her and teaching her to tap-dance.[33]

Poitier was ready to fill the emptiness with work, and since *In the Heat of the Night* had no director or script yet, he would soon head for Seattle to begin shooting a movie for Sydney Pollack, a thirty-one-year-old TV director making his first feature. The project, *The Slender Thread,* was based on a *Life* magazine article by Shana Alexander that had been transformed by writer Stirling Silliphant, the man behind CBS's popular *Route 66,* into a melodrama about a suicide hotline worker who tries to help a depressed woman (played by Anne Bancroft.) Poitier may have found the role appealing because it had nothing in particular to do with the "Negroness" of his life, but there turned out to be a saccharine ideology behind his casting after all—the notion that if a black man in mid-1960s America could explain to a desperate woman why life was worth living, the film would be all the more believable. Poitier was, as always, an amiable collaborator, and he was willing to push himself even when the material didn't challenge him—he brought his own acting coach to Seattle to help him figure out how to play his big scenes with nothing but a telephone receiver as his costar. But *The Slender Thread* wouldn't prove to be much better than his other recent films, despite its energetic director. "You have to take Dramamine to watch that movie," says Pollack. "I was trying so hard to shake off the stigma of television that everything was moving and zooming and panning. I didn't know what the hell I was doing."[34]

In the middle of the party, and yet, as always, standing at a cocked eyebrow's distance from it, was Mike Nichols. Once again an immigrant in a new land, he surveyed the tribal rituals, the lapses of etiquette, the deferences and courtesies and small humiliations of this hothouse of West Coast privilege and restlessness, and filed them away for future use. At one point in the evening, he wandered from the crowd and found himself under the canopy of a huge tree around which part of the tent had been set up. A small knot of revelers was slouched around the trunk, and when

Nichols approached, one of them looked up at him and said, "Are you having a good time in L.A., Mike?"

Nichols responded in his slow deadpan, "Yes. Here under the shadow of this great tree, I have found peace."

The laugh he got came from Buck Henry. Henry knew Nichols's work, but not the man himself; although as children they had briefly overlapped at New York's Dalton School, and Henry had performed improv with a group called the Premise at around the same time Nichols and May were gaining a following at the Village Vanguard, their paths had never crossed. As Nichols remembers it, Henry picked up his little jab at Big Sur–meets-India mysticism and ran with it. "We started laughing," Nichols says, "throwing some of that shit back and forth. I had found a buddy."[35]

The party broke up into smaller groups that straggled away at dawn, with the younger guests who had stayed on as long as there was fun to be had now asleep, stretched out on mattresses in the house or on the veranda as the tents came down. The older guests had retreated earlier, back to their homes in Beverly Hills and Brentwood, perhaps amused and perhaps alarmed at their first extended glimpse of the inheritors of their kingdom. Vadim and Fonda, in each other's arms, looked out at the ocean and back at the revelry's debris. Vadim thought it looked like a movie. But not a Hollywood film. More like something by Fellini or Antonioni,[36] unresolved and inchoate, that would leave everyone walking out of the theater talking and wondering what would happen next.

PART TWO

NINE

Every time he made a movie that fell short of his hopes, Stanley Kramer felt "a kind of pain that starts somewhere near the groin and goes up to the chest, as though you're having a heart attack in your stomach."[1] Lately, he was feeling it again. His latest film, an all-star adaptation of Katherine Anne Porter's novel *Ship of Fools,* was due to open on July 29, and Kramer could already recognize the onset of the sickening deflation of his own expectations. How could it have been otherwise when, by his own admission, he "had dreamed it would be a great accomplishment, a definitive motion picture showing what the medium can be" and not merely "a good piece of work that didn't quite fulfill our aspirations"?[2]

In 1965, Stanley Kramer was, at fifty-one, as enshrined a member of the Hollywood establishment as anyone in the movie business, and there was probably not an active producer or director who would have hated that description more. Kramer had been making movies since the late 1940s. He had started as a producer, overseeing Mark Robson's *Home of the Brave,* an adaptation of an Arthur Laurents play that dealt with racism in the American military. Kramer went on to produce *The Men* (Marlon Brando's movie debut), *High Noon, Death of a Salesman, The Member of the Wedding,* and *The Caine Mutiny* in the space of a few years. His movies were emblematic Hollywood prestige projects, and he made sure his name and reputation were so firmly associated with them that by the mid-1950s, moviegoers already knew what a Stanley Kramer movie was—something serious and charged and significant and edifying, if not necessarily innovative or aesthetically unsettling. In the 1955 movie-biz melodrama *The Big Knife,* Jack Palance, playing a down-on-his-luck movie star, barks at his wife (Ida Lupino), "You know that this industry is capable of turning out good pictures—pictures with guts and meaning!" "Sure, sure," she replies, "and we know some of the men who do it! Stevens, Mankiewicz, Kazan, Huston, Wyler, Wilder . . . Stanley Kramer!"

In the mid-1950s, Kramer decided to step behind the camera himself and start directing. "Stanley's drive has always been to be the boss, the man who wants it done his way," his longtime associate George Glass later said. "The time came in the industry when directors took greater control over picture making than ever before. So Stanley, in my opinion, decided if that was where the action was, that was where he'd be, by God."[3] He loved tackling topics that would make news—racism in *The Defiant Ones,* the threat of nuclear annihilation in *On the Beach,* the Holocaust in *Judgment at Nuremberg*—but, as many of his own friends and colleagues, including Norman Jewison, put it, "Stanley was a better producer than he was a director,"[4] and once he was in the director's chair, he continued to think like a producer, concentrating on the overall package rather than the shaping of individual scenes, performances, and moments. "Guts and meaning" was a label he would have loved, although he sometimes undercut himself by being too willing to trumpet the presence of both qualities in his films. Kramer wanted credit for the politics and moral rectitude that he believed gave his pictures weight and significance, but while he understood that great movies had to be more than the sum of their issues, he didn't always know how to get them there. He didn't possess what came naturally to many of the directors he admired—an unforced sense of pacing or camera placement or a particularly visual imagination—and the screenplays for his films (which he did not write) often omitted nuance, surprise, and specificity in favor of a stentorian sense of the wrongness of things that all right-thinking people already agreed were wrong: racism, the threat of nuclear annihilation, the Holocaust.

Kramer was respected within the world of old Hollywood as a reliable filmmaker and a staunch civil libertarian. In 1960, he had defied a demand from the American Legion that producers not hire "Soviet-indoctrinated" writers, calling the organization's stance "reprehensible,"[5] a position that was not without some risk in a business still very much in the chokehold of McCarthyism. The movies he made were manna for the Academy—his producing career had brought him four Best Picture nominations by the time he won the Academy's 1962 Irving Thalberg Award, essentially a lifetime achievement honor for a producer—and they were revered by middle-brow reviewers. When *Judgment at Nuremberg* opened in 1961, *The New York Times'* Bosley Crowther pronounced it "persuasive" and said "it manages to say so much that still needs to be said."[6]

But Crowther, typically, never managed to explain what exactly he had needed to be persuaded about, and Kramer's appetite for matter over art made him into something of a whipping boy for the critical intelligentsia. In 1965, Pauline Kael, who had not yet been hired by *The New Yorker* but was building a reputation as a pugnacious contrarian as eager to pick fights with her rivals as she was to tear down the movies they supported, launched a blistering attack on Kramer, using the arrival of *Ship of Fools* as her pretext. She mocked him, not entirely unjustly, for his tendency to sound self-important and chest-thumping in interviews. His reputation, she said, was "based largely on a series of errors." She twitted him for mistaking storytelling that "represents a blow for or against something" for "art." She took apart his films one by one, calling them "irritatingly self-righteous," "messianic," and "feeble intellectually"; she belittled the "original sin meets Mr. Fixit" style of his plots. "Kramer asks for congratulations on the size and importance of his unrealized aspirations," she concluded. "In politics a candidate may hope to be judged on what he intends to do, but in art we judge what is done. Stanley Kramer runs for office in the arts."[7]

If François Truffaut exemplified, as Robert Benton and David Newman had written in *Esquire*, "Style over Content," Kramer and his films epitomized Content over Style—the "Old Sentimentality" of the Eisenhower era. The label was particularly painful for a director who, unlike many in his generation, was an open-minded advocate of the new directions world cinema was taking in the 1960s and an avid fan of Fellini, Kurosawa, and Antonioni.[8] Kramer had a hard time understanding how critics like Kael could give him so little credit for ambition, especially since his films were sometimes more controversial than those who belittled him acknowledged. His adaptation of *Inherit the Wind* had been picketed at many theaters; some southern movie-house chains wouldn't play *The Defiant Ones,* in which escaped prisoners Tony Curtis and Sidney Poitier were shackled together as an ironclad symbol of interracial brotherhood. And the critics who charged that Kramer's movies pandered to what they considered to be a good-liberal consensus ignored the reality that most of the films he directed were financial failures. "All the people who say 'Messages are for Western Union' really don't mean it," he said. "They mean, 'Messages that don't make money are for Western Union.' "⁹ While *The Defiant Ones,* thanks to its very low budget, squeezed out a small profit, *Inherit the Wind* lost almost 90 percent of the $2 million that it cost, *On the Beach* ended up in the red, and despite its Best Picture Oscar, *Judgment at Nuremberg* lost money as well.¹⁰ How, wondered Kramer, could Kael believe that he was viewed as "some sort of savior"¹¹ when he wasn't even filling up the pews? And how could other critics fail to see Kramer the way he saw himself, as a lifelong outsider, an independent producer who "took on the establishment *within* the Hollywood firmament"?¹²

Kramer wasn't humble, and he knew his weakness for grandiosity in print made him an easy target. In an interview on the set of *Inherit the Wind,* he proclaimed, "In *The Defiant Ones* we dealt with the problem of race. *On the Beach* . . . concerns the big question, the Bomb. And now I'm dealing with what I consider the third major problem today, freedom of speech and, more important, freedom of thought."¹³ But in person, people found Kramer disarming; they were often surprised to discover that the slender man behind the big talk was soft-spoken, witty, and self-aware. And his fiercest detractors might have been surprised, or at least amused, to hear the director's own assessment of his work and his motives. Kramer once told an audience that he chose to direct "because I'm arrogant and I have an ego and I enjoy it."¹⁴ But he almost always ended up disappointed in himself and his movies, particularly those he made in the 1960s. After *Judgment at Nuremberg,* he produced 1962's *Pressure Point,* a drama about a black psychiatrist (Poitier) treating a white racist (Bobby Darin). "It isn't an even match," he admitted. "You know from the start that Poitier must win . . . you can blame me for undertaking the project before [thinking] it through completely." In 1963, he produced *A Child Is Waiting*, with Judy Garland as a teacher caring for an autistic boy. "When you attempt a subject [that] difficult and delicate . . . you had better be sure that what you're making will be just about the best picture of the year. This one wasn't," he wrote. When Kramer, in a change of pace, directed 1963's *It's a Mad Mad Mad Mad World*, he intended, quite sincerely, to make the funniest comedy in the history of motion pictures, and decades later, he still expressed disappointment that his "silly dream" yielded a film that "just had too much of everything."[15]

Kramer thought *Ship of Fools*, a portent-filled *Grand Hotel* about the various travelers on a ship bound for Germany in 1933, offered all the ingredients for a prestige blockbuster. Instead, its reception was fairly typical: respectful but not ecstatic reviews, eventual Oscar nominations, and only middling box office. In 1962, when Kramer had started working on *Ship of Fools*, his decision to make the film at Columbia instead of United Artists, which had been his base of operations for several years, made headlines.[16] Three years later, his cold streak at the box office was so protracted—even *It's a Mad Mad Mad Mad World*, which audiences loved, was so costly that it wouldn't make much of a profit—that his switch in studios no longer seemed to mean much.

When *Ship of Fools* opened, Kramer was feeling particularly heavy-hearted; he knew the film might have represented his last chance to work with Spencer Tracy. Tracy was sixty-five and had been in poor health for years; after the deaths of Clark Gable and Gary Cooper within months of each other in 1960 and 1961, he was seen by many as one of the last links to the first generation of sound-era male movie stars. In the past several years, Tracy had acted infrequently, and almost exclusively for Kramer, who had directed him in *Inherit the Wind*, *Judgment at Nuremberg*, and in a tiny role in *It's a Mad Mad Mad Mad World*. When Kramer first read Abby Mann's script for *Ship of Fools*, he knew he wanted Katharine Hepburn to play the role of an angry, neurotic alcoholic—a showpiece character turn that captured Hepburn's interest immediately. But Hepburn would do the film only if Kramer agreed to give Tracy what amounted to the male romantic lead, the role of the ship's doctor. Kramer resisted; Tracy was far too old to play the part and too frail as well. When Hepburn realized that

Kramer wouldn't cast Tracy, she decided not to make the film;[17] her part went to Vivien Leigh, and Tracy's went to Oskar Werner, who was more than twenty years his junior.

Ship of Fools did provide Kramer with one happy memory; on the set, he met Karen Sharpe, the woman who would become his third wife and who, by the time the film opened, was already his biggest cheerleader. "I used to get angry with him because he'd say, 'It's not as good as I dreamed it.' It's *never* as good as you dreamed it, I'd tell him. You have to make compromises—the sun doesn't go down at the right time, so you lose that shot you envisioned. Or the actor that you hired because you loved him suddenly says he can't say your favorite line in the movie. You have to make compromises when you're working with people. And I don't think Stanley was completely happy with anything he ever made."[18]

Kramer shook off his disappointment and went back to work. He had long wanted to make a movie about war—perhaps even *the* movie about war—and he started looking for a book about Vietnam to adapt. With the exception of George Englund's prescient Marlon Brando drama *The Ugly American* in 1963, Hollywood movies had barely touched on the war in Southeast Asia. But in 1965, as President Johnson increased the number of American soldiers in South Vietnam from 23,000 to 184,000 and a national antiwar movement began to gain traction, Kramer wanted to mark the subject as his territory. He acquired the rights to a novel called *Seek Out and Destroy* and made a public announcement that he was planning a major take on the Vietnam War, but he felt there was no need to rush.[19] His next movie was to be an adaptation of MacKinlay Kantor's 1955 Civil War novel, *Andersonville,* a script he had already spent three years developing. He would have time for Vietnam later.

That summer, Mike Nichols was ready to get out of Los Angeles. For weeks he had been on the Warner Brothers lot, filming interiors for *Who's Afraid of Virginia Woolf?*; now, he was, at least physically, taking the movie away from the studio, returning to the East Coast to film part of *Virginia Woolf* on the campus of Smith College in Northampton, Massachusetts. Nichols welcomed the time on location, out from under what felt like Warner's watchful and suspicious eye, and his two stars were proving to be game and reasonably focused. Richard Burton found himself looking at rushes for the first time since the beginning of his career, while Taylor would throw herself into each day of work and then enjoy whatever local entertainment she could find, pursuing it in her characteristic not-quite-incognito style. When a reporter came to visit the production in New England in search of Taylor, Burton informed him dryly, "Elizabeth's gone to see *What's New, Pussycat?* with ten policemen."[20]

Nichols was no longer the new guy; he was the boss, successful lion tamer to two of the world's least controllable celebrities and fearsome taskmaster to everyone else. On the set, he would push Taylor and Burton until she would break down in tears and he would be too shaken to come out of his dressing room,[21] and they would still return the next day eager for more. Burton wrote in his diary that Nichols was one of only two men he had met (the other was Noël Coward) who had "the capacity to change the world when they walk into a room. They are both as bland as butter and as brilliant as diamonds." And he was delighted that a director who had never stepped behind a camera and was still learning how to use lenses wasn't even a little afraid of the biggest star in movies. "I have actually seen people shiver as they cross the room to meet Elizabeth. What the hell is it?" he wrote. ". . . I know that we are both dangerous people, but we are fundamentally very nice. I mean we only hurt each other."[22] Nichols had just as loyal an ally in Taylor, who was never one to overpraise her own movies or performances and who knew that *Who's Afraid of Virginia Woolf?* was the best role she had ever had; she was determined not to hold back, no matter how painful the process or unflattering the results. "I think many people probably will be shocked," she said at the time, "but they'll stay, not run out of the theater the way they're doing at *The Sandpiper,*"[23] her most recent, and at that time most dreadful, on-screen romantic pairing with Burton.

The shoot at Smith unfolded in an atmosphere of mild urgency, politely expressed by the college's administrators, who requested that the production be packed up and gone by the time Smith's young ladies arrived for the fall 1965 term. That was the least of the pressures Nichols faced. Though he was delighted to be away from Hollywood, the exigencies of working for a studio, and handling movie stars, and spending a great deal of money (Taylor received $1.1 million and Burton $750,000),[24] caused constant tension. And Ernest Lehman, whom he had started to think of as "the so-called writer-producer who was neither producer nor writer," had become an adversary. Nichols had discarded one embellishment in his script after another, beginning with "a title sequence [that] included [Burton's character] George going for a walk and coming upon two dogs fucking. And it said in parentheses, 'This must be beautifully shot.' Anthea Sylbert, who later became my costume designer, said, 'I know just how to do that! Afghans and lots of fans!' "[25] When Nichols and Lehman crossed swords, Nichols almost always got his way, but his victories had a price: Feeling excluded from the bond Nichols had formed with his actors, Lehman simply stepped away from any conflict that arose. "This bunch would not only shoot it, they would edit it, cut it, premiere it, distribute it, and sell it to television without telling me," he grumbled to a reporter on the set.[26]

With Lehman declining to run interference with the studio, Nichols had to defend every decision and delay himself. There were plenty of the latter: Taylor and Burton, as cooperative as they were, had a propensity for non-negotiably long, boozy lunches, and although Nichols had hand-picked Haskell Wexler (who would win an Oscar for his work on the film) to replace Harry Stradling as his cinematographer, their relationship was less than congenial; Nichols couldn't believe the amount of time Wexler and his crew spent lighting each shot. Unsurprisingly, the film ended up going thirty days over schedule. "Mike was going crazy," said Sam O'Steen, *Virginia Woolf*'s editor, later. "He'd walk around saying, 'Cocksuckers, I hate their fuckin' guts. . . .' "[27] At the same time, Nichols backed Wexler consistently when the studio complained about the shadowy, unglamorous look of the rushes, and Wexler, though he would butt heads with Nichols, was impressed by his ability to draw strong work from his cast.

Nichols himself wouldn't be hurried, and he occasionally felt the brunt of his crew's impatience. As the shoot wore on, Meta Rebner, the script supervisor and a formidable southern belle who was intimidated by no one, warned Nichols that he was losing the confidence of some of the union guys on the set.* If he cared, he didn't let Rebner know it. In fact, he may have taken a little longer than necessary with the next setup[28] just to remind everyone involved that there was only one person in charge of this movie and to drive home the point that if he wouldn't let Jack Warner push him around, then anyone else who went up against him would surely be fighting a losing battle.

It was during the shooting of *Who's Afraid of Virginia Woolf?* that Buck Henry started to get to know Nichols better. Henry was a good friend of George Segal, who was playing Nick, and he visited the set often. As he spent more time with Nichols, a friendship sparked between them, and they began to talk about *The Graduate*. "I remember Mike saying, 'Read this book and see what you think of it,'" says Henry. "As soon as I read it, I got the point. It didn't take more than ten pages to know that this was something really interesting and to see where all of our lives were intersecting. I think that Larry Turman and Mike and I *all* thought that we were the protagonist of the book. We were all roughly the same age, we'd all gone to the same kinds of schools, we all sort of liked the same movies, and we all got the same jokes. But hiring me was a leap of faith on Mike's part. He was really just going on personality and *Get Smart,* which I wouldn't have thought would be a direct line to *The Graduate.*"[29]

Henry became the movie's fourth screenwriter and started from scratch with a new draft that retained much of the book's dialogue but transformed the character of Benjamin Braddock in some crucial ways. Charles Webb had been Benjamin's age when he wrote the novel, and with perhaps too little authorial distance, he had allowed Benjamin to personify the confusion, arrogance, and uncertainty of a pampered twenty-two-year-old who hadn't yet figured out a direction for his life but knew he wanted it to point away from his parents. On the page, Benjamin's ungainly sense of moral severity can become smug; the first time he tries to break off his affair with Mrs. Robinson, he writes her a note in which he says to her, "I don't know if you were ever taught the difference between right and wrong or not, but since I was, I feel a certain obligation to it."[30] Early in the

---

*Rebner would go on to serve as script supervisor on both *In the Heat of the Night* and *The Graduate*.

novel, Webb's grasp of Benjamin's sexual inexperience seems to falter and give way to a bluster that feels inorganic; questioned by his father after he takes a hitchhiking trip to northern California, Benjamin tells him that most of the people who gave him rides were "queers . . . I averaged about five queers a day" and makes a point of adding, "One queer I had to slug in the face and jump out of the car."[31] And despite Webb's skillful use of dialogue to portray Benjamin's anxiety, the character is, in moments of physical action, a cipher—a hostage to the novel's spare descriptive style who is rarely described as doing more than frowning, blinking, waving his arms, or nodding his head. After a fight with Elaine, Webb writes, "Benjamin stared at her until she was finished screaming and then continued to stare at her for a long time afterwards while she lifted her hands up from her side and put them over her face to cover it and then finally brought them slowly back down and held them in front of her."[32]

Henry did his writing alone, although he discussed the story and characters with Nichols constantly, and with Turman as well. Some choices were easy: Benjamin's apparent homosexual panic, his brief adventure fighting forest fires, and his dalliances with prostitutes, which all came early in the novel and seemed poorly connected to the rest of the narrative, would be omitted. ("I think I tried writing [the hitchhiking]," said Henry, "and over a period of time, we dropped it.")[33] But Henry and Nichols also altered the novel's tone. "I had a feeling that in real life, Benjamin Braddock was not a person you'd want to know now," says Henry. "He's a bit of a prick—he doesn't give anybody much of a chance."[34] As the story of Benjamin, Elaine, and Mrs. Robinson passed from the hands of a novelist in his early twenties into the custody of a writer and director who were both in their mid-thirties, it became both more detached and more sympathetic. Henry's screenplay took Benjamin's earnest, surly struggle to be better than the people around him less seriously than the novel does, and it emphasized the richly funny tension between his human appetites and his stern self-condemnation as a "filthy degenerate."[35] "Even though I felt I was Benjamin Braddock, Benjamin Braddock is a pain in the ass in the book," says Turman. "What we excised was the stuff that made him a pain in the ass."[36]

Henry found Benjamin most engaging in his moments of deepest befuddlement or awkwardness—the initial seduction scene, the mortifying birthday party at which he is forced to parade for his parents' friends in a deep-sea-diving suit, the episode in which he can barely bring himself to secure a hotel room for his first assignation with Mrs. Robinson. "I knew the book could make an interesting film, because it not only had scenes, it had places for the camera to go, which a lot of books don't have," he says. With that in mind, Henry shaped Benjamin's terrified journeys into the unknown—the bedroom, the bottom of the swimming pool, the hotel cocktail bar—into comic set pieces, and deemphasized his somewhat exhausting tendency to tell off everyone around him. He cut long passages of dialogue in which Benjamin, strangely irritated, tries to talk Elaine into marrying him, and he also dropped a groaner of a moment in which he tells his parents that he wants to spend his life with "simple honest people that can't even read or write their own name."[37] A scene in which Benjamin humiliates Elaine on their first date by taking her to a strip club and then explains his behavior by saying, "Ever since I've been out of school I've had this overwhelming urge to be rude all the time," remained in the movie and stood in effectively for many moments in Webb's novel in which Benjamin succumbed to that urge.

By favoring Benjamin's bumbling attempts at moral rigor over his cold, sour narcissism, Henry and Nichols located *The Graduate*'s comic center in his complete failure to live up to his own standards, and, unlike Webb, they came up with an ending in which it's not clear if Benjamin triumphs by meeting those standards or by discarding them. In one of the screenplay's few actual alterations of the novel's plot, Henry and Nichols agreed that Benjamin would now interrupt Elaine's wedding seconds *after* their vows were exchanged, not before. Webb hated the revision because he felt that breaking up a marriage stained Benjamin's good character,[38] but the futility of his quest for goodness was exactly what Henry and Nichols wanted—and getting to the church in the nick of time was the kind of cliché they were striving to avoid.

Nichols and Henry also knew that *The Graduate* offered a great comic opportunity to dissect a certain stratum of vulgar new-money West Coast culture that movies had not yet exploited for laughs, probably because so many of the people who made them were too close to that culture to recognize anything funny about it. Their version of Benjamin's story would be a poisoned arrow aimed from New York toward the heart of Los Angeles. "*The Graduate* is filled with all the stuff you can wring out of the upper middle class," says Henry. "That hadn't been very evident in American films for a long time. There were so many movies where you didn't know what people did for a living, but they lived so well. I had an idea to do a shot of an airplane coming in over L.A., and we would see all the swimming pools, and they would merge into one big pool." Henry "knew L.A. as well as I knew New York. My mother came from L.A.—we went out almost every year, and we lived there from 1941 to 1945, while my father was overseas." And Nichols, though a relative newcomer to Los Angeles, "got stuff awfully fast," says Henry. "It doesn't take him more than a few moments to understand the behavior of whatever society he's in."[39] Together, they started thinking of Benjamin as a product of WASPy overprivilege in a society devoted to it.

In choosing to root the script so firmly in contemporary Southern California, Nichols and Henry solved another problem: They brought *The Graduate* up-to-date. Eisenhower was barely out of office when Webb had first gotten the idea for his novel, but five years later, generational wars that had previously focused on an antipathy toward consumer culture and conformity were now being fought on different fronts. Nichols and Henry were not especially interested in making a "sixties" movie (had the label or its meaning even existed in 1965), but they didn't want to make a comedy with one foot still planted in the previous decade, either. Henry, in particular, was so worried about the script sounding dated that he came close to dropping the line that became the movie's first big laugh, when a middle-aged businessman offers Benjamin just a single word of advice about his future (a scene that's not in the novel). "I worried about 'Plastics' for a while," Henry said, "and even talked to Mike about it, saying, are we too old-fashioned, with what was a sort of fifties . . . society way of complaining about falseness? But I couldn't ever think of a better word for him to say." [40]

TEN

Years later, when *Doctor Dolittle* was finally about to be released, Arthur Jacobs would, with a straight face, say that he and 20th Century-Fox had rejected Vincente Minnelli, John Huston, and William Wyler as directors before settling on the man who finally got the job, Richard Fleischer. The claim was classic Jacobs: one part truth to two parts hyperbole. Minnelli, who had never really been intimately involved with the movie's development, left *Dolittle* before Leslie Bricusse had signed to write the screenplay, and the famously unrushable Wyler, who Jacobs felt sure "would take fifty takes of every shot and the picture would end up costing thirty-five million," wasn't seriously approached. But John Huston was, and for a while, the director, who had been working on *The Bible* for 20th Century-Fox, was interested. "Darryl [Zanuck] wanted Huston," Jacobs said, "but I felt there was enough temperament with Rex."[1] Jacobs got his way, but not before an overture had been made to Huston that had to be retracted with embarrassment and a collectively agreed-upon lie. The fib, Richard Zanuck decided in a cable to Jacobs, would be to tell Huston that "we have run into certain legal difficulties with basic material and have decided not to proceed until we have resolved those difficulties. Please tell Bricusse to stick to this story."[2]

Richard Fleischer was not a marquee director; he was, recalls one colleague, "a nice man, and a man they could control—easy in that the studio knew he wouldn't give them any trouble." He had the confidence of Dick

Zanuck, who at twenty-four had gotten his start as a producer on Fleischer's 1959 fictionalization of the Leopold and Loeb murder trial, *Compulsion*; having just used Fleischer on the science-fiction adventure *Fantastic Voyage,* Zanuck knew that he was capable of handling what promised to be an elaborate physical production. Fleischer, the son of groundbreaking animator Max Fleischer, was known as a patient and pleasant director, so there was little chance of a clash of egos, and he was eager for the job. In his cigarillo-scratched rasp, Arthur Jacobs told Fleischer the same thing he had told Bricusse—that the job would change his life.

Dick Zanuck and Jacobs were both pleased with the work Bricusse had done on the *Dolittle* story line, and ecstatic about his speed. By July 14, 1965, he had turned in an elaborately detailed eighty-two-page treatment for *Doctor Dolittle,* with demos of four songs and lyric fragments for many others. Bricusse had concocted a promising opening sequence that involved Dolittle riding through the jungle on a giraffe to visit a crocodile with a toothache.[3] And his treatment had also solved a problem with the story of *Doctor Dolittle* that could have led to disaster—the patronizing colonialism and racism of some of the source material. Though the depiction of Africans in Hugh Lofting's first Dolittle book, which was published in 1920, was not vicious and would have shocked nobody in post–World War I England or America, it was, by contemporary standards, appalling. *The Story of Doctor Dolittle* features a voyage to Africa that leads to an episode between the doctor and Bumpo Kahbooboo, the son of the King of Jolliginki, who yearns for Dolittle to turn him into a white man so that the woman he loves will return his affection. Dolittle first asks if it would be enough to dye his hair blond, but when Bumpo insists on a full transformation, the doctor creates a potion that turns Bumpo's skin white, at which point Bumpo "sang for joy and began dancing around." As Dolittle sails away, he says, "I am afraid that medicine I used will never last. Most likely he will be as black as ever when he wakes up in the morning. . . . Well, well!—Poor Bumpo!"[4] In later books, Bumpo leaves Africa to attend Oxford, and Lofting uses his malapropisms (and, at one point, his interest in cannibalism) as comic relief. (These segments of the books, with Christopher Lofting's approval, were deleted and rewritten in the 1980s.)[5]

Bricusse kept Bumpo but dropped the skin-color-transformation episode and his mangled syntax and introduced the character after he'd completed his Oxford education; since Jacobs and Fox owned the rights to all twelve Dolittle books, he could cherry-pick plot points from any volume. Bricusse's version of Bumpo was likable enough to bring Fox an early casting coup: The studio had gotten Sammy Davis Jr. to commit himself to the role. Davis had long been a fixture in Rat Pack movies and on television, where sooner or later, every western and cop series had an episode that called for a black guest star. In late 1964, Arthur Penn directed him in the Broadway musical adaptation of the Clifford Odets play *Golden Boy,* and the result was a hit show for which Davis received a Tony nomination. Getting him to agree to costar in *Dolittle* before they even had a completed screenplay was news that could be used to attract more talent and a sign to Jacobs and Zanuck that they had chosen their new writer wisely.

Bricusse's treatment surmounted one major hurdle when it received the enthusiastic approval of Hugh Lofting's widow, who called his work "a complete surprise . . . he has caught the spirit of the Doctor himself. The lyrics are . . . right in the vernacular of Dolittle. I predict nothing but success."[6] But a more forbidding potential obstacle loomed in Rex Harrison, whose rejection of either Fleischer or Bricusse could scotch the whole enterprise. Harrison, basking in the afterglow of his Academy Award and awaiting the start of production on Joseph Mankiewicz's Volpone variation, *The Honey Pot,* had installed himself in his villa in Portofino and was completely aware that he now held the project's future in his hands. Accordingly, Fleischer and Bricusse, with Jacobs coming along as a sort of marriage broker, were dispatched to Italy and told, in essence, to pitch themselves.

Harrison could be hard on directors, especially younger ones. A few years earlier, when Norman Jewison had directed him in a TV variety show, Harrison greeted him by saying, to nobody in particular, "He looks like a paperboy." "My God, he was a pain in the ass," recalled the usually unflappable director.[7] When Fleischer arrived in the dining room of the Hotel Splendido with Bricusse, Jacobs, and two of Harrison's agents, the star first asserted his authority by showing up ninety minutes late to lunch.

Fleischer was forty-eight, old enough to know how to handle the vanity of an aging leading man, and decided to gamble on a joke. "I'm sorry," he said to Harrison, "but I just don't think you're right for the part."

After a long and blood-freezing moment, the silence was broken by a laugh from Bricusse. And then Harrison laughed as well. "Perhaps you're right," he replied affably.[8] "Nice chap, good chap," the star told Arthur Jacobs later.[9] Fleischer had the job.

Bricusse's memories of his own "audition" are less happy. Harrison, he wrote, was "charm itself to my face and as trustworthy as a crocodile behind my back."[10] "I believe the idea of Leslie coming to Portofino will be most fruitful,"[11] Harrison had written to Jacobs. But once there, Bricusse found himself at the mercy of a star who had expected to be working with Alan Jay Lerner and was not about to let go of his disappointment quickly.

In the days after their lunch at the Splendido, Harrison summoned both Bricusse and Fleischer to his home at the Villa San Genesio to talk about any aspect of *Dolittle*, large or small, that crossed his mind. Harrison was a serious drinker whose moods lurched and careened as his level of intoxication rose; his much younger fourth wife, actress Rachel Roberts, suffered from suicidal depression and violent mood swings that were exacerbated by blackout drinking;[12] she had accompanied Harrison to the initial getting-to-know-you lunch and ended up, as Bricusse recalls it, drunk and barking like a dog in an impromptu audition to provide animal voice-overs for the movie. Harrison had not yet signed off on Bricusse and had questions—or, rather, accusations—about his lyrics. When Bricusse arrived at the villa, Harrison began by expressing particular unhappiness about a line in "Talk to the Animals": "If people asked us, can you speak in rhinoceros / We'd say 'Of courserous, can't you?' " Rhinoceros and "of courserous," Harrison noted, do not rhyme.

When Bricusse replied that the song was supposed to be humorous, Harrison snapped, "A humorous song is meant to be funny. This isn't funny," then added, "Oh God protect me from fucking puns. . . . The point is that it doesn't fucking rhyme!"[13]

If Harrison never quite assented to the hiring of Bricusse during those first meetings in August 1965, he didn't reject him outright, either. Bricusse wasn't required to turn in a completed script until the end of the year, and Harrison, who was about to have his hands full with the shoot of *The Honey Pot*, was content to wait until then to make his decision. Besides, he had a more pressing matter to address with Jacobs and his new director: He wanted them to fire Sammy Davis Jr. "I don't want to work with an *entertainer*," he told them. "I want an actor. A real actor, not a song-and-dance man." Fleischer and Jacobs's attempts to talk Harrison out of his antipathy toward Davis only caused the actor to dig in more deeply and to raise the stakes on the spot: He wanted Sidney Poitier to play the role. Impervious to the reasonable arguments made by Jacobs and Fleischer that they weren't certain if Poitier could sing or dance, or if he would be willing to take a supporting part, Harrison finally laid down an ultimatum: Sidney Poitier was in or Harrison was out. Jacobs, wrote Fleischer later, "would have loved to be able to tell Rex . . . go screw yourself, but he couldn't. There was just too much at stake."[14]

Bricusse flew back to Los Angeles to continue working on the script, and Jacobs and Fleischer glumly returned to New York, where they managed to set up a meeting with Poitier. The actor had just finished *The Slender Thread* for Sydney Pollack and was looking for a project he could fit in while *In the Heat of the Night* was being developed. The two men pitched him hard, selling him on Harrison's appetite for an "actor" rather than an entertainer and offering him $250,000.[15] Poitier had recently finished three small, serious, black-and-white movies—*The Bedford Incident*, *A Patch of Blue*, and *The Slender Thread*—none of which had been released yet and all of which seemed like minor films. In the wake of the vast success Fox was having with *The Sound of Music*, he may have been attracted to the prospect of a big payday for a small role—in Bricusse's treatment, Bumpo appeared only in the last third of the movie—that would offer him a chance to reach a wider audience. Poitier accepted their proposal but made it clear that his agreement was contingent on a meeting with Leslie Bricusse. Elated, Jacobs promptly agreed to fly Bricusse to New York for a lunch date at Poitier's favorite restaurant, the Russian Tea Room.

A few hours after they met with Poitier, Jacobs and Fleischer were due at the Majestic Theatre for an evening performance of *Golden Boy*, and Sammy Davis Jr. knew they were coming to see him; they were all planning to have dinner together afterward. As the two men sat in the audience, feeling like executioners, Davis, charged with excitement, sang, danced, and even threw in an ad-lib about Rex Harrison as a sort of secret nod to Jacobs. When the show ended, they went to Davis's dressing room, listening to him talk with great enthusiasm about his ideas for Bumpo. The dressing room door then opened to another visitor: Sidney Poitier.

Neither Jacobs nor Fleischer had mentioned to Poitier that he would be replacing Davis during their pitch meeting. Poitier looked at them. They looked back at him. Fleischer, frozen in place, assumed Poitier would think they were trying to sell Davis on the same role. Davis had no idea anything out of the ordinary was going on. And Poitier gave nothing away. He simply paid his respects to Davis and left the theater.

At a dinner that Fleischer later described as "a nightmare . . . very mafioso," Jacobs asked Fleischer to leave the table while he broke the news to Davis himself. Fleischer stood watching at a distance as, in his words, "this wonderfully talented, delightful elf [had] his dream blown to smithereens. . . . I could tell from watching Sammy's face exactly where he was in the story." Davis, understandably hurt and angry, told Jacobs he intended to make the incident public, go to the NAACP, and sue Harrison personally.[16] By the next morning, Poitier had heard what happened and changed his mind about playing Bumpo. Davis was a friend; taking a role away from him would be disloyal. But Poitier insisted on keeping his date with Bricusse, and by the following week, when they met, the actor had presumably managed to smooth things over and confirmed that he would costar in the movie after all.

On September 28, Rex Harrison, all charm, wrote Jacobs from the Italian set of *The Honey Pot* (then called *Tale of the Fox*), "I was very delighted to hear of the possibility of Sydney [*sic*] Poitier for Dr. Doolittle [*sic*]. . . . I would have thought it was worth going to any lengths to get him for the part as he would be so fresh and exciting for it." Harrison didn't take long to offer some further suggestions: For the role of Emma Fairfax, which Bricusse was creating as a romantic female lead, he suggested one of his *Honey Pot* costars, Maggie Smith, a rising London stage actress who at thirty had made just a few movies. "I feel that she might be awfully good for the girl. She has rather a prim quality, and, of course, is able to acquire a period quality." Harrison's letter also contained a barbed reminder that he could pull the rug out from under *Dolittle* at any moment: "How is Leslie proceeding with the lyrics and music? He has, I know, got a couple of months more before he has to produce it, but I am naturally anxious." And he warned Jacobs against any further casting decisions that might involve what he had called "entertainers"—in other words, anyone whose singing and dancing might call attention to Harrison's deficiencies in those areas. "I think once we get anybody who is musical comedy in the film," he wrote, "it is dead."[17]

By the time Bricusse turned in the first draft of his screenplay on October 22, the runaway success of *The Sound of Music,* which had been in theaters for seven months, was so apparent that every studio in Hollywood was pushing hard to get a giant road-show musical, or two, or three, into production. Warner Brothers was actively developing *Camelot,* the film it hoped would be the next *My Fair Lady;* Disney was planning to follow *Mary Poppins* with *The Happiest Millionaire;* Columbia had bought the rights to the Broadway shows *Funny Girl* and *Oliver!;* MGM had commissioned six new songs from Irving Berlin for a biopic called *Say It with Music;* UA was adapting *How to Succeed in Business Without Really Trying.* Alan Jay Lerner's *On a Clear Day You Can See Forever* had just opened on Broadway that week, and the rights were going to Paramount; and Universal could boast the biggest casting catch of the year, having secured the services of Julie Andrews for *Thoroughly Modern Millie.*[18] Nowhere was the urgency greater than at Fox, where *The Sound of Music* had almost single-handedly undone the damage wrought by *Cleopatra.* So it was hardly a surprise that when Dick Zanuck and Arthur Jacobs read Bricusse's script, their orders to him were simple: Make it bigger.[19]

In part, Jacobs meant that literally: *Doctor Dolittle* would have to run at least two and a half hours in order to merit an intermission and a reserved-ticket, road-show-style release. Some members of the Fox team disagreed with that strategy: Mort Abrahams, who was to serve as the movie's associate producer, wondered whether the material was strong enough to make *Dolittle* a must-see event for parents and children, an audience that any road-show release needed to be successful.[20] David Brown, who had left New American Library to become Zanuck's associate in New York, was analyzing the musical boom with more wariness than many of his colleagues; he noted that musical budgets were growing fast and that the pictures tended to perform poorly in markets outside the United States, an area of revenue that was already considered critical by the 1960s.[21] But Jacobs and Zanuck persisted with their more-is-more vision. *Doctor Dolittle* was going to be shot on the Fox lot in Los Angeles, on location in England, where they intended to find a town to double as Puddleby-on-the-Marsh, and in the Caribbean. The studio wanted Poitier's role enlarged with a major new sequence, a flashback to Bumpo at college early in the picture, to give them more bang for their $250,000.[22] And although he no longer had any hope of signing Julie Andrews, Jacobs was still hoping for big names to fill out the remaining principal roles in the cast: Emma Fairfax and the doctor's merry Irish friend Matthew Mugg.

As Fox started pulling deal memos together—the studio agreed to pay Fleischer $300,000 plus 5 percent of the net profit and $7,500 for every week the film ran over schedule,[23] and Harrison, over and above his salary, was to receive a rising percentage of the gross if the film became a hit[24]—Jacobs continued to hunt for talent. Looking for an Emma Fairfax, he went to New York in an unsuccessful effort to woo Barbra Streisand ("Forget about her," Dick Zanuck wrote after her agents asked for $500,000).[25] He then began talks with Hayley Mills, the very popular child star of Disney's *Pollyanna* and *The Parent Trap* who was, at nineteen, attempting a transition into young adult roles. Mills's participation would have been a tremendous boon in marketing the movie to kids, so much so that Fox was willing to offer her $300,000 and billing equal to Rex Harrison's.[26]

For the role of Matthew, Harrison, who was continuing to make his feelings known on everything from casting to Jacobs's choice of cinematographer, was enthusiastic about David Wayne, a character actor and TV mainstay in his early fifties who had been a familiar face since the Katharine Hepburn–Spencer Tracy comedy *Adam's Rib* in 1949. Danny Kaye and Bing Crosby were also among the names that had been floated.[27] But Jacobs wanted a younger leading man, and an obvious candidate presented himself in Bricusse's creative partner, Anthony Newley, who at thirty-four was just wrapping up a run on Broadway in their flop, *The Roar of the Greasepaint—The Smell of the Crowd,* and was eager to relocate to Los Angeles with his wife, Joan Collins, and their two small children. After some push and pull over his salary, Fox signed him to play Matthew for $200,000,[28] and the Newleys relocated to Bel Air, where Collins reentered the Hollywood social scene she loved with the vigor of an Olympic athlete.

Newley's hiring was bound to inflame Harrison, who had already made clear his distaste for musical theater actors and younger male costars, but at the moment, his mood was plummeting for other reasons. Joseph Mankiewicz's first script for *The Honey Pot* had been too innovative and bizarre for United Artists—the characters in his original screenplay included Production Code censors who were to show up periodically during the movie itself to delete unacceptable material—and to Harrison's disappointment, he had redrafted the film as a far more conventional dark comedy by the time shooting began. Mankiewicz fired his first cinematographer; the second died suddenly during the shoot; Rachel Roberts, upset that Maggie Smith had won the role she wanted in the film, was spiraling into deep depression and barbiturate abuse, and Harrison and Mankiewicz, by this point, felt, in the words of Mankiewicz's agent, Robert Lantz, "enough residual contempt [for each another] to last a lifetime."[29]

At the moments when Harrison was able to turn his attention to *Dolittle*, he did so with irritation and volatility. Fleischer had found a picturesque English town called Castle Combe to serve as Puddleby, Dolittle's home village, but in November, Harrison told Jacobs and Fleischer that he didn't want to have to shoot the film in England; before agreeing to Castle Combe, he forced Fleischer to go on a pointless location-scouting trip to Ireland. The towns he found there, he told Harrison, were "depressing, faceless places, more suitable for a Great Potato Famine story."[30] (Castle Combe itself was far from ideal; a National Weather Institute memo sent to Fox warned the studio months before the shoot that the sun shone only five days a month during the summer,[31] but in the manic optimism that preceded the production of *Dolittle*, the news was ignored.) Harrison also insisted that he be allowed to perform his own songs live on the set rather than lip-synching to tracks that would be recorded before the start of production, a costly whim that nobody at Fox thought was likely to yield any usable scenes. "Everything Rex did and said indicated that he was very hesitant about saying yes," says Mort Abrahams. "He wasn't happy with the book, with the score, with the script."[32]

Harrison's inconsistency bewildered Jacobs and Zanuck, who could barely keep pace with his mood swings. On December 7, his discontentment boiled over. Laurie Evans, Harrison's agent in London, called Arthur Jacobs to tell him that Harrison had read Bricusse's screenplay and was rejecting it. Jacobs was floored. "He would like to get out of his commitment," he wrote in a memo to Zanuck. "He claims it was not written for him. It is not what his fans expect of him. He claims it is for a small round man like Edmund Gwenn. He said he will not do prat falls. He said he will not be part of a trio. He said he will not be sung to [by other actors]. . . . Laurie said that Rex said, 'Why don't you get Cary Grant to do it and let me out?' . . . I said I was totally amazed, stunned and shocked and would get back to him."[33]

Five days later, Dick Zanuck received a more serious and troubling critique of the script—a thirteen-page memo from his own father. Darryl Zanuck, in his sixties, was still a fiercely competitive man, and his son's relationship with him was, in some ways, an extended Oedipal wrestling match (literally so when the younger Zanuck was a kid and he and his father would go at it every weekend, each trying to pin the other to the ground).[34] He had given his son a studio to run, but even though he now spent most of his time in New York or Europe, he still held on to his own authority and oversight. As Dick became more self-assured in his position, his father gave him a freer hand, but when he chose to step in, he did so with formidable force. Fox's willingness to throw good money after bad on *Cleopatra* had almost destroyed his studio and cost hundreds of people their jobs, and the elder Zanuck was not about to let that happen again. "Since this is the most expensive project on our entire program we have got to be positive that the final script will be a masterpiece," he wrote. "This story can become great only if it is really funny and delightful from beginning to end . . . and if the musical numbers are outstanding. . . . In *Doctor Dolittle* we do not have any genuine suspense, no danger and no conflict. . . . This leaves us then with comedy and music as our foundation. It will only reach the top brackets if we are almost continually funny, delightful, and musically superior . . . you could eliminate almost any one of the individual episodes and you would not miss it, particularly in the last half of the screenplay. These are facts that must be analyzed even if they cannot all be 'cured.' "

Darryl Zanuck's lecture to his son continued with a reminder that he had been in the movie business since Rin Tin Tin was a star and thus spoke from experience when he wrote, "It is my belief that you will not be able to do more than half the 'animal scenes' that are written into the script." The production, he warned, was bound to be "a hell of a mess." He told his son that animal trainers always overpromise good results, that the film was too long, that Bumpo's dialogue was flat (adding, "I have never seen Sidney Poitier in a comedy"), and that a scripted encounter with a pirate ship would only raise the budget and should be eliminated.

Zanuck's conclusion was grim: "I am deeply concerned about the overall cost," he wrote. "This is a big physical picture with enormous mechanical problems . . . it is absolutely essential that every episode we photograph remain in the picture. This is not a film where you can afford to overshoot." Of *Dolittle*'s planned June 1966 start date, he wrote, "Since I must speak frankly I believe you are taking a hell of a gamble. . . . I know of no motion picture that needs more careful and expert preparation than this one. When you deal with a number of almost uncontrollable items, it goes without saying that you have to <u>know</u> exactly what you can and what you can't do from a practical standpoint, otherwise it can be an economic disaster." The memo was signed "D.F.Z."[35]

Dick Zanuck's response, which was sent a few days later by cable, was amiable but firm. He reassured his father that they planned to make changes in the script, but he insisted on keeping the pirate ship sequence and calmly concluded, "Despite the multitude of problems and difficulties I do feel that we will be prepared by July First."[36]

Father and son were in agreement on only one point: Rex Harrison, without knowing it, had finally overplayed his hand. The actor's tyrannical irascibility had pushed his employers to the breaking point. "He will drive us all to an asylum," Darryl Zanuck wrote. For the first time, the Zanucks and Jacobs began a fresh discussion: What if Rex Harrison wasn't in *Doctor Dolittle* after all? Over the next several days, the three men started talking over a new list of names. What about Alec Guinness? Too much of an "art-house star," said Darryl Zanuck. "All the boys here [in New York] are dead set against Peter Sellers," he added. "And they are also not in favor of Jack Lemmon . . . while he is a star he is an out-and-out comic and a far cry from the character of Doctor Dolittle."[37]

Darryl Zanuck was intrigued by the idea of Peter Ustinov, but his son resisted the suggestion, wanting to protect Richard Fleischer from another star who was thought to be uncontrollable by directors. During these discussions, Harrison's agents, oblivious to the deep trouble in which their client now found himself, were cabling Arthur Jacobs wanting to know whom he was planning to hire to rewrite Bricusse's script, music, and lyrics and conveying Harrison's wish that Alan Jay Lerner be wooed back to the film, or perhaps Frank Loesser.[38]

In the last week of December, the Zanucks finally found their new leading man: He had been in front of their noses for almost a year. Christopher Plummer, star of *The Sound of Music*, would be hired to replace Harrison. The studio offered Plummer $250,000[39] and also spent a great deal of money to buy out his contract for Peter Shaffer's Broadway play *The Royal Hunt of the Sun*, in which he had been starring since October. By the time Harrison himself got wind of what was happening, he was too late. On December 30, he cabled Dick Zanuck himself, pleading ignorance of his agent's most recent demands. "Personally consider am fully committed Dolittle," he wrote frantically. "Can we not clear this up personally?"[40]

The next day, Dick Zanuck sent a telegram to Harrison assuring him that it was nothing personal at all. "From the very beginning you were always our number one choice," Zanuck wrote. "I am extremely gratified to receive your wires which express your attitude of honor and integrity. . . . Really Rex I am dreadfully sorry that things have turned out this way."[41] Then he fired him.

ELEVEN

The weekend that Warren Beatty contacted Robert Benton and read the script for *Bonnie and Clyde* also brought the opening of the film he had let slip away, *What's New, Pussycat?* Buoyed by the combination of Peter O'Toole and Peter Sellers, the movie became a substantial hit for United Artists; except for *Goldfinger* and the three blockbuster musicals that were still dominating American screens, *Pussycat* was the highest-grossing film of 1965.[1] But the final product contained only shreds of the idea that had attracted Beatty in the first place—the notion of turning a man who was unsuccessfully juggling relationships with several different women into a comic hero. "I know Woody [Allen] didn't agree with me on this," says Beatty. "His point of view was always, if you're successful with women, what's the problem? But even after my bad experience on *Pussycat,* I still thought the compulsive Don Juan could be a basically sympathetic character."[2]

Soon after the movie opened, Beatty found, by accident, a writer who agreed with him. Like so many young filmmakers in the mid-1960s, Robert Towne was working for Roger Corman—he had written 1964's *Tomb of Ligeia,* the last in a long series of luridly enjoyable Edgar Allan Poe horror films starring Vincent Price that American International Pictures had been turning out for years. Towne and Beatty shared a psychotherapist, and their friendship began to develop after they met in his waiting room. Towne was working on a rewrite of a western in which Corman wanted Beatty to star, and Beatty, though he wasn't particularly interested in the project, liked the writing.[3] He began to talk to Towne about his idea for what he called "an updated version of Wycherly's *The Country Wife*—a guy pretends to be gay, but he's really getting more action than anybody. In [the 1960s] if you were a hairdresser, people assumed you were gay. So we talked about making the guy a hairdresser and began to work on it."[4] In its early stages, the screenplay was called *Hair*; eventually it became *Shampoo*.

As that project began what turned out to be a decade-long gestation, Beatty kept his eye on *Bonnie and Clyde*. François Truffaut's unexpected return to the film rekindled the hopes of Elinor Jones and Norton Wright for a couple of months during the summer, but Truffaut's idea for how to make it seemed, suddenly, to be disappointingly close to the vision Jean-Luc Godard had expressed that *Bonnie and Clyde* should be shot quickly, cheaply, and without any big names. Alexandra Stewart, despite her distinct French Canadian accent, would be fine for Bonnie, he insisted. And when Wright suggested they get in touch with Paul Newman about playing Clyde, Truffaut replied that Newman would make the film "too important and disproportionate. . . . .Scooter Teague [Anthony Teague, an actor who had played a tiny role in *West Side Story*] and Robert Walker [Jr.] seem to me adequate for the two male parts."[5] And Elinor Jones's belief that United Artists would jump at the project now that Truffaut was ready to commit himself proved unfounded. "He was not considered by United Artists someone who could make money," she said. "David [Picker] always backed it—but he needed [Krim and Benjamin's] approval. He couldn't pull it together himself. And they didn't want it."[6]

Once it became clear to Truffaut that there was no way *Bonnie and Clyde* could be shot before *Fahrenheit 451* (which was to be made by Universal), he lost interest in the movie altogether, and at the end of August, he dropped out for the second and last time.* The movie Robert Benton and David Newman had conceived as an American version of a French New Wave film had now lost both of the directors who inspired it, and the Nouvelle Vague itself, by late 1965, was no longer the repre-

---

*After six years of waiting, Truffaut was finally able to start shooting *Fahrenheit 451* in January 1966; after its indifferent reception, he never directed another film in English.

sentation of cinema's future that it had seemed to be two years earlier. The fickle attention of American audiences was shifting decisively from France to England, in particular to the brittle, contemporary, sexy London comedies—*Darling, Alfie, The Knack, Morgan*—that were creating a new generation of stars.

Jones and Wright had three months left on their option, and they made some halfhearted runs at directors, hoping to attract, among others, Philippe de Broca, who had directed 1964's farcical *That Man from Rio*.[7] Having been turned down by every major studio they had approached, they also contacted producer Claude Giroux to see if an independent company, Allied Artists, might be interested in the film.[8] But Jones and Wright both knew their chance to make *Bonnie and Clyde* had probably passed. At one point, Jones began to wonder if there was a problem with the script that she just wasn't seeing. "I thought, maybe it has to be rewritten. And Bob and David said no, and they were right."[9]

In the fall of 1965, Beatty made a single attempt to get in touch with Elinor Jones, calling her in New York and leaving a message. Jones ran across the hall to tell her brother (who had, with his wife, moved into an apartment across from the Joneses). "We thought, hey, this is terrific— when he calls back, we'll say, let's get into business together," says Wright. But they never heard from Beatty again. "Why did he call?" says Jones. "It's a mystery to me. I think he found out, after that call, that the option was up in two months and just waited us out."

Jones and Wright went to see Arthur Penn's *Mickey One* that September at the third annual New York Film Festival, where it was coolly received. Wright thought it was "a turkey of a movie—one of Penn's few."[10] Beatty's concern during the long Chicago production that the movie was "too fucking obscure" turned out to be well-founded. "*Mickey One* is a strange and sometimes confused offbeat yarn which is going to need careful nursing if it is to make real impact at the wickets," warned *Variety*'s reviewer.[11] But Columbia Pictures was ready to cut its losses on the film, and it snuck into (and out of) theaters three weeks later. "The morning after *Mickey One* opened, I called the studio and said, how did it do?" says Beatty. "They said, it did thirteen dollars. I said, is that good?"[12]

On November 27, 1965, Jones and Wright's option on *Bonnie and*

Clyde lapsed. The same day, Beatty bought Benton and Newman's script, paying them $75,000.[13] The producers were disappointed but not angry. "My reading of it is that Beatty moved, professionally and with alacrity, once the option expired," says Wright.[14] "He did what a smart producer would do." When Jones saw the movie two years later, "I was very proud," she recalls. "I knew that we had done all we could. We believed in Bob and David's screenplay, and seeing the movie, I knew we had bet on the right horse."[15]

That fall, when Sydney Pollack's suicide hotline movie *The Slender Thread* had its first preview in Encino, its screenwriter, Stirling Silliphant, was sitting in the audience. In the network TV universe, Silliphant was famous, regarded on the same level as Paddy Chayefsky or Rod Serling. An adulatory *Time* magazine profile in 1963 titled "The Fingers of God" had called him "television's thinking man"[16] and noted that he now commanded $10,000 to write an hour of episodic drama, a fee that added up quickly since Silliphant was, by any standards, extraordinarily productive. In the first season of *Naked City,* his innovative, textured police drama, he wrote thirty-one out of thirty-nine episodes himself; by the early 1960s, he had turned his attention to *Route 66,* a series about two young men traveling across the country in a Corvette. The show, though it had a couple of continuing characters, was really an anthology that allowed Silliphant to explore any themes that grabbed his attention—he had a particular taste for politically chancy, forward-looking topics—within the space of an hour, creating a new set of guest characters and conflicts every week (he later referred to the show as "a dramatization of my personal four-year psychiatric exhumation of all the shit that was bubbling inside me").

Silliphant had written a handful of feature films in the late 1950s, but, consumed by work on his television shows, which brought him a seven-figure annual income, he hadn't had a big-screen credit since the 1960 horror movie *Village of the Damned* when he completed *The Slender Thread.* "Stirling was the most prolific writer in the world," says Pollack. "He used to write on toilet paper when he was in the bathroom, literally. He was extremely fast and extremely facile—so facile that he could sometimes go off in crazy directions. He could write on a plane, in a waiting room, on napkins, and he didn't know where it came from. He was a very mystical guy, and he thought his own talent was mystical." On *The Slender Thread*, Pollack had eventually brought in his own writer, David Rayfiel. "I was lying and hiding the rewriting going on with David, but when Stirling found out, he wasn't upset or possessive. He just said, 'Fantastic, can we get him to do some more?' "[17]

Silliphant had been attracted to the idea of writing a script that paired Sidney Poitier and Anne Bancroft in a drama in which "race was totally ignored [because] neither hero nor heroine could see each other." But the gimmick, which might have been able to sustain an episode of *Route 66*, proved too flimsy for a feature-length film, and far from ignoring race, it also made the story disconcertingly similar to *A Patch of Blue*, another drama in which a white woman drew strength from Poitier without actually seeing him. As he watched the preview of *The Slender Thread*, Silliphant later said, "It was clear the picture was NOT giving off sparks." The man sitting next to him felt it as well. "A bomb, huh?" he said. "A fucking bomb, from start to finish," Silliphant replied. "I doubt that [a] single person in America will ever bother to buy a ticket."[18]

The man next to Silliphant turned out to be Sidney Poitier's agent, Martin Baum, who told him, "I want you to know something: Sidney doesn't blame you for this picture." Then Baum gave him a piece of advice: Get another screenplay assignment fast, before this turkey opens and word about it starts to spread. Two days later, Baum arranged a meeting between Silliphant and Walter Mirisch at which Mirisch gave him John Ball's novel *In the Heat of the Night*.[19] When Mirisch had first purchased the book, he intended the writing job to go to Robert Alan Aurthur,[20] a friend of Poitier's who had written an episode of *The Philco Television Playhouse* for the actor that was so well received, it became a feature with Poitier, 1957's *Edge of the City*. But Aurthur hadn't worked out, and Mirisch, on Baum's recommendation, turned to Silliphant.

Anyone taking on the challenge of adapting Ball's novel would have a great deal of work to do, since *In the Heat of the Night*, on the page, was a far cry from the story it became on the screen. Ball's basic outline was workable and remains recognizable in the finished film: Virgil Tibbs, a black police officer, is waiting for a train in a small southern town, having just visited his mother, when a murder occurs. After first being questioned as a suspect, Tibbs reveals his profession and stays on to work with the grudging, racist, and suspicious local police force to help solve the case.

But the way in which Ball had fleshed out the story and characters would have to be completely discarded. Ball had first conceived the plot of *In the Heat of the Night* back in 1933 and had written the novel in 1960; it took him four years to find a publisher.[21] Virgil Tibbs was already, by 1965, a retrograde character whose placid reaction to a racially charged situation was far too outdated for Poitier to play, or for any moviegoer who would choose to see this film in the first place to believe. On screen, Poitier was a master at keeping a lid on his anger while letting his audience know it simmered just beneath the surface of his characters, but Tibbs, in the novel, seems to be almost completely untroubled and to have no interior life at all. In Ball's novel, the character of Police Chief Gillespie is a minor one; the murder victim (and the reason for his killing) is different; and En-dicott, the white tycoon who rules the small town, is a friendly, pro–civil rights progressive. Tibbs himself is imagined almost completely from the outside, often from the perspective of Officer Sam Wood (the character eventually played by Warren Oates): "The Negro climbed out and submit-ted without protest when Sam seized his upper arm and piloted him into the police station," writes Ball.[22] Tibbs, in the novel, explains his investiga-tive techniques with inexhaustible patience and pages-long loquacity; the mystery concludes with him gathering all the suspects in a room and, like Mr. Moto or Agatha Christie's Hercule Poirot, laboriously detailing the path of his deductive reasoning until the guilty party is identified. "You're a great credit to your race," Gillespie tells Tibbs. "I mean, of course, the human race." Tibbs then asks Gillespie if he might be allowed to sit on the "Whites Only" bench until the train comes to take him away. Gillespie grants his permission, and the novel ends.[23]

Silliphant knew that any successful version of *In the Heat of the Night* would have to dispense with viewing Tibbs as nothing more than "the Negro"; a character who submitted to insults without protest and asked permission for everything was not one he wanted to write. On Decem-

ber 15, 1965, just a week before *The Slender Thread* opened, Silliphant
turned in a seventy-six-page treatment in which he started to reimagine *In
the Heat of the Night* as a civil rights drama. "I do <u>not</u> want [Tibbs] to have
come from Pasadena, California," as he does in Ball's novel, Silliphant
wrote. "I want Tibbs to have come out of Harlem, to have fought and bled
and suffered his way out of a crushing environment." Silliphant felt he
should be a New York City homicide detective first-class and "a far more
sophisticated, experienced human being than anybody out of Pasadena."
And, he added, "I want Tibbs to have an ulcer."[24]

In relocating Tibbs, Silliphant wasn't just making the story's North-
vs.-South tension more geographically explicit; he was responding to the
news. In the civil rights movement, the galvanizing event of early 1965 had
been the march in Selma—a call-to-action moment for many in the movie
business, who started writing checks, raising money, holding benefits at
Hollywood nightspots like the discotheque the Daisy,[25] and publicly iden-
tifying themselves with the cause. But by the summer, the riots in Watts
had begun to shift the battlefront of civil rights away from the inequities
in the South (where most of the major legal battles had by then been
won) and toward the frustration, poverty, and anger of inner-city black
Americans. "We shall overcome," the rallying cry of 1963,[26] had given way
to "Burn, baby, burn!"[27] in just two years, and since the film industry was
beginning to realize how far behind current events its movies had fallen
regarding race relations, there was every chance that a screenplay ripped
from today's headlines was going to feel embarrassingly outdated by the
time it reached theaters. In November, as Silliphant began working on his
treatment, *The Autobiography of Malcolm X* was published to wide attention and acclaim, and accounts of black rage, not just of black oppression,
began to make their way onto the evening news. The serene unflappability
of Virgil Tibbs, a gentle black visitor to a town full of racists, would no
longer be credible in a motion picture. Of course Tibbs would have to be
angry. And the cause of his rage, in Silliphant's treatment, would be woven
right into the southernness of the locale. Noting that in the novel, Endicott is "a 'nice' guy," he wrote, "The only Southern 'heavy' in the book . . .
is a councilman . . . who tells Gillespie to get Tibbs the hell out of town.
In the book this threat is never fully developed. . . . I believe we must build

and dramatize this threat against Tibbs so that it lies behind and ahead of every scene. . . . I want to change the book's George Endicott into a worthwhile enemy."

Under the heading "The Negro Community of Wells" (the town in the novel), Silliphant remarked, "I feel that the author of *In the Heat of the Night* may never have spent a night in, let alone lived in or around, a Negro community, so underdeveloped is his subtext in this area. . . . I want to write a larger sense of the community and Tibbs within it." He also announced his intention to reduce the importance of Officer Sam Wood and in turn to reshape the character of Gillespie, who in Ball's novel is a tall, lean thirty-two-year-old with only nine weeks on the job, into a second main character and Tibbs's primary adversary. Silliphant knew that a northern black detective squaring off against a southern sheriff would be far more dramatic than a polite Negro from Pasadena repeatedly explaining his actions to a low-level beat cop.

Not all of Silliphant's ideas for *In the Heat of the Night* made sense; some were awful. He was writing fast and off the top of his head, as was his custom, and he didn't censor himself. Sometimes his mystical bent got the better of him; nothing else could explain his proposal for a scene in which Tibbs, interrogating a woman who serves as the town's abortionist, would pull her into an confrontation in which he "digs into his cultural African past" and essentially challenges her to an all-night voodoo duel "using their minds and their eyes."[28] But in the overall thrust of his approach, Silliphant had already gone a long way toward turning Ball's story line into a viable movie and Virgil Tibbs into the most sophisticated iteration of the black outsider, burning with rage but always keeping cool, that Sidney Poitier had yet played.

As Silliphant started to write *In the the Heat of the Night*, Mirisch was still looking for a director, and Norman Jewison was lobbying for the job. Nothing in Jewison's background or résumé suggested any particular kinship with either the detective genre or a hard-edged story about civil rights; he was a native of Canada, and like many directors then in their thirties, he had come up in television, directing episodes of Judy Garland's short-lived variety series for CBS. In 1962, Jewison got his first chance to make a feature, a throwaway comedy for Universal called *40 Pounds of*

Trouble with Tony Curtis and Suzanne Pleshette. The studio signed him to a seven-picture deal and intended to keep him busy; on his second movie, he was paired with Universal's biggest star, Doris Day, on *The Thrill of It All*, a quintessentially early-1960s spoof of network TV, Madison Avenue, and suburban domesticity on which Jewison put what he called the "genuine hatred for commercials and their interruptions of the television shows I had been producing for CBS" to adroit use.[29] The movie, in which James Garner costars, may be the best of Day's films from that period.

Universal liked what it saw enough to put Jewison right back to work on another Day picture, 1964's *Send Me No Flowers*, the last of the three comedies she made with Rock Hudson. The film had a weaker script than *The Thrill of It All*, and Jewison was beginning to chafe; he hadn't spent a decade paying his dues in television only to end up directing feature films that looked and read like sitcoms. For the first time, he started to turn down assignments; "I was fed up with being a hired hand," he wrote.[30] Jewison said no to two more comedies, *Goodbye Charlie* and *Sex and the Single Girl*, before giving in and making a fourth, *The Art of Love*, with Dick Van Dyke. Not until the first preview did he realize that "I had directed my first bomb." Jewison had recently seen Stanley Kubrick's *Dr. Strangelove* and left the theater both thrilled by the movie and profoundly depressed that "my life was being wasted on these commercial comedies where everyone ended up happy and went to the seashore."[31]

In late 1964, Jewison got a lucky break, engineered in part by his agent, William Morris's canny and powerful Abe Lastfogel (who also worked with Arthur Penn and Warren Beatty). A long-forgotten clause in Jewison's contract with Universal set a deadline by which the studio had to inform him it was exercising its option for a fifth movie. Jewison, counseled by Lastfogel, sat quietly by and let the deadline pass. By the time Universal realized it had made what amounted to a clerical mistake, Jewison was free of his contract[32] and jumped at the first drama he was offered, MGM's *The Cincinnati Kid*. The circumstances couldn't have been much worse: The movie, a poker table version of *The Hustler* in which Steve McQueen was to play a young cardsharp facing off against a veteran, had already chewed through five writers (including Paddy Chayefsky and Ring Lardner Jr.); its other leading man, Spencer Tracy, had bowed out on the advice of his doctors just two weeks before shooting was to begin, and only four days into production, the director, Sam Peckinpah, had shot a nude scene without the authority of Martin Ransohoff, his producer.[33] Ransohoff was not a prude; he had already battled Geoffrey Shurlock and the Production Code (and lost) over a very brief nude scene in *The Americanization of Emily* earlier in the year.[34] But he thought Peckinpah was a loose cannon and hated his footage. Peckinpah was fired; Jewison came in with less than a week to prepare, and although the film he made was no masterpiece, he got considerable credit for pulling together a coherent story and focused performances under difficult circumstances.

For Jewison, *The Cincinnati Kid* was the movie that "made me feel I had finally become a filmmaker."[35] It also marked the beginning of a significant professional relationship between the director and Hal Ashby, whom Jewison hired to edit the movie. Jewison and Ashby teamed up again on his next film, *The Russians Are Coming, the Russians Are Coming,* a dark comedy about cold war paranoia that brought him to UA and the Mirisches. This time, Jewison was careful not to be trapped, as he had been at Universal; he signed a deal with Mirisch for just two pictures, for each of which he would be paid $125,000 plus 25 percent of the profits; his contract guaranteed him a voice in development, casting, and editing.[36]

At $3.9 million, *The Russians Are Coming* was a little more expensive than the average studio comedy, but Mirisch was justifiably optimistic about its commercial prospects, and Jewison had earned some leverage with him. He heard about *In the Heat of the Night* while *Russians* was in postproduction and was immediately interested. Mirisch tried to dissuade him, telling him the film was too small; the producer didn't intend to spend nearly as much on this picture as he had on *Russians,*[37] and he may have wanted Jewison to direct a bigger property, *How to Succeed in Business Without Really Trying.* He also let Jewison know that *In the Heat of the Night* would have to be shot on the Goldwyn lot. In the mid-1960s, the issue of "runaway production," the ever rising percentage of studio films that were shot outside of Hollywood (and often outside of the United States), was inflaming tempers and unsettling studio economics,[38] and

Jewison—who had no intention of shooting *In the Heat of the Night* on the lot—decided not to press the point yet. Mirisch gave him the job.

In January and February 1966, Silliphant began turning his outline into a first-draft screenplay that was in some ways stronger than his treatment and in other ways a retreat from it. As planned, Virgil Tibbs had been relocated from Pasadena—but not to Harlem; now, for reasons that the script never made clear, he came from Phoenix, Arizona. Chief Gillespie had become more central to the plot and his backstory had been fleshed out, but, introduced as "a tall, hard-bodied man in his mid-thirties"[39] stepping out of the shower wearing only a towel, he was still more Paul Newman than Rod Steiger. Silliphant had made good on several of his ideas: The story now focused more on the working relationship between Gillespie and Tibbs; the unrelenting oppression of southern racism, including repeated references to Tibbs as a "nigger," was now threaded throughout the script and worked into scenes involving the mayor and the city council; a subject in which Tibbs befriends a black family in Wells had been developed; and the character of Endicott had been turned into a villain. In what was to become a pivotal scene, set in an orchid hothouse, he slaps Tibbs in the face and, wrote Silliphant, "Tibbs responds instantly, slapping him back as hard—or possibly harder, the blow virtually rattling Endicott's head."* In this draft, Silliphant included the idea that Endicott's elderly black butler, seeing the returned slap, immediately "begins to tremble and pray," to which Tibbs snaps, "Don't pray for me! Pray for them!"

But the first draft of *In the Heat of the Night* was also replete with missteps that demonstrated the limitations of Silliphant's speed writing. In describing Tibbs, the screenplay seemed to revert to the novel's white-man's-eye view of him: The first time we see the character, Silliphant presents him from Sam Wood's perspective as "a Negro, in his late twenties . . . but here's a strange thing—this Negro is well-dressed, despite the

---

*In his memoir *The Measure of a Man,* Sidney Poitier writes that Silliphant's script originally called for Tibbs to respond to Endicott's slap with a disdainful stare and then walk out and that he insisted to Walter Mirisch that Tibbs return the slap instantly. But the scene Poitier rejected may have only been an idea that was discussed, since the second slap appears to have been in Silliphant's screenplay as early as its first draft.

heat, with a shirt and tie. . . . His nose seems the nose of an aristocratic white man, the line of his mouth slender and well-formed." (The equation of black refinement with atypical facial features, which came directly from Ball's novel, was, thankfully, a notion that did not survive later rewrites.) Tibbs, in Silliphant's first draft, was still a big talker, albeit far less deferential and courtly, and the screenplay hit every beat of the murder mystery plotline so explicitly that it ran to 166 pages, a blueprint for a movie that would run two hours and forty-five minutes. Silliphant had eliminated one of the novel's wittiest exchanges, in which Gillespie barks, "Virgil is a pretty fancy name for a black boy like you. What do they call you around home where you come from?" and Tibbs replies, "They call me Mister Tibbs." He had employed some gimmicky shorthand to establish Tibbs's intelligence, having him carry around *The Philosophy of Jean-Paul Sartre.* He had made Endicott a vicious bigot but also given him a long speech in which he explains, "You can't legislate tolerance." And Silliphant's portrait of a South Carolina black family didn't feel any more believable than Ball's: When Tibbs starts explaining his profession to a local garage mechanic's kids, their father says, "You gon' spook those chillen!"

Silliphant's first version of *In the Heat of the Night* ended with a handshake between Gillespie and Tibbs, a moment Gillespie pointedly avoids at the end of the book. The screenwriter had been able to eradicate the novel's timeworn sentimentality about race—the idea that black people could be worthy of admiration only if they were better than everyone around them, a stereotype that tied in closely to the exceptionalism that had both shaped and constricted Poitier's career. But what replaced that idea was no less of a platitude—the concluding image (unintentionally echoing *The Defiant Ones*) of a white hand and a black hand clasped together. The final shot embodied a notion that all problems could be solved if two men just got to know each other as people—it may have been politically spurious, but at least it was more contemporary and less condescending than Ball's ending.

Jewison, however, knew that the script had a long way to go. Silliphant later joked about the finesse with which the director handled him. "He called me and said, 'Stirling . . . I have never read a first draft which is so brilliant. I want you to know that I'm not going to change a word.' . . . I was so honored and flattered, I was in a euphoric state for about a week. . . . I called Norman and we had lunch, and I said, 'I'm troubled by your easy acceptance of the script. What I'd like to do is go over it page by page.' Norman said, 'It really isn't necessary, Stirling, but since you insist . . .' He takes his script out of the briefcase, and I see that it is bristling with paper clips, one on almost every page.' "[40] Jewison, it turned out, had some notes. And Silliphant, the fastest writer in Hollywood, found himself working on the screenplay every day for the next six months. "Stirling always said I told him it was brilliant and then months later he was still working on it," says Jewison. "But it wasn't that. We were living in a difficult time for race relations, and I wanted him to dig deeper. What were Virgil's feelings about race? What were Bill Gillespie's? That's where he still had to go."[41]

TWELVE

Arthur Penn was in New York City directing Robert Duvall and Lee Remick in the Broadway play *Wait Until Dark* when, for the third time in three years, he turned down an invitation to direct *Bonnie and Clyde*. This time, the offer was coming from Warren Beatty, whose argumentative collaboration with Penn during production of the ill-fated *Mickey One* had only increased his affection for the director. Penn liked Beatty as well. "Nothing on *Mickey One* was personal," he says. "We remained friends."[1] Beatty thought Penn's affinity for the French New Wave made him a natural choice for the film, but Penn had no interest in directing *Bonnie and Clyde* or any other movie. *The Chase* was about to open to poor reviews, and the experience of having Sam Spiegel take the movie away from him in the editing room, eight years after Warner Brothers had done the same thing on his first picture, *The Left Handed Gun,* had convinced Penn he wasn't meant to work in the movies at all. He had one Hollywood commitment remaining—a deal to direct a project about an ancient Native American and George Custer called *Little Big Man*—but otherwise, he intended to remain in New York and concentrate on directing Broadway plays and forming a repertory theater company in the Berkshires. "I was sick of movie shenanigans," he said later, "and mostly sick of myself for abdicating responsibility."[2] From now on, he told *The New York Times,* "I won't touch anything I can't control to the end."[3]

Soon after Beatty bought Benton and Newman's screenplay, he had to put his search for a director on hold; he had agreed to return to London in early 1966 to star in *Kaleidoscope,* a slapdash caper film about an elaborate card game scam that was intended to capitalize on the success of films like *Charade* and *Topkapi* as well as the public appetite for James Bond–like heroes scampering along ledges in scenic European locations. The blockbuster opening of the fourth Bond film, *Thunderball,* in December 1965 had only increased the urgency every studio felt to mount some competition; 20th Century-Fox had James Coburn in *Our Man Flint,* Columbia was beginning the Matt Helm series with Dean Martin, and even United Artists, the home of 007, was trying newcomer Michael Caine as a sort of unglamorous, bespectacled anti-Bond in *The Ipcress File. Kaleidoscope* was Warner's unmemorable attempt to get in the game. "The shoot was great fun, very jolly," says Susannah York, who replaced Sandra Dee as Beatty's costar a few weeks before production. "It was a shame the movie didn't really live up to the script."[4]

Beatty's colleagues on *Kaleidoscope* recall him as a funny and rambunctious presence during the shoot. "Warren is a great flirt, and if you're up for it, that's great," recalls York. "But I was pretty newly married at the time, and he was still with Leslie Caron, and while I enjoyed his company on the set, sometimes I sort of had to put him down a wee bit."[5] In fact, Beatty's relationship with Caron was coming to an end during production— a split he later said left him "with enormous, overwhelming sadness"[6] —and his mind seemed more on moviemaking than on romance. Before he could even try to get a studio to finance *Bonnie and Clyde,* he had a couple of key decisions to make, and while acting in *Kaleidoscope,* he made the first of them. Despite his initial interest in Bob Dylan and his later insistence that he did not intend to star in the film when he bought the script, Beatty does not appear to have given serious consideration to casting any other actor as Clyde Barrow; by the time he finished *Kaleidoscope* in March, he was committed to playing the role. That, at least, clarified two things for him: As a first-time producer who was also the film's star, he could not consider directing *Bonnie and Clyde* as well, and Shirley MacLaine was now, obviously, out of the running to play Bonnie Parker.

While Beatty was in Europe, he met briefly with Jean-Luc Godard, mostly as a courtesy to Benton and Newman,[7] who were not quite ready to give up their dream of making the first American French New Wave movie. But Beatty didn't start thinking seriously about a director until he returned to the United States. In the decades since *Bonnie and Clyde* was released, a myth of rejection has been attached to the film, often burnished in the retelling by the moviemakers themselves; the project was said to have been turned down by every director, by every actress, by every studio. But, as Beatty says, "sometimes turndowns are not so clear. . . . You talk to somebody, and something doesn't spark, so you don't really follow it up and then you talk to someone else. So I guess it's somewhat of a misspeak to say they all turned me down."[8] However, it's easy to imagine that polite indifference would have felt like rejection to Beatty, and once he settled in Los Angeles and started meeting with directors, he found himself in a position that was as unfamiliar professionally as it was personally: lots of first dates that ended with handshakes and pleasant good-nights.

In his talks with directors, Beatty knew he was at a disadvantage: He was a twenty-nine-year-old actor with a spotty track record who was declaring his intention to become a producer at a time when only a handful of actors, all much older and more experienced, took those reins. Even his friends warned him he was making a mistake: "They would say to me, 'Why are you producing this? You're a movie star. What's it going to say: "Produced by *Warren Beatty*"?' Kirk Douglas could do that. But not conventional, pretty movie stars."[9]

In the five years since his debut in *Splendor in the Grass* had won him access to anyone in old or new Hollywood, Beatty had done his homework and learned his movie history. The first director he pursued was George Stevens, whose career, which began when he worked as a cameraman on Laurel and Hardy silent shorts, had spanned two-thirds of the history of the American movie business. Stevens had made comedies (*Alice Adams, The Talk of the Town*), melodramas (*Penny Serenade*), action-adventures (*Gunga Din*) and, in the 1950s, three films, *A Place in the Sun, Shane*, and *Giant,* that some critics viewed as a thematic trilogy that explored American ambition, expansion, and longing. That was as much of a through line as anyone then looking to trace a pattern in Stevens's work was able to discern. His reputation as a consummate, versatile craftsman was unimpeachable, but he was as far from Truffaut or Godard as it was possible to get: At sixty-one, he was part of Hollywood's unapologetic old guard. As a director who tried to tailor himself to each movie rather than use his films to express an overriding personal vision, he was of little interest to auteurist critics or to New Wave directors. Nonetheless, "Warren had a real fascination with Stevens," says Robert Benton. "He was one of the first names he mentioned."[10]

Beatty may have looked at Stevens's films of the 1950s and seen his gift for bringing out greatness in actors like Montgomery Clift and for pulling better work out of performers like Alan Ladd and Rock Hudson than anyone knew they had in them. "Warren spent a long time talking to George Stevens about doing the picture," says *Bonnie and Clyde*'s script supervisor, John C. Dutton, who had worked with the director on *The Greatest Story Ever Told*. "I'd see the two of them walking up and down Sunset Boulevard—they'd have dinner someplace on the Strip and then walk, and Warren would talk about the picture."[11] But in early 1966, Stevens was not in a state of mind to attempt a fresh approach to moviemaking. He had worked for six years on *The Greatest Story Ever Told*, planning a version of the life of Christ that would be stripped of pageant and spectacle, a counterpoint to the extravagant epics of Cecil B. DeMille. But Stevens, a deliberate worker who liked to shoot and reshoot scenes from all possible angles, took so long to make the movie that religious films passed out of fashion; by the time the 225-minute picture lumbered onto screens in early 1965, Pier Paolo Pasolini's spare and stark *The Gospel According to St. Matthew* had dazzled European critics, and Stevens's film was derided for being as stiff and old-fashioned as anything by DeMille.

After that, Stevens seemed to dig in his heels and rail against an industry that was changing more quickly than he could. In 1965, he filed a $2 million lawsuit against Paramount and NBC, charging the network with the "dismemberment" and "emasculation" of *A Place in the Sun* by planning to air it with commercial interruptions and claiming that Paramount had violated his right to control the film's editing by selling it to a network.[12] Stevens's suit came at a moment when Hollywood's older directors felt particular enmity toward television, possibly because a new generation of TV-trained directors was asserting itself in the movie business. Otto Preminger had recently filed a similar suit over *Anatomy of a Murder*, and

William Wyler sided publicly with Stevens in his claim against NBC, urging his colleagues at a Directors Guild dinner to join the "fight to keep our films from being mutilated on television."[13] But Stevens's lawsuit was shot down,[14] and he turned away from the industry. Beatty's attempt to woo him for *Bonnie and Clyde* came to nothing, and he reluctantly moved on.

In the weeks that followed, Beatty talked to at least a half dozen other directors. The conversations all led nowhere. He tested the waters with Wyler (like Stevens, a giant of the Hollywood establishment and a director for whom auteurists had little use at the time). He approached the sharp, modern filmmakers he had gotten to know while shooting *Promise Her Anything* and *Kaleidoscope* in London, discussing *Bonnie and Clyde* with both Karel Reisz, whose comedy *Morgan: A Suitable Case for Treatment* opened in the United States in April 1966, and John Schlesinger, whose 1965 film, *Darling,* had been among the best-reviewed films of the year. Beatty also discussed the movie with Brian Hutton,[15] a young American director who had just completed *The Pad and How to Use It* (a comedy based on Peter Shaffer's *The Private Ear,* the companion piece to the one-act play Mike Nichols had almost filmed, *The Public Eye*).

Robert Towne, though he had no official role in *Bonnie and Clyde* yet, had become a close friend of Beatty's and an articulate champion of Benton and Newman's screenplay, and he accompanied Beatty to many of the meetings. But Towne's impassioned take on the script didn't move any directors. "I remember at one point in the meeting—and this was typical of a lot of the interviews—Brian Hutton turned to me and said, 'What do *you* think is so special about the movie?'" says Towne. "And I remember saying that this was something new in movies, that it may have been putatively a gangster movie, but that it was nothing like *They Made Me a Criminal* or *I Am a Fugitive from a Chain Gang* or *You Only Live Once,* all of those movies in which sociological issues were at the forefront and sympathy was enlisted because of the characters' circumstances. This script eschewed that, and it was also a very bold use of what the French had been doing that at the same time transcended mere admiration for them and did something different. I certainly went on at some length. And he looked at me and said, 'Well, that's what you *say* is in it, that's what you may *think* is in it, but it's just in your mind. It's not in the script.' And that little scene was replayed many, many times. After a while, I just kept quiet."[16]

Some directors may have shied away from *Bonnie and Clyde* because Beatty made no secret of his intention to serve as a hands-on producer. "My producing point of view came, really, when I was a kid," he says. "The great advantage I had in getting famous when I was twenty-one was that I knew, very well, Sam Goldwyn, David Selznick, Sam Spiegel, Arthur Freed, Jerry Wald, Pandro Berman—so as a producer, I felt, I'm responsible for the movie. I started it, and I'm going to finish it, and if you're going to be a director on a movie that I do, you better know you're gonna have to put up with that."[17] But Beatty himself may have held back from making any director a firm offer because he still hadn't taken Penn's rejection as a final answer. In the late spring of 1966, Beatty met with Sydney Pollack about the movie. "I was quite serious about wanting to do it," says Pollack, "but Warren was very honest with me. He said, 'Look, I don't know yet whether this is going to work out, but if it does work out and Arthur wants to do it, I'm going to do it with Arthur.' "[18]

Beatty returned to New York and decided to make one final run at Penn, telling Abe Lastfogel, the William Morris agent they shared, that he was going to lock himself in a room with Penn until he agreed to direct *Bonnie and Clyde*.[19] Lastfogel stepped in and set up a lunch between the two men at Dinty Moore's. "I didn't stand a chance," Penn wrote later. "Warren can be the most relentlessly persuasive person I know. . . . I had capitulated by the time Warren had finished his complicated order for a salad."[20] In truth, Penn had also looked at the script and found his own door into it for the first time. "I had seen it as this romantic legend all the way through. But then I thought, this is really a story about the agricultural nature of the country. Those banks out there [that Parker and Barrow robbed] were farmers' banks, and then the farmers couldn't pay their mortgages, and eventually the banks took over the farms. . . . Well, all of that was not in the script. But I thought it could be."[21] Imagining *Bonnie and Clyde* as a canvas on which he could depict American social and economic injustice sparked Penn's excitement, and he knew that however contentious their relationship might become, Beatty would agree not to take the movie away from him during postproduction. He felt the script still needed work, but he was, finally, ready to sign on as *Bonnie and Clyde*'s director.

"Arthur was my first choice not only because I knew him, but because I *could* get into an argument with him," says Beatty. "So when he said he would make the movie, I said, 'I want to have one agreement—that if we make this movie, we will have an argument every night. If we don't have anything to argue about, I want to find something to argue about, because there's always something that can be better or can be thought about more.' That's what I wanted the dynamic to be."[22]

Penn agreed. And over the next several months, both men had no trouble keeping their promise.

Two weeks after Richard Zanuck fired Rex Harrison from *Doctor Dolittle*, he rehired him. The showdown had benefited no one, with the exception of Christopher Plummer, who didn't have to miss a single performance of *The Royal Hunt of the Sun* on Broadway and still pocketed $87,500 in severance pay just for signing a contract.[23] Harrison had misbehaved throughout the fall of 1965 in part because his marriage was at a point of dire crisis: During the production of *The Honey Pot*, Rachel Roberts had attempted suicide by taking an overdose of pills after a fight with him. "Rex was in a temper. Abuse flowed. I drank brandy. I came home to emptiness and ice, and swallowed Seconal," she wrote in her journal.[24] Joe Mankiewicz helped keep the episode out of the press. Given the strain Harrison had been under, Zanuck was willing to offer him a second chance. "Rex was a tough guy to deal with," he says. "He could be mean-spirited and very excitable, and he'd have a few drinks and fly off the handle. And on top of it all, he was an egomaniac at the height of his clout. But when he heard about Christopher Plummer, he temporarily turned into a human being again and begged his way back. And from that point on, I had him."[25]

Harrison's good behavior, however, bore a striking resemblance to his bad behavior. He still had little use for Leslie Bricusse or his screenplay; when the two men met in late January, Harrison gave him a set of notes on the *Dolittle* script that left Bricusse frustrated and bewildered. "Mr. Harrison would like the character of Dolittle to be more like Henry Higgins, a man of 'amusing irritability,' to quote his own phrase," Bricusse wrote to Arthur Jacobs after the meeting. "This represents a total change of mind from the meetings in Portofino when he 'didn't care what the character was like so long as he wasn't like Henry Higgins.' . . . This basic change will necessarily have far-reaching effects upon the existing screenplay." Among the other revisions Harrison was requesting were the addition of an opening sequence in London showing Dolittle "as a fashionable Harley Street consultant, bored with life," the creation of a new underwater sequence in which Dolittle would be shown taking the pulse of an octopus, and more than a dozen other significant and expensive changes.[26]

In Los Angeles, as Bricusse worked on expanding the script, 20th Century-Fox's moneymen made their first attempt to create an itemized budget for *Doctor Dolittle*. Jacobs's original projection that the film would cost $6 million had given way to news that stunned the studio: The movie was now expected to cost $14.4 million.[27] Suddenly, Darryl Zanuck's warning that his son could be headed for "economic disaster" seemed alarmingly plausible. "After *The Sound of Music* became the biggest picture of all time, we were really back in business, I was suddenly hailed as, you know, boy genius, and we were off to the races," says Dick Zanuck.[28] But even Zanuck's optimism had limits, and he told Jacobs to cut $2 million out of the budget, and quickly, since the start of production was less than six months away.

Even as *Dolittle*'s costs were rising, the studio allowed Harrison to indulge for nearly two months in what turned out to be a drunken whim. On one of his visits to Italy to discuss the film with his star, director Richard Fleischer met Harrison and Rachel Roberts, both of whom were already intoxicated, in their suite at the Excelsior Hotel in Rome. Harrison, whom Fleischer wrote was "working himself into a frenzy of insecurity," insisted that he wanted Bricusse replaced by different songwriters.[29] He first suggested Betty Comden and Adolph Green and then brought up Michael Flanders and Donald Swann, a comic songwriting team who had been performing in their own revues in England for the last ten years. Fleischer, Harrison, and Roberts then went out to a local restaurant called the White Elephant for an evening that ended in utter chaos when Roberts, who had begun indulging her penchant for barking like a dog as soon as they entered the establishment, brandished a knife at her husband, and Fleischer hurried them out and poured them both into a cab.[30]

Fleischer had to baby-sit Harrison through every mood swing. "The 'Talk To The Animals' number is a hang-over from the old character of Dolittle which I described as a sort of wet-nurse [and] wanted at any price to get out . . . the song to Sophie [the seal] is still <u>quite impossible for me to handle</u> . . . again utterly lacks humour," he wrote to his director after their Portofino meeting. Harrison was convinced that Bricusse was trying to write songs that could become stand-alone hits. "He can do that with his partner, Newley," he snapped. "I don't think I <u>have</u> a number yet." Besides Flanders and Swann, Harrison also wanted Comden and Green to write him some songs: "Please try and explain this complicated artistic truth to Dick [Zanuck]," he wrote. "I cannot do any more work on any of this material. It just isn't <u>any fun</u>."[31]

Fleischer, by now, knew how to handle his star. "I've spent the day mulling over your letter and after analyzing it carefully . . . I have decided that the sky wasn't falling after all," he wrote back. "Leslie is capable of coming through for you." Fleischer wasn't a huge fan of the music he was hearing, either. "I'm praying that Flanders and Swann will come to the rescue . . . even partially," he wrote. "[But] the situation, while urgent, doesn't call for the pressing of the panic button." Asking the studio chief who had fired Harrison just two months earlier to hire still more songwriters would, he reminded his leading man, open a "Pandora's Box."[32] Harrison quieted down quickly.

Nonetheless, Jacobs went along with Harrison's demand that Flanders and Swann be signed to prepare an alternate score for *Doctor Dolittle* while Bricusse continued his own work. The duo spent a month writing songs, most of which were *My Fair Lady* knockoffs tailored to Harrison's limited range. One, called "I Won't Be a King," included a wink to the actor himself, ending with the lyric "Lash me to an eagle / I won't be regal / Lock me in an attic / I shall still be most emphatic that I / Won't be / I can't be / I daren't be / I shan't be a king! / And another thing: I couldn't bear being called 'Rex'!"[33] When they presented their songs to a sober Harrison in April, the actor quickly realized he didn't dislike Bricusse's tunes so much after all, and he sent them packing.

While Fleischer kept Harrison at bay, Jacobs assembled the rest of *Dolittle's* cast and crew, hiring Herbert Ross and Nora Kaye to choreograph the film's big numbers[34] and Ray Aghayan to design the costumes. His negotiations with Hayley Mills had fallen apart, but Jacobs had found a strong substitute to play Emma Fairfax: Samantha Eggar, a twenty-six-year-old auburn-haired Englishwoman who had recently starred as a kidnapping victim in William Wyler's *The Collector*. Eggar and Wyler clashed repeatedly during the shoot; Wyler said that directing the young actress was "like carving soap,"[35] and Eggar didn't hide her feeling that he was a withholding, punitive martinet who had made her first time on a Hollywood set "sheer hell." But the result impressed critics and audiences alike; as her $250,000 deal to star in *Doctor Dolittle* was closing,[36] she received a Best Actress Oscar nomination for *The Collector*. Jacobs was so happy to get her that he didn't even worry about the fact that Eggar couldn't sing; he just added the need to hire a voice double to one of the to-do lists he carried around on index cards.

"At that time, I was under contract to Columbia and Paramount," says Eggar, "and I didn't have a green card," which limited the number of days she could live and work in the United States each year. "Every five months, my husband and my child and I would have to move out of the country, with a new house rented by the studio every time I came back. I can't believe the kind of life we led." When Eggar got the *Dolittle* offer, she had just left her month-old baby to travel to Tokyo, where she was starring opposite Cary Grant in what turned out to be the actor's final film, *Walk, Don't Run*. "Given the toll that took on my health and my psyche, I don't think I realized the scope of *Doctor Dolittle*, the size and responsibility, at the time I signed the contract. . . . I never got that message."[37]

Eggar had no idea that her twenty-six-week commitment to *Doctor Dolittle* would eventually double, but in one regard she was already well prepared for the production. A few years earlier, she had signed to costar with Harrison in an adaptation of Graham Greene's play *The Living Room*. "Everything was fine until the first day of shooting, and on the first day,

Rex walked out—just as he had walked out of many other commitments that he had made. He doubted himself, always. Regardless of being such a brilliant light comedian, he had this gross insecurity about himself. So I already knew this side of him—I had had a Rex experience."[38]

For two weeks in February, 20th Century-Fox struggled to cut *Dolittle*'s budget. When Donald Pleasence asked for $60,000 to play a supporting role in the film and Robert Morley wanted $50,000,[39] Jacobs was told to hire the less-known Peter Bull for $11,000.[40] The animal-training budget estimate fell by $300,000, a cut that was predicated on wild optimism about the ease of working with parrots, pigs, and chimpanzees. And the pirate ship sequence that Dick Zanuck had insisted remain in the script a couple of months earlier was jettisoned as well. But the single biggest piece of cost cutting was one that had the potential to cause a terrible embarrassment: Zanuck and Jacobs decided to eliminate the character of Bumpo, writing Sidney Poitier out of the film altogether and saving themselves his salary, which, given the new, longer production time that *Dolittle* would require, had risen from $250,000 to $400,000.[41]

At the same time that Leslie Bricusse, who hadn't been told of the studio's sudden change in plans, was turning in a new draft of the script in which he had followed Jacobs's orders to enlarge Bumpo's role, Fleischer was complaining that the Bumpo sequences were "extraneous nonsense,"[42] and Zanuck and Jacobs were fretting over how to handle the firing of America's only Oscar-winning black actor. In addition to the certainty that the decision would enrage Harrison, who had insisted on Poitier's casting, their blunder would bring the film unwelcome publicity, and they would probably have to spend far more to pay off Poitier than it had cost them to end their two-week dalliance with Christopher Plummer. As it happened, Jacobs and Zanuck got lucky: Poitier had never signed his contract. A few weeks after they decided to cut him from the film, Poitier's agent, Martin Baum, brought up some minor sticking points in his deal for *Dolittle*. Jacobs flatly refused to give an inch, hoping to force an artificial confrontation, and his strategy worked: Poitier quit. That saved the producer from having to send out a press release that he had drafted in which he was ready to fall on his sword, admitting that "we simply had a script which ran well over four hours" and noting that the role of Bumpo would have to shrink so much that "it would have been an imposition to insist that Mr. Poitier continue in it."[43]

Poitier himself could have chosen to make Fox's sloppy treatment of him public, but by the time his *Dolittle* deal came undone in April, he was probably happy to be rid of the film. The actor had not had high hopes for any of the three pictures that opened at the end of 1965, and he was right about *The Bedford Incident* and *The Slender Thread,* which received indifferent reviews and did little business. But the third movie, MGM's *A Patch of Blue,* was surprising everyone by becoming the biggest box office success of his career. Poitier had agreed to a substantial salary cut, taking just $80,000[44] in exchange for 10 percent of the gross to star in director Guy Green's low-budget black-and-white drama about a black man who befriends a teenage blind white girl (Elizabeth Hartman) and then runs afoul of her slatternly, racist mother (Shelley Winters). His decision paid off handsomely when *A Patch of Blue* returned $6.8 million to the studio. In promoting the movie, MGM followed the *Lilies of the Field* playbook to the letter, selling the film as a parable of racial understanding in the press while soft-pedaling anything that could offend southern theater owners or audiences. Print advertisements for the film showed Hartman swinging gaily around the trunk of a tree, with a tiny head shot of Poitier placed as far away from her as possible,[45] and MGM's endorsement of racial understanding proved to be somewhat flexible; the studio willingly cut eight seconds from all prints of *A Patch of Blue* that showed in the South,[46] excising what would have been the first time a black man kissed a white woman in a major Hollywood film.

A Patch of Blue turned Poitier into a first-tier national movie star. Despite *Variety*'s concern that the film would have "possible limited appeal in Dixie,"[47] the movie was his first to do big business in cities like Atlanta, Houston, and Charlotte,[48] playing well in both black and white neighborhoods. Most critics felt that the mawkish material was elevated by the performances and shared Judith Crist's conviction that the movie showed Poitier "at the peak of his abilities . . . the embodiment of a man secure within himself."[49] But many also expressed impatience with seeing the actor forced into one more turn-the-other-cheek characterization. White liberals were especially eager to take on the mantle of black rage: "The caricature of the Negro as a Madison Avenue sort of Christian saint, self-less and well-groomed, is becoming a movie cliché nearly as tiresome and, at bottom, nearly as patronizing as the cretinous figure that Stepin Fetchit used to play," wrote Brendan Gill in *The New Yorker.* "Negroes must find it extremely irritating."[50] "The implicit moral is that affection between a Negro man and a white girl is all right so long as the girl is blind, ignorant, undeveloped and 18 years old," complained the reviewers for *Film Quarterly.* "We will have got somewhere when she's a bright 25-year-old who knows what she's doing."[51]

The critics who argued that *A Patch of Blue*'s take on race relations was hopelessly behind the day's headlines never mentioned that the film had to be bowdlerized in order to play in half the country. Nor did they acknowledge that they stood an ideological world apart from some of their own colleagues. In the widespread shock that followed the Watts riots, some white commentators and cultural critics started to articulate a ludicrous position of evenhandedness, attempting to advance the notion that in 1966, the problem of antiwhite anger could be reasonably discussed in the same breath as the issue of civil rights for black Americans. Positioning itself above what it decided were the orthodoxies of both sides, *Saturday Review* praised *A Patch of Blue* for refusing to "imply that racial tolerance is wholly 'one-sided' "[52] (a message that is nowhere to be found in the movie itself). Meanwhile, members of the Ku Klux Klan were picketing the Memphis theater showing the movie, calling it "ungodly" and complaining that "the nigger's name [is] above the white woman's on the marquee." The protesters were far outnumbered that day by moviegoers.[53]

In the winter and spring of 1966, Poitier, thanks in part to the persistence of Harry Belafonte, was becoming a more visible and audible political activist. He and Belafonte went to East Harlem to talk to four thousand grade school students for what was then called Negro History Week;[54] the two men paid the bail for five protesters, including SNCC chairman John Lewis, who were arrested for picketing against apartheid at the South African consul general's office in New York;[55] and Poitier made a guest appearance in *The Strollin' Twenties,* a CBS special produced by Belafonte that was a rarity for network television, a proudly Afrocentric history of entertainment in Harlem.

But when it came to acting challenges that would take him in new directions, Poitier was, perhaps for the first time, as hamstrung by the restrictions he placed on himself as by the limitations of the material he was given. After fifteen years of being Hollywood's exception to the rule, he either would not or could not see himself as anything other than a role model. He could barely suppress his weariness with material like *A Patch of Blue* ("I don't think anyone familiar with American social life could construe [it] as being representative," he said), but when opportunities to shake off his plaster-saint image presented themselves, he turned away. That summer, Poitier entertained an offer to play *Othello* in an NBC special, a role that surely would have been the most challenging of his career. After weeks of indecision, he dropped out, claiming defensively that the role "bored me"[56] and that he didn't want to play a black man who was "a dupe."[57] "If the fabric of the society were different, I would scream to high heaven to play villains. But I'll be damned if I do that at this stage of the game. Not when there is only one Negro actor working in films with any degree of consistency. It's a choice," he said. "A clear choice."[58]

THIRTEEN

In the mid-1960s, there were two kinds of young actors working in New York theater: the type that Hollywood's East Coast casting directors thought were handsome enough to recruit for movies and the type that weren't. Those in the first group—square-jawed, symmetrically attractive men like George Peppard, James Farentino, and John Phillip Law—were approached by the studios early in their stage careers and in many cases signed multifilm contracts and were thrown into one movie after another to see if the transplant would take. In rare instances, as was the case with Warren Beatty and Robert Redford, the bet paid off well enough to justify all the times that it didn't. The second tier of actor was understood to be a victim of genetic bad luck, someone who, whatever his talent, could never be groomed or reshaped or prettified into a movie star and was left behind to ply his trade in New York. The studios assumed that actors who looked or sounded like Robert Duvall, Gene Hackman, Jon Voight, and Alan Arkin would be of little interest to the American public; they might be useful in a comic or supporting role now and then, but nothing more.

Dustin Hoffman was in a third category: He was the kind of actor who couldn't get work at all. Hoffman had grown up on the West Coast; he dropped out of Santa Monica City College to come to New York in the late 1950s.[1] Despite the fact that his parents had named him, aspirationally, after the silent-movie cowboy star Dusty Farnum, he had no illusions about the sorts of roles that he would be able to get. "At that time, there was not necessarily an anti-Semitic, but certainly an antiethnic code," he says. "If you got *Back Stage* [a New York theater trade paper], the casting notices said Leading Men, and then Juveniles, and Leading Ladies, and then Ingenues. And then, next to that, it said Character Leading Men, Character Juveniles. And that word—'character'—meant that you were not attractive: You were the funny-looking person next to the good-looking person in high school. And everybody knew it."[2]

For five years, Hoffman scraped together a bare subsistence living in New York City. He got a handful of tiny parts, mostly one-shot guest appearances on New York–based TV series like *The Defenders, The Nurses,* and *Naked City.* "And I only got those because Bob Duvall was a favorite with Marion Dougherty, the casting agent," he says. "He would read for her, and I'd be waiting outside, and as he'd leave, he'd say, 'Marion, cast him, he's good!' So I got a couple of little parts, but that was it. Bob, at least, got the lead as the villain on a lot of those shows. If I had a scene, I was lucky."[3] Hoffman worked as a waiter, as a toy demonstrator at Macy's, as an attendant at the New York Psychiatric Institute, and as the only male typist in the steno pool at the Manpower temp agency. When jobs got really scarce, he would sleep on Gene Hackman's kitchen floor.[4] And on the few occasions when he was able to get an audition, he was turned down every time.

"Dusty did something I could never do," says Susan Anspach, a friend from those years, "which is that he kept hanging in there through rejection after rejection, year after year after year after year."[5] That may have been due less to Hoffman's faith in himself than to his natural tenacity and unwillingness to back down. "I got kicked out of acting class when I was twenty years old because I screamed at the teacher when she started talking to me in the middle of a scene," he said later. "I had a big fight with Lee Strasberg in my first class with him. . . . .I have never felt unbrave."[6]

Nonetheless, by the beginning of 1965, Hoffman was twenty-seven, seriously demoralized by his inability to land an acting job, and considering a change in careers. He signed on to work for Ulu Grosbard as an assistant director and assistant stage manager on Grosbard's production of *A View from the Bridge,* which featured Duvall, Voight, and Anspach in the principal roles. "I had reached a point, when I was doing *View from the*

Bridge, when I decided, I'm not gonna act anymore—to the extent that you can quit something you're not doing," says Hoffman. "I thought, maybe I'm gonna become a director or something."[7] But he couldn't quite let go of the hopes that had brought him to New York in the first place. Anspach, who met him during that production, recalls a lunch for the cast and crew of the play at which he told her with bravado, " 'You know, if I were older, I'd be playing Bobby's part.' And I said, 'Sure, right, Dusty.' And he said, 'What do you mean!? I'm fuckin' talented! Ask Bobby! He'll tell you himself!' I said to Bobby, 'Is he putting me on? He's the sweep-up guy!' And Bobby said, 'No, it's true, he's the most talented guy among all of us.' "[8]

Hoffman impressed Grosbard, who told Arthur Miller that the actor might make a good Willy Loman one day. (In his memoir, *Timebends,* Miller wrote, "My estimate of Grosbard almost collapsed as, observing Dustin Hoffman's awkwardness and his big nose that never seemed to get unstuffed, I wondered how the poor fellow imagined himself a candidate for any kind of acting career.")[9] When *A View from the Bridge,* a one-act version of which had failed on Broadway ten years earlier, opened, it began a highly successful two-year run that gave many of the people involved a degree of job security for the first time in their lives. "Ulu would let me leave to do other plays, and they'd flop, and then I'd come back," says Anspach. "Bobby Duvall did the same thing."[10]

Grosbard encouraged Hoffman, who was now rooming on and off with Duvall, not to give up on acting and got him an audition for *Harry Noon and Night,* a play by Ronald Ribman that was to be staged in Hell's Kitchen at St. Clement's Church by the American Place Theatre, which was then in its first season. The role for which Hoffman read was Immanuel, a handicapped, cross-dressing German who was living with an American soldier in the ruins of Berlin after World War II. "He just walked in off the street," says Ribman. "And we knew instantly he was Immanuel."[11]

"I think I tended to relax a little after *View from the Bridge,*" says Hoffman. "So I did a very nutty audition—this hunchbacked gay Nazi guy with a limp. And I was outrageous enough to get the part. Wynn Handman [co-founder of the American Place Theatre] came up to me years later and said, 'You put a lot of that into *Midnight Cowboy,*' and I said, 'Hmm, maybe, I don't know.' "[12]

The production, in which Hoffman costarred with Joel Grey, was small—the American Place could afford to give it a run of just three weeks, and "we did it with the understanding that it was not to be reviewed," recalls Ribman.[13] But Hoffman, thrilled to have won a role at last, threw himself into preparing for the part with years of pent-up desire to prove what he could do if someone gave him a chance. Arthur Miller arranged for him to spend an evening with his daughter's German baby-sitter so he could find an accent for his character. "She was from Munich, so we got together and I suggested that she say all my lines into a tape recorder. I remember I used to continually make passes at her. Every once in a while as she was recording, I'd kind of get my hand going down her arm and try to sneak it over, and she would say, 'I don't *need* dis ting!' " The baby-sitter was unyielding, but Hoffman did leave with a workable sound for Immanuel and, although he spoke no actual German, decided to try out his accent in the Upper East Side neighborhood then known as Germantown for its stretch of German restaurants, stores, and candy shops. "I'd go there, and I used to sit at a bar, and someone would talk to me in German, and I would say, 'I'm sorry, but the only way I'm gonna learn English is to keep speaking it.' And it worked—they believed it."[14]

Despite the play's short run, Hoffman's performance generated considerable word of mouth among a small group of devoted theatergoers and professionals. Mike Nichols and Buck Henry both made a point of going to see him. "He played a crippled German transvestite, and I believed all three, no question," says Henry. "It wasn't enough for either of us to say, 'Let's get this guy for *The Graduate*,' but it was enough so that I realized, 'Oh God, this guy can do a lot of stuff.' "[15] Ribman was excited by the play's reception and went ahead with plans that he had made with another producer to move *Harry Noon and Night* to a theater in the East Village for an open-ended engagement. But Hoffman, to everyone's surprise, decided not to continue with the show. "He never told me why he left," says Ribman, "but it's my impression that maybe he felt he had a better offer."[16] Joel Grey left the cast as well (he was replaced by Robert Blake), and *Harry Noon and Night*'s commercial run lasted just four days, leaving Ribman angry at what he felt was Hoffman's ingratitude.

Hoffman's better offer wasn't for a new role, but simply for a steadier and more reliable income from working in the theater, a luxury he had sought for years and wasn't ready to abandon for a part in a play that might not last. He went back to work for Grosbard, who offered him a new job on his production of Frank Gilroy's *The Subject Was Roses,* which had won the Tony Award for Best Play in the summer of 1965. Grosbard gave Hoffman the chance to stage-manage the production and also to serve as standby for the young male lead (a role originated by Martin Sheen and then being played by Walter McGinn).

In the fall, Wynn Handman began planning the American Place Theatre's 1965–1966 season with the company's co-founders Michael Tolan, an actor, and Sidney Lanier, an Episcopal priest who felt his mission was to bring theater to St. Clement's Church. Ribman was working on a new piece called *The Journey of the Fifth Horse* that would be ready in the spring, but the first play they planned to produce that season was William Alfred's *Hogan's Goat,* a drama about an Irish family in 1890s Brooklyn. Handman and director Frederick Rolf were struggling to cast the female lead, the angry, maltreated wife of the play's main character, when a striking actress with high cheekbones and regal bearing walked in to read for them. "We saw a lot of actors," Handman says. "Among them was this woman, Faye Dunaway. When she auditioned, I thought she was very talented and beautiful. The director said, 'She'll do this when it's a movie, but not onstage.' I said, 'No, let's give her a call back.' "[17]

Dunaway, an intensely ambitious and volatile young woman, projected a glamour that was almost entirely self-invented; she was the daughter of an army man with little money who had moved his family from Florida to Arkansas to Texas to Germany to Utah when she was growing up. She had arrived in New York in 1962 as a twenty-one-year-old graduate of Boston University and had made herself known quickly. Within two days, she had signed a year-long contract as a replacement in the cast of the Broadway play *A Man for All Seasons;* soon after, she met Lenny Bruce, who was beginning his skid into legal battles and drug abuse, and began a brief affair with him. In 1963, Dunaway auditioned for Elia Kazan and made such a strong impression on him that the director invited her to join the repertory company he and producer Robert Whitehead were forming at Lincoln Center. When Kazan directed Arthur Miller's play *After the*

Fall, about his marriage to Marilyn Monroe, on Broadway in 1964, he chose Dunaway to understudy his own wife, Barbara Loden, as Maggie, the play's female lead. Dunaway would study Loden's performance every night from the catwalk, wondering if she could match it and if she would be given the chance to try. She started to feel anxious and depressed and went into analysis.[18] "I thought that I had talent . . . but I was frightened that I wouldn't be able to shape it into something that was exceptional," she wrote in her autobiography. "The very things that drove me to succeed as an actress—my need and wish and desire for perfection—were also the things that worked against me in trying to find my own happiness."[19]

During its two years under Kazan's stewardship, the Lincoln Center rep company, which also included Martin Sheen, Frank Langella, Hal Holbrook, and Jason Robards Jr., [20] was a hothouse of talent, tension, and neurosis, as thirty actors working closely together committed themselves to the idea of ensemble work but also chased the spotlight. "In those days, all the Method actors, the Actors Studio people, would say, you have to experience everything," says John Phillip Law, a member of the company. "To assign somebody to do a scene with somebody else was almost to say, 'Jesus, go home and fuck 'em, and then come back and try to make something real happen.' And of course, Faye shows up for our scene one day and says right off the bat, 'Oh, I had a dream about you last night!' So we had our little roll in the hay. But it was no big deal—it was just how things worked then." Law, who went on to act in *The Changeling* and *Marco Millions* with Dunaway while they both worked for Kazan, remembers her work as extraordinary. "Faye was a little jealous of Barbara Loden, who she felt was getting her parts because of Kazan. But even then, it was clear she was a wonderful actress."[21]

Dunaway was offered a contract to join the cast of the daytime soap opera *The Guiding Light*, but she turned it down. ("In New York, if you did a soap or a TV ad, you'd never admit it," says Dustin Hoffman. "It meant you weren't serious.")[22] When Handman was casting *Hogan's Goat*, Dunaway had just suffered the first setback of her brief career; Kazan and Whitehead, whose ambitious Lincoln Center productions had received mixed reviews and done only modest business, were dismissed, and their replacements fired Dunaway and many of the other actors Kazan had mentored. When Handman saw Dunaway, he knew she was just one good role away from being noticed by the studios. He and Frederick Rolf hired her to play Kathleen, a challenging, emotional role that required the actress to rail drunkenly against her husband and fall down a flight of onstage stairs to her death in every performance. *Hogan's Goat* opened to excellent reviews in November 1965, and nobody was shocked when Dunaway was spotted by a scout for producer Sam Spiegel. "Dustin Hoffman was someone I would never have guessed would end up on a poster in girls' bedrooms," says Handman. "But Dunaway becoming a movie star? That didn't surprise me at all."[23] Three months after *Hogan's Goat* opened, she left the play to make her first film. By the spring of 1966, Dunaway had signed long-term contracts with both Spiegel and Otto Preminger and had turned down a chance to test with Michael Caine for the sequel to *The Ipcress File, Funeral in Berlin.*[24] "I longed to do great work," she said, "and since you must be famous to get those opportunities, I wanted to be famous."[25]

In February, Dunaway left for Florida to star in *The Happening,* an uneasy combination of comedy and crime drama, for Spiegel and *Cat Ballou* director Elliot Silverstein. She was paid $25,000 for her role as a bored wild child who joins a group of hippies on a housebreaking escapade. Dunaway was able to resist the romantic advances of her notoriously insistent producer, but there was no escaping the intention of her director to transform her physically into "the cookie-cutter blond bombshell" that he wanted for the movie.[26] "The role called for a more kittenish kind of girl," says Silverstein.[27] In 1966, "kittenish" didn't mean brunette, and the director insisted that Dunaway bleach and tease her brown hair into a blond mane and wear a padded bra and costumes that exposed as much skin as possible. Dunaway started starving herself, fearful about what "acres of bare midriff"[28] would look like on a movie screen, and did her best to turn herself into what everyone was telling her she had to become. "I understood from her hair and makeup people that she was quite upset," says Silverstein. "There were a lot of emotions." Dunaway, after two years with Kazan, wasn't used to working fast, without any discussion. "I'd say, 'Faye, the sun is fading, we have to move on,'" says Silverstein. "She was upset, but then she'd be fine. Most of the time she just walked right in and did it."[29]

Hogan's Goat continued without Dunaway, and Handman began to hold auditions for the American Place's spring production, *The Journey of the Fifth Horse*, Ribman's adaptation of Turgenev's *Diary of a Superfluous Man*. "I'm sitting in the theater next to Wynn," says Ribman, "and in walks Dustin Hoffman, *again,* on an open call. He says, 'I'm terribly sorry for what I did [on *Harry Noon and Night*], and I hope it won't interfere with you letting me read for the part.' One impetus I had was to grab him by the seat of his pants and throw him out. But he was terrific."[30]

Hoffman wanted to play Chulkaturin, a young nobleman dying of tuberculosis. But Handman and Ribman steered him toward the play's other main role, a "character leading man" part, and cast him as Zoditch, a pinched, fussy proofreader who is forced to confront the tininess and circumscription of his own life while reading Chulkaturin's diary. Rip Torn and Susan Anspach were cast in the other lead roles, and the play went into rehearsals under the direction of Larry Arick. The level of tension in the room was intolerable almost from the first day. "Rip had a lot of problems with the director," says Ribman. "He would sit there when Larry Arick was giving notes and hold a newspaper in front of his face—that kind of juvenile behavior. And he and Dustin and Susan became a kind of trio."[31]

Arick, for his part, was unhappy with Torn's behavior and was just as frustrated with Hoffman's tentative performance and uncompromising working methods. "Dusty did a good audition, but then, like any good actor, he let everything go and started from scratch," says Anspach. "How do you play a character who's full of rage but too repressed to show it? It took a while for him to figure out how to show that without spelling it out. By the second week, they were sure they hired the wrong guy. By the third, they were ready to fire him. By the fourth, they had offered the part to another actor behind his back." The actor, Albert Paulson, was a friend of Torn's, and Torn asked him not to take the job, telling him, "Please, this guy's gonna be brilliant, he needs a break, string them along, don't turn it down or accept it until it's too late and they have to keep him."[32] Torn was able to protect Hoffman, but not himself. Just a week before the play was to open, communication in the rehearsal room broke down entirely. "We had a few choices," says Michael Tolan. "We could remove the director, Dustin, or Rip. Wynn Handman and I decided that the easiest thing to do was replace Rip."[33]

Tolan stepped into Torn's part himself, and Handman postponed the opening to give the cast a few extra days of rehearsal. "At that time, Dustin was a very difficult actor to work with," says Tolan, "because he had such an intense sense of capital-T 'Truth' that he found it very difficult to give a performance. He was hardly talking above a whisper in his scenes because he wouldn't commit to anything that he thought would be false."[34] One afternoon, at the peak of his frustration, Hoffman cut short a rehearsal by saying, "Nobody likes me!" and walked out. "He just left for several hours—maybe to talk to his analyst—and when he came back, he was more confident," says Ribman.[35] But his performance still wasn't making any impression. "Wynn, Larry, and I got together and said, 'What the fuck are we gonna do here?' " says Tolan. "At the final dress rehearsal, we said, 'Dustin, we can't hear you past the second row of the theater. And he said, 'What do you want me to do, shout?' And we said, 'Yes!' And suddenly, he gave the performance that he'd been working on for weeks. He'd been getting there all along."[36]

When *The Journey of the Fifth Horse* opened on April 21, 1966, Hoffman received his first review as a professional actor, from Stanley Kauffmann in *The New York Times,* who wrote, "This portrait of a repressed, clerkish tyrant is sharply outlined and vividly colored. . . . It is an able comedian's performance."[37] Other critics were even more enthusiastic; although *Journey* ran for just ten days, Hoffman won the Obie Award as the season's best off-Broadway actor, the first time the prize had been given since George C. Scott won it three years earlier. An abridged version of the play was filmed for National Educational Television, the forerunner of PBS, and Ribman and the producers quickly made plans to transfer the production to a commercial run at Greenwich Village's Circle in the Square. But shortly after the television taping was completed, Hoffman, just as he had done a year earlier, decided to drop out of the play, and the transfer was canceled. "The play was optioned, and Dustin Hoffman just walked out," says Ribman. "And I think that was the last time I saw him."[38]

"They talk about Oscar-itis," says Hoffman. "Well, I guess I got Obie-itis. I won the award, and I didn't work for six months."[39]

Hoffman had given his first preview performance in *Journey* the night after the 1966 Academy Awards ceremony. Like most New York theater actors, he professed not to care much about the Oscars. "There really was a red-state blue-state feeling," he recalls. "New York was Arthur Miller. Hollywood was *Bonanza*."[40] That year, the ceremony served primarily as an exercise in studio self-affirmation, an announcement from the Hollywood establishment that it was celebrating a year of having succeeded in doing what it had been built to do, which was to put out big, long movies that made lots of money. *The Sound of Music* won Best Picture and was probably the most critically scorned film in a dozen years to take the top prize. The night's other big winner, MGM's *Doctor Zhivago*, was an expensive, epic road-show presentation that was doing such massive business that voters permitted themselves to ignore the many critics who noted that the movie fell well short of David Lean's *Lawrence of Arabia*.

The ten Oscars won by *Zhivago* and *The Sound of Music* represented a defiant ratification of old-fashioned picture making and a preference for defending familiar turf over breaking new ground. But the threat to old Hollywood was evident right in the nominations, which seemed to emanate from England and New York as much as from Los Angeles. For Best Actor, Hoffman was rooting for Rod Steiger, a New Yorker who had crossed successfully into Hollywood with his Method training intact; he was nominated for his performance as an emotionally deadened Holocaust survivor working in Harlem in Sidney Lumet's *The Pawnbroker*, which epitomized the kind of uncompromising East Coast filmmaking the studios wouldn't touch. It was left to Samuel Z. Arkoff and James Nicholson's exploitation company, American International Pictures, to distribute the movie, an odd fit on a slate of 1965 releases that also included *How to Stuff a Wild Bikini* and *Die, Monster, Die!*

One Best Picture nominee came straight out of the New York theater-television nexus—a cheaply made black-and-white adaptation of the play *A Thousand Clowns* that starred Jason Robards Jr. and Martin Balsam. Another nomination went to John Schlesinger's tough-minded swinging-London comedy-drama *Darling,* which turned Julie Christie into an international celebrity and a fashion sensation and gave Embassy's Joseph E. Levine, whom everyone enjoyed belittling as a noisy New York importer of Italian schlock and European art-house films, his first-ever Best Picture contender. Only eight of the twenty acting nominations went to Americans, and the night's big old-guard moment—the "surprise" presentation of an honorary Academy Award to the show's host, Bob Hope, who had already been given four other honorary Oscars—was so anticlimactic that *Time* magazine said the telecast (the first time the Oscars aired in color) "made *The Beverly Hillbillies* look good."[41]

Warren Beatty, back from shooting *Kaleidoscope,* was present to hand out an award, as was one of the actresses he was still considering as a possible Bonnie Parker, Natalie Wood. Another presenter, Yvette Mimieux, had drawn the interest of United Artists' David Picker,[42] who was still interested in making *Bonnie and Clyde* and also wondering who could play the female lead. That evening, Beatty watched yet another potential Bonnie, Julie Christie, take home the Best Actress prize. A few weeks earlier, he had met Christie for the first time in England as they both stood on a receiving line to greet Queen Elizabeth II at the royal premiere of *Born Free,*[43] and he couldn't get his mind off the woman who was to become his lover and frequent costar in the 1970s. "I had met Julie Christie. Oh boy, had I met her," he says. "We had lunch at Shepperton [Studios in England]. I thought she would be, physically, very good for the part. Bonnie was petite, and it struck me as more dramatic to have this petite thing be so tough. But she was British, so that just wasn't going to work."[44] In any case, Beatty knew there was no point in casting Bonnie until he had a deal with a studio, and that meant shopping the project to the same people who had already turned it down.

In Los Angeles to begin rehearsals and song prerecording for *Doctor Dolittle,* Rex Harrison, the previous year's Best Actor winner, showed up at the Santa Monica Civic Auditorium to present Christie with her award. Among the actresses she beat were Julie Andrews, who had been Arthur

Jacobs's first choice for *Dolittle*'s female lead, and Samantha Eggar, who, carefully counting the number of days she was allowed to spend in the United States, had returned to attend the ceremony and begin preparations for *Dolittle*. Sidney Poitier was not present that evening; both of his costars in *A Patch of Blue,* Elizabeth Hartman and Shelley Winters, had been nominated, but he had not. The Best Actor slot he might have gotten went instead to Laurence Olivier's blackface performance in *Othello*. Despite Poitier's own misgivings about playing the part, it was hard not to feel that Olivier's nomination was undoing whatever symbolic progress had been made in giving Poitier an Oscar two years earlier, especially since Olivier was being honored for an overripe, pop-eyed filmed stage turn that *The New York Times'* Bosley Crowther had called an "outrageous impression of a theatrical Negro stereotype. He does not look like a Negro. . . . He looks like a Rastus or an end man in an American minstrel show. You almost wait for him to whip a banjo out."[45] And what was Poitier (or any other black actor) to make of Pauline Kael's patronizing assertion in *McCall's* that she "saw Paul Robeson and he was not as black as Olivier is. . . . Possibly Negro actors need to sharpen themselves on white roles before they can *play* a Negro"?[46]

The evening's glummest attendee was probably Stanley Kramer. *Ship of Fools* had been nominated for eight Academy Awards, including Best Picture, but Kramer, whose direction of the movie had come in for stinging criticism in many reviews, was not among the Best Director nominees, and his own gloomy assessment that the film had fallen short of greatness had not been contradicted by its mediocre grosses or by the bad night it was having (it won awards in the black-and-white categories for Cinematography and Art Direction, but nothing else). Kramer also had to contend with the bleak news that his bad run at the box office had just put an end to his next project, *Andersonville*. An ambitious, large-scale battlefield drama could never be made within the $3 million budget ceiling that Columbia had imposed on Kramer, and longtime ally Mike Frankovich had let him know that his studio had now decided not to bankroll the movie at all, even though he had been working on it for nearly four years. For the first time since he had become a producer, Kramer had nothing on his plate.

In the audience, Rod Steiger sat nervously waiting for the Best Actor category. Two rows in front of him was Lee Marvin, who, as he was taking his seat, turned around and joked that he was planning to wait until Steiger's name was announced, then trip him on his way to the stage.[47] Steiger was an actor's actor, but not, by any stretch of the imagination, a movie star. Reviewing him in *The Pawnbroker,* Judith Crist called him "a brilliant and bravura actor whose performances . . . are unforgettable but who, of course, just doesn't rank at the box office the way a Rock Hudson or a Heston does."[48] He had been nominated once before, for playing Marlon Brando's brother in *On the Waterfront*. But in the decade since, Steiger's career had drifted; he made a number of unmemorable movies, then showed up in a few television series. In the early 1960s, fed up with his inability to get work in the United States, he and his wife, actress Claire Bloom, moved to Europe,[49] where he worked for the Italian directors Francesco Rosi and Ermanno Olmi.

Steiger had a major role in *Doctor Zhivago,* which was by far the biggest hit of his career, but it was his work in *The Pawnbroker,* which he had finished more than two years earlier, that marked a triumphant homecoming for the actor—that is, once the film reached the United States. The brutal, small-scale character study had been developed for MGM, but after the studio demanded that the script be softened, independent producer Ely Landau decided to finance the $1.2 million film out of his own pocket. When Sidney Lumet took over as director during preproduction after Landau fired Arthur Hiller, Steiger had already been cast. Lumet's initial reaction was disappointment. "That was my one hesitation in taking it," says Lumet. "I knew Rod. We had worked together in live television, and I liked his work. But I felt he was a rather tasteless actor—awfully talented, but completely tasteless in his choices."[50] Steiger's Achilles' heel was what even his own wife recognized as his tendency to go over the top; Bloom wrote that he could "be all over the place, out of control, no sense, just the spewing out of a scene" on the first take.[51] "The *New York Post* used to have a columnist named Max Lerner, a really cantankerous fool," says Lumet. "A friend of mine, the scenic designer Boris Aronson, was once asked why he didn't like Lerner. And he said, 'For five cents, he gives you too much.' I felt that way about Rod."

Lumet, if he had had his way, would have cast James Mason as the haunted camp survivor, but Steiger ended up surprising the director. "During rehearsals, we talked about how important the repression of the character's feelings was, and Rod was more than willing to go that route," says Lumet. "And he worked out just fine."[52] When *The Pawnbroker* made its debut in June 1964 at the Berlin Film Festival—an especially meaningful venue given its subject matter—it received a sustained ovation, and Steiger won the Best Actor prize for what many hailed as the performance of his career. But the movie was rejected by every studio in Hollywood because of less than five seconds of footage—a scene in which a black prostitute exposes her breasts to Steiger's character, whose memory flashes, in a split-second shock cut, to his late wife, also bare-breasted, in the concentration camp. Lumet had decided not to film a "protection shot" (an alternate take of the scene without nudity): "I figured, what the hell, it's private money, we're all working for next to nothing, and I'll just dump the problem on Landau."[53] But the Production Code's ban on nudity was absolute. Without a PCA seal from Geoffrey Shurlock, and its nonsecular equivalent, an approval rating from the Legion of Decency (by then called the National Catholic Office for Motion Pictures), no major company would touch the picture. Landau, to his credit, refused to remove the footage, and *The Pawnbroker* remained unseen in the United States for almost a year after its Berlin premiere.

At the urging of his colleague Joe Mankiewicz, Lumet took the then unusual step of appealing Shurlock's decision to the Motion Picture Association's thirteen-member board. Mankiewicz himself was a member of the appeals committee, and thanks to his impassioned lobbying, in March 1965 *The Pawnbroker* became the first movie with bare breasts to receive Code approval, with the Code announcing that it was "to be viewed as a special and unique case." Notwithstanding Shurlock's insistence that the decision was, as *The New York Times* dryly put it, "an unprecedented move that will not, however, set a precedent,"[54] the reversal was the first of a series of injuries to the Production Code that would prove fatal within three years. And the National Catholic Office's decision to stand firm and give the movie a "Condemned" rating was just as damaging to its own authority; for the first time, the Catholics were pointedly belittled by other religious film advocacy groups. The Broadcasting and Film Commission of the National Council of Churches gave *The Pawnbroker* a best picture award, and the editor of the newsletter the *Christian Advocate* wrote in defense of the nude scene, "Anyone obtaining salacious pleasure from those terrifying moments is already dead to the rest of life, and hardly a subject for further stimulation."[55]

Steiger's work in the film moved *Life* magazine to praise his "endless versatility"[56] and *The New Yorker*'s Brendan Gill to write, "By a magic more mysterious . . . than his always clever makeup, [he] manages to convince me at once that he is whoever he pretends to be."[57] Steiger was considered, along with *Ship of Fools'* Oskar Werner, a front-runner for the Oscar, and his visibility in *Doctor Zhivago* could only help. When Julie Andrews opened the envelope and announced that the winner was Lee Marvin for *Cat Ballou*, Steiger, according to one account, "momentarily choked."[58] Marvin was a well-liked actor who, after years of playing heavies, had delighted and surprised audiences by giving a deft comic performance in the western spoof. He went home the winner, and Steiger and Claire Bloom went back to their hotel, miserable. "I can't say I was happy about it," he said. "I think I wound up telling *her* not to feel so bad."[59] Soon after, Steiger took a role in *The Girl and the General*, a minor Italian antiwar comedy, and returned to Europe. His comeback had stopped short of either an Academy Award or a single job offer from Hollywood.

FOURTEEN

teiger wasn't Norman Jewison's first choice to play *In the Heat of the Night*'s Bill Gillespie. Jewison wanted George C. Scott, an actor against whom Steiger often found himself competing for roles. But Scott was already committed to playing a rascally southerner in a con-artist comedy called *The Flim-Flam Man* that Larry Turman was producing while he waited for *The Graduate* to come together, so Steiger got Walter Mirisch's next offer[1] and signed on to the film for $100,000, half of what Sidney Poitier was receiving.[2] By the time he did, Gillespie had been transformed from the tall, lean lawman of John Ball's novel into a physical incarnation of the southern sheriff—older, bigger bellied, more confrontational—that ten years of television news stories about civil rights unrest had made familiar to everyone in America.

Gillespie's makeover wasn't the only change that Jewison brought to the screenplay once he started working with Stirling Silliphant. By the time Silliphant turned in his final draft, the plot, the characters, and the racial conflict that pulsed beneath every scene had all been both stripped down and sharpened. The story's setting had been moved from South Carolina to Mississippi, and Tibbs was no longer from Arizona, but from Philadelphia, making the two police officers explicit stand-ins for the attitudes and politics of North and South. Virgil's line "They call me Mister Tibbs," a punch line in the novel that Silliphant had dropped in the first draft, was reinstated, but with anger this time[3]—it was now the verbal roundhouse wallop that Silliphant knew would mark the moment "the film explodes into life."[4]

In Silliphant's earlier draft, Tibbs faced an ingrained, pervasive culture of southern racism again and again. Jewison encouraged the writer to refocus his attention on the way in which prejudice can play out between two people rather than between one man and an entire town (a plot gimmick that Silliphant had already deployed in too many episodes of *Route 66*). He pushed Silliphant to cut scenes in which Tibbs was the target of official bigotry, including one in which he was made to wait outside of a whites-only hotel, and to trim any sequence that might distract moviegoers from the push and pull between the two main characters. That relationship reaches its climax in a scripted scene in which Tibbs visits Gillespie's run-down home for a drink and the sheriff begins to open up to him. "Thirty-seven years old," he says, "no wife, no kids . . . scratching for a living in a town doesn't want me. Fan I have to oil for myself . . . desk with a busted leg . . . *this* place. Know something, Virgil? You're the first person who's been around to call. Nobody else has been here . . . *nobody* comes."[5] (Although Jewison, Poitier, and Steiger all later claimed that the dialogue in the house was largely improvised on the spot—and, in fact, it was fleshed out considerably during the production—Silliphant always insisted that he had written the scene, and dated drafts of the script bear out his account.)

"There's no doubt what the film is about," says Jewison. "We knew people would be aware of it from the very beginning, from the way Tibbs is treated when he's arrested."[6] But the director worried that long speeches and explicit message moviemaking would be ruinous to *In the Heat of the Night*, as would the depiction of Gillespie as an overdrawn Deep South racist. In the final draft, Silliphant dramatically reduced the number of times the word *nigger* was used, particularly by Gillespie. Lines like "Now what's a northern nigger doing in South Carolina?" became "Now what's a northern colored boy doing down here?"[7] With each alteration, Gillespie evolved from an unreconstructed Bull Connor to a man who was, although prejudiced, one step smarter and less bigoted than the rednecks around him and self-aware enough to be slightly on his guard in Tibbs's presence;

he's someone who knows that the rules are beginning to change. The final draft of *In the Heat of the Night* still contained enough uses of "nigger" to trouble Geoffrey Shurlock, who wrote in a Production Code memo to the filmmakers that while the presence of the word was "quite valid . . . unnecessary repetition could prove objectionable. We urge that you eliminate one or two uses."[8]

At the same time, Silliphant and Jewison toughened their depiction of Virgil Tibbs, paring away so much of his dialogue that he became, by the final draft, someone who uses silence, withholding, and watchfulness as a weapon. In some ways, the changes were designed to tailor Tibbs to Poitier's special talent for controlled anger while allowing him to take a stride forward from *Lilies of the Field* and *A Patch of Blue* into a hipper, more contemporary persona. ("Where you going?" Gillespie asks at one point as Virgil walks away from him. "Where Whitey ain't allowed," snaps Tibbs.) The accommodationist Negro of Ball's novel was disappearing, in part because Silliphant and Jewison knew it was already outdated and in part because Poitier, who had a good deal of influence in the shaping of Tibbs's character during the screenwriting process, was no longer interested in playing the role of an appeaser.

Many of the refinements were structural rather than political. "I never spent a great deal of time talking to Stirling about prejudice or racism," Jewison says. "We were more concerned with the construction of the mystery."[9] In particular, the two men zeroed in on the main weakness of Ball's novel—the murder case at its center was not particularly intricate or complex, and its solution hinged on the clumsy last-minute introduction of new information. Silliphant made a few changes in the mystery itself, generally for the better; the murder victim was changed from a music promoter planning a local concert to a northern liberal industrialist who had come south to build a factory in the town. But he and Jewison decided to build suspense simply by omitting as much information about the case as they could without rendering the narrative incomprehensible. "If the crime story were plotted as the alphabet," Silliphant said, "from A to Z, how much of it could we pull out and play off screen? We kept A and jumped to F, then from F to L. . . . The result of this withholding . . . was to compel the viewer to invest attention in the least detail. Maybe there was a clue in the look Gillespie gave Virgil—maybe not. But we'd better watch and see."[10]

By July, Poitier felt that Silliphant's screenplay—twenty-six pages shorter than his first draft[11]—was "a very forward-looking piece of material"; what had begun as a police procedural had been reimagined as a racially charged dual character study effectively disguised as a whodunit. *In the Heat of the Night* now had a script Jewison wanted to shoot, and just in time, he had acquired the clout to do it his way. A month before Silliphant delivered his draft, *The Russians Are Coming, the Russians Are Coming* opened and, somewhat unexpectedly, became the best-reviewed movie and biggest hit of Jewison's career. The success of *Russians*, which had been shot largely on location, gave Jewison the power to go to Mirisch and tell him that for the sake of authenticity, *In the Heat of the Night* would have to be shot in the South, not on a studio lot. Mirisch agreed.[12]

Sidney Poitier did not. His memories of being tailed by Klansmen the previous summer while visiting Mississippi with Harry Belafonte were vivid, and horror stories were beginning to come out of Louisiana, where the racially mixed cast of Otto Preminger's *Hurry Sundown* was enduring harassment and death threats, the film's black actors were being turned away from restaurants and hotels, and a crew member was chased out of a local Laundromat by someone who didn't want him using it to wash the black cast members' hotel bedsheets.[13] "You can cut the hostility with a knife," said Diahann Carroll on the set. "Down here, the terror has killed my taste for going anywhere."[14] Poitier's fears were not unjustified, since his own family had recently been menaced. On June 6, James Meredith, who had become famous as the first black student at the University of Mississippi, was shot as he began a "March Against Fear" from Memphis to Jackson. Meredith recovered, and a couple of weeks later, Poitier's ex-wife, Juanita, held a fund-raising reception for him at the Pleasantville, New York, home the couple had shared. When she did, a cross was burned on her lawn.[15] Poitier, now America's most recognizable black actor, was not about to turn himself into an even bigger target. "Sidney didn't want to go below the Mason-Dixon line," says Jewison. "There was no goddamn way he'd do it."[16]

On June 1, 1966, Jack Valenti, a forty-four-year-old former Texas advertising executive who had become a special assistant to Lyndon B. Johnson, left his White House post to head the Motion Picture Association of America. The MPAA had had only two presidents since its founding in 1922: Will Hays, the architect of the 1930 Production Code that still governed the content of Hollywood movies, and Eric Johnston, whose death in 1963 had left the organization rudderless for almost three years. The MPAA had many functions, the most economically significant of which was to operate as the movie industry's lobbying arm in Washington. But at the moment Valenti took over, the association was consumed by the issue of censorship, and in particular by its oversight of the failing and outmoded Production Code. While Code administrator Geoffrey Shurlock was still systematically ticking off the number of uses of "hell" and "damn" in every script and informing producers by letter what lines, scenes, and even gestures would have to come out of their screenplays, American filmmakers were rising in insurrection not only against the Code's restrictions, but against its very existence.

As Valenti began work, the crisis over the Code was coming to a head so quickly that there was little time for deliberation. For decades, control over the content of Hollywood films had been split three ways, in an unofficial power-sharing arrangement between the studios themselves (via the Code), religious organizations such as the National Catholic Office for Motion Pictures and the Episcopal Committee for Motion Pictures, and censorship boards whose standards varied capriciously by city and state and which were generally overseen by local police departments. As a result, films with potentially inflammatory subjects would sometimes end up playing in a checkerboard pattern across the country: For instance, it took two years and a fight that went to the Georgia Supreme Court before the Oscar-winning *Room at the Top*, about an extramarital affair, could be shown in Atlanta.[17] The system was intended to encourage self-censorship by the studios: The more stringently they governed their own product, the less risk they would run of a religious anti-Hollywood groundswell or of having to fight costly legal battles to get their movies shown. Until the last few years, that had given Shurlock near absolute power, no matter how many decades behind the times some of the Production Code's statutes were. In 1961, when he had reviewed the script for *West Side Story* and ruled that words like "schmuck" and "S.O.B.," and even a phrase as mild as "he's hot" would have to be deleted from Stephen Sondheim's lyrics, UA had no choice but to comply." Even as late as 1964, the Code was able to veto the movie title *How to Murder Your Mistress* in favor of the somehow more acceptable *How to Murder Your Wife*.[18]

But the Code's rigidity had recently begun to work against it. The influx of European films, some with nudity, that weren't produced by studios and didn't require a Code seal had created a double standard; local theaters, meeting the demands of their audiences, were increasingly willing to show movies without Code approval, as well as those that had been branded with the Catholic rating of "Condemned." The double standard didn't apply only to sex: Dated and rarely enforced Code provisions against things like "trick methods shown for concealing guns," "illegal abduction," and the depiction of any "notorious real-life criminal" who had not been punished for his crimes[19] had turned Hollywood's rule book into a bizarre patchwork of policies, some rigorously enforced and others routinely ignored. Distributors were challenging local censorship boards in courts across the country and almost always winning, while conservative and religious organizations were calling for the Code to be abolished altogether and replaced by film ratings,[20] an idea that the studios resisted, believing it was a first step toward outright censorship. The studios had reason to distrust the motives of those who were calling for a classification system; the only "ratings" for films at the time were handed out under the aegis of the National Catholic Office for Motion Pictures, which classified movies on a scale based not on age appropriateness, but on degree of moral turpitude, up to and including condemnation. The National Catholic Office was blunt about its desire for a ratings system that would keep movies with adult subject matter out of many theaters altogether.

Valenti knew the Code was preposterous, but he worried that a ratings system might bring even bigger problems; he correctly surmised that film ratings would result in more freedom rather than less, since once a movie could be designated as being for adults, it could offer unapologetically adult content. That, he feared, would lead to more clashes with municipal censorship boards or a fight against church leaders that Hollywood was desperate to avoid. But he knew that in its present form, the Code was doomed. The 1965 decision to approve the nudity in *The Pawnbroker* because of the film's high quality had created an untenable loophole, suggesting that one standard existed for good films and another for ordinary ones. Although the studios had always cooperated with Shurlock, they had no interest in allowing him to judge their movies on merit.

Valenti and Louis Nizer, who had signed a five-year contract to serve as the MPAA's senior counsel,[21] hadn't even unpacked their boxes when Jack Warner decided to use Mike Nichols's *Who's Afraid of Virginia Woolf?* to finish what *The Pawnbroker* started. Although the first time they saw the picture, Warner and his executives had famously reacted by saying, "My God, we've got a $7.5 million dirty movie on our hands,"[22] Nichols had jockeyed skillfully behind the scenes to keep much of its profanity intact. The vast circle of New York friends he had acquired in the years since he had starred with Elaine May on Broadway proved to be a critical asset; *Virginia Woolf* won a perfectly choreographed private endorsement from Jacqueline Kennedy, who, at Nichols's request, attended a small screening and made sure to say, within earshot of a key member of the Catholic film board, "Jack would have loved this movie."[23] After extensive internal debate, the National Catholic Office gave *Virginia Woolf* a rating of A-IV, "morally unobjectionable for adults, with reservations."[24] This coup, which allowed the film to escape not only a "C" (Condemned) rating, but a "B" ("morally objectionable in part for all"), would put even more pressure on the Production Code authority to approve the film.

Jack Warner then came up with his own preemptive way of undercutting the Code. On May 25, 1966, he announced that *Who's Afraid of Virginia Woolf?* would be released with the label "For adults only" and that theaters would have to sign contracts agreeing not to admit minors without adult accompaniment.[25] While newspaper ads for independent or foreign movies had carried "adults only" labels for years, the label was used as a racy tease, not as a studio-approved enforceable restriction. Warner's maneuver, which effectively created the "R" rating two years before a ratings system existed, unsettled Geoffrey Shurlock. Shurlock was now seventy-one and had enjoyed extraordinary influence over the years; at one point, he was even able to order Alfred Hitchcock to reshoot the opening scene of *Psycho*. But his investment in the Code was rooted more in a desire to protect his own power than in any innate prudishness. When Warner Brothers bought *Virginia Woolf,* Shurlock had warned them that there was unacceptable language on 83 pages of the script.[26] But after Warner's decision, Shurlock knew his own standing was at stake and decided not to risk a public defeat. For the first time ever, he declined to make any ruling and privately advised Jack Warner to end-run him and take *Virginia Woolf* straight to the Code's appeals board.[27] That jury, led by Valenti, who had spent just ten days in his new job, approved the movie using the same pretext they had offered for *The Pawnbroker*, announcing that they would not have given the seal to "a film of lesser quality" and warning that "this exemption does not mean that the floodgates are open."

But of course, it meant exactly that. Valenti had already stated that he had serious questions about "the entire philosophy of self-censorship,"[28] and in his first week running the MPAA, he ordered a complete overhaul of the Production Code—which, he said, Shurlock would continue to administer. (Shurlock quickly announced that he thought *Virginia Woolf* was "marvelous" and had simply been following the rules by withholding a seal.)[29] The *Virginia Woolf* experience, said Valenti, "was Fort Sumter . . . it revealed to me that the past was done. I wasn't quite sure what the future was going to be."[30] But he was sure of one thing: After a heated hours-long private meeting in which he, Nizer, Jack Warner, and Warner's New York distribution chief, Ben Kalmenson, had dickered over every single profanity in the movie before it even went to the appeals board, he said to Nizer, "I'm not going through that again. I'm not going to spend my life sitting in . . . offices and saying, 'I gotta take out one "shit" and one "screw."' This is crazy."[31]

If Warner had any worries that the controversy over *Who's Afraid of Virginia Woolf?* would endanger its profitability, they were quickly allayed. The trade paper *Variety*, which used to headline its major reviews with a prognostication about the film's box office, simply and accurately wrote of its prospects, "Big."[32] They weren't wrong; *Virginia Woolf* became the second-highest-grossing film of 1966, trailing only *Thunderball*, as the lure of seeing Elizabeth Taylor and Richard Burton behind closed doors doing something suitable "for adults only" proved irresistible. Reviews were stellar, with many critics pointedly endorsing Warner's use of a warning label and to applauding the license it would give Hollywood filmmakers to tackle rougher material.

Nichols was once again the man of the moment, but not an especially happy one. Jack Warner had treated him badly during postproduction of *Virginia Woolf*. Nichols had wanted the film's composer, Alex North, replaced with André Previn; when he pushed too hard, Warner bristled and had him barred from the editing room with only a day or two of work left.[33] North's score stayed in, but Nichols had won almost every other battle. Still, his first Hollywood movie had left him battered and exhausted, and he found the overwhelming praise for his movie debut disorienting. "I am . . . upset by good reviews. . . . I get to feeling very unreal and very undeserving," he told the *Today* show.[34] Nichols was now becoming as famous as many of the people he directed and too busy for his own comfort. Production of *The Graduate* was supposed to start in the fall; he had just signed to direct the movie version of Joseph Heller's *Catch-22*, which was to start shooting the following summer; and with the first three Broadway plays he directed all still running, he had also agreed to stage his first Broadway musical, a trio of one-acts by the composer and lyricist of *Fiddler on the Roof* called *Come Back! Go Away! I Love You!* (later retitled *The Apple Tree*). In early 1966, ABC decided to make him the focus of an hour-long special, *The Many Worlds of Mike Nichols*.[35] There turned out to be too many worlds: Nichols decided to retreat. He canceled the special, pushed *Catch-22* further into the future, and postponed production of *The Graduate* until the spring of 1967.

Throughout the summer of 1966, *Who's Afraid of Virginia Woolf?* shared its place atop the box office with *The Russians Are Coming, the Russians Are Coming*. The cold war comedy was several shades lighter than *Dr. Strangelove* had been, thanks largely to its droll, playful script by William Rose, a writer with fifteen years of screen credits who was nonetheless something of an enigma to the studios. Rose spent very little time in Los

Angeles; many people in the industry weren't exactly sure whether he was American or English. In World War II, he served under Canada's Black Watch regiment in Europe, later reenlisting for the United States.[36] In the 1950s, he had won Oscar nominations for writing two English comedies, *Genevieve* and the Alec Guinness classic *The Ladykillers*; by the 1960s, he was spending most of his time in England's Channel Islands, where he lived on the isle of Jersey with his wife, Tania. Rose was actually a native of Jefferson City, Missouri, albeit one who preferred to view America, and his chosen industry, from as great a distance as possible. "Bill got very nervous when he came to Hollywood," says Norman Jewison. "He hated Hollywood. When the plane landed he would break out into a sweat. He was not good with studios or anything."[37]

In 1963, Rose had written the screenplay for Stanley Kramer's *It's a Mad Mad Mad Mad World*. Kramer liked Rose's work, and the two became friends; Rose then began to work on *Andersonville* for him. When Columbia pulled the plug on Kramer's plan to make the film, Rose happened to be in Los Angeles visiting him. After dinner at Kramer's home, the director recalled walking Rose out to his car when Rose brought up an idea for a screenplay he had been considering about racial intermarriage in South Africa. "I said, off the top of my head, 'Why don't you set it in the United States?'" wrote Kramer in his memoirs. " 'Oh, sure,' replied Rose. 'They'd name it picture of the year, at least in Harlem.' "[38] (Rose's memory of the project's origin was somewhat different and probably more accurate; he later said that he never conceived of setting the story in South Africa and had had the idea for an American comedy of intermarriage since at least 1960; documents show that he had his agent pitch the premise to Kramer as early as the summer of 1962.)[39]

Guess Who's Coming to Dinner, although it would be widely publicized by its studio as a taboo-shattering comedy, was not the first American movie to depict an interracial relationship. In 1964, director Larry Peerce's low-budget *One Potato, Two Potato*, about a white divorcée (Barbara Barrie) who marries a black man (Bernie Hamilton), had been released by the independent distributor Cinema V; the film had shown at the Cannes Film Festival, played throughout the United States, including the South (although primarily in black neighborhoods), and won an Oscar nomination for its screenplay. And audiences, at least in the North, had just seen the first stirrings of another interracial romance in A *Patch of Blue*.

Nonetheless, Kramer was certain that building an entire movie around the topic would put him on dangerous ground. He and Rose quickly talked through a plot that sounded like the premise of a very old-fashioned drawing room comedy: An affluent white couple, proud liberals in late middle age, would have their political and personal principles put to the test when their daughter walked through the door with a black fiancé. The premise was thin—little more, really, than the expansion of the then-familiar line "But would you want your daughter to marry one?" that had been applied by WASP America to Catholics, then to Jews, and then to blacks over the last thirty years. Rose brought a veteran screenwriter's sense of structure to the piece, talking it through with Kramer first on long walks through Beverly Hills and in meetings at the Beverly Wilshire[40] and later when Kramer flew overseas to Jersey. Expanding on the plot's original quartet, he added characters—a winsome monsignor who could call the bride's parents on their hypocrisies, the groom's father and mother, who had reservations of their own about the proposed wedding, and the white family's loyal and suspicious black maid—and he compressed the plot's chronology: A story line that Kramer had originally imagined would unfold over two or three days was now to take place in twelve hours and be built around a single suspenseful question: Would the father of the bride grant permission for the marriage or not?

Kramer and Rose tangled over every plot point of *Guess Who's Coming to Dinner*. "It was a love-hate relationship," recalls the director's widow, Karen Kramer. "They really were very competitive and could be quite combative. Bill was an egotist, and he was also an alcoholic. Stanley was smart and clever and quippy, and he could also be a bit of a put-down artist—he could really nail you if he wanted to, and when Bill would get out of line, Stanley would go after him and they'd both get really angry. I think Stanley would always say that Bill was a brilliant writer, but he was a very difficult person. They'd really get into it with each other, and Stanley would always win, which would make Bill furious."[41]

At the time he started working on the screenplay, Rose was in his early fifties; he had been away from the United States for a long time, and judging by his earliest plot outlines for the movie, his knowledge of the American civil rights movement was about twenty years behind the news. A treatment he wrote for *Guess Who's Coming to Dinner* describes one minor character as "a sexy little colored girl" and Tillie the housekeeper as "a tough but lukewarmhearted darkie"; later, he took pains to write Tillie's dialogue in dialect, having her say "sumpin," "jest," "sposed," and "lissen."[42] And the beginnings of Afrocentrism and discussions of cultural identity among black Americans were huffily dismissed by him in a few lines. Rose was still appalled that Cassius Clay had, in 1964, changed his name to Muhammad Ali, so much so that he mentioned it in his treatment. Declaring that Dr. Prentice, the black fiancé, was the grandson of slaves, he wrote, "Prentice isn't at all ashamed of [being called] Prentice. Nor does he really care who he might have been, or what he might have been called, somewhere in the Continent of Africa."[43]

Kramer managed to comb out some, though by no means all, of the screenwriter's condescensions and stereotypes. But he was, characteristically, thinking more like a producer than a director and insisted that Rose play it safe in one significant area: "I wanted the prospective black bridegroom to be a person so suitable that if anyone objected to him, it could only be due to racial prejudice," he wrote.[44] Kramer was sure that if Prentice had any flaws at all, bigots in the audience would seize on them as a reason to disapprove of the marriage, but in seeking to avoid that trap, he fell right into another one: the return of the exceptional Negro, a character type that had by then become so familiar that even white critics were beginning to react against its persistence. In Rose's script, Prentice became not just a doctor, but an Ivy League–educated potential Nobel laureate who worked for the United Nations on worldwide health missions. Kramer's insistence on stacking the deck so heavily in favor of Prentice changed everything about the movie. The answer to the question "Guess who's coming to dinner?" now had to be Sidney Poitier, the only black actor Kramer thought that white America would find believable as a superachiever.

"Casting is destiny," says Warren Beatty. "Particularly in movies, because casting *is* character—and character is plot. Casting really controls story. One guy would do a thing, another guy wouldn't. And if you're the guy in the close-up, character acting isn't going to help—you either are that guy, or you aren't."[45] If that is the case—and it's hard to find a movie from the mid-1960s in which it is *more* the case than *Guess Who's Coming to Dinner*—then Stanley Kramer had a serious problem once Rose finished his script. The movie, he felt, would be unfilmable, and unfinanceable, if he couldn't sign the three principal actors he wanted. The film couldn't simply be about a nice white couple welcoming a nice black son-in-law; it had to be about the screen's most famous romantic duo symbolically opening their arms to its biggest black star. And that didn't look likely: Sidney Poitier was busy—and, for the first time in his career, expensive. Katharine Hepburn had all but officially retired. And Spencer Tracy was dying.

FIFTEEN

Jack Warner's office overlooking his studio's Burbank lot was designed for genuflection. Warner was not a tall man, and he had his desk built on a platform raised eight or ten inches above the carpet, with two small stairs behind his chair. " 'Look up at me—don't look down at me'—that was the message," says Joel Freeman, who worked for Warner in the mid-1960s.[1]

For years after the release of *Bonnie and Clyde,* a story persisted that Warren Beatty got down on his knees in front of the man who had run the studio since its founding in 1918 and begged him to finance the film. The anecdote, which Beatty himself kept alive for a while, made its way into *Time* magazine at the end of 1967, vividly ornamented with the detail that the actor "prostrated himself before the old man, dug his nose in the rug, and moaned, 'Look, Jack, please do what I say. I won't waste your money.'" Warner's putative reply: "Get up off the floor, kid. You're embarrassing me."[2] Long after Warner's death in 1978 and Beatty's eventual denial that the incident ever occurred, this particular piece of what Beatty calls "the apocrypha surrounding the movie"[3] survived, probably for two reasons: It sounds like something he would have done, and it sounds like something Jack Warner would have enjoyed.

"If Warren did do it," says Robert Benton, "it wouldn't have been the first time. He was prone to do that with people."[4] Supplication was just another weapon in Beatty's arsenal of strategies, to be deployed as needed.

He used it with Robert Towne during *Bonnie and Clyde*'s long shoot in Texas, when Towne wanted to go back to Los Angeles for a few days. "He literally got down on his knees and said, 'Oh, please don't,' " recalls Towne. "Well, what can you say to that but 'Okay, I won't'? No one can know the depth of that man's persuasiveness. It wasn't an illustration of how important I was to the project, but of the lengths to which he would go to make anything he wanted to happen happen. He says, 'Save me! Rescue me!' And I suspect somehow that was not the least of his seductive charm when it came to women."[5]

Nor would it have been the first time that Jack Warner had experienced—or relished—that kind of flattery. Warner, at seventy-three, was proud of the power he had consolidated over so many decades in charge and unselfconscious about exercising it. He had had things his own way for fifty years, even when it cost him his relationships with his own brothers. He liked his subordinates—and that included the men who worked most closely with him—to call him "Mr. Warner" or "Chief" or "Colonel"[6] (an essentially honorary designation he had picked up in exchange for producing anti-Nazi films during World War II)[7]—but never "Jack." "I've often thought of the studio as a palace that had everything but a moat," says Richard Lederer, who worked as Warner's head of advertising in New York. "There were gates within gates within gates. Warner lived like a king, and Warner Brothers was his kingdom, even if it was a kingdom that, at that point, churned out nothing but crap."[8] And anyone who wanted to get his way with the boss knew that self-abasement, tears, and outright pleading often worked. In 1966, around the time Beatty paid him a visit, Jack Warner was immersed in the planning stages of what was by far the most expensive movie on his 1967 slate of releases, *Camelot.* Even though the Lerner and Loewe musical had received mixed reviews and was by no means an unqualified success on Broadway, Warner was so convinced that director Joshua Logan's film version would follow in the path of *My Fair Lady* that he planned to put his own name on the movie as producer for only the second time in ten years. Alan Jay Lerner had recovered well enough from his tabloid divorce and the disaster of his involvement with *Doctor Dolittle* to write the script, but it was wildly overlong. When Joel Freeman, who was to function as *Camelot*'s producer in everything but name,

went into Warner's office to tell him that the movie would run a draggy
three hours as written and that the screenplay needed to be cut, Warner
agreed, and Freeman went to tell Lerner, who was waiting in a downstairs
office.

"An hour or so later, I walk back into Jack's office," says Freeman.
"Kneeling in front of his desk was Josh Logan, with tears in his eyes. I
thought, 'Uh-oh.' Logan got up, never said a word to me, and walked out
the door. I said, 'What was that all about?' And Jack said, 'Executive decision. Leave the script the way it is.' I said, 'What are you talking about?
You just agreed to all these cuts—you *know* it's too long.' And he walked
me outside his office to a window, looked out, and pointed to a water tower
with the studio insignia. He said, 'What does it say? When it says *Freeman
Brothers,* you can decide how long it should be.' "[9]

The water tower routine was a favorite of Jack Warner's, although it's
safe to say that nobody had ever responded to it the way Warren Beatty
did. When Warner, during a lunch with the actor, pointed to the tower,
Beatty paused for a moment and said, "Well, it's got your name, but it's
got my initials."[10]

"I *think* Jack Warner found me funny," Beatty says. "But I think something about me also scared him—I don't know if something had once happened with another actor, but he never wanted to be in a room alone with
me. But all the stories about me not being able to get *Bonnie and Clyde*
financed—they're not true. I didn't have to beg, because I had offers from
three studios. Well, two, and something I could have turned into an offer,
but I didn't want to be misleading."[11]

For a time, Beatty considered trying to finance the film himself. "Originally, he thought he would be able to come up with the budget for the
movie out of his own pocket," says Elaine Michea, who worked as his assistant on *Bonnie and Clyde* for more than a year. "This was when he was
thinking it was going to be much less expensive. We worked together trying
to see how little we could make it for. He was very frugal—he lived well,
but he didn't throw money away."[12] Once Beatty abandoned that plan and
started making the rounds with the script, not everyone was interested in
working with him. He was considered, as *Time* put it, "an on-again, off-
again actor who moonlighted as a global escort,"[13] and the studios greeted

the news that the "sullen, difficult, stubborn performer who fouled up [scripts] with his demands for rewriting" and "quarreled with directors" was planning to become a producer "with only slightly more enthusiasm than that summoned up for the announcement that Ross Hunter would produce a third Tammy picture,"[14] said *Life* magazine.

Beatty's confidence as he walked into one executive suite after another was disarming. "We went into a meeting . . . and Warren said, 'This is what they're gonna ask, this is what we're gonna say,' and he was right. He's a great wheeler-dealer," Benton and Newman told Rex Reed.[15] But some studio chiefs couldn't begin to comprehend Beatty's enthusiasm for the heavily annotated screenplay he was pitching. "That's one that I kick myself in the ass for," says Richard Zanuck, who, deep into preproduction on *Doctor Dolittle* at the time, had no interest in having Beatty make the movie at Fox. "Warren came over and presented me with the script, and we had lunch in my office. It was like 250 pages long and had all these different-colored pages—blue, red, gray, green. I said, 'What *is* this?' I read it, and I didn't have the belief that I should have had in Warren. That was one of my big mistakes."[16]

United Artists' David Picker, who had tracked the project since Elinor Jones had pitched it to him, still wanted to make the movie, but *Bonnie and Clyde* had gotten more expensive since the first time he'd heard about it. Harrison Starr, the associate producer of *Mickey One* who had talked about producing the movie with both Truffaut and Godard, was for a time working with Beatty and Penn, hoping to serve as production manager on the film. He talked to the two men in Texas, where they were scouting potential locations, and then went to New York to discuss terms with Picker. "I was foolish," says Starr. "He said, 'What can you make it for?' And instead of giving him the lowest price, I thought, 'I'll give myself some room.'" Starr suggested a budget of $1.75 million. Picker countered at $1.6 million, and by the time he was able to convince his bosses to back the movie, Beatty had moved on, and UA and Starr were out of the picture.[17] "I can only tell you that when that deal blew up, it broke my heart," says Picker.[18]

"I almost made the movie at United Artists," says Beatty. "But I had a better offer, and I liked Jack Warner." Warner Brothers ended up offering Beatty a $1.8 million budget, still well below the average for a studio picture, and Beatty agreed to take a lower-than-usual combined acting/producing salary of $200,000 in exchange for 40 percent of the film's profits.[19] No kneeling or begging was necessary, largely because of the efforts of two supporters of *Bonnie and Clyde* at the studio, Richard Lederer and production chief Walter MacEwen. Lederer read the screenplay and thought it was "terrific"; he knew it would represent a welcome departure for what he called "a very conservative studio that put out one terrible movie after another. Nobody seemed to realize that the audience was changing and we'd better change, too."[20] Lederer knew that Ben Kalmenson, the New York–based head of distribution and one of Jack Warner's closest colleagues, could persuade Warner to make the movie. Kalmenson had worked with Warner for twenty-five years, and Jack Warner took his advice seriously. Warner also liked to use Kalmenson as a bad cop: When Warner would reject projects, he would often tell producers that "New York" had told him they wouldn't be able to sell their movie to audiences.[21] Lederer walked Beatty down to Kalmenson's office with the script. "Kalmenson said nice things," says Lederer. "But I knew that the minute we left, he picked up the phone and told Jack Warner not to make the movie."[22]

"The decision [to green-light *Bonnie and Clyde*] was made by Walter MacEwen," says Beatty. "Jack Warner never got into it."[23] But it wasn't that simple: MacEwen liked the script very much, but he had worked for Warner for decades; he tended to make his case for or against a project and then defer to his boss's wishes, and he knew that Warner would need a good deal of convincing. The studio had made Beatty famous with *Splendor in the Grass,* and Jack Warner was still angry that Beatty had backed out of *Youngblood Hawke* and refused to star in *PT 109.* "Warren wasn't a favorite of Jack Warner's," says MacEwen's assistant Robert Solo. "He thought Warren was uppity. The man was, at the time, pretty stuck in his ways. He ran the studio, but he was more subject to the whims of actors and directors than he had been twenty years ago, and he didn't like it. So anybody who didn't play ball his way, he didn't want anything to do with. We tried very hard to talk Warner into it." MacEwen had his own concerns: Geoffrey Shurlock would soon weigh in with a Production Code memo calling various scenes "unacceptably brutal," "excessively gruesome," and "grossly animalistic."[24] But he liked the project, and he and Solo enlisted Martin Jurow, Warner's head of European production, to lobby Jack Warner as well. Solo also used his connection with Jack Schwartzman, who was his neighbor and Beatty's attorney; he would secretly coach Schwartzman on what to say during the time Schwartzman was negotiating the deal's fine points with the studio's head of business affairs.[25]

What may ultimately have convinced Warner to make the movie was, ironically, his own poor judgment: He was convinced that *Kaleidoscope*, the forgettable little thriller Beatty had made with Susannah York, was going to be a hit for the studio, and he knew from the film's producer, Elliott Kastner, that the actor had behaved himself on the set, allowing production to wrap on time and on budget. By the end of August, Warner "was comfortable that he would have limited financial exposure," says Solo,[26] and he agreed to make *Bonnie and Clyde* without even reading the screenplay. A month later, when he did look at the script, he expressed bitter regret. Warner wasn't put off by the movie's innovations (which he couldn't see on the page). On the contrary, he thought the story was decades out-of-date, nothing more than a relic of a slightly disreputable genre his own studio had pioneered and used up in the 1930s. "I can't understand where the entertainment value is in this story," he wrote to Walter MacEwen. "Who wants to see the rise and fall of a couple of rats. . . . I don't understand the whole thinking of Warren Beatty and Penn. We will lose back whatever we happen to make on *Kaleidoscope* . . . this era went out with Cagney."[27]

If *Bonnie and Clyde* escaped Jack Warner's close scrutiny until it was too late for him to reverse himself, the distraction of *Camelot* was at least partly responsible, and Warner was hardly alone among studio chiefs in neglecting the rest of his films in order to concentrate on a single big-ticket entertainment that could prove to be the next *Sound of Music*. At Fox, Dick Zanuck was presiding over a lineup of movies being planned for release in 1967 that included several potential box office successes: *Hombre,* a western that would reunite Paul Newman with his *Hud* director, Martin Ritt, an adaptation of Jacqueline Susann's best seller *Valley of the Dolls,* and *Two for the Road,* a sophisticated bittersweet comedy about marriage starring Audrey Hepburn and Albert Finney that a more relaxed Production Code had finally made it possible to green-light. But in the summer of 1966, everything was taking a backseat to Arthur Jacobs's mammoth effort to get *Doctor Dolittle* off the ground.

Zanuck had succeeded in shaving $2 million from the budget, although Rex Harrison had thrown a tantrum and threatened to quit when he learned he wasn't going to be working with Sidney Poitier after all.[28] But Fox's attempts to economize were almost completely undone in the next couple of months, as the start of production approached. Work at Jungleland, the animal-training facility in California, was proving more arduous than anyone had anticipated, since, in addition to teaching a rhino, a giraffe, and several hundred chimps, pigs, birds, mice, sheep, cows, squirrels, chickens, and parrots to perform tricks, the handlers had to spend time simulating the noisy conditions and flashing lights of a studio soundstage in order to accustom the animals to being on a set.[29] The American Humane Association (AHA) was taking an interest, writing detailed memos about the script to the studio. ("When Bellowes . . . flings the skunk away from him," AHA director Harold Melniker reminded Fox politely after reading the script, "the use of a dummy skunk is in order.")[30] And for every item that had been extracted from the budget in the spring, another had taken its place, pushing the film's price tag past $14 million once again. The new cost estimate included $276,000 more for animals, real and mechanical; an additional $226,000 in previously unforeseen expenses for the location shoot in England; $72,000 more for sets; $20,000 to pay Harrison's personal public relations agent; a voice double to sing Samantha Eggar's numbers; a trainer who was up to the six-month task of trying to teach Chee-Chee, the chimpanzee (and his three stand-ins), to cook bacon and eggs in a frying pan; and $97,000 in projected overtime costs for the services of Leslie Bricusse,[31] who had to redraft an entire script without Poitier's character and make almost endless revisions to keep Harrison happy.

That was proving impossible. After his ill-considered attempt to select his own team of songwriters for *Doctor Dolittle,* Harrison had finally reconciled himself to working with Bricusse, but the fact that Bricusse's best friend, Anthony Newley, had come on to the project as a costar sent him into fits of anger and paranoia. He was sure that Newley and Bricusse were working together in Beverly Hills, shaping the script into a showcase for their talents and rewriting it to diminish his own role.[32] Harrison wasn't entirely wrong to think that Newley's casting meant that the part of Matthew would be expanded. And his disdain for Newley was predictable—he had as little use for a British song-and-dance man as he had had for Sammy Davis Jr., whom he had dismissed as an "entertainer." But undisguised prejudice, well-known among those who had worked with Harrison before, was also a factor. Before and during *Doctor Dolittle*'s production, Harrison would disparage Newley, sometimes to his face, as a "Jewish comic" or a "Cockney Jew."[33] Newley was braced for it and, at least at the beginning, too excited about working on the film to care. In April, when he and the cast began learning the movie's choreography in Los Angeles, he wrote exuberantly to his friend Barbra Streisand, who was then performing in *Funny Girl* onstage in London, "We started rehearsing the dances for 'Dr. Dolittle,' or as it's known amongst the Hebrew elements, 'Dr. Tagoornicht'!!* I shall have the pleasure of working with that well-known anti-Semite, Rex 'George Rockwell' Harrison,"[34] he added, referring to the head of the American Nazi Party.

Throughout rehearsals, Bricusse sequestered himself in his home office in Beverly Hills, rewriting and refining the script, changing song lyrics, and trying to meet the demands of his star, Arthur Jacobs, and Fox. He was beginning his second year on the job and tiring of it. "I am desolated that I was not with you at the Grove last night," he wrote after turning down an invitation from Newley and Joan Collins. "The strain of 'Dolittle' has been beginning to show lately, but I do so desperately want it to be good. This is our first cinematic outing in Hollywood, Newberg, so how can I expect you to be as good as I want you to be unless I give you something to be good with? Deep down beneath several crusts of misery that have been heaped on to me during the past few months is the same happy, laughing idiot we all used to know and love."[35]

**Goornicht is Yiddish for "nothing"; Newley was punningly translating the title.

Much of that misery came at Harrison's hands. Whatever the actor's other faults, laziness was not among them, and he besieged Bricusse with questions, requests, and revisions. To Harrison's credit, he was taking his role as Doctor Dolittle seriously; he filled a June 1966 draft of the script with handwritten notes, some of them directions to himself ("very real despair," he jotted next to one of his lines), some of them suggestions that Bricusse incorporate more dialogue from Hugh Lofting's books, and some of them sharp-eyed notations of lapses in logic. Harrison was a close reader and circled lines in which his character seemed to be repeating himself; he also had an experienced performer's sense of what would and would not work once he was on the set interacting with actual animals. "It is no good taking a chance that something [funny] will happen," he wrote of a scene in which Dolittle was to stroll through his menagerie. "Each animal cannot do the same thing. . . . Think cockerel is important. Perhaps the cockerel doesn't approve of Dolittle. I feel that it [will be] the reaction of the animals [that] gets the laugh—not what Dolittle does so much."[36]

Harrison was willing to shorten his own lines or suggest that the camera cut away from him in order to make a joke work, but he was unable to contain his jealousy and contempt when he came to any scene or speech in which Newley's character had a lot to do. "All the quips of Matthew are impossible and unanswerable and hold up the scene," he complained of one exchange. "These unanswerable set ups are monotonous," he wrote, dashing out lines twenty pages later.[37]

But many of Harrison's instincts were wrong and costly—Bricusse had to waste an entire draft accommodating his insistence that Dolittle be depicted as a sophisticated London physician before he admitted the idea was a dead end.[38] And even as Harrison was slowing everyone down, his agent, Laurie Evans, was demanding that the actor be guaranteed $75,000 for three weeks of overtime, a situation that Arthur Jacobs apoplectically called "disaster and blackmail."[39] An excitable man on the calmest of days, Jacobs was now beginning to suffer physically from the stresses of *Doctor Dolittle*; in the spring, he was hospitalized for what he told his colleagues was surgery for "some rather irritating sinus condition."[40] But Jacobs, a forty-three-year-old hyperactive overweight chain-smoker, was really beginning to suffer from heart problems. When he was released from the hospital, he apologized to Harrison for missing a meeting in New York, saying only that he was under doctor's orders not to travel.[41] In the next month, he pushed ahead, hiring crew members, fighting the picture's rising costs, and telling no one that he was seriously ill.

In late June, the *Doctor Dolittle* crew flew to England to set up shop in Castle Combe, a small town in Wiltshire that proudly advertised itself as "the prettiest village in England," a designation it had won from the British tourist bureau. With Barnumesque brio, Jacobs started talking up the production in the press, ordering the staging of a photo opportunity in which Chee-Chee and Polynesia the parrot would "greet" Harrison upon his arrival in London,[42] and boasting that the movie would use 1,150 animals, 480 of them for the "Talk to the Animals" sequence alone ("He does the number and the camera slowly pulls back showing 480—I mean *four eight oh!*—animals standing there," he announced with delight), and "the biggest publicity and merchandising campaign ever."[43] Jacobs was somewhat more restrained when discussing the budget, telling one reporter the movie would be made for $12 million and another that the final cost would be somewhere between $11 million and $15 million.[44] In fact, *Doctor Dolittle* was already moving briskly past the $15 million mark, in part because of a colossal miscalculation: Nobody at Fox had realized that the hundreds of animals that had been trained in California would have to be quarantined as soon as they were shipped to England. An entirely new troupe of birds and beasts had to be found and trained on the spot, while the Jungleland animals were returned to California to be held for use on the studio lot.

Castle Combe welcomed the production with a combination of suspicion and delight. Residents were not happy when Jacobs's crew decided the village wasn't quite pretty enough and went through the town tearing down Coca-Cola signs and antennae. They were temporarily mollified when Jacobs got Fox to pay for a community antenna to bring the quaint little town what it really wanted—better TV reception. But when Jacobs had his construction team dam the local trout stream and fill it with artificial seaweed and rubber fish in order to make it deep enough to pass as a river on which Dolittle could set sail, grumbling gave way to sabotage.[45]

On June 27, before the actors arrived, Sir Ranulph Twisleton-Wykeham-Fiennes, a twenty-two-year-old baronet, and another man were arrested for trying to set fire to an outhouse with a can of gasoline and blow up the sandbag dam. His goal, he announced, was to stop "mass entertainment from riding roughshod over the feelings of the people."[46] (Fiennes, a distant cousin of the actor Ralph Fiennes, later became a well-known explorer and writer and was briefly considered as a possible replacement for Sean Connery when Connery quit the James Bond series in 1967.) The baronet's unsuccessful attempt at vandalism did no real damage to the production.

As Richard Fleischer put it, "It is the weather, not the bombs, which has made life intolerable."[47] Of the two months the *Dolittle* production spent in Castle Combe, all but five shooting days were either shortened or canceled altogether because of the constant downpours—a condition about which the studio had chosen to ignore all warnings.[48] "Big rain," says Samantha Eggar, reading from her diary entries at the time. " 'More rain. . . . Rained all day. . . . Whiled away the time with Pat [Newcomb] and Tony [Newley] and the Rosses [Herb Ross and Nora Kaye]. . . . Poured all day. . . . Pouring again.' It's on every page."[49]

"Castle Combe is a gorgeous place, but everywhere you walked there was either cowshit or mud," says Ray Aghayan, the film's costume designer. "It rained every day except the one day we needed it to rain—we had to shoot that day with phony rain."[50]

Even on the rare occasions when the weather was forgiving, the animals were not. Shooting with animals that had barely been trained was "not easy," said Ross, who had been brought over to stage the musical sequences. "The script just says, 'Swans do something,' and we have to see what they do."[51] The fields where many of the animals were kept became so saturated with rain that they turned into swamps. The rhinoceros got pneumonia. In his autobiography, Harrison wrote that the animals became "restless and angry" ("I was bitten by a chimp, a Pomeranian puppy, a duck and a parrot"), that their trainers were occasionally abusive, and that shooting was "inordinately slow." Even a shot as simple as one in which Dolittle addresses a few lines to an attentive parrot and squirrel who are standing on a railing became a nightmare when the recalcitrant squirrel wouldn't stay still. When crew members tried to wrap tiny wires around its paws and then attach the wires to the rail with tacks, the squirrel became understandably agitated. The production broke for lunch, and Fleischer, furious, went off to find a local veterinarian to find out how the squirrel could be sedated. In the afternoon, trainers filled a fountain pen with gin and fed it to the squirrel drop by drop. Finally, Harrison wrote, they got "a few seconds of film showing the squirrel . . . nodding and swaying" before it passed out cold.[52]

The cast and crew greeted each new catastrophe with gallows humor. "We are deep in the heart of British Occupied Wiltshire making a grand Todd-AO Classic—'Dr. Dolittle,' " Newley wrote to a friend. "You will probably be seeing it in 1984!"[53] But a generational rift quickly developed, with Harrison and Fleischer on one side and Newley and Eggar on the other. Harrison, wrote Fleischer, thought the younger actors were "twits when they clowned around on the set and disturbed his concentration."[54] But Harrison was so consistently unpleasant to Newley that the younger actor had little reason to make things easier for him.

As *Doctor Dolittle* fell further behind schedule with every day of rain, Dick Zanuck voiced his support for the production, and his father backed him up, at least publicly. Although 20th Century-Fox had lost $39 million during the catastrophic era of *Cleopatra* in 1962, it had reported an $11.7 million profit for 1965. Darryl Zanuck may have grumbled that "stars today think nothing of asking $500,000 to $750,000. . . . I used to make entire pictures—good ones—for that!"[55] but he wasn't about to change the think-big strategy that had brought the studio *The Sound of Music*.

Jacobs, however, found himself under increasing pressure. He was already thinking ahead to the Los Angeles shoot, trying to book Maurice Binder, creator of the famous title sequences for the James Bond movies, to shoot *Dolittle*'s opening credits without any principal actors, using the animals that had been sent back to Jungleland;[56] he was replacing cast members on the spot (Richard Attenborough stepped into a role that was originally to be played by character actor Hugh Griffiths with barely a week's notice); and, most pressingly, he was trying to decide whether the production should tough it out in Wiltshire or cut its losses. At first, Jacobs had leaned toward keeping the *Dolittle* crew in England well into

September, but as the weeks dragged on, he realized it was time to give up. Doctor Dolittle's elaborate house and yard would have to be meticulously reconstructed on a soundstage in Los Angeles. In mid-August, he and Fleischer decided to shut down the production, and his health got worse. Jacobs fought an ongoing battle with Fox about what the studio considered his overuse of limousine drivers, telling them that "I have been in the hospital and I am not allowed to carry heavy suitcases."[57] But as production in England wrapped, there were some days he was so ill that he couldn't even get out of bed in his suite at the Savoy Hotel in London. "Arthur would always insist he had indigestion," said director J. Lee Thompson, a friend. "But we knew it was heart trouble. He was not a well man."[58]

SIXTEEN

In the summer of 1966, Norman Jewison and Hal Ashby began working together on preproduction for *In the Heat of the Night*. Ashby was an editor by trade; he had learned his craft working under the veteran film cutter Robert Swink, assisting on William Wyler's *Friendly Persuasion* and *The Children's Hour* and also on George Stevens's *The Diary of Anne Frank* and *The Greatest Story Ever Told*. By the time Jewison met him, Ashby had gotten his first job as lead editor, on Tony Richardson's *The Loved One*; the professional bond that began when he edited Jewison's *The Cincinnati Kid* was cemented when the two teamed up on *The Russians Are Coming, the Russians Are Coming*.

Although Ashby's only credit on *In the Heat of the Night* is as its editor, he was, by every other definition, what would now be considered a co-producer; his work with Jewison was, according to cinematographer Haskell Wexler, the single most important creative partnership on the movie, and it started before a foot of film had been shot. Ashby was a rarity in mid-1960s Hollywood: a day-in, day-out pothead who was also a workaholic. Although at thirty-six he was at least a generation older than the kids who were converging on Haight-Ashbury and beginning to preach the gospel of Timothy Leary, Ashby, an ex-Mormon raised in Utah, grew his blond hair long, wore beads, and was the first in his crowd to tune in and turn on. But, at least at that point in his career, he did it without dropping out. "In those days, there was a kind of bohemian aspect to filmmaking," says Jewison. "We worked on a Moviola, and the cutting room had that pungent smell—the smell of film. And everybody smoked a little pot. It was a very relaxed atmosphere. Hal was a hippie. But I've never seen anyone so obsessed with film. At nine o'clock at night, I'd say, 'Hal, I have to go, I've got kids, I've got a wife, we've been working all day, I've got to go, and *you've* got to go. Now come on.' And he'd say, 'Hey, man, I know what, let me take another whack at this, we can tighten it.' And I would come back and he would have slept there all night. He went through five wives that way."[1]

For all his aging-flower-child eccentricity, Ashby had serious ambitions, and he was up front with Jewison about his desire to get away from the Moviola and start directing his own movies. But until that happened, he reveled in the opportunity to work under the wing of the director, who considered him a "younger brother." Ashby became a jack-of-all-trades on *In the Heat of the Night*; he served as liaison between Jewison and Mirisch, he helped to fill out the movie's supporting cast with casting director Lynn Stalmaster and supervised the hiring of a crew, he worried over story points in Silliphant's script, he nudged Jewison when he was falling behind in duties like location scouting, and he made suggestions for shots that he was already anticipating putting together in the editing room.

Ashby and Jewison were deep into prep work for the shoot when Sidney Poitier left for London; while he was waiting for *In the Heat of the Night*'s late September start of production, he snuck in another movie, almost as an afterthought. The entire budget of Columbia's *To Sir, with Love* was a rock-bottom $640,000. The project, based on a 1959 novel by Guyanese writer E. R. Braithwaite, had been kicking around for years—Harry Belafonte had once considered playing the lead[2]—and it's likely that Mike Frankovich decided to make the film only because he had a professional relationship with both Poitier and producer-director-writer James Clavell, whose novel *King Rat* had been adapted into a reasonably well-received drama for the studio in 1965. Poitier's role in *To Sir, with Love* was a chance for him to play the flip side of *The Blackboard Jungle*. This time, he would be an idealistic but sharp teacher who manages to make an enduring impression on a group of surly but not terribly menacing British teenagers. Even the studio, wrote Poitier, felt the script was "too soft, too sweet, too sentimental." But at a time when the actor's every decision—most recently his tentativeness about whether to play Othello—subjected him to public scrutiny and interrogation, Poitier may have relished the chance to escape from the Central Park West apartment where he now lived in solitude; and from American racial politics altogether. The shoot took up just a few weeks, and Poitier, though he felt Columbia's budget was "offensively meager," agreed to a salary of just $30,000 in exchange for a percentage of the overall gross.[3]

While Poitier was filming at England's Pinewood Studios, Jewison was traveling through the Midwest, looking for a location that could be visually convincing as Wells, the sleepy southern hamlet described in Ball's novel and Silliphant's script, but would still satisfy his star's requirement that *In the Heat of the Night* be shot north of the Mason-Dixon line. He finally settled on Sparta, a tiny Illinois town south of St. Louis near the Missouri border that had everything the screenplay required except a cotton plantation, an essential location that nobody wanted to write out of the script. Jewison gambled that once production got under way in Illinois, he would be able to convince Poitier to head south to cotton country for at least a few days of work; meanwhile, he concentrated on finding ways to keep the budget as low as Walter Mirisch wanted. Making a movie on location with two well-paid stars for significantly under $3 million meant cutting corners wherever doing so wouldn't hurt the movie; the town of Wells was renamed Sparta, for instance, just so the production wouldn't have to pay crew members to repaint the name on the local water tower.[4] Economizing also meant using unknown actors in smaller parts, and that meant looking to New York theater and television. For the role of Harvey Oberst, the drifter who becomes Sheriff Gillespie's primary murder suspect, Jewison had considered several young actors, including Jon Voight; he was about to cast Robert Blake when Lynn Stalmaster met Scott Wilson, a lean, handsome twenty-four-year-old Georgia native who had never made a movie before. Stalmaster and Jewison were looking for an actor who was physically fit enough for a long, complicated chase sequence. "At the time, I was parking cars in Los Angeles at the first topless place in California," says Wilson. "It did a brisk lunchtime business as guys would drive up, jump out of their cars, run in, and run out again. You had to park their cars up in the hills and run back and forth, up and down, so I was in good running shape." Wilson auditioned the day before Blake was to be offered a contract and won the job on the basis of a cold reading in which he knew nothing about the character he was playing.[5]

For most of the other roles, Stalmaster turned to actors he had used in TV shows. William Schallert, who played the town's racist mayor, was a veteran of *The Patty Duke Show*. Anthony James, another suspect in the film, had read for a small part in the western series *Death Valley Days*, and his lanky, intense look stuck in Stalmaster's mind. Many of the actors, including Warren Oates, who was hired to play Officer Sam Wood, had been cast by Stalmaster in *Slattery's People*, a politically progressive CBS drama about urban politics that was well reviewed but canceled in 1965 after one season. (Oates beat out a pair of actors Stalmaster cast regularly throughout the early 1960s, Ed Asner and Gavin MacLeod.)[6]

The sole exception to Jewison's decision to populate the cast with lesser-known performers was Lee Grant, who was signed to appear in two short but important scenes as the murder victim's widow. Fifteen years earlier, Grant had won an Oscar nomination for her film debut as a shoplifter in William Wyler's *Detective Story*, only to have her movie career destroyed by the blacklist. As was the case with many Hollywood victims of McCarthyism, says Stalmaster, "we were able to bring her into television, mostly in New York. In the days of shows like *Ben Casey* and *Slattery's People*, there were people, directors like Sydney Pollack and Leo Penn and Mark Rydell, who abhorred the abuses of the time and would hire these people."[7] In 1966, the effects of the blacklist were still being felt: Members of the Writers Guild of America were battling with the studios over the issue of withholding credit from writers who had taken the Fifth Amendment about their political beliefs,[8] and directors were in federal court, fighting their own guild's requirement of an anti-Communist loyalty oath.[9] For Jewison, who was such a committed liberal that a friend once joked that "if Norman gets reincarnated, he'll want to come back black and Jewish and blind,"[10] casting Grant was a chance to rectify an injustice. At the time she was hired for *In the Heat of the Night*, Grant had just won an Emmy for the TV soap opera *Peyton Place*, but she had not worked in a major role in a studio film for more than ten years.

Bonnie and Clyde was also heading toward its first day of production, but now that Arthur Penn was aboard, Robert Benton and David Newman's screenplay was being rewritten, and in one of its final overhauls, Clyde Barrow became unambiguously heterosexual. How and why the ménage à trois between Clyde, Bonnie, and their male getaway driver was eliminated from the script months after Benton had warned Beatty that its inclusion was non-negotiable (and after Beatty had assured him that he wouldn't flinch at playing a bisexual character) remains a matter of dispute even after forty years. "It never occurred to me to tamper with that," says Beatty. "It would have been a sign of some sort of chickenheartedness. When Arthur decided to do the movie, he said, 'I want to make a change.' I said, 'I would think that'd be the *last* thing you want to change,' and he said, 'No, I think it dissipates the passion between Bonnie and Clyde.' And I agreed with him. I think that if you have somebody going in two directions at once, it's a different can of peas. What does the character want? It's the thing you have to ask in any picture."[11]

"We had been working with Arthur in Stockbridge, Massachusetts, on rewrites for about a month," says Benton, "and Arthur said, 'First of all, I want you to understand something. This is not coming from Warren, it's coming from me. There are two problems. One is that you haven't written the emotional complexity of this [three-way] relationship. And two, people will say, "Of course they're gangsters—they're a bunch of sexual freaks."' The moment we took it out, I knew it was right. What Arthur was saying was, you can only take the audience so far. In most gangster movies, there's a moment when the audience can stand outside, at arm's length from the characters. We were very careful *not* to do that. We wanted their affection for the characters to remain."[12]

But others recall Beatty himself as having an aversion to Clyde's bisexuality. Mart Crowley, author of *The Boys in the Band*, had worked briefly for Natalie Wood in the mid-1960s and knew Beatty through her. "I remember running into Warren in the Daisy nightclub one night, and I said, 'Listen, Clyde Barrow was gay—are you gonna do anything about that?' And the sense I got from him was, 'Are you kidding? That's not the kind of picture we're doing.' "[13] And Newman wrote soon after the film's release that "Warren was adamant about [the bisexuality] being removed for two reasons, the first being that it was not such a terrific thing for his image and the second being that it 'just wasn't working,' "[14] a point he reiterated in 1997.[15]

Penn may have claimed responsibility for the decision in order to protect Beatty, but he also wanted to solve what he called the problem of "the script turning too dark too early, when they introduced this big, oafish third figure that Bonnie was hitting on while we were dealing with Clyde's homosexual tendencies."[16] No matter who ultimately made the call, it must have been completely obvious to everyone involved at the time. To imagine otherwise would be to ignore the reality that a homosexual or bisexual protagonist in a Hollywood movie was then unthinkable, and the makers of *Bonnie and Clyde* knew it. The Production Code had maintained a complete ban on the subject until a few years earlier and now permitted homosexuality to be depicted only as an "aberration."[17] When homosexual characters began to show up in a handful of studio movies, they were seen only as mincing, effeminate sissies in comedies and as murder or suicide victims in dramas like *Advise and Consent* and *The Children's Hour*. Characters who were incidentally gay, or heroic and homosexual, simply didn't exist, nor did any kind of movement to lobby for more positive portrayals.[18] In a lengthy essay published at the beginning of 1966, *Time* magazine (whose movie critics used the word *fag* in their reviews without a second thought) spoke for and to much of America when it called homosexuality "a pathetic little second-rate substitute for reality, a pitiable flight from life . . . it deserves no encouragement, no glamorization, no rationalization, no fake status as minority martyrdom, no sophistry about simple differences in taste—and above all, no pretense that it is anything but a pernicious sickness."[19] The following year, when Mike Wallace's CBS report *The Homosexuals* aired after three years of preparation, the documentary's subjects were photographed in silhouette and the tone was so clinical and grim that one reviewer wondered whether even a moment could have been spared for "the minority viewpoint that homosexuals are just as normal as anyone else."[20]

By insisting on the ménage à trois and introducing it early in the film,

Benton and Newman knew that they might damage something that was just as important to them—an arc of audience identification in which moviegoers would take Bonnie and Clyde's side at the outset and have bonded to them by the time their adventures turned disorientingly dark and violent. The writers liked the idea of weaving a sexual component into Clyde's frustration and appetite for violence, and Penn's suggested solution—that they make Clyde impotent—"fit right in with all that phallic gun stuff," wrote Newman.[21] Beatty thought impotence worked better than bisexuality, but he pushed Penn for a scene, late in the movie, in which Clyde finally manages to complete sex with Bonnie; Penn resisted but ultimately gave in.[22]

Its politics aside, the decision to eliminate the ménage à trois benefited the script in other ways; it allowed Benton and Newman to rewrite the character of C. W. Moss, the wheelman. A thick, dull stud-for-hire in the first version of the screenplay, he now became a puckish, slightly dopey kid brother—this "lovable little guy," says Penn—an important comic element in the movie's lighthearted early scenes and an ideal part for Michael J. Pollard, a friend of Beatty's from their days working together in the play *A Loss of Roses* and on the sitcom *The Many Loves of Dobie Gillis*. "The only other person I ever thought about was Dennis Hopper," says Beatty. "I thought he would be funny, and a very good actor. But Michael J.—you just look at him and he's fun."[23]

Beatty and Penn turned to New York for the rest of *Bonnie and Clyde*'s cast, populating the film almost entirely with inexpensive stage actors. For the role of Buck's nervous, chattery wife, Blanche, Beatty had been interested in Elia Kazan's wife, Barbara Loden,[24] but Penn wanted Estelle Parsons, an actress who had worked in television (including as a cub reporter for the *Today* show) but had had only one tiny movie role. "I was not having a good career at that moment," says Parsons, who had packed up her New York apartment and two children in order to join a San Francisco repertory company, only to have the job fall through before she got there. "I was doing a Murray Schisgal play with Gene Hackman and Dusty Hoffman up at Stockbridge, for Arthur [at the Berkshire Theatre Festival]. . . . I was thinking, what am I doing in this ridiculous business? I really do tragicomedy, and nobody hiring for a rep company wanted that. But Arthur's rehearsal technique was so exciting, it really turned me around. It was impossible to work for him and not be 100 percent fully engaged. I would have gone anywhere with him." Parsons signed on to play Blanche for $5,000. For the role of Clyde's brother, Buck, she suggested her stage costar Hackman—"People always thought we must be lovers because we had the same rhythm, the same way of acting," she says. "And of course, Gene wanted to be a movie star, always."[25] Penn was enthusiastic about him, and so was Beatty, who had shared a scene with Hackman in Robert Rossen's *Lilith* and came away thinking, "This guy's such a good actor, he's making me look good."[26] And Penn brought in Evans Evans and Gene Wilder, with whom he had worked at the Actors Studio, to play a young couple briefly swept up in the Barrow gang's joyride.[27]

The ensemble Beatty and Penn pulled together was made up of newcomers and outsiders, and the crew was light on experience as well: Neither Theadora Van Runkle, the costume designer, nor Dean Tavoularis, the production designer, had made a film before. "I waited three hours to meet Warren Beatty, and he breezed in and the first thing he said to me was, 'Sorry, kid, you can't do the movie—I talked to the Costume Designers Guild and you're not in the union,'" says Van Runkle. "So I did something uncharacteristic—I leapt across the room and grabbed him by his shirt and said, 'I've got to do the movie!' He said, 'Okay, okay,' and got the head of the guild on the phone, and they swore at each other for about half an hour, and I was in."[28] Editor Dede Allen had overseen the cutting of only a few films, but they included Kazan's *America America* and Rossen's *The Hustler*, which was enough of a recommendation for Beatty. The sole veteran behind the scenes was Burnett Guffey, a sixty-one-year-old cinematographer who had begun his career as an assistant cameraman in 1923 and had shot more than eighty films, among them *All the King's Men, From Here to Eternity,* and *Birdman of Alcatraz*. Guffey had been nominated for four Academy Awards and won once, but these days, he went where the work was, whether it was episodes of *Gidget* or Dean Martin's Matt Helm movies. "My impression was that people were down on their luck," says Parsons. "It was more or less like doing an independent movie. I mean, Gene hadn't done much, I had not really done a movie before, Warren and Arthur had done that *Mickey One,* so they were both kind of down . . . and Faye had not really done anything, or anything that people had seen."[29]

Dunaway was among the last of *Bonnie and Clyde*'s principals to be cast. Beatty had thought a great deal about his former lover Natalie Wood and discussed the part of Bonnie Parker with her more than once. "Here's how out of touch I was with the movie world," says Van Runkle. "When Warren said he wanted to cast Natalie Wood, I said, 'No, she can't be Bonnie—she doesn't have enough class!' "[30]

A reunion of the two stars of *Splendor in the Grass* would have gone a long way toward selling the film to audiences, and Wood, though her romantic relationship with Beatty was long over, was interested. "All during the time I was directing her in *This Property Is Condemned*," says Sydney Pollack, "she was trying to decide whether to do it or not. That's how I met Warren. He kept after her."[31]

But Wood's emotional state was fragile, and Robert Towne was quietly urging Beatty to look elsewhere. "I remember feeling that he should not go back to Natalie, and I'm sure I expressed that, because I felt that this script really needed someone different," he says. And Beatty himself stopped short of directly asking Wood to take the part. "There is that point," says Towne, "when he would have just thrown himself at a prospective Bonnie's feet and said, 'Please do it, you're the only one.' I don't know that he ever did that—I don't know that he ever felt it."[32]

Beatty looked at Sharon Tate, the young starlet who was about to be cast in *Valley of the Dolls*. He wondered if Ann-Margret might be good for the part, or perhaps Carol Lynley, who had just played Jean Harlow in a biopic and might have had the right period look. And he gave serious consideration to Jane Fonda, who years earlier had been François Truffaut's first idea for the role. "I thought that Jane would be very, very good in it," says Beatty. "But Jane had worked on *The Chase*, and because that was not a good experience either for her or for Arthur, that sort of negated that."[33]

"We talked about Jane Fonda, but she seemed too sophisticated," says Penn. And for the director, Fonda's fame, which was on the rise after the success of *Cat Ballou*, also worked against her: "I didn't want a movie star."[34]

"Warren has an incredible way of making you *think* he's offering you a part . . . and then not using you—and you never feel you've been rejected," Fonda told Beatty biographer Suzanne Finstad. "That's a gift."[35]

Beatty and Penn both say the only actress to receive a firm offer from them before Dunaway was Tuesday Weld—and she turned them down. Beatty had worked with Weld years earlier on *Dobie Gillis* when she was still a teenager; she was now a twenty-three-year-old new mother whose almost doll-like beauty and unconcealable streaks of wildness and neurosis might have made her a fascinating Bonnie. But she was nursing, overwhelmed by parenthood, and didn't want to travel to Texas for the shoot. And, says Penn, "she didn't like the script."[36] ("I refused to do *Bonnie and Clyde*," she fretted later, "because down deep I knew it was going to be a huge success.")

By the time Dunaway's name came up, Beatty and Penn were out of options, and the excited ingenue who had been signed to two multipicture contracts just six months earlier had already had a bruising introduction to the realities of Hollywood moviemaking. Dunaway's debut in *The Happening* had been reasonably smooth, if somewhat rushed, but when she went from that into Otto Preminger's southern melodrama, *Hurry Sundown*, in which she had a supporting role as the wife of a dirt farmer, the shoot turned into an ordeal that left the actress badly shaken.

Preminger had assembled an impressive young cast, including Michael Caine, Jane Fonda, Robert Hooks, and Diahann Carroll, for the Louisiana shoot, "right in the heart of Ku Klux Klan territory," Dunaway wrote. For Fonda, the besieged production represented a step in her political awakening: "I was still using the term *Negro* while the African-Americans in the cast were calling themselves black," she wrote. "I listened to conversations between Robert Hooks, Beah Richards and others . . . about a burgeoning 'black nationalism' . . . a growing sense that blacks had only themselves to depend on."[37] But for Dunaway, the shoot tapped into her innate competiveness: "Jane was the May Queen in this film. She was the bigger star, and Otto wanted her to be the main star of this movie," she wrote.[38] And Dunaway learned the hard way that Preminger's reputation as a monster with actors was well earned. He was "autocratic and dictatorial," she wrote. "It is difficult to understand the depth of the rage until the full force of it is turned directly on you." When Preminger exploded at her one day "like a mad dog," Dunaway kept her cool, finished her work on the movie, went back to New York, and told her lawyer to do whatever he had to do to get her out of the remainder of her multifilm contract. "It cost me a lot of money," she wrote, "not to work for Otto again."[39]

It's not clear how Dunaway came to the attention of Beatty and Penn. Some people have said that publicist John Springer, a confidant of Beatty's, first suggested her. Theadora Van Runkle remembers sitting in a meeting where Beatty "scooted this catalog of actresses across the table and I opened it to Faye's picture and saw her and said, 'There's the girl you should cast!' She was perfect for the spirit of the thirties and the spirit of the sixties."[40] In her autobiography, Dunaway writes that it was Penn who got in touch with Creative Management Associates' David Begelman and asked to meet her, although earlier, when she had wanted to audition for Fonda's role in *The Chase*, she couldn't get past Penn's casting director, who said she "didn't have the face for movies."[41]

Neither of Dunaway's first two films was scheduled to open for several months, so Beatty and Penn asked Columbia if they could look at footage of Dunaway in *The Happening*, and they liked what they saw enough to fly her to Los Angeles. But the woman who walked into Beatty's suite at the Beverly Wilshire Hotel bore little resemblance to the blond, gaunt Bonnie Parker of *Bonnie and Clyde*. Dunaway had gained weight during the making of *Hurry Sundown*; her appearance in the film, in which she gave a vivid, impassioned performance, was womanly, full-hipped, appropriately unglamorous. That evening, Dunaway shuttled between Beatty's penthouse and Penn's room several floors below; each man claims to have convinced the other to hire her. "I had a long meeting with her, and I was impressed by her energy and intelligence," says Beatty. "And I also felt her toughness, which I thought was dramatic and funny." Knowing how many times Penn had watched him blow hot and cold about an actress, Beatty called him and said, " 'I've gotta introduce you to an actress who I *don't* think I want in the movie, but you should meet her because you'll really like her.' An hour later, he calls me and says, 'I met Faye Dunaway. I think I want her in the movie.'"[42]

Penn's account is slightly different. "It got a little testy between Warren and me, because I had seen Dunaway in *After the Fall* in New York.

Warren had a sense about her, that she was difficult, I think that was part of it. I don't know what it was, but it made him keep her at a distance. But she was clearly beautiful and a damn good actress. And Benton and Newman were there, we were all up in Warren's suite, and it got to the push-comes-to-shove point, and the three of us wanted Dunaway. And at that point Warren said all right."[43]

As Dunaway was coming on to *Bonnie and Clyde*, Benton and Newman were stepping away from the film. The project they had begun three years earlier had launched their careers; they now had a musical, *It's a Bird . . . It's a Plane . . . It's Superman*, on Broadway and a suspense drama in the works for Universal. For weeks, they had been traveling to Stockbridge, rewriting the script for Penn, and they had reached a dead end. "Benton and Newman, by then, were just exhausted," says Penn.[44]

"Arthur said to me at one point, 'Look, I like these guys a lot, but would I be letting you down terribly if I don't do the movie?'" says Beatty. "This was in July of 1966, and I think we started in October! So, rather than be graceful, I said, 'Yes, you would be letting me down—what the hell are you talking about?'" Beatty asked Penn if he wanted to work with Lillian Hellman or Arthur Miller on the script, offering to get in touch with them. Penn, not looking for a wholesale rewrite, said no.[45] Then Beatty suggested that Robert Towne step in. Towne had already been serving as Beatty's unofficial adviser on the movie; he had been a strong advocate for getting rid of the three-way: "Now they're all in bed together, now they're in bed separately—it took *Jules and Jim* a whole movie to resolve a ménage à trois *without* any gangster stuff going on," he had said. Penn agreed to sit down with him and talk through the screenplay. When the two men met, says Towne, "I think it probably was within two to three weeks, maybe a month at most, of the time that the production actually went to Texas."[46]

Towne told Penn he thought the screenplay was still too episodic and suggested a vital reordering of scenes late in the movie. In Benton and Newman's script, Parker and Barrow interrupt their crime spree so that she can visit her mother; in the following scene, the gang picks up a young mortician and his girlfriend and chats with the terrified couple for a while before dropping them off on an empty road. Towne suggested reversing the scenes; Bonnie's revulsion at the scent of mortality once she realizes that she is in the car with an undertaker would now lead directly to her desire to see her mother one last time, and the change would suffuse the last third of the movie with a sense that death was approaching inexorably. He also suggested a substantial rewrite of the exchange with Bonnie's mother, which Beatty says "had been sort of a plateau, the kind of scene that would give you a great opportunity to go to the candy counter."[47] Towne made a case for darkening the moment dramatically; in his revision, when Bonnie dreamily suggests that she and Clyde might soon move closer to her family, her elderly mother replies, "You try living three miles from me and you won't live long."

"Look, anybody who sees this movie is going to know what's going to happen at the end—they're going to get killed," Towne recalls telling Penn. "There's no mystery involved in that. So the only dramatic element you're going to have is *when* they're going to get killed. That's a potential element of suspense, and as a corollary, is there something that will need to be resolved between Bonnie and Clyde before that death that people are looking forward to?" Penn and Towne both felt that Clyde's continuing struggle with impotence could serve as an unresolved, barely stated plot thread connecting the scenes, and Penn liked Towne's argument that the end of the movie needed "a sense of the roads that they were traveling down closing off, so that there was only one end to the road that was coming." By the end of the meeting, Penn asked Towne to sign on.[48]

Benton and Newman walked away with no rancor; Towne had been an early booster of their script with Beatty, and they knew that he wouldn't rewrite them casually. "I honestly don't know who the 'auteur' of *Bonnie and Clyde* was," says Benton. "I can't tell you that it was us, or Warren Beatty, or Arthur, or Towne, who was a very important part of the process. I don't know."[49]

Towne worked quickly and made plans to travel to Texas for daily on-set rewrites. Van Runkle started making the costumes; Dean Tavoularis went to Texas to look at locations. As the days until the start of production dwindled, Beatty's temper occasionally flared. Warner Brothers was pressuring him to go to New York to do publicity for *Kaleidoscope,* a thousand decisions still needed to be made, and his inclination toward slowness and deliberation as an actor was at war with the sense of urgency he felt as a first-time producer. "Warren's anger, when it came, was intense," says Van Runkle. "He walked in once when I was fitting Faye with the dress she's wearing when she first comes on screen and said, 'You don't know what you're doing, do you!' And I said right back, 'No, I don't!' I was just a kid— I just guessed and did it."[50]

Neither Beatty nor Penn needed any reminders to fulfill the pledge they had made to have an argument every day. "I remember being in the car with him," Beatty says, laughing. "We pulled up to a stop sign on Sunset, and I said, 'Let's have an argument! What do you think the biggest casting problem in the movie is?' And he said, 'You!' He told me to stop thinking about the production and start thinking about playing the part. And he was right."[51]

But Beatty knew just how closely and skeptically his decision to oversee production of a movie before his thirtieth birthday was being watched by his colleagues. "He was hammered so many times by so many people," says Towne. "Sometimes I think that reassuring him that he was on to something was as important a contribution as any that I made, because so many people did not feel that way."[52]

"From the first day of shooting, I felt there was one thing I could never run away from in this film," said Beatty. "No matter what was wrong with it, I was gonna step up and take the complete blame. For a change, there wouldn't be any cop-outs."[53]

SEVENTEEN

Norman, since I talked to you this afternoon, I've become so god-damned, furiously frustrated from anger I don't know what to do except sit here at this typewriter and rant and rave," wrote Hal Ashby to Norman Jewison on October 5, 1966. "To think Walter [Mirisch] would put this kind of pressure on you is beyond the realm of my comprehension. . . . I guess *Russians* wasn't enough to prove you are an honorable and responsible man. I swear to Christ what do you have to do."[1]

Almost every day, a new letter from Ashby would arrive in the hotel in Belleville, Illinois, that served as headquarters for Jewison and the cast and crew of *In the Heat of the Night*. The film was two weeks into production; the director and his sixty-man team would drive thirty-five miles to Sparta every day for the shoot. "We were the biggest thing in Sparta," Haskell Wexler recalled later. "It was like the carnival coming! Guys had [girls] stashed, some of them had wives . . . there were a lot of dramas . . . mostly because we were exotic and exciting and they were vulnerable and stupid and had nice boobs and didn't know anything about predatory northern city people."[2] But while some in the town may have been dazzled, nobody involved in the movie itself was likely to mistake *In the Heat of the Night* for a glamorous, free-spending Hollywood production. Certainly not the local extras, who were paid all of $1.50 a day ("It beats cleaning house," said one);[3] or the worn-out, constantly chilled crew, who had been passing around the same head cold for weeks;[4] or Sidney Poitier and Rod Steiger, whose only star treatment on location consisted of space heaters in their dressing rooms,[5] or the younger actors, who had to pretend they were sweating through a humid summer evening in the Deep South when in reality the nights in Sparta were so cold that they had to keep ice chips in their mouths in order to prevent their breath from showing up on camera, spitting them out just before each take.[6] Jewison was doing what he could to keep costs down—most of the younger actors, even those in major supporting roles, were working for $100 a day[7]—and he was pushing through the shoot under difficult circumstances: His producer, Walter Mirisch, who never came to the set, was hundreds of miles away in Los Angeles, and so was Ashby, his closest ally. Mirisch was pressuring him about the already low budget; Ashby was running interference as well as he could; and Jewison was left to make every decision himself, serving as his own uncredited line producer.[8]

Jewison had arrived in Belleville in early September to start preparing for the movie, relying on Ashby, whose commitment to recreational drugs didn't seem to impede his skill as a superb detail man, to take care of every loose end: the selection of blouses and wigs for Lee Grant, the name of the movie that would appear on the marquee of the Sparta Cinema House ("Walter suggested *How to Succeed* [*in Business Without Really Trying*]," he wrote to Jewison, "as it is scheduled for release about the same time as *Heat*"), even whether a Sony or a Zenith radio should be used in the background of a scene. As Jewison combed through the screenplay one last time before the actors arrived, Ashby tried to chase down the answer to every one of his questions and anticipate those that he hadn't yet asked: "DEADIES," one of his letters began. "I did check with the coroner's office since we talked and he said 99 out of a hundred times when somebody is done in the eyes are open. Not wide open mind you, but you can most certainly tell they are open." Ashby went on to explain—and to illustrate—the way the film's makeup men should simulate the pooling of blood in the corpse.

The inimitable shorthand psychedelic patois of Ashby's daily memos, which were usually festooned with two or three salutations and pseudonymous sign-offs (he called himself everything from "lonesome luke" to "Capt. Ashby/Ret"), sometimes made him sound like a free-associative LSD adventurer: "The above typographical-marginal errors are a direct result of a malady (non-zymotic, fortunately) closely akin to bad brains," he once wrote without elaborating. But nothing escaped Ashby's attention: He was a persistent dramaturge ("pages 91 to 94 . . . I'm still concerned . . . it just seems too pat and convenient"), a conscientious editor who thought ahead ("Scene 5—Sam in car in front of diner—remember to get some kind of signing-off deal at end"), and, when needed, a cautious cheerleader: "Saw some good dailies today and would say a few words, but there are many words necessary. . . . For the moment, know I left the projection room with a smile. Bye, bye black evil moon. Love, me yah yah." On the rare occasions Ashby became angry, it was on Jewison's behalf. "When I look at our dailies, and see the extra quality—I'm talking about those values which can not be evaluated—and then hear what you told me today I feel like I'm going crazy," he wrote to Jewison after his quarrel with Mirisch. "If there is anyone you want me to kick in the shins or bite, please let me know."[9]

The extra quality Ashby was talking about in the footage Jewison was shipping from Belleville may have been exactly what alarmed Mirisch, since, from his first day working on *In the Heat of the Night*, Haskell Wexler was determined to shoot the film in a style that had never been seen in a color Hollywood movie. In 1966, the industry's long-held principle that black and white connoted serious, gritty reality and color suggested spectacle or frivolity was finally crumbling; black-and-white films were falling victim to the ubiquity of color television and the changing tastes of moviegoers. A handful of movies were still shot in black and white, but only if the budget was extremely low, or a veteran director who was uncomfortable with color was digging in his heels, as Billy Wilder did on *The Fortune Cookie*,[10] or the use of color would reveal a flaw (for instance, the artificiality of Elizabeth Taylor's makeup in *Who's Afraid of Virginia Woolf?*).

In the Heat of the Night was Wexler's first chance to shoot in color. After the indoor confinement of *Virginia Woolf*, he was hungry to try new techniques and more than ready to eschew the stiff, floodlit, immobile framing to which many of Hollywood's older cinematographers had clung as they switched from black and white. Wexler admired the jagged, shadowy work that Raoul Coutard had been doing for Jean-Luc Godard, and

he wanted his camera to move with the jolt and immediacy of photojour-
nalistic footage. Setups were jerry-rigged on the spot: For a scene in which
Scott Wilson's character runs through the woods pursued by dogs, Wexler,
holding the camera himself, knelt on a platform made of two-by-fours.
Four crew members carried him and dodged low-hanging branches as they
tore past the trees alongside Wilson, sometimes racing backward through
thick brush. "I remember being very impressed by him," says Wilson. "I
thought, damn, that fucking guy could get his eye poked out."[11] For a shot
in which Wilson was to run across train tracks just ahead of an onrushing
locomotive, Jewison and Wexler didn't have the money to hire a train to
arrive on cue, so they would just tell Wilson to start sprinting as soon as
he heard the railroad whistle and hope that he wouldn't run out of camera
range.[12] In the climax of the chase scene, in which Wilson tears along
a bridge trying to cross the Mississippi River to Arkansas, Wexler used a
zoom, giving the shot a semidocumentary feel. The effect was that of a
gunsight training on its target, with a rough, grainy quality that evoked the
Zapruder film, a technique that would be appropriated by action-movie
directors and cinematographers throughout the 1970s.

Wexler's technique was no less innovative in the movie's dialogue sequences. *In the Heat of the Night*'s palette—inky black nighttime scenes
with patches of dull greenish or reddish illumination—was a violation of the
shadowless, picturesque aesthetic that had ruled Hollywood color movies
for decades. The visual motif Wexler created was harsh, murky, resolutely
unscenic—a portrait of darkness with a few isolated spots of light that was
very much in tune with Jewison and Silliphant's decision to keep the film's
murder mystery elliptical and the town's atmosphere heavy with intangible
menace. Wexler and Jewison have both said that his low-light technique
was at least in part a cost-saving measure, and their do-it-yourself approach
is evident even in the film's opening shot, in which the lights of a train
reaching Sparta first appear as an abstract array of colors penetrating an
overwhelming blackness. The striking effect was achieved by the cheapest
means imaginable: Wexler held a piece of screen door in front of the lens,
focused on it, and then slowly adjusted his focus to the locomotive.[13]

But Wexler's choices for *In the Heat of the Night* were never simply
expedient: The bland light of a diner, the lonely glow of an empty train

platform, and the institutional bleariness of a police station were all given sharp, specific looks—and so, for once, was Sidney Poitier. Unlike almost all of his colleagues at the time, Wexler knew that white and black actors shouldn't be lit the same way. The low light he used throughout *In the Heat of the Night* was designed in part to make his star's facial features completely clear; Poitier had often been the victim of thoughtless over-lighting designed for white actors that added glare to his face and rendered his expressions indistinct, but here, Wexler and Jewison made sure that every unspoken thought that played across his lips and eyes would read on camera and be visible to moviegoers.

In the Heat of the Night was Poitier's twenty-sixth movie, and the material had been developed expressly for him, but he was still taken aback by what he encountered when he arrived in Illinois. By his own admission, Poitier hadn't had a part that really challenged him for years, and although he and Rod Steiger had been casually friendly for some time, he was un-prepared for the Method-driven intensity that Steiger was bringing to the role of Gillespie. Steiger's physical transformation alone was startling; he had soared past 230 pounds and was packing on more every night, as Jewison enthusiastically pushed him to eat two dinners and a piece of banana cream pie at Sparta's only diner. Jewison also urged Steiger to chew a wad of gum in every scene, and although the actor initially resisted, he came to love it.[14] "Norman Jewison said, 'Try it for one day, do it for me, will you?' " he said. "And what I found was, by the rhythm of my chewing . . . slow, fast, or what have you, I could tell the audience what my character was thinking and feeling. . . . When things get exciting, he chews faster. When he really gets shocked, *everything* stops, including the chewing."[15] With his big gut hanging over a sheriff's belt, his yellow-tinted glasses, and his black chukka boots, Steiger looked the part and was living it as well, eating, walking, thinking, and talking like Gillespie around the clock. He had worked out a ripe, flavorful southern accent that he used both on and off camera. When script supervisor Meta Rebner, a Mississippian who, as the former mistress of William Faulkner, came by her knowledge of dialect honestly, would tell him, "Mistah Steigah, in the South, we pronounce ouah *t*'s. You may say whatevah you like, but we pronounce ouah *t*'s!" he'd growl, "Nobody's gonna tell me how I talk!"[16]

One day, Steiger showed up on the set an hour before his makeup call, already wearing Gillespie's costume, which he took back to the hotel with him every night. "I said, 'What are you doing here so early?'" recalls assistant director Terry Morse. "He said, 'I don't know. . . . I just didn't like the idea that I didn't *need* to be here.'"[17] "Much of my acting depends on sheer terror of failure," he said later. "I'd be so ashamed to be bad, I couldn't stand it."[18] It took Poitier only a couple of days to realize that his costar was poised to walk away with the movie.

At first, Poitier was tense and slightly guarded, all the more since his habitual restraint couldn't have been more at odds with Steiger's well-known tendency to come out of the gate wild on the first take. "He was a little nervous with Rod, because he felt he was over-the-top," says Jewison. "When Rod got angry, it's like you released Al Pacino or a Doberman pinscher. I remember near the beginning of shooting, Rod drives up to a diner and gets out and slams the door. And he slammed the door so hard the car shook. After the take, I said, 'Cut, okay, I'd like to do one more from a slightly different angle.' And Sidney came to me and said, 'Are you gonna let him do that?!' I said, 'Sidney, don't worry about Rod. I will always do more than one take, and the performance will be controlled in editing. You just concentrate on what *you're* doing, because I don't want you to get lost here.' Sidney was challenged by Rod and was shocked by the fact that Rod was not afraid to play a bigot."[19]

Instead of reacting with hostility, Poitier decided to push himself harder. He watched the technique of his costar with growing admiration. In fifteen years, he had never worked with an actor like Steiger. "His approach to his work fascinated me," Poitier wrote. "Working or not, he would remain completely immersed in the character of that Southern sheriff. I was astonished at the intensity of his involvement. . . . Throughout the making of the film I sensed that I was on the threshold of discovering what acting really is."[20]

Poitier's own breakthrough working on *In the Heat of the Night* came during the night-long filming of the scene in which Gillespie shares a drink with Tibbs and the two men warily recognize each other as intelligent and lonely kindred spirits—a scene that ends when Gillespie, embarrassed by his own vulnerability, abruptly remembers himself and angrily shuts out

Tibbs's gesture of sympathy. In an early draft, Stirling Silliphant had made the abrupt transition too explicit, having Gillespie snarl, "Don't treat me like *I* was the nigger!" His rewrite was more subtle, but both actors still felt there was more to explore in the exchange. A thunderstorm had blown into Sparta, and the drumming of the water on the tin roof of the set delayed the shoot for hours. While Jewison, Steiger, and Poitier sat in a parked car trying to stay warm and waiting for the skies to clear, they talked about possible improvisations, with Meta Rebner in the backseat taking notes on the dialogue. Although they eventually filmed the sequence largely as Silliphant had written it, Poitier and Steiger found they shared an exploratory spirit, and as they allowed themselves to think and speak as they imagined Gillespie and Tibbs would, they came to like and trust each other. Steiger tried out his theory that the characters had in common "respect for their manhood and professionalism, their refusal to lie, their refusal to be insulted. So they were brothers that way."[21] Poitier, meanwhile, came down hard on himself for "pretending, indicating, giving the *appearance* of experiencing certain emotions, but never, ever, really getting down to where real life and fine art mirror each other."[22] By the end of that night's shoot, a bottle of whiskey had been emptied and a deeper friendship had been cemented.[23] "There had been something missing in the film until then," says Jewison, "and working on that scene provided it."[24]

By the time Lee Grant arrived in Illinois, Poitier was, for the first time in years, energized by the work he was doing. Grant's ex-husband, Arnold Manoff, a screenwriter whose blacklisting had derailed her career as well as his own, had died a year earlier, and the actress threw herself into her two scenes as a grieving widow with pent-up pain and Method specificity, even asking that a strand of hair be placed in a brush she was holding that was supposed to have belonged to the murder victim. "I was the perfect candidate to play that woman at that moment," she says. "I came to that set with real baggage, and while it was not a subject I needed to go anywhere near as a person, as an actress it was a gift. And Sidney was totally clued in—we improvised, we connected as if there were a magnetic field between us. Working with him was like ballroom dancing."[25]

As Poitier started finding his own way into his character during the autumn he spent in Sparta, it became all too easy for him to put himself inside the anger, isolation, intelligence, and impatience of Virgil Tibbs. When Silliphant pared down the screenplay, a subplot he had originally planned about Tibbs's growing friendship with a local black mechanic and his family had all but disappeared, so Poitier was virtually the only black man on set. He was, as ever, pleasant and collegial to his co-workers; one weekend, he took the entire cast on a road trip to St. Louis, where Harry Belafonte was performing a concert with Nana Mouskouri. But on many evenings, Poitier kept to himself as much as possible, sitting alone during meals, watching the white men around him from a distance. During one dinner break, recalls William Schallert, "I was sitting at the table with the actors playing the town council members, and one of the guys was talking about what his character would say, and he used the word *nigger*. Sidney Poitier overheard and came up to us, and he was very offended by it. Poitier wasn't thin-skinned, but he was keeping himself on edge. It was a misunderstanding and was cleared up easily, but it was indicative of a kind of heightened sensitivity."[26]

Poitier had pushed Jewison to cut as many uses of the word as he could, but he knew that it had to stay in the movie, and, helped by his costar, managed to draw on his own disgust and rage for his performance. "He and Rod Steiger developed a really good rapport," says Terry Morse. "We were on this little jail set for a scene between the two of them. We would do a master shot, and then Rod's close-up, and then Sidney's— and for Sidney's close-up, Rod would feed him his lines off camera with exactly the same intensity, just as loud and as fiercely as he had in his own close-up, and he would say, *'Nigger!'* just to get his eyes popping out. And it worked. After they were done, they grabbed each other and just laughed."[27]

Poitier also came to trust Jewison, and when the director asked him if he would be willing to travel to Dyersburg, Tennessee, for a week to shoot the scenes in which Gillespie and Tibbs drive past a cotton field and then confront the racist industrialist who practically owns the town, he agreed. Poitier had told Jewison about his brush with white racists in Mississippi—in fact, Jewison added a scene in which white drivers rear-end Tibbs's car and nearly run him off the road after he heard about Klansmen following Poitier and Belafonte—and the director promised him that the shoot would be done quickly, with no publicity, and with heavy security. "I promise you'll be protected," he said, "and I promise you we'll all stay together."[28]

Jewison booked the four actors he needed and the skeleton crew he planned to use into the Dyersburg Holiday Inn. Even in November 1966, "there was no other place we could find that accepted black people," he recalls. "The Holiday Inn only did because it was a national chain that had an integrated policy by then." The threat they all felt once they arrived in Tennessee was not imaginary. "Man, that was an experience for all of us," says Jewison. "Nobody down there knew what we were doing, but the moment they found out the movie was about a black detective and they saw Sidney Poitier in an expensive suit . . . it upset people. There were pickup trucks circling the hotel at night, people getting drunk, driving into the courtyard, that kind of thing."[29]

"Sidney was getting very uptight, and it was beginning to affect his concentration," said Steiger, who stayed in a room that was connected to Poitier's. "We'd go into a restaurant and they wouldn't say anything, but they'd put down the plate so loudly and rudely they wouldn't have to."[30] One night, a drunk in a pickup truck screeched into the hotel parking lot and started banging on doors, shouting that he was trying to find his wife. Poitier told Jewison he was sleeping with a gun under his pillow. "The first one who comes through my door," he warned the director, "I'm gonna blow him away." Jewison, having discovered that the local police were unwilling to provide any security, got a couple of Teamsters to scare the young man off and quickly made plans to scale back the shoot and get his cast and crew out of Dyersburg as quickly as possible.[31]

In the sequence shot in Tennessee, Haskell Wexler used long, slow pans to fill the frame with an archetypal southern landscape, as Gillespie and Tibbs drive down an empty stretch of road past a field where black workers in rags are picking cotton. "None of that for you, huh, Virgil?" Gillespie mutters, looking at them. Poitier looks at him with a calibrated expression of disbelief and resignation. Jewison didn't want the driving scene to use rear-projection photography; he needed to capture Poitier actually looking at the field workers. He shot quickly and unobtrusively. "We were not welcome," says Terry Morse. "Usually, whenever you go on location, the people from the town show up to see who's there. But we didn't even have to keep crowds away during the cotton scene. They just didn't want to see us. And we didn't want to be there. As we approached the mansion, we saw some cattle next door that we decided we wanted in the shot, and the owner of the cattle said, 'Just tell me when you want to shoot, and I'll move them so that they can be on camera.' So we were getting ready to do the shot, and I told him. And he turned around and yelled, 'Hey, nigger! Move those cattle over!'"[32]

The next scene Jewison filmed is *In the Heat of the Night*'s dramatic centerpiece. An elderly black butler named Henry ushers the two men into a greenhouse belonging to Mr. Endicott (played by Larry Gates, a New York television actor), a wealthy white bigot whom Tibbs believes knows something about the murder. What begins as a polite exchange of remarks about orchids turns ugly when Endicott compares the flowers to black people, who he says also require special "care and feeding." When Tibbs coolly asks him a question that makes it clear he considers him a suspect, Endicott walks up to him and gives him a backhand slap across the face. Tibbs returns the slap instantly, and hard.

Endicott staggers backward, then turns to Gillespie. "You saw it?" he says.

"I saw it," Gillespie replies.

"What are you gonna do about it?" says Endicott.

Gillespie's answer: "I don't know."

"We only did the slap twice," says Jewison. "I remember telling Sidney, 'You can let him have it as long as you don't whack him right across the ear.' And Larry Gates was wonderful. He said to Sidney, 'Don't worry about it—you hit me!' And they hit each other pretty good!"[33] But as the scene progressed, it was, surprisingly, Steiger who ran into trouble. He tried saying "I don't know" a dozen different ways. The line "drove Rod crazy," wrote Jewison. "Nothing he did with that short sentence made him happy. . . . 'Rod,' I said, 'the reason you say 'I don't know' is because you really *don't* know what to do. . . . It's a situation you've never confronted before.' . . . We tried the scene again, and Rod said the line as if Gillespie . . . has come to a turning point in his life."[34]

The grace note of the scene is delivered, silently, by Endicott's butler, who stands still, holding a tray of lemonade, and witnesses both slaps. After Tibbs and Gillespie leave, he looks at Endicott and exits with a magnificently ambiguous shake of his head. In an unheralded piece of casting, the butler was played by Jester Hairston, a sixty-five-year-old actor, songwriter, and choral arranger. Hairston's grandparents had been slaves; he had attended Tufts University, worked with Ethel Waters, helped to conduct the choir for the all-black musical *Green Pastures*, and spent sixteen years on the radio show *Amos 'n' Andy*. Hairston had suffered through every indignity show business could throw at him. "I was a native running around [in *Tarzan* pictures] with a ring in my nose," he told an interviewer later. "I was a witch doctor." On screen, the way Hairston shakes his head at Endicott connotes grave disapproval without specifying its target. But personally, Hairston knew exactly how he felt. "I looked as if to say to him, 'You old son of a bitch . . . ' I was disgusted with him smacking Sidney like that." It was a slap that Hairston had waited his entire career to see a black man return in kind.[35]

"We had a couple of pickup shots left to do down there," says Terry Morse. "But after that day, Norman said to Sidney, 'Let's get out of here—we can do some of these shots back in L.A.' And we got on a plane that night."[36]

EIGHTEEN

While Sidney Poitier was finishing *In the Heat of the Night*, Stanley Kramer was courting his costars for *Guess Who's Coming to Dinner*, which he now planned to direct in early 1967. Pulling the project together required a kind of diplomatic gamesmanship at which Kramer, as a veteran producer, was an expert: His plan was to convince Poitier that he already had Spencer Tracy and Katharine Hepburn lined up, tell Tracy and Hepburn that Poitier was eager to make a movie with them, inform Columbia Pictures that all three stars were ready to go, and conceal the full extent of the film's potentially controversial subject matter from the press until the contracts were executed and the money was committed.[1]

Kramer had approached Poitier before the actor left New York for Illinois, meeting him at the Russian Tea Room and pitching William Rose's script almost apologetically by saying, "Look, the revolution is only a backdrop with a thing like this. This is an inventive comedy, an . . . entertainment."[2] Kramer knew that Poitier would consider the chance to work with Tracy and Hepburn a much bigger inducement than the role of Prentice, which in Rose's most recent draft amounted to little more than a straight man around whom the other characters fluttered, stammered, and panicked. Poitier, who had almost never been offered an opportunity to act with stars of Hepburn and Tracy's generation and caliber, had hesitated only briefly. "I'm not in their league," he told Kramer. "I'd get stagestruck and forget my lines."[3] Nevertheless, he quickly agreed to take the part.

Kramer's steeper challenge would be to coax Hepburn and Tracy out of a retirement that neither of them had actually planned. Hepburn was fifty-nine in 1966; she had made just one picture, Sidney Lumet's *Long Day's Journey into Night,* in the last eight years. After the film's completion, she had drifted away from the movie business to spend time nursing Tracy, who was now sixty-six and had been in failing health for as long as Kramer had known him. "Spencer was sick—seriously sick—on every movie he and Stanley made," says Karen Kramer.[4]

What the American public knew, or thought it knew, about Hepburn and Tracy's relationship was, even in the mid-1960s, the result of years of meticulous image crafting by the old-Hollywood studio machine and a compliant press corps. People knew that the couple had made eight movies together, starting with 1942's *Woman of the Year.* They knew that Tracy was married, and Catholic, and long estranged from his wife, Louise. And they knew, if they were avid enough followers of the movie business to read fan magazines and gossip columns, that Hepburn was his companion and that she stoically refused to make their relationship evident in any way that might embarrass Tracy or his wife. It takes a remarkable degree of finesse and public relations savvy to earn respect for the discretion with which you conduct an affair that everyone seems to know all about, but Hepburn had, over the years, become a skillful curator of her own image. Rumors about her relationship with Tracy had been printed in tabloids since the late 1940s, but by the early 1960s, they began to seep into the legitimate press as well. A 1962 profile of Tracy in *Look* magazine was the first to suggest that he and Hepburn shared an "unorthodox private life" and that he was given to unexplained disappearances and bouts of gloom and anger.[5] Although Tracy did not speak about his relationship with Hepburn, his participation in the piece suggested his tacit approval of the information it contained. Other magazines pointedly refused to pick up on the story, but by 1963, the widely syndicated Hearst columnist Dorothy Kilgallen was writing openly about them: "Katharine Hepburn could have her choice of several important Broadway plays, but she's turning down all New York offers to stay near ailing Spencer Tracy in Hollywood. Her devotion to him for more than two decades has been absolutely self-less."[6] Hepburn rarely gave interviews in the early 1960s, nor did she speak publicly of her relationship with Tracy at that time, but sympathetic references to her self-denial and devotion still found their way into print with regularity.

Kilgallen's item was both true and incomplete. The public did not know that Tracy had been a blackout alcoholic for decades, that MGM had long kept a fake ambulance and paramedic costumes on hand in case the studio needed to haul him out of restaurants or public places when he threatened to cause a scene,[7] that Hepburn and Tracy may both have been bisexual,* and that the passionate affair that was alluded to with increasing frankness by columnists and interviewers was in reality an on-again, off-again union that had become, by the mid-1960s, a kind of platonic quasi-marriage between old companions. Nonetheless, Hepburn and Tracy's closeness and affection were not simply a cover story for less acceptable realities; by the time Kramer approached the couple with *Guess Who's Coming to Dinner,* she really was looking after him, living in a bungalow near his on George Cukor's estate, cooking him meals, and trying to rouse his spirits and keep him alive.

Tracy looked and felt fifteen years older than he was. Thirty years of drinking had ravaged him; he had suffered from heart disease for ten years, he had ongoing respiratory problems, and he had spent much of his adult life fighting through periods of annihilating depression. In 1963, after making *It's a Mad Mad Mad Mad World* for Kramer, he had been hospitalized for two weeks with what the press was told was pulmonary edema but may have been a heart attack,[8] and it had taken a year for him to recover. In 1965, he went into the hospital for prostate surgery and, again, nearly died; during his six weeks in intensive care, both Hepburn and Louise Tracy were at his bedside, each making sure she never overlapped with the other.[9] When Tracy was finally released from the hospital, he went back to his bungalow; in the last year, he had almost never ventured out of the

---

*The sexuality of Hepburn and, especially, Tracy remains a matter of controversy. In *Kate: The Woman Who Was Hepburn* (New York: Henry Holt, 2006), William J. Mann gives a scrupulously researched and balanced account of Hepburn's relationships with women and reports that Tracy may have had sex with men; the vehement disdain with which this possibility was greeted by some critics says much about the persistence of romantic embellishment that attaches itself to the history of Hepburn and Tracy and about the difficulty of sorting out fact, fantasy, and self-invention in their lives, especially since Hepburn herself, as she got older, proved to be such a deft retailer of all three.

house.[10] He couldn't even bring himself to watch old movies on TV. "I'm about the only one left," he said. "I can't watch Clark, and I can't watch Bogie. Maybe I'm just too conscious of time passing, especially since I got so ill. But I simply can't watch them. I'm too uncomfortable."[11] His discomfort was physical as well; there were days when he could barely catch his breath.

Hepburn had, as Kilgallen wrote, turned down work to be with Tracy, but not much had been offered; although her contemporaries Bette Davis, Joan Crawford, and Olivia de Havilland were all getting regular (if increasingly demeaning) work thanks to the spate of Grand Guignol horror movies that followed the success of *Whatever Happened to Baby Jane?*, Hepburn's record at the box office had always been spotty, and she had had only a couple of popular successes, 1951's *The African Queen* and 1959's *Suddenly, Last Summer* (the latter of which she loathed), in the last twenty years. Tracy, despite his illnesses, had been more visible in the last decade than she had; he and Hepburn both wanted to work, and he had been sober for years, but now he worried that his alcoholism had destroyed his ability to remember lines.[12] John Ford, an old friend, had offered Tracy a role in his 1964 western, *Cheyenne Autumn,* and Hepburn a part in 1966's *7 Women,*[13] but Tracy's poor health and Hepburn's unwillingness to be away from him prevented either of them from taking a job.

By the time Kramer approached Tracy, the director wrote in his autobiography, "I knew I would have to hurry . . . his health had deteriorated to such a degree that he spent most of his time . . . not bedridden, but house-ridden. He seemed to have too little energy left for normal exertion."[14] Tracy liked Kramer, and neither he nor Hepburn bore any ill will toward the director for not having used Tracy in *Ship of Fools;* he clearly would not have been able to play the role even if Kramer had given it to him. Kramer knew just how, and how hard, to pressure the actor. "Stanley could talk to Spence like they were brothers," says Karen Kramer. "No matter what Stanley was presented with [in terms of Tracy's health], he'd say, 'I'm gonna do it with him—we'll make it work.' Even in *Judgment at Nuremberg,* when the studio wanted James Stewart, Stanley would say, 'No, it has to be Spencer.' "[15] Other directors and producers assumed that Tracy was simply no longer functional; at the time Kramer approached him, the only other call he had gotten for a job was from William Dozier, the producer of ABC's campy, popular *Batman* series. "[He] said, 'Didn't I have a grandchild who'd get a kick out of seeing Grandpa as a cameo on *Batman*,'" grumbled the actor. "Wasn't even one of those villain things."[16]

Kramer urged Tracy to get out of the house and try some fresh air and exercise, a suggestion the actor brushed aside. He then told Tracy about the plot of *Guess Who's Coming to Dinner*, and the role he wanted him to play, Matt Drayton, a not-as-liberal-as-he-thinks-he-is newspaper editor in San Francisco. Tracy liked the story but insisted he couldn't take on that substantial a part. Years later, Kramer would tell one of Tracy's biographers that he roused the actor's competitive spirit by shrugging off his refusal and telling him that he would approach Fredric March (with whom Tracy had costarred in *Inherit the Wind*) instead.[17] If Kramer did say that, it was a bluff on which he never would have followed through; he was too aware of the iconic value that Tracy and Hepburn together would bring to the movie. "Stanley didn't want to do the movie without Spencer in it," says Karen Kramer. "But this time, Spencer said, 'I'm not well—I'm not gonna do it.' And Stanley said, 'So what are you going to do—sit there and rot in that chair? Or are you going to get up and do something that means something? If you're going to die, die *doing* something.'"[18]

It was Hepburn who cast what amounted to the tie-breaking vote by agreeing to costar in the movie herself and telling Kramer she would work on convincing Tracy to take the role. Kramer felt that "there might be two or three actresses who might be able to do this part," including Vivien Leigh,[19] but he and Rose knew that only Hepburn could deliver Tracy to them, and they had threaded a great deal of flattery into the script they showed her, introducing her character as "a woman of extraordinary grace, with a quality of charm beyond a hack's powers of description and a strange imperishable beauty so finely and precisely drawn that it would take an Augustus John to define it. She makes us realize that a part of Joey's luck is that one day she'll be like her mother."[20] Hepburn was sold. Tracy was embarrassed by his own fragility, but knowing that both Hepburn and Kramer would protect him on the set by keeping his working hours to a minimum each day, he finally gave in.[21] On September 26, 1966, *The New York Times* announced that "one of Hollywood's legendary

filmmaking teams and close friends in private life" would "come out of retirement" to costar with Poitier in the film.[22] Part of the immense amount
of anecdotal embellishment that accumulated around *Guess Who's Coming to Dinner* in the years after its release was the suggestion that Kramer
somehow tricked Columbia Pictures into bankrolling the movie by refusing to reveal its subject to the studio or by telling Columbia's board of
directors that the film was about an intermarriage between a Christian
and a Jew. In truth, Columbia knew exactly what the movie was about.
The studio expressed some mild concern about how *Guess Who's Coming
to Dinner* would play in the South, but, as Walter Mirisch had done when
he was planning *In the Heat of the Night*, they calculated that by keeping
expenses low, they could make back their money if the movie performed
strongly in other parts of the country. The picture's "racial theme" was announced right along with the casting. As long as Kramer kept his budget
under $3 million, he would be able to make his movie.

The often repeated account of what followed in the months before the
production of *Guess Who's Coming to Dinner* illustrates Kramer's aptitude
for turning the story behind a movie's production into a dramatic struggle
designed to enhance the reputation of the film itself. As Hollywood lore
has it, once Columbia found out that the film was about interracial marriage, the studio decided it had to be scuttled and used Tracy's poor health,
which rendered him uninsurable, as an excuse to cancel the production.
Only at the last minute was Kramer able to save the film by going to Hepburn and telling her that he would agree to defer his entire salary if she
would defer hers; their pact thus reduced the financial risk to Columbia
and essentially shamed the studio into proceeding.

But it's hardly likely that Mike Frankovich or Columbia's board of directors, looking at the millions of dollars that had been earned by MGM's
interracial relationship drama *A Patch of Blue*, would suddenly have been
stricken with terror at the subject matter of a Stanley Kramer movie. What
really happened seems to have been a matter of business negotiation
rather than high drama. The studio was legitimately worried about Tracy's
health, and about the money it might lose if he died during production
and Kramer had to recast the role with another actor. But by early November 1966, deal memos were already in place that reduced Columbia's

risk considerably. Tracy was to receive top billing and be paid $200,000, not a cent of it up front—he would receive $50,000 upon completion of principal photography, $75,000 a year later, and the balance a year after that. He would not be covered by cast insurance, and, in a line that suggests how well-known in the industry Tracy's alcoholism, sudden disappearances, and relationship with Hepburn had become by then, the studio noted that "we have agreed to delete the morals clause per Tracy's previous contracts." Hepburn was to receive $150,000 in three installments; like Tracy, she would see no money until the end of production. Hepburn also agreed to shoulder the expenses caused by any delays in shooting because of Tracy's health and to surrender her own salary entirely if the film had to be reshot with another actor, even if she chose to remain in her role. Poitier, already a bigger box office star than either of them, was offered the richest deal in the cast: $225,000, with weekly expenses that would bring his pay up to $250,000, plus a guarantee of 9 percent of the film's profits and billing above Hepburn.[23]

For producing and directing *Guess Who's Coming to Dinner,* Stanley Kramer would be paid $500,000. When Tracy's health worsened suddenly in early 1967, Kramer agreed to defer that payment until completion of principal photography. It was money he needed badly, since the years of financial failures in the 1960s had affected him personally: Kramer's net worth at the end of 1966 was just over $100,000.[24] His gesture did save the film, but it made a less vivid anecdote than the story of Katharine Hepburn taking his suggestion and making a gallant last-minute sacrifice—when in fact the deferral of her salary was a pragmatic business decision she had made on her own months earlier. It was an impression Hepburn herself never chose to correct.

The same week that Columbia announced the cast of *Guess Who's Coming to Dinner,* Jack Valenti unveiled the drastic overhaul of the Production Code that he had promised when he took office in the summer. The Code had barely recovered from the blow it had been dealt by *Who's Afraid of Virginia Woolf?* when it lost another battle, this time with Paramount, over the British film *Alfie,* a dark comedy in which Michael Caine played a young, caddish Brit bedding one London "bird" after another. In the movie, one of Alfie's conquests becomes pregnant and has an abortion, a violation of a Code regulation that specifically prohibited abortion as a plotline. Geoffrey Shurlock had denied the film a Code seal, but the Code's review board had overruled him, and once again, the National Catholic Office for Motion Pictures, now worried that even its own diocesan newspapers were giving good reviews to films it had rated "Condemned," had decided to pass the movie with a rating of "A-IV" ("morally unobjectionable for adults—with reservations").[25] Like *Virginia Woolf, Alfie* was now headed toward a Best Picture nomination, and the old Code was looking more irrelevant every day.

A revised set of standards sounded like a step in the right direction, but it took only the length of a single press conference to reveal that Valenti's new Code was going to create at least as many problems as it would solve. The overhauled Code did offer one significant innovation, formalizing a new designation: "Suggested for Mature Audiences." The new label was the first official step in changing the spectrum of self-regulation from "approval" and "disapproval" into a system aimed primarily at providing information to parents—in essence, the "Mature Audiences" tag invented a class of films that could be approved without being deemed suitable for children.[26] But in every other regard, the revised Code merely disguised old problems with new language. Every screenplay would still have to be submitted to the Code authority and judged using an unintentionally hilarious multipage chart called "Analysis of Film Content." "Check this column if professional character is *inefficient* and *dishonest* in the performance of his professional duties," it read. "Is violence depicted? If so, in which form?" Diligent readers of the screenplay for *Guess Who's Coming to Dinner,* for example, would then be able to choose from Shooting, Knifing, Sword Play, Strangling, Torture, Fist Fight, Flogging, War, and Other.[27] The new Code was shorter, but only because it replaced specifics with generalities—ten semicommandments with vague phrasing along the lines of "The basic dignity and value of human life shall be respected and upheld," "Illicit sex relationships shall not be justified," and "Indecent or undue exposure of the human body shall not be presented."[28] When reporters started asking for definitions of "illicit," "indecent," and "undue,"

Valenti, Shurlock, and Louis Nizer all but admitted that the lack of clarity was intentional, a means of allowing filmmakers more latitude while at least temporarily maintaining the Code's putative final word on content. "Could bare breasts be deemed indecent in one film and decent in another?" Valenti mused in front of the assembled press. "Yes."[29]

That answer sealed the new Code's fate before it was even applied to a single film. By trying to retain the notion that movies could win approval by following a single set of rules while admitting that each case would be a judgment call, Valenti invited every filmmaker to push the envelope on the basis of artistic merit. The blurriness of the new Code was certainly good news for Mike Nichols and Buck Henry, whose plans for *The Graduate* included a scene in which Mrs. Robinson, completely nude, would lock Benjamin Braddock in her daughter's bedroom. "Shock cuts" to Mrs. Robinson's bare breasts, each lasting just a fraction of a second, would have been unimaginable three years earlier, when Larry Turman bought Charles Webb's novel; now, for the first time, it might be possible to make the adult sex comedy that Nichols had seen in the material all along.

But that fall, *The Graduate* seemed scarcely any closer to the start of production than it had been a year and a half earlier, when Nichols had temporarily left it behind to make *Virginia Woolf*. Nichols, Turman, and Henry were still stumbling over the casting of the family they had come to refer to as the Surfboards; partly because Webb himself was tall, light-haired, and preppy-looking, they had never quite been able to clear their minds of a certain WASP prototype. "Blond, all the way," says Buck Henry. "Sand in the genes, the roar of the ocean—the ideal young couple. We talked about more names than I could remember in ten years. We literally had the master blond list."[30] Over and over, they would return to the idea of Doris Day and Ronald Reagan as the Robinsons and, as Benjamin and Elaine, Robert Redford and Candice Bergen, visually unsurpassable representations of the sun-kissed Southern California children of overprivilege whom Nichols and Henry were so intent on skewering. Nichols had liked Redford since directing him on Broadway in *Barefoot in the Park* and had offered him the role of Nick, the young professor, in *Who's Afraid of Virginia Woolf?* Redford disliked the character's weakness and declined the film,[31] one in a series of poor choices he had made in the last couple of years: In *Inside Daisy Clover,* he costarred with Natalie Wood as a bisexual actor whose bisexuality was snipped out of the film's final cut,[32] and his back-to-back performances in the southern dramas *The Chase* and *This Property Is Condemned* had done little for his reputation. Now his movie career seemed to be on the upswing again: He had just finished the movie version of *Barefoot in the Park* opposite Jane Fonda, and he had tested with Bergen for the role of Benjamin Braddock, which he wanted badly.

Nichols, who had championed the idea, surprised himself by turning the actor down. "We were friends, we had done *Barefoot,* I was playing pool with him, and I said, 'I'm really sad, but you can't do it. You can't play a loser,' " says Nichols. "He said, 'Of course I can play a loser!' I said, 'You can't! Look at you! How many times have you ever struck out with a woman?' And he said, I swear to you, 'What do you mean?' He didn't even understand the concept. To him, it was like saying, 'How many times have you been to a restaurant and not had a meal?' "

But the problem was as much with Nichols as with Redford. "I couldn't be satisfied," says the director. "Whoever Benjamin was, I couldn't find him. I thought I was looking for someone who could handle the comedy and that *that* was the problem. But everyone I'd see, I'd think, 'He doesn't look like Benjamin.' Whatever the fuck I was looking for."[33]

Nor was the *Graduate* team making any headway casting Mrs. Robinson. As it had for Benton and Newman on *Bonnie and Clyde,* the influence of *Jules and Jim* loomed large for Nichols and Turman, and at one point they approached Jeanne Moreau, ready to reimagine Mrs. Robinson as a Frenchwoman. She said no. "I refused the part—the woman who is jealous of her daughter," she said later. "When I think about it, it was a mistake."[34] Nichols never considered Elizabeth Taylor ("She would have been way too young, but also superhuman—Mrs. Robinson had to be human and full of flaws").[35] He was still tantalized by the image-demolishing impact of casting Doris Day, but Day's husband and manager, Marty Melcher, wouldn't even show her the script.[36] And he was very serious about giving the role to Patricia Neal, the Oscar-winning costar of *Hud.* But Neal was still recovering from two devastating strokes she had suffered in early

1965 while filming John Ford's 7 *Women*,* and felt she wouldn't be up to such a demanding part.[37]

The strangest and saddest encounter Nichols had was probably with Ava Gardner, who was then coming to the end of her years as a self-invented movie siren. Gardner was only forty-three but already seemed like a relic of a fading Hollywood universe. "I was in New York, and my secretary said, 'Mike, Ava Gardner's calling.' I picked up the phone and a secretary said, 'Mr. Nichols, Miss Gardner's on the phone. And Mr. Nichols, this is *your* call.' I said, 'Excuse me?' And she said, 'This is your call. *You* are calling Miss *Gardner*.' I said, 'Okay. . . .' She got on the phone and said, 'I want to see you! I want to talk about this *Graduate* thing! Come and see me! We're at the St. Regis. Come at two.' I hung up, the phone rings, it's her secretary again, and she says, 'Uh, Mr. Nichols, we're at the *Regency*.' I thought, 'Oh God, this is gonna be hard.'

"There was this huge suite, and there were actual lounge lizards, like in bad movies of hers, guys with slicked-back hair and pinstripe suits and cigarettes—quite a lot of them. And to my horror, as I walked in, she said, 'All right! Everybody out! Out! Out! I want to talk to my director.' And I thought, 'Oh, help.' She sat at a little French desk with a telephone, she went through every movie star cliché. She said, 'All right, let's talk about your movie. First of all, I strip for nobody.' I said, 'That's fine, I don't think that's a problem, Miss Gardner.'" Then the actress's demeanor abruptly changed, as if she were letting a mask fall away. She said, 'You know, the thing is . . . I can't act. They've all tried. Huston, all of them. I just can't act.' I said, 'I beg to differ. I think you're a great movie actress.' She said, 'No, I just can't.' I never forgot it. She really got to me. But, obviously, she couldn't be Mrs. Robinson."[38]

With nobody yet cast, Nichols returned to Broadway and spent the fall of 1966 at the Shubert Theatre, directing Alan Alda, Barbara Harris, and Larry Blyden in the musical *The Apple Tree*. Nichols brought in Herbert Ross to help stage the numbers and could at least take comfort in the fact that somebody else's movie was in bigger trouble than his own: After six

---

*Ford replaced her with Anne Bancroft.

months, Ross was still working on *Doctor Dolittle* for Arthur Jacobs and was increasingly grim about the ordeal. "He was dividing his time," says Nichols. "He'd come to New York and he'd work, say, Friday, Saturday, Sunday, and half of Monday, and then he'd go back to Los Angeles and the movie. One week he flew off, and we were rehearsing the next day, and suddenly he comes back strolling across the stage. I said, 'Herbert, what happened?' And he said, 'We're postponed for three days. The giraffe stepped on his cock.' "[39]

The giraffe, just before his rumored injury, had made the cover of *Life* magazine in a publicity coup engineered by Jacobs that showed a cheerful Rex Harrison astride the animal, doffing his top hat to the camera. The image was planned as the centerpiece of the ad campaign for *Dolittle,* even though the movie was not scheduled to open for more than a year. The story inside acknowledged the film's high budget but made little mention of the troubles that had beset Richard Fleischer and his crew.[40]

In Los Angeles, the *Dolittle* team was pressing on—but without Jacobs. In early October, as he was preparing to leave London, the producer suffered a major heart attack. Get-well wishes and telegrams poured into the hospital, not just from his colleagues on the movie, but from Elizabeth Taylor, Richard Burton, and many in both old and new Hollywood who had gotten to know Jacobs during his years as an endearingly manic PR whiz. "Please stop running around like a man who hasn't got a picture to produce," Anthony Newley wrote to him. "Take this warning seriously," Leslie Bricusse cabled. "You have so much to look forward to in your life and your career. Everything you have worked for is now happening. You just have to be here to enjoy it." Dick Zanuck cabled Jacobs, telling him to get well by thinking about beautiful women. Jacobs, who had been single all his life but was now enjoying the company of a pretty, much younger aspiring actress named Natalie Trundy, told Zanuck that that's what had gotten him into trouble in the first place. "Then think of ugly girls," Zanuck cabled back.[41]

Jacobs's physicians told him he needed to lose weight, and he took their advice, but he wasn't willing to listen to any other warnings. "The first thing he said to the doctor was, 'How soon can I have a drink and a cigarette?' " says Trundy. "The doctor said, 'Mr. Jacobs, you may have a drink, but don't smoke.' But as soon as he could, he got the nurses to go downstairs and get him a pack of cigarettes."[42]

Jacobs pushed hard to keep his illness out of the press[43] and to get back to the set of *Dolittle* quickly. Doctors finally allowed him to leave London, arming Trundy with "a bottle of nitroglycerin tablets to put under his tongue and a packet of something like Demerol that I was supposed to inject him with in case he started to falter on the plane."[44] For several weeks after Jacobs returned to the United States, he was ordered to stay at home in bed, a wise move since what he would have seen on the Fox lot was a chaotic production that was falling further behind each day. "One of the main sets was Doctor Dolittle talking to the animals in his home," recalls set decorator Stuart Reiss, "and in case the animals made a mess, which they did, whether it was a bird or a cow, we had to have the set built on a slant so it could drain. We had laborers standing by with brooms constantly. All of the fabrics had to be plastic or painted so they wouldn't stain. The furniture had to look upholstered, but we couldn't use wool. Every night we had to take everything out and hose it down, drain it, and dry it. And we had to have duplicates of everything, even the walls, in case a big animal backed up into it or kicked it."[45]

The smell, both of animal waste and of the gallons of ammonia used to clean the sets, was unbearable, as was the nonstop noise. Birds were tethered to rails, but several of them escaped, flying up into the netting at the top of the soundstage, where they became entangled and rescue was impossible. The actors were enduring terrible conditions as they shuttled between the Fox lot and the Jungleland ranch, where some shooting was now being done on the sets where the animals had been trained, to avoid the expense of rebuilding them in the studio. "I loved being around the animals," says Eggar, "especially Gyp the dog and Chee-Chee the chimpanzee—well, one of the Chee-Chees. But then the trainers got hepatitis [from being bitten by animals] three times. So we were always being jabbed with these enormous great big long injection needles."[46]

A degree of rancor was beginning to become apparent even in the *Dolittle* media blitz. Bricusse broke what had been a tacit code of silence by calling Rex Harrison a "bully" and a "snob" in a *New York Times* interview and also by remarking, "Last week the producer called me up and said blandly, 'Cut $1.5 million out of the budget by Thursday.' "[47] That may have been true, but by the fall of 1966, *Doctor Dolittle*'s budget was, despite Jacobs's entreaties, going up, not down. When the crew had returned from Castle Combe, they had hoped to finish everything they needed to shoot on the lot and then fly to St. Lucia, the Caribbean island that was to double for Africa, where Doctor Dolittle sails on his ship, the *Flounder*, in the second half of the movie. But wrapping the California shoot in time had become impossible; they would now have to leave for St. Lucia in October, shoot there for several weeks, and return to Los Angeles one more time to complete the movie on the lot in early 1967.

Some at 20th Century-Fox advised scrapping the St. Lucia shoot altogether, since the island did not offer a climate that was any more welcoming than Castle Combe's had been. "I think it is essential . . . that we consider ways and means of doing some of the Flounder work on the stage [in Los Angeles]," warned Stan Hough, the head of Fox's Production Department, in a September memo. "Even if we go to St. Lucia, I think it is very possible, in view of the weather reports . . . that we would be forced to do some shooting back here."[48] Hough's warnings were ignored; Fleischer wanted as much of *Dolittle* shot on location as possible, and an advance team flew to St. Lucia in mid-October, with the actors preparing to follow them at the end of the month. Harrison would live on a yacht, where he would be joined by Rachel Roberts, and Anthony Newley made plans to bring his wife, Joan Collins, and their two young children on what sounded like a pleasant tropical adventure. A telegram from unit production manager William Eckhardt quickly dissuaded him. "Recommend Newley should not bring children," he wrote. "Insect terrible from very wet summer STOP everyone covered in welts and sores two people bad infections from bites STOP six people ill last week from dysentery." The cable went on to implore Fox's L.A. office to charter a small cargo plane and send twelve dozen cans of insect repellent immediately.[49]

The shoot in St. Lucia turned out to be even more of a horror than the crew had anticipated, and not just because of the swarms of stinging insects, or the tropical storms that seemed to shut down production every second day, or the fleas that lived in the sand that the *Dolittle* crew had found on a remote part of the island and trucked to the set by the ton because they liked its pinkish color.[50] As filming in St. Lucia dragged on, Harrison sank into an especially foul temper, and the rift between him and his younger costars was now irreparable. "I often had a wonderful time with Rex," says Eggar. "I mean, yes, he was unkind and vitriolic and very mean-spirited, but he was also very funny—until, of course, he turned on me, too. Rex separated himself from all us. In St. Lucia he rented a beautiful three-masted schooner that sat off in the bay while we were all in the hotel, and that was his fault. I mean, part of it was an age thing—he did think that we were incredibly stupid and called us that many times."[51] Newley became a particular target of Harrison's: Insults like "Cockney Jew" and "sewer rat" started to fly more frequently.[52] At one point months into the St. Lucia shoot, Fleischer was filming a scene with Newley on the water; Harrison ruined the shot by steering his schooner into camera range and refusing to move it for two hours.[53]

"That was more why we ganged up on him," says Eggar, "his despicable treatment of Tony. Tony's relationship with Leslie [Bricusse] played like the black night in Rex's psyche. . . . He didn't have a friend, and he didn't have anyone to bounce his fears off of. And as with all insecure bullies, they lash out. It's only once you stand up to them that they back down. And nobody stood up to him."[54]

"Rex was a terrific asset," says producer Mort Abrahams. "but you never knew which Rex you were meeting in the morning when you came to the set. He was so volatile."[55]

Harrison's mood only seemed to worsen once Roberts, still drinking heavily and more unstable than ever, flew down from New York. When Geoffrey Holder, who had been hired to play William Shakespeare X (an altered, greatly abridged reconception of the character of Bumpo), arrived on the island, he was already on his guard: The Trinidad-born actor-director-choreographer had little patience for any behavior that had a whiff of British colonialism or racism. Roberts was rude to him almost immediately ("I don't have to talk to you, do I?" she asked him by way of introduction), and during a cocktail party given for the cast and crew on Harrison's yacht, Holder had a run-in with a young member of Harrison's entourage. "I'm standing on the deck, all dressed up, and I see St. Lucians loading a banana boat with bananas. And this English girl says to me, 'How do you like being on *this* side of the boat?' Well, what could I expect."

Harrison and Roberts spent most evenings boozing and brawling, and their high-volume showdowns, which carried across the water, became the subject of daily gossip. "She was an alcoholic, he was whatever he was, and they were fighting like cats and dogs. The caretakers of the seals would come running out thinking the animals were making noise, but it was Rex and Rachel," says Holder.[56] One night, Roberts faked a suicide attempt by leaving her shoes on the deck, wrapping her clothes around a log, screaming, and throwing it into the bay;[57] on another evening, she got drunk and jumped into the water, swimming as fast as she could toward the seal tank with the intention of freeing them. "We should have taken out an insurance policy against your fucking wife!" Jacobs later told his star.[58]

By late November, the shoot was already estimated to be thirty-nine days behind schedule,[59] and Fleischer and Mort Abrahams started making plans to postpone even more of the remaining production until what would now be an extended Los Angeles shoot at the beginning of 1967. Most of the actors got sick at least once in St. Lucia; William Dix, the ten-year-old English boy playing Matthew Mugg's pal Tommy Stubbins, got the flu, and Newley was hit particularly hard. "I told you don't drink [the] water," Joan Collins cabled him. "Shape up, ace!"[60] Newley missed so many days that at one point Jacobs wrote to him, "One more illness and Norman Wisdom steps in . . . with new music by Lionel Bart."[61] Even a scene as innocuous as the movie's planned finale, in which Dolittle and his friends were to sail away in a giant pink sea snail, managed to generate a catastrophe when local St. Lucians, whose children had recently been plagued by a persistent gastrointestinal illness caused by freshwater snails, took the construction of the giant snail ship off the beach as an insult and threw rocks at it.[62]

Jacobs, still on the mend, was alarmed by some of the footage he was seeing as it was shipped back to Los Angeles. He told Abrahams that he was "devastated" by the garish plastic look of the sea snail, complaining, "How is it possible to go so far wrong from what we saw in the prop shop? Even in black and white long shots it does not look right, so certainly in seventy [millimeter] it will look worse."[63]

Bricusse, vacationing on Dorado Beach in Puerto Rico and happy not to be a part of the "Devil's Island existence"[64] his friend Newley was enduring on St. Lucia, was finally free of *Doctor Dolittle* after eighteen months of work—at least, so he thought. Dick Zanuck, impressed with his endurance and flexibility, offered him a job writing the screenplay for Fox's other big 1967 production, *Valley of the Dolls,* but Bricusse passed;[65] "247,659 pages of screenplay and four thousand songs," he told Jacobs, were enough for him.[66] But he had time to draft one more number, just for the eyes of the eternally optimistic producer whom everyone called Apjac, to be sung to the tune of *The Sound of Music*'s "Sixteen, Going on Seventeen":

> The budget's sixteen,
> Going on seventeen
> Apjac, it's time to think
> Better beware
> Be canny and careful
> Apjac, we're on the brink.
>
> When it was thirteen
> Going on fourteen
> Everyone wore a smile.
> Let's stop pretending—
> You started spending—
> Like it was out of style.
>
> Totally unprepared were you
> For rain in Castle Combe
> Timid and shy and scared are you
> When entering Zanuck's room
> To tell him
> Now it's nineteen going on twenty
> Please will you sign those checks?
> Though this film is costing us plenty
> Most of it goes to Rex![67]

NINETEEN

In his room at the North Park Motor Inn in Dallas, Robert Towne spent most of his evenings writing. Every morning, he waited in the motel parking lot with the rest of *Bonnie and Clyde*'s cast and crew for the buses to come and drive them several miles to that day's location. The farther they got from Dallas, the more arid, semiabandoned hamlets they'd find—each with its hollowed-out two-story buildings, a beauty parlor, and a luncheonette opening onto a mostly empty town square, all of which were largely unchanged since the depths of the Depression.[1] "Pilot Point Is Proud to Have Been Selected to Participate in 'Bonnie and Clyde,'" cheered one local newspaper ad, in which local businessmen pooled their dollars to run a picture of the present-day town in order to reassure readers that it was now "peaceful."[2] "All the young people had left," says Estelle Parsons. "These towns were really finished. Each one had one coffee shop, full of old men, just sitting around."[3]

Sometimes Arthur Penn and Warren Beatty would find themselves shooting near the same streets where, thirty-three years earlier, Bonnie Parker and Clyde Barrow had become famous. Bystanders would shyly introduce themselves, and every one of them had a story: The middle-aged woman in white gloves was a little girl who saw Bonnie and Clyde run out of the bank and jump into their getaway car; the man standing off to one side waiting to meet Penn was Clyde Barrow's nephew Duryl. What had seemed to Robert Benton and David Newman to be a story carved out of

the French New Wave and American pop-cultural debris—gangster movies, detective magazines, comic strips—was, to the local Texans who kept
showing up, just a part of their history, a brush with notoriety that had
taken place not so long ago. "Life was shaping art," Towne wrote later.
"Warren and Faye were not working on Bonnie and Clyde. Bonnie and
Clyde were working on them."[4] Towne wasn't doing a lot of on-the-spot
rewriting, although on many afternoons he'd leave shooting early to go
back to the motel and fine-tune a scene that Penn and Beatty were planning to film the next day.[5] "Robert, why don't you come down to Dallas
while we're doing the movie?" Beatty had said to him. "We can work on
Shampoo while we're there."[6] It had sounded like a reasonable idea. But
as the autumn days rolled by and *Shampoo* remained largely untouched,
Towne started to realize why he was really in Texas: His job was to listen
to Beatty and Penn fight.

"I can be obnoxious," says Beatty. "And I knew that I would be hard
to take in a one-on-one dialectic with Arthur, that finally he would say, 'I
just can't take it anymore.' Three heads are better than two, because if
two people disagree, it's more possible for it to become personal. You need
someone to say, 'Hey, schmuck!' So Robert really was very helpful when
we were kicking things around. He made the arguments, which I would
prefer to call discussions, very productive."[7]

"I would call it fighting," says Estelle Parsons. "Every morning we
would go to work, and Warren and Arthur would fight for half an hour
or an hour. We would be all ready to go and they would start serious,
professional, artistic fighting. I remember that when Gene [Wilder] and
Evans [Evans] came to do their scene, Gene said, 'My God, is this movie
ever going to get made? What's going on here? What are they doing?' We
laughed because we were so used to this happening that we'd forgotten
they did it by then. And those fights—the creative energy of them—were
so important to the movie."[8]

"Was it tense? Are you kidding? It was excruciating!" says script supervisor John Dutton. "Beatty used to ask these questions of Penn that
would sound silly, but there was always something behind it. He was fish-
ing for something."[9]

Beatty had tried to plan his entire career by studying the work of directors he admired, but as *Bonnie and Clyde*'s producer, suddenly he was feeling impatient with auteurism. "To attribute [movies] wholly to their directors—not to the actors, not to the producer, not [to] the leading lady . . . well, that's bullshit!" he fumed. "Those pictures were made by directors, writers, and sound men and cameramen and actors and so forth, but suddenly, it's 'Otto Preminger's *Hurry Sundown*.' . . . It's not healthy."[10] Beatty and Penn's discussions often concerned aspects of the script as small as which word in a line should be emphasized or as unquantifiable as the tone of a particular moment. A flourish, a camera angle, a reaction, a grace note—no issue was too trivial to stop both men in their tracks. "What else is making a movie," Beatty said, "except attention to detail?"[11]

Although he was Penn's boss, Beatty knew better than to tell him how to direct, at least most of the time. "He was always at Arthur Penn's ear about everything," says production designer Dean Tavoularis. "The wardrobe, a dolly shot, when to change a setup—he was hands-on, a very active producer. But I would never describe it as unfriendly."[12] Frequently, the conflicts would be put on hold only because shooting had to begin or the day would be lost completely; that night at dinner, Beatty and Penn would start again, often calling Towne over to step in and to take notes. "They were burning the midnight oil on that thing," says Dutton. "They'd come out with new pages every day."[13]

Penn and Beatty's relationship during the shoot never fractured; although Penn says that "very difficult situations emerged almost daily," Beatty usually knew when to quit pressing a point, perhaps because there was no producer around to stop him but himself. "The fact that Warren had nursed this material, that it was within his control, paradoxically allowed him to give up control more easily to a director," says Towne. "He picked Arthur, and he trusted Arthur more easily than he would have if he had had to just show up for a director as an employee—he had done that before, and it hadn't worked for him."[14]

Penn and Beatty had far more to contend with than their own disputes: *Bonnie and Clyde* was not one of those shoots in which a remote location and a lack of local entertainment foster a spirit of camaraderie. Estelle Parsons was quarreling with her on-screen husband, Gene Hackman, who was nursing his own resentments and grudges. The maverick Tavoularis was at loggerheads with the crusty, aging cinematographer Burnett Guffey. And Faye Dunaway's taut nerves and shaky emotional state were evident to everyone from the day she showed up on the set.

When Dunaway was cast, Penn and Beatty had worried about the weight she had put on during her unhappy stretch working for Preminger, and Penn told her she'd have to slim down. Just hours before Dunaway met Penn and Beatty, she had been at the beach with director Curtis Hanson, then a young film journalist and photographer, and the photographs he had taken of her that day convinced Beatty and Penn that they had made the right choice. "She was very overweight," said Hanson, "but the way I shot her, backlit with her hair back, she looked softer and thinner." But the actress, having been turned into a blond sex kitten for *The Happening* and then a drab farmwife for *Hurry Sundown*, was already insecure about her appearance, and the suggestion that she might not be physically attractive enough to play Bonnie was devastating to her. ("She doesn't look like much," an indifferent Beatty told Hanson when she was cast.)[15] In the few weeks before production started, Dunaway worked relentlessly to lose twenty-five pounds. By the time she arrived in Texas, she was rail-thin and both physically and emotionally fragile. "She went on a starvation diet," says Penn. "I mean, not eating anything."[16]

In her autobiography, Dunaway insists that she "spent weeks walking around my apartment and working out wearing a twelve-pound weight belt, with smaller weights around my wrists,"[17] but several people who worked with her on *Bonnie and Clyde* say she was also taking diet pills, a far more common way for an actress to lose weight in the preaerobics era. "What she went through . . . " says Theodora Van Runkle. "Once I took one of her diet pills and I stayed awake for *days*. You couldn't have any fat on you at all—it was just awful. So for actresses back then, it meant diet pills, water-retention pills, all that stuff. And remember, she was next to Warren, who was terribly pretty himself. It wasn't easy for her."[18] Beatty's assistant Elaine Michea remembers that Dunaway lost so much additional weight during the shoot that Van Runkle's costumes for her had to be resewn. " 'Fadin' Away.' That's what we used to call Faye on the set, she was so thin," says Dutton.[19]

Dunaway didn't have a lot of friends on the set; she blew hot and cold with the crew depending on her mood, and they noticed. Her self-absorption worked both for and against her. On screen, she seems almost electrically charged as Bonnie, deeply in touch with the character's restlessness, her desire to escape from her slow life and into a fast car, her hunger for thrills, her need to dramatize herself, and the speed with which her giddiness can turn to terror or anger; she channeled whatever anxiety or fear she was feeling off camera right into her performance. "I often say that the last role I played that really touched me and where I was able to access what I really am was Bonnie," she said thirty-five years later, "which is kind of sad when you think about how early in my career that was."[20] At its strongest, Dunaway's connection to the "yearning, edgy, ambitious southern girl who wanted to get out" was uncanny. "I knew everything about wanting to get out," she wrote. "Arthur . . . said he always felt in working with me that my talent was crying out for expression, and I was crying out for fame."[21] But Dunaway tried everyone's patience getting there. "Nobody was too keen on Faye," recalls Parsons. "We were all kind of annoyed with her. We'd be ready to do a shot, and Faye would need the makeup woman. We'd be all set to roll, and oops, Faye would have to have her hair combed. There was a lot of that. We'd go in early to get made-up, five or six in the morning, and she'd be there with rock and roll blaring. Listen, that was the way she kept herself going. She's got a temperament, but I love her, and I understand the way she is. Don't get me started on being a woman in a situation like that."[22]

Dunaway's lowest moment came after the first time Arthur Penn showed dailies to the cast. The actress had never seen herself on screen before—when she began shooting *Bonnie and Clyde* in the fall of 1966, she hadn't even had an opportunity to look at footage of herself in *The Happening* or *Hurry Sundown*. The rushes were "the first time I ever got a sense of how I must look to other people," she wrote.[23] The experience demolished what little confidence she had; she broke down, overwhelmed by the feeling that she was "ugly," and spiraled into a three-day depression during which she sat "silent, sullen, morose" in a hay field, talking to no one. (By some accounts, she was briefly hospitalized.)[24] "After that, I sort of closed the dailies," says Penn. "Actors can't look at themselves—all they can see is flaws. I have never done it again."[25]

When Dunaway emerged from her despair, she was somewhat less mercurial and more focused on business—including her interactions with Beatty, which surprised almost everyone who assumed that, given the actor's track record, a romance with his costar would be a foregone conclusion. "He was acting and he was producing," says Tavoularis. "That was what he had his mind on."[26] Even when talking about their sex scenes, Beatty kept his flirting in check. At the end of a long day's shoot, Dunaway and John Dutton were relaxing at the North Park Motor Inn when Beatty, his mind already on the next day's schedule, said to her, as if checking off items on a list, "We need to talk about the before-fuck and the after-fuck."[27] That was about as romantic as things got. "We had a tacit understanding that we'd simply remain friends," said Dunaway later.[28]

"Listen, she was . . . I . . . I like anybody who's working hard," says Beatty. "She was never dismissive or bored. I think it was hard for her. Because she was not used to this, and I think she saw that something was maybe gonna happen here. You get all tense if you're a thoroughbred and you know it's a big race. But you put the result first."[29]

To some extent, Beatty had only himself to blame for the less-than-cheerful atmosphere on *Bonnie and Clyde*, since he had assembled a creative team with nothing to lose, but also little reason for optimism. "Get 'em when they're down!" says Towne. "Gene [Hackman] didn't have anything going on, Arthur had just come off some damn mess [*The Chase*]. Warren's attitude very often was, Get somebody who's really talented at a point when they're going to be more pliant or malleable than they might otherwise be. And very often that's after a shaky or bad experience."[30] Beatty himself had just taken another pounding: *Kaleidoscope*, his attempt at a Bond-lite caper, had not fulfilled Jack Warner's prophecy of success. Worse, it had only reinforced its leading man's status as a pretty-boy actor in search of an identity. "Beatty tries so hard to act like Sean Connery that once or twice he almost develops a line in his face," smirked *Time*'s reviewer.[31] Any hope that a hit for Beatty might have loosened the studio's purse strings when it came to *Bonnie and Clyde* was gone: The film was budgeted so tightly that there wasn't even money for Van Runkle to come to the set, and other than the costumes worn by Beatty and Dunaway, the clothes came straight out of the studio's warehouse of used goods. "I wore

"The boys": *Bonnie and Clyde* screenwriters David Newman (left) and Robert Benton in New York City. *Warner Bros./Photofest*

"I was still the only one": Sidney Poitier backstage with Anne Bancroft at the Academy Awards after winning the Best Actor Oscar for *Lilies of the Field* in 1964. *Julian Wasser/Time Life Pictures/ Getty Images*

Warren Beatty cocks his pistol: "At a certain point," says Robert Towne, "no one can know the depth of that man's persuasiveness."
Condé Nast Archive/Corbis

Dunaway as Bonnie: "You see people who are great beauties and never get anywhere," says costume designer Theadora Van Runkle. "This was *style*."
Warner Bros./Photofest

Beatty, Dunaway, and Arthur Penn on the *Bonnie and Clyde* set. "There was nobody who was saying, 'Hey, it's just a movie, what do you want from me?' " says Beatty.
Warner Bros./Photofest

The final "dance of death" took days to choreograph and shoot as Penn struggled to avoid making it either "bang, bang, you're dead" or "just benign lyricism".
Warner Bros./Photofest

Norman Jewison, Rod Steiger, and Sidney Poitier confer over the script on the set of *In the Heat of the Night*. *United Artists/Photofest*

"The natural temptation to make [Tibbs] a repository of superhuman virtue has been sternly repressed by Poitier", wrote *Life*'s Richard Schickel. But Andrew Sarris disagreed, calling him "heroically inoffensive". *John Springer Collection/Corbis*

Steiger, in full costume and as heavy as Norman Jewison could make him, with Poitier at the Sparta train station. *John Springer Collection/Corbis*

Tibbs gives as good as he gets to Endicott (Larry Gates) in a sequence that stunned movie-goers. "He slaps Tibbs. Tibbs slaps him back. Now it's eyeball to eyeball", Stirling Silliphant wrote in the script.
Nate Cutler/Globe Photos

Doctor Dolittle producer
Arthur P. Jacobs with his
wife, Natalie Trundy,
whom he married just a few
years before his death.
Nate Cutler/Globe Photos

Dolittle screenwriter/
composer Leslie Bricusse
with Sammy Davis Jr.,
who was originally slated
to costar in the film
with Rex Harrison.
Nate Cutler/Globe Photos

The shot of Harrison riding a giraffe got *Doctor Dolittle* a *Life* magazine cover a year before the film opened but bored test-screening audiences. *The Kobal Collection/20th Century-Fox*

"How do you like *our* jungle?": Harrison and wife Rachel Roberts in St. Lucia on the set, much of which later had to be rebuilt in Los Angeles. *Bettman/Corbis*

Anthony Newley; wife Joan Collins; and one of the many chimps trained to play Chee-Chee at a *Dolittle* premiere. *Bettman/Corbis*

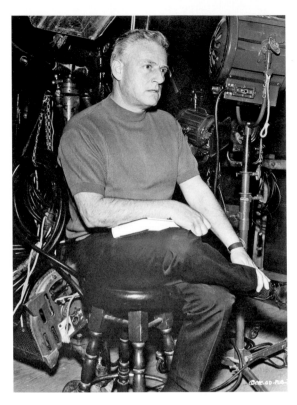

Stanley Kramer at the helm of *Guess Who's Coming to Dinner*. "There was always that traumatic thought," says Katharine Houghton, "of, Is there going to be another day?"
Bettman/Corbis

Katharine Hepburn's Joanna Drayton greets the family: (from left) Houghton, Poitier, Roy Glenn, and Beah Richards.
Underwood & Underwood/Corbis

Hepburn and Tracy on the set, in a posed "candid" with Hepburn in the position she favored during the shoot—lower in the frame than Tracy and with a hand casually covering her neck. *Bettman/Corbis*

A visibly frail Tracy with Hepburn in the last scene he shot for *Guess Who's Coming to Dinner*, just three weeks before his death. *Bettman/Corbis*

The last moment audiences saw of the screen's most famous romantic couple as Hepburn listens to Tracy's climactic monologue.

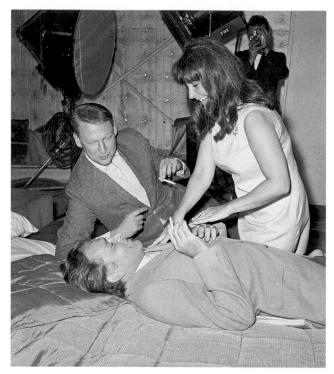

Mike Nichols clowning with Richard Burton and Elizabeth Taylor on the set of *Who's Afraid of Virginia Woolf?* Burton called the director "as bland as butter and as brilliant as diamonds". *Bettman/Corbis*

"Maybe I was kidding myself, but I felt I knew exactly what I was doing": Nichols directs a scene from *The Graduate*. *Embassy Pictures/Photofest*

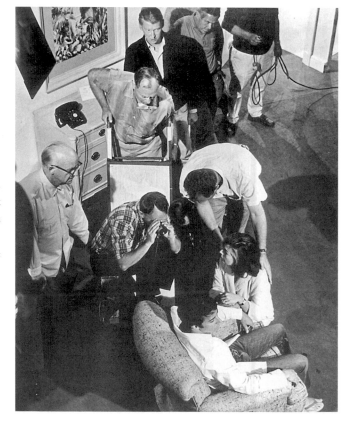

Dustin Hoffman and Anne
Bancroft (lit and made up to look,
respectively, a decade younger and
a decade older than they were).
Neither actor was shown dailies
during production.
John Springer Collection/Corbis

"They become their parents",
Nichols told moviegoers who
wanted to know what
happened to Benjamin and
Elaine (Katharine Ross)
after the credits rolled.
The Kobal Collection/Embassy

Screenwriter Buck Henry, who stepped in to play the hotel desk clerk when William Daniels,
who was originally cast, asked if he could play Hoffman's father instead.

New York Times movie reviewer
Bosley Crowther in 1960.
Photofest

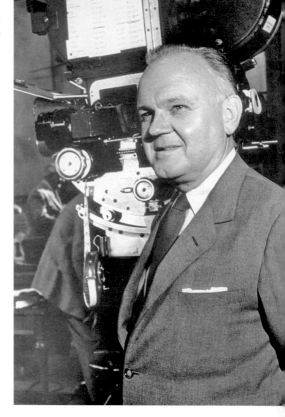

Pauline Kael at home, shortly
after she won the job as one
of the *New Yorker*'s two lead
film critics. *Martha Holmes/Time
Life Pictures*

Jack Valenti, shortly before he left
his job as an aide to President
Johnson to assume leadership of
the Motion Picture Association
of America. *Francis Miller/Time Life
Pictures/ Getty Images*

At the end of 1967, with *The Graduate* just arriving in theaters, Hoffman picks up his weekly unemployment check in Greenwich Village. *Bob Gomel/Time Life Pictures/Getty Images*

Beatty and Dunaway at the *Bonnie and Clyde* premiere in Paris, where the "Bonnie look" inspired a copycat fashion craze. *Bettman/Corbis*

Hoffman, with Eugene McCarthy's daughter Ellen as his date, takes his seat at the 1968 Academy Awards in front of fellow nominee Gene Hackman and his wife. *Bettman/Corbis*

Dame Edith Evans, a Best Actress nominee for *The Whisperers*, backstage after presenting Hal Ashby with the Best Film Editing Oscar for *In the Heat of the Night*. *Bettman/Corbis*

Best Director winner
Mike Nichols with
presenter Leslie Caron.
Bettman/Corbis

The acting winners, minus one: Rod Steiger, Estelle Parsons, George Kennedy, and director
George Cukor, who accepted for the absent Katharine Hepburn. *Photofest*

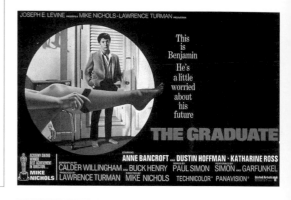

Two publicity campaigns
that worked—and one that didn't.
*Credits (clockwise): Warner Bros./Photofest,
United Artists/Getty Images, Alan Band/
Keystone/Getty Images*

Barbara Stanwyck's jodphurs," says Parsons, "and Dorothy Malone's skirts, whatever was left over from other movies." When the weather got colder in Texas, Elaine Michea had to go to local bargain-basement stores just to find winter coats for the crew.[32]

During *Bonnie and Clyde*'s long night shoots, the actors occasionally found time for a relaxing moment or two. Dunaway, at least for a while, discovered a kindred spirit in Michael J. Pollard. Dunaway's onetime lover Lenny Bruce had died of a heroin overdose a few weeks before production began, and Pollard had been a fan; one night after Bruce performed, the two men had shared a taxi uptown and Bruce suggested they shoot up together (Pollard declined, saying he'd rather stick to Jack Daniel's). Pollard and Dunaway bonded, playing Bob Dylan's recently released *Blonde on Blonde* on the phonograph all night long and cracking each other up with old Bruce routines.[33] But laughter was the exception to the rule. Parsons and Hackman kept to themselves. "I was a loner," she says. "I was so close to Arthur Penn, and Gene didn't have that—he was so competitive with Warren, so upset that I was so in love with working for Arthur. I would come out of my trailer crying and sobbing and run to Arthur saying, 'I don't know why Gene is so mean to me!' It's easy for me to be hysterical. Maybe that's why I didn't find Blanche hard to play."[34]

The actress Morgan Fairchild, who at the time was a sixteen-year-old Texan named Patsy McClenny who had gotten herself a job as Bonnie's driving double when Penn discovered that Dunaway couldn't work a stick shift, hung out with the stunt crew and, whenever she could, watched Beatty work. "It was very interesting to watch a young, beautiful, elegant man be the one in power," she says. Fairchild eavesdropped as much as she could, listening to Penn and Beatty argue about the "ring of fire, ring of fire, ring of fire. I didn't know what it was until I found out they were trying to figure out how to do the scene in which they wake up and the house is surrounded by cops. They talked about how to edit it, frame it, put it together, and I hung on every word."[35]

Penn's desire to break away from the bloat and tedium of most period movies in the mid-1960s was reaffirmed when he took a road trip to a Dallas theater to see an early screening of Robert Wise's *The Sand Pebbles*. After the success of *The Sound of Music*, Wise had carte blanche at 20th

Century-Fox; he brought his first cut of the movie about U.S. Navy men in 1926 China down to Texas himself and sat directly behind Penn, who watched with a look of polite interest frozen onto his face for three and a half hours. "I couldn't blink, I couldn't yawn!"[36] he said as he left the rented theater.* The movie was massive, ponderous, "important"—everything that Hollywood costume dramas had been for more than a decade—and it served as a reminder of the mission statement that Benton and Newman had laid out three years earlier: to make *Bonnie and Clyde* a film "about what's going on now."

Penn infused the movie with as much contemporary resonance as it could contain: He made the sexual psychodrama of Clyde's struggle with impotence as vivid as possible, despite Beatty's insistence that "the Freudian nature of [Bonnie and Clyde's] relationship puts me to sleep,"[37] using everything from suggestive cuts to crotch-level camera placement to imply that he was a man who wasn't in control of his gun. He pushed Robert Towne to rewrite, again and again, a scene in which the Barrow gang traps Frank Hamer, the lawman who has been tracking them, and Bonnie humiliates him by kissing him on the mouth:[38] They had to seem not like just a group of criminals tormenting a Texas Ranger, but like a band of antiauthority counterculture kids flipping off the Establishment. Penn liked the notion of Bonnie and Clyde as agrarian Robin Hoods who rob banks but not farmers, a notion made explicit in a couple of the film's stickup scenes. He held tenaciously on to one sequence in which a group of starved-out Okies welcome the injured couple as comrades in poverty, and another in which Clyde hands a gun to a black farmhand and allows him to shoot out the window of a foreclosed house. The scene suggested an alliance against the Man that crossed racial lines, even though Clyde's anachronistic lack of racism in the movie owes more to the progressivism of the 1960s than of the 1930s. After *Bonnie and Clyde*'s release, Penn proudly told *Cahiers du Cinéma* that black audiences looked at the characters and "said, 'This is the way to go, baby. Those cats were all right.' They really understood,

---

* Hal Ashby had a similar experience during production of *In the Heat of the Night,* when he went to see another Fox epic, John Huston's *The Bible.* "Great God in Heaven," he wrote to Norman Jewison, "I hope we never kid ourselves into trying something like that."

because in a certain sense the American Negro has the same kind of attitude of 'I have nothing more to lose.' "[39]

He had plenty of allies in his one-foot-in-each-decade approach. Towne knew just how much he could tweak Benton and Newman's dialogue without breaking with period reality altogether. And Van Runkle, after Beatty vetoed her perfectly in-period sketches of Bonnie and Clyde (with marcelled hair for her and a close-cropped center part for him), came up with a look that nodded both to the 1930s and, in Dunaway's straight hair, form-hugging skirts, and beret, to contemporary fashion and the French New Wave.

Penn's only real nemesis was Burnett Guffey, who after forty years in the business of lighting, framing, and shooting scenes didn't want to end his career with a movie he was sure would look ugly and amateurish. Guffey was a popular and respected leader within the Cinematographers Guild—he was known as "Six-Day" Guffey for his effort to prevent guild members from having to work seven-day weeks[40]—and he wasn't accustomed to being told how to do his job. Before shooting started, he summoned Dean Tavoularis to his room at the North Park. Tavoularis had violated a cardinal rule of old-guard art direction: He'd chosen rooms with low ceilings to serve as the locations where the Barrow gang hid out. But he wasn't about to give in and change them. "They hired me because they wanted a new approach," he says. "I found that totally to my liking, to rebel against the *Pillow Talk,* Hollywood movie look. I hated those narrowly framed back-lot street shots. I was more interested in what directors like Sidney Lumet were doing." For *Bonnie and Clyde*'s interiors, "I had looked at rooms in places like Waxahachie, and I knew what a modest house looked like—I wanted those old ceilings with old wallpaper on them to be visible," he says. "When I got to Bernie Guffey's room, he came to the door wearing a silk robe and holding a Scotch and soda, and he offered me a drink. He didn't say anything about the ceilings, the challenges of hanging lights in a small room, but I knew that's what he was thinking. He was sizing me up, waiting to hear if I knew what I was doing. It was very clear—I was just a little chick, and he was a veteran."[41]

Penn pushed Guffey, and Guffey pushed back. The director didn't want overlit scenes; he wanted soft-focus, filtered, almost foggy light in the sequence in which Bonnie reunites with her family in the Texas sand-hills; he wanted the same level of sophistication in a color movie that European cinematographers were bringing to black and white;* and he wanted some of the outdoor scenes to have the on-the-fly feeling of the Nouvelle Vague. "The famous scene where they were running in the fields and the light changed—Bernie hated that," says Tavoularis. "He hated flash, or lens flare, or bumps. Having the light change in a shot was, to him, a taboo—but why? Maybe it's great! Maybe it's dramatic! He hated anything like that."[42]

"It was really the lack of light that upset Bernie," says Beatty. "He was an older man—he wanted to use a lot of light, and Arthur did not. Arthur's influences were—well, one very strong influence was his brother [pho-tographer Irving Penn]. Arthur would say, 'Here's the light,' and Bernie would say, 'Well, this is not gonna play well in the drive-ins!' " Finally, after one too many confrontations with Penn, Guffey quit. The cast and crew were told he had suffered a heart attack. "It was not a heart attack," says Beatty. "It was an I-can't-do-it attack."[43] Another veteran, sixty-two-year-old Ellsworth Fredericks, took his place. Fredericks had shot for Joshua Logan and William Wyler, but "it was impossible," recalls Parsons. "The shots were so conventional that it became like a typical Hollywood movie. The guy would set up a shot, and Arthur would just throw up his hands."[44] After a few days, Penn had new respect for how hard Guffey had been struggling to take the look of the film in the direction he wanted, and Guffey returned to work.

As the shoot progressed, the violence and morbidity of *Bonnie and Clyde* became, more than ever, the focus of Penn's attention. The blood-shed in the movie, the intensity of which had never been seen in a studio film, was built right into the language of Benton and Newman's script. The

---

* Ingmar Bergman was an admirer of Penn's work on *Bonnie and Clyde,* but he disapproved of Penn's decision to shoot in color. "There's a sensual erotic charm in color, when properly used," he said. ". . . But I think color spoils a film like *Bonnie and Clyde.* That was a film, if any, which ought to have been shot . . . in coarse-grained black-and-white tones." At the time of his remark, Berg-man had not yet shot a color movie. (Bergman, quoted in *Bergman on Bergman,* by Stig Björkman, Torstenn Manns, and Jonas Sima, translated by Paul Britten Austin [New York: Touchstone/Simon & Schuster, 1973], p. 227.)

two writers had, by design, placed the story's most jolting moments of violence in the middle of episodes of comic incompetence: When Clyde holds
up a grocery store to impress Bonnie, he's suddenly overwhelmed by a
giant butcher who literally lifts him off the ground and tries to attack him
with a cleaver; "in blind fury, he pistol-whips the BUTCHER'S head with
two terrific swipes," they wrote. When Bonnie and Clyde rob their first
bank, their getaway is slowed because their simpleton accomplice C. W.
(Pollard) has decided to parallel-park their escape car in a tight spot. That
leaves time for a white-haired bank official to leap onto the back of the
car. As the passengers, the bystanders, and the tires are all screaming, a
panicked Clyde shoots him, and "the face of the man explodes in blood."[45]
Penn loved the moments in which rural ineptitude fractures into horror
and was determined to find a visual language that would shock moviegoers out of their laughter. When Clyde shoots the teller, he turns directly
to the camera for an instant before firing; Penn then cuts on the sound of
the gunshot to his victim's blood-soaked face, and we have the sickening,
split-second impression that the bullet has spiderwebbed two pieces of
glass—the back windshield and the lens of the man's spectacles.

   Beatty and Penn argued for much of the production about Penn's desire to include a scene that wasn't in the script, in which Bonnie and
Clyde, shortly before their death, act out their own demises in a ghoulish
private pageant. "I had a place for a scene just before the end in which I
thought—to my chagrin as I say it now—that Bonnie might have wanted
to perform her own death, something that grew out of the romantic idea
she had about herself, a kind of overembellished funeral with a movie
star look, and that was what I kept pressing for," says Penn. "It was a
colorful idea, but too elaborate. Warren didn't like it at all, and neither
did Towne."[46]

   After Penn gave up on the notion, he started concentrating on the
movie's most technically difficult scene, Bonnie and Clyde's death in a
hail of bullets that seem to come from every direction at once. Benton
and Newman's screenplay called for just five seconds of "rapid, deafen-
ing" gunfire and noted that "at no point during the gunfight do we see
BONNIE and CLYDE in motion. . . . We never see BONNIE and CLYDE
dead." Penn had something else in mind even before production started;

the way he visualized the sequence was what finally convinced him to make the movie earlier in the year, when he had been working with Benton and Newman in Stockbridge and wavering about his decision to direct.

"I just woke up one day in the country and thought, gee, I can see the ending," he says. "Not the benign, lyrical thing that I had thought, but something spastic and balletic. It has to do something extraordinary, something that makes them into a legend."[47] During the shoot, Penn mapped out the final scene, drawing for inspiration on Akira Kurosawa's *The Seven Samurai*, the Zapruder film, *Breathless*, and his own finale for his first movie, *The Left Handed Gun*, in which he had used different film speeds to intensify the image of Paul Newman's Billy the Kid shooting a man out of his boots. The summer's riots were on his mind; so was the war in Vietnam, which in the two months that *Bonnie and Clyde* had been shooting had become the subject of increasing pessimism in the nation's press and of major public protests, including the rally at the Pentagon that Norman Mailer later memorialized in *The Armies of the Night*. Penn wanted as much political resonance in the scene as it could comfortably contain, an ambush that would, as Richard Gilman later put it in *The New Republic*, "mount up to an image of absolute blind violence on the part of organized society, a violence far surpassing that which it is supposed to be putting down."[48]

The final sequence in *Bonnie and Clyde*, which includes sixty shots in less than a minute, took longer to film than anything else in the movie. Penn used four cameras for every setup, each one filming from the same angle but running at a different speed. He extended the gunfire from five seconds to twenty-five; he rigged Beatty and Dunaway with dozens of squibs and blood packets that would be set off when Beatty squeezed a pear that Clyde was eating;[49] he attached a piece of prosthetic scalp to Beatty's head that an off-screen makeup man would pull off using an invisible nylon thread (a subliminally fast moment designed expressly to evoke memories of the Kennedy assassination); he tied one of Dunaway's legs to the gearshift of the car so that she would eventually be able to fall dead according to "the laws of gravity" without hurting herself; and he devised separate pieces of choreography for Beatty, who is quickly knocked onto the dusty road by bullets, and Dunaway, who dances like a marionette behind the steering wheel, unable even to fall over as the bullets jolt her in every direction. "There's a moment in death when the body no longer functions, when it becomes an object and has a certain kind of detached ugly beauty," he said. "It was that aspect I was trying to get."[50] Penn mapped out every shot in advance, including the fast, flashing sequence of close-ups in which Beatty and Dunaway realize what's happening and lock eyes. The elaborate setup of the squibs meant he had time to film the scene from only two angles each day. On the fourth afternoon, he was done.[51]

Penn and Beatty had kept costs down at the beginning of the shoot; Benton and Newman's lawyer had even had to write a letter after filming started reminding the production that they still hadn't been paid most of what they were owed for the screenplay and that "the boys need it very badly."[52] But as the weeks continued, Beatty and Penn's long discussions, their attention to detail and shared taste for multiple takes, Dunaway's skittishness, and the logistical complexities of filming a period movie on location had wreaked havoc with the schedule. The ever changing combination of night shoots and early-morning calls had exhausted the cast; Pollard had to have a tattoo painted on his chest for many scenes and would often lie there sound asleep while makeup designer Bob Jiras did his work.[53] As long as they were in Texas, and as long as the footage from *Bonnie and Clyde* was being sent to editor Dede Allen in New York, Beatty and Penn were free from studio interference; Warner Brothers would be forced either to keep sending money or to shut down the production and lose everything it had spent. Nevertheless, "there was always a sense of something between a request and a threat about our need to come back to the studio," says Tavoularis.[54] "Jack Warner was having apoplexy when we were *three* days over," says John Dutton. By the end of the Texas shoot in December, "we were [weeks] over schedule and well over budget. And then he clamped down."[55]

Walter MacEwen had worried since production began about being beaten to screens by another Depression-era gangster movie, *The St. Valentine's Day Massacre,* that Roger Corman was directing for 20th Century-Fox; he wanted *Bonnie and Clyde* in theaters by the summer of 1967 without fail. "Stay as sweet as you are," he wrote to Beatty at the beginning

of the shoot, "[and] complete the goddamn show on schedule."[56] And Jack
Warner could barely muster enough enthusiasm to send the traditional
first-day-of-filming cable to Arthur Penn. "Every good wish on the start of
your picture," he wrote. "Know you will bring production in on schedule.
And for the budget," he added, before crossing the last four words out.[57]
"Warner was so pissed off that they were in Texas," says Walter MacEwen's
assistant Robert Solo. "He'd say, 'Why aren't they on the lot? Why do they
have to be in Texas? Mike Curtiz could shoot on the lot! Mervyn LeRoy
could shoot on the lot! What's wrong with these guys?' He would rant and
rave and carry on every day. Finally, he forced them to come back."[58]

   Bonnie and Clyde moved to Burbank for its final weeks; the technical requirements of filming the driving sequences would eventually have
forced the production onto a rear-projection stage in any case. Since so
much of the movie is set in the very crowded getaway car, all five principal
actors were there as well as Gene Wilder and Evans Evans. "If the movie
had been shot just a couple of years later," says Penn, "there would have
been no need for rear projection. But the terrain of the road was just too
rough for those cameras and the sound equipment, so we had to go to
the lot."[59] Jack Warner had gotten his wish; the film was now nominally
under his control, although he hadn't seen the unprecedentedly bloody
and brutal footage that Dede Allen and her assistant, Jerry Greenberg,
were beginning to cut together. Obsessed with *Camelot*, he hardly paid attention to *Bonnie and Clyde*. When he did, he expressed little enthusiasm.
"We had shot one scene in Dallas—the scene where Buck, the brother, is
first seen with Clyde . . . about fifteen times," said Beatty. "When we got
back to Hollywood, we did some over-the-shoulder shots—all of this same
scene. We had about 125,000 takes . . . and this was the one day, of all
the goddamn days, that Jack Warner picked to come and see the rushes.
He came up to me afterward and said, 'Hey, kid, Bogart wouldn't do that.
You think Errol Flynn would put up with that many takes? For Christ's
sake, kid!' "[60]

   On the film's last day of production, the seventy-four-year-old studio
chief found an opportunity for one last assertion of authority. "There had
been a long tradition at Warner Brothers, with their B movies, that Jack
Warner would give them a time frame and then come down to the set,

no matter how far along they were, and say, 'Your picture wraps tonight.' That became sort of legendary," says Penn. "Well, we finished *Bonnie and Clyde* on a Friday and we were having a wrap party, but the photographs that open the movie—the stills—we were gonna do without the crew, in a studio off the lot. And we kept the costumes for them. So here's this wrap party going on, and Jack comes down and says, 'You finish tonight.' And lo and behold, we were forced right then to do the stills, while the crew was sitting there eating and drinking. It was, I guess, an exercise in power for him. But it was also a last hurrah."[61]

PART THREE

TWENTY

The two girls were naked. That fact alone represented three problems. *Naked* was, of course, the first problem; even if there had been no other issues, *naked* was a deal breaker all by itself. *Girls* was the second problem; not women, but girls. Wasn't one of them, one of the two that were giggling and wrestling and rolling around the floor naked, supposed to be a teenager, perhaps not even of the age of consent? And *two* was a problem; two girls together, with everything that might suggest to a moviegoer. Not to mention the presence of the male photographer whose clothes they were tugging off, who was happily diving into the action, threatening to become naked himself. Three naked young people, tumbling and laughing and thrashing and clearly about to have sex in several different combinations.

And then there was the scene in which the photographer stood over Sarah Miles, locking eyes with her, while another man thrust into her.

This was not possible.

The first letter that Geoffrey Shurlock sent to MGM had been polite but firm. Nobody at the studio could say they hadn't been warned; they had been warned as far back as March, before the movie had even been shot. "As you know, nudity is prohibited under the Code," Shurlock had reminded the studio, as if any reminder were necessary. "We notice that the story calls for Thomas to have a sex relationship between two teenagers. This . . . would not be approvable." And the scene in which he just . . .

watches? "This suggestion seems to us to verge on the pornographic."[1] Shurlock had warned MGM again in April, after the movie's title had changed from *The Shot* to just *The Antonioni Picture*; this time he had used stronger language, phrases like "heightening the degree of offensiveness" and "unacceptably irreverent."[2] And he had tried one more time in July,[3] but by then it was too late, because *Blow-Up*, as it was now called, was shooting all over London in the summer of 1966, and the old Code, thanks to *Who's Afraid of Virginia Woolf?* and *Alfie*, was already on its way out. By the fall, when the movie was completed and edited, Shurlock was overseeing the new, more relaxed Code, which everyone knew was a half-hearted attempt to maintain the integrity of a system that still demanded a certain toeing of the line by studios while giving filmmakers a little more room. A *little* more room. Not room for bare teenage breasts and three-ways and a man trying, as Shurlock put it, "to incite the girl into a state of orgasm."[4]

This time, Shurlock knew that he had Jack Valenti in his camp. Valenti was liberal, he was open-minded, he had sided with Warner Brothers and against the Code on *Virginia Woolf*, and he admired Antonioni, but, he said, "I don't believe that everything that's put into a film by a man of quality is sacrosanct. . . . We've got to draw the line somewhere."[5] And the National Catholic Office for Motion Pictures, even with a more permissive advisory board now in place, would certainly condemn the film. So Shurlock knew that MGM would have to yield: The studio needed to get a Production Code seal somehow. For a while toward the end of 1966, negotiations seemed possible. MGM even approached Shurlock for an ex parte discussion: What if the studio agreed to release *Blow-Up* with the "Suggested for Mature Audiences" label that had recently become an official part of the Code? Would that do the trick?[6]

It would not. The two girls were still naked.

Time was running out, which was bound to work in the Production Code's favor. It was the end of November. *Blow-Up* was booked to open at New York City's Coronet Theater on December 18. And Antonioni was apparently willing to make some cuts. A few seconds here, a few frames there. Cuts would, of course, be the best way to solve this. A small, willfully difficult art movie that would be seen by only a handful of East and

West Coast cinephiles wasn't worth the rupture of a system that had been in place for decades or the demolition of a new set of guidelines that had barely been road-tested.

On December 17, Shurlock and Valenti handed down their final decision. *Blow-Up* would not receive a Production Code seal.

The next day, MGM opened the movie anyway. The technicality the studio used was an insult in itself: It simply invented a new company, "Premier Production Company, Inc.," which was not bound by the authority of the Code, and released the movie under that banner.[7] The lion didn't roar before the movie started—the lion wouldn't have roared anyway, since MGM had decided to retire it a couple of months earlier in favor of a new, "mod" solarized lion graphic[8] that its executives believed would appeal to young people—but the impact was the same. *Variety*'s reviewer predicted that Antonioni's film would never go into general release and complained that "it goes far beyond the limits of good taste, thru nudie action and play which undoubtedly will be found offensive by many."[9] MGM didn't even bother to get an official ruling from the National Catholic Office for Motion Pictures before the movie opened; by the time they gave *Blow-Up* a "C" rating in early January, their condemnation was moot. The movie was a smash: It played not just in New York and Los Angeles, but everywhere in the United States, in Michigan and Minnesota and South Carolina and Vermont, returning a huge profit to the studio. Ten years of steady art-house releases by upstarts and masters of the New Cinema from Europe had created what critic Stanley Kauffmann called a "Film Generation" whose conversation was no longer confined to cocktail parties and thoughtful essays in the kinds of magazines that published thoughtful essays: "Everyone in Zilchville [saw] *Blow-Up*," wrote Kauffmann, "not just the elite."[10]

Blow-Up began 1967 by throwing a stick of dynamite into the middle of the movie business, and the fifty-four-year-old Antonioni, a saturnine man given to pronouncements on the order of "I hate my films and do not wish to talk about them,"[11] suddenly seemed to be the unlikely leader of what, for the first time, looked like a full-out revolution. A few theaters across the country were unwilling to show the movie without a Code seal; other exhibitors eagerly stepped in to take their place. The reviews, for the most part, were raves: In *The New York Times,* Bosley Crowther wrote favorably about *Blow-Up* four times in less than a month and pointedly asked, "Why should a picture as intelligent and meaningful as this one be stigmatized by the Production Code people and condemned without any appreciation by the National Catholic Office of Motion Pictures? . . . I would say that, in this instance, both organizations have committed a grievous error."[12] Crowther had been at the *Times* for twenty-seven years; he was known as an aesthetic conservative and was belittled by many of his colleagues for his sludgy, malaprop-riddled writing style and his middlebrow primness. But Crowther also had a long-standing and passionate aversion to anything that smacked of censorship, and he was a writer who was more than comfortable with the clout his particular pulpit gave him. His sustained praise for *Blow-Up* served notice that the country's most powerful newspaper had lost its patience with the Production Code in any form.

Blow-Up's success, though it enhanced MGM's bottom line, only increased the atmosphere of uncertainty and paranoia that seemed to pervade the major studios at the end of 1966. When Arthur Penn remarked that Jack Warner's eleventh-hour seizing of the reins on *Bonnie and Clyde* was a last hurrah, he meant it literally; in November, Warner had sold a third of his shares in Warner Brothers to Eliot Hyman's production company Seven Arts, and the industry knew it was just a matter of months before Hyman took over completely.[13] Warner's decision, along with the sudden death of Walt Disney on December 15 at sixty-five, would leave Darryl Zanuck at 20th Century-Fox as the only mogul from Hollywood's golden age still in power. United Artists was also being sold; days after Warner's decision to go into business with Seven Arts, UA entered formal negotiations to become a subsidiary of the Transamerica Corporation,[14] an insurance company that had in recent years become a diversified conglomerate, albeit one with no experience in the entertainment business. MGM itself was facing a proxy fight in February 1967,[15] and the trade papers were full of talk that a French bank was beginning a takeover bid for Columbia Pictures.

The studios seemed to be under siege, and the men running them felt cranky and bewildered—torn between continuing to fight the enemy (which, at various times toward the end of 1966, they identified as runaway production, color TV, the new morality, and the influence of European directors and filmmakers) and trying to profit by allying with their adversaries. The studios' relationship with television networks was proving particularly nettlesome. The public appetite for theatrical movies on TV was insatiable—in 1967, they aired on at least one network every night of the week but Monday and sometimes drew more than 50 percent of the viewing audience. While the studios were making fortunes by selling packages of their films to the networks, they were also holding movies back: As the year began, MGM rejected a $10 million TV offer for *Gone With the Wind* and decided to rerelease it theatrically instead.[16] With a collective sense of uncertainty and alarm about what the moviegoing public now wanted, many studios clung to the past, announcing plans to put *The Alamo, Spartacus, The Longest Day,* and *The Greatest Show on Earth* back in theaters, too.[17] The choice of long, massive visual spectacles was no accident; with the conversion of all television shows to color, the only enticements that Hollywood still had to offer movie fans that they weren't already getting at home were size, scope, length, and lack of commercial interruption.

But the studios couldn't ignore the fact that their current product was held in almost universally low regard. Embarrassments seemed to come at every turn; when the 1966 Venice Film Festival announced its selections, it bypassed traditional studio product completely, choosing instead the Roger Corman biker-exploitation movie *The Wild Angels,* an American International Pictures melodrama about a barely disguised version of the Hells Angels that ended with a drug-saturated orgy in a church. The fact that the picture starred Peter Fonda and Nancy Sinatra seemed only to underscore Corman's generational nose-thumbing at what Hollywood's old guard viewed as its obligation to export its best possible image to the rest of the world. *The Wild Angels* was hardly *Easy Rider;* Corman and AIP staked out a shrewd middle ground that was characteristic of the period, making sure that the film was officially appalled by the behavior of its drunken, brawling, sex-mad bikers while giving audiences a good, long, passably lurid look at every one of their misdeeds. After the movie grossed forty times its $360,000 budget, the major studios held their noses and quietly started making plans to produce imitations. At the beginning of 1967, any possible loss of corporate dignity was giving way to bottom-line realities—and there wasn't much dignity left to lose, anyway. "Experience has long since prepared us to accept the uncomfortable fact that the best work in motion pictures—the most intelligent, progressive, astute and alert to what is happening to people—is being done abroad,"[18] wrote Bosley Crowther before announcing that his list of the ten best films of 1966 would include only two studio movies set in America, *Who's Afraid of Virginia Woolf?* and *The Russians Are Coming, the Russians Are Coming*.

Mike Nichols and Norman Jewison spent much of the first part of 1967 running into each other on the awards circuit, as both their films came in for year-end honors. On one evening that quickly earned a spot in the annals of awards ceremony horror stories, they both found themselves in attendance at the Directors Guild of America banquet, where they were among the ten nominees. Walter Matthau, the awards presenter, took the stage to announce that the winner of the guild's Best Director award was Nichols for *Who's Afraid of Virginia Woolf?* Nichols, genuinely startled, got up and made a long, heartfelt acceptance speech, then returned to his seat with his plaque. When Matthau returned to the podium, he announced with some embarrassment that he had misunderstood his presenting task—and that each of the ten nominated directors was to receive the plaque that Nichols had just accepted. The Best Director winner, he then announced, was Fred Zinnemann for *A Man for All Seasons*. A mortified Nichols somehow managed to laugh it off.[19]

After leaving Tennessee, Jewison had wrapped *In the Heat of the Night* in Los Angeles on a note of confidence. His two stars finished the production as friends, and newcomer Scott Wilson had, thanks in part to Sidney Poitier's urging,[20] gotten a major break that would only increase his stock; just as the movie finished, he and Robert Blake—the actor Wilson had essentially replaced as *In the Heat of the Night*'s vagrant suspect—had been cast over such big names as Paul Newman and Steve McQueen as murderers Dick Hickock and Perry Smith in Richard Brooks's high-profile adaptation of Truman Capote's *In Cold Blood* for Columbia. The news, and the year of publicity that would precede its release, could only help *In the Heat of the Night* get noticed.

Jewison spent the Christmas holidays in Sun Valley, Idaho, skiing with his wife and kids, only to wind up in a local emergency room when one of his sons broke a leg on the slopes. The concerned father sitting across from him in the hospital waiting room, waiting to hear about his own son's broken leg, was New York's junior senator, Robert F. Kennedy. The two families began chatting, and Kennedy offered Jewison some encouraging words about his movie, telling him he thought the moment was right for a film about a black detective in the South and promising to mail him research from his Senate office about southern race relations, which he did. "Timing is everything," Jewison says Kennedy told him, "in politics, art, and life."[21]

Other studios now had the same idea: Just before Jewison's ski trip, producer Samuel Goldwyn Jr. announced that he had acquired the rights to seven of Chester Himes's detective novels featuring the Harlem cops Grave Digger Jones and Coffin Ed Johnson, and Jewison knew that feelers had gone out to Poitier and Harry Belafonte to play the leads.[22] But without a director or a script, he also knew there was no possibility the project would reach screens before his own film. With little to worry about, Jewison was ready to spend some time with Hal Ashby in the editing room and to start planning his next film for the Mirisch Company, a light-spirited, sexy comedy-drama about a master thief called *The Crown Caper* (later retitled *The Thomas Crown Affair*). He had wanted Elizabeth Taylor and Richard Burton to star,[23] but after the huge success of *Virginia Woolf*, they were freer than they had ever been to choose the films that struck their fancy and embarked on what would turn out to be an ill-fated year of conspicuous consumption and bloated international productions, beginning with Franco Zeffirelli's leaden adaptation of *The Taming of the Shrew*.

As 1967 began, Nichols was considerably less cheerful than Jewison; he was beginning to wonder if *The Graduate* had taken so long to come to fruition that it was in danger of being rendered irrelevant by movies that were already beating it to the finish line. In Los Angeles, he and Buck Henry went to see a movie about a young man who rejects the oppressively bourgeois lifestyle of his parents to take his first timid and neurotic steps into a new world of free-spirited sexuality. The film, an $800,000 comedy called *You're a Big Boy Now,* was the MFA thesis project of Francis Coppola, a twenty-seven-year-old UCLA graduate student who had been getting steady work as a screenwriter for Seven Arts (he had written drafts of *This Property Is Condemned, Is Paris Burning?,* and *Reflections in a Golden Eye*).[24] The movie and its brash director were now being hailed as the first piece of evidence that the widespread emergence of film school programs might have something to offer Hollywood. *You're a Big Boy Now* also suggested a glimmer of a new business model for cheap color movies; thanks to a lucrative presale to network TV, the film was already guaranteed to make a profit. Coppola, wrote critic Hollis Alpert, is "new generation, new breed, possessed of talent, boldness, drive; and . . . now has the chance to prove his genius," adding, "Chances that might otherwise not have been taken, because of their commercial risk, are now quite feasible, especially if the film can be in color."[25] Henry and Nichols left the theater glumly convinced that the movie they had just seen "had clearly and totally pre-empted *The Graduate,*"[26] wrote Turman. Even Nichols's usually droll press interviews started to betray his depression as he temporarily lost his perfect pitch. "I'm doing it better than anyone, and I can't do it at all," he complained. "I'm a fraud."[27]

Nichols and Turman weren't getting much encouragement from Joseph E. Levine, the Embassy Pictures czar who had agreed to finance the movie but now, in a temporary cash crunch, was threatening to pull the plug. The large and youthful audience that was turning *Blow-Up* into a hit did not impress the indefatigably lowbrow producer. "Some of these films are liked by the critics and no one else," he told a group of college students while getting an honorary degree. "Antonioni, Truffaut, Resnais, Fellini are known to maybe only 1 percent of filmgoers. Antonioni is getting to be better known because of *Blow-Up,* but before that, mention the name Antonioni and most filmgoers would think it was some kind of Italian cheese."[28]

Levine told Turman not to count on him for *The Graduate*'s budget, sending the producer on a frantic series of return visits to all of the studios that had rejected the project in the first place. "He said he couldn't do it—he doesn't have the money," says Turman. "And there are no secrets in Hollywood. So, 'secretly,' 'surreptitiously,' I sent it back out to *everyone.*

For a second time. And they all turned it down again. The problem was, nobody got the book. Nobody liked it. I don't even think Joe Levine got it, but he saw it as a chance to rub shoulders with class, to do something that would contradict his image as the king of trash."[29]

One problem for the studios may have been Nichols's persistent inability to find the actors he wanted, a dilemma that bewildered the director himself. "It's the hardest thing I've ever tried to cast," he told a reporter at the beginning of 1967. "These people are so far removed from stock characters."[30] In early January, Turman announced a "nationwide talent search" for a twenty-two-year-old actor to play Benjamin, a halfhearted attempt at a Scarlett O'Hara–style publicity spin for what was essentially a bicoastal open call for résumés and head shots.[31] At the same time, they finally nailed down one of the principals. "I was walking on the Paramount lot," says agent Leonard Hirshan, "and on the first floor, an office window opened and Larry Turman stuck his head out and said, 'Can you come in here for a minute? I want you to meet Mike Nichols.' I go in and they say, 'We're very interested in Anne Bancroft for a role in this picture *The Graduate*.' . . . So I said, 'Give me a script,' and the rest is history. I got her $200,000, which was a nice salary at that time."[32]

"I had dated Annie a little bit, long before this," says Nichols. "She was certainly a beautiful, exciting, wonderful, angry young woman. Which I happened to like. But it took us a long time to think of her. Now, one of the reasons I didn't think of Annie is the famous thing that she was too young [Bancroft was thirty-five when she was cast]. But then we decided it didn't matter."[33] Nichols, having just aged the thirty-three-year-old Taylor into a hardbitten middle-aged drunk, knew he could do the same for Bancroft, and besides, says Turman, "she was a name. Not a blockbuster name, but a name Hollywood knew, and a name I could get for a price."[34]

Turman and Nichols seemed to be inching closer to signing a Benjamin, especially after the director started to realize a built-in problem with his casting strategy: "I discovered that boys who really were that age couldn't get the distance to get rid of the self-pity and . . . have an *attitude* toward that point in one's life,"[35] Nichols said. Once they started looking at older actors, Charles Grodin, a thirty-one-year-old TV and theater performer with a growing list of credits, impressed them both with a very sharp reading. "Grodin got very close," says Nichols. "His reading was hilarious, he's brilliantly talented, and he understood the jokes. But he didn't look like Benjamin to me."[36]

"Chuck Grodin gave the best reading," says Henry. "And maybe one of the best readings I've ever heard in my career, so funny and interesting. He thinks we offered him the part—I don't think we did. But I don't remember his screen test, whereas Dustin's was really memorable."[37]

It was Nichols who first asked to see Hoffman, remembering his performance a couple of years earlier in *Harry Noon and Night* off Broadway. In mid-1966, Nichols had auditioned him for the musical *The Apple Tree*. Hoffman lost the part to Alan Alda, but shortly after that, he had a true breakthrough success as a New York stage actor for the first time in his career. The vehicle was a comedy by Henry Livings called *Eh?*, a British import in which Hoffman was playing a distractible teenage night watchman. "The play went through two directors, neither of whom wanted me," says Hoffman. "The first one wanted me to 'do' David Warner, who had done the play in London." He told Hoffman to go see Warner in the Vanessa Redgrave movie *Morgan: A Suitable Case for Treatment* and simply duplicate the performance. "Of course, I reacted negatively to that," says Hoffman. To the actor's amazement, Theodore Mann, the artistic director of New York's Circle in the Square Downtown, where *Eh?* was being staged, kept Hoffman and fired the director. "The second director wanted a kind of camp performance," says Hoffman, "and I don't do camp very well. I don't think it's funny. I do farce, but I don't do camp. So he fired that director, too." The third director Mann chose was Alan Arkin, who hit it off with Hoffman immediately but, says Hoffman, "was so afraid that this play wasn't going to be a hit that he didn't use his real name" in the program or on the posters.[38]

When *Eh?*, with staging credited to the pseudonymous "Roger Short," opened in October 1966—two nights before Nichols's *The Apple Tree*—it was an instant sellout hit, and Hoffman, whom *The New York Times'* Eliot Fremont-Smith called "one of the most agile and subtly controlled comedians around,"[39] was suddenly a local sensation. A follow-up rave by Walter Kerr comparing the twenty-nine-year-old actor to a young Buster Keaton cemented his success.[40] Now, Hoffman was also turning up on television with regularity, and not just in one-line roles. He starred in adaptations of *The Journey of the Fifth Horse* and Maxwell Anderson's *The Star Wagon* that aired within a week of each other on public television and in a couple of ABC specials as well. "It's funny—I don't think Mike ever saw me in *Eh?*," says Hoffman. "He was *the* hot director, so if he had come, I would have remembered."

Hoffman was sent the script for *The Graduate* and a copy of Charles Webb's novel and sat in his apartment on West 11th Street reading both. On his coffee table was *Time* magazine's recent "Man of the Year" issue: at the end of 1966, the editors had selected "The 25 and Under Generation." The drawing on the cover focused on a blondish, square-jawed young white man with the determined, clear-eyed mien of a future Apollo astronaut. Hoffman looked at the illustration and tossed aside the screenplay. "I thought, *that's* your guy. I reacted against all of it. I didn't want to read for it. I was right. Nichols was wrong. I was not in any way right for that part," Hoffman says. "I thought, are these people having a breakdown? The guy's name is Benjamin *Braddock,* he's like six feet tall, he's a track runner."

After eight years of trying, Hoffman, at twenty-nine, finally had the career he thought he wanted. "I had this kind of chutzpah, this New York coffeehouse-and-Kerouac-and-Ginsberg thing: You weren't there to 'make it,' you were there to be an artist," he says. "That conceit kind of propelled me. I thought, I'll work off Broadway for the rest of my life and I'll be very happy and I'll have a nice apartment, and I'm not going to screw it up by making a Hollywood movie and being miscast, even though I respected the director."

Hoffman got a call from Nichols, who was still in Los Angeles doing screen tests. "Nichols said to me, 'Did you like the script? Did you think it was funny?'" says Hoffman. "And I said, 'Yeah, very much.'"[41] Taking a couple of days off from *Eh?*, the actor flew to Los Angeles in mid-January to test with Katharine Ross, a dark-eyed, strong-jawed twenty-six-year-old contract player at Universal who reminded Nichols of his first wife (Barbara Hershey and Kim Darby were among the other actresses who had read for Elaine).[42] Although potential Benjamins and Elaines had read for Nichols and his team separately, Nichols preferred to screen-test them in pairs. Hoffman was whisked through a quick meeting with Bancroft—"It was all 'How do you do?' 'How do you do?'—a blur to me," he says—and then into the makeup room. "It was awful. I had only two or three days to memorize ten pages, and I'm a slow memorizer—I tried to do it on the plane. And then my memory jumps to the makeup chair, and, you know, feeling 'What am I doing here?' while they tried to turn my face into an Aryan. I remember Nichols saying, *kind of* kiddingly, 'What can we do about his nose? What can we do about his eyebrows?' I think they plucked me. It was his sly kind of humor, but it wasn't helping me."

Hoffman was then marched onto a soundstage that contained a bed, Katharine Ross, and a crane on which a camera was mounted. "He had a *crane,*" says Hoffman. "How many screen tests use a crane? Maybe he was working something out—it was only his second movie. Or maybe he was trying to see whether I could do a movie at all—'Can the kid sustain?' All I know is that through lack of sleep, makeup chair paralysis, and nerves, I couldn't get through it." Nichols did take after take, coaching Hoffman, trying to relax him, taking breathers. It was going badly—so badly that Ross began to tense up as well. "He looks about three feet tall, so dead serious, so humorless, so unkempt," she thought. "This is going to be a disaster."[43] At one point as the hours dragged on and the two sat wearily on the bed, Hoffman reached over and pinched her bottom, trying to relax her or perhaps energize himself. She spun around in cold anger. "Don't you *ever* do that!" she said. "I'm in the wrong place," he thought. As Nichols seemed to shift his attention to Ross, Hoffman got even more clenched and inexpressive.[44]

"He was just sitting like a lump," says Nichols, "not visibly doing much, which of course I'm usually crazy about. But it was a hard day." Nichols was impressed by Ross—"I thought, this is her, this is how I want Elaine to look, she even knew what to wear"[45]—but less sure about Hoffman. After twelve hours, it was over. Hoffman shook hands with the director, "and Nichols's hand was so damp that I really got nervous because I realized how nervous *he* was." Hoffman shoved his hands back into his pockets; when he pulled them out again, several subway tokens flew out. "Here, kid," said an exhausted and annoyed crew member, picking them up. "You're gonna need these."

Hoffman flew back to New York, where his costars in *Eh?*, Elizabeth

Wilson and Alexandra Berlin, were anxious to hear if they were going to lose their leading man. He told them not to worry.[46] In Los Angeles, enthusiasm wasn't running much higher. "I looked at it, and it was just this ugly boy playing the part, and I thought, 'Ugggh,'" Nichols's editor, Sam O'Steen, said later.[47] "There was no 'Eureka!'" says Nichols. That is, until they printed the screen test and watched Hoffman on film. "He had that thrilling thing that I'd only seen in Elizabeth Taylor," says the director. "That secret, where they do something while you're shooting, and you think it's *okay*, and then you see it on screen and it's five times better than when you shot it. That's what a great movie actor does. They don't know how they do it, and I don't know how they do it, but the difference is unimaginable, shocking. This feeling that they have such a connection with the camera that they can do what they want because they own the audience. Elizabeth had it, and by God, so did Dustin."[48]

"With that, in one fell swoop, we lost all the blonds we were thinking about," says Buck Henry. "I remember Mike said, 'I have the rationalization for Dustin—he's a genetic throwback. Somewhere in the genes of these people, there was some twisted dark pirate uncle, and that gene got passed on to Dustin. His whole appearance suggests that he doesn't belong in that laboratory full of blond gods.'"[49]

A few days later, Hoffman got a call from his agent telling him to phone Nichols. It was a snowy Sunday morning, and Hoffman had walked to the Upper West Side apartment of his girlfriend, a ballet dancer named Anne Byrne, to make breakfast with her. "Anne was cooking eggs at one end of the apartment, and I was on the line at the other, and there was a typical Nicholsian pause, and he said, 'Well . . . you got it,'" says Hoffman. "And I didn't say a word, except maybe thank you. And he said, 'You don't seem very excited.' And I said, 'Oh no, yeah, thanks.' All I knew was that I was working with the greatest director of my life and that he was about to make the biggest mistake. I hung up the phone and looked at my girlfriend and said, 'I got it,' and there was this terrible, sad moment when she said, 'I knew you would.' It was heavy. Laden with potential regret that this was going to break us up.'"[50] Ironically, Hoffman was now going to have to turn down a second movie role—one that had been offered to him by the husband of his new costar, Bancroft. Mel Brooks was also working for Joe

Levine; he too had seen Hoffman's performance as *Harry Noon and Night*'s German transvestite and now wanted him to play a Nazi playwright in his new comedy, tentatively titled *Springtime for Hitler*. "I thought he was the most original, spectacularly funny guy," says Hoffman, "and I had to call him up and say, I can't do it."[51]

Nichols brought Hoffman to meet Levine in his New York office on a rainy afternoon. The financier was not impressed with Nichols's choice of star. "The windows leaked when it rained," Levine said years later. "Mike pushed him through the door with a towel in his hand. I thought it was the plumber who had come to fix the leaks. I pointed to the window that was leaking and said, 'It's over there.'"[52] But Hoffman, at least, came cheap: He would cost Levine just $750 a week.[53] His casting was announced in February 1967; production would begin in April, after he returned from Italy, where he had agreed to spend a few weeks shooting an ultracheap comedy called *Madigan's Millions*. A couple of days after the news broke that an unknown young New York actor would star in *The Graduate*, the Academy Award nominations were announced. Nichols's adaptation of *Who's Afraid of Virginia Woolf?* led the field with thirteen, and suddenly Joe Levine realized that he had the money to make *The Graduate* after all.

TWENTY-ONE

I must say that I haven't known any colored person particularly well," Katharine Hepburn told a journalist during the making of *Guess Who's Coming to Dinner*. "I've never had one as a friend."[1] Somewhat more remarkably, given the length of her career, Hepburn had never had a black actor as a colleague, either: She had not shared an extended scene with a well-known African American performer since 1935's *Alice Adams*, in which her character watched helplessly as a housemaid played by Hattie McDaniel made a shambles of her attempt at a fancy dinner party. So in early 1967, when Hepburn and Spencer Tracy invited Sidney Poitier over to Tracy's cottage for a getting-to-know-you dinner party, it was an unofficial dress rehearsal for the awkwardness of the comedy they were soon to play out collectively on screen.

In the decades after *Guess Who's Coming to Dinner*, Hepburn developed and cultivated a reputation as a strong-minded Yankee liberal and social progressive—the trousers-wearing iconoclast who was a feminist before the word existed, the high-minded blue blood whose mother had been a pioneering suffragist, the actress who, at least on screen, would confront intolerance with chin-up common sense. But Hepburn's off-screen politics, such as they were, emanated from more personal and often contradictory standards: Mixed in with her professed approval of independence and strong will was a streak of unreconstructed prudishness, an appetite for indignation, a high level of arrogance, and, in many cases, astonishing naiveté. When Poitier was first taken to meet the actress at her Los Angeles home, he encountered the tough, unsmiling Hepburn that many journalists met in the 1970s and later—the one who knew her own reputation and inwardly delighted in letting people know that they were being judged and, sometimes, found wanting. "Every time I spoke, every response I made, I could imagine a plus and minus column, notations in her mind," he wrote.[2]

But Poitier encountered a far milder version of Hepburn when he arrived at Tracy's home a few days later for a meal she had cooked. As many who knew the couple have noted, Hepburn submerged her personality when she was in Tracy's presence: She would mute her own power and authority and become deferential and doting, letting Tracy take center stage every time. There is a sameness to the anecdotes about Tracy and Hepburn in the 1960s that has little to do with their on-screen sparring, in which she usually gave as good as she got and then some. The stories, often told as examples of her devotion and their mutual affection, generally come with an undertow of anger and abusiveness; they begin with Hepburn expressing an opinion about something and end with Tracy snapping at her, belittling her, cutting her down, or telling her to be quiet.[3]

Poitier knew that Hepburn and Tracy were on unfamiliar terrain just trying to get through a dinner with a black man who wasn't serving them. Although he permitted himself some private irritation—"If it had been Paul Newman they were going to do a movie with, would they have checked him out so thoroughly?" he wondered—he made as many allowances as he could for two stars who struck him as "exceedingly decent people."[4] Still, one can only imagine his polite smile as he listened to Hepburn feel her way toward some sort of position on contemporary race relations, a subject on which her tone-deafness could be stunning. "I made a picture in Africa," she told an interviewer at the time, "and I know that there is one characteristic the Negroes have which is wonderful and basic: the desire and ability to make people feel wonderfully about themselves. . . . I think that when the bulk of them get out of the rut they've been kept in, they're going to snag all the public relations jobs because they're brilliant about remembering people. When you drive into New York . . . there's a colored policeman at the [bridge] who says, 'Miss Hepburn, you're back.

How nice.' . . . This quality is straight out of the jungle; they had it in the jungle when I made *The African Queen*."[5]

After the dinner was over and the guests moved to the living room, Tracy told some well-rehearsed anecdotes about his old movies, and Hepburn, according to Poitier, would "listen to each with wide-eyed fascination, as if she were hearing it for the first time." When she would interrupt, Tracy would cut her off with, "Oh, Katie, just shut up and let me tell the story."[6] By the end of the dinner, Poitier knew that he had passed whatever test he had just been asked to undergo.

Hepburn decided she officially approved of Poitier, albeit on her own cringe-inducing terms. What the actress intended as a gush of praise for her new colleague—"I can't consider Sidney as a Negro; he's not black, he's not white, he's nothing at all as far as color is concerned"[7]—represented exactly the attitude that was bringing Poitier under increasingly direct fire from social critics and movie reviewers alike. Much of the anger was coming from black progressives, who were starting to use Poitier's weakness for playing cardboard heroes as a means to attack Hollywood's unwillingness to create stronger black characters. In an essay titled "And You Too, Sidney Poitier!" in his 1966 manifesto, *White Papers for White Americans,* Calvin Hernton complained, "Why can't Sidney Poitier . . . make love in the movies? . . . By desexing the Negro, America is denying him his manhood." Hernton went on to accuse Hollywood of a "systematic attempt to castrate" Poitier or, worse, to make him play "faggots."[8] At the same time, there was no shortage of white commentators who were eager to use Poitier as a vehicle to peddle their own noxious stereotypes. "Where is the Negro American life depicted in movies as it's lived by American Negroes? Where's the child desertion and illegitimacy, the policy games and the bag women?" wrote Burt Prelutsky in the *Los Angeles Times.* "Do you think for a moment that you will ever go to a movie and see Sidney Poitier father an illegitimate child, live off his woman's earnings or mug an old Jew on the subway?" Concluding that "the pendulum" had swung too far, he labeled Poitier a "Negro in white face."[9]

Poitier, always conscious of playing to the center of the American moviegoing audience, knew that the center was starting to move, and he was trying to move along with it. He used his growing influence to urge Stanley

Kramer and William Rose to toughen his character in *Guess Who's Coming to Dinner*, and they added a scene in which Prentice privately confronts his own father about his resistance to the marriage, one of only two moments in the movie when the audience is permitted to overhear a snatch of conversation between two black characters without a white observer present. But Poitier was still hamstrung by three unsolvable problems: Kramer's insistence that his character be so far above reproach that Tracy and Hepburn would not be able to, in her words, consider him as a Negro; the screenplay's gimmicky contradiction of a man independent enough to propose an interracial marriage after a whirlwind courtship but so timid and traditional that he leaves the final decision to his fiancée's father; and the fact that Kramer and Rose wanted the young woman herself to be a blank slate, a middle-aged man's idealization of innocent yet contemporary mid-1960s girlhood.

To that end, they cast the film's final principal role with Katharine Houghton, an untried twenty-one-year-old actress who was the daughter of Hepburn's sister Marion Hepburn Grant. Houghton was, in most ways besides genealogy, an unlikely choice; she had suffered from a severe bout of rheumatic fever as a teenager and went through her adolescence with what she calls "a very limited physical life. . . . I had been told initially that I would be in a wheelchair by the time I was twenty-one, or dead, so I was always feeling that I was living on borrowed time." Houghton began acting in student films while at Sarah Lawrence College, realizing that in the short takes required by movies, nobody would be able to see her pronounced limp or "put it together that I was an invalid."[10] Kramer always maintained that Houghton was initially suggested to him by Carl Reiner, who was making *Enter Laughing* at Columbia while Kramer was casting and had auditioned her for the comedy, but it's clear that Hepburn's enthusiasm about her niece played a decisive role. Hepburn had, after all, gotten Tracy to do the film, and Kramer knew how much he owed her, although the debt, of course, was never expressly called in. Throughout the making and release of *Guess Who's Coming to Dinner*, everyone involved stuck to the same story—Kramer was charmed by the young actress, dumbstruck by her resemblance to Hepburn, and he chose her completely on his own. Clearly, his hand wasn't forced: As a producer, he knew exactly the human-interest magazine stories Houghton's presence would generate. " 'This is a family,' " Kramer's wife, Karen, told him, " 'Why not take the niece? There's a great publicity factor here, with "Aunt Kate" and Katharine Houghton. Why don't you do it?' I was newly married, and we're sometimes most effective at that moment. So he took her."[11] But there is no doubt about Hepburn's advocacy and involvement: Behind the scenes, she oversaw and approved every detail of Houghton's contract, which came to a grand total of $6,000 and included an option for four more films for Columbia at preset, modest salaries.[12]

Kramer had looked at other young actresses for the role of Poitier's fiancée; he was interested in Mariette Hartley but didn't think she was a good physical match for Hepburn, and he approached Samantha Eggar, whose high cheekbones and auburn hair would have made her a more than credible choice as Hepburn's daughter.[13] But even though production on *Guess Who's Coming to Dinner* was not scheduled to begin until March, Eggar saw no end in sight to *Doctor Dolittle*. She also would have been fifty times as expensive as Houghton, and with Tracy's health appearing to worsen by the month, Columbia was not about to do anything to increase its financial risk. "There was nothing hypothetical about it," says Houghton. "Because Kate was my aunt, I knew, of course, that Spencer really was dying and that it was becoming a dire crisis."

Just how dire became clear only a few weeks after Tracy and Hepburn's dinner with Poitier. In February, as the last sets at Columbia were being built and some of the supporting actors were coming onto the lot to sign their contracts, Tracy collapsed at his home, so sick from a buildup of fluid in his lungs that paramedics had to come and give him oxygen. He recovered after a few days but told Kramer he didn't think he was up to doing the movie. The director was in San Francisco, already beginning to shoot the scene that opens the film, in which Poitier's and Houghton's characters arrive at the airport from a vacation in Hawaii. "I called Kate, and she said the film had been canceled," says Houghton. "I thought, well, I had one day—that was fun."[14] Production was postponed for a few weeks. It was then that Kramer agreed to put his half-million-dollar salary in escrow and also told Tracy that he wouldn't make the movie without him. Columbia, looking at a reduced budget (including $71,000 in insur-

ance for Tracy that was now canceled), stayed on board.[15] Tracy rallied
and a few days later felt well enough to step back into the project and announce that *Guess Who's Coming to Dinner* would be his seventy-eighth
and, he said, final film.[16]

Eggar wasn't wrong about *Doctor Dolittle;* what had originally been planned
as a brief reunion of the cast for the final shoot in Los Angeles stretched
into four more months of production. The delays caused by both the natural and man-made disasters of the location shoots in Castle Combe and
St. Lucia had forced the re-creation of lengthy segments of the movie
on the 20th Century-Fox lot, and although Richard Fleischer insisted in
interviews that the film's budget was holding steady at $15 million,[17] $18
million was closer to the truth. With panic about *Dolittle*'s expenditure
and schedule now almost pointless, Jacobs and the studio started killing
the messengers; shortly after film editor Marjorie Fowler warned the producer that any guess about a timetable for editing *Dolittle* "quite possibly
carries the same validity as a tea-leaf reading," she was fired.[18]

Rex Harrison and Rachel Roberts, set up in a mansion in Beverly Hills,
were both drinking more heavily than ever in what Roberts later called a
period of "real disintegration."[19] "They had rented a house that my godfather, Jean Negulesco, used to own," recalls Natalie Trundy, who was by
then Arthur Jacobs's fiancée. "There was one night when Rachel Roberts
was so drunk that the police picked her up—she had run away, and they
found her crawling through the grass, trying to get home. And Rex used
to come to the set in the morning with about five martinis in him. It was
pathetic."[20] The couple's problems were becoming dangerously public:
They showed up disheveled and disoriented at a tribute to George Cukor
one night, Harrison with his toupee stuffed in his jacket pocket; on another occasion, Harrison appalled a room full of the Hollywood establishment—among them William Wyler, Billy Wilder, Jimmy Stewart, and their
wives—at a party at the Los Angeles restaurant the Bistro, singing obscene
lyrics about his penis to the tune of "I've Grown Accustomed to Her Face"
while Roberts, who was not wearing underwear, did handstands.[21]

By the end of the shoot, several of the cast members were barely on speaking terms with their star. For Geoffrey Holder, the last straw came in February, when the Ethiopian emperor Haile Selassie came to Los Angeles to visit the set of *Dolittle* during a week-long trip to the United States. The day he visited the set, Fleischer was filming one of the many sequences set in Africa that had originally been planned for St. Lucia. "Selassie was very quiet," says Holder, "and his coolness and composure made Rex look *short*. And Rex couldn't stand it when he wasn't the center of attention—you can't even say that it was *My Fair Lady* that went to his head, because it was all there already. So we meet Haile Selassie, and do you know what Rex had to say to him? 'Uh . . . how do you like *our* jungle?' *Our* jungle! What a bitch he was."[22]

Nevertheless, Harrison, as the key selling point of *Doctor Dolittle*, still wielded extraordinary power on the production. Long after Anthony Newley had filmed one of his songs, Harrison insisted that it be taken away from the character of Matthew and be reshot with Dolittle singing instead, and Jacobs assented.[23] At the same time, Dick Zanuck was still concerned that the film wasn't big, spectacular, or special enough; at great expense, he commissioned two new songs and rehired Bricusse, who thought he had seen the last of Harrison and animals months earlier, to write them.[24] When the movie finally finished production, Harrison had one last bombshell for Jacobs: Having insisted on performing all of his songs live during the movie's production, he now announced that he wanted to rerecord them. Lionel Newman, the head of Fox's music department, was furious, calling Harrison's latest whim "a crock of shit," but he got his way, and even Newman had to admit the results were an improvement.[25]

Doctor Dolittle finally wrapped in April, with little fanfare or ceremony for its exhausted crew. Zanuck and Jacobs both knew that their main job on the movie until it opened in December would be salesmanship, regardless of whether the product was worth selling. In *Variety*, a huge ad announced that reserved-seat tickets for the first nineteen weeks of the movie's premiere run at New York City's Loews State Theatre, which was to begin on December 21, 1967, were available at sky-high prices ranging from $2.50 to $4.00,[26] and Richard Fleischer began shrewdly positioning the movie for an Academy Awards campaign by giving an interview in which he called for the abolition of the annual prizes given by the Directors Guild, the Writers Guild, and various craft unions on the grounds that they diminished the impact of the Oscars.[27]

Dolittle's astonishing final cost[28]—$29 million after the then astronomical $11 million marketing budget was factored in*—should have been enough to make the blood of any studio executive run cold. But in the spring of 1967, blind belief in the future of the movie musical reached an apex of irrational exuberance. Universal Pictures had just opened *Thoroughly Modern Millie,* a long, silly 1920s pastiche put together by producer Ross Hunter for $7 million when he couldn't get the rights to the stage musical he really wanted to adapt, *The Boy Friend.*[29] Hunter had paid top dollar to secure Julie Andrews, whose success in both *The Sound of Music* and *Mary Poppins* had made her the biggest box office star in the country at the end of 1966, according to a survey of theater owners. When director George Roy Hill insisted on cutting what he called "20 minutes of meaningless cream puff"[30] from the movie, Hunter fired him and restored the footage, bringing *Millie* back up to a bloated but road-show-friendly 153 minutes, complete with an overture and an intermission. The movie may have been dreary, but it was also critic-proof; *Millie* eventually grossed $40 million worldwide, making it the studio's biggest hit in five years. If Universal, a company that in the late 1960s was widely and justly regarded as inept at both the making and the selling of movies, could find its feet with a musical, the possibilities for other studios seemed limitless. As *Millie* took off at the box office, Dick Zanuck reunited Andrews with her *Sound of Music* director, Robert Wise, and put the three-hour musical *Star!* into production for release in 1968. Warner Brothers, awaiting the fall release of its own musical behemoth, *Camelot,* decided to repurpose that film's magical-forest set and hired Francis Coppola to shoot *Finian's Rainbow* on it.† And Buena Vista decided to take its Fred MacMurray

---

* In 2007 terms, the film's total cost would have been in the neighborhood of $190 million.

† Coppola's assistant on the movie was twenty-three-year-old film school student George Lucas, whose first film, then called *THX 1133-4EB,* Coppola had promised to produce if *Finian's Rainbow* turned out to be a hit. "If suddenly they don't want me," Coppola told reporter Joseph Gelmis just before *Rainbow* opened, "then George has got a problem."

comedy *The Happiest Millionaire* and expand it into a massive 164-minute reserved-ticket musical, the company's first attempt ever to make a road-show movie that could play huge theaters like Radio City Music Hall at higher ticket prices.

A heart attack, a budget that had tripled, and a production that had lasted ten months had not deterred Arthur Jacobs from investing his energy in another movie musical or from working with Rex Harrison again. Jacobs sold MGM on a musical version of its 1939 drama *Goodbye, Mr. Chips* and flew to Portofino, where Harrison and Roberts had fled as soon as *Dolittle* wrapped, to try to convince him to take the role that had won an Oscar for Robert Donat. When Harrison passed, Jacobs moved on to Peter O'Toole without missing a beat; he then returned to the Fox lot, where he had a new movie going into production. Science fiction was a genre that had almost no box office traction in the 1960s; audiences enjoyed the more outlandish technological excesses of the James Bond movies, but "flying saucer" adventures were part of a B-picture genre that was more than a decade out of style. What Stanley Kubrick was planning with MGM's *2001: A Space Odyssey* was still a mystery: Studio head Robert O'Brien had said only that "it won't be a Buck Rogers type of space epic,"[31] and Kubrick, who had been working on the film since 1964 and had kept it in postproduction for a year while he worked on the special effects, wasn't talking. Most studios avoided sci-fi altogether, but Dick Zanuck had had some success with Richard Fleischer's *Fantastic Voyage* and was willing to green-light another space travel film as long as Jacobs agreed to stick to a tight $5 million budget. A month after *Doctor Dolittle* wrapped, cameras started to roll on *Planet of the Apes*.

TWENTY-TWO

"The first, put-together version [of a movie] is like a suicide note," Arthur Penn has said, only half-jokingly. "It has no rhythm, it's flaccid, excessive—there *are* no 'emerging qualities.' " In the spring of 1967, Penn was, at least, able to experience the mild despair he was feeling on his own terms; *Bonnie and Clyde* was being cut in Manhattan, away from the prying eyes of the studio, and he and Beatty were working at their own, deliberate pace while Dede Allen was giving them both a master class in what can be accomplished—and rectified—in postproduction. The skills of a great film editor are almost always invisible, and when Allen's work on *Bonnie and Clyde* is discussed, the focus tends to be on her split-second cross-cutting in the shoot-out that ends the movie or the breakneck robbery getaway scenes. But Allen's contribution was far more nuanced than the creation of a couple of showpiece sequences. Allen, who has called herself a "gut editor—intellect and taste count, but I cut with my feelings"— was almost peerless in her ability to focus on "character, character, character":[1] She had visited the set for a few days to get a sense of what Penn and his cast were trying to accomplish and returned to her Moviola with a sense of what to bring forth in each actor. Allen knew just how long she could hold a shot of Beatty to reveal the insecurity beneath Clyde's preening; she seemed to grasp instinctively that sudden cuts to Dunaway in motion would underscore the jagged, jumpy spirit of Bonnie Parker and that slow shots of Michael J. Pollard's C. W. Moss would mimic his two-steps-behind mental processes. And Allen cut *Bonnie and Clyde* with an eye and ear for the accelerating pace of the story, making the building of its panicky momentum her priority.

Allen and Penn shared an admiration for the suggestive, almost sensual editing of French New Wave movies: The sequence in which Bonnie first sees Clyde's pistol—a series of disembodied shots of her moist lips and flashing eyes, his gun at his waist, her lips parting in excitement as her mouth plays over the rim of a Coca-Cola bottle, her hand tentatively reaching over to fondle his gun, and a couple of close-ups of his distracted, detached expression—conveys Bonnie's charged, troubled sexual appetites and Clyde's uneasy relationship to his own body purely through the rhythm of shot selection and cutting. Beyond that, Allen proved instrumental in shaping the performances of a group of actors who, aside from Beatty, were largely new to film and whose work could vary wildly from take to take and within single takes as well. "Dede is enormously sensitive to a good, well-acted moment," says Penn. "A lot of actors owe a great deal to her."[2]

That may have been especially true of Dunaway, whose performance as Bonnie was full of brilliant, quicksilver flashes that had to be selected carefully from takes in which her nerves got the better of her. The help came at a critical moment for the actress. The fact that she had been cast in three films in quick succession had won her a spate of "It girl" publicity, but as Penn and Allen were editing *Bonnie and Clyde,* Dunaway's first two movies opened to receptions that were indifferent or worse. Elliot Silverstein's *The Happening* never quite decided whether it was supposed to be a lark about youth culture or a crime thriller; it opened early in the year, just as the idea that 1967 was to be a "Summer of Love" was gathering currency, and its portrait of hippies as "menacing" hoods already seemed quaint and silly, two steps behind the romanticization of Haight-Ashbury, LSD, and human be-ins. And *Hurry Sundown* was a disaster; no trace of comprehension of the very real contemporary racism that the cast and crew had experienced in making the film under the shadow of the Klan in Louisiana had rubbed off on the movie itself. When Paramount released Otto Preminger's long, turgid melodrama, which showcased a depiction of southern race relations that included a group of black farmhands spontaneously bursting into song on a porch, reviewers moved into shoot-to-kill mode. "Gather roun', chillun, while dem banjos is strummin' out 'Hurry, Sundown' an' ole Marse Preminger gwine tell us all about de South," wrote Judith Crist, saying it "stands with the worst films of any number of years."[3] Even *Variety*, which rarely had a negative word to say about any expensive studio picture, shook its head at "the darkies-are-a-singin' discredited racial stereotype."[4] Dunaway's brief, strong performance was completely overshadowed by near unanimous contempt for the "awful glop of neo–Uncle Tomism"[5] that defined the movie as a whole.

Then Dunaway got a lucky break: Norman Jewison, having been turned down by Elizabeth Taylor, Julie Christie, and Brigitte Bardot, was still looking for an actress to star opposite Steve McQueen in *The Thomas Crown Affair*. Jewison hadn't been any more impressed by *The Happening* or *Hurry Sundown* than critics or audiences had been, but when Allen and Penn offered to show him sequences of her performance in *Bonnie and Clyde*, he was sold. Everyone else took some convincing. "Nobody *knew* Faye Dunaway," said Jewison. "She wasn't hot."[6] Even McQueen accepted his decision only grudgingly and replaced the nickname—"Fadin' Away"— that Dunaway had acquired on Penn's set with a crueler version. According to cinematographer Haskell Wexler, McQueen was so sure his new leading lady was headed nowhere that he wrote her off as "Done Fade-Away."[7]

While Jewison prepared to shoot *Thomas Crown*, he experienced his first real lapse of optimism about *In the Heat of the Night*. Postproduction had, he felt, been going smoothly; he had brought in the movie for just over $2 million,[8] and he and Hal Ashby had been working together in the editing room for weeks, fine-tuning each scene, stripping away anything that felt extraneous—including almost every moment that remained of Virgil Tibbs's relationship with a black family in Sparta ("I sure resented being preached at like that," Jewison's own secretary told him after she saw the scenes).[9] Together, they whittled the finished film to a taut 110 minutes. Jewison had liked the jazz-inflected scores of Sidney Lumet's *The Pawnbroker* and Sydney Pollack's *The Slender Thread*, so he hired the same composer, thirty-three-year-old Quincy Jones, to score *In the Heat of the Night*; Jones suggested that they sign Ray Charles to sing a bluesy, mood-setting title song over the opening credits.

In the spring, the Mirisch Company scheduled the film's first sneak preview, and Jewison and Ashby took a print to San Francisco, a city they chose for its hip, liberal, antiauthority moviegoing audience. "In those days, we used to do real sneak previews," says Jewison, "on a Friday or Saturday night. After the audience had already seen a film, we'd say, 'If you want to stay, we have another movie to show you.' And that's what we did on *In the Heat of the Night*." The audience watched quietly as the first few scenes of the movie unfolded—the discovery of a dead body on Sparta's main drag in the middle of the night, the introduction of Virgil Tibbs as he's hauled into the police station for questioning, and his first encounter with Chief Gillespie. "When Steiger said to Poitier, 'What do you do up there in Philadelphia to make that kind of money?' and Poitier answered, 'I'm a police officer,' " says Jewison, "the audience went nuts. But with *laughter*. They were stamping their feet, they thought it was so funny." The laughter came again, in a tremendous wave, when Poitier spoke his signature line, "They call me *Mister* Tibbs!" and Jewison's heart sank completely. As the movie ended, he walked out of the theater dazed and sorrowful, with Ashby trailing behind him.

"I thought I had made a film that had a little bit of humor," says Jewison, "but not a comedy. I was devastated. Truly devastated. I said to Hal, 'Oh, my God. What have we done here?' "

Ashby was unfazed. A proud hippie, he was more in touch than Jewison was with an emerging post-*Strangelove* generation of moviegoers who weren't interested in earnestness but got the barbed sociocultural joke of a smart black cop waiting with ever-decreasing patience for a backward southern sheriff to drag his carcass into the modern world. They weren't laughing at the movie, he told Jewison; they were just grooving on the humiliating comeuppance Poitier was handing to Steiger in every scene. "You don't understand," he told Jewison. "They were enjoying the film. They were into it. They *get* it." Jewison wondered if the movie needed a major recut; Ashby suggested losing a couple of lines here and there, but nothing more. Jewison returned to Los Angeles with serious misgivings. But he was able to console himself with one reaction. "Even in San Francisco," he said, "when we got to the scene where Endicott slaps Tibbs and Tibbs slaps him right back, there was suddenly no sardonic or ironic feeling in the audience. There was a gasp, an intake of breath throughout the theater that was almost palpable. From the white audience and the black audience. They didn't take that as a joke. And at that moment, I knew we had them."[10]

In March, Mike Nichols assembled the cast of *The Graduate* on a Los Angeles soundstage for what was to be an almost unheard-of luxury for a small film: three weeks of rehearsal, during which the actors would have a chance to explore their characters, improvise scenes, and feel their way into relationships while Nichols shaped them into an ensemble. Dustin Hoffman, Anne Bancroft, and Katharine Ross took their places at a long table, scripts in hand, as did the rest of the actors Nichols had hired: Elizabeth Wilson, who had costarred with Hoffman onstage in *Eh?*, was to play his mother; William Daniels, another theater veteran who had just finished starring in a short-lived sitcom overseen by Buck Henry called *Captain Nice*, would play Benjamin's father, though he was just ten years older than Hoffman; and Gene Hackman, fresh from *Bonnie and Clyde*, had won the role of Bancroft's husband, the unsuspecting Mr. Robinson. Nichols's brain trust was also present: Buck Henry, editor Sam O'Steen, and production designer Dick Sylbert. And, as Warren Beatty had done on *Bonnie and Clyde,* Nichols completed the mix with a veteran cinematographer. Robert Surtees came to the project with three Academy Awards, thirty-five years of experience, and a résumé that had included some of the most difficult productions of the last several years: William Wyler's *The Collector,* Arthur Penn's *The Chase,* and, most recently, *Doctor Dolittle,* from which he had gotten an early parole in order to join Nichols's crew. O'Steen, remembering Nichols's sometimes stormy relationship with Haskell Wexler on *Virginia Woolf,* warned Surtees that Nichols was going to push him hard,[11] but Surtees couldn't imagine that *The Graduate* would offer him any more of a challenge than a thousand animals had. While the actors worked, Sylbert would scout locations in Los Angeles[12] and Surtees would begin to map out shots, with O'Steen serving as a sounding board for Nichols and consulting along the way, just as Ashby had done for Jewison on *In the Heat of the Night.*

"Don't do anything," Nichols told his cast before they opened the script. "Don't push. Don't try to perform. This is just for us."[13] And then they turned to page 1, starting with one of the very few scenes in Henry's screenplay that did not make it into the finished film, an overexplicit prologue in which Benjamin the valedictorian, in cap and gown, reads his speech in front of thousands of classmates. "What is the purpose of these years, the purpose for all this demanding work, the purpose for the sacrifices made by those who love us?" he asks. As he builds to the answer, he begins to panic; he can't remember it. Wind rustles the pages on the lectern; perspiration begins to bead on his brow. The audience stares at him expectantly. "The purpose is . . ." he says, searching for the word as the pages of his speech blow away. "There is a reason, my friends, and the reason is . . . ," he trails away, pouring sweat. He never finds the answer.

Two hours later, the actors got to the last moments of Henry's original screenplay, in which Benjamin and Elaine, fleeing from the church, jump onto a bus. "Let's go. Let's get this bus moving!" Benjamin says to the driver.[14]

The bus was not moving. The panic Benjamin expressed in the movie's first scene had, by the end of that morning, spread to the entire table of actors. "That day," says Hoffman, "I'll never forget. That movie just fell right on its ass. By the time that reading was over, there was a glumness on everybody's faces. The same expression. And I remember Nichols just saying, 'Okay, let's break for lunch, and then we'll come back and start rehearsal.' "[15]

"I don't think there was a lot of love in the room," says Buck Henry. "Dustin was very withdrawn. And when Anne started working, I don't know what was wrong, but I thought, Lord, there's no Mrs. Robinson in there that I know of."[16]

Hoffman's initial struggle wasn't surprising; his character was the center of the movie, his grueling screen test just weeks earlier had felt like a giant vote of no confidence, and he still worried that he had been miscast as a young superachiever in a romantic triangle. As he began rehearsals, every bit of his meager off-Broadway theater experience was telling him to hold back, refuse to commit himself, and wait until later in the process to discover the character. "That's why we never got jobs, me and Hackman

and Duvall!" he says. "Duvall would say, the ones that get the jobs, what
you see at the audition is what you get. Whatever they did to get the part,
that was it—that was the character. But we would try to develop a character, and when we didn't know what it was going to be, we were taught to
do zero, it'll come to you, just read the lines."[17]

Bancroft's troubles were harder to decipher. By 1967, she was an experienced film actress who, after her Academy Award in 1963, had moved
on to a challenging role as an unhappy woman heading toward her third
marriage and sixth child in the British drama *The Pumpkin Eater,* written by Harold Pinter, and won another Oscar nomination. But the kind
of movie stardom she might have expected in the five years since *The
Miracle Worker* had eluded her; in the early and mid-1960s, the era of sex
comedies, westerns, and war films, Hollywood didn't have much use for an
actress with her kind of dark, brittle strength. Playing the bored, alcoholic
wife of a successful businessman, she seemed lost, disconnected from
the character's intelligence and suffocating ennui. "I wasn't seeing upper
middle class in her performance," says Henry. "I was seeing lower middle
class, or upper lower class. It took them a while. But that's what rehearsals
are for, and she and Mike both knew how to use it. It made me admire her
more that she had to climb out of someplace to get there."[18]

"Do you like my character?" the irritated actress asked Nichols after a
few days of rehearsal.

"No, not at all!" said Nichols. "She's much too nice! She doesn't sound
like that."

"*Why* isn't she nice?" said Bancroft.

"I can't tell you," said Nichols. "I don't know why. But I can do it
for you."

"All right," said Bancroft. "Let me hear it."

Nichols read her one of Mrs. Robinson's lines—"Benjamin, will
you drive me home?"—with as much frosty, deadpan neutrality as he
could muster.

"Oh!" she said. "I can do *that.* I know what that is. That's *anger.*"[19]

"Annie was tough," says Elizabeth Wilson. "I don't think she was a
happy camper from the first day I worked on the film. She had a sort of
aloofness—she wanted to be left alone to work on her character and to

think whatever she had to think. It made sense for her to do that, but it wasn't easy."[20]

"Annie wasn't Mrs. Robinson," says Nichols. "She was very different. But she also had this tremendous anger—*that* was real, that was her power. Years later, we were all together for some anniversary of *The Graduate*, and we were encouraged by some studio or other to reminisce. And every time someone would say something about how much fun it was, she would contradict them, almost harshly. She would say, 'No, it wasn't like that, it wasn't such a wonderful time, we worked *hard!*' Afterwards, I said to her, 'We remember everything differently, but I have to ask you, do you remember the moment when you said, "That's anger!" the same way I do?' And she said, 'Yes, word for word—and sometimes I think I've never lost the anger since then.' Which I think was sort of true."[21]

"One of Mike's great gifts is as a *casting* director," says Wilson. "He can somehow pick up on the essence and spirit of a person, and study it, and then tap into it."[22] For Bancroft, that meant unlocking her rage. For Hoffman, it meant exploring, and more than once exploiting, his awkwardness, his stubbornness, his embarrassment, and his dreadful certainty that the experience of making *The Graduate* would end in humiliation for him, an anxiety that had, in a way, started the moment Nichols peered at Hoffman in the makeup chair and asked, "Can't we do something about his nose?" One afternoon, reporter Betty Rollin watched as Nichols took the actors through a rehearsal of the scene in which Mrs. Robinson sits in Benjamin's car and warns him to stay away from her daughter. Nichols had Hoffman and Bancroft push their chairs together and sit side by side, looking straight ahead. "You threaten him with something so terrorizing that you know he has to do what you want," Nichols told Bancroft.

"Oh, I have so much anger I can't breathe!" said Bancroft, exhilarated.

"Now, Dusty," said Nichols, turning to Hoffman. "It's like you just won an award, say, for that [Italian] picture you just did, and I say, 'Listen, I have permission from SAG to see that you never work again.'" Hoffman just nodded, the blood draining from his face.

The barbs Nichols aimed at the young actor could sting, especially when they focused on his appearance: "Oh, I'm so sick of that shirt off," he said, sighing, when Hoffman started undressing to rehearse a bed-room scene with Ross. "It's not like he's Bardot."[23] Hoffman had already endured an early round of publicity that focused, sometimes caustically, on his "extraordinarily ordinary" looks and a childhood that had included "braces on the teeth, polyps in the nose, acne on the skin."[24] But Hoff-man thrived on the push and pull with his director. "The rehearsal period was the greatest experience I've ever had in terms of film, bar none," he says. "What he did was what I had always heard directing should be. I remember when we were rehearsing the hotel scene [in which Benjamin beds Mrs. Robinson for the first time], he took me into a corner and said, 'Do you remember the first time you had any action at all?' And I said yeah. It was a sweater feel. I was in junior high school, playing the piano, doing Al Jolson in blackface, if you can believe that, and this girl was in the show, and we were waiting to be called. And we're kind of attracted to each other, but I can't get too close to her because of the blackface. And somehow, at one point, I put my hand on her breast.

"Mike said, 'Let's do the scene again, and do that to Annie. Don't tell her. Just find a place to do it.' So I go up behind her, and just as she takes her sweater off, I put my hand on her breast. And she was brilliant. She just looked at it, and then went back to her sweater, taking a stain out of it or something. And I started to break [into laughter]. I took my hand off her breast, and I turned away and thought, I'm gonna get fired, because breaking is the worst thing you can do. I turned my back on her and Nich-ols and walked over to the wall and started banging my head against it. And he goes into hysterics. He said, '*That's* in the movie.' "[25]

Nichols would constantly come up with new questions for Hoffman: Do you think Benjamin's a virgin? Did you have any idols when you were growing up? How would you play this scene if you were twelve years old and Mrs. Robinson were in her twenties? What would Benjamin do if he went over to the Robinsons' for a barbecue? "He was talking the talk that I'd been learning for years," says Hoffman. "It was exhilarating."[26]

But several other cast members still felt mystified about *The Graduate*. They found the chilly tone of Henry's screenplay jarringly bleak for what seemed, in its plot contours, to be a fairly standard dirty joke—the one about the nice boy, the nice girl, and the predatory older woman. "We all knew Mike's reputation," says William Daniels. "He had done *Barefoot in the Park,* so when you looked at the script for *The Graduate,* and thought, 'Here's a New York director who does light comedies,' you looked at it in a certain way. We assumed it was a light comedy about Anne Bancroft and the young boy. But in the second week of rehearsal, Mike said to us, 'I'm thinking of using these two kids for the music—one tall and one small.' And he put on 'The Sound of Silence.' Well, I completely turned around. Suddenly, I realized, hearing the music, that this was going to be told entirely through Dustin's eyes. And that was something I hadn't seen before. All of a sudden, the film felt more significant."[27]

At the end of the second week of rehearsals, the room was still tense and unsettled, and Nichols's frustration focused on one actor. "Gene Hackman and I were in a studio men's room," says Hoffman, "with about four or five urinals separating us. We were both taking a pee. And I said, 'How do you think it's going today?' And he said, 'I think I'm getting fired.' 'Fired! What are you talking about? You're not getting fired.' And Gene just said, 'He doesn't like what I'm doing.' We were two old friends. We had gone to acting school together. It was hard."

Nichols fired Hackman that afternoon. "It's very simple," the director says. "He was too young. Gene was wonderful about it—he has never been a particularly easygoing guy, but he's always been amazing about that." Nichols replaced him with Murray Hamilton, seven years Hackman's senior. Hackman put up a brave front, but privately, says Elizabeth Wilson, "he was devastated. Gene had refused to learn his lines, maybe that was it. I don't know why, but we were all told to learn the lines for rehearsals, and Gene didn't." The cast had no inkling that it was about to happen, and with only two weeks remaining before the start of production, everybody's guard went up. "I was kind of in a state of shock when I heard," says Buck Henry. "Everyone became very dour that day. And I thought, 'Oh God, is this the beginning of everything coming apart?' "[28]

TWENTY-THREE

Stanley Kramer didn't schedule more than a day or two of rehearsals for *Guess Who's Coming to Dinner*. Even if Spencer Tracy's health had allowed him to participate in any kind of extended preproduction, the actor would have found the idea of rehearsing for a movie as ludicrous as if Kramer had asked him to improvise or to base his emotional reaction in a particular scene on a childhood memory. Tracy understood anxiety and fear but scoffed at what he saw as the better-acting-through-neurosis style of the Brando generation and their followers, and he found the notion of interior exploration laughable. He was not a soul-searcher; whether or not he ever actually said that the secret of acting was to know your lines and not bump into the furniture, the frequency with which the remark was attributed to him was no accident. Tracy had an extreme distaste for what he saw as unmasculine oversensitivity in performers; he didn't even like to do a second take most of the time and would often end the first one by shouting to the cameraman, "Did you get that?" He had managed to make movies his way for nearly forty years, and on *Guess Who's Coming to Dinner,* Kramer accommodated him with a production style that, in most ways, owed more to 1947 than to 1967. The large hilltop home of Matt and Christina Drayton, the affluent couple Tracy and Hepburn were playing, was built entirely on the Columbia lot, including a veranda with a not particularly convincing painted backdrop of the San Francisco Bay into which was screwed a small flashing red bulb that was intended to indicate a ship in the distance. The lighting, by sixty-three-year-old cinematographer Sam Leavitt, obliterated every shadow. The costumes were not bought off the rack, as designers for contemporary movies increasingly preferred to do for the sake of realism, but were sketched and constructed expressly for the film by Jean Louis. "As a young person, I thought that was very strange," says Houghton of the sunshiny little frocks and gloves she was made to wear. "They were clothes that were out of another time and place, things I'd never wear in thirty years!"[1] And the driving scenes were done with the careless, blurred backgrounds that had been typical of process photography for decades. As his critics often noted, Kramer was probably the least visual thinker among Hollywood's major filmmakers of the time; shooting a movie, for him, was primarily a matter of assembling a group of actors and executing the words in a script.

By the time production began on March 20, Kramer had spoken privately to many members of the cast and crew and explained how the forty-five-day shoot would proceed. Tracy would be available for only two to four hours every day, starting at 10:00 A.M.; by 2:00 P.M. at the latest, he would be on his way home. Kramer and Leavitt would shoot his scenes first, and master shots in which he had to appear in the same frame as other actors would be prioritized, as would his close-ups. In group scenes, other members of the cast would have to be willing to save their own close-ups, answers, and reactions to Tracy until after the actor had left, with script supervisor Marshall Schlom feeding them Tracy's lines from behind the camera. On days when Tracy was well enough to work, his scenes would move to the top of the schedule. On days when he wasn't, which might occur with no warning, the rest of the cast would have to be prepared with no notice to shoot scenes that didn't involve him.[2] A story was planted with columnist Dorothy Manners in which she cooperatively explained that the set would be closed to most journalists because it's "very small . . . barely enough room for the technicians" and dismissed Tracy's recent physical collapse as "never as serious as it sounded. . . . A new maid became frightened when Spence had difficulty due to a chronic nasal congestion."[3]

"The whole film was terribly precarious," says Houghton. "The operative dynamic throughout was in trying to make this work for Spencer, so we all became teammates in that. Stanley must have been under extraordinary tension, but he was not the kind of person to show it. He had so many other responsibilities on the film that he couldn't afford to even think about the idea that Spencer might just drop dead, that he might not live to make it the next day. Spencer himself was very philosophical about the whole thing—he almost seemed to be the least worried about it. Kate, of course, was a nervous wreck."[4]

Guess Who's Coming to Dinner got under way in an atmosphere of artificial good cheer, as the imperative of making a movie temporarily forced everyone to put aside their fears. Tracy's presence was spectral; he had enough vitality to get through a couple of shots a day, but no more; except for a few pleasant exchanges with Poitier, whom he genuinely liked, he lacked the stamina even to chat with his costars or the crew, leaving the set between scenes to lie down in his trailer. As for Hepburn, she strode onto the lot the first morning, hungry to be back before the cameras for the first time in six years, and immediately started driving Kramer crazy. She paced the perimeter off the Draytons' living room, asserting her ownership of the set, inspecting the furniture. Why were the cords for all the lamps so visible? Cords running across the floor were vulgar; in her own home, she concealed them by tucking them under the rugs. Could someone get on that? She peered through the viewfinder. The fireplace looked just awful; it would have to be replaced. And what was that hat Kathy was wearing? It looked terrible. Now, about the first scene, a brief exchange between her character and Poitier's—what angle was he planning to shoot it from? Kramer finally blew up and asked her just who was running the show. "Now, now, Stanley," she said. "Let's not lose our equilibrium. I'm only trying to keep the set alive so everyone won't go to sleep."[5]

Hepburn's bulldozer energy exhausted Kramer, but it had a purpose: She was letting him know that he wasn't going to be able to get through the movie without her, and she may have been using manic activity to keep her alarm about Tracy's weakness at bay. Hepburn put in marathon days on *Guess Who's Coming to Dinner*—attending to Tracy and his needs every morning, getting him home in the afternoon, returning to the lot to shoot the scenes that didn't involve him, and then spending two hours every evening coaching her game but awkward niece through her role, after which she would run lines with Tracy, who was fearful about his failing ability to memorize his dialogue.[6] If the price for that level of commitment was her meddling, it was a trade-off Kramer was willing to make. "When she signed for the film, she said, 'I bet I'll bug you—I bet I'll drive you crazy,'" he told a reporter. "I said, 'I bet you will too, and I'll tell you how I'll live with it. Go ahead and bug me, drive me crazy—I'll let you know, but don't stop doing it.' Katie . . . is not always right, in my opinion, but she's right 60 percent of the time."[7] On a grouchier day, speaking to another writer, he revised that figure down to 50 percent.

Some natural insecurity was also playing on Hepburn's nerves: The actress, who celebrated her sixtieth birthday during the production, was being filmed in color under garish light for the first time in ten years, and she worried about her neck, her age spots, her wrinkled hands, her sun-damaged skin. Hepburn developed a self-protective strategy in which, in scene after scene, she would suggest blocking that positioned her face lower in the frame, where she believed the light was less harsh. "I'm not really vain," she insisted, "but I don't think people want to see me look like a corpse, or a monkey."[8] Tracy had no patience for her contrivances. He let every wrinkle show and even refused to wear makeup in the movie; when someone would try to powder his forehead, he would push him away with a look of disgust, calling it "nonsense."[9] When Hepburn entered for one scene and dipped low to kneel beside him, hiding her neck, Kramer recalled later, "it really teed Spencer off. He said, 'What the hell are you doing now?' She said, 'Spencuh, I just thought . . .' And he said, '*Spencuh, I just thought . . . ,*' imitating her Bryn Mawr accent. 'Go out and come in like a human being, for Christ's sake!' "[10] "Kate, why don't you talk like a person?" he snapped at her on another day. "You talk like you've got a feather up your ass!"[11] Hepburn would just smile and swallow whatever she was thinking. "In many ways, she was all about pleasing the men," says Karen Kramer, "acquiescing and making them feeling comfortable and almost being a doormat."[12]

On most days, Tracy's energy would evaporate quickly. "They used a very old-fashioned kind of lighting that took forever," says William Mead, who played a delivery boy in the film (he's billed as "Skip Martin"). "I remember Spencer Tracy getting very impatient between takes because they had to light everything within an inch of its life."[13] The more he felt his strength ebbing, the more he made Hepburn the target of his abuse. "Why don't you just mind your own goddamn business, read the lines, do what he says, and just get on with it," he would tell her when she started to argue with Kramer.[14]

As irritated as he would become with Hepburn, Tracy also knew that she was creating a buffer zone between him and the production, whisking him away for naps, telling Kramer that she thought the last take was perfect when she sensed he was tiring, making sure that he always had a glass of milk filled with ice cubes at hand (by then, despite Tracy's long history of alcoholism, he apparently restricted himself to milk during the day and a single beer at night). He was kinder when talking about her than when talking to her. "Do you notice she's the same with everybody—how she tries to help people?" he told a reporter in one of the rare interviews he gave during the production. "She helps little Kathy, she helps Cecil Kellaway . . . she helps me, she helps you. . . ."[15] Hepburn, though endlessly solicitous with Tracy, was a drillmaster with her niece, warning her, "I can see the wheels turning!"[16] whenever she thought Houghton was slowing down a scene, and ordering her to be home for dinner every night. While rehearsing a scene in which Joey Drayton runs downstairs to greet her mother, Houghton tripped on the staircase and sprained her ankle badly. Hepburn unsentimentally told her to soldier on. "Poor Kathy," she remarked. "Think of what would have happened if she'd broken something and had to be replaced. After losing this opportunity, there'd be just one goddamn thing for her to do—kill herself."[17]

Had she been a more experienced actress, or made her debut in a less troubled production, Houghton might have felt freer to articulate her own misgivings about playing a character who, on screen, seems so oblivious to the realities around her that, as many critics pointed out, it's hard to imagine what Poitier's character sees in her. "In the original script," she recalls, "there was a wonderful scene in which the girl gets to say to her father, 'I don't understand what's wrong with you—you brought me up to believe that a person's worth is not based on the color of their skin, but on what they are intrinsically. If anything, I'm not worthy of *him*, because he's a world-famous doctor and I'm young and haven't done anything!'" says Houghton. "For me, that scene *saved* me as a character, because I really did think, why on earth would he be interested in this girl unless she has something to say for herself?"

Kramer strongly disagreed; he believed that the naiveté of the blind girl in Poitier's *A Patch of Blue* had made her affection for a black man more palatable to white audiences, and two years later, he didn't believe moviegoers were ready for anything more challenging. "The day came when Spencer and I were going to do our big scene," she recalls, "and just before we shot it, Stanley said to me, 'I want you to know I may not use this. You don't know America the way I do,' he said. 'The American public will accept a girl's blind love for this man, but they won't forgive you if you go into this relationship with open eyes.' Well, I thought it was cuckoo, but because of the circumstances, I didn't know how hard I could push. How was this going to affect me, was this a good career move, blah blah blah—*afterwards* I had a lot of thoughts about that. But it's amazing what the traumatic event of being close to someone with a serious illness can do. That was our world. Nothing else mattered."[18]

The on-screen reunion of Tracy and Hepburn generated a tremendous amount of interest in the press, and despite the preemptive announcement that the set would be closed, Hepburn surprised everyone involved in the movie by making herself more available to reporters than she had ever been. In the 1940s, her exchanges with journalists were often combative; in the 1950s, around the time of *The African Queen*, she began using selected interviews to shape an image of herself as tough, indomitable, and indifferent to the vicissitudes of Hollywood. At sixty, Hepburn could be forbidding—"Bunk about the-public-has-a-right-to-know!" she barked. "They haven't got the right to know anything—not until forty or fifty years from now!"[19] But on *Guess Who's Coming to Dinner*, she apportioned generous helpings of her carefully honed personality to writers from *Look*, from *Life*, from *Esquire*, and from *The New York Times*; she cooperated with a promotional book being written about the stars of the movie; she toured reporters around the set, chatted away about any number of topics, and began to shape a new image—funnier, more talkative, full of loose-cannon opinions, stridency leavened by a measure of self-deprecation—that would carry her through the next thirty years. In part, the change came about because Hepburn was genuinely surprised and touched at the affection journalists suddenly seemed to feel for her after years in which she hadn't worked. "She'd always had an adversarial relationship with the press and enjoyed it, but I think on *Guess Who's Coming to Dinner* she found she could have an unadversarial relationship with the press and enjoy it, too," says Houghton. "This was a reemergence from her cocoon after five or six years. But she was also very aware that Spencer was going, and that made her vulnerable in a way that didn't involve her ego as much as all of the previous moments in her career—it really wasn't about *her*. Heretofore, she would have been much more concerned about 'Kate,' about what impression Kate Hepburn was making, her caprices, her image, was she going to be a success? But this film was probably the most personal film she made, and it opened a door for her into a new way of relating to the public."[20]

Hepburn took one journalist after another and gave them exactly what they wanted: good copy. She railed against sexual frankness ("Elia Kazan's book [*The Arrangement*, about a middle-aged married man who takes a mistress] is the most REPULSIVE point of view about sex"); about the new European cinema ("I saw *Blow-Up* and thought it an absolute bunch of claptrap . . . a lot of twaddle that winds up with a lot of poor, wretched, underfed things playing tennis WITHOUT a ball");[21] about the uselessness of psychiatry, a favorite and tellingly persistent theme of hers; about Jacqueline Susann's *Valley of the Dolls* ("straight pornography"); and about her loathing for on-screen nudity (especially when it featured "people with bosoms smaller than mine"). When she heard herself becoming too prissy or sour, she could switch gears immediately: Suddenly she would sing the praises of daring British movies like *Georgy Girl* or *Alfie*, remarking, "I think it's too bad that we can't, in this country, compete with that market and produce a picture that doesn't have to appeal to so many people." She started finding a useful tone of endearing self-disparagement ("I suppose people may be rather fond of me as they are of an old building").[22] And most surprising, she talked about Tracy in warmer and more personal terms that she had ever allowed herself to use publicly, even taking a cheerfully conspiratorial tone with visiting writers. "Listen, I'll be the easy one to get—I gab a lot," she told *Look*. "It's Spencer we have to work on. He gets melancholia if he thinks too much about the past." In talking about Tracy, Hepburn may have revealed more of the complexity of their relationship than she realized. Describing their on-screen sparring, she said, "The woman is always pretty sharp and she's needling the man, sort of slightly like a mosquito . . . and then he slowly puts out his big paw and slaps the lady down, and that's attractive to the American public." She even said to Tracy, in front of a writer, "I'm the most necessary person on this here set. I'm just here for you to pick on." Above all, she always remembered to sell the movie, telling reporters that she believed interracial marriage would soon become routine and letting them know that "there's no bunk in our movie—we play tennis WITH the ball."[23]

The emergence of a new, more open Hepburn was a result of some genuine softening on her part, but it was also the end product of what one reporter called a "minuet" of careful negotiations;[24] the visits were orchestrated by Columbia Pictures and by Howard Strickling, MGM's longtime publicity chief and the man who had successfully kept Tracy's problems out of the press for twenty years. Reporters from approved publications arrived on the set with an understanding that no rumor of Hepburn and Tracy's personal relationship, whatever it was, was to make its way into print; old-Hollywood decorum was to be observed. Accordingly, Hepburn and Tracy had separate trailers and dressing rooms. "Even then," says Marshall Schlom, "they always played it very low-key. She would go to her dressing room, but then she would bring lunch to his."[25] When the press was present, everyone knew their roles. Houghton was called in for interviews and struck the right note of pert enthusiasm and unflappability. Poitier was gracious and modest, trotting out a story—as did Kramer—that he was so nervous about his first time acting with stars of Hepburn and Tracy's magnitude that Kramer had to send them home and let Poitier say his lines to empty chairs. Tracy's illness seems a far more likely explanation of that anecdote than Poitier's nerves, but, says Houghton, "there was always a facade. There was just no way anybody was going to betray what was going on at the time with the seriousness of Spencer's fragility."[26]

For Poitier, *Guess Who's Coming to Dinner* felt, in some ways, like a creative step backward after the revitalizing challenge of his work with Rod Steiger on *In the Heat of the Night*; his character, Prentice, was the film's straight man, a paragon of accomplishment and good manners who

existed primarily to generate comic reactions in the characters around
him. "In this film we are first and foremost, it seems to me . . . presenting entertainment with a point of view," he told a reporter, expressing his
reservations as politely as possible. "I really don't quite understand what I
think of it in racial terms."[27]

Poitier's reticence was unsurprising. William Rose's script offered a
good deal of genuinely funny social comedy revolving around Tracy and
the spectacle of, as Cecil Kellaway's monsignor put it, "a broken-down
old phony liberal [coming] face-to-face with his principles." But when the
movie aimed for a more direct and contemporary take on race, the results
were hopeless. In the first scene in the movie to feature two black characters talking to each other, the Draytons' suspicious maid, Tillie, corners
Prentice while she's out of earshot of her employers and confronts him
about his intentions. "I got something to say to you, boy!" she says. "You
think I don't see what you are? You're one of those smooth-talkin' smart-ass
niggers just out for all you can get with your black power and all your other
troublemaking nonsense. And you lissen here! I brought up that chile from
a baby in her cradle and ain't nobody gonna harm her none while I'm here
watchin'! You read me, boy?" Isabel Sanford, hired for $600 a week to play
Tillie,[28] would go on to become well-known to TV viewers a few years later
as part of the cast of *All in the Family* and *The Jeffersons*; she played the
scene with tremendous comic vigor, and Kramer himself added the "black
power" line as a fainthearted nod to the news,[29] but nothing could save the
scene from the mammy clichés of a screenwriter who was completely out
of touch with the civil rights movement and who couldn't even imagine
Poitier's character would have a word of reaction to the dressing-down.
And Poitier had rarely had to say a worse line than Prentice's jab at his
own father (Roy Glenn): "Not until you and your whole lousy generation
lay down and die will the weight of you be off our backs. . . . You think of
yourself as a colored man—I think of myself as a *man*." The screenplay
was surely to blame for that moment, but in part, it echoed words Poitier
himself had spoken just a year earlier; talking about his role in the western
Duel at Diablo, he had said, "I play a guy, not a Negro."[30]

In fact, Kramer had taken pains to smooth out anything that might
disturb white moviegoers. In an early draft of the script, Rose had had

Prentice's father tell off Matt Drayton: "Calm down? Now, listen, you better let me tell you something. Have you got any idea at all of what a Negro doctor in the United States is up against?" He goes on to say that marriage to Joey would mean "throwing away everything he's ever done or ever <u>hoped</u> to do! I mean he would be <u>ruined</u>!" Kramer crossed it out.

The dissonance between the cloistered world of *Guess Who's Coming to Dinner* and the racial maelstrom of 1967 America became impossible to ignore when actress Beah Richards arrived on the set to film her scenes as Prentice's mother. Richards was a well-regarded stage actress and a deeply committed political activist who wrote a column for the civil rights publication *Freedomways*; by 1967, J. Edgar Hoover's FBI had been keeping a file on her for sixteen years. At forty-six, she was just seven years Poitier's senior, but she usually played characters who were older than her actual age—"I was everybody's mother, from Sidney's to James Earl Jones's," she said. Richards was furious about the lack of opportunities offered to African American performers, and she wasn't alone: Months after she had won a Tony nomination for James Baldwin's 1965 play, *The Amen Corner*, her director, Frank Silvera, took out a trade ad complaining that since the nomination, she had received only a single acting offer, "one day's work as a maid." Just a few months earlier, she had played opposite Poitier in *In the Heat of the Night* as the character Stirling Silliphant had once imagined as a sort of voodoo abortionist. She had made just $2,500 for the role[31] and never knew when—or if—another offer would be coming. Now she was put in a synthetic gray wig and dressed in pearls, white gloves, and a modest hat; her character was made to look like a loyal old housekeeper who has just come from a president's funeral. Prentice's mother was meant to embody the kind of soft-spoken, well-kept, epitome-of-dignity little old black lady who Kramer and Rose thought would put white audiences at their ease, but having to return to the kind of role that had made her into what one reviewer later called "the best sweet-and-sensitive Negro mother in all of show business," Richards was openly unhappy. Her speech to Spencer Tracy was, in the words of her friend Ossie Davis, a reminder that " 'These children are in love, and love is all that we need to consider.' . . . Now, Beah knew that was a lie. . . . At the same time, it was a chance at that level to make any statement at all, so she made it with authority."[32]

Richards brought great delicacy and restraint to her scenes, especially to her poignant and exquisitely performed speech to Tracy about how old men can no longer remember or understand passion, but by the end of her work on the movie, says Houghton, "I felt that she hated all of us. She was a formidable presence and a very angry person. She never misbehaved in any way. But I felt that there was no way, as a young white woman, that I could ever be redeemed in her eyes. And I totally understood that, and I didn't think the film really did a whole lot to ameliorate that situation. It was a big reality check—it must have been horribly difficult for her to even get those lines out."

As for Poitier, he felt more resigned than angry. The "Negro in white face" article and the increasingly personal attacks from black writers on his choices of roles had stung. "He was very, very kind to me," says Houghton. "He would talk to me when we were waiting for shots to be set up, but what I remember him talking about most was that he was tired of acting. He wanted to become a director—he felt that that was the only way he would be able to bring more black people into the business and tell different stories. He felt that as an actor, he had contributed as much as he could."[33]

By early May, Tracy was in such rapid decline that he was missing entire days and working as little as six hours a week.[34] "The on-the-set situation is tenser than tense," associate producer George Glass wrote to a journalist. "Tracy fell ill over the past weekend and failed to show for yesterday's big scene, shooting of which will occupy all this week." Hepburn was on guard at every moment; when Glass brought John Flinn, Columbia's director of publicity, onto the set, she berated him for allowing a "stranger" onto the production. When Glass explained who Flinn was, Hepburn, he wrote, "was taken about as far aback as she ever goes (an inch or so)."[35]

Kramer had worked around Tracy as much as possible, bringing in a body double for angles in which only his back was seen; as the shoot progressed, even the effort of standing exhausted his star, "and when he tired," Kramer said, "it came quickly." "He huffed and he puffed," said Schlom. "He had difficulty even walking up a short flight of stairs."[36] But there would be no way to fake the actor's big scene—a climactic monologue in which Matt Drayton summarizes every argument for and against racial intermarriage that the other characters have made and then grants his blessing to his daughter and future son-in-law. The speech, which unfolds virtually uninterrupted over the last eight minutes of the movie, is a skillful and touching piece of screenwriting in which Matt wrenchingly articulates his love for Christina and then works his way toward a benevolent conclusion. The final words in the monologue blended Kramer's taste for heartfelt speechifying with Tracy's warm, commonsensical voice almost perfectly: "As for you two and the problems you're going to have, they seem almost unimaginable. . . . There'll be a hundred million people right here in this country who will be shocked and offended and appalled by the two of you. . . . You will just have to ride that out, maybe every day for the rest of your lives. You can try to ignore those people, or you can feel sorry for them and their prejudices and their bigotry and their blind hatreds and stupid fears, but where necessary, you'll just have to cling tight to each other and say, screw all those people." (Just before production, Geoffrey Shurlock had warned Kramer that such a "coarse and vulgar expression" would not be approved "in a picture of this caliber," but Kramer and Rose had kept it in, knowing Shurlock no longer had enough power to take it out.)[37]

"Spencer Tracy never fluffed a word," Poitier wrote later. "Every person on the soundstage that afternoon became engrossed with [his] character as that remarkable actor did his job. . . . It was hypnotic watching that man pick up the pace here, slow it down there, take a pause here, smile there . . . all of it making sense—all of it believable. There was applause when he finished."[38] Poitier's words represented a warm and deeply felt appreciation of Tracy's talents, but also a beatification that bore little resemblance to the actual, far more arduous shooting of the speech. Kramer, aware of Tracy's memory problems and his difficulty breathing, broke the scene into tiny pieces and shot it over six full days, shooting a great deal of coverage of the other actors.[39] He wanted Tracy on his feet for most of the scene, and Tracy badly wanted to deliver a strong performance for him. "Lots of people around here keep telling me how great I am, but you

notice how it's Stanley who puts me to work," he told his friend Garson
Kanin. "I tell him my life expectancy is about seven and a half minutes,
and he says 'Action!' "[40]

Summoning the little strength he had left, Tracy rose to the occasion,
delivering one of his tenderest and most fully felt performances and letting the speech unfold with the relaxed cadence and rueful half-smile of a
man who knows he's made any number of mistakes but is seeing his own
life and marriage clearly for the first time in years. There were no more
afternoons off; that week, he put in six- and seven-hour days, pushing
through one segment of the scene after another. In the monologue's most
famous moment, he talks about his love for Christina. "Old?" he says of
himself. "Yes. Burned out? Certainly. But I can tell you, the memories
are still there—clear, intact, indestructible, and they'll be there if I live to
be a hundred and ten. . . . In the final analysis," he says, "the only thing
that matters is what they feel for each other. And if it's half of what we
felt," he says, turning to Hepburn, whose eyes are glistening with tears,
"that's everything."

Hepburn's tears were, for all the real emotion behind them, a measure
of her remarkable control. (In the script, Rose simply wrote, "Is Christina
weeping quietly? I don't know.")[41] Kramer was stunned by her ability, in
"seven, eight, nine successive takes of a scene, [to] make the teardrop
drop on the same line each time. . . . She was just fantastic the way she
could do that."[42] It takes nothing away from Tracy's thoughtfulness and
timing as he worked his way through the speech to note that the sequence
audiences eventually saw was a triumph of editing as well as of acting. "To
keep him appearing dynamic and healthy in that scene was the greatest
challenge," says editor Robert C. Jones. "To keep him seeming vibrant
meant going through a lot of film and cheating a lot of things, carefully
picking lines that were usable and deleting those that weren't, using a line
of dialogue from take three over a picture from take four. . . . Stanley gave
me a lot of room to do that and permission to cut to Katharine Hepburn
or one of the other actors so that we could just pick Tracy's best delivery
of a line regardless of what the camera was doing. We went through it for
weeks and weeks. And I think Tracy's health actually added something to
the performance—a kind of vulnerability he hadn't had before."[43]

Tracy finished the monologue on May 19, 1967, just five days before the end of production on *Guess Who's Coming to Dinner*.[44] He had one more scene to shoot, but his relief was palpable. "I've been looking over the script," he told his director. "You really don't need me after tomorrow. If I die on the way home, you and Kate are in the clear. You'll get your money." The next day, he returned, visibly haggard, for his final scene— a process shot in which he and Hepburn take a drive to get some ice cream. It was a simple sequence that demanded little more from him than his physical presence and a bit of easy dialogue. When his work was complete, assistant director Ray Gosnell turned to the crew and said, "Ladies and gentlemen, this was Spencer Tracy's last shot." "When he said that," says Karen Kramer, "Stanley cried. It was the first and last time I ever saw him cry." As the crew burst into applause, Tracy didn't say anything. He just stepped out of the prop car, smiled broadly, waved, and walked slowly off the soundstage. Kramer watched him go and then said softly, "That is the last time you will see Spencer Tracy on camera."[45]

Tracy went home and returned to the same chair in which he had been sitting a year earlier when Kramer had talked him into making the movie. The wrap party was three days later. Hepburn attended and made a speech in which she described herself as "everlastingly grateful," telling the crew, "Your help . . . made a hell of a lot of difference . . . to Spence."[46] Tracy didn't feel up to a party; instead, he picked up the telephone and called his friends. "I did it!" he said. "I've finished the picture! And I was betting against myself all the way."[47]

TWENTY-FOUR

ustin Hoffman paced the lobby of the Ambassador Hotel in downtown Los Angeles, about to relive the worst nightmares of his early adolescence. Mike Nichols was getting ready to shoot a scene in which Benjamin, with growing panic, attempts to book a room for his first tryst with Mrs. Robinson and tries desperately to improvise a lie he can tell to an inscrutable desk clerk. The concierge was to have been played by William Daniels, but when Daniels lobbied Nichols to give him something more to do in the movie, the director bumped him up to the role of Benjamin's father, and Buck Henry stepped behind the reservations desk instead.[1]

"Have you ever done anything like this?" Nichols said to Hoffman while they rehearsed the scene.

"I don't think so," Hoffman said, feeling himself start to freeze up.

"Let's think," Nichols said, persisting. "Did you ever go anywhere that unnerved you?"

Hoffman reached into his memory. "When I was a kid, I could never buy rubbers if it was a female behind the counter," he told Nichols. "I would go into a drugstore, and if it was a man, I could ask him very quietly, could I have some prophylactics? But many times, just as I got to the counter, the man would move away and a woman would be there. And in midsentence, I'd have to think of something else."

"Okay," said Nichols. "When you're going to get the room, you're walking in to get rubbers. And Buck is a female pharmacist."[2]

Hoffman didn't need much help to access his anxieties. Weeks into shooting *The Graduate,* he was so nervous that he even worried about his ability to manufacture nervousness on camera. And his relationship with Nichols was a complicated one; the more he opened up to Nichols, the more ammunition he gave his director to get under his skin and toy with his blackest fears. "I get to you sometimes, don't I?" Nichols asked him. "You just kind of clam up when I do."

"In New York I blow my top when things aren't going right," said Hoffman. "But here I go to the other extreme."

"That's no good. Just tell me to go to hell," said Nichols.

"I can't do that," said Hoffman. "You're the director."[3]

The shoot at the Ambassador that day was turning out to be particularly hard for Hoffman. "I had been having a difficult time with my parents," he says, "but they wanted to come watch, and I finally acquiesced. I figured it would be okay—there would be a lot of people there, and they could stand behind a rope." Hoffman's father, Harry, was a movie fan; in the early 1930s, before his son was born, he had worked at Columbia Pictures as a prop master and set decorator. "I never heard about any of that stuff growing up," says Hoffman. "But later I found out that he had really wanted to direct after watching Frank Capra work."

Before the scene started, Hoffman excused himself to go to the bathroom. At least once a day, before the cameras rolled, Nichols would give him the same humiliating reminder: "Don't forget to clean the inside of your nose." Hoffman stared at himself in the mirror, wondering, probably for the hundredth time, why Nichols had cast him. When he came out of the restroom, he saw his father standing next to Nichols, chatting with him. "It was the nightmare thing that every kid experiences," says Hoffman. "He had gone under the rope! I went over to them and he was saying, 'Mike, you know, you're not shooting this right. . . .'"

Hoffman went through the epic production of *The Graduate,* which shot for almost one hundred days, on a razor's edge between elation and terror. He was thrilled when he came up with something that made Nichols laugh. "He ruined more than a few takes by cracking up," says the actor. "But I guess he wasn't laughing enough, because once we started shooting, I never thought I was doing a good job. I've heard and read since then that he wanted to keep me in a constant state of tension, but I think he had really bitten off more than he could chew. He knew he shouldn't have cast me, and I think that's what was plaguing him."

In the course of a single day, Nichols could both reinforce the confidence of his hypersensitive star and demolish it. "I never had the feeling he was happy with what I was doing," said the actor. "He'd throw out a cookie occasionally, but I always felt like a disappointment. He'd walk around the entire time saying, 'Well, we'll never work together again, that's for sure.' "[4] Sometimes his direction to Hoffman was as simple as, "Act less. What you think is nothing will, on a big screen, be something." At other moments he was brutal, using the ear for perfect delivery he had honed in his years onstage to withering effect. "One time, I tried something in a scene and he said to me, 'What were you *doing*?' " says Hoffman. "And I said, 'Well, I made a choice. . . .' And he said, slowly, 'I see. Well, the next time you get a thought, do the opposite.' " But Nichols also knew when his star needed a boost: "I remember sitting with Katharine Ross in a car and Nichols letting me hear him say to the DP [Robert Surtees], 'He reminds me of Montgomery Clift.' He could relax me in an instant . . . or not. That was Mike."[5]

"To me, it seemed easy, all of it," says Nichols. "It all sort of fell into place. Maybe that's the rosy glow of memory talking, but I don't think so." If Nichols felt relaxed as production began, the reason was probably that, as he puts it, "I saw the whole thing—I knew what the movie was."[6] In that, he was a minority of one. "There were a lot of temperamental people," says Buck Henry, "a lot of actors who weren't coming from quite the same place."[7] And some of the director's crew felt at a loss as well. "When we were given the script," says Joel Schiller, who worked as an assistant production designer under Dick Sylbert, "I read it and said to Dick, 'What *is* this?' It didn't seem to be anything. Dick just shrugged and said, 'Mike'll probably play it for comedy.' "[8]

But the studiously blasé Sylbert knew Nichols was up to something more ambiguous. Long before he started to scout locations and design sets, he had had a number of conversations with Nichols about giving *The Graduate* a hard, gleaming modernist look—the new-money sheen of California wealth. "California is like America in italics," Nichols said at the time, "a parody of everything that's most dangerous to us."[9] In the mid-1960s, most American sex comedies were shot quickly, cheaply, and with as little sex as possible: films like *Divorce American Style* and *A Guide for the Married Man* drew their color-filled art direction, their camera blocking, and their punch-line-driven sense of pace from TV sitcoms. For *The Graduate,* Sylbert wanted a colder, more muted palette, something that would represent Nichols's and Buck Henry's desire to refract Los Angeles through a prism of East Coast amusement and light contempt. Henry's script even specified that the costumes were to embody "California Contemporary Sport Style: the adults in styles infinitely too young for them, the children in styles infinitely too old for them."[10] And Nichols decided to omit the opening scene of Benjamin's graduation in part so that he could begin with him on an airplane, allowing the first line of the film to be the pilot's voice-over: "Ladies and gentlemen, we're about to begin our descent into Los Angeles." "It's a statement of theme that you don't really hear, even though it's perfectly loud and clear," says Nichols. "It's my thesis, but it's invisible, which is just the way I want it."[11]

Sylbert started by thinking about the Robinson and Braddock homes while driving around Beverly Hills with Schiller, who photographed every ostentatious new faux-whatever mansion with a swimming pool that he could spot. Since Benjamin's and Elaine's fathers were partners in the same company, Sylbert told Schiller that "they'd probably buy the exact same everything and charge it against the business. We've got to see how much we can make the houses look alike."[12] But in Sylbert's final design, the relationship between the two homes became dialectical: The Braddock home was largely in white and full of right angles—an environment for bright, sunny, square people. The Robinsons' house, by contrast, was full of shiny black surfaces and sensual curves, a nighttime lair for predatory animals, with a glassed-in, overgrown garden off the living room. Sylbert decided to literalize the idea of Mrs. Robinson as a wild beast, luring Benjamin toward his moral doom, in the appearance of Bancroft herself, down to the suggestion of a wild stripe in her hair. "In those days, you had a long time to plan these things," says Nichols. "And Sylbert, who was a complicated man but a great art director, had so much fun with the beast in the jungle, as we used to call Mrs. Robinson, and her leopard underwear and her zebra-striped thing and her jungle plants. At one point, I was actually going to have an ape go through that garden, and then I thought, no, better just leave it lay. He even came up with the idea of seeing the bra strap marks—her tan—which they elaborately and carefully made up."[13]

Nichols and Henry both knew that *The Graduate,* if it worked, would convey, in its very texture, what Henry called "the disaffection of young people for an environment that they don't seem to be in synch with, the idea that Benjamin doesn't fit with ocean boys, with people his age, with his parents, with his girlfriend. Nobody had made a film specifically about that."[14] Accordingly, Nichols sought to have Benjamin constantly cut off from the movie's other characters either by water or by glass. From the opening scenes, in which Benjamin sits gloomily in front of an aquarium, to the final sequence, in which he is trapped behind a huge glass panel in a church as he tries to stop Elaine's wedding, Nichols and Sylbert wanted Benjamin to be shot through or against clear but impenetrable surfaces as often as possible, as if he were trapped in a fishbowl. It was an aesthetic that caused no end of difficulty for Robert Surtees. "Cinematographers absolutely didn't want to shoot with glass back then because it would catch too many reflections," says Schiller. "Usually, when we built a window or a glass door, we'd just put an inch and a half of glass around the sash to fake a full window reflection, but Dick wouldn't go for that. He said to Surtees, you're gonna have glass in the windows and glass in the doors and you're gonna figure out how to do it and you're gonna get an Academy Award nomination."[15]

Surtees had begun his career as an assistant cameraman on the 1931 RKO film *Devotion;* he had shot epics and melodramas and musicals and westerns, but little besides Wyler's *The Collector* that would have been described as visually innovative. What Nichols wanted from him sounded preposterous; "I asked for such peculiar things," he recalls. In the scene in which Elaine confronts Benjamin in the tiny apartment he has rented in Berkeley, Nichols wanted to use a long lens. "Surtees didn't say to me, 'But that has no meaning.' He would figure out a way to do it. He took out the entire wall of the apartment and we shot the scene from all the way across the stage."[16]

Surtees later said, "I needed everything I learned in the past thirty years to shoot *The Graduate*."[17] He had no choice. Though he may have grumbled privately, the cinematographer knew that, at sixty, he was the newcomer on the set, the stranger facing the tight-knit troika of Nichols, Sylbert, and editor Sam O'Steen, and that if he resisted their approach, he would find himself isolated and written off as a fogy from another generation. So he made it work. "Not only did he fall all over himself to do things he hadn't done, but he would show me things that I didn't know I was allowed to do," says Nichols. Unlike many of his contemporaries, Surtees was especially interested in the subtleties of lighting. "Look at the sequence in which Benjamin and Mrs. Robinson are at the bar in her house, and then she says, 'Would you like to see Elaine's portrait?'" says Nichols. "They go upstairs, and we have, 'Mrs. Robinson, you're trying to seduce me,' and then Benjamin hears Mr. Robinson come home and he runs back downstairs. When we come downstairs, back to the bar, the lighting is entirely different from the first time we were there—it's a dark and scary place because Mr. Robinson is scary and drunk, and she's *really* scary when she comes in. I said, 'How can we do this? How can we change the light in this room when nothing has changed?' and Surtees told me, 'It's all right that it's different. You're allowed to do that in movies. How the lights were when they left the room is beside the point—it's a new scene now.' He knew all those things, and he taught them to me beautifully."[18]

"Whatever Mike said, he got his way," says Hoffman. "They built the Robinsons' house on the set, the whole house, so you could open doors into rooms—there was a full bathroom even though it wasn't in the script, because you didn't know what Mike might want. I remember walking out of that hallway, and for some reason, he couldn't get the camera through. And he said, 'How long will it take to get these walls down?' On a regular set, it would be nothing, but it was a fully built *house*. 'Well, it might take a couple of days,' they said. And he said, 'All right, then we'll wait.'"[19]

Waiting became the rule. Nichols would not be rushed on *The Graduate* any more than he had allowed his producer or his crew to hurry him along on *Virginia Woolf*; he was more than willing to use all of the capital he had earned with his first film's success as long as Joe Levine, who had rented a soundstage at Paramount for the production, kept footing the bill. For Hoffman, who returned to his room every night at the Chateau

Marmont as spring turned into summer and his weeks on *The Graduate* turned into months, exhaustion began to set in. The day he was filming the sequence in which Elaine slaps Benjamin in the face, Nichols didn't like what Katharine Ross was doing. At several points during the shoot, he struggled with the young actress's inexperience, as well as with her natural reserve. When Ross was shooting the scene in which Elaine finds out that Benjamin has been sleeping with her mother, "he wanted me to be crying," said Ross later, "and I couldn't . . . and I always felt sort of disappointed in myself."[20] "She's driving me fucking crazy," Nichols complained to O'Steen, "she can't do it, she doesn't have it."[21] That day, nothing she did could please him. Patiently, he filmed take after take. Fifteen hard slaps later, Hoffman felt a stinging pain in his ear. The next day, he got into his deep-sea-diving gear for the swimming pool scene; when he jumped into the pool, he felt as if his head were going to explode. He emerged from the water, blood pouring from his ear. Working on the film became an endurance contest, a test of his mettle. When the doctor examining his torn eardrum asked him how he liked making a movie, he replied weakly that the food on the set was good.[22]

Bancroft's mood also darkened as the shoot went on. There were mornings she was hungover, and on some days she had such painful menstrual cramps that she couldn't get out of bed. "She would just lie there in agony," says Elizabeth Wilson. "And we'd reschedule around her."[23] The self-loathing beneath Mrs. Robinson's glacial exterior wasn't a completely foreign emotion for the actress who, before her success in *The Miracle Worker,* struggled to make it as a Hollywood ingenue and had essentially been washed out of the movie business for a few years. Sometimes the role seemed to come naturally to her; on other days she'd keep the character at arm's length, almost refusing to connect with her. The scene in which Mrs. Robinson and Benjamin lie in bed and he begs her to have a conversation with him took days to film; in the draft of the screenplay that Nichols shot, it was almost a one-act play in miniature, fifteen minutes of uninterrupted dialogue (much of it straight from Charles Webb's novel) in which Benjamin almost cruelly forces Mrs. Robinson to open up and learns that she was pregnant when she got married, that she once loved studying art, and that she wants him, above all, to keep clear of her daughter. He turns on her and calls her a "broken-down alcoholic," gets dressed, and starts to leave; the exchange ends with a grim reconciliation as the two of them start to undress again for sex and Benjamin mutters defeatedly, "Let's not talk at all." In rehearsals, Nichols and Bancroft had talked extensively about what the scene meant. "When Benjamin says, 'Art, huh. I guess you kind of lost interest in it over the years,' and she says, 'Kind of,' that's the key," he told her. "That's it. She just hates herself for having gone for the money, and she's punishing herself with everything she does." Bancroft understood him completely, but weeks later, when they were ready to shoot the scene, "she just tossed it off," says Nichols. "I said, 'Annie! Don't you remember our conversation about this beautiful, crucial moment?' She kind of casually said, 'Oh shit, yeah, I forgot.' And then she did it perfectly. For me, it was central. For her, it was just a line reading."[24]

That rueful back-and-forth between the characters, punctuated by stage-style blackouts as they keep turning the lights on and off, was the only scene in *The Graduate* that Nichols and Buck Henry still didn't feel they had gotten right once production began—it was too long, too diffuse, and its two-character, one-set, dialogue-based style seemed to belong on the stage, not on screen; it threatened to stop the flow of the rest of the movie. As Hoffman and Bancroft spent every working day in bed, feeling their way through round after round of bitter dialogue in which Bancroft had to play almost every moment with her back to Hoffman and the camera trained mercilessly on her face, gloom hung over the set. "We were not allowed to see rushes," says Hoffman. "And I think one of the big reasons was Mike couldn't let people see them and not let Annie in, and he didn't want her to see how badly he was lighting her, to make her look older. But I used to have lunch in the commissary at Paramount, and I knew when they were screening it, so I would look through the slit in the door and see a little slit of myself on screen and get very excited."[25]

By June, when Nichols and his cast and crew drove to La Verne, California, where Dick Sylbert had found a modern-looking church in which they could shoot the film's climax, they were so happy to get out of the studio that the several days on location felt almost like a field trip. Hoffman acquired his first groupie, a local girl who would hang out near his trailer and flirt with him between takes. "Beautiful, thin, a real *shiksa* goddess," he says. "I think Nichols took that as a sign—at least somebody found me attractive. And it didn't get past me, either!"

The weather was scorching, Bancroft fainted during the scene in which everyone was pushing to get out of the church and had to be given oxygen and sent home, and the minister who had agreed to let Nichols film there was "very unhappy," says Hoffman, "like they always are after they agree to have a movie come shoot and then see the reality after they say yes and everything starts to get the shit beat out of it." When Nichols started to film Benjamin pounding on the glass wall, trying to get Elaine's attention as she stands at the altar saying her vows, the huge pane of glass began to shake ominously, and the reverend yelled, "Everybody out! Out, out, out!" Trying to save the shoot, Nichols conferred with Hoffman—"the only time during the entire movie he asked me to compromise," he recalls—and asked if he could think of any other way to get Elaine's attention. Hoffman came up with the idea of spreading his arms apart and just tapping on the glass tentatively with his open palms. "The clincher was the reviews all saying this was Benjamin's Christ moment," says Hoffman. "It was a fix. That's all it was. You gotta love critics."[26]

As production of *The Graduate* rolled through its third month and into its fourth, Joe Levine started pressuring Larry Turman to wrap it up. "Levine may have chewed the producer's ass out," Sam O'Steen said later, "but at that point he was biting the bullet and pretty much left Nichols alone."[27] "It was endless," says Elizabeth Wilson, "many, many, many, many takes, as if they had all the time in the world, and then reshoots. There was one point when I was finished and back in New York, and a call came that they were adding a scene with Dustin and Bill Daniels and me. I remember when I walked back onto the set, Mike really seemed up to his neck in something. I said to him, 'Well, you always wanted to be a director,' and he said grimly, 'Ha ha ha.' "[28] When the pressure got to Nichols, he rarely let it show, but few who worked for him found the production an easy experience. Nichols greeted each day with a serene opacity that, depending on what he was seeing and feeling as work got under way, could transform incrementally into warm affection or icy disdain without any dramatic change in his demeanor. ("Never let people see what you feel," he had learned growing up, "because it gives them too much power.")[29] As had been the case on *Virginia Woolf,* his crew, not his cast, felt the brunt of his anger when it came. "One of the things in my life that I'm saddest about and most ashamed of," says Nichols, "is that when we were shooting on the Sunset Strip, stealing a shot of Benjamin and Elaine walking toward the strip club, I said something snotty, as I often did to the crew. And I heard Bob Surtees say to them—it wasn't meant for me to hear—'It's okay. It's not going to be much longer.' And I thought, oh, man, how could I have been such a shit that this man I revere feels that way about me? But I was."[30]

When he had decided to make *The Graduate* three and a half years earlier, Nichols thought he knew exactly what his satirical targets were. "I said some fairly pretentious thing about capitalism and material objects, about the boy drowning in material things and saving himself in the only possible way, which was through madness," he recalls. But the deeper he got into the shoot and the more intensely he pushed Hoffman past what the actor thought he could withstand, the more Nichols realized that something painful and personal was at stake, and always had been, in his attraction to the story. "My unconscious was making this movie," he says. "It took me years before I got what I had been doing all along—that I was turning Benjamin into a Jew. I didn't get it until I saw this hilarious issue of *MAD* magazine after the movie came out, in which the caricature of Dustin says to the caricature of Elizabeth Wilson, 'Mom, how come I'm Jewish and you and Dad aren't?' And I asked myself the same question, and the answer was fairly embarrassing and fairly obvious: Who was the Jew among the goyim? And who was forever a visitor in a strange land?"[31]

Nichols—the immigrant, the observer, the displaced boy who once said that one of the first two sentences he learned in English was "Please do not kiss me"[32]—finally understood why it had taken him years to settle on an actor to play Benjamin. "Without any knowledge of what I was doing," he says, "I had found myself in this story." And in Hoffman, he had found an on-screen alter ego—someone he could admonish for his failings, challenge to dig deeper, punish for his weaknesses, praise to bolster his confidence, and exhort to prove every day that he was the right man for the role. By the time the actor got into Benjamin's Alfa Romeo to shoot the montage in which he drives across the Golden Gate Bridge to find Elaine,* "I don't think they really cared whether I lived or died," Hoffman says, laughing. "There was a helicopter and a remote, and the direction I got was, 'Pass every car.' Traffic was moving fast, and I would hear on the walkie-talkie, 'Just drive.' I remember thinking, I can't get hurt—this is only a movie!"

Late in the shoot, Hoffman was ragged, wiped out, short-tempered. "It was rough going," he says. "It was long and it got much longer. I don't think I ever went out. I came home, and I'd study for the next day." His misery was manifest when he walked onto the set.

"What's the matter?" said Nichols, taking him aside.

"I'm tired," said Hoffman.

Nichols didn't say anything for a moment, then replied in a quiet, explanatory tone. "Well," he said, "this is the only chance you're ever going to have to do this scene for the rest of your life. When you look back on it, do you really want to say, 'I was tired'?"[33]

Nichols might as well have been talking to himself. "There's no question I was in the grip of some *thing*," he says. "Part of me knew what I was doing in terms of the outsider and so forth, but another part of me, a part that I had no inkling of, must have known that I would never get material so suited to *me* again. I knew all about it. Without even knowing I knew."[34]

---

* In the movie's one famous gaffe, Benjamin is shot driving in the wrong direction on the bridge.

TWENTY-FIVE

On June 10, 1967, Spencer Tracy woke up at 3:00 in the morning, got out of bed, walked to his kitchen to make a cup of tea, and collapsed, dead from a heart attack. The official story, swiftly constructed for the next day's newspapers, was that Tracy's body had been discovered by the housekeeper who worked for George Cukor, on whose property he had lived; she then called Tracy's brother and a physician. Tracy's wife, Louise, and their two children arrived next, followed by Cukor, Katharine Hepburn, and Tracy's business manager.[1] This fiction was in all likelihood the handiwork of Howard Strickling, the longtime guardian of Tracy's reputation at MGM and a friend of Louise Tracy's who escorted her to the funeral.[2] Decades later, after the death of Tracy's widow in 1983, Hepburn began to offer, with increasing frequency and detail, her own account of the last night of Tracy's life. She had run a wire from a buzzer that was by his bedside to a speaker in the room where she was sleeping; she heard him fall, heard the teacup shatter, found him dead, and called Phyllis Wilbourn, her assistant and closest companion. Hepburn asked Wilbourn to take all of her things out of the house before Tracy's family showed up; then she changed her mind and put them all back in. When Louise Tracy arrived, she and Hepburn quarreled briefly over what suit Tracy would be buried in. "You know, Louise, you and I can be friends," Hepburn said she told her a few days later. "Well, yes," said Tracy's widow. "But you see, I thought you were only a rumor."[3] Hepburn's decision to wait until Louise

Tracy's death to tell her side of the story was an act of discretion, but one that contained an element of self-protection; by the time she began to talk about—and to embroider on—her own relationship with Tracy, Hepburn had outlived almost everyone who could have contradicted her.

Six hundred people attended the funeral service for Tracy at Hollywood's Immaculate Heart of St. Mary Roman Catholic Church. Stanley Kramer and his wife, Karen, had been in Las Vegas, celebrating the end of production of *Guess Who's Coming to Dinner*, but they flew back immediately after Hepburn called them.[4] Kramer served as one of Tracy's pallbearers, along with Cukor, Jimmy Stewart, Garson Kanin, John Ford, Frank Sinatra, producer William Self, and Abe Lastfogel, Tracy's agent at William Morris.[5] Hepburn, in her car, followed Tracy's hearse until it reached the church, then turned around and drove home. "Of course, the minute it was over, the inside group went back to her house and told her everything," says Karen Kramer.[6]

Hepburn's decision not to go to the funeral was consistent with the way she had managed to give the public glimpses of her relationship with Tracy for many years while saying nothing about it: Her behavior represented an act of self-denial and dignified restraint that still managed to be conspicuous and public. She had made nine movies with him, including his last; while her attendance at the church alongside much of old Hollywood might have raised some eyebrows, she must have known that her absence would be highlighted in every story that covered the service. In many of those reports, she was upgraded from "a friend of many years" to "the actor's longtime companion." Even *The New York Times*, in its tribute to Tracy, noted that "in personal crises, she invariably appeared near him" and "maintained a vigil at his bedside" when he had been hospitalized.

The death of the man whom the *Times* called "one of the last screen titans of a generation"[7] was greeted with a flood of sentiment and sorrow that was unusual for the period; in 1967, critics and the entertainment press could be callous, even cruel, to anyone they felt had overstayed his welcome. Earlier in the year, when seventy-seven-year-old Charlie Chaplin released the catastrophically stiff and awkward *A Countess from Hong Kong*, his first film in more than a decade, reviews had been brutal, not only about the movie but about the man himself: *Time* magazine's piece was titled "Time to Retire,"[8] and in *The New Yorker*, Brendan Gill had sneered that he "shows us not a trace of his former genius."[9] Three days later, when Orson Welles's *Chimes at Midnight* opened in New York, the *Times'* Bosley Crowther compared the two movies and wrote, "Chaplin . . . should not have tried to make *A Countess from Hong Kong* or anything else at his age! . . . It would have been so apt and charitable if someone could have saved these two men from the embarrassment of their hopeless follies," and called Welles's movie "a disgusting indulgence."[10] Neither director ever completed another dramatic feature. But Tracy, perhaps because he had seemed to care so little for his image or appearance over the years, was one of the few older actors whose appeal was multigenerational; even younger moviegoers eager to dismiss anyone they thought was "phony" claimed him as their own. In the language of the Old Sentimentality–vs.– New Sentimentality paradigm that Robert Benton and David Newman had created in *Esquire* back in 1964, Tracy was like Humphrey Bogart—the rare figure who made the jump from Old to New by making it appear that "a man can both care and not give a damn."[11]

Tracy's death immediately raised the profile of his final movie, which was not due to open for six more months: Magazines and newspapers that had sent reporters to the set of *Guess Who's Coming to Dinner* rushed their stories into print early. *Life* asked Stanley Kramer to write a first-person tribute to Tracy; Garson Kanin began warming up to write a book-length "intimate memoir" that would retail a wildly romanticized version of Hepburn and Tracy's relationship by penning a tribute in *The New York Times; Look* published a photo portfolio; *Esquire* called its Hepburn profile "The Last of the Honest-to-God Ladies." The enshrinement of Hepburn and Tracy as the first couple of the screen—"perfect representations of the American male and the American female," as she herself put it, with little apparent irony—was ordained within a week of his death, as was the valedictory affection with which his last screen appearance would be greeted.

Lost in all the tributes was a remarkably timed piece of news that went unmentioned in stories about the movie: On the day Tracy was buried, the Supreme Court handed down its decision in the case of *Loving v. Virginia*, ruling that laws forbidding racial intermarriage in sixteen states were unconstitutional in that they violated the equal protection clause of the Fourteenth Amendment. The case had taken almost a decade to reach the Court. It began in 1959 when Richard Loving, a white man, and Mildred Jeter, a black woman, were sentenced to a year in jail for marrying each other, a term that was suspended on the condition that they leave the state of Virginia. (In his initial decision, the trial judge remarked that God had made His will manifest by putting different races on different continents.) The Warren Court examined Virginia's law, which forbade intermarriage only if one of the parties was white, and concluded that it was "invidious racial discrimination . . . designed to maintain White Supremacy"; the Court also ruled that "the freedom to marry has long been recognized as one of the vital personal rights essential to the orderly pursuit of happiness by free men."[12] When William Rose had written *Guess Who's Coming to Dinner* a year earlier, he had included a line in which Prentice's father tries to talk his son out of the marriage by saying, "In sixteen or seventeen states you'd be breaking the law!" Kramer kept the line in the movie, but as of June 12, it was no longer true.

The landmark *Loving v. Virginia* decision might have received more attention had it not arrived at a moment when history was unfolding with breathtaking speed. The same day, news broke that President Johnson would, the next morning, announce the nomination of Thurgood Marshall to the Supreme Court; meanwhile, the networks' evening newscasts were filled with the aftermath of the Six Days' War, which ended on June 10 and had transfixed much of America. On *The Graduate*, crew members were late to location shoots because they pulled their cars over to the side of the freeway, listening to reports that Israel had decisively won what *Life* magazine called "the astounding war." *Time*, which had headlined its June 9 cover ISRAEL: THE STRUGGLE TO SURVIVE, came back a week later with a heroic portrait of Moshe Dayan and the headline HOW ISRAEL WON THE WAR. And at Warner Brothers, Israel's victory had an extremely peculiar collateral effect: It helped save *Bonnie and Clyde*.

In early June, Warren Beatty and Arthur Penn took their movie to New York to screen it for Warner's head of advertising, Dick Lederer, and distribution chief Ben Kalmenson. Lederer loved it, just as he had loved the screenplay. But Kalmenson thought it was worthless. "Benny really hated it," says Robert Solo, who was just about to leave his job as assistant to Jack Warner's deputy Walter MacEwen. "He'd say, 'Warren doesn't mean anything to audiences,' and that was it. He was a crotchety, opinionated guy, a real old distribution hand, basically a jumped-up film salesman. He thought it was a cheap gangster movie, he wanted to bury it, and he did."[13] Lederer lobbied hard to get the movie booked into Manhattan's Cinema I, one of four first-run theaters on Third Avenue between 59th and 60th streets, a stretch of real estate so important to review-driven movies well into the 1980s that it came to be known in the industry as "the Block." He talked about the value of a red-carpet premiere on the East Coast. Kalmenson wouldn't hear of it; he booked the movie into two far less prestigious theaters, one near Times Square, the other in Murray Hill. He thought so little of *Bonnie and Clyde* that when he handed out a schedule of Warner Brothers' summer releases to his distribution team, the picture wasn't even listed.[14]

Beatty and Penn then took the print to Los Angeles to show it to Jack Warner, but by the time they got there, Kalmenson had delivered his verdict to Warner himself, confirming what his boss had feared when he read the script—the movie was nothing but a bloody retread of the 1930s gangster movies they used to make that were just one step up from Poverty Row. "Warner listened to Kalmenson," says Solo. "He's the man who was responsible for Jack Warner selling his stock in the studio to Seven Arts. He was really friendly with [Seven Arts head] Eliot Hyman, and Hyman kept wanting to buy the studio, and Kalmenson talked Warner into it. It was really against Warner's better judgment, because after that, he was done. He had the money, but he didn't have his studio."[15]

Jack Warner was already livid about the amount of time Penn, Beatty, and Dede Allen had taken editing the movie; he had threatened repeatedly to pull their funding during postproduction, to stop paying the rent on the New York editing rooms, to take the movie out of their hands.[16] "It won't be long before I should be leaving," he fumed, wondering why he was spending his last weeks at the company he co-founded "waiting around for geniuses to make up their minds, which I am not going to do."[17] In the spring, he had told Walter MacEwen, Penn and Beatty's biggest champion in the upper ranks, to crack down on the "thoughtless" director and producer: "If they are going to sit around we will end up with a slow, repetitious picture and anything Beatty is in will go on and on. This is the story on actors cutting pictures."[18] Even MacEwen was beginning to lose his patience; Beatty and Penn had insisted on editing the movie in New York against his wishes; they had delayed a small but critical reshoot until mid-May; and they were pushing past the limits of even a liberalized Production Code ("eliminate depiction of fellacio [*sic*]," an appalled Mac-Ewen jotted down, trying several different spellings after watching footage of Dunaway sliding out of frame while in bed with Beatty). In addition, Beatty, whether out of insecurity or annoyance at the difficulties Dunaway had caused during the shoot, had dug in for months in resistance to her agent's demand that she be billed above the title, a star-making flourish that the studio thought would help launch her. Beatty didn't give in until the studio started exploring whether it had legal standing to take the movie away from him altogether. "Would prefer not yielding to threats," he calmly cabled MacEwen before finally giving in. "In any case you are the boss."[19]

When Penn and Beatty walked onto the lot, they reentered a world that seemed frozen in time. "Studio life in 1967 was very much the life it had been for years and years and years," says Sid Ganis, one of a new generation of executives who moved from New York to Los Angeles after Seven Arts' takeover. "It was still the old guard, lots of old guys with great stories about their old successes. But they had all been there for twenty-five years. Jack Warner still had an office and still had his desk with the three steps up to where he sat. But it was the end of an era."[20]

Publicly, Warner was celebrating his approaching seventy-fifth birthday by announcing, "I feel 14!" watching dailies from the production of Francis Coppola's *Finian's Rainbow*,[21] and telling reporters, "I intend to go on doing what I am doing. If I quit now, where would I go? What would I do?"[22] But the truth was that Warner had given away his power and had only the trappings left; just a few weeks after his confident pronouncements, he would resign as production chief.

Warner was spending more and more of his time at home, and Penn and Beatty brought the print to his private screening room, with Walter MacEwen and a couple of publicists in tow. "If I have to get up and pee,"

Warner told Penn, "I'll know it's a lousy movie." "Well, he was up before the first reel," says Penn. "And several times after that."[23] Penn sat there, his mood black, feeling that he had made "the most diuretic film in human memory."[24] "He didn't like it, didn't understand it, didn't get it, and Benny Kalmenson had already seen it and proclaimed it a piece of shit, so that was that," Penn says. Warner took in *Bonnie and Clyde* with the eyes, the ears, and the taste of an angry, cut-off man and hated everything about it. The vintage photographs at the beginning were too blurry; the sound was too low; the dialogue was too muffled. "What the hell was that?" he said. "That's when Warren tried his wonderful line, 'It's an homage to old Warner Brothers gangster movies,' and Jack sort of perked up and said, 'What the fuck's an *homage*?'" says Penn. "It was the beginning of a dark time, because it was clear that if he didn't like it and Kalmenson didn't like it, it was gonna get dumped."[25]

In the days that followed, Beatty tried a bluff, suggesting to Kalmenson that if the studio was so unhappy with the movie, he would gladly buy it back from them himself. Then the Six Days' War broke out. By its end, Jack Warner was in full triumphalist mode. "Jack was very aroused," Beatty told the *Los Angeles Times*, "because Israel had done well and he'd raised more money for Israel than anyone in town."[26] At the end of the war, Warner was so exhilarated that he called the studio's employees together on a soundstage so he could address them one more time as their leader. A few days earlier, he had announced that despite Seven Arts' takeover, the company would continue to be named for him and his family. In a defiant mood, the pugnacious old man wasn't about to sell off anything, even a movie he suspected was worthless.

The same week, Columbia Pictures opened Sidney Poitier's schoolteacher drama, *To Sir, with Love*. The studio's expectations were minimal, especially since reviews were tepid, and critics who had praised Poitier for rising above his material in movies like *Lilies of the Field* and *A Patch of Blue* were now going after him for choosing these roles in the first place. "One hankers for the character he played in *The Blackboard Jungle* instead of the point-making prigs he takes on now," complained Penelope Gilliatt in

The New Yorker. "If the hero of this Pollyanna story were white, his pieties would have been whistled off the screen. . . . The fact that he is colored draws on resources of seriousness in audiences which the film does nothing to earn."[27] And Hollis Alpert, writing in *Saturday Review,* remarked that he was tired of seeing a "consistently desexualized" Poitier turn himself into "an ever more solid symbol, a minority figure who must eventually triumph . . . while making prejudice seem lowly and nasty."[28]

Columbia didn't realize that Poitier had been building a tremendous audience base thanks to television, where his movies were showing up more frequently. Until 1965, home viewers had rarely seen black performers on TV outside of guest shots on crime dramas, singing and dancing appearances in variety shows, or *Amos 'n' Andy* and *Beulah* comic stereotypes, but the emergence of Bill Cosby in *I Spy* and, a year later, Greg Morris in *Mission: Impossible* brought a new kind of self-assured African American star into American living rooms and tapped a previously unrecognized viewing audience. During the 1966–1967 season, *Variety* described Poitier as "redhot in TV ratings," pointing to huge numbers for telecasts of *Lilies of the Field* and *The Long Ships* as well as for the actor's appearance on a variety show celebrating the history of black humor.[29] When *To Sir, with Love* opened, the studio found out that Poitier was not only review-proof, but a much bigger star than anyone in the movie business had guessed. The film was an immediate and sustained hit that played for months and made the actor a rich man. His deal to take just $30,000 up front in exchange for 10 percent of the gross turned out to be one of the biggest paydays an actor had ever engineered. In Poitier's contract, Columbia had stipulated that his yearly take would be capped at $25,000 for as many years as it took to pay him in full. The studio realized it would have to revise that deal when *To Sir, with Love* took in so much money that it would have taken eighty years to fulfill the contract's terms.

Poitier himself agreed with some of the criticism of *To Sir, with Love*. "The guys who write these parts are white guys, more often than not," he said at the time. "And there are producers to deal with who are also white, and a studio with a board of directors, also white. So they have to make him—the Negro—kind of a neuter. . . . You put him in a shirt and tie . . . you make him very bright and very intelligent and very capable . . .

then you can eliminate the core of the man: His sexuality."[30] For the first time, Poitier decided to channel his frustration into producing: He made a deal with ABC, which was then launching a motion picture division, to produce and star in *For Love of Ivy,* which would mark the first mainstream romantic comedy about a black couple's relationship.[31]

The success of *To Sir, with Love* was good news for United Artists, which had chosen the beginning of August as a release date for *In the Heat of the Night* and was counting on Poitier's growing popularity to boost the chances of a movie for which the studio had planned only a modest publicity campaign. UA seemed remarkably short on inspiration when it came to selling Jewison's movie; the ideas it sent out to local publicity teams felt almost deliberately designed to avoid any mention of race, conflict, or civil rights. "It's a natural for stores selling air conditioners!" UA suggested. "Don't Lose Your Cool In the Heat of the Night. . . . Reverse angle, for cooler nites, is 'When Winter Winds Blow, Sleep "In the Heat of the Night" with (furnace, fuel, or heater tie-in).'" Some posters carried the tagline "They got a murder on their hands. They don't know what to do with it"; other ads featured a still from a seconds-long shot of a strategically concealed nude woman from an early scene and built an entire campaign around her, with the slogan "She always traipses around with the lights on. Somebody sure oughta make her stop it!"[32] No poster mentioned race at all. Jewison, who was in Boston shooting *Thomas Crown,* saw the posters for the first time when he passed the Music Hall and, not for the first time, complained bitterly to UA.* "I hate to keep flogging a dead horse," he wrote, "but the picture deserves a little better than this."[33]

United Artists had not had a hit all year and was counting on one movie, the James Bond adventure *You Only Live Twice,* to turn its bottom line around. The fortunes of the Bond franchise had grown exponentially with each installment, and a new Bond rip-off opened almost every month, but just before the massive success of *Thunderball* in early 1966, another studio decided to take direct aim at the value of UA's hot-

---

* Jewison's relationship with the Mirisch Company was friendly but often tense; the original contract the company offered him to direct *In the Heat of the Night* had so many points that were objectionable to him that he didn't officially sign the deal to make the movie until it had already been in theaters for a month. Jewison ultimately agreed to a salary of $200,000 plus a share of the profits.

test property. *What's New, Pussycat?* producer Charlie Feldman owned the rights to Ian Fleming's first Bond novel, *Casino Royale,* the only 007 story that producers Harry Saltzman and Cubby Broccoli hadn't acquired. Feldman initially approached Saltzman and Broccoli about going into partnership with them; when they stiff-armed him, he decided to make a bigger, wilder, more expensive Bond movie than any that had come before and took the project to Columbia. Creatively, *Casino Royale* was a disaster of fascinatingly outsize proportions: Six different directors and at least seventeen screenwriters (including, at various points, Woody Allen, Ben Hecht, Joseph Heller, Terry Southern, and Billy Wilder) were swallowed by Feldman's $12 million sinkhole, an incoherent spoof involving a half-dozen would-be Bonds played by, among others, David Niven and Peter Sellers, that was condemned as "total chaos,"[34] "unfunny burlesque,"[35] and "a frightful mess"[36] by the very people who made it.

Feldman oversaw a comically disjointed production during which scenes were sometimes written just to utilize elaborate sets that had been built for other purposes or to work in actors who happened to be in London for a few days, but he nonetheless succeeded in getting *Casino Royale* into theaters two months before *You Only Live Twice*. Abetted by a slogan that sold its gimmick effectively ("*Casino Royale* Is Too Much . . . For One James Bond!") and an eye-catching psychedelic poster of a nude woman covered in tattoos, the movie drew huge initial crowds. Bad word of mouth spread quickly, but Columbia had made its money (the film was the third-highest grosser of the calendar year) and done its damage. When *You Only Live Twice* finally arrived, audiences were oversaturated by Bond and his rivals. Even the film's nominally topical plotline, the space race, had been chewed up and parodied by everything from the sitcom *I Dream of Jeannie* to Don Knotts in *The Reluctant Astronaut*. *Time* magazine's critic called the movie a "victim of the same misfortune that once befell Frankenstein: there have been so many flamboyant imitations that the original looks like a copy."[37] The comparison was not lost on Sean Connery, who had already given his producers notice that he would not play Bond again. "The whole thing has become a Frankenstein monster," he complained. "The merchandising, the promotion, the pirating—they're thoroughly distasteful."[38] UA could take some consolation in the fact that the movie managed to outgross *Casino Royale,* but for the first time, the franchise started to contract instead of expand—*You Only Live Twice,* the studio's most expensive Bond film yet, grossed significantly less than *Thunderball* and signaled a dip in Bond's drawing power that would not turn around until the late 1970s.

The notion of a summer movie season as a business model wasn't yet formed in the 1960s, but in 1967 the studios began to grasp that there was money to be made by releasing movies with broad appeal while their potential audience was on vacation or out of school. Two weeks after *You Only Live Twice* opened, just in time for the July Fourth holiday weekend, MGM released *The Dirty Dozen* across the country and made the Bond film look puny. For twenty years, World War II movies had been a reliable box office staple, but they had begun to run out of steam as their plots became repetitive and moviegoers grew bored with their drab, earnest storytelling. The studios were still putting out several war movies every year, but there hadn't been a truly crowd-pleasing entry in the genre since 1963's *The Great Escape.* When *Dirty Dozen* director Robert Aldrich read seventy-year-old Nunnally Johnson's original script about twelve thuggish criminal soldiers in military prison who are melded into a ragtag unit and given a mission to bomb a German château, he thought it "would have made a very good, very acceptable 1945 war picture. But I don't think that a good 1945 war picture is a good 1967 war picture."[39] He hired the German-born screenwriter Lukas Heller to overhaul the screenplay and made a picture that was far more gory and violent, and far less interested in conventional military heroics, than any action movie Hollywood had produced about World War II. *The Dirty Dozen*'s antiauthoritarian message appealed to war movie buffs who wanted an unsanitized look at tough guys in combat, but it also found a tremendous audience of moviegoers in their twenties who had generally stayed away from the kinds of war movies their parents liked. "We got on a wave that we never knew was coming: not a wave, a tidal wave," said Aldrich. "Younger people by the bushel thought it was an antiestablishment movie."[40]

If United Artists had any doubts about whether moviegoers were ready to accept an angrier black man on screen than they had seen before, the success of *The Dirty Dozen* erased them. One of the film's most popular characters was played by former NFL fullback Jim Brown. Aldrich treated Brown's role carefully in some regards: Where almost every other member of the dozen has a record of irredeemable criminality, audiences were told that Brown's character had been jailed for attacking a group of white men, "cracker bastards" who had tried to castrate him. After thus preemptively exonerating Brown from any real wrongdoing, the script went on to turn his character into an anachronism in every respect. He's a street-talking separatist who sounds nothing like a jailed GI in the 1940s. When he's first told to join the unit, he declines, shrugging: "That's your war, man, not mine."

Aldrich denied that his intentions in making the movie were explicitly political: "When we planned *The Dirty Dozen* in 1965 do you think for one moment we knew that by the time the film came out the French kids would be in revolt and Americans would be sick of Vietnam so the mood would be just right for our picture? Rubbish,"[41] he said. But he admitted that the film's climax, in which Brown's character throws bombs down a ventilator shaft and burns a group of trapped Germans alive, was intended to discomfort audiences by evoking the use of napalm. The scene was shocking, in part because almost no Hollywood movie had yet made even an oblique reference to the Vietnam War and in part because Aldrich had found a way to make an audience cheer a lone black man killing a huge group of white people. Jim Brown could have been the embodiment of Stokely Carmichael's declaration in the spring of 1967 that "black people are now serving notice that we'll fight back."[42]

The Dirty Dozen became the year's biggest box office hit, and its unmistakable Vietnam-era resonance might have gotten more attention had it not opened at a moment when the news was filled with the war at home. On July 12, after John Smith, a black taxi driver in Newark, was seen being physically dragged into a police station after a minor traffic violation, two hundred protesters gathered outside the precinct; the assembly dissolved into an unruly ramble in which store windows were broken and a few Molotov cocktails were thrown. Two days later, state troopers and National Guardsmen moved into the city, an overreaction that was met with escalating violence. By July 17, 1,200 people had been jailed, 600 injured, and 23 killed; H. Rap Brown became famous that week when he called for "guerrilla war on the honkie white man."[43] The following weekend, Detroit exploded into riots and looting after a raid on illegal gambling dens; another 1,200 people were arrested, and four thousand fires were set. Again, federal troops rolled into the city. Even as President Johnson was increasing the number of American soldiers in Vietnam to nearly a half million, worries about the war were temporarily overshadowed by stories about "the fire this time," hugely exaggerated reports of property damage (the $25 million of wreckage caused in Detroit was widely reported as $500 million)[44] and a storm of "Who says it can't happen here?" editorials.

The poor, angry black man from the ghetto, ready to loot, shoot, and kill, became as much of a focus for the fears of Middle America—and of Middle American media—as the acid-tripping hippies and runaways pouring into San Francisco had been a month or two earlier; and Sidney Poitier, on a press tour for *In the Heat of the Night*, found himself asked again and again to denounce the rioters or ally with them, to identify himself politically at a moment when the ground was constantly shifting. "You ask me questions that pertain to the narrow scope of the summer riots," he seethed into a bank of microphones. "I am artist, man, American, contemporary. I am an awful lot of things, so I wish you would pay me the respect due."[45] "He was the only black leading actor out there for fifteen years," said Lee Grant later. "It was a terribly unfair responsibility for him . . . he was carrying this alone, and it was not a burden that he welcomed."[46]

But the relentless call for Poitier to become a political spokesman was also an indication of his growing cultural significance; *To Sir, with Love* was becoming Columbia's biggest hit since *Lawrence of Arabia*, and *Variety* called Poitier "the only Negro which myriads of Americans feel they know and understand . . . a symbol of the thoughtful, efficient Negro whose technological knowhow (no dropout, he) enables him to help, compete with, and, when necessary, show up whites." In a season during which the country was "stained by ugly race riots," the paper said, Poitier was now so popular that if he declines a role, "they rewrite the part for a white actor!"[47] Poitier heard that quasi compliment many times in 1967, usually from people who hadn't an inkling of the condescension that was built into it, and generally responded by politely acknowledging that, yes, he had heard that people were saying that, and quickly moving on to another subject. During the press junket for *In the Heat of the Night*, he was barely asked anything about his work; instead, he had to compose answers to questions about whether it was inherently offensive to depict black people in a cotton field in the movie. At one point, he was required to list other talented black actors for an indignant reporter from Boston who didn't believe she knew of any. (Although *I Spy* had been on the air for two years, he had to spell the name "Cosby" for her.)[48]

When *In the Heat of the Night* opened in New York on August 2, critics, perhaps inevitably, treated the movie as if it had been hatched overnight in response to the long, bloody summer, and most of them approved of what they saw. Although the film had nothing to do with race riots, Bosley Crowther announced that "the hot surge of racial hate and tension as it has been displayed in many communities this year . . . is put forth with realism and point," praising "the crackling confrontations between the arrogant small town white policeman . . . and the sophisticated Negro detective with his steely armor of contempt and mistrust."[49] A number of critics besides Crowther strained to find parallel flaws in Tibbs and Gillespie, unwilling to see *In the Heat of the Night* as anything other than a movie in which the black man needs to learn a lesson, too: *Time* magazine praised it for showing "that men can join hands out of fear and hatred and shape from base emotions something identifiable as a kind of love,"[50] and *Life* called it "a fine demonstration that races can work together."[51] Pauline Kael liked the film but hated the tone of most of its positive reviews; she had been relieved to discover that Jewison hadn't made a "self-righteous, self-congratulatory exercise in the gloomy old Stanley Kramer tradition" but complained that too many of her colleagues praised it "as if it had been exactly the kind of picture that the audience was so relieved to discover it wasn't."[52]

A few prominent critics dissented strongly. Andrew Sarris's dismissal of the movie as a "fantasy of racial reconciliation"[53] was echoed by *The New Yorker*'s Penelope Gilliatt, who was then in a relationship with Mike Nichols and had seen a screening of the movie during production of *The Graduate*. The film, she said, "has a spurious air of concern about the afflictions of the real America at the moment. . . . There is a predictable night interlude when the rivals suddenly come together and speak for a second of their common loneliness, thus tritely demonstrating that we are really all the same, though I can't think of any really first-rate film, play or book that isn't unconsciously dedicated to the fact that we are all inconsolably different."[54] The most pointed criticism *In the Heat of the Night* received stemmed from the decision Jewison made early in the development of Silliphant's screenplay to strip away scenes in which Tibbs faced the systemic racism of a small southern town and to boil down the movie's racial politics to a single relationship. "Jewison and . . . Silliphant are running on the premise that movies can correct the world by describing it incorrectly,"[55] the critic Ethan Mordden wrote later. And *Esquire*'s Wilfrid Sheed remarked, "If that were all Mississippi amounted to it wouldn't take much courage to march down there; one Poitier per town would soon bring the rascals to their senses. . . . Our peoples will work this thing out some day. Yeah, sure."[56]

The vast majority of reviewers weighed in with strong praise for the movie and its two stars, with the *New York Daily News* claiming that "nobody but an actor of Poitier's stature could have characterized [the] Negro detective with any amount of forcefulness"[57] and *Newsweek*'s Joseph Morgenstern writing that "Poitier, who could be ruling the roost if parts were handed out on the basis of talent instead of pigment, gets a rare opportunity to demonstrate the full sweep of his powers."[58] The *Chicago Sun-Times* and *The Boston Globe* both suggested that Steiger was headed for an Academy Award.[59] But Poitier—and what he represented—was also coming under harsher scrutiny. "He is not a Negro before being a man. He is a Negro instead of being a man," wrote Sarris in the *Village Voice*, dismissing the movie as "liberal propaganda. . . . Nowadays . . . Negroes are never condemned in the movies. Their faults, if any, are tolerated as the bitter fruits of injustice, and thus their virtues are regarded less as the consequences of free choice than [of] puppetry. . . . All that is expected of the Negro . . . is that he be inoffensive, and Poitier [is] heroically inoffensive. . . . It is not Poitier's fault that he is used to disinfect the recent riots of any lingering racism. It is his destiny to be forbidden the individuality to say 'I' instead of 'we.' "[60]

Sarris underestimated how unusual *In the Heat of the Night* would look to most moviegoers. Audiences reacted so strongly to the chance to see

Poitier fight back, and the politics behind it, that *In the Heat of the Night* soon acquired the jokey nickname "Super-Spade Versus the Rednecks."[61] And, as Jewison had predicted, the scene in which Virgil Tibbs delivers a backhand slap to the face of a white racist became a galvanizing moment. "Sidney and I used to go to the [Capitol] Theater in New York to see the scene," Steiger said later. "You could hear the black people say, 'Go get 'em, Sidney!' and the white people going, 'Oh!' And we used to break up. We could tell how many white and how many black were in the theater."[62] Anthony James, the young actor who had made just $100 a day to play the counterman in a Sparta diner who turns out to be involved in the murder, went to Grauman's Chinese Theatre in Los Angeles and listened to the gasps. "I have young African American friends who have seen the movie, and they don't really notice the scene now," he says. "But at the time, it was really startling."[63]

In almost every movie house, the slap drew cheers. "Applause in the movies . . . seems to have some belligerence in it, an assertion of will," wrote Renata Adler in *The New York Times*. "People applaud at movies, I think, because they want to insist on seeing more of something. . . . The enthusiasm for [Poitier's] small act of violence also contains a strong awareness of his real situation. He is playing once again, patiently, angrily, that young Negro . . . which he has managed to turn, over the years, into a kind of deliberate, type-cast, reverse racial stereotype. . . . This reinforces the sense of outrage at the abuse which, until the point of the liberating slap, he has had to take in role after role. . . . The reaction is shock and pure relief."[64]

TWENTY-SIX

"Oh shit," Arthur Penn said to himself. "Here we go."

It was August 5, the second day of the 1967 Montreal Film Festival, the Saturday morning after a capacity crowd of two thousand at the Expo Theater had attended the opening night premiere of *Bonnie and Clyde* and responded with laughter, cheers, and clearly heartfelt applause. Penn and Beatty, listening to the response, knew the movie had had exactly the effect they hoped it would. At a press conference, the director calmly fielded questions about the picture's comedy, violence, antiheroism, and "relevance," all of which had gotten the first-nighters buzzing. "I don't think the original Bonnie and Clyde are very important except insofar as they motivated the writing of a script and the making of the movie," he told reporters. The film's approach, he explained, was that, at a time when "very rural people were suffering the terrors of a depression . . . Bonnie and Clyde [became] folk heroes, violators of the status quo. And in that context, one finds oneself . . . confronted with the terrible irony that we root for somebody . . . who, in the course of [a] good cause, is called upon to commit acts of violence which repel us." Penn spoke about the "constant correlative" of humor and bloodshed and explained that as the movie unfolds, "the murders get less and less funny because they begin to be identified with the murderers. . . . With respect to *Bonnie and Clyde* and my other films . . . I would have to say that I think violence is a part of the American character."[1]

After the press conference, Penn saw Bosley Crowther, the *New York Times* critic who delighted in being a kingmaker—and sometimes an executioner—at international film festivals. Crowther had been at the Expo Theater the night before, and he was appalled; the audience's enthusiastic reaction and Penn's pro-insurrection rhetorical flourishes in front of reporters had only affronted him more. "He sort of warned me that he was really going to attack it," says Penn, "and I thought, well, here it comes."[2]

Bonnie and Clyde was scheduled to open in New York City on August 13—a Sunday—but Crowther couldn't contain his wrath even for a week. Immediately after Penn's remarks, he filed a dispatch that ran in the *Times* the next day. "Hollywood moviemakers seem to have a knack of putting the worst foot forward at international film festivals," he began. "Now they've done it again." *Bonnie and Clyde,* he fumed, "whips through the saga of the cheapjack bandits as though it were funny instead of sordid and grim." And while he sullenly acknowledged that most of those in attendance had liked the movie, "some more sober visitors from the United States," whom he did not identify, "were wagging their heads in dismay and exasperation that so callous and callow a film should represent their country in these critical times."[3] Five days later, Crowther went after the movie again, claiming it had sullied the festival for him and was even tarnishing the image of Expo 67. "Was the audience reaction a true expression of appreciation for the film or . . . a sort of rocking along with a form of camp?" he wondered.[4] By the time he filed his official review on opening day, his indignation had swollen into outrage. *Bonnie and Clyde,* he wrote, "is a cheap piece of bald-faced slapstick comedy that treats the hideous depredations of that sleazy, moronic pair as though they were as full of fun and frolic as the jazz-age cut-ups in *Thoroughly Modern Millie*." He called the performances "ridiculous, camp-tinctured travesties" and said he found the violence "as pointless as it is lacking in taste."[5]

Crowther's displeasure with the film came as less of a surprise than the ferocity and persistence of his attacks on it. After twenty-seven years on the job, he was a staid traditionalist with a harrumphing aversion to anything he found "sensationalistic" and a particular distaste for violence that went unpunished on screen. As far back as *The Killers* in 1946 and *White Heat* in 1949, he chided Hollywood for its eagerness to make movies about criminals and worried that the industry's emphasis on "malevolence" and "sadistic thrills" would generate "unhealthy stimulation"[6] in moviegoers, whom he viewed as an impressionable and easily corrupted stratum of consumer society. In the month before *Bonnie and Clyde* opened, the success of *The Dirty Dozen* had shocked Crowther; he called Aldrich's movie "astonishingly wanton . . . a studied indulgence of sadism that is morbid and disgusting beyond words."[7] And he had been equally horrified by two other recently released films that demolished the tradition of the western as thoroughly as *The Dirty Dozen* had upended the war-movie genre. Sergio Leone's *A Fistful of Dollars* had opened in Europe in 1964, and its sequel, *For a Few Dollars More,* had followed in 1965. But only in the last few months had the films, which introduced movie audiences to TV cowboy Clint Eastwood, reached the United States; in 1967, United Artists released them in rapid succession in order to build an audience for the third picture in the series, *The Good, the Bad and the Ugly.* Crowther had little fondness for moral ambiguity; he felt that Leone's movies, which featured Eastwood as a gunslinger who keeps his allegiances to himself and which UA's executives crowed "made money beyond all our hopes,"[8] were "constructed to endorse the exercise of murderers" and offer "fantasies of killing contrived . . . for emotional escapism."[9] Shortly before *Bonnie and Clyde*'s opening, he wrote a column called "Movies to Kill People By" that began, "Something is happening in movies that has me alarmed and disturbed. Movie-makers and moviegoers are agreeing that killing is fun." He concluded by calling *The Dirty Dozen* and the Leone pictures "as socially decadent and dangerous as LSD."[10] One of the last reviews he filed before leaving for Montreal to see *Bonnie and Clyde* was a pan of Roger Corman's *The St. Valentine's Day Massacre,* which had beaten Penn's film into theaters by just a couple of weeks and which, he wrote, "artificializes and confuses the tawdry history it is supposed to relate."[11]

In person, Crowther, according to his colleagues at the *Times* and his contemporaries in movie criticism, was a mild, soft-spoken gentleman, not lacking in perspective or a sense of humor. But in print, huffiness and sanctimony would often get the better of him. "The film critic is performing a function akin to a pastor—he is a counselor of a community about the values of a picture," he told Richard Schickel, then the reviewer for

Life. "[*Bonnie and Clyde*] is immoral, and we have to say so."[12] Unfortunately for Crowther, whenever he took umbrage at something, his prose, which was never smooth to begin with, would gnarl itself into incomprehensibility. "He was very amiable," says Joseph Morgenstern, who was then beginning his job as *Newsweek*'s movie critic. "But he was a know-nothing, fuddy-duddy, Puritan, turgid writer. Remember Arthur Krock, the *New York Times* columnist? There was a joke that nobody ever finished reading a whole Arthur Krock column. The same could have been said of Crowther, although he was immensely powerful, and people did read far enough to know what he thought."[13]

In 1967, the opinion of *The New York Times'* film critic didn't represent the last word on a movie, but it did tend to start the conversation, and Crowther's triple attack on *Bonnie and Clyde* was especially damaging because it echoed the contempt in which Jack Warner and Ben Kalmenson already held the movie. If they had been indifferent to its fate before, the *Times* certainly offered no reason for them to change their minds. And Crowther was hardly alone in his assessment; *Time* magazine handed the assignment of critiquing *Bonnie and Clyde* to its music reviewer, Alan Rich, who snidely dismissed Beatty's "long-unawaited debut as a producer" as "a strange and purposeless mingling of fact and claptrap."[14] When it first opened, *Life* didn't bother to review it at all. Even Andrew Sarris, a champion of the Nouvelle Vague films that had inspired the screenplay in the first place, had mixed feelings about the movie, saying it "oscillates between the distancing of period legend and the close-ups of contemporary psychology."[15] "Sarris's review, which was not good, was very smart," says Robert Benton. "He said, this is a self-conscious movie, and he was right to note that the New Wave had created a kind of self-consciousness that would mark the American films that were about to come out. But it was a pretty devastating time."[16]

When Joe Morgenstern went to Warner Brothers' Fifth Avenue screening room to watch *Bonnie and Clyde* for *Newsweek*, he was rattled to find Beatty sitting in the back row next to him. "I felt that he was trying to peer at my notes," he says. "It was a little unnerving, but that's not really an excuse." Morgenstern went back to his office and filed what he called a "pissy" review,[17] in which he wrote that although the movie had "interesting" elements and "some beauty, suggestions of humanity and even some legitimate humor," it devolved into "a squalid shoot-'em-up for the moron trade . . . *In Cold Blood* played as a William Inge comedy."[18]

"I got it wrong," he says. "I was not ready for the violence and kind of shrank from it." Morgenstern didn't give much thought to his piece after he filed it; "however upset or disoriented I had been by the movie," he says, "in my mind, that was all the more reason for me to move on." But as Friday approached, Morgenstern found himself suggesting to his wife, actress Piper Laurie, that they see it in a theater. "She looked at me kind of peculiarly and said, 'I thought you didn't like it.' This was on the weekend—my review wouldn't be published until Monday. And I said, somewhat illogically, 'Well, *you'll* like it—the costumes, the Flatt and Scruggs music. . . .' We went to see the movie that afternoon, and the audience just went crazy. It had a big crowd, despite Bosley Crowther's review. I just got this cold sweat on the back of my neck and thought, 'Oh shit, I've missed the boat.' I turned to my wife, who loved it, and said, 'Do you have anything to write with?' and she found a pad and pen, and I started frantically taking notes. I suddenly realized what I had missed."[19]

Morgenstern was too late to prevent his review from running, but that Monday, when it hit newsstands, he walked into the office of *Newsweek* editor Osborn Elliott, told him with a nervous attempt at casualness that he had "some other thoughts" on *Bonnie and Clyde,* and asked him if he could write about it again. "The only thing I was thinking about at that point was digging myself out of a hole that I'd fallen into. I was a deeply troubled soul that week. I thought I could get away with just a reconsideration, not a retraction. But I started to write, and I was as blocked as I've ever been. And then I thought, 'I've gotta come clean.' And I wrote the lead of the new piece." A few days later, Morgenstern and Laurie had dinner with Pauline Kael, who was then working on a long article about the movie for *The New Republic,* where she had been freelancing recently. "Pauline wasted no time in telling me smugly, 'You really missed the boat,' and I said, trying my best to imitate her smugness, 'Well, I may have more to say,' already knowing what I had written."[20]

"Last week this magazine said that *Bonnie and Clyde,* a tale of two young bank robbers in the 1930s, turns into a 'squalid shoot-'em-up for

the moron trade' because it does not know what to make of its own violence," Morgenstern's second review began. "I am sorry to say I consider
that review grossly unfair and regrettably inaccurate. I am sorrier to say
I wrote it." Morgenstern went on to praise "scene after scene of dazzling
artistry . . . [that] has the power to both enthrall and appall." The film,
he wrote, "makes a cogent statement . . . that violence is not necessarily
perpetrated by shambling cavemen or quivering psychopaths but may also
be the casual, easy expression of only slightly aberrated citizens, of jes'
folks." And the movie's audience, he added, was "enjoying itself almost to
the point of rapture."[21]

Morgenstern's mea culpa—"my Andy Warhol moment," he says
wryly[22]—was infinitely more valuable to *Bonnie and Clyde* than a mere
rave would have been: Suddenly the studio had a controversy it could
exploit. "After the first set of reviews, I thought, it won't even last a week
in theaters," says Robert Benton. "But when Joe Morgenstern changed his
mind, that pivoted it. It made news—and from there, the movie started
to have a life of its own."[23] When *Bonnie and Clyde* first opened, Warner
Brothers had run an ad with quotes from the critics who had seen the film
in Montreal and liked it—Judith Crist, whose enthusiastic recommendation had gotten the movie into the festival in the first place and who wrote
about it for *Vogue,* Gene Shalit in *Ladies' Home Journal,* and *Cue's* William
Wolf. (The film also drew support from an unlikely quarter: "It works,"
wrote the reviewer for the *Catholic Film Newsletter.* "You can say it should
not. You can insist it does not decide what it is: semidocumentary, ballad,
love story, social comment, comedy, psychological study or tragedy. But it
works.")[24] But now the studio had something juicier to sell—a movie that
had made a critic think twice.

In the weeks that followed, Crowther's unwillingness to let up on *Bonnie and Clyde* began to backfire; his obstinacy turned what had been long-
simmering annoyance with him into open warfare. Crowther had been
disdained by many of his colleagues for years. In 1963, his slack-jawed
rave for *Cleopatra,* about which he repeatedly used the word *brilliant,*
had been publicly mocked by Sarris and had even drawn groans from
within the *Times*; the paper's movie business reporter Murray Schumach

complained to his bosses that the review was just one more example of Crowther's tendency to coddle big, expensive studio films, and editors Arthur Gelb and Turner Catledge were embarrassed by the fulsomeness of his praise for a film that they themselves thought was overblown trash.[25] In the last year, critics had begun to mass against Crowther, not for his determinedly middlebrow taste, but for his propensity to bully anyone who didn't share it. Crowther's contempt for a small movie could kill it in its first week and sometimes prevent it from even *having* a first week. When he saw Orson Welles's *Falstaff* (*Chimes at Midnight*) at the 1966 Cannes Film Festival, he made his hatred of the picture so plain that its U.S. distributor, the small company Peppercorn-Wormser, tried for almost a year to avoid opening it in New York. ("Crowther, Please Stay Home," *Variety* pleaded in a story about his ability to keep audiences away from art-house movies.)[26] When *Falstaff* finally arrived, many critics found Crowther's review malicious. In the *Village Voice,* Sarris called him a "power-oriented critic. . . . What I object to is the implication that he is going to punish the distributors for bringing *Falstaff* to America against his express wishes." He added that Crowther "can call [Welles] old-fashioned and dated and used-up, as if critics stayed young forever and only directors became senile."[27]

"He was a very good man, especially on civil rights and politics, but he had a withering effect on foreign films and art films," says Sarris. "As films got more difficult, he gave courage to people who wanted to believe that if a movie was difficult to understand, it probably wasn't any good. That was particularly pernicious. But I was involved in a lot of critical feuds back then, and being at the *Times* and having a kind of philistine-ish style, he was an easy target, and we took advantage of it."[28]

In late 1966, Sarris, Morgenstern, John Simon, Hollis Alpert, and seven other reviewers formed the National Society of Film Critics, an awards-giving group intended to counterbalance the New York Film Critics Circle, which at the time was dominated by Crowther and a number of stodgy hacks from daily newspapers who tended to follow his lead. (In the National Society's first year, its membership awarded Best Picture and Best Director to *Blow-Up,* while the New York group gave its top prizes to *A Man for All Seasons.*) When Crowther aimed his fusillade at *Bonnie and*

Clyde, he suddenly found himself the target of increasingly personal and public counterattacks. Praising its treatment of violence as "thoughtful and piercing," *The New Yorker*'s Penelope Gilliatt, among the first major critics to review the movie positively, wrote that *"Bonnie and Clyde* could look like a celebration of gangster glamour only to a man with a head full of wood shavings."[29] And Sarris, though he was not a particular fan of the film, went after Crowther, too: "To use the pages of the *New York Times* for a personal vendetta against a director and actor one doesn't like is questionable enough. To incite the lurking forces of censorship and repression with inflammatory diatribes against violence on the screen is downright mischievous. . . . The slanders in the *Times* emerge as exercises in dull spite."[30] By the end of August, *Variety* had taken notice and wondered if Crowther's negative review had "hurt the cause of serious filmmaking in America by shooting down a work of art. . . . These concerns over violence might spark a return to the . . . days of movie-making when every 'commercial' picture had to make an explicit statement of its point."[31]

Whatever his other failings, Crowther had not called for a return to a more restrictive Production Code in any of his pieces. He had in fact spent thirty years fighting film censorship harder than almost anyone else in his profession; his reviews were even cited in the 1952 Supreme Court decision that ruled that movies were protected by the First Amendment.[32] He was stunned and hurt by accusations that he was advocating a return to a more restrictive era, and he lashed out. Even the *Times* began to exploit the controversy, running a flurry of letters from readers who called Crowther "blinded" and "insensitive" and excitedly praised *Bonnie and Clyde* as "deep—deep" and "a totally new thing—it's real and unreal."[33] Crowther responded with a fourth attack, expressing bewilderment at the "upsurge of passionate expressions of admiration" for a "deliberately buffoonized picture" that he felt was defined by a "kind of cheating with the bare and ugly truth." He concluded by digging himself a deep rhetorical hole, comparing *Bonnie and Clyde* to a movie that attempted to treat Lee Harvey Oswald or Adolf Hitler sympathetically.[34] "There came a certain point when the more he went after us, the more we enjoyed it," says Benton. "Bosley Crowther was far from the worst critic out there, but what he wasn't prepared for was something that would undermine the good, traditional, craftsmanlike, 'well made' movie, not only morally, but stylistically. It pushed some button in him. And it became impossible for him to stop."[35]

Then Pauline Kael stepped into the fray. After *The New Republic* rejected her *Bonnie and Clyde* piece, she took it to William Shawn at *The New Yorker*, which ran the essay, at its full length of seven thousand words, in its October 21 issue. Kael had written one long article for the magazine before—an essay on how television ruins and distorts movies, a favorite hobbyhorse of cinephiles in the mid-1960s[36]—but this was the first time she had taken on a single film for the magazine, and it was unmistakably an audition. At forty-eight, Kael had been putting together a living by talking and writing about movies for fifteen years; she had begun on the West Coast, writing film notes for Berkeley revival houses and making funny, combative appearances on San Francisco radio shows. By the mid-1960s, she was already so well-known in film circles for her pieces in *Partisan Review* that, after *McCall's* fired her, *Newsweek* ran a story discussing the growing "Kael cult." An attention getter by instinct, Kael relished any opportunity to position herself as the informal, gut-driven voice of sanity rising in opposition to whatever she defined as the current orthodoxy. While she was on the West Coast, she wrote, "I razzed the East Coast critics and their cultural domination of the country"; [37] now that she had come east, she chose more specific adversaries.

Kael knew that she could get herself noticed by picking a fight, as she had done a few years earlier when she went after Andrew Sarris with a piece in *Film Quarterly* that mocked him and twitted American auteurist critics for elevating what she felt was disposable work by minor talents to the status of art.[38] On the page, she was a mass of theoretical contradictions—a snob who railed against elitism, an epicure who boasted of her taste for vulgarity, an undeniably auteurist champion of her own pet directors who mocked auteurism in others, and a critic who so enjoyed writing in reaction against her colleagues that her desire to be iconoclastic at all costs sometimes clouded her judgment. But she was also the wittiest and most provocative writer that the field of film criticism had ever produced, and her article on *Bonnie and Clyde* put her at the center of an ongoing con-versation about American movies over which she presided for the next fifteen years.

From its first sentence—"How do you make a good movie in this coun-try without being jumped on?"[39]—Kael's impassioned, forceful defense of *Bonnie and Clyde,* which she identified as the gateway to a new kind of American moviemaking, was as much about the film's detractors as it was about the film itself. "*Bonnie and Clyde* brings into the almost frighten-ingly public world of movies things that people have been feeling and say-ing and writing about," she began. "And once something is said or done on the screens of the world, once it has entered mass art, it can never again . . . be the private possession of an educated, or 'knowing' group." She applauded the movie's violence as central to its meaning: "It is a kind of violence that says something to us; it is something that artists must be free to use. . . . Will we, as some people have suggested, be lured into imitating the violent crimes of Clyde and Bonnie because Warren Beatty and Faye Dunaway are 'glamorous'? . . . It's difficult to see how, since the characters they play are horrified by it and ultimately destroyed by it. . . . *Bonnie and Clyde* needs violence; violence is its meaning." She brushed off complaints about historical inaccuracy and bad taste as irrelevant. And she left little doubt as to whom she meant when she said, "Too many people—including some movie reviewers—want the law to take over the job of movie criticism; perhaps what they really want is for their own criti-cisms to have the force of law."

Kael's statement that "the whole point of *Bonnie and Clyde* is to rub our noses in it, to make us pay our dues for laughing," her understanding that "we don't take our stories straight anymore—*Bonnie and Clyde* is the first film demonstration that the put-on can be used for the purposes of art," and her awareness of the "eager, nervous imbalance" in which the movie intended to hold its audience all seemed uncannily in synch with the intentions of Robert Benton and David Newman. It was no accident. Though she didn't disclose it in the piece, she had taken the screenwrit-ers out to lunch before writing her essay[40] and gotten an earful of their motives, their admiration for the French New Wave, and their storytelling strategy. Her remark that "though one cannot say of *Bonnie and Clyde* to what degree it shows the work of Newman and Benton . . . there are ways of making guesses" was deeply disingenuous but very much in line with her pooh-poohing of "the new notion that direction is everything." Unsurprisingly, she made it clear that she didn't see the movie as Arthur Penn's accomplishment, although she praised him for the staging and editing of the dance-of-death sequence, which she called "a horror that seems to go on for eternity, and yet . . . doesn't last a second beyond what it should."

Kael's piece marked a decisive shift of the critical consensus on *Bonnie and Clyde* against Crowther and won her the job as one of *The New Yorker*'s two permanent film reviewers; she replaced Brendan Gill, sharing duties with Gilliatt in six-month shifts that began in early 1968. But her rave did not, as has often been claimed, turn *Bonnie and Clyde*'s fortunes around. For one thing, Kael was uncharacteristically late to the brawl; the movie had already been open for two months by the time her article appeared. In its two New York engagements and one Los Angeles theater, it was continuing to do strong, steady business and was also doing well in single-screen bookings in Chicago, Denver, and Baltimore. But Warner Brothers had little faith in the picture's ability to draw a broader audience. On October 4, the studio grudgingly began what it called a "midwest saturation" run, actually a barely publicized test release in which *Bonnie and Clyde* was booked in thirty-five theaters in and around Kansas City and Omaha.[41] With little in the way of support or promotion from the studio, the results were predictably unimpressive. Just as Kael's piece reached readers, Warner Brothers all but gave up. On October 10, the studio pulled the movie from the Forum, the New York theater where big crowds were still lining up to see what all the fuss was about, and replaced it with the Elizabeth Taylor–Marlon Brando melodrama *Reflections in a Golden Eye*.

Bonnie and Clyde's failure at the box office was overshadowed by what the trade papers were calling "Sidney Poitier Month."[42] In September, *In the Heat of the Night* and *To Sir, with Love* were, respectively, the number one and number two movies in the country. Though not a blockbuster, after eight weeks in release, *Heat* had easily earned back its $2 million budget and was on its way to what would be a healthy U.S. gross of about $7.5 million by the end of the year.[43] In October, *To Sir, with Love,* a much bigger hit that was then in its fourth month in theaters, took over the top spot again.[44] *Box Office* magazine now ranked Poitier as the fifth-biggest star in Hollywood, ahead of Sean Connery and Steve McQueen.[45] His drawing power was a shock to an industry that had, until recently, treated his employment in movies as something akin to an act of charity, and Hollywood greeted his new popularity with an orgy of self-congratulation, treating it as a further affirmation of the progress that his Oscar a few years earlier had purported to signify.

But just as Poitier's success was being widely heralded, he was the subject of a frontal assault in *The New York Times.* On Sunday, September 10, the newspaper ran an essay by Clifford Mason, an African American aspiring playwright who occasionally wrote theater criticism, called "Why Does White America Love Sidney Poitier So?"—a sustained attack not just on Poitier's roles, but on the actor himself. Mason cited *A Patch of Blue* ("Probably the most ridiculous film Poitier ever made . . . he's running his private branch of the ASPCA, the Black Society for the Prevention of Cruelty to Blind White Girls, the BSPCBWG"), *The Bedford Incident* (in which he played "a black correspondent who went around calling everyone sir. Did anyone ever see Gary Cooper or Greg Peck call anyone sir when they played foreign correspondents?"), and *To Sir, with Love* ("Instead of putting a love interest into a story that had none, they took it out"). Mason called Poitier's career "a schizophrenic flight from historical fact that [imagines] that the Negro is best served by . . . taking on white problems and a white man's sense of what's wrong with the world. . . . All this Mr. Poitier endures, and more, without a murmur of protest. . . . In all of these films he has been a showcase nigger.

"White critics will . . . applaud every 'advance' in movies . . . as so much American-style democratic goodwill," wrote Mason. "Gradualism may have some place in politics. But in art it just represents a stale, hackneyed period." Poitier, he predicted at the end of his tirade, would never break free of roles in which he was "nonplussed by white arrogance . . . but, because of his innate goodness, finally [makes] that fateful decision to solve the problem for 'them,' good nigger that he is."[46]

Times editor Seymour Peck's decision to publish the article with its racial epithets intact was a minor radical-chic moment, a way of inviting an angry black man into the homes of the paper's white readers, but its real effect was to expose, and deepen, the rift that had grown between Poitier and a younger, more militant black cultural intelligentsia. The week after the article ran, Poitier was attending a high school play in Harlem at the request of a friend, and Mason sat next to him, introduced himself, and asked if he had read the piece. "I want[ed] to say, 'Yes, mother-fucker, I read your article,'" wrote Poitier in *This Life*. "Instead I say, 'Oh, yes, I did.' Period."[47] Poitier was determined to avoid a confrontation, but he couldn't let go of his anger for months. He was terribly wounded by the story and furious at Mason's decision to lay "the film industry's transgressions at my feet," but at the same time, he knew the arguments Mason was making represented the thinking of a portion of black America that was tired of compromises and half measures and was growing larger and stronger by the day. He paced his living room, reading the piece aloud and complaining to his friends, "Some day people will realize that I'm doing my part. . . . How long do you think I'd last if I came on like Stokely Carmichael or Eldridge Cleaver?"[48] "It was crushing to him to be attacked as an Uncle Tom," says Katharine Houghton. "That kind of thing just tore him apart."[49]

Forty years later, Mason expresses a degree of regret about the article. "I was trying to inject a sense into my own people that we have to be less happy about *seeming* advantages instead of real achievement," he says. "But I sort of jumped all over Sidney because I wanted him to be Humphrey Bogart when he was really Cary Grant. I wanted him to be a personality type that he wasn't, and that, of course, was unfair. But that role that Sidney always played—the black person with dignity who worries about the white people's problems—you don't play that part over and over again unless you're comfortable with that kind of suffering."[50]

Mason's article, Poitier said later, started a "deluge" that steadily eroded his image among young black Americans and critics on the left. His acceptance by white moviegoers was used as evidence of how out of step his movies were with the needs and frustrations of his own people. Even journalists sympathetic to Poitier were starting to portray the actor as being aloof from the contemporary realities of the late 1960s; almost every profile and article made a point of referring to his Central Park West penthouse and its luxurious trappings, as if he were at an ivory-tower remove from the revolution taking place in the streets below. And the new level of success Poitier had achieved opened a floodgate of resentment among his own colleagues, who had kept silent when he himself was still struggling for parity with white movie stars but now demanded more from him than pleas for patience. Some of them wanted to know why doors weren't opening for more African American performers; to them, Poitier's career trajectory seemed to be creating new opportunities for no one but Poitier himself. "I'm tired of hearing Sidney say, 'I'll do this *some* time,'" said a black actor after sitting in Poitier's living room and listening to him argue that his success would eventually benefit everyone. "It's always *some* time. What's the matter with right now?"[51] Even Harry Belafonte, sometime friend, sometime rival, raised the possibility, however obliquely, that Poitier had sold out. "A lot of people have made their bargains with the devil," he told the *Los Angeles Times*. "Marlon has made his choice. Sidney has made his choice."[52] He didn't elaborate on what he thought those choices were.

"I represent ten million people in this country, and millions more in Africa . . . and I'm not going to do anything they can't be proud of," Poitier said at a press conference to promote the start of production of *For Love of Ivy*. "Wait till there are six of us—then one of us can play villains all the time. . . . First, we've got to live down the kind of parts we've had all these years." Poitier was referring, he said, to "frightened, bug-eyed maids and shuffling butlers."[53] But it was his own résumé of antiseptic, nonconfrontational role models that was drawing fire. The actor Brock Peters said publicly that Poitier's recent hits "don't go much further historically than, say, *The Defiant Ones* ten years ago"[54] and suggested that Poitier was complicit in his own on-screen desexualization.

For the first time, Poitier agreed to take a role that departed from his spotless image: He would play the leader of a group of black revolutionaries who masterminds a payroll robbery in Universal's *The Lost Man*. But while the mainstream press focused on the fact that he would receive a career-high $750,000 for the role,[55] Poitier felt a deep pessimism about his own prospects. If *In the Heat of the Night*'s Virgil Tibbs had not assuaged the critics who faulted him for his on-screen passivity, he had little doubt what they would make of *Guess Who's Coming to Dinner*. For fifteen years, Poitier had fought a battle for acceptance in an industry that was virtually closed to black people, and he had, just a year earlier, believed that *For Love of Ivy* would represent a giant step forward, a movie in which he could at last play a black man with a healthy libido and a romantic and professional life that had nothing to do with the white world. Now, he sensed it would be too little, too late. Throughout the fall of 1967, as one story after another appeared celebrating his breakthrough in mainstream Hollywood, Poitier felt, with growing certainty, that "my career as a leading man in Hollywood was nearing its end."[56]

TWENTY-SEVEN

The Mann Theatre in Minneapolis was a good-luck charm for Dick Zanuck. In 1965, he and Robert Wise had flown to Minnesota with a print of *The Sound of Music* for a sneak preview at Ted Mann's big road-show playhouse. The city was in the middle of a blizzard so terrible that Zanuck and Wise wondered if anybody would show up. "A sneak was still a real sneak back then," says Zanuck. "You didn't advertise the picture, but you tried to pick a theater that was showing a similar movie so that you'd get a friendly audience, and we'd usually leak what movie we were showing to a local disc jockey to get the word out." Zanuck cheered up a little when he saw a long line of Minnesotans lined up outside the Mann, bundled against the snow but determined to get in. The movie got a standing ovation before its first intermission. "We were all delirious," he says. "We came back to the hotel and waited in my suite, Bobby Wise and some of the executives and distribution guys, everyone from the picture. We got drunk and we waited for the comment cards to arrive." About four hundred audience members had written down their reactions. "Getting that many was a good sign," says Zanuck, "because when they like the picture, they'll take the time to write a card. By the time we got them, we were all pretty smashed. We divided them up and everybody started reading them off: 'Excellent! Excellent! Excellent! Excellent! Excellent!' In my pile, there was one 'Very Good.' I was so tanked up that I got enraged— I wanted to call Ted Mann and find out if there was any way of tracing who could have possibly written the card. We were living in such a stupefied world with that kind of hit."[1]

By September 1967, when Zanuck, Arthur Jacobs and Natalie Trundy, Richard Fleischer, Leslie and Yvonne Bricusse, and the Fox brass all flew up to Minneapolis to preview *Doctor Dolittle* in the same theater, stupefaction, superstition, and liquor seemed to be an appropriate set of operating principles when it came to the fate of the movie. For the last several months, Zanuck had allowed the journalist John Gregory Dunne to have access to all but a few meetings and conversations at 20th Century-Fox for a book he was planning to write on a year in the life of a movie studio, and Jacobs, who had recovered from his heart attack and thrown himself into micromanaging every aspect of *Dolittle*'s release, proved to be irresistible material for Dunne. Jacobs had lost thirty pounds since his illness but was otherwise the same chain-smoking, hard-drinking, fast-talking operator that he had always been. Dunne captured him proudly tooling around the Fox lot on a golf cart, showing off his new sports car, and boasting about the $12 million that fifty licensees had committed to promoting *Dolittle* on everything from cereal boxes to bottles of chocolate soda. He witnessed Jacobs's zeal in pushing Fox's "song plugger" Happy Goday to get dozens of singers to record songs from the movie before its release, including Bobby Darin, Andy Williams, and Tony Bennett. Goday even convinced Sammy Davis Jr., who apparently had gotten over his hard feelings about being dropped from the film two years earlier, to record an entire album of *Dolittle* music.[2]

Finishing the movie had dragged on into midsummer, as Lionel Newman, the cantankerous head of Fox's music department, tried to fix one dead spot in the picture after another by patching scenes together with a score he had never much liked in the first place. Newman treated Jacobs with semiaffectionate contempt: "Hello, lardass," he would say when the producer showed up on the recording stage. "Listen, lardass, is there any chance we can get a longer shot in the percussion sequence?" Newman particularly disliked "Talk to the Animals," which he called a "lousy song";[3] in fact, nobody who had worked on the film thought much of it. Most of the *Dolittle* team assumed that the breakout single from the movie would be the ballad "When I Look into Your Eyes"—that is, if listeners could ignore the fact that in the movie, Harrison croons the love song to a seal that he had dressed as an old lady just before he flings the animal over a steep cliff into the ocean, presumably sending her on a long plunge toward freedom.

In Dunne's 1969 book, *The Studio*, a classic of movie business reportage, he offers a bleakly funny account of the moment that everybody's hopes for *Doctor Dolittle* came crashing to earth. The Fox team had set off for Minnesota with high expectations and immense anxiety. "All I know is that when we go to Minneapolis, I'm going to take along a big bottle of Miltown and slip it into all that vodka you drink so much of," Jacobs's fiancée, Natalie Trundy, told him.[4] The collective nervousness was more than understandable. *Dolittle* had become Fox's most expensive movie since *Cleopatra*. Although Darryl Zanuck didn't fly out for the screening, everyone else at Fox was there, filling three rows of the theater.

Dick Zanuck knew the movie was in for trouble as soon as he saw the audience, which included almost no children. He hoped that perhaps what he was witnessing was just a reflection of the fact that it was a night-time screening. Perhaps word hadn't gotten out that they were showing an adaptation of a children's classic, because if it had, and this was an indication of the lack of interest kids had in it . . . The lights went down, and the movie, which ran close to three hours, began. In Dunne's description, the audience was "unresponsive" and "muted." "The second half of the picture did not play much better than the first," he wrote. "When the house lights came on, the only prolonged clapping came from the three rows where the Studio people were sitting."[5]

By the time Zanuck and his twenty-eight-man team returned to their rooms at the Radisson, it was painfully obvious that *Doctor Dolittle* was no *Sound of Music*. On the surface, the comment cards might have seemed encouraging: 148 moviegoers rated the movie "Excellent," 76 rated it "Good," and 42 called it "Fair." ("Poor" was not offered as an option.)[6] But Zanuck knew the results were terrible: A massively expensive movie that almost half of its first audience declined to label as excellent was all but doomed. As is often the case after a bad preview, gloom quickly gave way to an atmosphere of frantic, hypercheerful rationalization. Kids would turn the movie into a hit, if kids could just be gotten into the theater, and their enthusiasm would spread to their parents! This wasn't a death sentence, just a heads-up that they could make the movie even better! The problem wasn't the movie, it was the audience—it was just a dead house! The problem *was* the movie, but it was nothing that couldn't be fixed with a few trims here and there—it wouldn't take much to guarantee that the next set of comment cards wouldn't include the phrase *Too long,* which seemed to be an issue for a surprising number of people.

The Fox team left Zanuck's suite and went back to their own rooms, where they got a few hours of sleep, or tried to. "There was no point," says Zanuck. "Nobody could sleep." At 5:00 in the morning, Zanuck called them all back to his room. It was time for a more sober, no-bull round of decision making.[7] Even though the image of Rex Harrison riding a giraffe had made the cover of *Life* magazine, the long prologue in which it appeared would have to go. Leslie Bricusse would write a new song for Anthony Newley to sing with a group of kids, something that would enliven the movie's second half and underscore its appeal to young viewers. Richard Fleischer was tasked with spinning the preview results to Rex Harrison, who was apt to use any bad news as an excuse for a drunken tantrum and whose cooperation would be needed at various premieres and benefits to promote the movie. They would find a way to salvage at least one shot of the giraffe. And then they would retest the picture. Preferably in a city as far from Minneapolis as possible.

Everyone returned to Los Angeles that afternoon comforted by the knowledge that at least they now had a game plan. But Dick Zanuck knew it wouldn't make a bit of difference. "When a picture previews badly, there's very little you can do," he says. "You can make it a better picture by putting some things in or taking some things out, but you can't save it. The hand has been dealt, and there's no way of putting the cards back in the deck."[8]

"This is to reassure you that there is absolutely no cause for any concern whatsoever," Fleischer wrote to Harrison in a three-page single-spaced letter in which he cheerfully described the preview as "a very enlightening experience" and then told his star every detail of every change they would have to make, most of which involved the removal of footage in which Harrison appeared. "When you [preview] an original musical, it is really a New Haven opening. . . . After a great deal of analysis and agonizing reappraisal we came to the conclusion that the main offender was our lovely prologue. . . . What we have done is to remove approximately 7½ minutes of film that were really slowing us down terribly."[9] Zanuck, Jacobs, and Fleischer ended up cutting a good deal more than that, peeling off verses from several songs that threatened to slow the movie's already leisurely pace to a crawl.

Harrison, predictably, exploded—he was particularly bitter about the trimming of his final song, "Something in Your Smile." "Cannot have music department butchering any characterization of Dolittle by eliminating verse," he cabled Zanuck. "Surely you cannot be in such time trouble that you cannot allow the leading character to round himself off and complete his statement."[10] Zanuck cabled Harrison back immediately, telling him that he had "sensed a restlessness during the verse" among audience members and assuring him that "the ending of the picture and your characterization plays much better without it." Attempting to calm his star, he reminded him that "as you know, I have ruthlessly cut Newley."[11] A somewhat mollified Harrison wrote back, "I see your point," but grumbled, "For two years I was promised a tour de force number . . . comparable to 'I've Grown Accustomed to Her Face' "[12] and never got it.

In late October, Zanuck previewed a shorter version of *Doctor Dolittle* in San Francisco with results that, as he feared, showed no change in the audience's response: The film's "Excellent" rating, which had been 56 percent in Minneapolis, was now 57 percent. One night later, he showed a significantly shorter cut in San Jose, and the "Excellent" rating improved to 63 percent.[13] Zanuck decided that the San Jose version, which ran 151 minutes, would be the final cut of *Doctor Dolittle*. By then, the internal cheerleading was ramping up again: Harrison suddenly announced that he was "relieved to have lost that number"[14] from the end of the movie, and Darryl Zanuck, who had bluntly warned his son two years earlier about the risks involved in making the picture, offered warm words of reassurance, telling Dick that "it is my prediction that even though at the beginning adult audiences may not break down the doors to get in it will eventually end up by having every child in America insist that their parents take them at least three times."[15]

By then, Dick Zanuck knew that they were all whistling past a grave-yard. In October, Warner Brothers had opened Joshua Logan's $17 million, three-hour *Camelot*, the pride of Jack Warner's retirement and a picture that the studio had once hoped would play first-run engagements of a year or more in some theaters. Reviews were largely terrible, with *The New York Times* slamming its "dull and pretentious patches of realism and romantic cliché" and "grossly whimsy-whamsey Disneyland setting"[16] and *Time* writing that the movie, "which should have opened up the drama, shuts it down instead. . . . Even the makeup seems to have been applied by an amateur."[17] But far worse news was the fact that audiences had absolutely no interest in going to see it—the film made back barely a third of its budget in domestic rentals. The Broadway pedigree that had created such high awareness for *My Fair Lady* and *The Sound of Music* did nothing for *Camelot*, which turned out to be one of the biggest financial failures of the late 1960s. Its demise sent a shudder through the major studios, which were in production or deep into preproduction with more than a dozen large-scale musicals that were slated to open between 1968 and 1970.

"You look back now and ask, how could you have been so stupid?" says Zanuck. "*Doctor Dolittle* was conceived in a period of euphoria. We were all riding a musical wave that we didn't realize was going to come crashing down on the beach all at once. Sure, there were probably signs and warnings out there, but you're already so committed financially and emotionally that it's very hard to pull the plug on these big undertakings. Thinking of it now, we should have sent the songs out before we made the picture to see if any of them worked! I like Leslie very much, but outside of one or two songs, there wasn't anything really spectacular." For Zanuck, there was no turning back: He had already committed 20th Century-Fox to *Star!* (which, he consoled himself, at least had Julie Andrews as one of its assets) and *Hello, Dolly!* (which at least had a familiar score). "But none of that mattered," he said. "When the big musical ended, it ended with a thud. And we got hit hard."[18]

As *Dolittle*'s opening approached, 20th Century-Fox was hit with another unpleasant surprise—a $4.5 million lawsuit brought by Helen Winston, the would-be producer whom Arthur Jacobs had aced out of the rights to the Dolittle books four years earlier.[19] Winston had seen the movie and taken note of a scene in which the animals around the doctor threaten to go on strike, a plot element that her screenwriter, Larry Watkin, had included in the draft of the movie she had tried to sell to studios back in 1962.[20] When news of the suit broke, "Arthur Jacobs called," remembers Hugh Lofting's son, Christopher, "and said, 'Helen is threatening us over this scene. We know it's bullshit, but can you tell us what book it's from?' I said, 'Arthur, I have bad news for you. She's right! It was never in the books.' We were all surprised because it had seemed like such a natural idea—Leslie had seen the script [that Winston commissioned], assumed it had come from one of the books, and put it in."[21]

Fox eventually settled with Winston. There wasn't time for the distraction of a lawsuit. Whatever trepidation Zanuck and his colleagues were feeling, they had a gigantically expensive movie to open and promote, records to sell, and premieres to stage around the world in as many cities as possible. At one point, they even wondered if they could get Harrison to attend the movie's opening in Lima if the Peruvian government agreed to bestow some honor on him ("I think I can get him, I don't know, the Condor of the Andes or something like that," suggested Fox's head of Latin American publicity).[22] As for Jacobs, his aspirations for the film had no ceiling—among his publicity talking points were "Vatican screening" and "Local Boards of Education to declare Doctor Dolittle Day and release children from school."[23] The veteran publicist-turned-producer was back in his element and, blithely disregarding the ominous mood around him, started planning *Doctor Dolittle*'s Academy Awards campaign.

While Mike Nichols was filming *The Graduate*, staying in a rented house that had once belonged to Cole Porter, and cutting himself off from everything that didn't lie within the universe of Benjamin Braddock, he fell into a morning ritual: He would get up very early, listen to *Sounds of Silence* or *Parsley, Sage, Rosemary and Thyme*, the Simon and Garfunkel LPs that his brother had sent him—the music he had fallen in love with during rehearsals for the movie—and then go to the Paramount lot to shoot for the day. He'd come home late at night, go to bed, get up, and play the same music the next morning. Only a few weeks into the shoot, he decided to follow the instinct he had had during rehearsals and approach Simon and Garfunkel. "This is your score!" he thought. "Listen to it! How could it have taken so long to figure it out?" Nichols got in touch with them, showed them footage of a few scenes he had put together, and asked them if they'd be interested in writing a new set of songs for the movie.[24]

The two singer-songwriters, both twenty-five and already highly successful, didn't jump at the chance—with credibility to protect, they sniffed at anything that might smack of a Hollywood sellout. "Paul and Artie were, as they were about everything back then, unenthusiastic," says Nichols. "But they consented—Paul consented—to write a few songs."[25] Leonard Hirshan, the agent who represented Simon as well as Anne Bancroft, struck a deal in which Simon would be paid $25,000 to submit three new songs to Nichols and Larry Turman, any two of which they would have the right to use in the movie.[26]

Long before production was over, Nichols was cutting sequences in his head to "The Sound of Silence" and "Scarborough Fair." A few weeks later, Simon turned in two new pieces. One, "Punky's Dilemma," was a comically acid-trippy daydream of a song that contained a nod to the alienation of living in Southern California; the other, "Overs," was a melancholy tune about the disintegration of a romance, a ballad that was intended to be, says Nichols, "for, or about, Mrs. Robinson." Nichols didn't think either song worked. "Have you got anything else?" he said.

"Paul and Artie went off for a few minutes and muttered to each other," says Nichols, "and then came back and sang 'Mrs. Robinson.' And I said, 'Well, *that*'s great!' Paul had been working on a song called 'Mrs. Roosevelt.' That's why Joe DiMaggio was in there—it was about icons of a certain generation. But he just dumped that and made her Mrs. Robinson."[27] ("There was no name in it," insisted Garfunkel in 1968. "We'd just fill in with any three-syllable name . . . and then Mike froze it.")[28] Nichols wove it into the movie in three repetitive fragments, each about a minute long, one containing only the metronomic beat of the song and the others using "dee di-di-di dee dee dee" in place of actual verses, since Simon

hadn't written any yet and there wasn't time to do more.* Only two lines
of the song are actually heard in the movie, and only one—"And here's to
you, Mrs. Robinson, / Jesus loves you more than you will know"—made it
into the finished single a year later.

"Mrs. Robinson," even in piecemeal form, solved one problem, giving
Nichols the jaunty, accelerating sound track he needed to glue together
a seven-minute series of scenes near the end of the movie in which Benjamin finds out about Elaine's wedding and tries to stop it. After production was over, he worked and reworked the sequence with Sam O'Steen
in his editing room overlooking Times Square. "We had real trouble with
that montage. We had sweated over that scene for a week or ten days—in
the script it was just a page," says Buck Henry. "There was a part we
just couldn't get connected until that song. The fact that the song stops
and then starts again still really irritates me, but it's a great sequence
of filmmaking."[29] However, Nichols still had no music to pull together a
five-minute, wordless montage earlier in *The Graduate*, an impressionistic
sequence that suggests both Benjamin's moral drift and his liberation from
the constriction of being an A student and a good son. As we watch him,
he floats lazily through the summer, drifting from bedroom to backyard,
continuing his affair with Mrs. Robinson, and lolling on an inflatable raft
in his parents' swimming pool, letting time glide by. The montage ends
with a dazzling seamless cut that had been written and storyboarded early
on in which Benjamin appears to simultaneously lift himself onto the raft
and onto Mrs. Robinson. In the editing room, Nichols and Sam O'Steen
had cut it to "The Sound of Silence," playing the song until it ended and
then moving directly into "April Come She Will," another track from the
Sounds of Silence album. The deeper they got into the obsessive, sixteen-
hour-a-day rhythm of life in front of a Moviola, the less able they felt to
let go of the songs they had chosen. " 'Hello, darkness, my old friend . . .'
was what was happening in Benjamin's head," says Nichols. "O'Steen and
I were beside ourselves, because we knew nothing else would work. We
felt that the song expressed the deep depression he'd been in since he got

---

*"Punky's Dilemma," "Overs," and a completed version of "Mrs. Robinson" with revised lyrics all
appeared on the duo's 1968 album, *Bookends*.

home, an emotional suicide that he commits by starting to fuck Mrs. Robinson. At a certain point, movies just decide what they need. So I finally just said, 'Can I buy it?' "[30]

The decision didn't seem brilliant, just strange. Movies in the 1960s didn't recycle pop hits, and "The Sound of Silence" was, by the time Nichols got to it, used up; it had already reached number one on *Billboard*'s charts in January 1966, and Joe Levine thought it was perverse to play it twice in forty minutes—first over the opening credits as Benjamin and his luggage, parallel objects on parallel conveyer belts, move through the airport, and then in the montage. But Levine relented once Nichols showed him the footage. "I ran it, and he said, 'I smell money!'" says Nichols, "thereby endearing himself to Paul Simon for all time."[31]

When he saw the completed film, however, Levine lost the scent of profitability as quickly as he had found it. Nichols had trimmed *The Graduate* to a very lean 106 minutes, remaking several scenes in the editing room; he had dropped 6 minutes from Hoffman and Bancroft's long, problematic bedroom conversation by cutting large passages of dialogue every time one of them turned the lights on or off. But Levine didn't see the movie he expected to see: Where was all the sex? By late 1967, *The Graduate* could have gotten away with far more than it was showing. The new Production Code was already collapsing, along with the authority of the National Catholic Office for Motion Pictures, which had condemned five studio movies during the year, from *Hurry Sundown* to *Reflections in a Golden Eye*, without hurting their box office a bit.[32] Over the summer, *Variety* had reported that it could no longer find a single major theater chain in the country that refused to play condemned films. Joseph Strick's adaptation of James Joyce's *Ulysses* had become the first widely reviewed release to use the word *fuck*, and both *Ulysses* and Peter Brook's *Marat/Sade* had shown a man nude from behind, something the Code and the Catholics had let pass because, as *The New York Times'* Vincent Canby explained, the National Catholic Office "believes that females and 'normal' males are not sexually stimulated by rear-view male nudity."[33] The MPAA was no longer drawing any lines in the sand; Jack Valenti was just months away from scrapping the Code entirely and replacing it with a ratings system.

The Graduate did have a millisecond of skin: a blink-and-you-miss-it nipple that belonged to Anne Bancroft's body double, used by Nichols as a shock cut from Benjamin's terrified face in the scene in which Mrs. Robinson traps him in Elaine's bedroom. (Bancroft, Hirshan, and her lawyer, Norma Zarky, had contractual veto power over not only whose nipple would be used, but how long it would appear on screen. They watched the footage together in a Los Angeles screening room and were then given copies so that if anything changed, said Hirshan, "what Anne had in the vault would be the evidence required to take appropriate legal action.")[34] But aside from that moment, the movie didn't look much like either a sex film or a comedy to Levine. How was he supposed to sell something so uncategorizable?

"There was a brouhaha," says Dustin Hoffman. "He wanted me and Anne to be naked in the poster. She was supposed to be sitting on the bed, and I would have my back to the camera so you can see my ass, and she's looking up at me. And the reason he wanted that is that he was thinking, 'All this movie's ever going to be is an art-house release, and if people think there's nudity, maybe they'll come.' Anne wouldn't do it, but the one who *really* wouldn't do it was Nichols."[35]

Levine set an opening date of December 21 for *The Graduate*, but he seemed more interested in talking to the press about *The Tiger and the Pussycat*, an Italian sex comedy Embassy had imported that starred Ann-Margret and Vittorio Gassman.[36] Nichols spent the fall directing Bancroft on Broadway in a revival of *The Little Foxes* that also featured George C. Scott, E. G. Marshall, and Beah Richards. Out of the editing room at last, he felt calm about his final cut—"I knew what I was attacking," he says, "and I felt the movie was just the way I wanted it."[37]

But the mood of his colleagues in the months preceding the opening was tense. Buck Henry was angry that Calder Willingham, whose draft of the screenplay had been discarded years earlier, had reappeared out of nowhere and demanded a Writers Guild arbitration for co-credit on the movie. Once he heard that Willingham was arbitrating, Peter Nelson, who had done a draft for Larry Turman years earlier, lobbied for credit as well. (William Hanley, who had also written a version, opted not to ask for a credit.) Since all three arbitrating writers had drafted screenplays that relied heavily on Charles Webb's original novel, the Writers Guild decided to credit the script to Willingham and Henry, in that order, even though Henry had started from scratch and says he "didn't know Calder Willingham existed until I had finished my work. Nobody told me there had been three previous writers. There's nothing of Willingham's in the film. I thought, what is this!? I can't believe it! Was I pissed off? Yeah, I was pissed off that I wasn't warned, although I should have asked—I just hadn't had enough experience. Willingham was a really good writer, so I have to believe he thought he wrote it in some way. But he got a bad reputation for that." Turman, who felt that he had "inadvertently helped Calder Willingham get a credit by telling him to put more stuff in from the book," was upset as well. "But," he says, "everyone knew Buck wrote the script."[38]

Levine started to screen the movie for his friends and people in the industry. The first showings didn't go well. "I particularly remember a screening at the Directors Guild," says Nichols. "I was sitting behind Elia Kazan, who may have been with Budd Schulberg. Kazan was the reason I was in theater—I saw *Streetcar* when I was in high school, and I never got over it. And I sat behind them, and there was a lot of rolling of eyes. He was obviously not liking it. I was so sad." Even some cast members were indifferent. "I was very annoyed because they had cut some things that Elizabeth Wilson and I had done together that I liked, only small things, but I probably had a chip on my shoulder," says William Daniels. "I certainly didn't sense that it was going to become a classic—I don't think anyone did until it opened." Wilson was working with Nichols on *The Little Foxes* as a standby for Bancroft when he invited her to a small screening of the film. "I'll be honest—it just didn't hit me the way I thought it was going to," she says. "*Now*, of course, I love it, but that day . . . It was so stupid of me, but I went back to rehearsal and just couldn't cover my disappointment and said something to Mike. He got pretty angry."[39]

For the first time, Nichols's calmness and composure began to fail him a little, as the single biggest gamble he had taken in casting the movie seemed to have fallen flat. "The first of the people who saw the movie would go up to him," says Henry, "and say, 'Oh, it's wonderful, Mike, so, uh, beautiful to look at—it's just a shame about the boy.' They had only derogatory things to say about Hoffman."[40]

Hoffman hadn't been invited to any of the early private screenings of *The Graduate*. After the movie wrapped on August 25, he had returned to New York City and the cocoon of his former anonymous life. He survived for a few months on the $4,000 he had saved while working on the picture and then registered for unemployment, lining up on East 13th Street every week to pick up a $55 check while he looked for acting jobs.[41] When he ran into Sam O'Steen on the street and asked him how the movie was going, O'Steen said to him, "I hope it's not too fast! Mike cuts really fast!" and hurried on. Turman, Nichols, and Henry had shielded him from the early bad buzz about his performance, so Hoffman had little idea what to expect when he heard the movie had been booked into a theater on East 86th Street for its first sneak preview before a paying New York audience. He and his wife-to-be, Anne Byrne, went in just before the film started and sat in the back of the balcony: "I remember being in this excruciating, claustrophobic state, and the picture starts, and the first shot is a close-up of me. I literally shook through the entire movie."

The house wasn't sold out, but it was pretty full. "I had no sense of whether it was working or not," says Hoffman. "I think there are laughs, but mainly I'm looking at scenes and thinking, 'I should have done that better.' And then it gets to the church, and what got me out of my self-flagellation is that I looked down, over the edge of the balcony, and these kids were on their feet, cheering for me to get away. They had gone wild."

The movie ended. Hoffman and Byrne hung back until they were sure that everyone had left. Then they got up and pulled on their coats. Hoffman turned up his collar, and they started walking down the stairs. The only audience member left was a small woman in her mid-sixties, holding the railing and making her way toward the exit door with a cane. It was Radie Harris, who had written the "Broadway Ballyhoo" column for *The Hollywood Reporter* since the 1940s. She turned to Hoffman, peered at him, and pointed her cane at his chest. "You're the man who played that part," she said.

"Yeah." Hoffman nodded.

"Your life is never going to be the same," she said, and walked out of the theater.

"It was her way of complimenting me, but it felt like a death sentence," says Hoffman. "We go outside to get a cab, and it starts to snow. And I was in such denial about what life was doling out that I looked up at the snowflakes and said to Anne, 'See that? *That's* real. That's the only thing.' I just wanted to wipe it all away."[42]

But whatever confidence the reaction at the sneak preview might have instilled in Hoffman was erased by the movie's premiere, an invitation-only event that Levine staged on both coasts a few weeks before *The Graduate* opened. In Los Angeles, Gregory Peck, Julie Andrews, Norman Jewison, Natalie Wood, and Roman Polanski and Sharon Tate were among those who turned out;[43] the list of New York celebrities who attended the movie and dinner dance at the Hilton was a testament to the breadth of Nichols's universe and included Diane Arbus, Myrna Loy, Sidney Lumet, Saul Steinberg, Burt Bacharach, Irene Selznick, Bobby Darin, Neil Simon, Peter Shaffer, and George Plimpton. Nichols came with Penelope Gilliatt; Hoffman brought Byrne.[44] "That night, the suits, the tuxedos, I can't remember a single laugh," says Hoffman. "It was disastrous. I saw a lot of Levine's friends there, and they all looked like, what is he doing on the screen? It should be Redford!"[45]

TWENTY-EIGHT

W arren Beatty knew he was terrible at promotion but terrific at personal persuasion. In the early 1960s, when he made his first movies and was just entering the public eye, being a difficult interview subject still had a kind of cachet for a young movie star: Mumbling, murmuring, squirming, and answering questions with questions signified a reputation-enhancing unwillingness to play the publicity game, a Brandoesque attitude that implied one was up to something more substantial than behaving like the latest compliant product of the Hollywood studio machine. But slouching and surliness didn't come any more naturally to Beatty than opening up, so generally he wouldn't say very much at all. The interminable pause followed by the distracted nonanswer became his signatures, and he took them to maddening extremes: Just before going down to Texas to shoot *Bonnie and Clyde* in 1966, he reluctantly agreed to sit down with Barbara Walters for a *Today* show appearance promoting *Kaleidoscope*. Not only did Beatty neglect to mention the movie, he slid away from Walters's questioning with answers so devoid of content that she told him, on the air, that she had never had a worse interview.[1]

But by the time *Bonnie and Clyde* opened, evasion was becoming passé; these days, top-tier celebrities were proving their seriousness by submitting to long, confessional, let-it-all-hang-out Q&As in *Playboy*. They were expected to unload about sex, revolution, and politics, to free-associate and rant, to spin out anecdotes about losing their virginity or dropping acid. Beatty couldn't do that; although there was no mistaking his inter-est in sex and politics, talking about them was another matter. So when *Bonnie and Clyde* began to fail, he decided to try to save the movie not by embarking on a round of interviews, but by working the system from the inside, alternately deploying charm and a strong arm, using each tactic one-on-one wherever he saw a chance.

Beatty traveled from city to city and theater to theater, checking pro-jector bulbs to see how *Bonnie and Clyde* looked, making sure that, per his specifications, projectionists turned the volume two calibrations higher than the standard wherever the film played,[2] talking to exhibitors and telling them how well it was doing in New York, how young audiences were excited about the movie and urging their friends to go, how if movie houses just kept the picture booked for one or two more weeks, they'd see the needle start to move in the right direction and have a long-running hit on their hands. He would show theater owners week-by-week revenue charts from neighborhoods where the film's business had improved dur-ing the course of its run. Beatty found this door-to-door salesmanship "demeaning,"[3] but he didn't let up. Before the London opening, he went to England and hosted a week of private midnight screenings for the city's tastemakers, the people he had gotten to know when he was living there with Leslie Caron. He drafted Benton and Newman to work on the ad campaign with Dick Lederer, who had written the great slogan "They're Young. They're in Love. And They Kill People." Finally, he worked Warner Brothers' executive suites on both coasts, determined not to let a change in management sink his movie.[4]

In some ways, Seven Arts' takeover of the studio benefited Beatty. Jack Warner no longer had a say in *Bonnie and Clyde*'s future, and Ben Kal-menson, who had never had much faith in Beatty as a star, found himself in a drastically reduced role in the new company and was soon to be bought out.[5] Meanwhile, Lederer, a Beatty ally, was given more author-ity over advertising and publicity.[6] While those involved in the film have often said that it was washed up by the end of October, two and a half months into its run, the numbers suggest that the movie was still per-forming strongly. *Bonnie and Clyde* had been a hit in Manhattan from the beginning, and in mid-October, Warner Brothers expanded it onto dozens of screens in the New York area, where it drew impressive crowds. For the month of October, it was the number three film in the country, a remarkable performance given its limited release.[7] "The movie found, even at the very beginning, an audience of moviegoers, and word was getting out," says Penn. "Lines began to appear at the box office [in New York], all these wonderful-looking kids of what was beginning to be the 1960s, probably smoking dope while they were waiting to get in."[8]

In November, *Bonnie and Clyde* faltered, but not because its potential audience had been exhausted: Warner Brothers simply stopped booking the picture into theaters. Despite its high grosses in New York, the studio took the disappointing results of its Kansas City test run as justification for a decision not to give the movie a wide release anywhere outside of New York. Even though *Variety* reported *Bonnie and Clyde*'s weekly take as "big" in Washington, D.C., "boff" in Chicago, and "robust" in Los Angeles, the picture had only one print in each city; Warners was essentially treating it as an art-house release everywhere but New York. In Los Angeles, *Bonnie and Clyde* played to steady business at a single theater, the Vogue, for eighteen weeks without ever going wider.

Beatty was furious about the way the new Warner regime was handling the movie, particularly because he believed it was being shoved off screens in favor of *Reflections in a Golden Eye*, a movie Seven Arts had produced before it acquired Warner Brothers and which Beatty now believed that company chief Eliot Hyman was treating preferentially. In November, *Reflections* was on 250 screens, far more than *Bonnie and Clyde*, despite the fact that audiences had demonstrated little interest in seeing Marlon Brando play a half-mad repressed homosexual army colonel married to Elizabeth Taylor. Even the way *Reflections* looked was being widely rejected; moviegoers responded so poorly to director John Huston's decision to desaturate the color and tint the entire picture brownish gold that in many cities they complained to theater managers and demanded their money back. After *Reflections* opened outside of New York, Warner Brothers spent a considerable sum of money recalling every print and having the picture reprocessed in normal, untinted Technicolor.[9]

If that kind of expense was being lavished on a film that had virtually no critical backing or popular word of mouth, Beatty wanted to know why

Bonnie and Clyde wasn't getting more attention, especially since the press was now almost completely on the side of his movie. Faye Dunaway was appearing in *Harper's Bazaar, Town & Country, Life, Vogue, Cosmopolitan, Paris Match,* and *Esquire;*[10] in November, a *New York Times* Style section reporter followed her as she previewed the spring 1968 collections, which were full of berets and knit pullovers clearly inspired by Theadora Van Runkle's costumes; Dunaway's "portrayal of Bonnie," the reporter wrote, "is causing a resurgence of interest in nineteen-thirties fashions."[11] Arthur Penn found himself becoming a go-to talking head on the subject of violence in the movies throughout the fall, as critics found themselves weighing *Bonnie and Clyde* and *The Dirty Dozen* against John Boorman's brutal, nihilistic *Point Blank*, Stuart Rosenberg's *Cool Hand Luke*, and Richard Brooks's *In Cold Blood*. Even publications like the *National Catholic Reporter* were issuing strong defenses of Beatty's picture, writing, "There is a grim irony in hearing critics scream bloody murder when finally presented with an approximation of the genuine article (where were their outcries when a whole society was being marinated in violence?)."[12]

In early December, sixteen weeks after *Bonnie and Clyde* opened, the movie made the cover of *Time* magazine. Robert Rauschenberg created a collage of images of Beatty and Dunaway, adorned with the headline THE NEW CINEMA: VIOLENCE . . . SEX . . . ART . . . Inside was a five-thousand-word story in which the magazine admitted that its own original, dismissive review was a "mistake," then went on to call the film "not only the sleeper of the decade but also, to a growing consensus of audiences and critics, the best movie of the year . . . a watershed picture, the kind that signals a new style, a new trend. . . . In the wake of *Bonnie and Clyde*, there is an almost euphoric sense in Hollywood that more such movies can and will be made."

In a national media universe then dominated by three networks and three weekly newsmagazines (*Life* and *Newsweek* were the others), the impact of the *Time* cover can scarcely be overstated; it marked the public birth of the idea of a New Hollywood—and to believe in it was, by definition, to view the rest of the movie business as an archaic and doomed enterprise. Although the magazine cited films as disparate as *In the Heat of the Night, Two For The Road, Blow-Up,* and the still-to-open *The Gradu-*

ate as examples of fresh, forward-looking filmmaking, the piece left little doubt about what was igniting all the excitement. To understand *Bonnie and Clyde* as "a commentary on the mindless daily violence of the American '60s" (something that didn't exist when Benton and Newman started writing the film) and to realize that movies were now allowed to "[cast] a coolly neutral eye on life and death and on humanity's most perverse moods and modes" was to ally oneself with the future of film; to carp about realism, historical verisimilitude, or the moral effect on an audience "torn between horror and glee"[13] was to be consigned to the past. *Bonnie and Clyde* was now not just a movie, but a movement—and sides were being chosen.

That gave Beatty all the ammunition he needed. It was clear that Seven Arts' Eliot Hyman had little stake in promoting a movie he had inherited from the Jack Warner era, and he may have been uncommitted to *Bonnie and Clyde* in part because Beatty's production company, Tatira, had been promised such a big share of the movie's profits (should there be any) that the upside for the studio was limited. Whatever the reason, Beatty wasn't having it—he confronted Hyman behind closed doors in an angry conversation during which he says he threatened to sue the new studio head. "I got tougher than I had been before," he says. "I said, 'I want you to put this movie back in theaters,' but beyond that, I felt I had a hand to play with Hyman, and I played it well." The cards Beatty was holding were apparently less important than the cards Hyman feared he was holding; Beatty never made it clear exactly what he was going to sue him for—it's likely that it had something to do with a potential financial conflict of interest regarding *Reflections in a Golden Eye*—but the brinkmanship worked. Hyman dispatched his new second in command, Joseph Sugar, to New York to meet with Dick Lederer. "Is this movie as great as you say it is?" Sugar asked.

"Yes," said Lederer, "and we almost destroyed it." Together, they began mapping out plans for a rerelease.[14]

At *The New York Times*, Bosley Crowther was still throwing as many punches at the movie as he could: When *Cool Hand Luke* opened, he called it "much more effective, for my taste, than the glossy pseudo-realism of *Bonnie and Clyde*."[15] But his battle was lost. In November, the paper's executive editor Turner Catledge called him into his office and told him, as gently as possible, that it was time for a new assignment. Crowther would remain the chief movie critic of the *Times* through the end of December, in order to allow him to compile his final "ten best" list and, one last time, to preside over the New York Film Critics Circle awards. After that, he would be asked to serve as a roving reporter filing stories from film festivals around the world, but his days as a reviewer would be over. Renata Adler, who had never worked as a film critic, was to replace him. "I was very fond of Bosley Crowther, but it had to be done," says Arthur Gelb, then the paper's culture editor. "We had to have someone who could look at movies from a fresh perspective. At the *Times*, they never fire you—they feel too guilty. They just put you on a different path and give you more money to soothe their guilt. But I know he felt humiliated."[16] After thirty-nine years on the paper's culture desk, Crowther had no choice but to accept the reassignment. His farewell piece was to be a column on *The Graduate*.

As Columbia Pictures planned its publicity campaign for *Guess Who's Coming to Dinner*, Sidney Poitier was largely unavailable, immersed in the filming of *For Love of Ivy*. That was just as well for the cautious studio, which decided to capitalize on the sentiment surrounding Spencer Tracy's death by centering its promotional efforts on Katharine Hepburn, who agreed to "introduce" her niece to the press in a series of carefully managed interviews. Then the movie got an unexpected boost from some front-page news. In September 1967, eighteen-year-old Margaret Rusk married twenty-two-year-old Guy Smith at Stanford University. Rusk was white; Smith was black; and Rusk's father was the secretary of state. When Dean Rusk learned of his daughter's engagement, he went to President Johnson and offered to resign rather than embarrass the administration, but he also made it clear that he intended to walk her down the aisle either way. Johnson didn't let him go; his presidency was so intertwined with Rusk's policy making that *The New York Review of Books* ran a front-page David Levine caricature of Rusk and the president depicting them as, respectively, Bonnie and Clyde.[17] The Rusk-Smith wedding was covered extensively by most newspapers and made the cover of *Time*, which could have been reading outtakes from the final speech William Rose had given Spencer Tracy when it proclaimed, "In a year when blackwhite animosity has reached a violent crescendo in the land, two young people and their parents showed that separateness is far from the sum total of race relations in the U.S.—that to the marriage of two minds, color should be no impediment." But the article also noted that the State Department had received hundreds of angry calls and letters, that many members of Rusk's family did not attend the wedding, and that Democrats were worried about possible political fallout for Johnson in the 1968 presidential election. The magazine quoted one woman as saying of Rusk, "It will serve the old goat right to have nigger grandbabies,"[18] and followed up with a letter column in which two correspondents approved of the wedding and two did not—one of whom argued that "the mongrelizing of races . . . would be more properly ignored."[19]

The wedding, even more than the *Loving v. Virginia* decision, brought the subject of interracial marriage to the forefront of the national conversation about race, with articles and editorials that typically focused on such issues as where "mixed" couples could live and what biracial children would have to endure and offered vague and uneasy prognostications about what intermarriage would "lead to". As late as 1965, a Gallup poll revealed that 72 percent of southern whites and 42 percent of northern whites remained opposed to intermarriage.[20] And Columbia Pictures had little interest in stirring up controversy; the studio's New York publicity office kept out of the press all stills in which Poitier was seen kissing Houghton, marking them with red X's and the word *HOLD*.[21]

Whatever else he thought critics might throw at him, Stanley Kramer was now certain that he wouldn't be accused of irrelevance, since there was still nothing approaching a national consensus on the subject. He was wrong. *Life* magazine's Richard Schickel was the first major critic to review *Guess Who's Coming to Dinner*, which opened on December 11, and he tore it apart, insisting that "as usual, Kramer is earnestly preaching away on matters that have long ceased to be true issues. . . . Where to begin discussing the ineptitude with which the nightmare is realized on the screen?" Schickel directly attacked the very decisions on which Kramer had built the movie—especially the choice to make Poitier's character "not just an ordinarily decent chap, but . . . a regular Albert Schweitzer," the contradiction inherent in a man of Prentice's passion and independence submitting to the will of his fiancée's parents, and the creation of Houghton's character as an "imbecile" oblivious to the effect her engagement would have on her family. Schickel exempted only Hepburn and Tracy from his contempt, writing that "for me, at least, their performances in this movie are beyond the bounds of criticism."[22]

"*Life* magazine was the gospel back then," says Karen Kramer. "We thought that review was going to kill the picture." Schickel's turned out to be only the first of several terrible notices for the movie, but even critics who couldn't stand Kramer's direction or Rose's stacked-deck storytelling were stopped in their tracks by Hepburn and Tracy. "Kramer is simply not a very good director," wrote Andrew Sarris. "The lumbering machinery of his technique is always in full view." But he was as swept up as everyone else by the couple's final moments together on screen, especially by the shot in which the camera seemed to catch Hepburn's tears during Tracy's monologue, which he called "a moment of life and love passing into the darkness of death everlasting . . . anyone in the audience remaining dry-eyed through this evocation of gallantry and emotional loyalty has my deepest sympathy."[23] *The New Yorker*'s Brendan Gill wrote as if there were no distinction at all between the actors and their characters: "When he turns to her . . . it is, for us who are permitted to overhear him, an experience that transcends the theatrical."[24] *Newsweek*'s Joe Morgenstern complained that "the film might have been made a decade or two ago with its painted sunsets, sclerotic photography, glaucomic process shots and plastic flowers pummeled by floodlights" but called Tracy and Hepburn "glorious actors playing very good parts."[25]

Only the oldest and mildest critics on the beat thought Kramer was up to anything revolutionary or dangerous. *Variety* was relieved that it was "non-sensational," "balanced," and (remarkably) "free of preaching."[26] The *New York Post*'s Archer Winsten, who had been reviewing movies since the 1930s, called it a "trip into the realms of living, breathing, fiery contemporary controversy," noting that "you can't say it couldn't happen here. The Dean Rusk family appears to have fronted for this very film."[27] Even

Crowther, who endorsed the movie warmly, admitted that it "seems to be about something more serious and challenging than it actually is" and wondered what Poitier's character could possibly see in Houghton's.[28]

But liberal writers united in savaging the compromises and stereotypes inherent in what the *Los Angeles Times*' Charles Champlin called its "safety-first approach."[29] The reviewer for *The Nation* announced that he walked out after twenty minutes.[30] In the *National Catholic Reporter*, Father Andrew Greeley titled his piece "Black and White Minstrels" and, flinching at Tillie the housekeeper's embarrassing punch lines ("Civil rights is one thing, but this here's somethin' else!"), he wrote, "Laugh? I thought I'd die."[31] And in *Harper's*, Robert Kotlowitz predicted the movie would face resistance "in both the South and in the Northern ghettoes. In the South . . . it will surface those ancient sexual anxieties about mixing the races; in the ghettoes . . . it can only insult its audience. I would not want to watch *Guess Who's Coming to Dinner* in a Watts or Harlem movie house, where it may well be stoned by young Negroes."[32]

As it turned out, Kramer's movie didn't run into trouble in the North, the South, the ghettos, or anywhere else; it was an immediate blockbuster, the highest-grossing movie Kramer, Hepburn, Tracy, or Poitier had ever made, and the biggest success in the history of Columbia Pictures. Where its critics received the film as a timid and neutered issue picture, audiences saw it as a benign, often very funny, and finally touching portrait of discomposure, a glimpse at every strained smile, awkward pause, and gentle groping toward humanity that would unfold if Sidney Poitier walked unannounced into the home of Katharine Hepburn and Spencer Tracy. Watching two of the most self-assured stars in screen history not know how to behave in front of a black man—which was exactly how the two of them, particularly Hepburn, had chosen to play it—may not have ignited any revolutions, but it made for a genuinely crowd-pleasing comedy. As Arthur Knight predicted correctly in *Saturday Review*, "the very elements that prevent it from coming to grips with its potentially explosive material are probably also the ones that would commend it to a wide audience."[33]

Neither Columbia nor the critics anticipated the breadth of the film's demographic appeal. Older moviegoers turned out in force to watch Hepburn and Tracy together one last time; younger audiences, among whom

Poitier had built a big following with the release of *To Sir, with Love*, showed up to see him again; and for the first time, black moviegoers were recognized as a massive force at the box office. Two weeks before *Guess Who's Coming to Dinner* opened, *Variety* published the results of a survey that showed that African Americans were going to the movies in numbers far greater than the studios had realized; in first-run theaters in large cities, they represented 30 percent of the audience. The figure, said the trade paper, "will perhaps astonish many white showmen . . . [but] this must . . . buttress the case for a more open-minded use of Negro actors. . . . It has become much too ironic to [rewrite] the part for a white actor if Sidney Poitier is not available or not interested."[34]

In the South, Kramer's movie was not, initially, a sure thing. The worry expressed in *Variety*'s review that "certain Dixie areas may not dig the film, sight unseen"[35] was well-founded, at least until a crush of popular demand overcame the institutional resistance of theater chain owners. Beah Richards's family had to travel to Jackson, Mississippi, to see the picture, since no movie house in their hometown of Vicksburg would show it.[36] One New Orleans theater owner showed the film but snipped out the brief shot of Poitier and Houghton kissing, a moment shown only in a rearview mirror as a cabdriver looks at them, annoyed.[37] And in several cities, the Ku Klux Klan planned rallies, protests, and even attacks on theaters showing the movie; a scheme to throw tear-gas canisters into one theater was canceled at the last minute only when Klansmen discovered that the movie house was showing *To Sir, with Love*, a movie that local Klan leader Donald Heath apparently found less objectionable.[38] But eventually, *Guess Who's Coming to Dinner* played everywhere, the few lunatic-fringe protesters were swept aside, and in at least one regard, it did make history: Questions about the southern financial viability of a movie starring a black actor were never raised again.

As the movie took off, critics were still shaking their heads at its love-conquers-all message, complaining that Kramer and Rose had dodged every real problem intermarrying couples might face by virtually deracinating Poitier. Citing the moment when Prentice tells his father, "You think of yourself as a colored man, I think of myself as a man," *The New Republic*'s Stanley Kauffmann wrote, "Surely more and more Negroes today reject this washing-out of color and insist on thinking of themselves as Negroes."[39] But what *Esquire*'s Wilfrid Sheed had called "the *Gentleman's Agreement* ploy, or, whoever thought that nice young man was a Negro?"[40] had worked. Anyone, no matter how racist they might be, could enjoy the movie and congratulate themselves on finding Sidney Poitier an accept-able member of the family.* Within a few weeks, even the title was part of the cultural lexicon. "Guess who's coming to dinner with the Rex Har-risons on Christmas Day?" wrote Radie Harris in *The Hollywood Reporter*. "Their colored maid, Ruby, that's who."[41]

Harrison and Rachel Roberts had had a rocky summer after the comple-tion of *Doctor Dolittle*. They returned to Portofino, where they spent time with, and quickly exhausted the patience of, Elizabeth Taylor and Richard Burton. During one long evening at the Burtons', Roberts sent their guests Tennessee Williams and director Joseph Losey running for the door when, in Burton's words, "she insulted Rex sexually, morally, physically . . . lay on the floor in the bar and barked like a dog . . . started to masturbate her bas-set hound." Even Burton, no stranger to alcohol and excess, was shocked. "Rex is fantastically tolerant of her drunken idiocies," he wrote in his diary after another incident a few days later. "She wouldn't last 48 hours with me and he's had it for seven years."[42] Harrison and Roberts spent the next couple of months miserably unhappy, filming an ill-considered version of Feydeau's *A Flea in Her Ear* together. By the time Harrison was called back into service by 20th Century-Fox for his final round of duties on *Doctor Dolittle,* he and Roberts were on better behavior. He drew the line at going to Peru, but he showed up, smiling and waving, for premieres in Paris, Scandinavia, New York, and Los Angeles. The Bricusses and the Newleys made the rounds as well. The guest lists weren't exactly a roll call of the New Hollywood—the Los Angeles roster included the Reagans, the Samuel Goldwyns, and Dean Martin[43]—and nobody at the studio was har-

---

*A couple of years later, Hal Ashby stuck a joke about what an easy out the movie provided for its white audience into his Harlem comedy, *The Landlord,* when Lee Grant, playing an upper-middle-class suburbanite horrified that her son is engaged to a black woman, tries to prove to him that she's not a racist by saying, "Didn't we all go see *Guess Who's Coming to Dinner* together?"

boring any illusions about what kind of critical reception awaited the picture. But Dick Zanuck and his lieutenants told themselves that it wouldn't matter—that if they just announced loudly and frequently enough how wonderful their "Christmas gift to the world" was, nobody would look too closely once they unwrapped the box. Reviewers, after all, had referred to Fox's last big musical repeatedly as "The Sound of Mucus," and it was now the highest-grossing film in history. Maybe it wouldn't matter what they thought this time, either. "We've got $50 million tied up in . . . *Dolittle, Star!* and *Hello, Dolly!*," Darryl Zanuck told John Gregory Dunne just before leaving for the London premiere. "Quite frankly, if we hadn't made such an enormous success with *The Sound of Music*, I'd be petrified."[44]

With Academy Awards season approaching, the trade papers were, in those days, especially leery about stepping on the prospects of any expensive studio picture, and *Variety* ran a hilariously timid review that carefully noted that "the overall entertainment value of *Doctor Dolittle* is rather hard to pinpoint" and asked, "Is it a 'good' motion picture? The answer varies according to what the individual expects for his money." While murmuring a few words of complaint about "some slow periods and some insufficiently defined plot elements," the paper swept aside its own objections and noted that over $400,000 of advance tickets had been sold in New York City alone, so the actual quality of the film might not matter. This wasn't irrelevant; if Fox could make *Dolittle* look like a hit for just a couple of weeks, releasing photographs of long lines and sellout crowds, road-show houses outside of New York might book it before word started to spread. "After a couple of years" in theaters, *Variety* predicted, *Dolittle* could even earn back its money.[45]

Those were about the last kind words that Arthur Jacobs's film received in the press. The reviews weren't scathing, but their yawning tone and the impression they conveyed of dullness and overkill was almost worse. "Children, shmildren," snapped Archer Winsten in the *New York Post*. "Let them go by themselves if they like it so much. I'm not going to pretend I wasn't bored itchy."[46] Critics had few kind words for any element of the picture, even Harrison: Bosley Crowther predicted that audiences would be "considerably surprised and put off by [his] characterization. It has the inevitable casual air and tone of voice of Professor Higgins in *My Fair*

Lady."⁴⁷ Faulting the "flaccid pop songs" and "special-effects monstrosi-
ties" (especially the giant pink sea snail about which Jacobs had worried
so much), *Time*'s reviewer remarked, "Somehow—with the frequent . . .
exception of Walt Disney— Hollywood has never learned what so many
children's book writers have known all along: size and a big budget are no
substitutes for originality or charm."⁴⁸ The comparison was apt: The same
week *Doctor Dolittle* opened brought the release of Disney's *The Jungle
Book*, the last animated feature in which Walt Disney himself had had a
hand, and there was no doubt about which picture critics, or children,
preferred. *Dolittle* couldn't even skate past the Disney film on the issue of
stereotyping: While some commentators on the left attacked *The Jungle
Book* as an encoded story about the importance of keeping the races separated, with each in its own part of the "jungle," *Dolittle*'s episode involving
what *Newsweek* called "dopey African tribesmen"⁴⁹ was not greeted any
more warmly. By the time *Dolittle* opened, word was also out about the
long-forgotten racism in Hugh Lofting's then unrevised books: The chairman of the New York City Commission on Human Rights asked for them
to be removed from a Harlem school library, calling them "not truthful as
to race" and "disparaging about Negroes."⁵⁰

Faced with its worst nightmare, a movie that, in the words of one
reviewer, was "neither light enough nor fantastic enough for children,
and . . . neither sophisticated enough nor adult enough for their elders,"⁵¹
Fox did what it could, but to little effect. Studio publicists touted the
film's $91,000 first-week gross on a single screen in New York, although
it was already clear that advance ticket sales were responsible for most of
that and would dry up quickly. With no way to refute the U.S. reviews, the
studio got *Los Angeles Times* columnist Joyce Haber, a sort of friend of the
Hollywood court, to run an item saying that the notices in London had
been the best for any American movie in ten years except for *Bonnie and
Clyde*. (Haber must have missed Penelope Mortimer's *Dolittle* critique in
the *London Observer*, in which she reported, "What a wretched, discon-
solate Scrooge I must be . . . under different circumstances, I probably
would have crept away in the interval.") Even the $11 million invested in
Dolittle product tie-ins was a disaster: "Merchandising has always been a
problem for *Doctor Dolittle*," says Christopher Lofting, "because you're

trying to sell a stuffed animal that looks like a dog, not a character. Many of the manufacturers got seriously burned on that movie."

Fox's decision to press forward with an Oscar campaign for *Doctor Dolittle* came partly because it had nothing else to push; the studio's other year-end release, *Valley of the Dolls*, was doing sensational business but had gotten reviews so spectacularly scornful that they made *Dolittle*'s look kind, and the two most acclaimed performances in Fox's 1967 lineup, Paul Newman as a grim gunslinger in Martin Ritt's western *Hombre* and Audrey Hepburn as a disenchanted wife in Stanley Donen's romantic seriocomedy *Two for the Road*, had been overshadowed when Newman's *Cool Hand Luke* and Hepburn's *Wait Until Dark* (both from Warner Brothers) became bigger hits. In recent years, no studio had been shrewder than Fox at working the Academy; using the large portion of the voting membership that it employed, the studio had muscled its way to Best Picture nominations for one borderline-or-worse movie after another, from *The Longest Day* to *Cleopatra* to *The Sand Pebbles*. The studio had no choice but to try again. In January and February, Fox booked sixteen straight nights of free *Dolittle* screenings at its theater on the lot,[52] and promised dinner and champagne to any voter who showed up.

TWENTY-NINE

The opening of *The Graduate* on December 20, the day after *Doctor Dolittle*, was not a banner moment in American film criticism. Pauline Kael called Nichols's technique a "bad joke" and compared it to a "television commercial."[1] *Time* magazine dismissed the movie as "alarmingly derivative and . . . secondhand" and called its director "a victim of the sophomore jinx."[2] And John Simon seethed at its "oversimplification, overelaboration, inconsistency, eclecticism, obviousness, pretentiousness . . . and sketchiness" as well as its "rock bottom" music.[3] But the movie's opening did allow Bosley Crowther to finish his duties at *The New York Times* with genuine enthusiasm and open-mindedness. "Suddenly, when the . . . prospects of an Oscar-worthy long shot coming through get progressively more dim," he wrote in his farewell piece for the paper, "there sweeps ahead a film that is not only one of the best of the year, but also one of the best seriocomic social satires we've had from Hollywood since Preston Sturges was making them." Benjamin Braddock, he went on, "is developed so wistfully and winningly by Dustin Hoffman, an amazing new young star, that it makes you feel a little tearful and choked-up while it is making you laugh yourself raw. . . . The overall picture has the quality of a very extensive and revealing social scan."[4]

However, even critics who loved *The Graduate* couldn't agree on exactly what was being revealed. "This is no mean picture whether taken as entertainment or as a social statement," wrote Archer Winsten in the

New York Post. "It demonstrates a youth movement that can be cheered or jeered, enjoyed or criticized. The point is that Nichols has come through with something distinctly new under the movie sun."[5] But what? *Variety's* reviewer called the picture "excellent" but felt that "Hoffman's achievements in school are not credible in light of his basic shyness."[6] And the National Catholic Office for Motion Pictures came up with a pained endorsement of the movie by claiming that "the bedroom scene where Ben tries to talk with his mistress" is "perhaps the best statement on film about how joyless a thing an affair can be," adding, "There is no mistaking the point."[7]

Younger reviewers, unsurprisingly, didn't think that was the point at all and didn't have to twist themselves into knots to find redemption in the movie. Twenty-five-year-old Roger Ebert, who had just won the top reviewing job at the *Chicago Sun-Times*, saw Benjamin as a hapless hero lost in "a ferociously stupid upper-middle-class California suburb. He would like the chance to sit around and think about his future for several months. You know—think?" He called *The Graduate* "the funniest American comedy of the year . . . because it has a point of view. That is to say, it is against something."[8]

What many of *The Graduate's* naysayers felt the movie was against was *them*—their standards, their notion of what a well-made picture should be, their ability to control a cultural conversation that they suddenly felt was slipping out of their grasp. Hollis Alpert wrote in *Saturday Review* that when older audiences went to see *The Graduate*, "it was almost as though they felt themselves personally attacked."[9] In *Life* magazine, Richard Schickel, who was then all of thirty-three, fretted that the movie might be the latest symptom of the "battle cry, 'Never trust anyone over thirty,'" and wrote of his alarm at the "growing tendency among my fellow fuds to ingratiate themselves with their adolescent critics by agreeing with them."[10] A tone of contempt and anger united many of *The Graduate's* negative reviews, possibly because the film's release marked the first time in many years that so many American moviegoers had felt the direct sting of a generational insult. David Brinkley, writing in *Ladies' Home Journal*, called the movie "frantic nonsense" but admitted that he had had a "heated argument" with his college-age son and his friends, who "thought *The Gradu-*

ate was absolutely the best movie they ever saw . . . they liked it because it said about the parents and others what they would have said about us if they had made the movie—that we are self-centered and materialistic, that we are licentious and deeply hypocritical about it, that we try to make them into walking advertisements for our own affluence."[11]

Those college kids—the ones who filled the theater where Andrew Greeley watched the movie and who "had absolutely no trouble throwing themselves into the story and laughed loudly at lines their parents would not have caught"[12]—turned out to be a far more potent force than any friend or foe of *The Graduate* anticipated. *Variety*'s initial prediction of "hot b.o. in the young market"[13] proved true, but it was easy for the studios, all of which had rejected the script out of hand, to rationalize its success at first: Kids were home from their campuses for Christmas break and needed something to see. But in January, when they went back to school, *The Graduate* really took off. An industry report at the beginning of 1968 revealed that 48 percent of all movie tickets in America were now being sold to filmgoers under the age of twenty-four;[14] in other words, the first wave of the baby boom generation had grown up. In the late 1950s and early 1960s, they had been kids and teenagers, and their tastes had reshaped pop music. But when it came to movies, the industry's biggest hits—cheerful musicals and family-friendly epics—had been, by and large, the films their parents had chosen for them.

Movies from *A Hard Day's Night* to *The Wild Angels* to Francis Coppola's *You're a Big Boy Now* had played with the idea already, but *The Graduate* was the first true blockbuster of the sixties to exploit the fracture—the "generation gap," in the endlessly repeated term of the moment—between those kids and their parents. Its impact was felt even in the White House, where Lynda Bird Johnson, the president's twenty-three-year-old daughter, had a furious fight with her father after she learned that her husband, Charles Robb, was bound for Vietnam; she consoled herself, sobbing, through a screening of the film.[15] As *The Graduate* grew at the box office, first becoming the number two movie in the country and then number one, where it stayed for months, its success shattered a long-standing Hollywood studio business model. Warner Brothers and United Artists both announced that they were rethinking their entire development slates and marketing tactics with an eye toward courting younger audiences and hiring younger filmmakers;[16] other studios quickly followed their example. "We must hypothesize . . . that there are at least two huge American audiences," wrote Alpert about the movie. "One made up of the seventeens to the twenty-fives, the other over thirty-five . . . one wonders which is the more mature."[17]

On December 28, fifteen members of the New York Film Critics Circle gathered to vote on their thirty-third annual prizes, marking the unofficial start of the 1968 awards season. The best-foot-forward, values-driven taste of Crowther, its chairman, had dominated the group for decades, and its membership did not yet overlap with that of the newer National Society of Film Critics; although the two groups would have many members in common in later years, in 1967 only *Newsweek*'s Joseph Morgenstern belonged to both. At the meeting, Crowther argued passionately against awarding Best Picture to *Bonnie and Clyde* and prevailed, but only by a hair. Initially, *Bonnie and Clyde* led the voting but lacked the two-thirds majority then required for a first-round win; by the sixth ballot, the New York critics chose *In the Heat of the Night* for Best Picture.[18] The group voted to give a special prize to Crowther for his years of service to the *Times*, but it came with a bitter pill: He'd have to watch David Newman and Robert Benton collect the Best Screenplay prize. Nichols was named Best Director for *The Graduate*, and Rod Steiger won the Best Actor award for *In the Heat of the Night*. Best Actress went to seventy-nine-year-old Edith Evans for her delicate performance as a London pensioner barely scraping by and tormented by loneliness and senility in *The Whisperers*, a black-and-white character study that had come and gone quietly earlier in the year.

A few days later, the eleven members of the National Society of Film Critics—"the anti-Crowther gang," as Andrew Sarris called them—convened in New York, where most of them lived, to vote on their second annual awards. It was not a sweet-tempered meeting of colleagues, and the movie that most divided the room was, predictably, *Bonnie and Clyde*. Critics either loved it—Kael, Morgenstern, and *Esquire*'s Wilfrid Sheed all chose it as the year's best picture—or left it off their ballots altogether. Sarris was just about to publish his landmark auteurist guide to directors, *The American Cinema*, which would become a defining work for a generation of dedicated moviegoers (or, in a coinage the press had just started to use, "film buffs").[19] He filled out his ballot with works by two of the directors whom he was about to install as members of what he called "the Pantheon"—Jean Renoir (whose 1932 comedy, *Boudu Saved from Drowning,* he counted as a new movie, since it had gotten its first New York release in February) and Howard Hawks, whose *El Dorado* Kael had derided as "exhausted," "tired," and a "studio job."[20] Sarris's picks were, in part, a way of thumbing his nose at his rival, now starting her new life at *The New Yorker.* "It's strange that we should have been pitted against each other that way so often," he says, "but I really didn't like her."[21]

In the end, *Bonnie and Clyde* came in second: The winner of the group's Best Picture and Best Director awards was Ingmar Bergman's *Persona,*[22] which had opened early in the year and drawn virtually no audience, even by the standards of foreign-language films, but had excited tremendous admiration. The praise crested with a long and influential essay by Susan Sontag in *Sight and Sound* in which she declared the film Bergman's masterpiece, somewhat mysteriously attacked its treatment by American critics (which had been almost entirely positive) as "paltry," and explained that their attempts to explain the movie in narrative terms were futile since it existed in a realm "beyond psychology."[23] Much of the awe for Bergman's film was mixed with a degree of befuddlement—"After seeing *Persona* twice, I still cannot be sure that I understand it,"[24] wrote John Simon, who nonetheless gave it his Best Picture vote—but the support for *Persona* was also a way of reaffirming the primacy of Europe in world cinema from a group that wasn't quite ready to recognize the first stirrings of a new American aesthetic.*

The National Society's *Bonnie and Clyde* partisans got the movie prizes for Best Screenplay and for Gene Hackman's supporting performance, and the group gave *In the Heat of the Night* awards for Steiger and for Haskell Wexler's cinematography. Although they awarded nothing to *The Graduate,* the film was very much on their minds. The group met to conduct its

---

*The National Society was, for years, dominated by critics for whom Bergman could do no wrong; the group gave him its Best Director prize again the following year for *Shame* and *Hour of the Wolf,* and two years after that for *The Passion of Anna.*

voting in the East Side apartment of Hollis Alpert, an ardent supporter of *The Graduate* who gave it his votes for Best Picture, Director, Actor, and Actress. Alpert's living room overlooked "the Block"—the street that housed the four Third Avenue theaters that were then among the most desirable in Manhattan. Joe Levine had succeeded in booking *The Graduate* into one of them, the Coronet. At one point, the critics took a break from bickering and balloting and stared out the window at the street below. The line of young, shaggy moviegoers was endless, snaking around itself again and again. "It wasn't lost on us," said Sarris. "The line looked different from other lines. It felt quite symbolic."[25]

The Academy Awards race was hardly a gentleman's game in the 1960s. If campaigning was less costly and public than in more recent years, it wasn't due to a sense of decorum as much as to the fact that the Academy itself was half the size it is today, much more heavily populated with rank-and-file studio employees, and thus easier to manipulate and control. Oscar prognostication was not yet a blood sport; each year, the movies that would be the subject of campaigns were selected by their studios and then essentially dictated to selected gossip columnists and writers from *Variety*, *The Hollywood Reporter*, and the *Los Angeles Times*, the only major publications that then took much notice of the nominating process. In due course, the papers would print dutifully unsourced reports on what pictures "people" were citing as contenders. In the middle of January, *Variety* ran a piece breathlessly calling the 1968 Academy Awards contest "the closest in years," citing a dozen contenders for Best Picture nominations.[26] But in reality, the contest for nominations was hardly extraordinary: Critics' awards and "ten best" lists had already made it clear that *In the Heat of the Night*, *Bonnie and Clyde*, and *The Graduate* were all headed for Best Picture nominations, and given Stanley Kramer's Oscar pedigree and the big business the film was doing, *Guess Who's Coming to Dinner* was a likely nominee as well. "The Academy was conservative then, and demographically, it leaned on the upwards side even more then than it does now," says Dick Zanuck. "It was not what you would call youth-oriented."[27]

The fifth Best Picture slot was genuinely up for grabs. Some studios had just a single movie to promote—at Fox, Zanuck was putting everything behind *Doctor Dolittle*, MGM was campaigning aggressively for *The Dirty Dozen*, and Universal had no hopes for anything other than *Thoroughly Modern Millie*. Warner Brothers and Columbia each boasted a deeper roster of potential nominees, leading *Variety* to speculate that both companies "could be hurt by too much good product."[28] Besides *Bonnie and Clyde*, Warner was also getting behind *Cool Hand Luke*, the thriller *Wait Until Dark*, *Camelot*, and *Up the Down Staircase*, and Columbia was campaigning not just for Kramer's film, but for *To Sir, with Love*, *The Taming of the Shrew*, and the film that many in the business thought was most likely to be the fifth nominee, Richard Brooks's well-received adaptation of Truman Capote's *In Cold Blood*.

From the moment *In Cold Blood* was published in *The New Yorker* in four installments in the fall of 1965 until the day Brooks's movie premiered more than two years later, the project was scarcely out of the headlines. Brooks, who wrote, directed, produced, and controlled every aspect of the film himself, had insisted on casting virtual unknowns—Robert Blake and *In the Heat of the Night*'s Scott Wilson—as killers Perry Smith and Dick Hickock, and he resisted more than one plea from the studio to use color, instead hiring the great young cinematographer Conrad Hall to shoot the film in black and white, which Columbia warned him would impair a possible sale to television. *Life* and *Look* sent photographers to the Kansas town where the film was shooting, noting that the murder scene at the center of the picture would be filmed in the very farmhouse where the killings of the Clutter family took place. The movie met with Capote's approval, a relief, said Brooks, since "if he had disliked it, he could have murdered us. . . . He can really sting like a hornet."[29] Instead, Capote made a point of praising it and hosted a premiere for eighty-five of his friends, including Bill and Babe Paley, Lee Radziwill, Mike Nichols, Katharine Graham, Leonard Bernstein, Arthur Schlesinger, and Alan Jay Lerner, while announcing to the press, "I just want it to open in a quiet way."[30]

That proved all too easy to achieve. In the wake of *Bonnie and Clyde*, *The Dirty Dozen*, the Leone/Eastwood pictures, and *Point Blank*, Brooks's restraint and visual discretion—he presented the crime only in flashback and shot the murders indirectly, averting the eye of the camera at pivotal moments—worked against the film with audiences. The long-standing argument that serious movies should be shot in black and white because color was inherently festive and trivializing had become unsustainable in the face of the past year's subtle, thoughtful cinematography in *Bonnie and Clyde*, *The Graduate*, and *In the Heat of the Night*, and the very thing critics admired about Brooks—his "admirable skill and good taste . . . without once showing the raw performance and effects of violence," in Crowther's words[31]—apparently kept moviegoers away. *In Cold Blood*'s approach felt derived from a vanishing aesthetic, an Old Sentimentality, or, as Andrew Sarris put it, "the kind of facile Freudianism that is supposed to have gone out in the forties."[32] The movie, which was made for just $2 million, returned a solid profit, but its earnest, unself-conscious storytelling, which reached its end with a stern, Stanley Kramer–esque denunciation of capital punishment, was too much a product of the Hollywood establishment to have any impact with the young moviegoers who were now dominating the marketplace, and Columbia undersold it, making no real push for nominations for either of its two leading men, despite spectacular reviews for both of them.

Crowther said a final good-bye to his colleagues on January 31 at Sardi's, where the New York Film Critics Circle handed out the prizes they had voted on a month earlier. Robert Benton, David Newman, and their wives finally got to meet the man who had worked so hard to keep audiences away from their work and in the process argued himself out of his job. "We made small talk about the weather or the food or the room," said Newman. "His wife came over, a white-haired woman, and he said, 'Dear, these are the young men who wrote *Bonnie and Clyde*. You know something? They're not so terrible after all.' "[33] Crowther ended up introducing the two men to the assembled audience, getting a big laugh when he took one last shot at the movie's departure from factual accuracy by dryly praising their "highly *imaginative* and indisputably *original* script." Sidney Poitier showed up to hand Mike Nichols his Best Director prize; Nichols thanked Dick Sylbert, Sam O'Steen, and Robert Surtees.[34] *In the Heat of the Night*'s Best Picture award was presented by Bobby Kennedy, who had expressed enthusiasm about the project to Jewison more than a year earlier. "See?" said Kennedy. " I told you the timing was right."[35] The

senator, just weeks away from announcing his candidacy for the Democratic nomination for president, got the night's biggest laugh by referring
to a hit movie that had just opened a few days earlier, remarking that a
remake of *The Good, the Bad and the Ugly* was already being planned "with
President Johnson, Gene McCarthy and myself. We haven't quite figured
out the casting on this last one yet."[36]

On February 20, when the Oscar nominations were announced, *Bonnie and Clyde* and *Guess Who's Coming to Dinner* led the field with ten
apiece; *The Graduate* and *In the Heat of the Night* received seven. All
four movies received nominations for their directors and writers, and collectively, they dominated the acting categories, taking thirteen out of the
twenty available nominations. The news that *Doctor Dolittle* had won nine
nominations, including one for Best Picture, was greeted with shock and,
from several quarters, outright disgust. Arthur Jacobs's prime-rib-and-free-
booze campaign of dinner screenings had worked; though the picture received no nominations for directing, writing, or acting, it edged past *In
Cold Blood* in the category that counted most. Richard Brooks was recognized with nominations for directing and writing, but he admitted that
his wife, actress Jean Simmons, was in a "state of fury" when she heard of
In Cold Blood's omission from the Best Picture race, and Truman Capote
went public with his outrage. "Anything allowing a *Dolittle* to happen is so
rooked up it just doesn't mean *anything*," he fumed. "The only three good
American films last year were *Bonnie and Clyde, The Graduate* and *In
Cold Blood. In the Heat of the Night* was a good bad picture. *Guess Who's
Coming to Dinner* is a bad movie that got there for sentimental reasons
and all that political stuff. I think it's unbelievable."[37]

Capote may not have helped his own cause. By awards season, his taste
for social exclusivity, gossip, and New York high life was already beginning
to overshadow his reputation as a writer; even Robert Benton and David
Newman participated in a swipe at his famously lavish Black and White
Ball in the December 1967 issue of *Esquire*, which featured eight celebrities on a cover adorned with the headline "WE WOULDN'T HAVE COME EVEN
IF YOU HAD INVITED US, TRUMAN CAPOTE!"[38] But Capote's complaint, even if
it smacked of poor sportsmanship, accurately reflected an East Coast consensus: *The Graduate* and *Bonnie and Clyde*, movies made by New York

directors, were the year's standouts (a feeling shared by the creative teams of both movies, who were friendly with each other). To support one film was to support both. *In the Heat of the Night* fell somewhere in the middle of the pack; the new cultural gatekeepers knew it was more about content than style but felt it was intelligently made and well crafted; *Guess Who's Coming to Dinner* was brushed aside as self-important silliness—"that old Hollywood thing of, 'Love us because at least our hearts are in the right place,' " says Penn;[39] and *Dolittle* made them apoplectic. "Believe me, nobody was more surprised than I was when we got a nomination for Best Picture," says Dick Zanuck. "How we got in there is amazing to me. But these things happen. And you know, Arthur Jacobs . . . it was a bonus to have a guy who had done that for a living mastermind the whole thing."[40] Jacobs had worked the voters—including the publicists, who then made up nearly 10 percent of the Academy's membership—with consummate skill. He knew that the craft branches—sound, editing, art direction, costume design, cinematography, and music—were small, clubby, and among the most averse to change, and he used the old-fashioned familiarity of *Dolittle* to score nominations in every one of those categories.

"It was all so silly," said a disgusted Academy member a couple of years later about the *Dolittle* free-dinner campaign. "All the editors standing around, knowing they had been bought."[41] When the *Los Angeles Times'* Charles Champlin said as much in print, Richard Fleischer wrote him a furious letter. Champlin wouldn't back down: "A good many factors other than merit enter into the voting," he wrote back to Fleischer. "If this impugns the integrity of the voters, then that's what I've done. If I were a Fox employee and was aware that my studio had however many million it is—$18? $19?—riding on a picture which needs all the box office help it can get, I'd think twice about *not* voting for it."[42]

The nominations made manifest the rift between old and new, New York and Los Angeles, European-style cinema and studio establishment picture making, that had seized the industry, and in many cases, the old guard decided to make a defiant last stand. Haskell Wexler's universally praised cinematography for *In the Heat of the Night* went unnominated, while Robert Surtees's work on *Doctor Dolittle* was included, a choice that *Variety* reported was "astonishing to industryites."[43] Surtees's work on *The*

Graduate was also nominated, as was fellow veteran Burnett Guffey's cinematography for *Bonnie and Clyde*. But *Bonnie and Clyde*'s Dede Allen was not nominated for her groundbreaking editing, nor was *The Graduate*'s Sam O'Steen. The *Los Angeles Times* called the double omission "a spleen-busting travesty" and "a tribute to the tenacity with which Hollywood's gerontocracy still controls its guilds."[44] Somehow, an obscure and completely unexceptional war movie directed by Cornel Wilde called *Beach Red* did make the cut. Its editor, Frank Keller, was apparently in the habit of buying many of his colleagues a round of drinks during Oscar season; his nomination was one of several that represented the triumph of Tammany Hall–style Oscar politicking. ("Ever hear of *Beach Red*?" cracked O'Steen later. "You never will.")[45]

Bonnie and Clyde's five stars—Beatty, Dunaway, Gene Hackman, Michael J. Pollard, and Estelle Parsons—would all be attending the Oscars as first-time nominees, as would Dustin Hoffman and Katharine Ross, who were nominated for *The Graduate* along with Anne Bancroft. Rod Steiger was up for Best Actor for *In the Heat of the Night*, and Spencer Tracy, Katharine Hepburn, Cecil Kellaway, and Beah Richards had all been recognized for *Guess Who's Coming to Dinner*. Richards had received no major film offers since making the movie and had gone back to working in theater, hoping to find steadier employment. Stanley Kramer cabled her, telling her that he "could not be happier about any nomination."[46] Beatty, Hoffman, Steiger, and Spencer Tracy, whose posthumous nomination was unusual but not unprecedented, would be competing for Best Actor with Paul Newman, who had won his fourth nomination in the category for *Cool Hand Luke*. That meant that the odd man out was Sidney Poitier, who ended the year without a nomination for any of the three hit movies in which he had starred. The trade papers muttered a few words of disapproval and blamed split voting.

THIRTY

Twenty-seven weeks after it opened, *Bonnie and Clyde* had become a phenomenon without ever turning into an actual hit. Warren Beatty and Faye Dunaway were greeted with delirious enthusiasm when the movie had its Paris debut; they and the Bentons and Newmans were driven along the Champs-Élysées to the premiere in vintage 1930s automobiles; Dunaway made the cover of *Newsweek*; and a spate of European pop ballads inspired by the movie climbed the international charts. But by the end of 1967, *Bonnie and Clyde* had returned just $2.5 million in rentals to Warner Brothers, barely enough to cover its production and marketing costs. In January 1968, after Beatty's behind-closed-doors confrontation with Eliot Hyman, the studio had quietly put the film back into a handful of theaters around the country with mildly encouraging returns. But not until the day after its ten Oscar nominations were announced did Warner give *Bonnie and Clyde* its first wide release. This time, the public was ready. Many of the same theaters that had knocked the picture off their screens after a week or two in the fall of 1967 now reported grosses for the re-release that were five and six times what the film had taken in originally.[1]

Bonnie and Clyde's sudden and immense box office success flabbergasted Warner Brothers, made Warren Beatty wealthy beyond his wildest hopes, and turned the movie into the narrow front-runner for Best Picture. Suddenly, the 1968 Oscar race had become a referendum on something more than the quality of the five nominated movies. *Bonnie and Clyde* and *The Graduate* were now automatically paired by many commentators, greater than the sum of their parts whether you loved them or loathed them. To their detractors, both movies were morally contemptible, smirky, and ripe for dismissal in the same language that critics on the right used when they wanted to write off hippies, political militants, campus organizers, and war protesters as nothing more than exemplifications of youthful laxity and bad manners. In John Simon's harangue against *The Graduate*, he called Benjamin and Elaine "a younger Bonnie and Clyde, not forced into crime, but just as specious in their heroism, and pitted against just as simplistically villainous a society."*

But to their supporters, the two films added up to a kind of joint statement on what the future of American movies could and should be. In early 1968, as the studios were still racing to catch up with the headlines, *Bonnie and Clyde* and *The Graduate* were both instantly understood by younger moviegoers as mirrors on the counterculture, even if they weren't quite products of it. (The two films ran "neck-and-neck," Richard Corliss observed in *National Review*, "in the Most Analyzed U.S. Film of the Decade sweepstakes.")[2] The collective determination to find "relevance" in both movies was, at least in part, wishful. A large, youthful audience, desperately impatient for films that reflected social upheaval in the way that music was already doing, finally had some evidence that American movies could speak their language. When they became campus favorites in the wake of *Bonnie and Clyde*'s success, Robert Benton and David Newman faced questions from students who, wrote Newman, thought it "was 'really about' police brutality. . . . Then there were the 'really about Vietnam' theorists and 'really about the race riots' crowd."[3] Benton and Newman may have been bemused when moviegoers interpreted *Bonnie and Clyde* as an encoded representation of events that hadn't even occurred when they had written it, but those readings of the film were only fulfilling the mandate the two screenwriters themselves had issued five years earlier when they declared that the movie had to be about "what's going on now." When they wrote *Bonnie and Clyde*, that had meant creating unconven-

---

*Simon also accused Mike Nichols of filling the movie with "little New York Jewish touches," although the lines he flagged as sounding inappropriately "Jewish" came directly from Charles Webb's novel.

tional love triangles, treating outlaw style as an act of rebellion, and encouraging moviemaking with a European texture; by the time the movie opened, "what's going on now" also meant viewing crime as a political statement about social and economic injustice and a righteous response to the corruption of the Establishment.

The degree to which the movie was taken as a call to rebellion surprised some of the people who had made it. "It was such a turnoff for me at that moment," says Estelle Parsons. "I gave all these interviews in which I said, I believe in the rule of law and how terrible it is that this movie is going to say the law is bad! I was briefly horrified that I'd been a part of it."[4] But Arthur Penn was delighted with the way *Bonnie and Clyde* had been appropriated as an instrument of protest. "The social temperament of people in the Depression was what I think young people were experiencing at that point about the Vietnam War," Penn says. "Instead of economics, it was, 'This war's going on, and we're in the path of it, and we don't know whether it's going to roll over us.' I recognized that feeling of broad pessimism from my own childhood."[5] With the arrival of *The Graduate*, *Bonnie and Clyde* had a companion piece, and each movie's reputation was elevated by the other: The two movies were allied as indictments of the status quo, and *The Graduate*'s depiction of alienation and disaffection as a legitimate response to the false values of society was every bit as resonant for young audiences as *Bonnie and Clyde*'s prescription of insurrection. "Bonnie and Clyde have ironic companions—from across the railroad tracks—in Ben and Elaine," wrote Robert Coles in *Trans-Action*. "They go off together in a bus, stared at incredulously, she in her wedding dress, he ragged and unshaven. . . . For all the world the accompanying music could now be that same light-hearted, confident, jazzy, racy score that carries us along with Bonnie and Clyde. Ben and Elaine will never be hunted down by the police, but things may well get increasingly scary and desperate. Men will continue to die from hunger, and the 'restlessness'* that Lyndon B. Johnson mentioned but quickly dismissed could linger on and worsen."[6]

---

*Coles was referring to Johnson's January 17, 1968, State of the Union address, in which he said, "Our nation is accomplishing more for its people than has ever been accomplished before. . . . Yet there is in the land a certain restlessness—a questioning."

At thirty, Dustin Hoffman was suddenly famous. It was disorienting; he
wasn't even close to ready for it. His number was listed; his address was
right there in the New York City White Pages. He would come home at
night and find mason jars of matzoh ball soup that had been left for him
on his stoop. Sometimes the nice Jewish girls who made the matzoh ball
soup were waiting there, too. Sometimes they were neither Jewish nor
"nice girls." One day he was walking down Fifth Avenue with his fiancée,
Anne, and they passed a beautiful young woman. She recognized Hoffman, looked through Anne, smiled at him, and lifted up her shirt. She
wasn't wearing a bra. "Sign me," she said.[7]

At first, nobody could let go of the fact that he didn't fit the physical
description of a movie star. Who was this young actor who, wrote Kathleen
Carroll in the *Daily News,* "looks as if the worries of the world rested on
his sawed-off body"?[8] Newspaper and magazine profile writers referred
to him as "Mr. Acne" and "Peter Schlemiel."[9] They called his looks "so
extraordinarily ordinary it's peculiar."[10] They made fun of his height and
the size of his nose. Most of the pieces did not, of course, say much about
him being Jewish. "They wouldn't do that," he says. "However, Rex Reed
had read an interview with me where I said I wasn't sure I wanted the part,
and he called me a creep. They could call me a creep but not a Jew."[11]
Nevertheless, the stories made their point: People with faces like Dustin
Hoffman's didn't become the kind of star that Hoffman was becoming.
"The press couldn't believe that a movie actor could look like that," says
Buck Henry, "and soon, *every* movie actor looked like that. His success,
and the fact that he became a heartthrob, radically changed the percep-
tion of who a leading man is."[12]

For a while, Hoffman got a lot of fan mail from people who thought he
and Michael J. Pollard were the same person. Then *The Graduate* became
such a phenomenon that there was no mistaking Hoffman for anyone
else—except, of course, for the character he played. In the spring of 1968,
Hoffman found himself turning into Benjamin in the opening scene of
the movie—a young man being bombarded with insistent congratulations
for an achievement with which he himself wasn't even sure whether to be

impressed. "I was an object," he says. "No one knew my name. I wasn't a human being to them. I was the Graduate."[13]

"I would see him on television, on various immensely vulgar shows, having Israeli starlets flirt with him and having moronic interviewers ask him unanswerable questions," said Nichols that year, "and he seemed exactly like the boy in the picture."[14]

"It's Nichols' victory, not mine," Hoffman would tell people. "Nobody will ever take such care with lighting on me again, I'm sure, but I don't have much feeling of personal accomplishment about it."[15] Nobody really listened; they loved him, and if he didn't love himself, they wrote it off as part of his endearing-neurotic shtick. He was the hot kid of the moment; the fact that he wasn't a kid was as irrelevant as the fact that his moment had taken ten years to arrive. Old showbiz types wanted to meet him, *needed* to meet him, tried to *claim* him, had to introduce him to everybody else they knew. At a party, Otto Preminger—purple-faced, effusive, bellowing—literally grabbed Hoffman by the scruff of his neck and pulled him over to say hello to his friends. Embassy Pictures sent him off to Philadelphia to go make a guest appearance on *The Mike Douglas Show*. Hoffman walked into the green room and saw the other guest, sitting in a chair, looking at himself in a makeup mirror, catching Hoffman's reflection behind him, and deciding not to turn around. It was Milton Berle. A couple of years earlier, Hoffman had met Berle briefly at Broadway's Longacre Theatre; he had checked Berle's coat. Now they were both stars. "Sorry, kid, forgive me, I can't get up," Berle rapped out, looking for a common language. "I just went to the dentist and I've got an impacted *cunt*."

What was being a celebrity supposed to feel like? Hoffman wasn't sure. He had made $750 a week on *The Graduate*; now, Embassy was paying him $500 a week to go from one city to another and talk about it, and paying his hotel bills as well. It didn't have anything to do with acting, but it was undeniably a good deal, and he didn't have another job yet. Perhaps *The Graduate* would prove, in the long run, to be merely an exception, a brief interruption of his quiet life in the theater. Hoffman was socially committed, progressive, responsible; he hooked up with Eugene McCarthy's presidential campaign, flying to various campuses with McCarthy's daughter Ellen in a small plane, telling kids to "Get Clean for Gene." But students didn't want to talk about McCarthy; they wanted to talk to Benjamin Braddock, the young man they felt was their standard-bearer. "I'd say to these kids, I'm not that character," says Hoffman. "I'm not your generation. I'm thirty years old. I'd get this look. They felt betrayed."

Embassy packed Hoffman off to the Golden Globe Awards, which in 1968 were beginning a period of particular disreputability, having just been banished from NBC over accusations that they had leaked the winners in advance. "No one went," says Hoffman. "I mean, no one. But they told me to go, and I went." He sat in the audience and watched John Wayne serve as master of ceremonies. "There was a wire that went from him all the way to the front door. He announced at one point that someone was going to help him open the envelopes, and Sally Field came down the wire as the Flying Nun." The most humiliating moment in life, he thought. Almost none of the winners were present. Hoffman's category came up—he was named Most Promising Male Newcomer. He went up to the stage. "I'm sorry I couldn't be here tonight," he said.[16] Everyone laughed. Hoffman went home, back to New York. He tried to stay normal, to feel normal. He didn't move, but he changed his phone number at his agent's insistence. He answered his fan mail—every single letter, he says. He started to get offers. He tried to keep his head on straight.

Some members of the young left turned on *The Graduate*, complaining that it was insufficiently down with the revolution. They treated it as a failed newsreel, a dishonest portrait of their lives that reflected only passivity. Why hadn't the movie acknowledged Vietnam War protests? Why hadn't it covered student demonstrations at Berkeley? "Nichols doesn't risk showing young people who are doing truly daring, irreverent things . . . to seriously challenge the way old people live," wrote Stephen Farber and Estelle Changas in *Film Quarterly*.[17] (Perhaps they were angry at Nichols's response to the question he was asked over and over throughout 1968 about what eventually happens to Ben and Elaine: "They become their parents.") Jacob Brackman (later Carly Simon's lyricist) wrote a twenty-six-page takedown in *The New Yorker*, a stream-of-consciousness rant in which he faulted the movie for, among other things, not including any black characters and never allowing Benjamin to call Mrs. Robinson by her first name.[18] "He said he wrote it while extremely high," says Buck Henry. "It must have taken a *lot* of marijuana."[19]

Charles Webb, then trying to get his second novel published, chimed in with his own complaint: He was still unhappy about Nichols and Henry's decision to allow Benjamin to wreck Elaine's marriage after her vows had been spoken. "In the book the strength of the climax is that his moral attitudes make it necessary for him to reach the girl before she becomes the wife of someone else," he wrote to Stanley Kauffmann. "In the film version it makes little difference whether he gets there in time or not. As such, there is little difference between his relationship to Mrs. Robinson and his relationship to Elaine, both of them being essentially immoral."[20] Forty years later, Webb says, "I cringe at the quote. . . . Was I really that priggish? Yes, I suppose I was. But then again, if I hadn't been locked so tightly into that world at the time [that I was creating the character], I suppose it couldn't have been conveyed in all its nuances."[21]

But most of the criticisms about the movie were overshadowed by the magnitude of its popularity. Even Brackman admitted that it had become "a nearly mandatory movie experience . . . that [crosses] the boundaries of age and class. It also seems to be one of those propitious works of art which support the theory that we are no longer necessarily two publics—the undiscerning and the demanding—for whom separate kinds of entertainment must be provided."[22]

The centrality of film culture for young America was becoming impossible to miss. Everyone suddenly wanted to be a director. Andy Warhol had already made the jump from graphic artist to experimental auteur. Norman Mailer was directing his own movies and writing about his enthusiasm for the medium. *Hair* was about to take up residence on Broadway, and the lyric to its jaunty "Manchester, England"—in which the show's hero "finds that it's groovy to hide in a movie" and daydreams about becoming Fellini, Antonioni, or Polanski—perfectly captured the degree to which a European film sensibility had become a signifier of American cool. What could be groovier? Suddenly, being a director had become its own form of rock stardom. By the spring, *The New York Times* was reporting that sixty thousand students across the country were enrolled in film classes at 120 different schools, a total that had doubled in a year, largely because "Mike Nichols and Jean-Luc Godard have become the heroes of many college campuses." The piece went on to remark that Hollywood studios were more willing than ever to look to film school programs for the next generation of talent. It noted in particular the case of twenty-three-year-old George Lucas, who "won't collect his master's degree from the University of Southern California until the summer [and] has already gone to work full time . . . at Warner Bros. as an assistant director."[23]

Stanley Kramer thought college students were the key. That spring, as the popularity of *Guess Who's Coming to Dinner* continued to grow, what should have been a triumphant moment for Kramer was undone by his own dissatisfaction and his hunger for something more. The reception of the movie by the general public was all he could have asked, but the reviews stung, especially since the film was being scorned by the very people he thought he'd made it for. Kramer wanted a hit, but he also wanted the approval of what he imagined was his antiauthority, anti-Establishment constituency. He couldn't understand why nobody saw any element of subversion in his decision to back the white parents into a corner by making their prospective black son-in-law flawless, which he stubbornly insisted was what made the whole thing work; he didn't know why critics couldn't see that you had to make certain compromises in order to sell your message to a wide audience. If the people who were attacking his movie as old-fashioned and clichéd knew that he was getting anonymous phone calls from racists, even death threats, surely he would get credit for the bravery and moral courage he felt it had taken to make the movie. What was in play was, in part, the pride of a producer-director who wanted personal credit to accompany his popular success, but Kramer's self-definition was also at stake: To let the movie be written off as a middle-aged, middlebrow white man's take on racism would have meant accepting that he was now, and had long been, a Goliath, not a David—a fully functioning part of the system rather than a squeaky wheel within it. From the moment it opened, *Guess Who's Coming to Dinner* needed no promotional help from anybody, but Kramer decided to jump into the fray anyway. He would take the movie from one campus to another, screen it for undergraduates, and talk about the issue of integration.

Kramer visited nine different colleges that spring. The decision proved to be crushingly misguided. Students couldn't have been less interested in a movie that felt to them like the same hand-wringing, hypocritical take on race relations that they had been hearing from their own parents for years. The *Harvard Lampoon* named Kramer's film the worst movie of the year in its annual awards.[24] What most students really wanted to talk about was *Bonnie and Clyde*. "I enjoyed it," said Kramer, straining for politeness, "but I don't know what it means. I lived through that period myself, and the picture doesn't really represent it."[25] Kramer flew to Chicago with Jack Valenti to speak to an audience of six hundred students at Northwestern University. Roger Ebert, who covered the speech, wrote that the undergrads "heartily roasted" the movie, calling it "a copout."[26] Why couldn't Prentice have been a postman, like his father? Why was the only interracial kiss shown through a rearview mirror? Why weren't Poitier's and Houghton's characters already sleeping together?

Kramer returned home, bitter and hurt. He wrote a piece about the tour for the Directors Guild of America newsletter in which he complained that students didn't have respect for George Stevens or William Wyler or John Ford anymore—they all wanted to be Godard. Kids had told him, he wrote, "that I made a film about a problem which the university student maintains does not exist." He seethed over the emerging dominance of a filmmaking approach that valued "emotional essence" over "content and form." He complained that all students wanted to see on screen was a "put-on" and that they didn't understand why Poitier's character had to be so "pure and simple." After he had heard enough kids belittling *Guess Who's Coming to Dinner* as sentimental—"oh, sentiment, the whipping boy of the film buff, 1968 version," he sneered back at them—he tossed in the towel, insisting that he felt "no great defeat" and lambasting "bogus intellectual critics" who would rather praise work by "creative cowards" than his own. Kramer held his head high, but by the end of his tour, he was reduced to defending his own movie as "an adventure into the ludicrous."[27] He later admitted that after his cross-country journey, he was "in torment. I agreed with the college students in some of what they were demanding . . . but I didn't understand why some of them were attacking me. I had been assaulting the establishment for forty years and now was being smeared with the same brush."[28]

"It wasn't a movie for people my age," says Katharine Houghton. "I don't think he realized it on the set. The real event of the film was the relationship between Katharine Hepburn and Spencer Tracy—that was what was going on for audiences. The love affair between the white girl and the black man? That was never given any reality. It was a fable."[29]

"Everything was happening fast in the '60s," Kramer wrote later. "Too fast for me."[30]

THIRTY-ONE

I hope to God I don't win," said Dustin Hoffman. "It would depress me if
I did. Every actor thinks about winning an Oscar. But I don't honestly
believe I've earned it for *The Graduate*." Hoffman didn't have a vote—
he wasn't a member of the Academy—but if he had, it would have gone to
Rod Steiger. "Without any question," he said. "He gave a performance that
had many colors and facets to it. That's what acting is all about."

In 1968, Oscar campaigning was relatively subdued even for the old
guard, and newcomers found it downright unseemly. A young actor like
Hoffman felt free to say publicly that he expected *Bonnie and Clyde* to
win Best Picture but that he didn't feel Warren Beatty's role had "prize-
winning dimensions"[1] without sounding like a bad sport. Caring too much
was undignified, not to mention emblematic of shallowness and false values; in fact, Gregory Peck, the Academy's president, was working overtime
just to convince the acting nominees to show up for the ceremony after
years of fashionable and conspicuous absenteeism. Aside from the generational contest that seemed to define the Oscars that spring, it was also the
first time since 1962 that all five Best Picture nominees were homegrown
and marked the strongest showing for American actors in a decade. As a
member of the Hollywood establishment whose liberal political creden-
tials made him appealing to the new, engaged generation of stars as well,
Peck was in an ideal position to make sure that attendance was high at the
fortieth awards ceremony; his campaign of telephone calls and personal

appeals got eighteen of the nineteen living acting nominees to promise they would show up. The lone holdout was Katharine Hepburn, who had dived back into work following Tracy's death and was in Europe shooting *The Lion in Winter* and *The Madwoman of Chaillot*. Hepburn had won a Best Actress Academy Award back in March 1934 and had stayed away; she had received eight nominations since then and lost every time, and she had no intention of making what she believed would be a pointless trip back to Los Angeles, but she did agree to host a filmed segment celebrating the Academy's first decade. By this time, journalists were all but referring to her as Tracy's widow: She "doesn't want to return to Hollywood and memories so soon," wrote Sidney Skolsky. "She is working and living out her life until it becomes a life again."[2]

Columnist Sheilah Graham mulled over the chances of all five women in the Best Actress race and dismissed Hepburn's shot at the prize with the remark "If we are giving awards for Kate's devotion to Spencer Tracy, then she will have been the winner."[3] But that kind of guesswork about the awards was the exception, not the rule. Academy Awards handicapping was confined largely to the *Los Angeles Times* and the gossip magazines and trade papers, where a consensus seemed to be emerging, though with less conviction than usual. "It used to be very straightforward," says Mike Nichols, only half-jokingly. "If you had been sick, or you were a shiksa playing a whore, you won—everybody knew the rules. And then it started to change a little."[4]

Rod Steiger was considered a runaway favorite for Best Actor; Hoffman and Beatty were too young to take the prize; and there was considerable sentiment that giving Spencer Tracy an award would be touching but pointless. Although one Hollywood broadsheet argued that Steiger "is looked upon here as just a 'commuter,' whereas Tracy was always the hometown boy,"[5] Stanley Kramer himself said shortly after the awards that he was "opposed to a posthumous Oscar . . . it would not have been right."[6] Best Actress was seen as a contest between Edith Evans for *The Whisperers* and Dunaway, who had supplanted Julie Christie as the fashion and magazine icon of the moment and whom her pleased *Thomas Crown Affair* costar, Steve McQueen, was no longer calling "Done Fade-Away." The runaway success of *The Graduate* would probably be recognized with an award for Nichols, who had already taken top honors from the Directors Guild. And there was a growing sense that *Bonnie and Clyde* was going to complete one of the most stunning turnarounds in movie history by taking home the prize for Best Picture. In March, the National Catholic Office for Motion Pictures—which had rated the movie "morally unobjectionable for adults, with reservations"—presented Beatty, Penn, and Warner Brothers chief Eliot Hyman with a special award, Best Film for a Mature Audience. *Variety* speculated that such recognition from a religious body would go a long way toward soothing the anxieties of Academy voters who were "nervous about the violence . . . and are concerned about the 'image of Hollywood' which might be created by giving it the top award."[7]

Violence, and popular entertainment's role in either promoting or preventing it, was very much at the center of industry discussions in the weeks after the Oscar nominations. Memories of the previous summer's urban riots and images of armed National Guardsmen rolling into American cities were still fresh, and on February 29, the National Advisory Commission on Civil Disorders—better known as the Kerner Commission—that President Johnson had appointed to study the causes of the rioting issued its famous report, warning that "our nation is moving toward two societies, one black, one white—separate and unequal" and unambiguously implicating "white racism" as a primary cause of the riots.[8] The report's call for sweeping social and economic reforms extended to Hollywood. THINK BLACK, shouted a trade-paper headline, noting the commission's conclusion that network TV "must hire Negroes, it must show Negroes on the air, it must schedule programs relevant to the black ghetto."[9] The story noted that four of the seventeen new shows scheduled to air that fall would have black actors in key roles, including *Julia,* a gentle comedy in which Diahann Carroll would play a middle-class nurse whose husband had been killed in Vietnam; it would be the first TV series ever to star a black woman who wasn't playing a maid.

Hal Kanter, *Julia*'s creator, was also the head writer of that year's Academy Awards, and Carroll, though her experience in movies was limited, was drafted to be an Oscar presenter, ensuring a plug for her upcoming show and also helping Peck in his attempt to make the ceremony look even slightly racially diverse. Louis Armstrong signed on to perform one of the nominated songs, *The Jungle Book*'s "The Bare Necessities." Sammy Davis Jr. committed to singing his popular hepcat version of *Doctor Dolittle*'s "Talk to the Animals." And in a coup for Peck, Sidney Poitier agreed to present the Best Actress award: "I was delighted I was not nominated," he insisted. "To sit in that hall knowing full well that you'll be one of the four losers is not very pleasant."[10]

The Reverend Dr. Martin Luther King Jr. called the Kerner Commission Report, which became an instant best seller,[11] "a physician's warning of approaching death, with a prescription for life." It was also, for the industry's bottom-liners, a blueprint for sound economic health. Now that Hollywood had some hard numbers about how essential black urban moviegoers were to the continued success of their product, they were quick to advocate reform; violence that shut down cities was bad for business. When King flew to Memphis at the end of March and a protest rally erupted into shooting and bloodshed, a curfew was imposed and the night streets were empty; *Variety*'s spin was that "showbiz [was] hit hard" economically by the local racial strife.[12]

On the night of Thursday, April 4, just before 7:30 p.m. on the East Coast, Walter Cronkite interrupted his own *CBS Evening News* broadcast with the bulletin that King had been shot and wounded.[13] Later that evening, most Americans learned that King was dead when the networks broke into their prime-time entertainment shows to cover the story and await a statement from President Johnson.

In some quarters of Hollywood, the first instinct was to say nothing, do nothing, change nothing. The Academy Awards were scheduled for 7:00 p.m. on Monday, April 8, at the Santa Monica Civic Auditorium; the show was to be broadcast live by NBC one day before King's funeral in Atlanta. At first, nobody at the Academy saw any reason for a postponement. But by Friday night, it became clear that if the Oscars proceeded as planned, the awards would be handed out to a largely empty house. Carroll, Poitier, Armstrong, and Davis had all notified Gregory Peck that they would not even consider participating in the ceremony if it took place before King's burial. Rod Steiger dropped out as well, and Mike Nichols, Norman Jewison, and Arthur Penn all told the Academy they'd be staying home, too.[14] "I certainly think any black man should not appear," Davis told Johnny Carson that evening on NBC's *Tonight Show*. "I find it morally incongruous to sing 'Talk to the Animals' while the man who could make a better world for my children is lying in state."[15]

Peck denied that pressure from black entertainers had anything to do with his decision, but he got the message. On Saturday morning, he hastily convened a meeting of the Academy Board of Governors. That afternoon, he announced that for the first time in the history of the Oscars, the ceremony would be postponed and would now take place two nights later, on Wednesday, April 10. The delay, and the cancellation of the Governor's Ball, said Peck, "reflects the deep respect of all Americans for Dr. King and the Academy's sorrow over his tragic death."[16] Margaret Herrick, the Academy's executive director, immediately sent telegrams to all of the nominees and presenters asking them to confirm their availability for that evening.[17] All four black performers said they would gladly participate. "There was never a doubt, after they made this very fine gesture, that we would be on the program," said Davis, adding that everyone "from the most extreme militants to the most moderate were thrilled that the picture industry finally did something for the black man as a whole."[18]

"Two days?" says Nichols, shaking his head. "That was all? *That* was what we thought was taking a big stand? But until then they really were going to go right ahead with it as planned."[19]

Over the weekend, prominent Americans started to converge on Atlanta, where a service for King was to be held at the Ebenezer Baptist Church on Auburn Avenue, followed by a four-mile march to the campus of Morehouse College, where over one hundred thousand assembled mourners would hear a eulogy. At the beginning of the week, there was no longer much talk of "getting back to normal"; the Johnson administration struggled nervously with the question of how to treat the death of an unelected leader whose assassination seemed to have torn open a na-

tional wound. Johnson sent Vice President Hubert Humphrey to represent him. Jacqueline Kennedy was in attendance; so was Richard Nixon.
Television networks preempted their schedules of game shows and soap
operas to carry three hours of funeral coverage; Major League Baseball
canceled its opening day. Ossie Davis came to speak, as he had done at
the funeral of Malcolm X three years earlier; Mahalia Jackson sat in a
pew in the church and wept, listening to the singing; Wilt Chamberlain,
Jim Brown, Jackie Robinson, and Rafer Johnson could all be seen in the
march. Norman Jewison, Haskell Wexler, and Hal Ashby flew to Atlanta;
so did Marlon Brando, who had co-hosted SNCC fund-raisers with Arthur
Penn in Hollywood.[20]

When Sidney Poitier arrived in the city, Harry Belafonte was already
there; he had flown Coretta Scott King from Memphis to Atlanta on his
own chartered plane. Belafonte, more than any performer of the time,
was as much activist as entertainer; he and his wife, Julie, were close to
the Kings, and he was perhaps the critical liaison between the civil rights
movement and the Hollywood community. For years, he and Poitier, who
were just nine days apart in age, had been brothers and rivals, competitors who were bound together by the uniqueness of their status in the
entertainment industry but sometimes pulled apart by the same struggles
that divided so many black Americans at the time: accommodation versus
action, confrontation versus compromise, patience versus protest. There is
little doubt that Belafonte had made Poitier into more of an activist than
he otherwise would have been—and little doubt that Belafonte thought
his friend could have done still more.

Poitier walked into a planning meeting of King's inner circle at which
Belafonte was advocating strongly for an additional commemorative event
in Atlanta, possibly a rally in a stadium to be held the night before the
funeral. Poitier spoke up in opposition, feeling it would be impractical
to plan a huge event on such short notice and that another large-scale
gathering might draw attention away from King himself. It was the wrong
moment for a conflict. Poitier, by far the more formidable cultural presence, had challenged Belafonte in the one arena where he was used to
preeminence. Belafonte's wife tore into Poitier in a way that made it clear
that resentment had been simmering close to the surface for some time.

Poitier won the point, but, at least temporarily, he had lost a friendship. "I just knew I had hurt him awfully," he wrote later. "After that day in Atlanta, Harry didn't speak to me."[21]

The next day, Poitier flew to Los Angeles, where the Oscars were back on schedule and everybody was pressing ahead. Nobody canceled; nobody declined to appear. Hollywood had made its statement, and now it was going to have its celebration. "Oh, there were so many phone calls beforehand," says Penn. " 'Are you going?' 'I'm not going.' 'Well, *I'm* not going!' 'Well, I'm not going, either!' And in the end, everybody who called me and said 'I'm not going' went." He laughs. "But I didn't go. I went once, for *The Miracle Worker*. That was enough."[22]

The only other major nonparticipant was far more surprising: Arthur Jacobs. The man who had worked so hard to make *Doctor Dolittle*, and then to secure a Best Picture nomination for it, had decided to stay away. One week earlier, Jacobs's newest movie, *Planet of the Apes*, had opened; it was already shaping up to be a major success. But Jacobs, perhaps sensitive about the charges that *Dolittle*'s nominations were all but bought by 20th Century-Fox, chose to avoid the spotlight. "He never wanted to go," says Natalie Trundy. "That was the shy part of him. We went to a party at the home of Lew Wasserman's then son-in-law and watched it on TV. After all that! Can you imagine?"[23]

In the bleachers outside the Santa Monica Civic Auditorium that night, eight hundred movie fans gaped at the red carpet arrivals. Army Archerd asked them to vote for their choices in the top categories by cheering: They picked *Bonnie and Clyde* for Best Picture, *Cool Hand Luke*'s Paul Newman for Best Actor, and Anne Bancroft for Best Actress.[24]

When Faye Dunaway walked in on the arm of her boyfriend, the photographer and soon-to-be director Jerry Schatzberg, a teenager in a T-shirt yelled, "Hey, Bonnie, where's Clyde?" She smiled and waved.

Inside, the mood was more sober. "The world has always looked to Hollywood for escape," Hal Kanter told the audience in a warm-up speech before the telecast began. "In our ceremonies tonight, we hope to provide a measure of relief to a nation which today has again begun the normal routine."[25] The tone was to be tranquilizing; the theme of the show was the fortieth anniversary of the awards, and the evening was meant to reflect Hollywood's sense of its own history, elegance, and importance. Whether by design or chance, the seating arrangement reflected the year's thematic division: The nominees for *Bonnie and Clyde*, *The Graduate*, and *In the Heat of the Night* were seated along one aisle; on the other were Cecil Kellaway, Audrey Hepburn, Carol Channing, Edith Evans, and George Kennedy.[26] Other than the stars who lined the aisles, the audience in the auditorium appeared to be, literally, old Hollywood: Peering anxiously from their seats as the camera panned their faces very briefly, the vast majority of attendees looked elderly, weary, and sour—a group of unenthusiastic Rotarians and their wives stuffed into formal wear for an evening of forced jollity.

Eastman Kodak, the telecast's sole sponsor, had made sure to prepare an array of commercials showcasing America's racial harmony, so after a long advertisement for X-ray film that featured a black radiological technician, the curtain rose on an incongruously ornate set meant to replicate a Louis XIV drawing room. Gregory Peck walked to the microphone. "Good evening, ladies and gentlemen," he began. "This has been a fateful week in the history of our nation. We join with fellow members of our profession and men of goodwill everywhere in paying our profound respects to the memory of Dr. Martin Luther King Jr. Society has always been reflected in its art, and one measure of Dr. King's influence on the society we live in is that of the five films nominated for Best Picture of the Year, two dealt with the subject of understanding between the races."

It was a good start. The room was quiet and tense, but there was a sense that Peck had navigated a difficult path between the cheery artificiality of the evening and the bleakness of the day's headlines with modesty and taste. Those qualities vanished the moment he introduced the evening's master of ceremonies, Bob Hope, "that amiable national monument who pricks the balloons of pomposity." Hope ambled out and made it immediately clear that he thought the two-day delay was much ado about nothing. "It didn't affect me, but it's been tough on the nominees," he said. "How would you like to spend two days in a crouch?" As Hope went on, talking about how "any delay really snarls up programming" and joking that Eastman Kodak's image would be hurt by "a show that took three days to develop," there was some uneasy laughter. Mike Nichols squirmed in his seat. "What I remember is that it felt like he was saying something to the effect of, 'Well, here we are after an absolutely needless postponement,'" he says. "And in that moment, he sort of became the enemy."[27]

As Hope continued, trotting through jokes about Bing Crosby and Zsa Zsa Gabor, it became clear that beneath the surface of his comedy was barely concealed reactionary anger. "A year ago we introduced movies with dirty words," he said. "This year we brought you the pictures to go with it." The telecast's director avoided audience reaction shots for the most part but caught Hoffman barely smiling ("I can't imagine nominating a kid like Dustin Hoffman," Hope said of the thirty-year-old. "He starred in a picture he can't get in to see"). The camera also spotted Beatty and Dunaway looking awkwardly ahead when Hope started in on their movie ("I don't know what the writers have been smoking this year . . . *Bonnie and Clyde* is about happy killers . . .").

The first award of the night, for Best Sound, went to *In the Heat of the Night*. Norman Jewison, who had gone into the ceremony not daring to hope for much, began to sense the evening might go well for him. When Patty Duke came out to read the Best Supporting Actor nominees, the camera captured *Bonnie and Clyde*'s Michael J. Pollard in a ruffled collar and Gene Hackman looking apprehensive; the winner was *Cool Hand Luke*'s George Kennedy, who got up and made a brief, abashed speech in which he thanked the Academy for "the greatest moment of my life." "I was favored to win in Las Vegas," recalls Pollard. "George Kennedy wasn't even going to come because he thought I was going to win. . . . Warren said, as soon as [I] didn't win, he knew it was going to go downhill from there."[28]

"George Kennedy!" says Arthur Penn. "Jesus!"[29]

As the night went on and the leaden *Camelot* started to rack up victories, Buck Henry, who was nominated for *The Graduate* and remembers feeling "a boredom and irritation so deep that the next time I was nominated I went straight to New York and stayed there," kept exchanging glances with Robert Benton and David Newman across the aisle. "We were old friends," he says. "We had worked together, and as the awards were given out and some old-guard person won over infinitely better work, we gave each other a look that said, 'We've had it—we're out of this race.'"³⁰

The evening was dying on its feet. Hope's material alternated between the overfamiliar and the inadvertently tasteless (he remarked that an usher was on his way to check "the lump in Warren Beatty's pocket" and introduced presenter Natalie Wood as "the most talented beauty who ever came out of the Woods"). The winners seemed almost embarrassed, confining their speeches to a sentence or two. The Best Cinematography Award went to Burnett Guffey, who had shot, then quit, and then returned to *Bonnie and Clyde*. It was the movie's first award of the night. "Thanks, everyone who helped me do it," said Guffey. "That's really all I can say." He walked off. The speech by L. B. Abbott, who won the Visual Effects Oscar for *Doctor Dolittle*, was even shorter. When Alfred Hitchcock, who had never won an Oscar, was presented with the Irving Thalberg Award by Robert Wise, he trundled to the microphone, said, "Thank you," and began to walk away. The gesture was so perfectly in keeping with the perfunctory tone of the night that the audience could no longer contain its laughter. Hitchcock seemed startled; he walked back to the podium as if he had suddenly remembered something important and added, "Very much indeed." The two Hollywoods seemed to be fighting each other to a draw; when Dustin Hoffman and Katharine Ross were brought out to present an award with Bob Hope, they looked as if they were trapped at a family dinner with an uncle they didn't like. "Hi, kids," said Hope, barely bothering to conceal his lack of interest. At one point, Martha Raye came out to read a telegram from General William Westmoreland, thanking the entertainment community for its USO shows. There was a smattering of polite applause. A film clip of *Gone With the Wind* ended with the Confederate flag flapping in the breeze. The audience greeted it with silence.

Many of the evening's early winners were from England, Canada, and France; the Best Foreign Language Film winner was Czech director Jiri Menzel's *Closely Watched Trains*. Menzel, enjoying the brief freedom of the Prague Spring, was there to accept. "Anne Bancroft sat right in front of me," says Dustin Hoffman, "and Mel Brooks sat right next to her, and he was driving her crazy. Every time they would announce a foreign nominee or winner and he would come down the aisle, Mel would say out loud,

'*Wacko!* Another *wacko!*' Anne was literally sinking in her seat, saying, 'Mel, please, jeez, stop!' "[31]

With very few reaction shots, and with the audience observing what was then a long-standing tradition of withholding its applause during the reading of the nominees, it would have been hard for television viewers to gauge the mood of the room as the first hour of the show unfolded, but the level of energy and anticipation rose somewhat when Walter Matthau came out to present the award for Best Supporting Actress. The camera cut from *Thoroughly Modern Millie*'s Carol Channing to *Barefoot in the Park*'s Mildred Natwick, then to Estelle Parsons, who was starring on Broadway in a struggling Tennessee Williams play, *The Seven Descents of Myrtle*, and had had no intention of going to the Oscars until her producer, David Merrick ordered her to take the night off and Warren Beatty sent her a plane ticket; Warner executive and future Academy president Sid Ganis was her escort for the evening.[32] Viewers then saw Beah Richards, the lone black acting nominee, staring stoically ahead; she had been shaken to her soul by King's assassination. "It was a terrible time," Richards said later. "I was kind of unconscious during the whole thing. I wasn't even 'there,' do you know what I mean? . . . I didn't know what anything meant."[33] Matthau read the name of the last nominee, *The Graduate*'s Katharine Ross, and then announced that the winner was Parsons, news that was greeted with the first cheers of the evening. Parsons covered her face, giddy, and ran to the stage. "Boy, it's heavy!" she said before going on to thank Penn, whom she called "my own particular genius" and "of course, Warren Beatty," who beamed from the audience as his film took home its second Oscar of the night.

In the Heat of the Night won its second award when Hal Ashby took the prize for Best Film Editing. Ashby had trimmed his long hair and beard but had forgone the white-tie dress code in favor of an ivory turtleneck and love beads. ("Groovy. Really groovy," Steve McQueen cabled him the next day.)[34] Ashby's brief plea that the industry "use all of our talents and creativity toward peace and love" was the closest thing to a political moment on the telecast since Peck's opening remarks; in fact, no presenter or winner alluded to King again until Peck himself, who was brought out to receive the Jean Hersholt Humanitarian Award and remarked, "It's a humbling experience to hear oneself described as a humanitarian at any time, but especially this week." He went on to make a brief plea that viewers show their support for the Southern Christian Leadership Conference, "with its nonviolent approach to our most pressing problems," by sending contributions to the Martin Luther King Jr. Fund. Peck exited to warm applause, and as the show moved into its next segment—a film clip of Rod Steiger and Sidney Poitier facing off at the Sparta train station—a sense developed that the evening was beginning to take a particular direction.

Leslie Bricusse was in England working on the musical version of *Goodbye, Mr. Chips* for Arthur Jacobs, so he missed Sammy Davis Jr.'s finger-snapping, hip-shaking rendition of "Talk to the Animals," which ended with Davis, in a nod to the new series *Laugh-In,* saying, "Sock it to me, sock it to me, sock it to me, bay-bee! Here come de judge, here come de judge . . ." ("Here come de judge," replied a somewhat bewildered Hope, hoping to ride the laugh.) Bricusse didn't realize that he had won the Best Song Oscar for the song that Rex Harrison couldn't stand until weeks later, when Davis, who accepted for him, handed him the statuette. When the composer received all the congratulatory calls and telegrams, he assumed he must have won for Best Original Score—an award he lost to *Thoroughly Modern Millie*'s Elmer Bernstein.[35]

A tin-eared, all-brass version of "The Sound of Silence" played as Leslie Caron came out to present the Best Director Oscar, which went to Mike Nichols—the only award *The Graduate* was to win that night. Norman Jewison held his breath as the winner was announced, then slumped back in his seat, feeling "terrible disappointment"[36] as Nichols took the stage to sustained applause. In his genial and low-key speech, Nichols said he shared the award with the people who worked on the film, smiled, and wished his mother a happy birthday. Inside, he says, "I was completely blank. I stopped thinking, I stopped feeling. I was Mister Anhedonia— I just had no pleasure in it. Back then, I was a) very spoiled, b) very neurotic, and c) I had a very impaired sense of reality. To me, the Academy Award meant that you ended up at the Beverly Hills Hotel at midnight feeling empty. I don't know where I was, but that night, I just wasn't there."[37]

Rod Steiger was so visibly nervous when he and Claire Bloom took the stage to announce the nominees in the two screenplay categories that their somewhat flat scripted banter got big laughs. He mumbled something about the Maharishi Mahesh Yogi, who, thanks in part to the Beatles, had become an international cult figure in the last year and was something of an obsession for him. "Are you ready?" Bloom asked him. "Your mind seems to be on something else." "I can't imagine what that could be," Steiger replied. *In the Heat of the Night*'s screenwriter, Stirling Silliphant, had told his friends and family not to expect much; he'd encouraged them to watch the telecast, although he warned them, "I feel I will be defeated by either *The Graduate* or *In Cold Blood*."[38] He was shocked to win. "I really have no speech," he said. "The Writers Guild doesn't permit us to do any speculative writing. I'm deeply grateful and very touched. Thank you, Rod, Norman, Walter, Sidney, everybody."

As Steiger and Bloom read the nominees for Best Original Screenplay, Robert Benton prepared himself. "All of our friends kept saying, 'You're gonna win, you're gonna win.' And David and I were so naive, we thought, 'They must know something!' It never occurred to us that all of the nominees had friends who were saying to them that *they* were going to win. . . . I sat up, I buttoned my jacket, I fixed my cuffs. And then they said, 'And the winner is . . .' And I stood up. And they said, 'William Rose for *Guess Who's Coming to Dinner*!' And I sat down, *fast*!"[39] Rose, still almost phobic about Hollywood, had not come to the ceremony; Stanley Kramer made a brief acceptance speech in his place.

Steiger's category was next; nominee Audrey Hepburn was the presenter. Publicly, Steiger had said that he expected the Best Actor award to go to Spencer Tracy and joked that if he won, his acceptance speech would be, "Ladies and gentlemen, please make your checks payable in cash." But he also admitted, "I want to win it. It's important. It gives you greater latitude in the business and a chance to get bigger and better parts. I just don't think I'll get it."[40]

"I remember he was wearing cowboy boots," says Dustin Hoffman, who was sitting across the aisle from him. "And he was tapping his feet the whole night. I knew I wasn't going to win, so I was pretty comfortable, but he wasn't. And when she said his name, he came out of his seat about three feet."[41] For the first time that night, the whole room erupted in cheers. Claire Bloom, watching her husband take the stage, looked touched and oddly sad. Steiger praised the Maharishi again. "I find it unbelievable. I find it overwhelming," he said. He thanked the Academy, Norman Jewison, and the public, then took a deep breath. "Fourthly and most importantly," he said, "I would like to thank Mr. Sidney Poitier for the pleasure of his friendship, which gave me the knowledge and understanding of prejudice in order to enhance this performance. Thank you, and we *shall* overcome." As he left the stage, the room was electrified. Steiger had broken form—bringing any political reference into an awards acceptance speech was still exceedingly rare in 1968—and had chosen the perfect moment to do it. As Bob Hope came out, the applause for Steiger continued. "It's a little tense out there, isn't it?" he remarked, waiting. Hope then introduced the next presenter: Sidney Poitier.

Whatever the nature of the sentiment that had been building all evening in the Santa Monica Civic Auditorium, Poitier's appearance immediately after Steiger's victory gave the night its emotional climax. Waves of applause, whistles, cheers, and bravos greeted him as he walked to the center of the stage. A point was being made—although whether the point was that Poitier should have gotten an Oscar nomination, or that the white attendees found the characteristics they believed Poitier embodied to be exemplary, or simply that Steiger's words had given everybody license to use Poitier as a conduit through which they could pay tribute to Martin Luther King, was left to the imagination and understanding of each viewer.

Poitier, with a steady gaze and a gentle smile, waited for the applause to subside, engaged in some scripted back-and-forth with Hope, and then read the nominees for Best Actress, announcing with a surprised grin that the winner was Katharine Hepburn. Trade papers the next morning called Hepburn's win the biggest surprise of the evening, but it was in keeping with a kind of last-stand traditionalism that had emerged over the course of the broadcast. George Cukor accepted for Hepburn, who was privately furious that Tracy had lost; nonetheless, she quickly sent a telegram of thanks in which she said that she felt the award was "a great affectionate hug from my fellow workers" and fascinatingly chose to add that her character was "a good wife, our most unsung and important heroine. I'm glad she's coming back in style."[42]

In the Heat of the Night had seemed to be a long shot for the Best Picture Oscar when the evening began, but by the time the last envelope was opened, nobody was particularly surprised. Walter Mirisch made a brief acceptance speech, and Bob Hope reappeared to push his way through some dreadful scripted equivocations to the effect that Adolph Zukor and Samuel Goldwyn "had at least one thing in common with the man from Atlanta—they had a dream," followed by a series of pieties: "United we stand, divided we fall. Rioting and indifference are equal sins. Everyone must face up to their responsibilities." After cryptically reminding the home audience that conquering prejudice is something "each of us must face . . . through our own way of life and our own station," he sent the winners and losers on their way.

"I think it had a lot to do with timing," says Norman Jewison of *In the Heat of the Night*'s victory. "I really think that *The Graduate* is a brilliant film, and *Bonnie and Clyde* is a brilliant film. We happened to arrive at a moment when people felt strongly about race."[43]

Silliphant, who was never entirely comfortable with his own award for the movie, agreed. The script won, he said thirty years later, not "for its craftsmanship, or for its unique and polished style of holding back, holding back, but [for] its black-white content. . . . Getting plaudits for *In the Heat of the Night* was like waving the American flag or pushing Mom's apple pie. It was just too damn easy to manipulate people with issues which for the moment [had] flagged their attention."[44]

"It was a surprise," says Nichols, laughing. "I was living with Penelope Gilliatt, and we loved *Bonnie and Clyde*. Who wouldn't? It seemed perfectly clear to me that it should be one of us, but what did I know?"[45]

"Listen, *In the Heat of the Night* was a really good, rousing melodrama," says Buck Henry. "And a movie that has a lesson to teach about brotherhood will trump everything every single time. Brotherhood does pay."[46]

Some people took the movie's success as a triumph against the new, a defeat of what one congratulatory telegram called "those smug ones who thought they had it in the bag."[47] "So much for the *Bonnie & Clyde-Graduate* night predictions," Silliphant's son wrote to him. "The champagne went down oh-so-well."[48] If anything, *In the Heat of the Night*'s five Oscars represented a temporary compromise between the generationally divisive *Bonnie and Clyde* and *The Graduate* and the dug-in fustiness that young moviegoers were mocking in their response to *Guess Who's Coming to Dinner.* "It was clear that the Academy collectively retains an inherent conservativism," said the *Los Angeles Times,* "being less than eager to endorse the value-questioning of *Bonnie and Clyde* or the daring plot turns of *The Graduate.*"[49]

It had been five years since Robert Benton and David Newman had started talking about *Bonnie and Clyde.* They were no longer upstarts; they, along with Beatty and Towne and Dunaway and Nichols and Hoffman, were among the charter members of what would become a new Hollywood establishment, a group whose ranks would swell over the next decade as they redefined studio movies. But the day after the Oscars, Benton says, "I think I was a little disappointed. Miloš Forman said to me years later, 'You get all this attention, and it's wonderful, but it's like getting run over by a train.' And I knew enough, by then, to know that there was a good chance I might never do anything that would get recognized again."[50]

Benton and Newman and their wives went home to New York, feeling that they had had their adventure. "We was robbed," Beatty had said, smiling, as he was leaving the Oscars that night. His line was picked up by everyone—*Bonnie and Clyde*'s detractors took it as sour grapes, while the film's fans understood it as nothing weightier than a wink. "Oh, I wish I had a nickel for every telegram we got afterwards saying, 'You wuz robbed!'" says Leslie Newman. "But my favorite one came from Jean-Luc Godard." After the Academy Awards, the man who had come within one conversation of directing the movie dashed off a cheerful cable to Benton and Newman. "Now," he wrote, "let's make it all over again!"[51]

As is the case with most Academy Awards ceremonies, there was less symbolism to be extracted from the evening than morning-after analysts might have imagined, and even that applied only to the Academy's taste in movies, not to the country's. The weekend after the Oscars, *The Graduate* and *Bonnie and Clyde* continued to be two of the most popular films in the United States. And *2001: A Space Odyssey* was already drawing large and curious crowds transfixed by Stanley Kubrick's intergalactic light show with its mesmerizing final visual metaphor—an ancient traveler, racked by the decrepitude of extreme age, crawling to the finish line of his life so that a starchild could be born. *What did it all mean?* moviegoers asked as they emerged into the light. Even Benton and Newman weren't sure. "Plotless? Or beyond plotting? . . . It matters not," they postulated in *Esquire*. "The debate is: Does it have anything to do with movies?"[52]

It had, of course, everything to do with movies. Hollywood, which had held insistently to its own ways for so long, was suddenly moving forward, impelled by the demands of an audience that had, in 1967, made its wishes for a new world of American movies so clear that the studios had no choice but to submit to them. The outsiders were about to take flight and to discover that the motion picture universe was now theirs to re-create, to ruin, or to rule.

EPILOGUE

At the end of 1968, *Variety* printed its annual list of the highest-grossing movies of all time. One-third of the top twenty had opened in 1967. Highest of all was *The Graduate,* which eventually became the third-most successful movie in history, surpassed only by *The Sound of Music* and *Gone With the Wind*. The movie ran in theaters for almost two years. *Guess Who's Coming to Dinner* became the eleventh-highest-grossing movie ever. *Valley of the Dolls* and *The Dirty Dozen* finished sixteenth and seventeenth, and *To Sir, with Love* was in a nineteenth-place tie with *Bonnie and Clyde*, which grossed more than six times as much in 1968 as it had in 1967, even surpassing the James Bond film *You Only Live Twice*. *In the Heat of the Night* was rereleased after its Best Picture win and finished its initial run with a solid worldwide gross of about $16 million, five times its production and marketing budget.[1] *Doctor Dolittle* returned just $3.5 million in rentals to 20th Century-Fox, less than 15 percent of its production and marketing costs.[2]

The success of the pictures in the class of 1967 focused Hollywood's attention on a new generation of moviemakers and moviegoers and heralded what is now seen as a second golden age of studio moviemaking that lasted roughly until the late 1970s, when audience tastes and demographics changed once again and the dawn of the summer blockbuster era generated a durable new economic model for the movie business. But old Hollywood—the Hollywood of producer- and studio-driven product intended to reach the widest possible audience—didn't disappear; it simply reinvented itself. Even at the height of the new-Hollywood revolution, when Altman and Coppola and Mazursky and Scorsese and Friedkin and Schlesinger were dominating the conversation, the studios were beginning to find a way of creating and selling their product that didn't depend so much on directors. In 1970, Universal, the last-choice studio for much of the previous decade, released *Airport*, the first movie in what soon came to be known as the "disaster" genre. It quickly became the most popular movie since *The Graduate*. Many of the films that followed it—*The Poseidon Adventure, The Towering Inferno, The Swarm*—were written by **Stirling Silliphant**, who died in 1996 at age seventy-eight.

By the spring of 1968, **Warren Beatty** had begun to develop an interest in John Reed and the Russian revolution. After the Academy Awards, *Variety* columnist Army Archerd reported that Beatty was "off to Mexico—'to get away from the phones.' And then maybe to London before his big opus—a film in Russia." That plan changed when Beatty became actively involved in politics for the first time, working on Robert Kennedy's presidential campaign. When he returned to acting later in 1968, it was as a last-minute replacement for Frank Sinatra in George Stevens's little-seen drama *The Only Game in Town*. Beatty turned down *Butch Cassidy and the Sundance Kid* for the chance to work with Stevens, and never regretted his decision. Throughout the early 1970s, he continued to collaborate intermittently with **Robert Towne** on the screenplay for *Shampoo*; they finally made the film in 1975, after Towne's breakthrough success with the screenplay for *Chinatown*. Seven years after that, Beatty got around to *Reds*.

Robert Benton and David **Newman** teamed up as screenwriters on several more projects, from 1970's *There Was a Crooked Man . . .* to 1982's *Still of the Night*, while also pursuing separate careers, Newman as a screenwriter and Benton as a writer-director. Benton went on to win three Academy Awards, for writing and directing *Kramer vs. Kramer* and for writing *Places in the Heart*. Newman died in 2003 at age sixty-six.

In late 1968, Arthur Penn directed *Alice's Restaurant*, an adaptation of Arlo Guthrie's eighteen-minute comic talking-blues song that was one of the first studio movies to deal explicitly with the anti–Vietnam War movement. Penn won a Best Director Oscar nomination for the film and followed it with *Little Big Man*, a project on which he had been working since before signing on to *Bonnie and Clyde* and on which he worked, once again, with **Faye Dunaway**. The success of *The Thomas Crown Affair* in 1968 made Dunaway one of the most sought-after young actresses in Hollywood; she followed the film by returning to work for her theater mentor, Elia Kazan, playing a thinly disguised version of Kazan's wife, Barbara Loden, in the director's widely panned adaptation of his own novel *The Arrangement*. Dunaway then joined Dustin Hoffman in *Little Big Man*, which was a major popular success.

In 1969, just two years after it acquired the company, Seven Arts sold Warner Brothers to Kinney National Service, an owner of parking garages. Later that year, **Jack Warner** left the company he and his brothers had founded. He produced only two more movies, *1776* and the long-forgotten *Dirty Little Billy*, both of which were released by Columbia Pictures. One of his last unrealized ambitions was to make a gangster movie the way it "should be made."[3] He died in 1978, soon after his eighty-sixth birthday.

Shattered by the assassinations of Martin Luther King Jr. and Robert Kennedy, **Norman Jewison** left the United States, turned in his and his family's green cards,[4] and moved to Europe after completing the film *Gaily, Gaily*. In 1969, Jewison made good on his promise to help his longtime friend and colleague **Hal Ashby** break into directing, producing Ashby's debut, the comedy *The Landlord*. The seven films Ashby directed in the 1970s received twenty-four Academy Award nominations. Ashby died in 1988. He was fifty-nine.

Jewison's next several movies, including the musicals *Fiddler on the Roof* and *Jesus Christ Superstar*, were made abroad. *Fiddler on the Roof*, which opened in 1971, was one of the last successful reserved-seat road-show musicals, which, in the few years since *Doctor Dolittle* and *Camelot*, had become a virtually extinct genre, a victim of changing tastes and the failure of *Hello, Dolly!*, *Star!*, *Goodbye, Mr. Chips*, *Paint Your Wagon*, *On A Clear Day You Can See Forever*, *Song of Norway*, *Sweet Charity*, *Half a Sixpence*, and *The Happiest Millionaire*.

After winning his Academy Award, **Rod Steiger** received only one offer for a major role during the next year. He talked of playing Macbeth onstage and of his ambitions to portray Ernest Hemingway, Thomas Wolfe, and Edgar Allan Poe in movies, but nothing came of it. "There was absolutely no explanation," wrote Claire Bloom. "It is just the luck of the game. Rod lay on the sofa in the living room and watched sports programs on TV."[5] Steiger fell into a deep depression; in what he later called his "dumbest career move,"[6] he turned down the one offer he got, which was for the title role in *Patton*. Steiger felt that had he starred in the movie, he might have had a chance at Marlon Brando's role in *The Godfather*. Steiger went on to appear in nearly one hundred more movies before his death in 2002. In 1999, thirty-three years after they worked together on *In the Heat of the Night*, Jewison cast him in a small role in *The Hurricane*, the story of Rubin "Hurricane" Carter.

In the summer of 1968, **Jack Valenti** decided to abandon the Production Code once and for all. Later that year, the Motion Picture Association of America unveiled its first movie ratings system, designating all films with a rating of G, M (Suggested for Mature Audiences), R, or X. The week that the first set of movie ratings was announced, Production Code chief **Geoffrey Shurlock** retired at the age of seventy-four; he died in 1976. The ratings system was revised several times thereafter; Valenti defended it zealously even after his retirement in 2004, after thirty-eight years running the MPAA. He died in 2007.

Richard Zanuck was forced out of his job running 20th Century-Fox at the end of 1970, after three years during which the studio lost over $100 million, despite the release of *Planet of the Apes, Butch Cassidy and the Sundance Kid, Patton,* and *The French Connection.* "What did me in was the big musicals," he says. "*Doctor Dolittle, Star!* and *Hello, Dolly!*—three bombs in a row. Unfortunately, that more than counterbalanced the great success of all the other pictures that I did. What can you do? Nobody had crystal balls."[7] Zanuck partnered with **David Brown,** one of the few 20th Century-Fox executives who had sounded a note of caution about movie musicals in the late 1960s, to form Zanuck/Brown Productions. Two of their first movies were *The Sting* and *Jaws.*

Mike Nichols and **Lawrence Turman** each received 16 percent of the profits from *The Graduate.* After its success, Nichols and **Buck Henry** reteamed as the director and writer of *Catch-22,* an $18 million adaptation of Joseph Heller's novel that began production in early 1969. The film was Nichols's first financial failure. Two weeks after the 1968 Academy Awards, **Joseph E. Levine** sold his company, Embassy Pictures, to the Avco Corporation for $40 million in stock. In the fall of 1968, the new company, Avco Embassy, released its first reserved-seat road-show film, *The Lion in Winter.* The movie was **Katharine Hepburn's** first picture after the death of Spencer Tracy and won her a second consecutive Best Actress Academy Award in the spring of 1969.

Nichols still owed Levine one more movie and rebounded from *Catch-22* by directing *Carnal Knowledge* for him in 1970. Levine resigned from Avco Embassy in 1974 to become an independent producer. He died in 1987.

Dustin Hoffman came back to New York after the Academy Awards. In the summer, he began work on his next movie, John Schlesinger's *Midnight Cowboy*. His salary rose from the $20,000 he had been paid for *The Graduate* to $250,000. In September, Hoffman returned to working in the theater, starring in the Broadway play *Jimmy Shine*. Elizabeth Wilson came to see the performance and have dinner with her "son." When she got into Hoffman's limousine after the show, "these young girls surrounded the car," she says, "and they started pushing it back and forth and shouting, 'We want you! We want you! We want you!' My God, they practically tipped the car over. It was like he was one of the Beatles."[8]

"What I'm trying to do is keep my feet on the ground," said Hoffman in 1968. "This sudden stardom stuff completely knocks you out of perspective." Hoffman visited his psychoanalyst twice a week.[9] In 1969, he married his longtime girlfriend, Anne Byrne.

"It's nice, and slightly frightening, and it's not going to last," said **Katharine Ross** of the dozens of offers that came her way after the success of *The Graduate*. "I want to do something that is really good. . . . But how do you decide as an actress what's really going to be good? I can't tell. If I saw a part with a lot of horseback riding, I'd say 'Hey, that's good.'"[10] Soon after, Ross signed to costar in *Butch Cassidy and the Sundance Kid*.

After *Guess Who's Coming to Dinner,* **Stanley Kramer** made six more movies before retiring. None were financial or critical successes. (The first of them, 1969's *The Secret of Santa Vittoria*, was the last screenplay written by **William Rose**, who died in 1987.) "Stanley would get an idea for something contemporary," says his longtime associate Marshall Schlom, "but by the time it would get to the screen, it was old news."[11] But the immense financial success of *Dinner* allowed Kramer to weather his failures; his share of the film's profits, which he received incrementally through the 1970s, totaled more than $4 million.[12] Kramer died in 2001 at the age of eighty-seven. Since 2002, the Producers Guild of America has given an annual award in his name, administered by his widow, Karen, to a producer "whose work illuminates provocative social issues." Among the winners have been *Good Night, and Good Luck, Hotel Rwanda,* and *An Inconvenient Truth.*

Katharine Houghton made a handful of films after *Guess Who's Coming to Dinner,* but "the movie showed me," she says, "that Hollywood was just not my calling, that the movies were not where it was gonna be for me, and that I should go back into the theater."[13] She continues to work as an actress and playwright.

Leslie Bricusse tried his hand at a movie musical one last time with 1970's *Scrooge.* The film was to star **Rex Harrison,** but two weeks before production was to begin, Harrison dropped out, citing illness. He was replaced by Albert Finney.

Richard Fleischer directed twenty-two more movies after *Doctor Dolittle,* none of them family musicals. He died in 2006 at age eighty-nine.

Unhappy with his new assignment at *The New York Times,* **Bosley Crowther** officially retired from the paper in September 1968 to take a consulting job with Columbia Pictures, but he continued to write about movies, publishing several books of criticism in which he revisited old films. In 1977, he returned to *Bonnie and Clyde.* In his reconsideration of the movie, he called it "clever and effective," admitted that Beatty and Dunaway brought "interesting and affecting emotional range" to their roles, and wrote that he now appreciated Arthur Penn's calibration of lightheartedness and bloody violence, which made the movie's climax "shattering and sad." *Bonnie and Clyde,* he concluded, was "a landmark. . . . No film turned out in the 1960s was more clever in registering the amoral restlessness of youth in those years."[14] Crowther died in 1981.

After *Doctor Dolittle,* **Arthur Jacobs's** career as a producer was saved by the huge popularity of *Planet of the Apes.* The film spawned four sequels, all of which he produced. In May 1968, soon after the Academy Awards, Jacobs married his girlfriend, Natalie Trundy; he found small roles for her in all of the *Apes* sequels. Jacobs never lost his enthusiasm for movie musicals. Undeterred by the failure of *Doctor Dolittle* and *Goodbye, Mr. Chips,* he went on to produce popular children's musicals based on *Tom Sawyer* and *Huckleberry Finn* in the early 1970s. In 1973, while working on the latter film, he suffered a fatal heart attack. He was fifty-one.

Shortly after the 1968 Academy Awards, **Sidney Poitier** was named the biggest box office star in America in a national poll of theater owners, the first time a black actor had ever held the top spot. He was, he told an interviewer, "totally free—owned by no man or woman."[15] It didn't matter; as Poitier himself had predicted, his days as a movie star were over. In the face of increasingly brutal and public attacks—"Even George Wallace would like that nigger," said H. Rap Brown after seeing *Guess Who's Coming to Dinner*[16]—Poitier retreated, by degrees, from the very public life that he had led. He gave fewer interviews, he spent less time in the United States, and while he continued to make movies for several more years (including two in which he reprised his role as Virgil Tibbs) before a twelve-year retirement from screen acting that began in 1977, none of them had the cultural or popular impact of the three films he made in 1967.

Poitier rarely spoke in detail of the pain he felt at being jeered as a symbol of accommodation to white America. Stanley Kramer urged him to keep working, to try not to think about the insults, to stay focused.[17] As ever, Poitier kept his own counsel. A couple of years after their rift, he and Harry Belafonte repaired their friendship; in 1972, Poitier stepped behind the camera for the first time to direct Belafonte in *Buck and the Preacher.* He went on to direct eight more movies.

In 1967, shortly before the release of *In the Heat of the Night,* Poitier told a reporter that he had always tried to "make a positive contribution to the image of Negro people in America" with the roles he had chosen. "I guess I was born out of joint with the times," he said. "I have not made my peace with the times—they are still out of kilter. But I have made my peace with myself."[18]

APPENDIX

1967 ACADEMY AWARD NOMINEES AND WINNERS

BEST PICTURE

Bonnie and Clyde, produced by Warren Beatty

Doctor Dolittle, produced by Arthur P. Jacobs

The Graduate, produced by Lawrence Turman

Guess Who's Coming To Dinner, produced by Stanley Kramer

In the Heat of the Night, produced by Walter Mirisch

BEST DIRECTOR

Richard Brooks, *In Cold Blood*

Norman Jewison, *In the Heat of the Night*

Stanley Kramer, *Guess Who's Coming to Dinner*

Mike Nichols, *The Graduate*

Arthur Penn, *Bonnie and Clyde*

BEST ACTOR:

Warren Beatty, *Bonnie and Clyde*

Dustin Hoffman, *The Graduate*

Paul Newman, *Cool Hand Luke*

Rod Steiger, *In the Heat of the Night*

Spencer Tracy, *Guess Who's Coming to Dinner*

Best Actress

Anne Bancroft, *The Graduate*

Faye Dunaway, *Bonnie and Clyde*

Edith Evans, *The Whisperers*

Audrey Hepburn, *Wait Until Dark*

Katharine Hepburn, *Guess Who's Coming to Dinner*

Best Supporting Actor

John Cassavetes, *The Dirty Dozen*

Gene Hackman, *Bonnie and Clyde*

Cecil Kellaway, *Guess Who's Coming to Dinner*

George Kennedy, *Cool Hand Luke*

Michael J. Pollard, *Bonnie and Clyde*

Best Supporting Actress

Carol Channing, *Thoroughly Modern Millie*

Mildred Natwick, *Barefoot in the Park*

Estelle Parsons, *Bonnie and Clyde*

Beah Richards, *Guess Who's Coming to Dinner*

Katharine Ross, *The Graduate*

Best Screenplay Written Directly for the Screen

Bonnie and Clyde, by David Newman and Robert Benton

Divorce American Style, by Norman Lear, story by Robert Kaufman

Guess Who's Coming to Dinner, by William Rose

La Guerre Est Finie, by Jorge Semprún

Two for the Road, by Frederic Raphael

Best Screenplay Based on Material from Another Medium

Cool Hand Luke, by Donn Pearce and Frank R. Pierson

The Graduate, by Calder Willingham and Buck Henry

In Cold Blood, by Richard Brooks

In the Heat of the Night, by Stirling Silliphant

Ulysses, by Joseph Strick and Fred Haines

Best Cinematography

Burnett Guffey, *Bonnie and Clyde*

Conrad Hall, *In Cold Blood*

Richard H. Kline, *Camelot*

Robert Surtees, *Doctor Dolittle*

Robert Surtees, *The Graduate*

BEST ART DIRECTION/SET DECORATION

John Truscott and Edward Carrere (art direction); John W. Brown (set decoration), *Camelot*

Mario Chiari, Jack Martin Smith, and Ed Graves (art direction);
Walter M. Scott and Stuart A. Reiss (set decoration), *Doctor Dolittle*

Robert Clatworthy (art direction), Frank Tuttle (set decoration), *Guess Who's Coming to Dinner*

Renzo Mongiardino, John DeCuir, Elven Webb, and Giuseppe Mariani (art direction); Dario Simoni and Luigi Gervasi (set decoration), *The Taming of the Shrew*

Alexander Golitzen and George C. Webb (art direction); Howard Bristol (set decoration), *Thoroughly Modern Millie*

BEST COSTUME DESIGN

Theadora Van Runkle, *Bonnie and Clyde*

John Truscott, *Camelot*

Bill Thomas, *The Happiest Millionaire*

Irene Sharaff and Danilo Donati, *The Taming of the Shrew*

Jean Louis, *Thoroughly Modern Millie*

BEST FILM EDITING

Frank P. Keller, *Beach Red*

Michael Luciano, *The Dirty Dozen*

Samuel E. Beetley and Marjorie Fowler, *Doctor Dolittle*

Robert C. Jones, *Guess Who's Coming to Dinner*

Hal Ashby, *In the Heat of the Night*

BEST SOUND

Camelot

The Dirty Dozen

Doctor Dolittle

In the Heat of the Night

Thoroughly Modern Millie

Best Original Song

"The Eyes of Love," music by Quincy Jones, lyrics by Bob Russell, *Banning*

"The Look of Love", music by Burt Bacharach, lyrics by Hal David,
    Casino Royale

"Talk to the Animals," by Leslie Bricusse, *Doctor Dolittle*

"The Bare Necessities," by Terry Gilkyson, *The Jungle Book*

"Thoroughly Modern Millie," by James Van Heusen and Sammy Cahn,
    Thoroughly Modern Millie

Best Original Score

Lalo Schifrin, *Cool Hand Luke*

Leslie Bricusse, *Doctor Dolittle*

Richard Rodney Bennett, *Far from the Madding Crowd*

Quincy Jones, *In Cold Blood*

Elmer Bernstein, *Thoroughly Modern Millie*

Best Scoring—Adaptation or Treatment

Alfred Newman and Ken Darby, *Camelot*

Lionel Newman and Alexander Courage, *Doctor Dolittle*

DeVol, *Guess Who's Coming to Dinner*

André Previn and Joseph Gershenson, *Thoroughly Modern Millie*

John Williams, *Valley of the Dolls*

Best Special Visual Effects

L. B. Abbott, *Doctor Dolittle*

Howard A. Anderson Jr. and Albert Whitlock, *Tobruk*

Best Sound Effects

John Poyner, *The Dirty Dozen*

James A. Richard, *In the Heat of the Night*

Best Foreign Language Film

Closely Watched Trains

El Amor Brujo

I Even Met Happy Gypsies

Live for Life

Portrait of Chieko

Best Animated Short
The Box
Hypothese Beta
What on Earth!

Best Live-Action Short
Paddle to the Sea
A Place to Stand
Sky over Holland
Stop, Look and Listen

Best Documentary Feature
The Anderson Platoon
Festival
Harvest
A King's Story
A Time for Burning

Best Documentary Short
Monument to the Dream
A Place to Stand
The Redwoods
See You At The Pillar
While I Run This Race

Irving G. Thalberg Memorial Award
Alfred Hitchcock

Jean Hersholt Humanitarian Award
Gregory Peck

Honorary Award
Arthur Freed

BIBLIOGRAPHY

The magazine, newspaper, and trade journal articles used in research for this book are too numerous to list here and can be found in individual citations in the end notes.

BOOKS

Armes, Roy. *A Critical History of British Cinema*. New York: Oxford University Press, 1978.

Arnold, Edwin T., and Eugene L. Miller Jr. *The Films and Career of Robert Aldrich*. Knoxville: University of Tennessee Press, 1986.

Baker, Robert K., and Dr. Sandra J. Ball, *A Staff Report to the National Commission on the Causes and Prevention of Violence: Volume 9: Mass Media and Violence* and *Volume 9A: Violence and the Media*. Washington, DC: U.S. Government Printing Office, 1969.

Baldwin, James. "The Devil Finds Work," in *James Baldwin: Collected Essays*. New York: Library of America, 1998.

Balio, Tino. *United Artists: The Company That Changed the Film Industry*. Madison, University of Wisconsin Press, 1987.

Ball, John. *In the Heat of the Night*. Originally published 1965. Reissue: New York: Carroll & Graf, 2001.

Bardsley, Garth. *Stop the World: The Biography of Anthony Newley*. London: Oberon Books, 2003.

Baxter, John. *Woody Allen: A Biography*. New York: Carroll & Graf, 1998.

Benedictus, David. *You're a Big Boy Now*. New York: Dutton, 1964.

Berg, A. Scott. *Kate Remembered*. New York: G. P. Putnam's Sons, 2003.

Bergman, Carol. *Sidney Poitier: Actor*. Los Angeles: Melrose Square Publishing Co., 1990.

Biskind, Peter. *Easy Riders, Raging Bulls: How the Sex-Drugs-and-Rock 'n' Roll Generation Saved Hollywood*. New York: Touchstone/Simon & Schuster, 1999.

Bjorkman, Stig, Torsten Manns, and Jonas Sima, trans. by Paul Britten Austin. *Bergman on Bergman: Interviews with Ingmar Bergman*. New York: Touchstone/Simon & Schuster, 1973.

Bloom, Claire. *Leaving a Doll's House*. New York: Little, Brown & Co., 1996.

———. *Limelight and After: The Education of an Actress*. New York: Harper & Row, 1982.

Bogle, Donald. *Toms, Coons, Mulattoes, Mammies & Bucks: An Interpretive History of Blacks in American Films*, 4th ed. New York: Continuum, 2002.

Bordwell, David. *The Way Hollywood Tells It: Story and Style in Modern Movies*. Berkeley and Los Angeles: University of California Press, 2006.

Bragg, Melvyn. *Rich: The Life of Richard Burton*. London: Hodder & Stoughton, 1988.

Branch, Taylor. *At Canaan's Edge: America in the King Years 1965–68*. New York: Simon & Schuster, 2006.

Brando, Marlon, with Robert Lindsey. *Brando: Songs My Mother Taught Me*. New York: Random House, 1994.

Brantley, Will, ed. *Conversations with Pauline Kael*. Jackson: University Press of Mississippi, 1995.

Bricusse, Leslie. *The Music Man: The Key Changes in My Life*. London: Metro Publishing, 2006.

Brooks, Tim, and Earl Marsh. *The Complete Directory to Prime Time Network TV Shows 1946–Present*, 3rd ed. New York: Ballantine, 1985.

Bruck, Connie. *When Hollywood Had a King: The Reign of Lew Wasserman, Who Leveraged Talent into Power and Influence*. New York: Random House, 2003.

Burrough, Bryan. *Public Enemies: America's Greatest Crime Wave and the Birth of the FBI, 1933–34*. New York: Penguin Press, 2004.

Capote, Truman. *In Cold Blood*. New York: Random House, 1965.

Carroll, Diahann, with Ross Firestone. *Diahann!* New York: Little, Brown, 1986.

Castle, Alison, ed. *The Stanley Kubrick Archives*. Germany: Taschen, 2005.

Cawelti, John G., ed. *Focus on Bonnie and Clyde*. Englewood Cliffs, NJ: Prentice-Hall, Inc., 1973.

Clarke, Gerald. *Capote: A Biography*. New York: Carroll & Graf, 1988.

Conrad, Peter. *Orson Welles: The Stories of His Life*. London: Faber & Faber Ltd., 2003.

Corman, Roger, with Jim Jerome. *How I Made a Hundred Movies in Hollywood & Never Lost a Dime*. New York: Random House, 1990.

Cowie, Peter. *Revolution!: The Explosion of World Cinema in the Sixties*. New York: Faber & Faber, Inc., 2004.

Crowther, Bosley. *Reruns: Fifty Memorable Films*. New York: G. P. Putnam's Sons, 1978.

Davidson, Bill. *Spencer Tracy: Tragic Idol*. New York: E. P. Dutton, 1987.

Davis, Deborah. *Party of the Century: The Fabulous Story of Truman Capote and His Black and White Ball*. Hoboken, NJ: John Wiley & Sons, 2006.

Davis, Francis. *Afterglow: A Last Conversation with Pauline Kael*. Cambridge, MA: Da Capo Press, 2002.

De Baecque, Antoine, and Serge Toubiana. *Truffaut*. Trans. by Catherine Temerson. New York: Alfred A. Knopf, 1999.

Dick, Bernard F. *Hal Wallis: Producer to the Stars*. Lexington University Press of Kentucky, 2004.

Dunaway, Faye, with Betsy Sharkey. *Looking for Gatsby: My Life*. New York: Simon & Schuster, 1995.

Dunne, John Gregory. *The Studio*. New York: Farrar, Straus & Giroux, 1969.

Eames, John Douglas. *The MGM Story*, 2nd rev. ed. New York: Crown, 1982.

———, with additional text by Robert Abele. *The Paramount Story: The Complete History of the Studio and Its Films*, rev. ed. New York: Simon & Schuster, 2002.

Edwards, Anne. *A Remarkable Woman: A Biography of Katharine Hepburn*. New York: William Morrow & Co., Inc., 1985.

Ewers, Carolyn H. *Sidney Poitier: The Long Journey*. New York: Signet/New American Library, 1969.

Finstad, Suzanne. *Warren Beatty: A Private Man*. New York: Harmony, 2005.

Fitzgerald, Michael G. *Universal Pictures: A Panoramic History in Words, Pictures, and Filmographies*. New Rochelle, NY: Arlington House, 1977.

Fleischer, Richard. *Just Tell Me When to Cry: A Memoir*. New York: Carroll & Graf, 1993.

Fleming, Ian. *Casino Royale*. Originally published 1953. New York: Penguin, 2002.

Fonda, Henry, as told to Howard Teichman. *Fonda: My Life*. New York: New American Library, 1981.

Fonda, Jane. *My Life So Far*. New York: Random House, 2005.

Fonda, Peter. *Don't Tell Dad: A Memoir*. New York: Hyperion, 1998.

Fraser-Cavassoni, Natasha. *Sam Spiegel*. New York: Simon & Schuster, 2003.

Frayling, Christopher. *Once Upon a Time in Italy: The Westerns of Sergio Leone*. New York: Harry N. Abrams, 2005.

Friedman, Lester D., ed. *Arthur Penn's Bonnie and Clyde*. Cambridge, UK: Cambridge University Press, 2000.

————, *Bonnie and Clyde*. London: BFI Publishing, 2000.

Gabler, Neal. *Walt Disney: The Triumph of the American Imagination*. New York: Alfred A. Knopf, 2006.

Geist, Kenneth L. *Pictures Will Talk: The Life and Films of Joseph L. Mankiewicz*. New York: Scribner, 1978.

Gelb, Arthur. *City Room*. New York: Marian Wood/G. P. Putnam's Sons, 2003.

Goldman, William. *The Season: A Candid Look at Broadway*. New York: Harcourt, Brace & World, 1969.

Goudsouzian, Aram. *Sidney Poitier: Man, Actor, Icon*. Chapel Hill: University of North Carolina Press, 2004.

Gray, Beverly. *Roger Corman: An Unauthorized Biography of the Godfather of Indie Filmmaking*. Los Angeles: Renaissance Books, 2000.

Grobel, Lawrence. *The Hustons: The Life & Times of a Hollywood Dynasty*, updated ed. New York: Cooper Square Press, 2000.

Guest, Val. *So You Want to Be in Pictures*. Surrey, UK: Reynolds & Hearn, Ltd., 2001.

Guralnick, Peter. *Careless Love: The Unmaking of Elvis Presley*. Boston and New York: Back Bay/Little, Brown, 2000.

————. *Last Train to Memphis: The Rise of Elvis Presley*. Boston and New York: Back Bay/Little, Brown, 1994.

Harrison, Rex. *Rex: An Autobiography*. New York: William Morrow & Co., Inc., 1975.

Hepburn, Katharine. *Me: Stories of My Life*. New York: Ballantine, 1991.

Hernton, Calvin C. *White Papers for White Americans*. Garden City, NY: Doubleday, 1966.

Himes, Chester. *For Love of Imabelle* (also known as *A Rage in Harlem*). Originally published 1958. New York: Signet, 1974.

Hirschhorn, Clive. *The Columbia Story*, London: Hamlyn, 1999.

————. *The Warner Bros. Story*. New York: Crown, 1979.

Hoberman, J. *The Dream Life: Movies, Media, and the Mythology of the Sixties*. New York: New Press, 2003.

Hoffman, William. *Sidney*. New York: Lyle Stuart, 1971.

Hotchner, A. E., and Doris Day. *Doris Day: Her Own Story*. New York: William Morrow & Co., 1975.

Hutchinson, Tom. *Rod Steiger*. New York: Fromm International, 2000.

Jablonski, Edward. *Alan Jay Lerner: A Biography*. New York: Henry Holt & Co., 1996.

Jacob, Gilles, and Claude de Givray, eds. *François Truffaut: Correspondence 1945–1984*. Trans. by Gilbert Adair. New York: Noonday Press/Farrar, Straus & Giroux, 1990.

Jewison, Norman. *This Terrible Business Has Been Good to Me*. New York: St. Martin's Press, 2005.

Kael, Pauline. *Deeper into Movies*. New York: Warner Books, 1980.

————. *5001 Nights at the Movies*. New York: Holt, Rinehart & Winston, 1982.

————. *For Keeps*. New York: Dutton, 1994.

————. *Kiss Kiss Bang Bang*. Boston: Atlantic Monthly Press, year unlisted.

Kantor, Bernard R., Irwin R. Blacker, and Anne Kramer. *Directors at Work: Interviews with American Film-Makers*. New York: Funk & Wagnalls, 1970.

Kaufman, Bel. *Up the Down Staircase*. New York: Prentice Hall, 1964; reissued by HarperCollins with a new introduction by Kaufman, 1991.

Kramer, Stanley, with Thomas M. Coffey. *A Mad, Mad, Mad, Mad World: A Life in Hollywood*. New York: Harcourt Brace & Co., 1997.

Lacy, Ed (pseudonym for Len Zinberg). *Room to Swing*. Originally published 1957. Reissue. Blackmask.com/Disruptive Publishing Inc., 2005.

Lambert, Gavin. *Natalie Wood: A Life*. New York: Alfred A.Knopf, 2004.

Lax, Eric. *Woody Allen: A Biography*. Da Capo, 1991.

Leaming, Barbara. *Katharine Hepburn*. New York: Crown, 1995.

————. *Orson Welles: A Biography*. New York: Viking Penguin, 1985.

Lewis, Roger. *The Life and Death of Peter Sellers*. New York: Applause Books, 1997.

LoBrutto, Vincent. *Stanley Kubrick: A Biography*. New York: Da Capo, 1999.

Lofting, Hugh. *The Story of Doctor Dolittle*. Originally published 1920.

————. *The Voyages of Doctor Dolittle*. Originally published 1922.

Lumet, Sidney. *Making Movies*. New York: Alfred A. Knopf, 1995.

MacCabe, Colin. *Godard: A Portrait of the Artist at Seventy*. New York: Farrar, Straus & Giroux, 2003.

Mailer, Norman. *The Armies of the Night*. New York: New American Library, 1968.

Mangan, Richard. *Sir John Gielgud: A Life in Letters*. New York: Arcade, 2004.

Mann, William J. *Kate: The Woman Who Was Hepburn*. New York: Henry Holt, 2006.

Manso, Peter. *Brando: The Biography*. New York: Hyperion, 1994.

McBride, Joseph. *Searching for John Ford: A Life*. New York: St. Martin's Press, 2001.

McCarthy, Todd. *Howard Hawks: The Grey Fox of Hollywood*. New York: Grove Press, 1997.

McGilligan, Patrick. *Jack's Life*. New York: Norton, 1995.

————, ed. *Backstory 3: Interviews with Screenwriters of the 60s*. Berkeley: University of California Press, 1997.

————, ed. *Backstory 4: Interviews with Screenwriters of the 1970s and 1980s*. Berkeley: University of California Press, 2006.

Miller, Arthur. *Timebends: A Life*. New York: Grove Press, 1987.

Miller, Eugene L. Jr., and Edwin T. Arnold, *Robert Aldrich Interviews*. Jackson: University Press of Mississippi, 2004.

Miller, Gabriel, ed. *Martin Ritt Interviews*. Jackson: University Press of Mississippi, 2002.

Mordden, Ethan. *Medium Cool: The Movies of the 1960s*. New York: Alfred A. Knopf, 1990.

Morris, Oswald, with Geoffrey Bull. *Huston, We Have a Problem: A Kaleidoscope of Filmmaking Memories*. Lanham, MD: The Scarecrow Press, 2006.

Mosley, Leonard. *Zanuck: The Rise and Fall of Hollywood's Last Tycoon*. Boston: Little, Brown, 1984.

Moss, Marilyn Ann. *Giant: George Stevens, a Life on Film*. Madison: University of Wisconsin Press/ Terrace Books, 2004.

Neal, Patricia. *As I Am*. New York: Simon & Schuster, 1988.

Newquist, Roy. *A Special Kind of Magic*. New York: Rand McNally & Co., 1967.

Nowell-Smith, Geoffrey, ed. *The Oxford History of World Cinema*. New York: Oxford University Press, 1996.

O'Steen, Sam, as told to Bobbie O'Steen. *Cut to the Chase: Forty-Five Years of Editing America's Favorite Movies*. Studio City, CA: Michael Wiese Productions, 2001.

Paris, Barry. *Audrey Hepburn*. New York: G. P. Putnam's Sons, 1996.

Parker, John. *Warren Beatty: The Last Great Lover of Hollywood*. New York: Carroll & Graf Publishers, Inc., 1994.

Parrish, Robert. *Hollywood Doesn't Live Here Anymore*. Boston: Little, Brown, 1988.

Phillips, Gene D. *Godfather: The Intimate Francis Ford Coppola*. Lexington: University Press of Kentucky, 2004.

Phillips, Gene D., and Rodney Hill, eds. *Francis Ford Coppola Interviews*. Jackson: University Press of Mississippi, 2004.

Poitier, Sidney. *The Measure of a Man: A Spiritual Autobiography*. San Francisco: Harper, 2001.

————. *This Life*. New York: Alfred A. Knopf, 1980.

Polito, Robert, ed. *Crime Novels: American Noir of the 1950s*. New York: Library of America, 1997.

Pym, John, ed. *Time Out Film Guide*, 14th ed. London: Ebury, 2005.

Rapf, Joanna E., ed. *Sidney Lumet Interviews*. Jackson: University Press of Mississippi, 2006.

Reporting Civil Rights: Part Two—American Journalism 1963–1973. New York: Library of America, 2003.

Reporting Vietnam: Part One—American Journalism 1959–1969. New York: Library of America, 1998.

Roberts, Randy, and James S. Olson. *John Wayne: American*. New York: Free Press, 1995.

Robinson, David. *Chaplin: His Life and Art*. New York: McGraw-Hill, 1985.

Rose, Frank. *The Agency: William Morris and the Hidden History of Show Business*. New York: HarperBusiness, 1995.

Rubin, Steven Jay. *The Complete James Bond Movie Encyclopedia*, 2nd rev. ed. New York: Contemporary Books, 2003.

Russo, Joe, and Larry Landsman, with Edward Gross. *Planet of the Apes Revisited: The Behind-the-Scenes Story of the Classic Science Fiction Saga*. New York: Thomas Dunne Books/St. Martin's Press, 2001.

Russo, Vito. *The Celluloid Closet: Revised Edition*. New York: Harper & Row, 1987.

Sarris, Andrew. *The American Cinema: Directors and Directions 1929–1968*. New York: Dutton, 1968.

Schickel, Richard. *Clint Eastwood*. New York: Alfred A. Knopf, 1996.

———. *Elia Kazan: A Biography*. New York: HarperCollins, 2005.

Schickel, Richard, and John Simon, eds. *Film 67/68: An Anthology by the National Society of Film Critics*. New York: Simon & Schuster, 1968.

Schumacher, Michael. *Francis Ford Coppola: A Filmmaker's Life*. New York: Crown, 1999.

Shadoian, Jack. *Dreams and Dead Ends: The American Gangster/Crime Film*. Cambridge, MA: MIT Press, 1979.

Sikov, Ed. *Mr. Strangelove: A Biography of Peter Sellers*. New York: Hyperion, 2002.

———. *On Sunset Boulevard: The Life and Times of Billy Wilder*. New York: Hyperion, 1998.

Silver, Alain, and James Ursini. *What Ever Happened to Robert Aldrich: His Life and His Films*. New York: Limelight, 1995.

Simon, John. *Movies into Film: Film Criticism, 1967–1970*. New York: Dell, 1972.

Simon, Neil. *Rewrites: A Memoir*. New York: Simon & Schuster, 1996.

Spoto, Donald. *A Passion for Life: The Biography of Elizabeth Taylor*. New York: HarperCollins, 1995.

———. *Stanley Kramer: Film Maker*. New York: G. P. Putnam's Sons, 1978.

Steinberg, Cobbett. *Reel Facts: The Movie Book of Records, Updated Edition*. New York: Vintage, 1982.

Stevens, George Jr., ed. *Conversations with the Great Moviemakers of Hollywood's Golden Age at the American Film Institute*. New York: Alfred A. Knopf, 2006.

Swindell, Larry. *Spencer Tracy: A Biography*. New York: NAL/World, 1969.

Sylbert, Richard, and Sylvia Townsend. *Designing Movies: Portrait of a Hollywood Artist*. Westport, CT: Praeger Publishers, 2006.

Thomas, Bob. *Clown Prince of Hollywood: The Antic Life and Times of Jack L. Warner*. New York: McGraw-Hill, 1990.

Thomas, Sam. *Best American Screenplays: First Series*. New York, Crown, 1986.

Thomas, Tony, and Aubrey Solomon. *The Films of 20th Century-Fox: A Pictorial History*. Secaucus, NJ: Citadel Press, 1979.

Thomson, David. *The Whole Equation: A History of Hollywood*. New York: Alfred A. Knopf, 2004.

Turman, Lawrence. *So You Want to Be a Producer*. New York: Three Rivers Press, 2005.

Vadim, Roger. *Bardot Deneuve Fonda: My Life with the Three Most Beautiful Women in the World*. Trans. by Melinda Camber Porter. New York: Simon & Schuster, 1986.

Valenti, Jack. *This Time, This Place: My Life in War, the White House, and Hollywood*. New York: Harmony, 2007.

Various authors. *Variety's Film Reviews: Volume 11, 1964–1967*. New York: R. R. Bowker, 1983.

Walker, Alexander. *Fatal Charm: The Life of Rex Harrison*. London: Weidenfeld & Nicolson, 1992.

———. *No Bells on Sunday: The Rachel Roberts Journals*. New York: Harper & Row, 1984.

Walters, Barbara. *How to Talk with Practically Anybody About Practically Anything*. Garden City, NY: Doubleday, 1970.

Wake, Sandra, and Hayden, Nicola. *The Bonnie and Clyde Book*. New York: Simon & Schuster, 1972.

Watson, Steven. *Factory Made: Warhol and the Sixties*. New York: Pantheon, 2003.

Webb, Charles. *The Graduate*. New York: New American Library, 1963.

Weddle, David. *"If They Move . . . Kill 'Em!": The Life and Times of Sam Peckinpah*. New York: Grove Press, 1994.

Weingarten, Marc. *The Gang That Wouldn't Write Straight: Wolfe, Thompson, Didion, and the New Journalism Revolution*. New York: Crown, 2006.

Wiley, Mason, and Damien Bona. *Inside Oscar: The Unofficial History of the Academy Awards*. New York: Ballantine, 1986.

Wolfe, Tom. *The Electric Kool-Aid Acid Test*. New York: Farrar, Straus & Giroux, 1968.

Young, Freddie, as told to Peter Busby. *Seventy Light Years: A Life in the Movies*. London: Faber & Faber, 1999.

Zeffirelli, Franco. *Zeffirelli: An Autobiography*. New York: Weidenfeld & Nicolson, 1986.

WEB-ONLY MATERIAL

http://members.tripod.com/~Puddleby/index.html (for information on Hugh Lofting).

Colville-Andersen, Mikael. "David Newman—Conversation at Hotel Chelsea." October 1, 1998. http://zakka.dk/euroscreenwriters/articles/david__newman__536.htm.

Dominus, Mark. "The Bowdlerization of Dr. Dolittle." Jan. 23, 2006. http://www.plover.com/blog/book/Dolittle.html.

"Entertainment: Rod Steiger on Surviving Hollywood." May 25, 1999. http://news.bbc.co.uk/1/hi/entertainment/352147.stm.

Kennedy, Randall. "*Loving v. Virginia* at Thirty." February 6, 1997. http:speakout.com/activism/opinions/3208-1.html.

King, Steve. "Literary Daybook, Jan. 14." January 14, 2003. http://archive.salon.com/books/today/2003/01/14/jan14/index.html.

McNeal, Jeff. "A Conversation with Rod Steiger." November 1, 2001. http://www.thebigpicturedvd.com/bigreport12.shtml.

VIDEOGRAPHY AND AUDIOGRAPHY

This list does not include the movies discussed in this book but is restricted to filmed and/or audio-taped documentary material.

American Masters: Sidney Poitier—One Bright Light, directed by Lee Grant, written by Prudence Glass, produced by Mary Beth Yarrow and Glass (a production of Thirteen/WNET in association with Joseph Feury Productions, copyright 1999).

Beah: A Black Woman Speaks, produced by Neda Armian, Jonathan Demme, LisaGay Hamilton, and Joe Viola; written and directed by Hamilton (Clinica Estetico, Ltd. and LisaGay Inc., copyright 2003).

Donen, Stanley, commentary track on *Two for the Road* (Twentieth Century-Fox Film Corporation LLC, copyright 2005).

Fresh Air, National Public Radio, March 22, 2002, interviews by Terry Gross with Dustin Hoffman, Buck Henry, and Mike Nichols.

The Goldfinger Phenomenon, directed by John Cork, produced and written by Mark Cerulli and Lee Pfeiffer; *The Making of Goldfinger*, written by Cerulli, produced by Cerulli and Pfeiffer, directed by Cork; and two commentary tracks (available on the special edition of *Goldfinger*, copyright 1995 MGM/UA Home Entertainment Inc.).

The Graduate at 25 and *The Graduate: One on One with Dustin Hoffman*, produced by New Line Home Video, interviewer and creative consultant Craig Modderno (New Line Home Video, copyright 1992, available on the special edition of *The Graduate*).

Inside Dr. No, written and directed by John Cork, produced by David Naylor and Bruce Scivally, *Terence Young: Bond Vivant*, written by Scivally, directed by Cork, and produced by Cork, Naylor, and Scivally; and commentary track (MGM Home Entertainment Inc., copyright 2000, available on the special edition of *Dr. No*).

Inside From Russia with Love, written and directed by John Cork, produced by Cork, David Naylor, and Bruce Scivally; *Harry Saltzman: Showman*, written by Scivally, directed by Cork, produced by Cork, Naylor and Scivally; and commentary track (MGM Home Entertainment Inc., copyright 2000, available on the special edition of *From Russia with Love*).

Inside You Only Live Twice, written and directed by John Cork, produced by David Naylor and Bruce Scivally; and commentary track (MGM Home Entertainment Inc., copyright 2000, available on the special edition of *You Only Live Twice*).

Jewison, Norman, with Lee Grant, Rod Steiger, and Haskell Wexler, commentary track on *In the Heat of the Night* (MGM Home Entertainment, Inc., copyright 2001).

King, Larry, *CNN Larry King Weekend: Interview with Rod Steiger*, CNN. Rebroadcast July 14, 2002.

———. *CNN Larry King Live: Interview with Katharine Houghton*. Broadcast June 19, 2003.

Leone's West, the Leone Style, Il Maestro: Ennio Morricone and The Good, the Bad and the Ugly, and *Reconstructing The Good, the Bad and the Ugly*, all directed and produced by Michael M. Arick (MGM Home Entertainment LLC, copyright 2004, available on the two-disc special edition of *The Good, the Bad and the Ugly*).

The Making of Thunderball and *The Thunderball Phenomenon*, written and directed by John Cork, produced by Lee Pfeiffer and Mark Cerulli; and two commentary tracks (MGM/UA Home Entertainment Inc., copyright 1995, available on the special edition of *Thunderball*).

An Opera of Violence, The Wages of Sin, and *Something to Do with Death*, produced by Enfys Dickinson and Philip Moores, directed by Lancelot Narayan (Paramount Pictures, copyright 2003, available on the two-disc special collector's edition of *Once Upon a Time in the West*).

A Poem in Images, and on-camera interviews with Bibi Andersson and Liv Ullmann, produced and directed by Greg Carson; commentary track by Marc Gervais; on the special DVD edition of *Persona* (MGM Home Entertainment LLC, copyright 2005).

Pontecorvo: The Dictatorship of Truth (1992), directed by Oliver Curtis; and *Marxist Poetry: The Making of The Battle of Algiers*; on the three-disc Criterion Collection edition of *The Battle of Algiers* (the Criterion Collection, copyright 2004).

Preminger: Anatomy of a Filmmaker, produced and directed by Valerie A. Robins (Otto Preminger Films, Ltd.; copyright 1991, available on the two-disc special edition of *The Cardinal*).

Psychedelic Cinema, produced and directed by Greg Carson, (MGM Home Entertainment Inc., copyright 2002, available on the DVD edition of *Casino Royale*).

Schickel, Richard, commentary track on the two-disc special edition of *The Good, the Bad, and the Ugly* (MGM Home Entertainment LLC, copyright 2004).

The Spencer Tracy Legacy: A Tribute by Katharine Hepburn, directed by Heeley; produced by David Heeley and Joan Kramer; written by John Miller (1986).

Sterritt, David, commentary track on *Le Petit Soldat* (Koch Lorber Films/Winstar Home Video, copyright 2001).

Steve McQueen: The Essence of Cool, written, produced, and directed by Mimi Freedman (Turner Classic Movies, copyright 2005, available on the two-disc special edition of *Bullitt*).

Webb, Charles, interviewed by Susan Stamberg, National Public Radio, November 8, 1976.

Who's Afraid of Virginia Woolf?: A Daring Work of Raw Excellence, Who's Afraid of Virginia Woolf?: Too Shocking for Its Time, and a July 29, 1966, *Today* show interview with Mike Nichols, on the two-disc special edition of *Who's Afraid of Virginia Woolf?* (Warner Bros. Entertainment and Turner Entertainment Co., copyright 2006).

NOTES

CHAPTER 1

1. Author interview (AI) with Robert Benton; Finstad, Suzanne. *Warren Beatty: A Private Man* (New York: Harmony, 2005).
2. *François Truffaut: Correspondence 1945–1984*, translated by Gilbert Adair (New York: Noonday Press/Farrar, Straus & Giroux, 1990), p. 172.
3. AI with Arthur Penn.
4. Schumach, Murray. "Movie Creativity in Europe Hailed." *New York Times*, April 13, 1961.
5. "French Say, 'It Ain't So, Bos,' as Many Dispute Critic's 'Quality Gap.' " *Variety*, December 26, 1962.
6. AI with Leslie Newman.
7. AI with Benton.
8. *The Gang That Couldn't Write Straight: Wolfe, Thompson, Didion, and the New Journalism Revolution* by Marc Weingarten (New York: Crown, 2006) provided useful background on the history of *Esquire* in the early 1960s.
9. AI with Benton.
10. Benton, Robert, and David Newman. "Lightning in a Bottle." In *The Bonnie and Clyde Book,* compiled and edited by Sandra Wake and Nicola Hayden (New York: Simon & Schuster, 1972).
11. AI with Benton.
12. Ibid.
13. Goldstein, Patrick. "Blasts from the Past." *Los Angeles Times*, August 24, 1997.
14. Benton and Newman, "Lightning in a Bottle," op. cit.
15. AI with Benton.
16. *Master Detective*, February 1945.
17. AI with Benton.
18. *Public Enemies: America's Greatest Crime Wave and the Birth of the FBI* by Bryan Burrough (New York: Penguin Press, 2004) was a valuable resource for background information on Parker, Barrow, and their confederates.
19. Text of the Production Code and subsequent revisions, reprinted in *Reel Facts*, updated ed., edited by Cobbett Steinberg (New York: Vintage, 1982).
20. AIs with Benton and Elinor Jones.
21. AI with Norton Wright.
22. Ibid.
23. AI with Jones.
24. AI with Penn.

25. De Baecque, Antoine, and Serge Toubiana, translated by Catherine Temerson. *Truffaut* (New York: Alfred A. Knopf, 1999), pp. 198–1999.

26. Reed, Rex. "Penn: And Where Did All the Chase-Ing Lead?" *New York Times*, February 13, 1966.

27. AI with Penn.

28. *François Truffaut: Correspondence 1945–1984*, pp. 220–223.

29. Crowdus, Gary. "The Importance of a Singular, Guiding Vision: An interview with Arthur Penn." *Cineaste*, March 22, 1993.

30. AI with Penn.

31. AI with Jones.

32. Menand, Louis. "Onward and Upward with the Arts: Paris, Texas." *The New Yorker*, February 17 and 24, 2003.

33. Letter from Helen Scott to François Truffaut, December 4, 1963, courtesy of Elinor Jones.

34. Menand, op. cit.

35. Letter from François Truffaut to Helen Scott, December 17, 1963, *Truffaut Correspondence*, p. 229.

36. Letter from Truffaut to Scott, January 1964 undated, *Truffaut Correspondence*, p. 234.

CHAPTER 2

1. Author interview with Warren Beatty.

2. Ibid.

3. Ibid.

4. Fonda, Jane. *My Life So Far* (New York: Random House, 2005), p. 198.

5. AI with Beatty.

6. Thompson, Howard. "Inge's Kansas Through a Kazan Kaleidoscope." *New York Times*, May 22, 1960.

7. Ibid.

8. Finstad, op. cit.

9. AI with Beatty.

10. Ibid.

11. Navasky, Victor. *Naming Names* (New York: Viking, 1980), pp. 302–304.

12. Finstad, op. cit., pp. 301–303.

13. AI with Robert Solo.

14. Thomas, Bob. *Clown Prince of Hollywood* (New York: McGraw-Hill, 1990), p. 239.

15. Finstad, op. cit., pp. 274–275.

16. *Variety's Film Reviews 1964–1967* (New York: R. R. Bowker, 1983). Review originally published in *Weekly Variety*, September 23, 1964.

17. Crowther, Bosley. " 'Nothing but a Man' and 'Lilith' Presented." *New York Times*, September 21, 1964.

18. AI with Beatty.

19. Ibid.

20. Ibid.

21. Finstad, op. cit., p. 314.

22. AI with Beatty.

23. Webb, Charles. *The Graduate* (New York: New American Library, 1963; reprinted by Washington Square Press, 2002).

24. Finstad, op. cit.

25. AI with Lawrence Turman.

26. Prescott, Orville. "Books of the Times: 'Talent Busting Out All Over.' " *New York Times*, October 30, 1963.

27. Nichols, Lewis. "In and Out of Books." *New York Times*, June 30, 1963.

28. Allis, Tim. "Post-*Graduate* Life Proves Unkind to Author Charles Webb—Footloose, Fundless and Looking for Help." *People*, October 24, 1988.

29. AI (by e-mail) with Charles Webb.

30. AI with Webb.
31. Webb, op. cit., p. 63.
32. AI with Webb.
33. Turman, Lawrence. *So You Want to Be a Producer* (New York: Three Rivers Press, 2005).
34. Bart, Peter. "An Ambition: To Make a Movie No One Else Would." *New York Times*, January 30, 1966.
35. AI with Turman.
36. Webb, Charles, interviewed by Susan Stamberg on National Public Radio, November 8, 1976.
37. Turman, *So You Want to Be a Producer*, op. cit.
38. AI with William Hanley.
39. The website http://members.triod.com/[tilde]Puddleby/index.html is a useful resource for information on the life of Hugh Lofting.
40. AI with Christopher Lofting, as are all comments attributed to him that follow.
41. Unfilmed screenplay for *Doctor Dolittle* by Larry Watkin, Arthur P. Jacobs Collection, Special Collections Department, Charles Von Der Ahe Library, Loyola Marymount University.
42. Bricusse, Leslie. *The Music Man: The Key Changes in My Life* (London: Metro Publishing Ltd., 2006), pp. 141–142 and 180.
43. Memo headed " 'Doctor Dolittle' Lawsuit," from Arthur P. Jacobs to Jack Schwartzman, September 7, 1966, Jacobs Collection.
44. AI with Lofting.
45. Dunne, John Gregory. *The Studio* (New York: Farrar, Straus & Giroux), 1969.
46. Archer, Eugene. "5 Million Film Offer Made for 'Fair Lady.'" *New York Times*, September 27, 1961.
47. Memo from Jacobs to Schwartzman, September 7, 1966, op. cit.
48. "Lerner to Write a Movie Musical; Will Do Script and Lyrics for 'Dr. Dolittle' Stories." *New York Times*, January 6, 1964.
49. Memo from Jacobs to Schwartzman, op. cit.
50. Harrison, Rex. *Rex: An Autobiography* (New York: William Morrow & Co., 1975), p. 193.
51. Walker, Alexander. *Fatal Charm: The Life of Rex Harrison* (London: Weidenfeld & Nicolson, 1992), pp. 299–306.
52. Memo from Jacobs to Schwartzman, op. cit.

CHAPTER 3

1. *Truffaut Correspondence*, op. cit., letter from François Truffaut to Helen Scott, January 1964, undated.
2. Author interview with Benton.
3. AI with Jones.
4. AI with Jones.
5. Letter from François Truffaut to Helen Scott, February 22, 1964, *Truffaut Correspondence*, op. cit.
6. AI with Jones.
7. Friedman, Lester D., ed. *Bonnie and Clyde*. (London: BFI Publishing, 2000), p. 11.
8. AI with Benton and Jones.
9. Benton and Newman, "Lightning in a Bottle," op. cit.
10. Ibid.
11. Original treatment with introduction courtesy of Elinor Jones.
12. AI with Benton.
13. AI with Jones.
14. *Truffaut*, op. cit., p. 211.
15. Benton and Newman, "Lightning in a Bottle," op. cit.
16. AI with Beatty.
17. Letter from Truffaut to Helen Scott, December 1964, p. 259, *Truffaut Correspondence*, op. cit.
18. AI with Harrison Starr.
19. AI with Beatty and Penn.

20. AI with Starr.
21. AI with Alexandra Stewart.
22. Ibid.
23. AI with Starr.
24. AI with Beatty.
25. Background on the history of United Artists can be found in *United Artists: The Company That Changed the Film Industry* by Tino Balio (Madison University of Wisconsin Press, 1987).
26. Balio, op. cit., p. 87.
27. Ibid., pp. 134–136.
28. Eames, John Douglas. *The MGM Story*, 2nd rev. ed. (New York: Crown, 1982), p. 310.
29. Thomas, *Clown Prince of Hollywood*, op. cit., pp. 260–261.
30. Records of Jacobs's meetings with Warner, Minnelli, Andrews, and Ira Steiner come from memo from Jacobs to Schwartzman, September 7, 1966, op. cit., Jacobs Collection.
31. Smith, Kenneth S. "Skouras Defends 'Cleopatra' to Stockholders." *New York Times*, May 16, 1962.
32. "Zanuck Succeeds Skouras as President of Fox." *New York Times*, July 26, 1962.
33. Alden, Robert. "Zanuck Dismisses 'Cleopatra' Chief." *New York Times*, October 24, 1962.
34. Archer, Eugene. "Zanuck Reports on Fox Finances." *New York Times*, February 21, 1964; Esterow, Milton. " 'Cleopatra' Termed 'Success.' " *New York Times*, March 27, 1964; Canby, Vincent. "Costly 'Cleopatra' Is Nearing Its Break-Even Point." *New York Times*, March 25, 1966.
35. "Zanuck Reports on Fox Finances," op. cit.
36. Archer, Eugene. "Zanuck Shuts Fox's Coast Studio; 300 Employees Are Suspended." *New York Times*, August 20, 1962.
37. Mosley, Leonard. *Zanuck: The Rise and Fall of Hollywood's Last Tycoon* (Boston: Little, Brown, 1984), p. 344.
38. AI with Richard Zanuck.
39. Ibid.
40. Memo from Arthur Jacobs to Jack Schwartzman, September 7, 1966, op. cit.
41. "Proposal," memo from William Morris Agency, 1964 undated, Jacobs Collection.
42. Memo from Arthur Jacobs to Richard Zanuck, May 29, 1964, Jacobs Collection.
43. Reference in letter of agreement between 20th Century-Fox and Apjac, May 24, 1965, Jacobs Collection.
44. Draft of 20th Century-Fox publicity materials, undated, Jacobs Collection.
45. Jablonski, Edward. *Alan Jay Lerner: A Biography* (New York: Henry Holt & Co., 1996).
46. Dunne, *The Studio*, op. cit., pp. 32–33.

CHAPTER 4

1. Author interview with Mike Nichols.
2. Background on Nichols's early life and career comes from "Profiles: Making It Real—How Mike Nichols Re-Created Comedy and Himself" by John Lahr, *The New Yorker*, February 21 and 28, 2000.
3. AI with Nichols.
4. Scheuer, Philip K. "Nichols: The Whiz Kid Whizzes Onward." *Los Angeles Times*, February 5, 1967.
5. Lahr, op. cit.
6. Smith, Gavin. "Mike Nichols Interview." *Film Comment* (May 1999).
7. Lahr, op. cit.
8. AI with Nichols.
9. Smith, op. cit.
10. Lefferts, Barney. "Now the Mike Nichols Touch." *The New York Times Magazine*, November 22, 1964.
11. AI with Turman.

12. O'Steen, Sam, as told to Bobbie O'Steen. *Cut to the Chase: Forty-Five Years of Editing America's Favorite Movies* (Studio City, CA: Michael Wiese Productions, 2001).

13. AI with Nichols.

14. AI with Hanley.

15. AI with Nichols.

16. Ibid.

17. Wiley, Mason, and Damien Bona. *Inside Oscar: The Unofficial History of the Academy Awards,* 10th anniversary ed. (New York: Ballantine, 1996), p. 360.

18. Ibid., pp. 362–364.

19. Poitier, Sidney. *This Life* (New York: Alfred A. Knopf, 1980), p. 253.

20. Goudsouzian, Aram. *Sidney Poitier: Man, Actor, Icon* (Chapel Hill: The University of North Carolina Press, 2004), p. 206.

21. Schumach, Murray. "Stars Join Drive Against Bigotry." *New York Times,* July 15, 1963.

22. ———. "Hollywood Cause." *New York Times,* August 22, 1963.

23. Wiley and Bona, op. cit., p. 360.

24. Poitier, Sidney. *The Measure of a Man: A Spiritual Autobiography* (San Francisco: HarperSanFrancisco, 2001), p. 107.

25. Pryor, Thomas H. "A 'Defiant One' Becomes a Star." *New York Times,* January 25, 1959.

26. Schumach, Murray. "Poitier Says Bias Exists on Coast." *New York Times,* August 19, 1960.

27. Background on Poitier's relationship with Diahann Carroll comes from Poitier's two autobiographies, cited previously, and from *Diahann!* by Diahann Carroll with Ross Firestone (New York: Little, Brown, 1986).

28. "Wailing for Them All," *Time,* April 24, 1964.

29. Ibid.

30. Schumach, Murray. "N.A.A.C.P. Assails the Movie Industry." *New York Times,* November 29, 1961.

31. ———. "Hollywood Wary on Charges by the N.A.A.C.P." *New York Times,* June 27, 1963.

32. Raymond, Jack. "Negroes Listed in D-Day Assault." *New York Times,* June 28, 1963.

33. "Richard Zanuck Surprised." *New York Times,* June 28, 1963.

34. Schumach, Murray. "N.A.A.C.P. Seeks Job Equality in Hollywood Film Companies." *New York Times,* June 26, 1963.

35. ———. "Producers Agree on Using Negroes." *New York Times,* August 22, 1963.

36. ———. "Negro Assistant Film Director Solves Problems of Protocol." *New York Times,* January 31, 1963.

37. ———. "N.A.A.C.P. Scores Film Labor Units". *New York Times,* June 1, 1964.

38. AI with Elizabeth Wilson.

39. Gould, Jack. "Honesty and Ad Libs Enliven Ceremonies; Academy Awards Show Has 'Rented' Look." *New York Times,* April 15, 1964.

40. Poitier to Sheilah Graham. *New York World-Telegram and Sun,* August 9, 1965.

41. "Poitier's Oscar Has Exhibs Whistling Dixie." *Variety,* April 22, 1964.

42. "Actor Tells Press Off." *Variety,* April 22, 1964.

CHAPTER 5

1. Author interviews with Robert Benton and Elinor Jones.

2. Postcard from David Newman to Elinor Jones, postmarked May 24, 1964, courtesy of Jones.

3. "Lightning in a Bottle," op. cit.

4. AI with Wright.

5. Ibid.

6. The account of Truffaut's meeting with Jones at the Algonquin comes from the author's interview with Jones and her own notes written after the meeting.

7. AI with Starr.

8. Newman, David, and Robert Benton. "The New Sentimentality." *Esquire,* July 1964.

9. Newman, David. "What's It Really All About?: Pictures at an Execution." In *Arthur Penn's Bonnie and Clyde*, ed. by Lester D. Friedman (Cambridge: Cambridge University Press, 2000), p. 39.
10. AI with Wright.
11. Ibid.
12. Letter from François Truffaut to Elinor Jones, September 7, 1964, *Truffaut Correspondence*, op. cit.
13. Letters from François Truffaut to Helen Scott, May 28, 1964, and August 19, 1964, *Truffaut Correspondence*, op. cit.
14. De Baecque and Toubiana, *Truffaut*, op. cit.
15. Steinberg, Cobbett. *Reel Facts: The Movie Book of Records, Updated Edition* (New York: Vintage, 1982).
16. AI with Jones.
17. AI with Wright.
18. AI with Starr.
19. AI with Wright.
20. AI with Jones.
21. AI with Newman.
22. AI with Jones.
23. This account of the meeting is based on interviews with Benton, Jones, and Wright.
24. AI with Starr.
25. AI with Henry.
26. Undated notes by Elinor Jones about her conversation with Helen Scott, probably on or about September 21, 1964, courtesy of Elinor Jones.
27. Ibid.
28. AI with Wright.
29. Undated notes by Jones about her conversation with Scott, op. cit.
30. AI with Newman.
31. AI with Benton.
32. AI with Turman.
33. *So You Want to Be a Producer*, op. cit., pp. 195–196.
34. Archer, Eugene. "Hunter of Love, Ladies, Success." *New York Times*, October 16, 1960.
35. AI with Nichols.
36. Weiler, A. H. "Miss Ross' 'Bus' Moves Toward Screen". *New York Times*, December 13, 1964.
37. AI with Nichols.
38. *So You Want to Be a Producer*, op. cit., p. 196.
39. AI with Henry.
40. AI with Nichols.
41. AI with Lumet.
42. AI with Turman.
43. *So You Want to Be a Producer*, op. cit., p. 196.
44. "Most Fans Think Antonioni Is a Cheese—Levine." *Variety*, May 24, 1967.
45. "Embassy to Film 'Graduate.'" *New York Times*, October 7, 1964.
46. Lefferts, "Now the Mike Nichols Touch," op. cit.
47. "The Nichols Touch," *Time*, November 27, 1964.
48. "Movie Rights to 'Virginia Woolf' Sold to Warners for $500,000." *New York Times*, March 5, 1964.
49. "Who's Afraid of Virginia Woolf?: A Daring Work of Raw Excellence." Documentary featurette on two-disc DVD reissue of *Who's Afraid of Virginia Woolf?* (Warner Home Video).
50. Fonda, Henry, as told to Howard Teichmann. *Fonda: My Life* (New York: New American Library, 1981), p. 283.
51. Leff, Leonard J. "A Test of American Film Censorship: 'Who's Afraid of Virginia Woolf?'" *Cinema Journal* 19, no. 2 (Spring 1980): 43.
52. "Movie Rights to 'Virginia Woolf' Sold to Warners for $500,000," op. cit.
53. "Who's Afraid of Virginia Woolf?: A Daring Work of Raw Excellence," op. cit.
54. Mike Nichols, commentary track on two-disc DVD reissue of *Who's Afraid of Virginia Woolf?*
55. AI with Nichols.
56. AI with Turman.

57. Leff, "A Test of American Film Censorship," op. cit., p. 44.
58. "Miss Ross' 'Bus' Moves Toward Screen," op. cit.
59. AI with Nichols.

CHAPTER 6

1. *Variety*, January 4, 1967.
2. Grobel, Lawrence. *The Hustons: The Life & Times of a Hollywood Dynasty*, updated ed. (New York: Cooper Square Press, 2000), pp. 532–533.
3. Picker, David. "How UA Bonded with Bond." *Variety*, May 3, 2005.
4. "Inside Dr. No." Written and directed by John Cork, produced by David Naylor and Bruce Scivally. DVD documentary on special edition of *Dr. No* (copyright 2000, MGM Home Entertainment Inc.).
5. Rubin, Steven Jay. *The Complete James Bond Encyclopedia*, 2nd ref. ed. (Contemporary Books, 2003).
6. Ibid.
7. "The Goldfinger Phenomenon," Directed by John Cork, produced and written by Mark Cerulli and Lee Pfeiffer. DVD documentary on the special edition of *Goldfinger* (copyright 1995, MGM/UA Home Entertainment Inc.).
8. "New York Sound Track," *Variety*, January 11, 1967.
9. Jablonski, *Alan Jay Lerner: A Biography*, op. cit.
10. "Lerner to Write a Movie Musical." *New York Times*, January 6, 1964.
11. Memo from Jack Schwartzman to Arthur Jacobs, February 25, 1965, Jacobs Collection.
12. Ibid.
13. Cable from Arthur Jacobs to Alan Jay Lerner, December 15, 1964, Jacobs Collection.
14. Memo from Schwartzman to Jacobs, February 25, 1965, op. cit.
15. Cable from Arthur Jacobs to Irving Cohen, January 15, 1965, Jacobs Collection.
16. Dunne, *The Studio*, op. cit., pp. 32–33.
17. Telegram from Arthur Jacobs to Alan Jay Lerner, January 25, 1965, Jacobs Collection.
18. Memo from Schwartzman to Jacobs, February 25, 1965, op. cit.
19. Cable from Richard Zanuck to Alan Jay Lerner, March 4, 1965, Jacobs Collection.
20. Cable from Owen McLean to Irving Paul Lazar, March 11, 1965, Jacobs Collection.
21. Cable from Arthur Jacobs to Alan Jay Lerner, April 8, 1965, Jacobs Collection.
22. Harrison, *Rex*, op. cit., pp. 208–209.
23. Letter to Arthur Jacobs from Frank R. Ferguson, resident counsel, 20th Century-Fox, Jacobs Collection.
24. Telegrams from Arthur Jacobs to Alan Jay Lerner, May 3 1967, and May 7, 1967. Jacobs Collection.
25. Goudsouzian, op. cit., p. 221.
26. "N.A.A.C.P. Weighs Movie Job Suits." *New York Times*, July 9, 1965.
27. Poitier, *This Life*, op. cit, pp. 279–283.
28. Ibid, pp. 268–269.
29. Thompson, Howard. "Why Is Sidney Poitier the Only One?" *New York Times*, June 13, 1965.
30. Barthel, Joan. "He Doesn't Want to Be Sexless Sidney." *New York Times*, August 6, 1967.
31. Goudsouzian, op. cit., p. 235.
32. Barthel, "He Doesn't Want to Be Sexless Sidney." op. cit.
33. Author interview with Kramer.
34. AI with Jewison.
35. Balio, op. cit., p. 180.
36. Ball, John. *In the Heat of the Night* (originally published by Harper & Row, 1965; reprint by Carroll & Graf, 2001).
37. Lacy, Ed (aka Len Zinberg). *Room to Swing* (originally published 1957; reprint by Blackmask .com, 2005).
38. "Poitier to Play Film Detective." *New York Times*, June 19, 1965.
39. AI with Walter Mirisch.

40. Canby, Vincent. "Poitier, as Matinee Idol, Is Handsomely Rewarded." *New York Times*, November 18, 1967.
41. "Poitier to Play Film Detective," op. cit.

CHAPTER 7

1. "Peter Hall Seeks Divorce from Miss Caron in London." *Associated Press*, June 17, 1964.
2. Letters from Warren Beatty to Charles K. Feldman, July 17 and 23, 1964, undated handwritten response from Feldman, Charles K. Feldman Collection, American Film Institute.
3. Ibid.
4. Memo from Charles K. Feldman, November 7, 1964, Feldman Collection.
5. Author interview with Beatty.
6. AI with Hiller.
7. John Lennon, interviewed by Sandy Lesburgh, May 9, 1965.
8. "London—The Swinging City." *Time*, April 15, 1966.
9. Bricusse, Leslie. *The Music Man: The Key Changes in My Life* (London: Metro, 2006).
10. Ibid.
11. Memo from Arthur Jacobs to Richard Zanuck, May 7, 1965, Jacobs Collection.
12. Ibid.
13. Bricusse, *The Music Man*, op. cit.
14. Memo from Arthur Jacobs to Richard Zanuck, May 7, 1965, op. cit.
15. Bricusse, *The Music Man*, op. cit.
16. AI with Leslie Newman.
17. AI with Wright.
18. AI with Penn.
19. AI with Wright.
20. Jones, W. D. "Riding with Bonnie and Clyde." *Playboy* (November 1968).
21. AI with Wright.
22. AI with Jones.
23. Benton and Newman, "Lightning in a Bottle," op. cit.
24. Undated typed notes, courtesy of Elinor Jones.
25. AI with Wright.
26. AI with Benton and Wright,
27. Finstad, p. 343.
28. Ibid.
29. Letter from François Truffaut to Elinor Jones, June 18, 1965, *Truffaut Correspondence,* op. cit.
30. AI with Jones.
31. Letter from Elinor Jones and Norton Wright to François Truffaut, June 5, 1965, courtesy of Elinor Jones.
32. Letter from François Truffaut to Elinor Jones, June 18, 1965, *Truffaut Correspondence,* op. cit.
33. AI with Jones.
34. AI with Beatty.
35. AI with Benton.
36. AI with Beatty.
37. Benton and Newman, "Lightning in a Bottle," op. cit.
38. AI with Newman.
39. Letter from Elinor Jones to François Truffaut, June 29, 1965, courtesy of Elinor Jones.
40. Letter from François Truffaut to Elinor Jones, July 2, 1965, courtesy of Elinor Jones.
41. AI with Beatty and Benton.

CHAPTER 8

1. LoBrutto, Vincent. *Stanley Kubrick: A Biography* (New York: Da Capo, 1999), p. 120.
2. Manso, Peter. *Brando: The Biography* (New York: Hyperion, 1994), p. 473.

3. Turman, *So You Want to Be a Producer*, op. cit., p. 84.

4. Author interview with Turman and Nichols.

5. AI with Nichols.

6. AI with Turman.

7. AI with Nelson.

8. Ibid.

9. Thompson, Tommy. "Raw Dialogue Challenges All the Censors." *Life*, June 10, 1966.

10. Madsen, Axel. "Who's Afraid of Alfred Hitchcock?" *Sight and Sound* 37. Cited in Jeff, Leonard J. "Play into Film: 'Who's Afraid of Virginia Woolf?'" *Theatre Journal* 33, no. 4 (December 1981): p. 457.

11. Leff, "Play into Film: 'Who's Afraid of Virginia Woolf?'" op. cit., p. 456.

12. Mike Nichols, commentary track for two-disc DVD edition of *Who's Afraid of Virginia Woolf?*

13. Ibid.

14. Sylbert, Richard, and Sylvia Townsend. *Designing Movies: Portrait of a Hollywood Artist* (Westport, CT: Praeger Publishers, 2006).

15. AI with Nichols.

16. Ibid.

17. Mike Nichols, commentary track, op. cit.

18. AI with Nichols.

19. Fonda, Jane, *My Life So Far*, op. cit., pp. 163–165.

20. Vadim, Roger, translated by Melinda Camber Porter. *Bardot Deneuve Fonda: My Life with the Three Most Beautiful Women in the World* (New York: Simon & Schuster, 1986), p. 242.

21. AI with Henry.

22. Fonda, Peter. *Don't Tell Dad*, p. 196.

23. Schumach, Murray. "Wyler Is Critical of Foreign Films; Director Assails Some for Glorifying Confusion." *New York Times*, April 27, 1964.

24. Fonda, *My Life So Far*, op. cit.

25. AI with Pollack.

26. McDonald, Thomas. "Presenting A Happy 'Act': Wagner and Wood." *New York Times*, June 14, 1959.

27. Fonda, Peter. *Don't Tell Dad*, op. cit., pp. 206–208.

28. AI with Penn.

29. Crowdus, "The Importance of a Singular, Guiding Vision," op. cit.

30. Reed, "Penn: And Where Did All the Chase-ing Lead?" op. cit.

31. Penn's frankness about his unhappiness with *The Chase* and about his experience working with Spiegel led to a minor controversy when he gave free vent to his frustrations in an interview with Rex Reed for *The New York Times* when the film opened. The week after the piece appeared, Penn wrote a letter, which the *Times* printed, in which he denied having said many of the things attributed to him. Reed, whose response was also printed, stood by the piece and suggested that Penn had "been threatened or scared out of his wits by one of his own big-studio Powers That Be." More than twenty-five years later, Penn, in an interview with *Cineaste*, gave an account of *The Chase* that confirmed his displeasure with the film, a view that he reiterated in his interview for this book.

32. Poitier, *This Life*, op. cit., pp. 276–277.

33. Vadim, *Bardot Deneuve Fonda*, op. cit., p. 242.

34. AI with Pollack.

35. AI with Nichols.

36. Vadim, op. cit., p. 243.

CHAPTER 9

1. Newquist, Roy. *A Special Kind of Magic* (New York: Rand McNally & Co., 1967), p. 44.

2. Kramer, Stanley, with Thomas M. Coffey. *A Mad, Mad, Mad, Mad World: A Life in Hollywood* (New York: Harcourt Brace & Co., 1997).

3. Letter from George Glass to Roy Newquist, May 10, 1967, Stanley Kramer Collection, UCLA.

4. Author interview with Jewison.

5. Schumach, Murray. "Kramer Defies American Legion over Hiring of Movie Writers." *New York Times*, February 8, 1960.

6. Crowther, Bosley. "The Screen: 'Judgment at Nuremberg.'" *New York Times*, December 20, 1961.

7. Kael, Pauline. "The Intentions of Stanley Kramer," September 1965. In *Kiss Kiss Bang Bang* (Boston: Atlantic–Little, Brown, 1968), pp. 209–213.

8. Kantor, Bernard R., Irwin R. Blacker, and Anne Kramer. *Directors at Work: Interviews with American Film-Makers* (New York: Funk & Wagnalls, 1970).

9. Ibid.

10. Balio, *United Artists: The Company That Changed the Film Industry*, op. cit., pp. 142–146.

11. Kael, "The Intentions of Stanley Kramer," op. cit.

12. Stevens, George Jr. *Conversations with the Great Moviemakers of Hollywood's Golden Age at the American Film Institute* (New York: Knopf, 2006), pp. 562–564.

13. McDonald, Thomas. "Hollywood 'Trial.'" *New York Times*, November 1, 1959.

14. Stevens, *Conversations with the Great Moviemakers of Hollywood's Golden Age at the American Film Institute*, op. cit., p. 572.

15. Kramer, *A Mad, Mad, Mad, Mad World*, op. cit.

16. Archer, Eugene. "Columbia to Get a Kramer Movie." *New York Times*, June 13, 1962.

17. Davidson, Bill. *Spencer Tracy: Tragic Idol* (New York: E. P. Dutton, 1987); and Leaming, Barbara. *Katharine Hepburn* (New York: Crown, 1995).

18. AI with Karen Sharpe Kramer.

19. Weiler, A. H. "On the Run Toward the 'Money.'" *New York Times*, December 19, 1965.

20. Thompson, Howard. "Unafraid of 'Virginia Woolf.'" *New York Times*, September 5, 1965.

21. Bragg, Melvyn. *Rich: The Life of Richard Burton* (London: Hodder & Stoughton, 1988), p. 206.

22. Ibid., p. 309.

23. Thompson, "Unafraid of 'Virginia Woolf,'" op. cit.

24. Bragg, *Rich*, op. cit., p. 204.

25. AI with Nichols. A different account can be found in "Play into Film: 'Who's Afraid of Virginia Woolf?'" (op. cit.), in which Leonard J. Leff cites an opening scene in an early draft by Lehman in which two dogs were shown fighting and notes that Jack Warner thought the scene was "good action," something he felt the dialogue-driven play needed.

26. "Elizabeth Taylor and Richard Burton: The Night of the Brawl." *Look*, February 8, 1966.

27. O'Steen, *Cut to the Chase*, op. cit.

28. AI with Nichols; Nichols on *Who's Afraid of Virginia Woolf* commentary track, op. cit.

29. AI with Henry.

30. Webb, *The Graduate*, op. cit., p. 102.

31. Ibid., p. 59.

32. Ibid., p. 182.

33. AI with Henry.

34. Ibid.

35. Webb, *The Graduate*, op. cit., p. 99.

36. AI with Turman.

37. Webb, *The Graduate*, op. cit., p. 49.

38. Alpert, Hollis. "'The Graduate' Makes Out." *Saturday Review*, July 6, 1968.

39. AI with Henry.

40. Henry, interviewed by Terry Gross, National Public Radio, 1997.

CHAPTER 10

1. Dunne, *The Studio*, op. cit., p. 33.

2. Cable from Richard Zanuck to Arthur Jacobs, July 28, 1965, Jacobs Collection.

3. "Treatment for Doctor Dolittle" by Leslie Bricusse, July 14, 1965, Jacobs Collection.

4. Lofting, Hugh. *The Story of Doctor Dolittle* (originally published 1920) and *The Voyages of Doctor Dolittle* (originally published 1922).

5. Author interview with Christopher Lofting.
6. Letter from Josephine Lofting to Bernard Silbert, July 20, 1965 (misdated July 20, 1964), Jacobs Collection.
7. AI with Jewison.
8. Fleischer, Richard. *Just Tell Me When to Cry: A Memoir* (New York: Carroll & Graf, 1993), pp. 238–239.
9. Dunne, *The Studio*, op. cit., p. 33.
10. Bricusse, *The Music Man*, op. cit., pp. 162–165.
11. Memo from Rex Harrison to Arthur Jacobs, July 22, 1965, Jacobs Collection.
12. Accounts of Roberts's struggle with mental illness and alcoholism come from Alexander Walker's *Fatal Charm: The Life of Rex Harrison* (op. cit.), from Walker's *No Bells on Sunday: The Rachel Roberts Journals* (New York: Harper & Row, 1984), and from interviews with those who knew her.
13. Bricusse, *The Music Man*, op. cit., pp. 166–167.
14. Fleischer, *Just Tell Me When To Cry*, op. cit., pp. 240–241.
15. Goudsouzian, *Sidney Poitier: Man, Actor, Icon*, op. cit.
16. Fleischer, *Just Tell Me When to Cry*, op. cit., pp. 243–246.
17. Letter from Rex Harrison to Arthur Jacobs, September 28, 1965, Jacobs Collection.
18. Bart, Peter. "Hollywood Finds Harmony Paying." *New York Times*, May 14, 1966.
19. AI with Mort Abrahams; see also Bricusse, *The Music Man*, op. cit.
20. AI with Abrahams.
21. AI with Brown.
22. Fleischer, *Just Tell Me When to Cry*, op. cit., p. 247.
23. Unsigned memo dated November 1, 1965, retroactive to August 30, 1965, Jacobs Collection.
24. Unsigned memo dated November 2, 1965, Jacobs Collection.
25. Handwritten initialed note by Richard Zanuck on memo from Owen McLean to Zanuck, Jacobs, and Fleischer, November 2, 1965, Richard Fleischer Collection, USC.
26. Letter from Owen McLean to Richard Zanuck, November 4, 1965, Jacobs Collection.
27. Undated handwritten note by Arthur Jacobs, Jacobs Collection.
28. Telegrams from L. Arnold Weissberger to Anthony Newley, November 18 and November 19, 1965, Anthony Newley Papers, Boston University; letter from Owen McLean to Richard Zanuck, November 22, 1965, Jacobs Collection.
29. Geist, Kenneth L. *Pictures Will Talk: The Life and Films of Joseph L. Mankiewicz* (New York: Scribner, 1978), pp. 351–352.
30. Letter from Richard Fleischer to Rex Harrison, November 22, 1965, Jacobs Collection.
31. Memo from National Weather Institute to 20th Century-Fox, December 6, 1965, Jacobs Collection.
32. AI with Abrahams.
33. Memo from Arthur Jacobs to Richard Zanuck, December 7, 1965, Jacobs Collection.
34. Mosley, *Zanuck: The Rise and Fall of Hollywood's Last Tycoon*, op. cit., pp. 235–236.
35. Memo from Darryl F. Zanuck to Richard Zanuck, December 12, 1965, Jacobs Collection.
36. Cable from Richard Zanuck to Darryl F. Zanuck, December 16, 1965, Jacobs Collection.
37. Cable from Darryl F. Zanuck to Richard Zanuck, December 12, 1965, Jacobs Collection.
38. Cable from Ted Ashley to Richard Zanuck, December 27, 1965, Jacobs Collection.
39. Fleischer, *Just Tell Me When to Cry*, op. cit., pp. 249–252.
40. Cable from Rex Harrison to Richard Zanuck, December 30, 1965, Jacobs Collection.
41. Telegram from Richard Zanuck to Rex Harrison, December 31, 1965, Jacobs Collection.

CHAPTER 11

1. Steinberg, Cobbett. *Reel Facts: The Movie Book of Records* (New York: Vintage, 1982), p. 24.
2. Author interview with Beatty.
3. AI with Towne.
4. AI with Beatty.
5. De Baecque and Toubiana, *Truffaut*, op. cit., p. 212.

6. AI with Jones.

7. Ibid.

8. AI with Wright.

9. AI with Jones and Wright.

10. AI with Wright.

11. *Variety*, September 8, 1965.

12. AI with Beatty.

13. AI with Benton.

14. AI with Wright.

15. AI with Jones.

16. "The Fingers of God," *Time*, August 9, 1963.

17. AI with Pollack.

18. Stirling Silliphant, interviewed by Nat Segaloff in *Backstory 3: Interviews with Screenwriters of the 60s*, edited by Patrick McGilligan (Berkeley: University of California Press, 1997), pp. 344–345.

19. Ibid.

20. "Poitier to Play Film Detective." *New York Times*, June 19, 1965, op. cit.

21. Ball, in press notes for *In the Heat of the Night*, Norman Jewison Collection.

22. Ball, *In the Heat of the Night*, op. cit., p. 17.

23. Ibid., pp. 172–173 and 185.

24. "In the Heat of the Night Character Notes and Step Outline," December 15, 1965, Stirling Silliphant Collection, UCLA.

25. Bart, Peter. "Liberals vs. Their Movies." *New York Times*, August 29, 1965.

26. Kenworthy, E. W. "200,000 March for Civil Rights in Orderly Washington Rally; President Sees Gain for Negro." *New York Times*, August 29, 1963.

27. Richardson, Robert. " 'Burn, Baby, Burn' Slogan Used as Firebugs Put Area to Torch." *Los Angeles Times*, August 15, 1965.

28. "Character Notes and Step Outline," Stirling Silliphant Collection, UCLA, op. cit.

29. Jewison, Norman. *This Terrible Business Has Been Good to Me* (New York: St. Martin's Press, 2005), p. 75.

30. Ibid., p. 87.

31. Ibid., pp. 92–93.

32. AI with Jewison.

33. Weddle, David. *"If They Move . . . Kill 'Em!": The Life and Times of Sam Peckinpah* (New York: Grove Press, 1994), pp. 258–261.

34. Schumach, Murray. "Producer Decries Movie Nudity Ban." *New York Times*, March 19, 1964.

35. Jewison, *This Terrible Business Has Been Good to Me*, op. cit., p. 114.

36. Balio, *United Artists: The Company That Changed the Film Industry*, op. cit., pp. 168, 185–187.

37. AI with Mirisch.

38. Bart, Peter. "Where the Action Isn't." *New York Times*, July 31, 1966.

39. This and all subsequent notes on this draft of the screenplay come from "In the Heat of the Night, First Draft" by Stirling Silliphant, dated "January–February 1966," Stirling Silliphant Collection, UCLA.

40. "Dialogue on Film: Stirling Silliphant." *American Film*, (March 1988).

41. AI with Jewison.

CHAPTER 12

1. Author interview with Penn.

2. Penn, Arthur. "Making Waves: The Directing of *Bonnie and Clyde*." In *Arthur Penn's Bonnie and Clyde*, edited by Lester D. Friedman (Cambridge: Cambridge University Press, 2000).

3. Reed, "Penn: And Where Did All the Chase-Ing Lead?", op. cit.

4. AI with York.

5. Ibid.
6. Reed, Rex. "Will the Real Warren Beatty Please Shut Up." *Esquire*, August 1967.
7. Finstad, *Warren Beatty: A Private Man*, op. cit., p. 356.
8. AI with Beatty.
9. Ibid.
10. AI with Benton.
11. AI with Dutton.
12. Bart, Peter. "N.B.C.-TV Is Sued by Film Director." *New York Times*, October 27, 1965.
13. ———. " 'Place in the Sun' Is Spared Scissors." *New York Times*, February 14, 1966.
14. "Stevens Loses Suit over His Film on TV." *New York Times*, May 24, 1967.
15. AI with Beatty.
16. AI with Towne.
17. AI with Beatty.
18. AI with Pollack.
19. Rose, Frank. *The Agency: William Morris and the Hidden History of Show Business* (New York: HarperBusiness, 1995), p. 295.
20. Penn, "Making Waves," op. cit.
21. AI with Penn.
22. AI with Beatty.
23. Letter and attachment from Frank H. Ferguson to Jack Schwartzman, with an executed copy of Christopher Plummer's termination agreement dated March 22, 1966, Jacobs Collection.
24. Walker, Alexander. *No Bells on Sunday: The Rachel Roberts Journals* (New York: Harper & Row, 1984).
25. AI with Zanuck.
26. "Notes on Proposed Script and Score Revisions Resulting from London Meetings with Rex Harrison," memo by Leslie Bricusse, January 1966, Jacobs Collection.
27. 20th Century-Fox internal memo from Stan Hough to Bob Daniel, January 11, 1966, Jacobs Collection.
28. AI with Zanuck.
29. Fleischer, *Just Tell Me When to Cry*, op. cit., pp. 252–257.
30. Ibid.
31. Letter from Rex Harrison to Richard Fleischer, March 7, 1966, Fleischer Collection, USC.
32. Letter from Richard Fleischer to Rex Harrison, March 11, 1966, Fleischer Collection, USC.
33. Sheet music with lyrics, by Michael Flanders and Donald Swann, circa March 1966, Jacobs Collection.
34. Letter from Owen McLean to Sandy Bresler at William Morris Agency, March 14, 1966, Jacobs Collection.
35. Reed, Rex. "Will They Dig 'Dr. Dolittle'?" *New York Times*, September 4, 1966.
36. 20th Century-Fox internal memo, February 18, 1966, Jacobs Collection.
37. AI with Eggar.
38. Ibid.
39. Morley's salary: Telegram from Jacobs to Fleischer, February 19, 1966, Fleischer Collection.
40. A memo from Stuart Lyons to Owen McLean dated February 9, 1966, stated that Bull would accept $4,000, but a Fox budget memo from February 18, 1966, indicated that his salary would be $11,600. Jacobs Collection.
41. Fox internal memo, Hough to Daniel, January 11, 1966, op. cit.
42. Fleischer, *Just Tell Me When to Cry*, op. cit., p. 257.
43. Ibid., pp. 258–259; undated press release by Arthur Jacobs, Jacobs Collection.
44. Canby, Vincent. "Poitier, as Matinee Idol, Is Handsomely Rewarded." *New York Times*, November 18, 1967.
45. Motion Picture Association of America promotional mailing for *A Patch of Blue*, New York Public Library for the Performing Arts.
46. Canby, Vincent. " 'A Patch Of Blue' Draws in South." *New York Times*, April 5, 1966.

47. *Variety*, December 8, 1965.
48. Ibid.
49. Crist, Judith. Review of *A Patch of Blue*. *New York Herald-Tribune*, December 16, 1965.
50. Gill, Brendan. "The Current Cinema." *The New Yorker*, December 25, 1965.
51. *Film Quarterly* (spring 1966).
52. Review of *A Patch of Blue*. *Saturday Review*, January 8, 1966.
53. "KKK, Freshly Laundered, Pickets 'Patch of Blue.'" *Variety*, May 11, 1966.
54. "Poitier, Belafonte Score Hit with East Harlem Students." *New York World-Telegram and Sun*, February 17, 1966.
55. "Belafonte & Poitier Bail 5 Held in Sit-In." *New York Post*, March 21, 1966.
56. Barthel, Joan. "He Doesn't Want to Be Sexless Sidney." *New York Times*, August 6, 1967.
57. Goudsouzian, *Sidney Poitier: Man, Actor, Icon*, op. cit., p. 252.
58. Barthel, "He Doesn't Want to Be Sexless Sidney," op. cit.

CHAPTER 13

1. Klemesrud, Judy. "Dustin Hoffman: From 'Graduate' to Ratzo Rizzo, Super Slob." *New York Times*, July 14, 1968.
2. Author interview with Hoffman.
3. Ibid.
4. Klemesrud, July 14, 1968, op. cit.
5. AI with Anspach.
6. Schwartz, Tony. "Dustin Hoffman vs. Nearly Everybody." *New York Times*, December 16, 1979.
7. AI with Hoffman.
8. AI with Anspach.
9. Miller, Arthur. *Timebends: A Life* (New York, Grove Press, 1987), p. 373.
10. AI with Anspach.
11. AIs with Wynn Handman, Ronald Ribman, and Michael Tolan all provided useful background about the early history of the American Place Theatre.
12. AI with Hoffman.
13. AI with Ribman.
14. AI with Hoffman.
15. AI with Henry.
16. AI with Ribman.
17. AI with Handman.
18. "Faye Dunaway: The Farmer's Granddaughter." *Look*, December 13, 1966.
19. Dunaway, Faye, with Betsy Sharkey. *Looking for Gatsby: My Life* (New York: Simon & Schuster, 1995), pp. 77 and 79.
20. Schickel, Richard. *Elia Kazan: A Biography* (New York: HarperCollins, 2005), pp. 407–417.
21. AI with Law.
22. AI with Hoffman.
23. AI with Handman.
24. Dunaway, *Looking for Gatsby*, op. cit.
25. *Los Angeles Times*, June 18, 1997.
26. Dunaway, *Looking for Gatsby*, op. cit., p. 96.
27. AI with Silverstein.
28. Dunaway, *Looking for Gatsby*, op. cit., p. 96.
29. AI with Silverstein.
30. AI with Ribman.
31. Ibid.
32. AI with Anspach.
33. AI with Tolan.
34. Ibid.
35. AI with Ribman.
36. AI with Tolan.

37. Kauffmann, Stanley. "Theater: Turgenev Tale." *New York Times*, April 22, 1966.

38. AI with Ribman,

39. AI with Hoffman.

40. Ibid.

41. "Ticky-Tack." *Time*, April 29, 1966.

42. AI with Elinor Jones.

43. Finstad, *Warren Beatty: A Private Man*, op. cit., photo insert.

44. AI with Beatty.

45. Crowther, Bosley. "The Screen: Minstrel Show 'Othello'; Radical Makeup Marks Olivier's Interpretation." *New York Times*, February 2, 1966.

46. Kael, Pauline. "Laurence Olivier as Othello." *McCall's*, March 1966.

47. Wiley and Bona, *Inside Oscar*, op. cit., p. 386.

48. Crist, Judith. "Over the Rainbow—Two Big 'Little' Films." *New York Herald-Tribune*, April 25, 1965.

49. Ward, Robert. "Hollywood's Last Angry Man: Rod Steiger Bites the Hand That Hasn't Been Feeding Him." *American Film*, (January–February 1982).

50. AI with Lumet.

51. Bloom, Claire. *Limelight and After: The Education of an Actress* (New York: Harper & Row, 1982), p. 154.

52. AI with Lumet.

53. Ibid.

54. Weiler, A. H. "Board Gives Seal to 'Pawnbroker.'" *New York Times*, March 29, 1965.

55. American International Pictures press release, April 29, 1966, *The Pawnbroker* file, New York Public Library for the Performing Arts.

56. Oulahan, Richard. *Life*, April 2, 1965.

57. Gill, Brendan. "The Current Cinema." *The New Yorker*, Jan. 24, 1965.

58. Wiley and Bona, *Inside Oscar*, op. cit., p. 389.

59. "Playboy Interview: Rod Steiger," *Playboy*, July 1969.

CHAPTER 14

1. Author interview with Jewison.

2. Salary sheets and cast contact information, Stalmaster Co., Norman Jewison Collection, Wisconsin Center for Film and Theater Research.

3. "In the Heat of the Night," drafts dated March 14, 1966, and July 5, 1966, Stirling Silliphant Collection.

4. Silliphant in *Backstory 3*, op. cit.

5. "In the Heat of the Night," draft dated March 14, 1966, op. cit.

6. AI with Jewison.

7. "In the Heat of the Night," draft dated March 14, 1966, op. cit.

8. Letter from Geoffrey Shurlock to Walter Mirisch, September 23, 1966, Production Code files, Margaret Herrick Library.

9. AI with Jewison.

10. Silliphant in *Backstory 3*, op. cit.

11. "In the Heat of the Night," draft dated July 5, 1966, op. cit.

12. AI with Jewison and Mirisch.

13. Accounts of the troubled production of *Hurry Sundown* appear in *Looking for Gatsby* by Faye Dunaway and *My Life So Far* by Jane Fonda, both previously cited, and in the documentary *Preminger: Anatomy of a Filmmaker*, produced and directed by Valerie A. Robins (copyright 1991, Otto Preminger Films, Ltd., available on the two-disc DVD edition of *The Cardinal*).

14. Reed, Rex. "Like They Could Cut Your Heart Out," *New York Times*, August 21, 1966.

15. "Cross Burned at Poitier Home," *New York Post*, June 21, 1966.

16. AI with Jewison.

17. Letter written by Walter Reade Jr. in advertisement, *New York Times*, July 9, 1961.

18. Bart, Peter. "Label Babel." *New York Times*, December 6, 1964.

19. Revisions to the 1930 Production Code dated December 20, 1938, and December 3, 1947.
20. Archer, Eugene. "Catholics Urge Movie Labeling." *New York Times*, December 7, 1962.
21. Canby, Vincent. "Czar of the Movie Business." *New York Times Magazine*, April 23, 1967.
22. Thompson, Thomas. "Liz in a Film Shocker." *Life*, June 10, 1966.
23. AI with Nichols.
24. Leff, "A Test of American Film Censorship," *Cinema Journal*, op. cit., p. 52. Leff's piece offers a fascinating and valuable account of the internal workings of the National Catholic Office for Motion Pictures, which rated films in the mid-1960s based on the combined input of two subgroups, the International Federation of Catholic Alumnae (IFCA)and a newly enlisted council of secular educators and businesspeople called the "Consultants." The Consultants outnumbered the IFCA members three to one. Although a majority of IFCA voters wanted *Virginia Woolf* condemned, the Consultants group, which had been assembled only in 1965, voted for the "A-IV" rating and carried the day.
25. " 'Virginia Woolf' to be Shown as a 'For Adults Only' Film." *United Press International*, May 25, 1966.
26. Leff, "A Test of American Film Censorship," *Cinema Journal*, op. cit., p. 43.
27. Jack Valenti, in *"Who's Afraid of Virginia Woolf?*: Too Shocking for Its Time," on two-disc DVD edition of *Who's Afraid of Virginia Woolf?*
28. Canby, Vincent. " 'Virginia Woolf' Given Code Seal." *New York Times*, June 11, 1966.
29. Thompson, "Raw Dialogue Challenges All the Censors," op. cit.
30. Valenti, in "Too Shocking for Its Time," op. cit.
31. Thomas, *Clown Prince of Hollywood*, op. cit., pp. 277–278.
32. *Variety*, June 20, 1966.
33. Thomas, *Clown Prince of Hollywood*, op. cit., p. 275.
34. Nichols on *Today*, July 29, 1966.
35. Adams, Val. "Mike Nichols's Career Prevents His Finishing TV Show About It." *New York Times*, June 2, 1966.
36. AI with Jewison.
37. Ibid.
38. Kramer, *It's a Mad, Mad, Mad, Mad World*, op. cit., pp. 217–219.
39. Affidavit of William Rose in *Plunkett v. Columbia*, 1973, with attached letter from Rose to Michael Zimring, July 13, 1962; also letter from Seymour Steinberg to M. Milo Mandel, July 18, 1966; Kramer Collection, UCLA.
40. Newquist, Roy. *A Special Kind of Magic* (New York: Rand McNally & Co., 1967), p. 34.
41. AI with Kramer. Rose's alcoholism is also mentioned in *Kate Remembered* by A. Scott Berg (New York: G. P. Putnam's Sons, 2003), p. 275.
42. Final draft, *Guess Who's Coming to Dinner*, February 15, 1967, Kramer Collection, UCLA.
43. Box 292, Kramer Collection, UCLA, cited in Goudsouzian.
44. Kramer, *It's A Mad, Mad, Mad, Mad World*, op cit., p. 219.
45. AI with Beatty.

CHAPTER 15

1. Author interview with Freeman.
2. Kanfer, Stefan. "The Shock of Freedom in Films." *Time*, December 8, 1967.
3. AI with Beatty.
4. AI with Benton.
5. AI with Towne.
6. AI with Solo.
7. Thomas, *Clown Prince of Hollywood*, op. cit., pp. 130–131.
8. AI with Lederer.
9. AI with Freeman.
10. AI with Beatty.
11. Ibid.
12. AI with Michea.

13. Kanfer, "The Shock of Freedom in Films," op. cit.
14. Thompson, Tommy. "Under the Gaze of the Charmer." *Life*, Apr. 26, 1968.
15. Reed, "Will the Real Warren Beatty Please Shut Up," op. cit.
16. AI with Zanuck. The screenplay that Beatty shopped around was actually 157 pages—significantly longer and more dialogue driven than the final shooting script.
17. AI with Starr.
18. AI with Picker.
19. AI with Beatty; "Warren Beatty Sues for Full Accounting on 'Bonnie & Clyde.'" *Variety*, June 9, 1971.
20. AI with Lederer.
21. Thomas, *Clown Prince of Hollywood*, op. cit., p. 184.
22. AI with Lederer.
23. AI with Beatty.
24. Letter from Geoffrey Shurlock to Jack Warner, October 13, 1966, Warner Bros. Collection, USC.
25. AI with Solo.
26. Ibid.
27. Letter from Jack Warner to Walter MacEwen, Jack Warner Collection, USC, cited in Goldstein and Finstad, op. cit.
28. Fleischer, *Just Tell Me When to Cry*, op. cit., pp. 260–261.
29. Walker, *Fatal Charm*, op. cit., pp. 332–323; and Dunne, *The Studio*, op. cit., p. 35.
30. Letter from Harold Melniker to Frank Ferguson, April 28, 1966, Jacobs Collection.
31. 20th Century-Fox budget memo for *Doctor Dolittle*, May 23, 1966, Jacobs Collection.
32. Fleischer, *Just Tell Me When to Cry*, op. cit., pp. 260–261.
33. Bardsley, Garth. *Stop the World: The Biography of Anthony Newley* (London: Oberon Books, 2003).
34. Letter from Anthony Newley to Barbra Streisand, April 6, 1966, Anthony Newley Collection.
35. Letter from Leslie Bricusse to Anthony Newley, April 20, 1966, Anthony Newley Collection.
36. "Doctor Dolittle—Second Revised Screenplay," by Leslie Bricuse, June 1966, with handwritten notes by Rex Harrison, Rex Harrison Collection, Howard Gotlieb Archival Research Center, Boston University.
37. Ibid.
38. Bricusse, quoted in *Fatal Charm*, op. cit., p. 331.
39. Telegram from Arthur Jacobs, recipient unclear, May 1966, Jacobs Collection.
40. Letter from Arthur Jacobs to Rex Harrison, April 5, 1966, Jacobs Collection.
41. Cable from Arthur Jacobs to Richard Fleischer, April 12, 1966, Jacobs Collection.
42. *Daily Telegraph*, June 21, 1966.
43. Bart, Peter. "At Last, Rex Harrison Agreed . . ." *New York Times*, June 19, 1966.
44. Ibid; "19th Century Fox." *Time*, July 8, 1966.
45. "19th Century Fox," *Time*, op. cit.
46. *Newsweek*, August 9, 1966.
47. "'Dr. Dolittle' Retreating from Britain." *Variety*, August 17, 1966.
48. Rex Harrison's biographer Alexander Walker writes in *Fatal Charm* that fifty-one out of fifty-six shooting days were marred by rain; in *The Studio*, John Gregory Dunne says it was fifty-three out of fifty-eight days.
49. AI with Eggar.
50. AI with Ray Aghayan.
51. Reed, "Will They Dig 'Dr. Dolittle'?" op. cit.
52. Harrison, *Rex*, op. cit., pp. 214–218.
53. Letter from Anthony Newley to Niels Larsen, July 6, 1966, Newley Collection.
54. Fleischer, *Just Tell Me When to Cry*, op. cit., pp. 262–263.
55. Canby, Vincent. "Now That Zanuck Is President, He Still Thinks Like a Producer." *New York Times*, July 6, 1966.
56. Letter from Arthur Jacobs to Mort Abrahams, July 28, 1966, Jacobs Collection.
57. Letter from Owen McLean to Arthur Jacobs, May 17, 1966, and memo from Jacobs to Mike Pagano, July 1, 1966, Jacobs Collection.

58. Russo, Joe, and Larry Landsman, with Edward Gross. *Planet of the Apes Revisited: The Behind-the-Scenes Story of the Classic Science Fiction Saga* (New York: Thomas Dunne/St. Martin's, 2001).

CHAPTER 16

1. Author interview with Jewison.
2. Poitier, *This Life*, op. cit., pp. 283–284.
3. Ibid.
4. AI with Jewison.
5. AI with Jewison, Stalmaster, and Wilson.
6. AI with Stalmaster, Schallert, and James.
7. AI with Stalmaster.
8. *Variety*, December 28, 1966.
9. Zion, Sidney E. "U.S. Court Voids a Loyalty Oath." *New York Times*, July 15, 1966; "Directors Guild Is Ordered to Drop Oath." *New York Times*, January 28, 1967.
10. Boaty Boatwright, quoted by Jewison, *This Terrible Business Has Been Good to Me*, op. cit., p. 133.
11. AI with Beatty.
12. AI with Benton and Penn.
13. AI with Crowley.
14. Newman, "What's It Really All About?" op. cit.
15. In Patrick Goldstein's oral history of *Bonnie and Clyde*, "Blasts from the Past" (*Los Angeles Times*, August 24, 1997), Newman is quoted as saying, "Our very first meeting with Warren, he came right out and said, 'I'm not playing a [homosexual].' He had plenty of aesthetic reasons, but he thought it would make him terribly unsympathetic to his audience."
16. AI with Penn.
17. An October 1961 amendment to the Production Code permitted "sex aberration" when treated with "care, discretion and restraint."
18. *The Celluloid Closet: Homosexuality in the Movies* by Vito Russo (New York; Harper & Row, rev. ed. copyright 1987) remains the most valuable single-volume treatment of this subject.
19. "The Homosexual in America." *Time*, January 21, 1966.
20. Gent, George. "TV: C.B.S. Reports on Homosexuals." *New York Times*, March 8, 1967.
21. Newman, "What's It Really All About?" op. cit.
22. AI with Penn.
23. AI with Beatty.
24. Ibid.
25. AI with Parsons.
26. AI with Beatty.
27. AI with Penn.
28. AI with Van Runkle.
29. AI with Parsons.
30. Ibid.
31. AI with Pollack.
32. AI with Towne.
33. AI with Beatty.
34. AI with Penn.
35. Finstad, *Warren Beatty: A Private Man*, op. cit., p. 362.
36. AI with Beatty and Penn.
37. Fonda, *My Life So Far*, op. cit., p. 171.
38. Dunaway, *Looking for Gatsby*, p. 110.
39. Ibid., pp. 111–115.
40. AI with Van Runkle.
41. Dunaway, *Looking for Gatsby*, op. cit., p. 120.
42. AI with Beatty.

43. AI with Penn.
44. Ibid.
45. AI with Beatty.
46. AI with Towne.
47. AI with Beatty.
48. AI with Penn and Towne.
49. AI with Benton.
50. AI with Van Runkle.
51. AI with Beatty.
52. AI with Towne.
53. Thompson, *Life*, April 26, 1968, op. cit.

CHAPTER 17

1. Letter from Hal Ashby to Norman Jewison, October 5, 1966, Hal Ashby papers, Margaret Herrick Library.
2. Haskell Wexler, commentary track on *In the Heat of the Night* (MGM Home Video, 2001).
3. Keller, Diane. "A Day 'In the Heat of the Night.'" *Southern Illinoisan*, October 9, 1966.
4. Letter from Meta Rebner to Hal Ashby, October 7, 1966, Ashby papers.
5. Author interview with Wilson.
6. AI with James.
7. Salary sheets and cast contact lists, Stalmaster Co., Jewison Collection, op. cit.
8. AI with Jewison and Morse.
9. Letters from Hal Ashby to Norman Jewison, September 14, September 21, September 25, September 28, October 5, and October 6, 1966. Ashby papers.
10. For more on Wilder's aversion to color cinematography, see *On Sunset Boulevard: The Life and Times of Billy Wilder* by Ed Sikov (New York: Hyperion, 1998), p. 469.
11. AI with Wilson.
12. AI with Jewison, Wilson, and Masterson.
13. Norman Jewison and Haskell Wexler, commentary track on *In the Heat of the Night*, op. cit.
14. AI with Jewison.
15. Rod Steiger, interviewed on thebigpicturedvd.com, 2001.
16. AI with Jewison.
17. AI with Morse.
18. "The Big Picture." *Los Angeles Times West Magazine*, April 7, 1968.
19. AI with Jewison.
20. Poitier, *The Measure of a Man*, op. cit.
21. Steiger, commentary track on *In the Heat of the Night*, op. cit.
22. Poitier, *This Life*, op. cit.
23. Hutchinson, Tom. *Rod Steiger* (New York: Fromm International, 2000).
24. AI with Jewison.
25. AI with Grant.
26. AI with Schallert.
27. AI with Morse.
28. AI with Jewison.
29. Ibid.
30. Steiger, commentary track for *In the Heat of the Night*, op. cit.
31. AI with Jewison.
32. AI with Morse.
33. AI with Jewison.
34. Jewison, *This Terrible Business Has Been Good to Me*, op. cit.
35. Jester Hairston, interviewed by James Standifer, August 4, 1980, University of Michigan School of Music Archives.
36. AI with Morse.

CHAPTER 18

1. Author interviews with Karen Kramer and Katharine Houghton.
2. Newquist, *A Special Kind of Magic*, op. cit., p. 39.
3. Kramer, *A Mad, Mad, Mad, Mad World*, op. cit., pp. 222–223. Poitier also alludes to his nervousness in *This Life*.
4. AI with Karen Kramer.
5. Davidson, Bill. "Spencer Tracy." *Look*, January 30, 1962.
6. Kilgallen, Dorothy. "The Voice of Broadway: Katy Hepburn Puts Spencer Ahead of Theatre." *New York Journal-American*, September 11, 1963.
7. Davidson, *Spencer Tracy: Tragic Idol*, op. cit., pp. 103–104.
8. Swindell, Larry. *Spencer Tracy: A Biography* (New York: NAL/World, 1969).
9. Leaming, Barbara. *Katharine Hepburn* (New York: Crown, 1995), p. 508.
10. Swindell, *Spencer Tracy: A Biography*, op. cit.
11. Unpublished transcript of Roy Newquist interview with Tracy, Kramer Collection, UCLA.
12. Davidson, *Spencer Tracy: Tragic Idol*, op. cit., p. 196.
13. Leaming, *Katharine Hepburn*, op. cit, pp. 507–508.
14. Kramer, *A Mad, Mad, Mad, Mad World*, op. cit., p. 219.
15. AI with Karen Kramer.
16. Champlin, Charles. "Tracy and Hepburn to Rekindle That Old Magic." *Los Angeles Times*, September 26, 1966.
17. Davidson, *Spencer Tracy: Tragic Idol*, op. cit., p. 206.
18. AI with Karen Kramer.
19. Unpublished transcript of Roy Newquist interview with Stanley Kramer, Kramer Collection, UCLA.
20. Undated early draft, *Guess Who's Coming to Dinner*, Kramer Collection, UCLA.
21. AI with Marshall Schlom.
22. "Hepburn and Tracy Will Co-Star Again." *New York Times*, September 26, 1966.
23. Internal salary memo, Columbia Pictures, November 11, 1966, and Columbia interoffice memo from Seymour Steinberg to M. Milo Mandel, Nov. 22, 1966, William Gordon Collection, Margaret Herrick Library.
24. Deposition by Stanley Kramer in *Joseph Than and Elick Moll v. Columbia Pictures Corporation*, November 20, 1969, Kramer Collection, UCLA.
25. Canby, Vincent. "Appeal by 'Alfie' Wins a Movie Code Certificate; Review Panel Votes to Waive Ban Against Mention of Abortion in Pictures." *New York Times*, August 3, 1966.
26. ———. "A New Movie Code Ends Some Taboos." *New York Times*, September 21, 1966.
27. Production Code Files, *Guess Who's Coming to Dinner* correspondence and "Analysis of Film Content," dated February 20, March 7, and March 16, 1967, Margaret Herrick Library.
28. "The Code of Self-Regulation: Standards for Production," reprinted in Steinberg, *Reel Facts*, op. cit., p. 406.
29. Canby, "A New Movie Code Ends Some Taboos," op. cit.
30. AI with Henry.
31. Nichols, commentary track on *Who's Afraid of Virginia Woolf?*, op. cit.
32. Lambert, Gavin. *Natalie Wood: A Life* (New York: Alfred A. Knopf, 2004), p. 224.
33. AI with Nichols.
34. Olsen, Mark. "Francois Ozon, Always a Leading Ladies' Man." *Los Angeles Times*, July 30, 2006.
35. AI with Nichols.
36. AI with Turman.
37. Neal, Patricia. *As I Am* (New York: Simon & Schuster, 1988), p. 290.
38. AI with Nichols.
39. Ibid.
40. "Debonair Rex Now a Celebrated Doctor." *Life*, September 30, 1966.
41. AI with Trundy; get-well cards and cables from Elizabeth Taylor and Richard Burton, Darryl Zanuck, Richard Zanuck, Anthony Newley, and Leslie Bricusse, Jacobs Collection.

42. AI with Trundy.
43. Memo from Arthur Jacobs to Pat Newcomb, November 16, 1966, Jacobs Collection.
44. AI with Trundy.
45. AI with Reiss.
46. AI with Eggar.
47. Bart, Peter. "He Grew Accustomed to Rex." *New York Times*, October 2, 1966.
48. 20th Century-Fox memo from Stan Hough to Jack Smith, September 6, 1966, Jacobs Collection.
49. Cable from William Eckhardt to Stan Hough, October 24, 1966, Jacobs Collection.
50. Bricusse, *The Music Man,* op. cit., p. 189.
51. AI with Eggar.
52. Fleischer, in Bardsley, *Stop the World,* op. cit.
53. AI with Holder.
54. AI with Eggar.
55. AI with Abrahams.
56. AI with Holder and Eggar.
57. Fleischer, *Just Tell Me When to Cry,* op. cit., pp. 262–263.
58. Walker, *Fatal Charm,* op. cit., pp. 334–335.
59. Cable, recipient unknown, November 21, 1966, Jacobs Collection.
60. Cable from Joan Collins to Anthony Newley, November 25, 1966, Newley Collection.
61. Cable from Arthur Jacobs to Anthony Newley, November 26, 1966, Newley Collection.
62. AI with Abrahams.
63. Memo from Arthur Jacobs to Mort Abrahams, November 22, 1966, Jacobs Collection.
64. Letter from Leslie Bricusse to Anthony Newley, November 24, 1966, Newley Collection.
65. Bricusse, *The Music Man,* op. cit., p. 190.
66. Letter from Leslie Bricusse to Arthur Jacobs, November 25, 1966, Jacobs Collection.
67. Undated, by Leslie Bricusse, Jacobs Collection.

CHAPTER 19

1. This chapter's account of the production of *Bonnie and Clyde* comes from interviews with Warren Beatty, John C. Dutton, Morgan Fairchild, Elaine Michea, Estelle Parsons, Arthur Penn, Michael J. Pollard, Robert Solo, Dean Tavoularis, Robert Towne, and Theadora Van Runkle, among others.
2. Advertisement, *Denton Record-Chronicle,* 1966 undated, Warner Bros. Collection, USC.
3. Author interview with Parsons.
4. Towne, Robert. "A Trip with Bonnie and Clyde." *Cinema,* III, no. 5.
5. AI with Towne.
6. AI with Beatty.
7. Ibid.
8. AI with Parsons.
9. AI with Dutton.
10. Beatty, to Curtis Hanson in Wake and Hayden, *The Bonnie and Clyde Book,* op. cit., p. 180.
11. Ibid., p. 179.
12. AI with Tavoularis.
13. AI with Beatty, Dutton, Penn, and Tavoularis.
14. AI with Penn and Towne.
15. Hebron, Sandra. "Curtis Hanson (part 2)." *Guardian,* November 16, 2002.
16. AI with Penn.
17. Dunaway, *Looking for Gatsby,* op. cit., p. 58.
18. AI with Van Runkle.
19. AI with Dutton and Michea.
20. "Faye Dunaway: Frank Words from a Cult Goddess," *Interview,* November 2002.
21. Dunaway, *Looking for Gatsby,* op. cit., pp. 131–133.
22. AI with Parsons.

23. Dunaway, *Looking for Gatsby*, op. cit., pp. 118–119.
24. Finstad, *Warren Beatty: A Private Man*, op. cit., p. 372.
25. AI with Penn.
26. AI with Tavoularis.
27. AI with Dutton.
28. Goldstein, "Blasts From the Past," *Los Angeles Times*, op. cit.
29. AI with Beatty.
30. AI with Towne.
31. "In the Cards." *Time*, September 30, 1966.
32. AI with Michea, Parsons, and Van Runkle.
33. AI with Pollard.
34. AI with Parsons.
35. AI with Fairchild.
36. AI with Dutton.
37. Beatty to Curtis Hanson, *The Bonnie and Clyde Book*, op. cit., p. 178.
38. AI with Towne.
39. Labarthe, Andre and Jean-Louis Comolli. "The Arthur Penn Interview." *Cahiers du Cinéma*, December 1967.
40. AI with Beatty.
41. AI with Tavoularis.
42. Ibid.
43. AI with Beatty.
44. AI with Parsons.
45. Benton and Newman's screenplay for *Bonnie and Clyde* is reprinted in its entirety in both *The Bonnie and Clyde Book* (op. cit.) and *Best American Screenplays: First Series*, edited by Sam Thomas (New York: Crown, 1986).
46. AI with Penn.
47. Ibid.
48. Gilman, Richard. "Gangsters on the Road to Nowhere." *The New Republic*, November 4, 1967.
49. Goldstein, "Blasts from the Past," *Los Angeles Times*, op. cit.
50. "The Arthur Penn Interview," *Cahiers du Cinéma*, op. cit.
51. Crowdus, "The Importance of a Singular, Guiding Vision," *Cineaste*, op. cit.
52. Letter from Floria Lasky to "HWF," October 12, 1966, Warner Bros. Collection, USC.
53. AI with Pollard.
54. AI with Tavoularis.
55. AI with Dutton. Daily production and progress reports from *Bonnie and Clyde* show that the production had fallen fourteen days behind schedule by December 10, the last day of the shoot in Texas; Warner Bros. Collection, USC.
56. Letter from Walter MacEwen to Warren Beatty, November 2, 1966, Warner Bros. Collection, USC.
57. Telegram from Jack Warner to Arthur Penn, October 12, 1966, Warner Bros. Collection, USC.
58. AI with Solo.
59. AI with Penn.
60. Thompson, "Under the Gaze of the Charmer," *Life*, op. cit.
61. AI with Penn.

CHAPTER 20

1. Letter from Geoffrey M. Shurlock to Robert Vogel, March 30, 1966, MPAA file, Margaret Herrick Library.
2. Ibid., April 27, 1966.
3. Ibid., July 19, 1966.
4. Ibid., April 27, 1966.
5. Gold, Ronald. "Valenti Won't 'Blow-Up' Prod. Code for Status Films." *Variety*, January 11, 1967.
6. Various memos, November 1967, MPAA file, Margaret Herrick Library. A November 9, 1966,

memo from Sidney Schreiber to Ben Melniker indicates that MGM actually solicited advice from the Code office about the viability of releasing the movie under a subsidiary company without a seal.

7. "Approval Denied to Antonioni Film." *New York Times*, December 17, 1966.
8. "M-G-M's Leo the Lion Is Cast as a 'Mod' Type." *New York Times*, September 20, 1966.
9. *Variety*, December 21, 1966.
10. Kauffmann, Stanley. "Some Notes on a Year with Blow-Up." In *Film* 67/68, op. cit., pp. 274–281.
11. Reed, Rex. "Antonioni: After the 'Blow-Up,' a Close-Up." *New York Times*, January 1, 1967.
12. Crowther, Bosley. "In the Eye of the Beholder." *New York Times*, January 8, 1967.
13. Sloane, Leonard. "7 Arts to Buy 33% of Warner." *New York Times*, November 15, 1966.
14. "United Artists' Sale Backed in Principle." *New York Times*, November 21, 1966.
15. Canby, Vincent. " 'Blow-Up' May Get New Code Review." *New York Times*, February 7, 1967.
16. *Variety*, February 15, 1967.
17. Ibid., March 1, 1967.
18. Crowther, Bosley. "The Ten Best Films of 1966." *New York Times*, December 25, 1966.
19. Author interview with Turman and Nichols; Turman, *So You Want to Be a Producer*, op. cit.
20. AI with Wilson.
21. AI with Jewison. In his autobiography, Jewison appears to misplace the conversation with Kennedy at the end of 1965 rather than at the end of 1966.
22. Weiler, A. H. "Success Spangled Simon" (third item, headed "Harlem Whodunits"). *New York Times*, December 4, 1966; a September 26, 1966, memo from Hal Ashby to Norman Jewison (Hal Ashby files, Margaret Herrick Library) indicates that the possibility of a movie series based on Himes's books was a matter of mild concern to both men.
23. Memo from Ashby to Jewison, September 14, 1966, Ashby Collection, Margaret Herrick Library, op. cit.
24. Useful background on Coppola's early career can be found in *Godfather: The Intimate Francis Ford Coppola* by Gene D. Phillips (Lexington: University Press of Kentucky, 2004) and *Francis Ford Coppola: Interviews*, edited by Phillips (Jackson: University Press of Mississippi, 2004).
25. Alpert, Hollis. "Off the Hook." In *Film* 67/68, op. cit., p. 111–112.
26. Turman, *So You Want to Be a Producer*, op. cit.
27. Bart, Peter. "Mike Nichols, Moviemaniac." *New York Times*, January 1, 1967.
28. "Most Fans Think Antonioni Is a Cheese—Levine." *Variety*, May 24, 1967.
29. AI with Turman.
30. Bart, "Mike Nichols, Moviemaniac," op. cit.
31. "Manhunt Is On for 'Graduate.'" *New York Post*, January 17, 1967; and "New York Sound Track." *Variety*, January 18, 1967.
32. AI with Hirshan.
33. AI with Nichols.
34. AI with Turman.
35. Day, Barry. "It Depends On How You Look at It." *Films and Filming* (November 1968).
36. AI with Nichols.
37. AI with Henry.
38. AI with Hoffman.
39. Fremont-Smith, Eliot. "Theater: What's That?" *New York Times*, October 18, 1966.
40. Kerr, Walter. "The Theater Looks at Our Times: 'Eh?'—No Security for Us?" *New York Times*, November 6, 1966.
41. AI with Hoffman.
42. Rambeau, Marc. " 'The Graduates' Undergraduate." *Los Angeles Times*, August 13, 1967.
43. Zeitlin, David. "A Homely Non-Hero, Dustin Hoffman, Gets an Unlikely Role in Mike Nichols' 'The Graduate.'" *Life*, November 24, 1967.
44. Ibid.
45. AI with Nichols.
46. AI with Hoffman.
47. O'Steen, *Cut to the Chase*, op. cit.

48. AI with Nichols.
49. AI with Henry.
50. Hoffman eventually told the story of the moment Nichols gave him the part to Neil Simon, who took the notion of an actor's success breaking up a relationship and, ten years later, turned it into the screenplay *The Goodbye Girl*.
51. AI with Hoffman.
52. "Dialogue on Film: Joseph E. Levine." *American Film* (September 1979).
53. AI with Hoffman.

CHAPTER 21

1. Newquist, *A Special Kind of Magic*, op. cit., p. 93.
2. Poitier, *The Measure of a Man*, op. cit., p. 121.
3. Author interview with Katharine Houghton, Karen Kramer, and Marshall Schlom.
4. Poitier, *The Measure of a Man*, op. cit., p. 122.
5. Newquist, *A Special Kind of Magic*, op. cit., p. 93.
6. Poitier, *This Life*, op. cit., pp. 285–286.
7. Newquist, *A Special Kind of Magic*, op. cit., p. 92.
8. Hernton, Calvin. *White Papers for White Americans* (New York: Doubleday, 1966), p. 64.
9. Prelutsky, Bert. "Hollywood's Negroes Mired in Stereotypes." *Los Angeles Times*, February 19, 1967.
10. AI with Houghton.
11. AI with Karen Kramer.
12. Columbia Pictures memo from Gordon Stulberg to Seymour Steinberg, January 30, 1967, *Guess Who's Coming to Dinner* production files, Margaret Herrick Library.
13. AI with Kramer and Eggar.
14. AI with Houghton.
15. Memo from Gordon Stulberg to Samuel Zagon, February 10, 1967, and memo to Zagon from Earl Kramer, March 22, 1967, Kramer Collection, UCLA.
16. Swindell, Larry. *Spencer Tracy: A Biography* (New York: NAL/World, 1969), p. 267.
17. "Location Delays, but 'Dolittle' Not Way Over-Budget." *Variety*, January 11, 1967.
18. Memo from Marjorie Fowler to Arthur Jacobs, December 15, 1966; Fox interoffice memo from Sam Beetley to Stan Hough, January 3, 1967; letter from Fowler to Jacobs, January 7, 1967, all from Jacobs Collection.
19. Walker, *No Bells on Sunday: The Rachel Roberts Journals*, op. cit.
20. AI with Trundy.
21. Walker, *Fatal Charm*, op. cit., p. 336.
22. AI with Holder.
23. Ibid.
24. Letter from Jack Schwartzman to Richard Zanuck, March 9, 1967, Jacobs Collection.
25. Fleischer, *Just Tell Me When to Cry*, op. cit., pp. 264, 270–271.
26. *Variety*, April 19, 1967,
27. "Fleischer: Other Awards Hurtful to Acad Oscars." *Variety*, April 12, 1967.
28 "20th's $11,000,000 Budget for 'Dolittle.'" *Variety*, September 13, 1967.
29. Bart, Peter. "Movies: A Sweet Young Thing." *New York Times*, July 17, 1966.
30. Davidson, Bill. "The Entertainer." *New York Times Magazine*, March 16, 1975.
31. Alpert, Hollis. "Offbeat Director in Outer Space." *New York Times Magazine*, January 16, 1966.

CHAPTER 22

1. Penn and Allen, speaking at an Academy of Motion Picture Arts and Sciences tribute to Allen in New York City, November 7, 2006.
2. Author interview with Penn.

3. Crist, Judith. *New York World Journal Tribune*, March 24, 1967.
4. *Variety*, February 15, 1967.
5. Crowther, Bosley. "The Significance of Sidney." *New York Times*, August 6, 1967.
6. AI with Jewison; also Archerd, Army. "Just for Variety." *Variety*, November 14, 1966.
7. Wexler, on commentary track for *In the Heat of the Night*, op. cit.
8. Interoffice memo from Harold J. Mirisch to Oscar Steinberg, August 23, 1967, Jewison Collection.
9. Memo from Nadine Phinney to Ashby and Jewison, January 13, 1967, Jewison Collection.
10. AI with Jewison.
11. O'Steen, *Cut to the Chase*, op. cit.
12. AI with Joel Schiller.
13. AI with Hoffman.
14. *The Graduate* by Buck Henry, *Best American Screenplays*, op. cit.
15. AI with Hoffman.
16. AI with Henry.
17. AI with Hoffman.
18. AI with Henry.
19. AI with Nichols.
20. AI with Wilson.
21. AI with Nichols.
22. AI with Wilson.
23. Rollin, Betty. "Mike Nichols: Wizard of Wit." *Look*, April 2, 1968.
24. Lester, Elenore. "Dustin's Shrinker Will Let Him Know." *New York Times*, March 12, 1967.
25. AI with Hoffman.
26. AI with Hoffman and Nichols.
27. AI with Daniels.
28. AI with Henry, Nichols, and Wilson.

CHAPTER 23

1. Author interview with Houghton.
2. AIs with Katharine Houghton, Robert C. Jones, Karen Kramer, and Marshall Schlom; also Assistant Director's Daily Production Reports, Kramer Collection, UCLA.
3. Manners, Dorothy. *Los Angeles Herald-Examiner*, March 22, 1967.
4. AI with Houghton.
5. Frook, John. "Hepburn Comes Back Big, Bringing a Niece Who Calls Her Aunt Kat." *Life*, January 7, 1968; Edwards, Anne. *A Remarkable Woman: A Biography of Katharine Hepburn* (New York: William Morrow & Co., Inc., 1985).
6. Berg, A. Scott. *Kate Remembered* (New York: G. P. Putnam's Sons, 2003).
7. Newquist, *A Special Kind of Magic*, op. cit.
8. Ibid.
9. Kramer, Stanley. "He Could Wither You with a Glance." *Life*, June 30, 1967.
10. Davidson, *Spencer Tracy: Tragic Idol*, op. cit.
11. Kramer, *A Mad, Mad, Mad, Mad World*, op. cit.
12. AI with Kramer.
13. AI with Mead.
14. Kramer, "He Could Wither You with a Glance", op. cit.
15. Hamilton, Jack. "A Last Visit with Two Undimmed Stars." *Look*, July 11, 1967.
16. Frook, "Hepburn Comes Back Big," op. cit.
17. Newquist, *A Special Kind of Magic*, op. cit., p. 62.
18. AI with Houghton.
19. Israel, Lee. "Last of the Honest-to-God Ladies." *Esquire*, November 1967.
20. Ibid.

21. Hamilton, "A Last Visit with Two Undimmed Stars," op. cit.
22. Newquist, *A Special Kind of Magic*, op. cit.
23. Hamilton, "A Last Visit with Two Undimmed Stars," op. cit.
24. Ager, Cecilia. "Katharine Hepburn: 'Come, I Want You to Meet My Niece.'" *New York Times*, June 18, 1967.
25. AI with Schlom.
26. AI with Houghton.
27. Newquist, *A Special Kind of Magic*, op. cit.
28. Salary memo, November 11, 1966, Gordon Collection, Margaret Herrick Library.
29. Handwritten note on early draft of William Rose's script, Kramer Collection.
30. Goudsouzian, *Sidney Poitier: Man, Actor, Icon*, op. cit., p. 246.
31. Salary sheets and cast contact lists, Stalmaster Co., Jewison Collection, op. cit.
32. The quotations from Richards, Davis, and Silvera, and valuable background on Richards's life and career, come from the documentary *Beah: A Black Woman Speaks*, produced by Neda Armian, Jonathan Demme, LisaGay Hamilton, and Joe Viola and written and directed by Hamilton (Clinica Estetico, Ltd., and LisaGay, Inc., copyright 2003).
33. AI with Houghton.
34. Assistant Director's Daily Production Reports, Kramer Collection, UCLA.
35. Letter from George Glass to Roy Newquist, May 10, 1967, Kramer Collection, UCLA.
36. AI with Schlom.
37. Letter from Geoffrey Shurlock to Mike Frankovich, February 20, 1967, Production Code Files, Margaret Herrick Library.
38. Poitier, *This Life*, op. cit., pp. 286–287.
39. AI with Jones, Karen Kramer, and Schlom.
40. Kanin, Garson. "Tracy: He Did His Job Before He Died." *New York Times*, June 25, 1967.
41. Final draft, *Guess Who's Coming to Dinner*, February 15, 1967, Kramer Collection, UCLA.
42. Kramer, in *Conversations with the Great Moviemakers of Hollywood's Golden Age at the American Film Institute*, op. cit., p. 572.
43. AI with Jones.
44. Assistant Director's Daily Production Reports, Kramer Collection, UCLA.
45. Kramer, *A Mad, Mad, Mad, Mad World*, op. cit., pp. 227–228; AI with Karen Kramer and Schlom.
46. Swindell, *Spencer Tracy: A Biography*, op. cit., p. 271.
47. AI with Kramer; also Kanin, "Tracy: He Did His Job Before He Died", op. cit.

CHAPTER 24

1. Author interview with Daniels.
2. AI with Hoffman.
3. The four-line exchange between Hoffman and Nichols comes from Zeitlin, "A Homely Non-Hero . . . ," *Life*, op. cit.
4. Williams, Michael. "Tales of Hoffman in 'The Graduate.'" *Los Angeles Times*, December 31, 1967.
5. AI with Hoffman.
6. AI with Nichols.
7. AI with Henry.
8. AI with Schiller.
9. Day, Barry, "It Depends on How You Look at It." *Films and Filming*, November 1968.
10. *The Graduate* by Buck Henry and Calder Willingham, in *Best American Screenplays*, op. cit.
11. AI with Nichols.
12. Ibid.
13. Ibid.
14. AI with Henry.
15. AI with Schiller.
16. AI with Nichols.

17. Brackman, Jacob. "Onward and Upward with the Arts: 'The Graduate.' " *The New Yorker*, July 27, 1968.
18. AI with Nichols.
19. AI with Hoffman.
20. Ross, in "The Graduate at 25." Produced by New Line Home Video, interviewer and creative consultant Craig Modderno (New Line Home Video, available on MGM Home Entertainment's 1999 DVD of *The Graduate*, copyright 1992).
21. O'Steen, *Cut to the Chase*, op. cit.
22. Ibid.
23. AI with Wilson.
24. AI with Nichols.
25. AI with Hoffman.
26. Ibid.
27. O'Steen, *Cut to the Chase*, op. cit.
28. AI with Wilson.
29. Lahr, John. "Profiles: Making It Real—How Mike Nichols Re-Created Comedy and Himself." *The New Yorker*, February 21 and 28, 2000.
30. AI with Nichols.
31. Ibid.
32. Lahr, "Profiles: Making It Real," op. cit.
33. AI with Hoffman.
34. AI with Nichols.

CHAPTER 25

1. Swindell, *Spencer Tracy: A Biography*, op. cit.
2. Davidson, *Spencer Tracy: Tragic Idol*, op. cit., p. 213.
3. Hepburn, Katharine. *Me: Stories of My Life* (New York: Ballantine, 1991); and Barbara Leaming, *Katharine Hepburn*, op. cit.
4. Author interview with Kramer.
5. "Spencer Tracy's Funeral Attended by 600 on Coast." *United Press International*, June 12, 1967.
6. AI with Kramer.
7. "Spencer Tracy Dies at Age of 67; A Hollywood Star for 37 Years." *New York Times*, June 11, 1967.
8. "Time to Retire." *Time*, March 31, 1967.
9. Gill, Brendan. "The Current Cinema: Triumphs and Defeats." *The New Yorker*, March 25, 1967.
10. Crowther, Bosley. "How Hath the Mighty?" *New York Times*, March 26, 1967.
11. Benton and Newman, "The New Sentimentality," op. cit.
12. *Loving Et Ux. v. Virginia*, 388 U.S. 1, Decided June 12, 1967.
13. AI with Solo.
14. AI with Lederer.
15. AI with Solo.
16. Memo from Jack Warner to Walter MacEwen, March 9, 1967, and telegram from MacEwen to Warren Beatty, April 5, 1967, Warner Bros. Collection, USC.
17. Memo from Jack Warner to Walter MacEwen, May 15, 1967, Warner Bros. Collection, USC.
18. Ibid., April 14, 1967.
19. Letter from Walter MacEwen to Warren Beatty, November 2, 1966; memo from Peter Knecht to Walter MacEwen, May 31, 1967; memo from Walter MacEwen to Benjamin Kalmenson, May 31, 1967; telegram from Warren Beatty to Walter MacEwen, undated; and handwritten notes by Walter MacEwen, also undated, all from Warner Bros. Collection, USC.
20. AI with Ganis.
21. "Jack L. Warner Rolls 'Finian's Rainbow'; He 'Starts Another Decade.' " *Variety*, June 28, 1967.
22. "World-Famous 'Warner Bros.' Name to Be Retained After 7A Merger; Jack L. Goes on Pro-

ducing." *Variety*, June 7, 1967; Francis Coppola's commentary track on *Finian's Rainbow* DVD (copyright 2005, Warner Bros. Entertainment Inc.).

23. AI with Penn.

24. Penn, "Making Waves," op. cit.

25. AI with Penn.

26. AI with Beatty; Goldstein, "Blasts from the Past," op. cit.

27. Gilliatt, Penelope. "The Current Cinema: The All-Right World." *The New Yorker*, June 17, 1967.

28. Alpert, Hollis. "The Admirable Sidney." *Saturday Review*, July 8, 1967.

29. "Poitier Redhot in TV Ratings." *Variety*, April 19, 1967.

30. Barthel, "He Doesn't Want to Be Sexless Sidney," op. cit.

31. "ABC Makes Feature Deals with David, Nelson, Maybe Poitier." *Variety*, June 14, 1967.

32. United Artists Pressbook for *In the Heat of the Night*, Jewison Collection, Wisconsin Center for Film and Theater Research.

33. Letter from Norman Jewison to Fred Goldberg, Jewison Collection.

34. Ken Hughes, quoted in *The Life and Death of Peter Sellers* (New York: Applause Books, 1997) by Roger Lewis, p. 205.

35. Woody Allen, quoted in *Woody Allen: A Biography* (Da Capo, 1991) by Eric Lax, pp. 222–223.

36. Wolf Mankowitz, quoted in *Orson Welles: A Biography* (New York: Crown, 1995) by Barbara Leaming, pp. 570–573.

37. "006 3/4." *Time*, June 30, 1967.

38. Bart, Peter. "Sean Connery Vows He's No Fan of James Bond's." *New York Times*, November 16, 1965.

39. Miller, Eugene L, Jr., and Edwin T. Arnold, eds. *Robert Aldrich Interviews* (Jackson: University Press of Mississippi, 2004), p. 50. Originally printed in *Sight and Sound* (Winter 1968–1969).

40. Silver, Alain, and James Ursini, *What Ever Happened to Robert Aldrich: His Life and His Films* (New York: Limelight, 1995).

41. Miller and Arnold, *Robert Aldrich Interviews*, op. cit., p. 104. Originally printed in *Movie* (Winter 1976–1977).

42. Branch, Taylor, *At Canaan's Edge: America in the King Years 1965–68* (New York: Simon & Schuster, 2006), p. 607.

43. Ibid., pp. 632–633.

44. *Time*, August 3, 1967.

45. Archival footage from *American Masters: Sidney Poitier—One Bright Light*. Directed by Lee Grant, written by Prudence Glass, produced by Mary Beth Yarrow and Glass (a production of Thirteen/WNET in association with Joseph Feury Productions, copyright 1999).

46. Lee Grant, on commentary track for *In the Heat of the Night*, op. cit.

47. Landry, Robert J. "Poitier: Negro Image-Maker—His 'Know How' over Rednecks." *Variety*, July 26, 1967.

48. Robinson, Barry. "Press Junketing with Poitier and Steiger." *Asbury Park Evening Press*, July 3, 1966.

49. Crowther, Bosley. "Screen: 'In the Heat of the Night,' A Racial Drama." *New York Times*, August 3, 1967.

50. "A Kind of Love." *Time*, August 11, 1967.

51. Schickel, Richard. "Two Pros in a Super Sleeper." *Life*, July 28, 1967.

52. Kael, Pauline. "Trash, Art, and the Movies." *Harper's* (February 1969).

53. Sarris, Andrew. "The Inoffensive Hero." In *Film 67/68*, op. cit., pp. 214–215. Originally printed in *The Village Voice*.

54. Gilliatt, Penelope. "The Current Cinema: Heated Bandwagon." *The New Yorker*, August 5, 1967.

55. Mordden, Ethan. *Medium Cool: The Movies of the 1960s* (New York: Alfred A. Knopf, 1990), p. 158.

56. Sheed, Wilfrid. "The Movie South." In *Film 67/68*, op. cit., p. 220. Originally printed in *Esquire*.

57. "In the Heat of the Night." *New York Daily News*, August 3, 1967.
58. Morgenstern, Joseph. "Red-neck and Scapegoat." *Newsweek*, August 14, 1967.
59. Jewison Papers.
60. Sarris, "The Inoffensive Hero," op. cit.
61. Ewers, Carolyn H. *Sidney Poitier: The Long Journey* (New York: Signet/New American Library, 1969).
62. Steiger, on *Larry King Live*, CNN, rebroadcast July 14, 2002.
63. AI with James.
64. Adler, Renata. "The Negro That Movies Overlook." *New York Times*, March 3, 1968.

CHAPTER 26

1. Penn, Arthur. "Bonnie and Clyde: Private Integrity and Public Violence—From questions at a Press Conference in Montreal 1967." In *The Bonnie and Clyde Book*, op. cit.
2. Author interview with Penn.
3. Crowther, Bosley. "Shoot-Em-Up Film Opens World Fete; 'Bonnie and Clyde' Cheered by Montreal First-Nighters," *New York Times*, August 7, 1967.
4. ———. "Screen: 8th Montreal Event Projects Weak Image." *New York Times*, August 11, 1967.
5. ———. "Screen: 'Bonnie and Clyde' Arrives." *New York Times*, August 14, 1967.
6. Crowther, cited in *Bosley Crowther: Social Critic of the Film* by Frank Eugene Beaver (New York: Arno Press, 1974), pp. 138–139.
7. Crowther, Bosley. "Screen: Brutal Tale of 12 Angry Men." *New York Times*, June 16, 1967.
8. "Don't Watch This Part, Honey—I'll Tell You When It's Over." *Esquire*, July 1967.
9. Crowther, Bosley. "Screen: 'For Few Dollars More' Opens." *New York Times*, July 4, 1967.
10. ———. "Movies to Kill People By." *New York Times*, July 9, 1967.
11. ———. "Reenacted Slaughter." *New York Times*, July 27, 1967.
12. Steele, Robert. "The Good-Bad and Bad-Good in Movies: *Bonnie and Clyde* and *In Cold Blood*." *Catholic World*, May 1968.
13. AI with Morgenstern.
14. "Low-Down Hoedown." *Time*, August 25, 1967.
15. Sarris, Andrew. *Bonnie and Clyde* review. *Village Voice*, August 24, 1967.
16. AI with Benton.
17. AI with Morgenstern.
18. Morgenstern, Joseph. "Ugly." In *Film 67/68*, op. cit., pp. 25–26.
19. AI with Morgenstern.
20. Ibid.
21. Morgenstern, "A Thin Red Line," in *Film 67/68*, op. cit., pp. 26–28.
22. AI with Morgenstern.
23. AI with Benton.
24. *Catholic Film Newsletter*, September 7, 1967.
25. AI with Gelb.
26. "Crowther, Please Stay Home." *Variety*, December 21, 1966.
27. Sarris, Andrew. "Humpty-Dumpty from Wisconsin." *Village Voice*, reprinted in *Film 67/68*, op. cit., pp. 72–73.
28. AI with Sarris.
29. Gillatt, Penelope. "The Current Cinema: The Party." *The New Yorker*, August 19, 1967.
30. Sarris, *Bonnie and Clyde* review, op. cit.
31. Gold, Ronald. "Crowther's 'Bonnie'-Brook." *Variety*, August 30, 1967.
32. Beaver, *Bosley Crowther: Social Critic of the Film*, op. cit.
33. "Movie Mailbag." *New York Times*, August 27, 1967.
34. Crowther, Bosley. "Run, Bonnie and Clyde." *New York Times*, September 3, 1967.
35. AI with Benton.
36. Kael, Pauline. "Movies on Television." *The New Yorker*, June 3, 1967.

37. ———. Introduction to *For Keeps: 30 Years at the Movies* (New York: Dutton, 1994).

38. ———. "Circles and Squares", *Film Quarterly*, 1963. The piece was a direct response to Sarris's "Notes on the Auteur Theory in 1962."

39. All quotations in this paragraph and the next are from Kael's *Bonnie and Clyde* review, *The New Yorker*, October 21, 1967.

40. Menand, Louis. "Onward and Upward with the Arts: Paris, Texas." *The New Yorker*, February 17 and 24, 2003.

41. Information on *Bonnie and Clyde*'s weekly box office performance and Kansas City/Omaha run comes from *Variety*, August 23, August 30, September 6, September 13, September 20, September 27, October 4, and October 11, 1967.

42. "September as Sidney Poitier Month; His 'Heat' and 'Love' Rate One, Two, Longruns Otherwise Dominant." *Variety*, October 4, 1967.

43. United Artists Inter-Office Memorandum to Norman Jewison, May 22, 1968, with attachment "Daily Accumulated Gross Receipts," Jewison Collection.

44. *Variety*, November 8, 1967.

45. Canby, Vincent. "Poitier, as Matinee Idol, Is Handsomely Rewarded." *New York Times*, November 18, 1967.

46. Mason, Clifford. "Why Does White America Love Sidney Poitier So?" *New York Times*, September 10, 1967.

47. Poitier, *This Life*, op cit., p. 336. In Poitier's two autobiographies, he misplaces the Mason article as appearing in 1969 (in *This Life*) or the early 1970s (*The Measure of a Man*) and mistakenly says it included an attack on *Guess Who's Coming to Dinner*.

48. Hoffman, William. *Sidney* (New York: Lyle Stuart, 1971), pp. 8–9.

49. AI with Houghton.

50. AI with Mason.

51. Hoffman, *Sidney*, op. cit., pp. 8–9.

52. Johnson, Pete. "Harry Belafonte—No Bargain with the Devil." *Los Angeles Times*, August 23, 1967.

53. Gold, Ronald S. "While He's Sole U.S. Negro Star Seen Regularly, Sidney Poitier Expects to Play Only Heroes." *Variety*, October 4, 1967.

54. "Brock Peters on Negro Skepticism; One Colored Star Hardly a Trend." *Variety*, December 20, 1967.

55. Canby, "Poitier, as Matinee Idol, Is Handsomely Rewarded," op. cit.

56. Poitier, *The Measure of a Man*, op. cit., p. 119.

CHAPTER 27

1. Author interview with Zanuck.

2. John Gregory Dunne, *The Studio*, op. cit.

3. Ibid.

4. Ibid.

5. Ibid.

6. Minneapolis preview results, Box 17, Jacobs Collection.

7. AI with Zanuck.

8. Ibid.

9. Letter from Richard Fleischer to Rex Harrison, September 25, 1967, Jacobs Collection.

10. Cable from Rex Harrison to Richard Zanuck, October 31, 1967, Jacobs Collection.

11. Cable from Richard Zanuck to Rex Harrison, undated, Jacobs Collection.

12. Cable from Rex Harrison to Richard Zanuck, undated, Jacobs Collection.

13. San Jose and San Francisco preview results, October 27, 1967, Jacobs Collection.

14. Cable from Rex Harrison to Richard Zanuck, November 10, 1967, Jacobs Collection.

15. Cable from Darryl F. Zanuck to Richard Zanuck, November 9, 1967, Jacobs Collection.

16. Crowther, Bosley. "Screen: 'Camelot' Arrives at Warner." *New York Times*, October 26, 1967.

17. "The Castle That Never Was." *Time*, November 3, 1967.

18. AI with Zanuck.

19. "Helen Winston in $4 1/2-Mil. Suit vs. 20th's 'Dolittle.'" *The Film Daily*, October 3, 1967.

20. Screenplay by Larry Watkin for Helen Winston Productions, Aug. 13, 1962, Jacobs Collection.

21. AI with Lofting.

22. Dunne, *The Studio*, op. cit.

23. Publicity and promotion notes, undated, Jacobs Collection.

24. AI with Nichols.

25. Ibid.

26. AI with Hirshan.

27. AI with Nichols.

28. Greenfeld, Josh. "For Simon and Garfunkel, All Is Groovy." *New York Times Magazine*, October 13, 1968.

29. AI with Henry.

30. AI with Nichols.

31. Ibid.

32. Canby, Vincent. "Filmmakers Show Less Fear of Catholic Office." *New York Times*, October 13, 1967.

33. ———. "A Growing Issue: Nudity in Movies." *New York Times*, April 20, 1967.

34. AI with Hirshan.

35. AI with Hoffman.

36. Frederick, Robert B. "'68: Levine's Year for Action." *Variety*, September 6, 1967.

37. AI with Nichols.

38. AI with Hanley, Henry, Nelson, and Turman.

39. AI with Daniels, Nichols, and Wilson.

40. AI with Henry.

41. Sullivan, Dan. "Newfound Stardom Worries Dustin Hoffman." *New York Times*, December 30, 1967.

42. AI with Hoffman.

43. *New York Daily News*, December 6, 1967.

44. The Graduate Supper Dance Seating Listing, *The Graduate* file, New York Public Library for the Performing Arts.

45. AI with Hoffman.

CHAPTER 28

1. Walters, Barbara. *How to Talk with Practically Anybody About Practically Anything* (New York: Doubleday, 1970), pp. 194–195.

2. Memo from Walter MacEwen Collection, Warner Bros. Collection, USC.

3. Thompson, "Under the Gaze of the Charmer," *Life*, op. cit.

4. Author interview with Beatty, Lederer, and Penn.

5. Gold, Ronald. "Kalmenson Outside Inside; Close to Jack L., but Not to W7." *Variety*, December 6, 1967.

6. "Dick Lederer to Reorg W7 Ad-Pub." *Variety*, November 1, 1967.

7. *Variety*, November 8, 1967.

8. AI with Penn.

9. "250 Tinted Prints Pulled as W7 Reverses Huston Re 'Eye.'" *Variety*, December 13, 1967; also Morris, Oswald, with Geoffrey Bull. *Huston, We Have a Problem: A Kaleidoscope of Filmmaking Memories* (Lanham, MD: Scarecrow Press, 2006), pp. 116–117.

10. Letter from David Foster of Allen Foster Ingersoll & Weber to Norman Jewison, December 14, 1967, Jewison Collection.

11. Morris, Bernadine. "Seventh Ave. Turns Soft at the Thought of Spring." *New York Times*, November 3, 1967; and "Hats On." *Time*, November 3, 1967.

12. Jacobs, Jay. "Bloody Murder." *The Reporter*, October 5, 1967.

13. Kanfer, Stefan. "The Shock of Freedom in Films." *Time*, December 8, 1967.

14. AI with Beatty, Lederer, and Penn.

15. Crowther, Bosley. "Style and the Filmic Message." *New York Times*, November 12, 1967.
16. AI with Gelb.
17. Hoberman, J. *The Dream Life; Movies, Media, and the Mythology of the Sixties* (New York: New Press, 2003), pp. 172–173.
18. "A Marriage of Enlightenment (Mr. & Mrs. Guy Smith/An Interracial Wedding)." *Time*, September 29, 1967.
19. Letters. *Time*, October 6, 1967.
20. Kennedy, Randall. "*Loving v. Virginia* at Thirty." February 6, 1997, http://speakout.com/activism/opinions/3208-1.html.
21. Hoffman, William. *Sidney* (New York: Lyle Stuart, 1971), pp. 9–10.
22. Schickel, Richard. "Sorry Stage for Tracy's Last Bow." *Life*, December 15, 1967.
23. Sarris, quoted in *Stanley Kramer: Film Maker* by Donald Spoto (New York: G. P. Putnam's Sons, 1978), p. 280.
24. Gill, Brendan. "The Current Cinema." *The New Yorker*, December 16, 1967.
25. Morgenstern, Joseph. "Spence and Supergirl." *Newsweek*, December 25, 1967.
26. *Variety*, December 6, 1967.
27. Winsten, Archer. " 'Guess Who's Coming' Bows Here." *New York Post*, December 12, 1967.
28. Crowther, Bosley. "Screen: 'Guess Who's Coming to Dinner' Arrives." *New York Times*, December 11, 1967.
29. Champlin, Charles. "Movie Reviews: 'Dinner,' 'Cold Blood' to Bow", *Los Angeles Times*.
30. *The Nation*, January 1, 1968.
31. Greeley, Andrew M. "Black and White Minstrels." *The Reporter*, March 21, 1968.
32. Kotlowitz, Robert. "Films: The Bigger They Come." *Harper's* (January 1968).
33. Knight, Arthur. "The Now Look." *Saturday Review*, December 16, 1967.
34. Beaupre, Lee. "One-Third Film Public: Negro." *Variety*, November 29, 1967.
35. *Variety*, December 6, 1967.
36. *Beah: A Black Woman Speaks*, op. cit.
37. Goudsouzian, *Sidney Poitier: Man, Actor, Icon*, op. cit., p. 287.
38. Hough, Hugh. "Poitier Film in Chicago Faced a Klan Gassing." *New York Post*, March 11, 1968.
39. Kauffmann, Stanley. Review of *Guess Who's Coming to Dinner. The New Republic*, December 2, 1967.
40. Sheed, Wilfrid. *Esquire*, date unavailable.
41. Harris, cited in *The Studio*, op. cit., p. 246.
42. Richard Burton's diary, June 1 and 4, 1967, quoted in *Rich: The Life of Richard Burton* by Melvyn Bragg (London: Hodder & Stoughton, 1988), pp. 239–240.
43. Invitation list for the Los Angeles premiere of *Doctor Dolittle*, Jacobs Collection.
44. Dunne, *The Studio*, op. cit., pp. 240–241.
45. *Variety*, December 20, 1967.
46. Winsten, Archer. " 'Dr. Dolittle' Opens at Loew's State." *New York Post*, December 20, 1967.
47. Crowther, Bosley. "Screen: That Grand Zoomanitarian, 'Doctor Dolittle,' Arrives For the Holidays on a Great Pink Snail." *New York Times,* December 20, 1967.
48. "Dr. Dolittle." *Time*, December 29, 1967.
49. Morgenstern, Joseph. *Newsweek*, date unavailable.
50. Van Gelder, Lawrence. "Racism Ascribed to Dr. Dolittle." *New York Times*, July 28, 1968.
51. Mishkin, Leo. "Rex Harrison Talks to Horses." *New York Morning Telegram*, December 20, 1968.
52. Memo from Jack Hirschberg to Arthur Jacobs, undated, Jacobs Collection.

CHAPTER 29

1. Kael, Pauline. "Trash, Art and the Movies." *Harper's* (February 1969).
2. "The Graduate." *Time*, December 29, 1967.
3. Simon, John. "Nulla Cum Laude." *The New Leader*, February 26, 1968.
4. Crowther, Bosley. "Film: Tales Out of School." *New York Times*, December 22, 1967; and "Graduating with Honors." *New York Times*, December 31, 1967.

5. Winsten, Archer. " 'The Graduate' at Lincoln, Coronet." *New York Post*, December 23, 1967.
6. *Variety*, December 20, 1967.
7. National Catholic Office for Motion Pictures newsletter, undated, *The Graduate* file, New York Public Library for the Performing Arts.
8. Ebert, Roger. "The Graduate." *Chicago Sun-Times*, December 26, 1967.
9. Alpert, Hollis. " 'The Graduate' Makes Out." *Saturday Review*, July 6, 1968.
10. Schickel, Richard. "Fine Debut for a Square Anti-Hero." *Life*, January 19, 1968.
11. Brinkley, David. "David Brinkley's Journal: What's Wrong with *The Graduate*." *Ladies' Home Journal*, 1968 (date not available).
12. Greeley, Andrew M. "Sons and Fathers." *The Reporter*, (February 1968).
13. *Variety*, December 20, 1967, op. cit.
14. "Over-50s Vote for Oscar's 'Bests' but Film Audience 48% Under 24." *Variety*, January 24, 1968.
15. Branch, *At Canaan's Edge*, op. cit., p. 747.
16. "UA Bridges Generation Gap." *Variety*, November 15, 1967; and "W7 Stress Upon Youth." *Variety*, December 6, 1967.
17. Alpert, " 'The Graduate' Makes Out," op. cit.
18. Skolsky, Sidney. "Hollywords and Picturegraphs." *Citizen-News*, January 3, 1968.
19. Canby, Vincent. "Repertory Holds 20 Film Classics." *New York Times*, March 9, 1966.
20. Kael, "Saddle Sore." Originally published in *The New Republic*, August 1967, reprinted in *Kiss Kiss Bang Bang*, op. cit.
21. Author interview with Sarris.
22. Information on individual ballots comes from *Film 67/68*, op. cit.
23. Sontag, Susan. "Persona." *Sight and Sound* (Autumn 1967).
24. Simon, John. Originally published in *The New Leader*, reprinted in *Film 67/68*, op. cit.
25. AI with Sarris.
26. Beaupre, Lee. "A Whisker-Close Oscar Race." *Variety*, January 17, 1968.
27. AI with Zanuck.
28. Beaupre, "A Whisker-Close Oscar Race", op. cit.
29. Richard Brooks, interviewed in *Conversations with the Great Moviemakers of Hollywood's Golden Age at the American Film Institute*, op. cit.
30. Carmody, Deirdre. "Capote and Friends See 'In Cold Blood' at Quiet Screening." *New York Times*, December 13, 1967.
31. Crowther, Bosley. "Screen: Graphic Quadruple Murder." *New York Times*, December 15, 1967, and "Of Color, Crime and Punishment." *New York Times*, December 17, 1967.
32. Sarris, Andrew. "Facile Freudianism." In *Film 67/68* pp. 64–66, op. cit.
33. Colville-Andersen, Mikael. "David Newman—Conversation at Hotel Chelsea." October 1, 1998, http://zakka.dk/euroscreenwriters/articles/david_newman_536.htm.
34. AI with Jewison.
35. "RFK Hands Critics Award to Mirisch; Nichols Broadens 'Auteur' Theory; Bos Crowther's 'Bon & Clyde' Wit." *Variety*, January 31, 1968.
36. "'Good, Bad and the Ugly.' " *Variety*, January 31, 1968.
37. Jennings, Robert C. "Oscar and the Generation Gap." *Los Angeles Times West Magazine*, April 7, 1968.
38. *Esquire*, December 1967, cited in *Party of the Century: The Fabulous Story of Truman Capote and His Black and White Ball* by Deborah Davis (Hoboken, NJ: John Wiley & Sons, 2006), pp. 248–249.
39. AI with Penn.
40. AI with Zanuck.
41. Harmetz, Aljean. "How to Win an Oscar Nomination, From 'Anne' to 'Z.'" *New York Times*, April 5, 1970.
42. Letter from Charles Champlin to Richard Fleischer, March 18, 1968, Fleischer Collection, USC.
43. "Annual Wonderment in Gotham: How-Come Those Oscar Folkways?" *Variety*, February 21, 1968.
44. Jennings, "Oscar and the Generation Gap," op. cit.

45. O'Steen, *Cut to the Chase*, op. cit.
46. Telegram from Stanley Kramer to Beah Richards, Kramer Collection, UCLA.

CHAPTER 30

1. Author interviews with Beatty and Towne; advertisement for *Bonnie and Clyde* listing specific theater grosses, *Variety*, March 6, 1968.
2. Corliss, Richard. "Film Chronicle: The Graduate." *National Review*, May 7, 1968.
3. Newman, David. "What's It Really All About?" in *Arthur Penn's Bonnie and Clyde*, op. cit.
4. AI with Parsons.
5. AI with Penn.
6. Coles, Robert. *Trans-Action* (May 1968).
7. AI with Hoffman.
8. Carroll, Kathleen. "Director and Star Shine in 'The Graduate.'" *New York Daily News*, December 22, 1967.
9. "The Moonchild and the Fifth Beatle." *Time*, February 7, 1969.
10. Lester, "Dustin's Shrinker Will Let Him Know," op. cit.
11. AI with Hoffman.
12. AI with Henry.
13. AI with Hoffman.
14. Day, "It Depends on How You Look at It," op. cit.
15. Sullivan, "Newfound Stardom Worries Dustin Hoffman," op. cit.
16. AI with Hoffman.
17. Farber, Stephen, and Estelle Changas. "The Graduate." *Film Quarterly*, (Spring 1968).
18. Brackman, Jacob. "Onward and Upward with the Arts: 'The Graduate.'" *The New Yorker*, July 27, 1968.
19. AI with Henry.
20. Webb's letter in response to a *New Republic* piece written by Kauffmann is cited in Alpert, " 'The Graduate' Makes Out," op. cit.
21. AI with Webb.
22. Brackman, "Onward and Upward with the Arts: 'The Graduate,'" op. cit.
23. Windeler, Robert. "Study of Film Soaring on College Campuses." *New York Times*, April 18, 1968.
24. Steinberg, Cobbett, *Reel Facts*, op. cit., p. 344.
25. Gilmour, Clyde. "Kramer, Self-Critic, in Bearpit." *The Telegram* (Toronto), June 8, 1968.
26. Ebert, Roger. "Interview with David Newman and Jack Valenti." *Chicago Sun-Times*, May 12, 1968.
27. Kramer, Stanley. "Nine Times Across the Generation Gap: 'On The Campuses Anything Less Than the Ultimate Is a Cop-Out'." *Action!* (March–April 1968).
28. Kramer, *A Mad, Mad, Mad, Mad World*, op. cit.
29. AI with Houghton.
30. Kramer, *A Mad, Mad, Mad, Mad World*, op. cit.

CHAPTER 31

1. "Tale of Hoffman." *New York Daily News*, April 7, 1968.
2. Skolsky, Sidney. "Oscar Show Dull, Then Bombshell." *Citizen-News*, April 11, 1968.
3. Graham, Sheilah. "How to Pick Oscar Winners." *Citizen-News*, April 11, 1968.
4. Author interview with Nichols.
5. Heffernan, Harold. "A Spark for Oscar Show: Tracy Honor Seen as 'Call from Grave." *Citizen-News*, February 9, 1968.
6. Kramer, quoted in *The Record*, July 18, 1968.
7. "Catholic Accolade May Soften Coast Fears of Giving Oscar to 'Bonnie.'" *Variety*, March 13, 1968.
8. Transcript of the National Advisory Commission on Civil Disorders report, February 29, 1968.

9. Michie, Larry. "TV Advised to 'Think Black.'" *Variety*, March 6, 1968.
10. Beigel, Jerry. "Peck Tells Behind-Scenes Story of Oscarcast Postponement." *Variety*, April 11, 1968.
11. Branch, *At Canaan's Edge*, op. cit., p. 706.
12. Brescia, Matty. "Show Biz Hit Hard by Memphis Race Riot; Damage Tops $500,000." *Variety*, April 3, 1968.
13. Bal, Vidula. "The Martin Luther King Assassination." Web site article for the Museum of Broadcast Communications, undated.
14. AI with Nichols and Jewison.
15. Bona and Mason, *Inside Oscar*, op. cit., p. 408.
16. "Oscar Presentation Postponed Because of National Mourning." *New York Times*, April 7, 1968.
17. Telegram from Margaret Herrick, Stirling Silliphant Collection, UCLA.
18. Beigel, *Variety*, op. cit.
19. AI with Nichols.
20. "King's Last March." *Time*, April 19, 1968; Jewison, *This Terrible Business Has Been Good to Me*, op. cit.
21. Poitier, *This Life*, op. cit.
22. AI with Penn.
23. AI with Trundy.
24. "Fans at Awards Younger Than Usual, and Very Enthusiastic." *Variety*, April 11, 1968.
25. Archerd, Army. "Hope, Hal Kanter Deftly Tickle Oscar Risibles." *Variety*, April 11, 1968.
26. This and all quotations from the show that follow come from a viewing of *The 40th Annual Academy Awards*," courtesy of the Academy Film Archives.
27. AI with Nichols.
28. AI with Pollard.
29. AI with Penn.
30. AI with Henry.
31. AI with Hoffman.
32. AI with Ganis and Parsons.
33. Richards, from *Beah: A Black Woman Speaks*, op. cit.
34. Ashby Collection, Margaret Herrick Library.
35. Bricusse, *The Music Man*, op. cit.
36. Jewison, *This Terrible Business Has Been Good to Me*, op. cit.
37. AI with Nichols.
38. Letter from Stirling Silliphant to Mrs. Leigh Silliphant, February 27, 1968, Silliphant Collection, UCLA.
39. AI with Benton.
40. "The Big Award." *Los Angeles Times West Magazine*, April 7, 1968.
41. AI with Hoffman.
42. Edwards, Anne. *A Remarkable Woman: A Biography of Katharine Hepburn* (New York: William Morrow & Co., Inc., 1985), pp. 320, 355.
43. AI with Jewison.
44. Silliphant, interviewed in *Backstory* 3, op. cit.
45. AI with Nichols.
46. AI with Henry.
47. Telegram from Steve Sekely to Stirling Silliphant, April 10, 1968, Silliphant Collection.
48. Letter from Stirling Silliphant Jr. to Stirling Silliphant, undated, Silliphant Collection.
49. Champlin, Charles. "Katharine Hepburn, Steiger, 'Heat of Night' Win Oscars." *Los Angeles Times*, April 11, 1968.
50. AI with Benton.
51. AI with Newman.
52. Newman, David, and Robert Benton. "The Movies Will Save Themselves," *Esquire*, February 1968.

EPILOGUE

1. Interoffice memo from Norman Jewison, July 3, 1968, Jewison Collection.
2. "List of All Time Box Office Champs" and "Big Rental Films of 1968." *Variety*, January 8, 1969; and "List of All Time Box Office Champs." *Variety*, January 7, 1970.
3. Thomas, *Clown Prince of Hollywood*, op. cit., p. 300.
4. Author interview with Jewison.
5. Bloom, *Leaving a Doll's House*, op. cit.
6. Gorman, Steve. "Oscar-Winning Actor Rod Steiger Dies at Age 77." *Reuters*, July 9, 2002.
7. AI with Zanuck.
8. AI with Wilson.
9. Klemesrud, "Dustin Hoffman: From 'Graduate' to Ratso Rizzo, Super Slob," op. cit.
10. Champlin, Charles. "The Graduate's Girl Friend." *Los Angeles Times*, January 22, 1968.
11. AI with Schlom.
12. Columbia Pictures memo, April 17, 1968; Columbia Pictures memo from Phil Leonard to Stanley Kramer, January 6, 1970; and letter from Edwin E, Holly to Sam Zagon, December 17, 1971, all from Kramer Collection, UCLA.
13. AI with Houghton.
14. Crowther, Bosley. *Reruns: Fifty Memorable Films* (New York: G. P. Putnam's Sons, 1978).
15. Sanders, Charles L. "Sidney Poitier: The Man Behind the Superstar." *Ebony*, April 1968.
16. Hoffman, *Sidney*, op. cit.
17. AI with Karen Kramer.
18. Barthel, "He Doesn't Want to Be Sexless Sidney," op. cit.

ACKNOWLEDGMENTS

My sincere thanks to the people who agreed to be interviewed for this book, and who, in many cases, shared not only memories but telephone numbers, diaries, journals, private collections, letters, and contracts. They are (billed alphabetically) Mort Abrahams, Ray Aghayan, Angela Allen, Susan Anspach, Warren Beatty, Robert Benton, Alexandra Berlin, Eileen Brennan, David Brown, Warren Cowan, Mart Crowley, Brenda Currin, William Daniels, John C. Dutton, Samantha Eggar, Morgan Fairchild, Joel Freeman, Sid Ganis, Arthur Gelb, Lee Grant, Wynn Handman, William Hanley, Buck Henry, Arthur Hiller, Leonard Hirshan, Dustin Hoffman, Geoffrey Holder, Katharine Houghton, Anthony James, Norman Jewison, Elinor Jones, Robert C. Jones, Karen Kramer, Larry Kramer, John Phillip Law, Richard Lederer, Christopher Lofting, Sidney Lumet, Clifford Mason, Peter Masterson, William Mead, Elaine Michea, Walter Mirisch, Joseph Morgenstern, Terry Morse, Peter J. Nelson, Patricia Newcomb, Leslie Newman, Mike Nichols, Estelle Parsons, Arthur Penn, David Picker, Sydney Pollack, Michael J. Pollard, Stuart A. Reiss, Ronald Ribman, Andrew Sarris, William Schallert, Joel Schiller, Marshall Schlom, Elliot Silverstein, Robert Solo, Lynn Stalmaster, Harrison Starr, Alexandra Stewart, Dean Tavoularis, Michael Tolan, Robert Towne, Natalie Trundy, Lawrence Turman, Theadora Van Runkle, Charles Webb, Elizabeth Wilson, Scott Wilson, Irwin Winkler, Norton Wright, Susannah York, and Richard Zanuck. A number of people agreed to speak to me on the condition that their names not be used, and although I chose not to quote them directly in the book, they have my gratitude for their time, their candor, and the useful background information and context they provided.

Much of the information in *Scenes from a Revolution* comes directly from archival documents, which were invaluable to my research, all the more since the period this book covers was one in which so much of Hollywood's business was conducted by memo, cable, letter, and telegram. I thank the following people and institutions for the access they provided and for their ongoing efforts to preserve and catalogue film history: the dedicated and resourceful staff of the New York Public Library for the Performing Arts at Lincoln Center; Ben Brewster and the staff of the Wisconsin Center for Film and Theatre Research at the University of Wisconsin-Madison; Ned Comstock, Sandra Lee, and Steve Hanson at the USC Cinema-Television Library and Archives of Performing Arts; J. C. Johnson and Alexander Rankin at the Howard Gotlieb Archival Research Center at Boston University; Neil Bethke and Cynthia Becht in the Archives & Special Collections Department of the Charles Von Der Ahe Library at Loyola Marymount University in Los Angeles; Jeff Rankin and the staff of the Charles E. Young Research Library Department of Special Collections at UCLA; Caroline Sisneros of the Louis B. Mayer Library at the American Film Institute; Brian Meacham of the Academy Film Archives at the Pickford Center for Motion Picture Study; Randy Haberkamp of the Academy Foundation in Los Angeles, and Barbara Hall and the staff of the Margaret Herrick Library of the Academy of Motion Picture Arts and Sciences at the Fairbanks Center for Motion Picture Study. (And a plea to all contemporary filmmakers: Archive your e-mail!)

For returning calls, answering my questions, offering good counsel, speaking up on my behalf, and/or pointing fingers in the right directions, thanks to Michael Abrams, Doug Aibel, Tino Balio, Bonnie Bartlett, Eyde Belasco, Michael Black, Paul Bloch, Leslee Dart, Claire Dippel, Carlo Eugster, Francesco Foggia, Martin Stephen Frommer, Selina Gomeau, Jeff Gardinier, Raja Gosnell, Lisa Gay Hamilton, John Lahr, Jeffrey Lane, Liz Mahoney, Camryn Manheim, Carri McClure, Wendy Morris, Sacha Newley, William B. Mann, Marion Rosenberg, Will Schwalbe, Chris Sherman, Michael Small, Steven Spielberg, and Bobby Zarem.

When I began this book four years ago, I was an editor at *Entertainment Weekly*. My work on *Scenes from a Revolution* spanned a period of multitasking, then a long leave of absence from the magazine, then a return in a different job, then my departure from *EW*, and finally another return as a columnist. I owe more of my colleagues there than I can possibly name an immense debt of gratitude for bearing with me along the way, and particular thanks to Rick Tetzeli for his remarkable support at every turn.

I'm grateful to Luke Janklow of Janklow & Nesbit for his passion, his perspective, and his willingness to take a chance on this project. Brian Siberell allowed me to interrupt many of his working days in order to draw upon his help and hospitality, and I feel fortunate to have had him in my corner. Michelle Kung provided resourceful and energetic research assistance down to the wire, both in New York and in Wisconsin. Michele Romero found and assembled the pictures for this book; she is a treasure of a photo editor, an original thinker about pop culture, and a great pal.

Without the wisdom, calmness, clarity, focus, and gentle hand on the wheel of my superb editor, Scott Moyers, I would not have been able to write this book. I will never be able to thank him sufficiently, or to express how meaningful Ann Godoff's vision and encouragement have been, from the first day we met to the finish line. My heartfelt thanks to the rest of the fantastic Penguin Press team as well, especially Laura Stickney, Tracy Locke, and Maggie Sivon.

The steadfastness and good wishes of Elly Eisenberg, Linda Emond, Oskar and Laurie Eustis, Dan Fierman, Owen Gleiberman, Betsy Gleick, Henry Goldblatt, Michael Mayer, Mary Kaye Schilling, Ben Svetkey, Ken Tucker, Roger Waltzman, and Jay Woodruff throughout this project have meant the world to me. And Lisa Schwarzbaum gets special billing—a title card of her own—for magnificence above and beyond the call of duty.

Finally, I thank my many families—the Harrises and Davises, the Wisniewskis, the Kushners, and the Deutschers—for their unconditional embrace, especially my brother David, one of the best guys I've ever known, and my husband, Tony, whose unfailing generosity with his eyes, his ears, his mind, and his heart sustains me every day.

INDEX